THE GUINNESS
WHO'S WHO OF

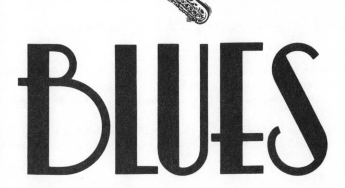

Mojo and Akoko
Best wishes for the future,
Niale "The Harp"

General Editor: Colin Larkin

Introduction by Neil Slaven

GUINNESS PUBLISHING

Dedicated to John Lee Hooker

First published in 1993 by
GUINNESS PUBLISHING LTD
33 London Road, Enfield, Middlesex EN2 6DJ, England

British Library Cataloguing-in-Publication data
A catalogue record for this book is available from the British Library

ISBN 0-85112-725-8

Reprinted 1994

Conceived, designed, edited and produced by
SQUARE ONE BOOKS LTD
Iron Bridge House, 3 Bridge Approach, Chalk Farm, London NW1 8BD
Editor and Designer: Colin Larkin
Picture Editors: Colin Larkin and John Martland
Editorial and production assistant: Susan Pipe
Special thanks to
Neil Slaven, Dave Laing, Ian Slater
David Japp, John Reiss, John Eley and Guy at L&S
Logo concept: Darren Perry

This book has been produced on Apple Macintosh computers
using Quark Xpress and Microsoft Word
Image set by L & S Communications Ltd

Printed and bound in Great Britain by The Bath Press

EDITORS NOTE

The Guinness Who's Who Of Blues forms a part of the multi-volume *Guinness Encyclopedia Of Popular Music.* A further 16 specialist single volumes are planned in the near future.

Also available:
The Guinness Who's Who Of Indie And New Wave Music.
The Guinness Who's Who Of Heavy Metal.
The Guinness Who's Who Of Sixties Music.
The Guinness Who's Who Of Jazz.
The Guinness Who's Who Of Seventies Music.
The Guinnness Who's Who Of Country Music.

Blues music has always been with us, and lovers of rock 'n' roll, jazz, pop, soul and heavy metal should be acutely aware of its important root to those genres. From the earliest days of the work song in the southern states of the USA the Blues has spoken volumes, sending its influences throughout America. In recent times their have been two boom eras for the music. The first started in the early 60s when white groups (mostly from the UK) played their version of the blues. Bands such as the Pretty Things, the Yardbirds, the Animals, the Rolling Stones and John Mayalls Bluesbreakers bought the names of Muddy Waters, Howlin' Wolf, Sonny Boy Williamson and John Lee Hooker to a popular audience. By the end of that decade as progressive music became the fashion, vast numbers of the bands began to play hard electric and improvisational blues. From the UK there were the Keef Hartley Band, Cream, Savoy Brown Blues Band, Fleetwood Mac, Chicken Shack, Taste and the Groundhogs. In America in addition to the influential Paul Butterfield Blues Band there were the Steve Miller Blues Band, Canned Heat and Electric Flag together with

the whole range of San Francisco bands who featured lengthy versions of blues-based songs. Much of the psychedelic music from the Grateful Dead, Jefferson Airplane, Quicksilver Messenger Service, Moby Grape and Big Brother And The Holding Company was blues in disguise.

Many of the blues masters enjoyed financially rewarding twilight years as they came out of the shadows to play alongside their younger contemporaries. A second resurgence is happening as I write. Recent albums by John Lee Hooker and Buddy Guy have been critically acclaimed resulting in vast sales. Hooker's outstanding *The Healer* has become the biggest selling blues album of all time. Artists such as Robert Cray, Gary Moore, John Campbell, Stevie Ray Vaughan and Jeff Healey have further extended the blues audience.

In selecting entries for this volume we have tried to cover all areas of blues music and not the obvious section, which is for purists only. Notable figures in the genre such as Paul Oliver would, I am sure, rather see and hear blues music played to a wide audience even if the artist in question happened to be born in Ripley, Surrey and not near the Mississippi delta. Suggestions regarding future additions for the next edition will be welcomed by writing to the Editor.

Most of the photographs in this volume were supplied by Tony Gale of Pictorial Press. The remaining plates were supplied by Neil Slaven pages 47, 67, 84, 124, 150, 240, 273, 305, 327 and 339 and David Redfern pages 21, 29, 69, 103, 178, 191, 193, 222, 258, 298, 302, 318, 330, 344, 360, 363 and 366.

The contributors for this volume were Alan Balfour, Keith Briggs, Neil Slaven, Tony Burke, Chris Smith, Dave Laing, Brian Hogg,

Alan Clayson, Johnny Rogan, Robert Pruter, Jeff Tamarkin, Colin Larkin, Ray Templeton, Pete Watson, John Eley and Dave Penny
I would like to thank, in addition to Neil Slaven, Tony Burke and his colleagues from *BRGT (Blues Rythem The Gospel Truth)* who were involved during the original preparation. To John Martland who joined us at a very difficult time and added great enthusiasm to the project.
To Susan Pipe for her now familiar super-efficiency in putting it all together at the end and holding things together during my enforced absence. To Ian 'Guitar' Slater for checking the master list. To John Reiss, David Japp and the legendary Freddy for making the working environment that much more secure. To Mark Cohen, always the vital link in the chain. To David Roberts, Sallie Collins and Sarah Silvé for their production work and for Donald McFarlan's receptive eardrum. Finally to Laura, Ben, Tom, Dan and Goldie, who can finally have a rest from listening to 'woke up this mornin' and 'my woman done gone and left me'.

Colin Larkin, February 1993

INTRODUCTION

It starts with the sound, the totality of the performance. A sound so unlike anything else that it fascinates from the first hearing, stirs recognition and a sympathy the listener didn't know he possessed. The words don't register at first, not at least on a conscious level, but the emotion does. The message is often simple, so simple that gradations of meaning only become apparent after the initial intrigue has subsided. The emotion can be palpable, so much so that when set alongside other forms of music, it seems as histrionic as grand opera. You've discovered the blues.

What is the blues? From the title of his autobiography, *I Am The Blues*, the answer ought to be Willie Dixon. And in one sense, it's true. As a studio musician and session supervisor for Chess and other Chicago blues labels during the 50s and 60s, Dixon wrote for, and worked with Muddy Waters, Howlin' Wolf, Otis Rush, Buddy Guy and Little Walter, to name but the most well-known of the city's teeming blues talent. With an ear for alliteration that marked the best of his compositions, Dixon averred, 'the blues are the roots and the other musics are the fruits'. Add to that Muddy Waters' 'The Blues Had A Baby And They Called It Rock 'n' Roll', and surely the point is made.

Brownie McGhee also put it succinctly, 'Blues is not a dream. Blues is truth.' John Lee Hooker, interviewed long before his elevation to Grand (and Wealthy) Old Man Of The Blues, said, 'It has more feeling than other music. When I sing these songs I feel them down deep and reach you down deep.' The recently deceased Johnny Shines, an eloquent, if not always grammatical apologist for the blues, was as apposite as McGhee, 'The blues are not wrote; the blues are lived'.

Most appropriately for the status of the blues today, J.B. Hutto delivered this visionary thought: 'The blues will never die because it's the original thing. It's coming back up from where they tried to stomp it down; it's coming back up again and it's gonna get better. Blues will be blues until the world ends.' But just what is the blues?

The blues is both music and the feeling that inspires it. Many scholarly treatises have faltered at the need to be specific. One eminent musicologist wrote a whole book about just one composition, only to admit at its end that, because of the fluid nature of the song's various components and the random approach adopted by its performers, there was no such thing as a definitive performance. Other writers, with a specific axe to grind, subverted their wide-ranging research in order to maintain their own contentions about just one blues singer.

The blues may be truth but there is not just one. There are many truths and all of them pertinent. The clearest analogy to make about the music's origin is to note how often the same scientific discovery is made almost simultaneously in widely separated locations. Music in its many forms, like research, represents the totality of what has preceded it. There came a point in time when the creation of a new musical form within the black communities of America became an inevitability. It was almost as if the blues, like gravity or the genetic code, was just waiting to be identified.

Willie Dixon liked to place the beginning of the blues in the Garden of Eden. Others, less fanciful, pointed to the days of slavery.

Booker White had been told by an ex-slave about men and women working in the fields, who would 'sing them songs so pitiful and so long'. Johnny Shines was more graphic: 'Just think of a little child standing at his mother's knee, crying "Mama, take me up". And she can't even look down at him. She's got to look the people in the eye who's gonna sell her and buy her. She can't even reach down and pick him up and nurse him. Now, those people had the blues.'

But the slaves didn't know that because the term didn't come into common parlance until the last decade of the 19th century. Much as the music it described didn't coalesce into the predominantly 12-bar format that became its most frequent setting until the first decades of the 20th century.

The story of how the blues came to be what it is, is too long and convoluted to be attempted here. The complex interaction of African and European musical traditions, the way in which European musical instruments and notation were imposed upon, or co-opted into, less formally structured African traditions, happened haphazardly over a century and a half. And, though the phrase has lost its power to impress, has been reduced almost to cliché, the blues was born out of oppression. To be treated like beasts of burden, casually abused at every opportunity, brutalised to such a degree that family values were totally negated, it is small wonder that the oppressed resorted to a coded behaviour that bound them together and bitterly celebrated their position at the bottom of a social order that barely recognised their existence.

Then again, there were moments when such bitterness could be transcended and spirits could be lifted to exalt existence. Black churches metamorphosed the Christianity that had been imposed upon the slave community into a joyful celebration of the freedom to come. And the blues could provide temporal relief from the harsh realities of black life that not even emancipation could affect.

There were other contributory factors in the emergence of the blues at the dawn of the present century. The momentum of life changed significantly in its first two decades. The unknown was no longer just over the horizon or a day away. Systems of communication brought events in far-off cities into the daily lives of farming communities. The telephone and the telegraph brought instant awareness across the entire continent. The expansion of the railroad system enabled the population to become more mobile.

More importantly for the current narrative, acquisition of musical instruments became easier with the formation of mail-order houses like the Sears, Roebuck Company. The means to make music, for so long the only form of passive resistance available to black people, was brought within the reach of even the poorest. Sales of guitars boomed. Mobility and portability were the order of the day.

Piano blues flourished alongside guitar blues but inevitably the piano's bulk precluded its easy transportation, making it appropriate for more permanent institutions such as gaming houses and brothels, which often amounted to the same thing. Official indifference to black life meant that such illegal establishments were condoned by the police as long as they remained in the black ghettos of major cities like St. Louis, Chicago and, particularly, New Orleans.

The last crucial element in the development of the blues was the advent of the phonograph. Recordings of black musical traditions were sparse to begin with, although the Dinwiddie Colored Quartet recorded six single-sided discs of gospel songs in the last days of October 1902.

The neon light of blues iconography points to Valentine's Day 1920 as the date on which the first blues record was made. In reality, Mamie Smith's 'That Thing Called Love' was an anodyne pop song, and even the innuendo of 'You Can't Keep A Good Man Down' on the b-side was gentle enough to be lost on those without the tuning apparatus to pick up the signal. 'Crazy Blues', which she recorded six months later, opened a floodgate that released a clutch of 'classic' female blues singers, most of whom already worked in vaudeville.

Inevitably, as 19th century minstrel shows had parodied black musical gatherings, as 'nigger' and 'coon' songs had conveniently distorted and sentimentalised white perceptions of black life, as the instrumental music from New Orleans called 'jass' had been appropriated by white musicians, the blues made its public debut as a performance art that bore only a distant resemblance to the realities that it was meant to reflect.

The dictates of commerce must always exploit the opportunities that are offered. An untapped and potentially huge market for 'blues' music had been identified and the recording industry targeted the black population with avaricious precision. As the 20s progressed, records by Smiths, Bessie, Clara and Mamie, Ida Cox, Lucille Hegamin and Alberta Hunter were eagerly consumed by all levels of the black community.

Companies like Okeh, Columbia and RCA Victor were joined by a number of smaller, independent labels that were either bought up by the majors or choked off for lack of adequate distribution. In order to feed and foster their profits, the majors cast ever widening nets, sending out talent scouts to summon musicians to their studios in New York and Chicago. In this way, less formal musicians who had never graced a theatre stage had the opportunity to address a wider (and more avid) audience.

One of the first 'country' blues artists to record was Papa Charlie Jackson, who played both banjo and guitar, but favoured the former on his first 1924 releases. The banjo was in fact an American adaptation of an African instrument and, with the violin, prevalent as the instrument of choice amongst black musicians until the ready availability of the guitar. Jackson was joined within a couple of years by such artists as Blind Blake, Blind Lemon Jefferson and Big Bill Broonzy.

As the 20s progressed, the companies' studio sessions were supplemented by mobile recording teams that criss-crossed the southern states to record musicians performing in regional styles not previously heard outside one town or community. As these records found their way into black homes across America, they sowed the seeds of familiarity that would choke the rich diversity of music that had flourished unchallenged over previous undocumented decades.

Listening to blues recordings of the 20s, that richness is immediately apparent. With even a brief acquaintance, it is possible to identify the spare, extended metres of Texas blues, the churning rhythm and bottleneck vocalisation of Mississippi blues, the grace and dexterity of Piedmont blues from the east coast states.

Initially, these records sold predominantly to city dwellers who accepted the music's variety with indiscriminate taste, perhaps remembering the music of their hometown or state. Outside the cities, each artist's recordings sold mainly to the communities familiar with the individual or the style. Sales continued to rise as the 20s were coming to an end. But, even though artists received meagre one-time payments and no royalties, it was just a matter of time before recording costs could no longer be justified by sales.

The 1929 Stock Market crash not only curtailed most blues recording activity, it also created a situation that called for a standardised approach. It was a rationale that would have been imposed in due course, the failure of the money markets only hastened its arrival. As the 30s began, companies like Okeh, Decca, Bluebird and Vocalion pared down their artist rosters to proven talents such as Big Bill, Leroy Carr, Walter Davis, Lonnie Johnson, Memphis Minnie and Tampa Red. Intensive sessions took place over a number of days, with a small group of reliable studio musicians going through the motions while a parade of star names passed before the microphone.

Instead of pursuing a policy of recording little and often, artists were called upon to cut as many as 18 songs at one session. The random brilliance that had been caught a decade before was reduced to a routine proficiency that relied on nuance and contrivance rather than inspiration. In the second half of the 30s, artists like Sonny Boy Williamson and Joe Williams reconnected with the conviction that city-dwelling sophisticates had lost or expunged from their work. However, Williamson quickly acquired the veneer of professionalism, while Williams, the eternal itinerant, shuffled back to the comfort of his independence.

The 30s was also the time of the Great Migration, as farming communities of the southern states were overturned by the arrival of machinery that replaced the gangs of field hands so necessary to cotton farming. Whole families moved to the industrial north, where expanding production called for a larger work force. Wages were not high by white standards but better than the subtle slavery of the sharecropping system.

These people entered a rigidly delineated social order, as rigorous as that of white society, that didn't want to be reminded of its country origins. They wanted their music to reflect their new-found affluence and improved standard of living. It was the era of the big bands of Duke Ellington, Count Basie, Chick Webb and Jimmy Lunceford. Chicago churches vied with one another for the spectacle of their services, the size and skill of their classically trained choirs.

Black communities were not necessarily imitating their white counterparts but they were trying to develop a sophistication that at least mirrored the white society of which they could never be a part. The old way of life that was celebrated in country blues had no place in black urban culture.

World War II brought a cessation to recording. War work ensured that industrial cities like Chicago, Detroit and Pittsburgh remained financial meccas for the black work-force. When the war ended, free enterprise and a ready supply of shellac brought both black and white entrepreneurs into the record business. Men like Syd Nathan, Fred Mendelsohn, Herman Lubinsky, Leonard Chess, the Rene brothers, Art Rupe, the Messner brothers, the Biharis and the Erteguns launched King, Savoy, Exclusive, Specialty, Regal, Aladdin, Modern and Atlantic.

The formulaic fodder churned out by the major companies to replace outmoded traditions was itself no longer what the public wanted. The electric guitar, in the hands of men like T-Bone Walker and Charlie Christian, revolutionised the sound of blues and jazz. The era of the big band came to an end, large orchestras were no longer economically viable for all but the most successful units. Into the void came small six and seven piece bands, led by men such as Joe Liggins, Roy Milton and Johnny Otis, who developed a form of blues-based jump music that they called 'rhythm and blues'.

In Chicago, the sound of amplified slide guitar played by Muddy Waters brought the vitality of Mississippi Delta blues to the city. Amplified guitars and harmonicas swept through the clubs and bars of the city's South Side. Labels like Chess, Chance, Parrot, J.O.B., United and States discovered a host of talent ignored by the larger companies. Released from the straight-jacket of formalised sessions, bluesmen such as J.B. Lenoir, Sunnyland Slim, Baby Face Leroy Foster, Johnny Shines, Homesick James and J.B. Hutto followed Muddy's lead.

Chess and its subsidiary, Checker, became the city's leading blues labels with a roster that included Muddy Waters, Howlin' Wolf, Little Walter, Jimmy Rogers, Eddie Boyd and Sonny Boy Williamson. Add to that, R&B performers like Chuck Berry, Bo Diddley, Etta James and Little Milton. Next in importance during the mid-50s was Vee Jay, with leading lights John Lee Hooker and Jimmy Reed, and a strong gospel catalogue that included the Swan Silvertone Singers and The Staple Singers.

West Coast blues tended to be less dramatic. Charles Brown's blues ballads and Amos Milburn's piano boogies were at the forefront of a more relaxed form of blues that entertained rather than confronted its audiences. What country blues there was, was dominated by Lightnin' Hopkins. T-Bone Walker inspired a new generation of bandleading guitarists, including B.B. King and Gatemouth Brown.

As the music proliferated, so its individuality was narrowed down to a small number of influential figures, most of whom have already been mentioned. By the end of the 50s, the torch that T-Bone Walker had lit and B.B. King had carried around the country, was picked up by younger men like Buddy Guy, Magic Sam and Otis Rush. They, in turn, kept their eye on popular music trends, intent upon reaching a wider market place than just the diminishing blues audience. But, having been ignored and marginalised in America for four decades, in the 60s the blues became a major influence on European popular music. British musicians like John Mayall, Eric Clapton and Peter Green, and groups such as the Rolling Stones and the Yardbirds, were at the forefront of a movement that took the music back to an America in need of re-education about its own heritage.

Beginning in 1962, and continuing for a decade, package tours of bluesmen and women travelled throughout Europe. Record labels sprang up in England, France, Italy and Scandinavia to record these musicians, and supply the growing demand for both contemporary blues recordings and reissues of classic recordings from all eras of the blues' development. Blue Horizon was created by producer Mike Vernon, responsible for recording artists such as John Mayall, Savoy Brown, Curtis Jones, Champion Jack Dupree, Eddie Boyd and Otis Spann, to spotlight British blues talent, led by Fleetwood Mac and Chicken Shack, and American bands like Rod Piazza's Bacon Fat.

White Americans, such as Paul Butterfield and Mike Bloomfield, formed bands of their own, and did what they could to promote and encourage the blues amongst other rock bands. Veteran bluesmen like Albert King, B.B. King, Muddy Waters and Howlin' Wolf, already heroes to the British bands, took their place alongside their young adherents at venues such as the Fillmore West in San Francisco, the Fillmore East in New York and Chicago's Kinetic Circus.

While Europe was giving the blues a new lease of life, it fell from favour in its own community. Soul music, which combined elements of the blues and mainstream popular music with gospel fervour, provided its audiences with songs that reflected their contemporary concerns in musical settings that weren't constrained to reiterate the past.

With an irony the bluesmen themselves recognised, the blues became more popular on college campuses than it was amongst their own people. Throughout the 70s, blues artists and their record companies tried to accommodate themselves to the parade of flamboyant musical trends consumed with ever-increasing rapidity by a clamouring public. The traditions that the blues represented were disparaged or ignored in the rush to be 'hip' or relevant. Black pride could not tolerate anything that evoked a subservient past, even though the blues was primarily a music of protest and reaction.

Into the 80s, record companies such as Alligator, Black Top, Blind Pig and Rounder catered to a predominantly white audience with product by both black and white artists. As the decade proceeded, the blues adopted an increasingly higher profile, aided by artists such as Eric Clapton and Stevie Ray Vaughan, who appealed to both blues and rock audiences. Each man took care to use his own success to foster the careers of men like Albert Collins, Buddy Guy and Robert Cray.

Cray and Joe Louis Walker represent a generation of black musicians that includes Kenny Neal, Larry Garner and Jay Owens, who can move between musical genres with ease, developing a repertoire that simultaneously pays homage to the background of the blues while it creates a new dialogue in tune with contemporary concerns. Alongside these men are performers like Charlie Musselwhite, William Clarke, Rod Piazza and Anson Funderburgh, whose command of the blues and respect for its traditions prevents their efforts from slipping into mere pastiche. In addition, there's Terry Garland, Sonny Landreth and John Campbell, all of whom have worked in a traditional blues setting but have chosen to broaden their scope with more original material.

Now, in the 90s, British companies such as Silvertone and PointBlank are prepared to promote blues records with the same investment and commitment that in the past has been lavished on pop music. The phenomenal success of John Lee Hooker, garnering Grammy awards, gold discs and Top 20 singles in his 70s has meant that the blues is no longer being treated as a train-spotting pursuit, fit only for teenage pensioners in duffel-coats.

Some of their number may have already flipped these pages to see if their pet obscurity has been enshrined. This book is not directed at them, though they're welcome to benefit from its information. Gathered within these pages is the most comprehensive biographical list of bluesmen and women from all stages of the music's recording history. It is not meant to be all-encompassing.

What this *WHO'S WHO OF BLUES* does reflect is the diversity within the music and the lives of artists, great and small, who've helped to shape one of America's few indigenous art forms. That it is no longer just an American art form is a testament to its power and influence and a guarantee that, in J.B. Hutto's words, 'Blues will be blues until the world ends.'

Neil Slaven
February 1993

References and suggested further reading:
Big Road Blues, David Evans (Da Capo, 1982), *The Blackwell Guide To Blues Records*, Edited by Paul Oliver (Blackwell, 1989), *Blues*, Robert Neff & Anthony Connor (Latimer, 1976), *Chicago Breakdown*, Mike Rowe (Eddison Bluesbooks, 1973), *The Devil's Music*, Giles Oakley (Ariel, 1983), *Red River Blues: The Blues Tradition In The Southeast*, Bruce Bastin (Macmillan, 1986), *The Story Of The Blues*, Paul Oliver (Barrie Cresset, 1969).

A

Abramson, Herb

b. c.1920, Brooklyn, New York, USA. A record collector from his teens, Abramson staged jazz concerts with Ahmet Ertegun and his brother Nesuhi in New York and Washington in the early 40s, while training as a dentist. He was also a part-time producer for National in 1944-47, working with Billy Eckstine and the Ravens. Abramson briefly ran the Jubilee and Quality labels with Jerry Blaine before he and Ahmet Ertegun set up Atlantic in 1947. Over the next five years, he and Ertegun worked as producers, promoters and distributors in building up the company into a leading R&B label. From 1953-55, Abramson did military service and on his return launched the Atco subsidiary, working with the Coasters, Clyde McPhatter, Bobby Darin and Wynonie Harris. However, tensions between the Atlantic team caused Abramson to sell his interest in Atlantic in 1957 for $300,000. He then set up labels such as Triumph, Festival and Blaze, which provided his only big pop hit 'Tennessee Waltz' by Bobby Comstock (1959). After those companies failed, Abramson continued as an independent producer, supervizing tracks by Gene Pitney, Don Covay and others. In the R&B field he recorded sessions by Elmore James, Tommy Tucker ('Hi Heel Sneekers' 1964), Titus Turner and Louisiana Red (Atco 1971).

Aces

Comprising Louis Myers, his brother Dave Myers and drummer Fred Below (b. 6 September 1926, Chicago, Illinois, USA, d. 13 August 1988, Chicago, Illinois, USA). The Aces became Little Walter's backing band in the early 50s (they were often called the Jukes on his records), and were one of the first electric Chicago blues bands to undertake major tours. Their swinging approach was extremely influential. In the 70s they visited Europe, recording accompaniments to blues artists such as Mickey Baker, Willie Mabon and Jimmy Rogers and made albums for Vogue, Black & Blues, and MCM, with special guests including Joe Carter and ex-Muddy Waters guitarist Sammy Lawhorn.
Albums: *Kings Of Chicago Blues Volume One* (1971), *The Aces With Their Guest* (1975).

Adams, J.T.

b. 17 February 1911, Morganfield, Kentucky, USA. John Tyler Adams learned blues guitar from his father; moving to Indianapolis in the 40s, he fell in with Scrapper Blackwell, and Mississippian Shirley Griffith, a fellow Chrysler employee who became his closest musical associate. Each accompanied the other, their twin guitars blending as impeccably on Mississippi blues standards like 'Big Road Blues', as on songster material like 'Kill It Kid' and 'The Hop Joint'. Adams was recorded in the early 60s, but was little heard of thereafter, although he was reported still to be partnering Griffith at the time of the latter's death in 1974.
Albums: *Indiana Avenue Blues* (1963), *Indianapolis Jump* (1976).

Adams, Woodrow

b. 1917, Tchula, Mississippi, USA. Although he earned his living driving a tractor in rural Mississippi, Woodrow Adams made enough records to give us a fascinating insight into the music of a non-professional Delta blues musician. He learned both harmonica and guitar during childhood, but was 35 years old before he made his first record. In all, he released three singles between 1952 and 1961. The first was extremely rough, unpolished performance in the Mississippi-based Chicago blues style of the time but by the time the third was released there was an attempt to update his sound to a more commercial R&B. None of these records enjoyed any success and Adams was still working on a plantation when researcher David Evans recorded a session with his band in 1967, part of which was later issued on an album.
Album: *Lowdown Memphis Harmonica Jam* (1976).

Akers, Garfield

b. c.1901, Mississippi, USA, d. 1959, Mississippi, USA. Akers was a lifelong friend and partner of Joe Callicott, the two of them taking turns to play lead and second guitar as they sang blues for parties and picnics in north Mississippi's De Soto County. Callicott was present on the two-part 'Cottonfield Blues', recorded in 1929; Akers was equally impressive on two solo titles cut the following year. His singing and playing are highly rhythmic, with a hypnotic guitar pulse under extended vocal notes. Akers' singing has been said to have the qualities of the field holler, but its lack of decoration belies this; rather it combines danceability with intensity of personal feeling.

Album: *Son House And The Great Delta Blues Singers* (1990).

Alexander, Alger 'Texas'

b. 12 September 1900, Jowett, Texas, USA. d. 16 April 1954, Richard, Texas, USA. A small, powerful man, Alexander was unusual among rural blues singers on record, in playing no instrument. He worked as a sectionhand when not making his living, (from about 1923 onwards) as an itinerant singer, and carried a guitar with him in case he should meet a potential accompanist for his resonant baritone. He recorded extensively between 1927 and 1934 with such sophisticated guitarists as Lonnie Johnson and Eddie Lang, whose style dovetailed brilliantly with his artless structurally unpredictable singing. Other collaborations included: the Mississippi Sheiks string band; jazz great King Oliver (a sadly unsuccessful collaboration); and guitarists (and fellow Texans) Dennis 'Little Hat' Jones, Willie Reed and Carl Davis. His songs articulate, as few others do, what life was like for black Texans in a world where poverty and racial oppression were dominant, and the prison system perpetuated slavery. Alexander went to prison in the 40s for singing an obscene song, but it seems likely that he knew prison life even before he came to record, for he sings about it in unusually explicit terms, and many of his blues have the cadences and, sometimes the texts, of worksongs. 'What he talked about, he lived it,' said Lowell Fulson, who travelled with Alexander in 1939. A solitary record made in 1950 is rendered almost unlistenable by the combined effects of lack of rehearsal and the syphilis that was soon to kill him.

Selected albums: *Texas Troublesome Blues* (1982), *Texas Alexander Volume 1* (1982), *Volume 2* (1983), *Volume 3* (1986), *Volume 4* (1987).

Alexander, Dave

b. 10 March 1938, Shreveport, Louisiana, USA.

Alexander began to play piano after hearing a record by Albert Ammons on the radio around 1945. His first professional appearance was in 1954; however, he joined the navy at the age of 17, was discharged in 1958 and moved to Oakland, California. He played all over the west coast, but in 1968 was badly wounded in a domestic quarrel and during his hospitalization he started writing his own material. In 1969 he recorded for World Pacific (featuring Albert Collins) and later made two albums for Arhoolie Records. He also recorded with L.C. Robinson. In 1976 he changed his name to Omas Hakim Khayyam and is now known as Omas The Magnificent. A versatile pianist and singer who mixes elements of jazz with his strong blues and boogie-woogie playing, his live show is a capsule of blues piano.

Album: *The Rattler* (1972).

Allison, Luther

b. 17 August 1939, Mayflower, Arkansas, USA. In his youth Allison sang with a family gospel group and moved to Chicago in 1951. Around 1957 he formed his own band to work on the west side. After a year the group disbanded and Allison went on to work with Jimmy Dawkins, Magic Sam, Freddie King and others until the mid-60s. In March 1967 he recorded a session for Bill Lindemann, later issued by the collector label Delmark. He toured California, recording there as accompanist to Sunnyland Slim and Shakey Jake Harris. He made his first album under his own name in 1969 and was one of the major successes of the Ann Arbor festivals of 1969 and 1970. In the early 70s he recorded for Motown subsidary label Gordy and since the late 70s he has spent much of his time in France, where he has a large and faithful following. He has since recorded for many labels, usually adequate live albums or studio sessions comprising funk or Jimi Hendrix and Rolling Stones influenced rock; however, when Luther remembers his roots, he is still an exciting bluesman.

Selected albums: *Luther's Blues* (1974), *South Side Safari* (1982), *Lets Have A Natural Ball* (1984), *Powerwire Blues* (1986), *Life Is A Bitch* (1988), *Love Me Mama* (1988), *Serious* (1988).

Allison, Mose

b. 11 November 1927, Tippo, Mississippi, USA.

Mose Allison

Allison began piano lessons at the age of five, and played trumpet in high school, although he has featured the latter instrument less frequently in recent years. His music is a highly individual mix of blues and modern jazz, with influences on his cool, laconic singing and piano playing ranging from Tampa Red and Sonny Boy 'Rice Miller' Williamson to Charlie Parker, Duke Ellington, and Thelonious Monk. He moved to New York in 1956 and worked mainly in jazz settings, playing with Stan Getz and recording for numerous companies. During the 60s Allison's work was much in evidence as he became a major influence on the burgeoning R&B scene. Pete Townshend, one of Mose's greatest fans recorded his 'A Young Man's Blues' for the Who's *Live At Leeds*. Similarly John Mayall was one of dozens who recorded his classic 'Parchman Farm' and Georgie Fame featured many Allison songs in his heyday with the Blueflames. Fame's nasal and understated vocal was similar to Allison's, as is Ben Sidran's style and voice. In the 80s he saw a resurgence in his popularity after becoming a hero to the new, young audience for modern jazz. Ultimately his work is seen as hugely influential; and this has to a degree limited the success of his own considerable recording career.

Selected albums: *Back Country Suite* (1957), *Mose Alive* (1966), *I've Been Doin' Some Thinkin'* (1968), *Hello There* (1969), *Universe* (1969), *Western Man* (1971), *Mose In Your Ear* (1972), *Your Mind's On Vacation* (1976), *Middle Class White Boy* (1982), *Ever Since The World Ended* (1983), *Lessons In Living* (1983), *Sings And Plays* (1991). Compilation: *Mose Allison Sings The Seventh Son* (1988).

Altheimer, Joshua

b. c.1910, Arkansas, USA. A virtual biographical blank, Altheimer was a pianist of distinction operating in the Chicago blues scene of the 30s. He never had a record issued under his own name but was well known for his work accompanying such artists as Big Bill Broonzy (with whom he worked for three years, 1937-40), Lonnie Johnson, Jazz Gillum, Washboard Sam (Robert Brown) and John Lee 'Sonny Boy' Williamson. Altheimer was not regarded as a great practitioner of boogie styles or display music, (although he could certainly rock when required to, he seldom took a solo), he was

always to be found in a band setting where his reliable and sometimes outstanding rolling piano work was most effective in underpinning some classic blues performances. What little information there is about his life will be found in Broonzy's book *Big Bill Blues* or Paul Oliver's *The Story Of The Blues*.
Album: *Chicago Blues* (1985).

Anderson, Jimmy

Little biographical information is available on blues harmonica player and vocalist Jimmy Anderson, despite the fact that he recorded as recently as the early 60s. It appears, however, that he was based in Baton Rouge, Louisiana, USA and all of his records were made for Jay Miller at his studio in Crowley. His records were influenced, almost to the point of impersonation, by the popular Chicago blues singer Jimmy Reed - the same high-pitched harmonica breaks and nasal whine in the vocals - but despite their derivative qualities they are good blues with a contemporary, upbeat sound. One single, 'I Wanna Boogie' and 'Angel Please' was issued on Miller's own Zynn label in 1962 and enjoyed some local success, and a further three were leased to Excello Records for wider distribution over the next couple of years. Nothing seems to have been heard from him since then.
Album: *Baton Rouge Harmonica* (1988).

Anderson, Pinkney (Pink)

b. 12 February 1900, Laurens, South Carolina, USA, d. 12 October 1974, Spartanburg, South Carolina, USA. For much of his life, Anderson was Spartanburg's most famous songster and medicine show huckster. He was 10 when he first learned to play the guitar in open tuning from Joe Wicks. He also earned money as a buck dancer on the streets of Laurens. In 1917 he joined 'Doctor' W.R. Kerr's medicine show, learning every facet of the calling and staying, with Peg Leg Sam as his straight man, until it ceased in 1945. When not on the road, he partnered Simmie Dooley, a blind guitarist from whom he learned to tune his guitar and play chords. In 1928 the pair recorded four titles for Columbia in Atlanta. One of the songs, 'Every Day In In The Week', also featured on a May 1950 session, recorded while Anderson was performing at the State Fair in Charlottesville,

and released in conjunction with titles by another Laurens musician, Blind Gary Davis. Anderson continued to work the medicine shows, teaming up with Baby Tate, until heart trouble forced his retirement in 1957. In 1961 he recorded three albums for Bluesville, each with a theme, blues, medicine show songs and folk ballads. Gradually deteriorating health prevented him from working. An album project for Trix, begun in 1970 was never realised.
Selected albums: *Carolina Blues Man* (1962), *Medicine Show Man* (1962), *Ballad And Folksinger* (1963).

Arnold, Billy Boy

b. 16 March 1935, Chicago, Illinois, USA. Arnold first played blues harmonica with Bo Diddley's group in 1950 and became a well-known figure in Chicago blues throughout the following two decades. Among those he accompanied were Johnny Shines and Otis Rush. With a serviceable singing voice and a harmonica style influenced by John Lee 'Sonny Boy' Williamson, Arnold recorded as a solo artist for local labels Cool (1953) and VeeJay (1955). In 1958 he led a group which included Mighty Joe Young and recorded for Mighty H. However, none of Arnold's records were as successful as the mid-50s hits of Bo Diddley such as 'Pretty Thing' and 'Hey Bo Diddley', to which he contributed the keening harp phrases. The most renowned of Arnold's own tracks is 'I Wish You Would' (VeeJay), which was adopted by British R&B group the Yardbirds, appearing on *Five Live Yardbirds* (1964). During the mid-60s blues boom, he cut an album for Prestige/Bluesville (1964), recorded with pianist Johnny Jones (a 1963 session which remained unreleased for 17 years). There was a later album for Vogue. Not forgotten by European blues enthusiasts, Arnold toured there in 1975 as part of the Blues Legends package, when he recorded two albums for Peter Shertser's UK-based Red Lightnin'.
Albums: *More Blues On The South Side* (1964), *Blow The Back Off It* (1975), *Sinner's Prayer* (1976), *Checkin' It Out* (1979, reissue), *Johnny Jones & Billy Boy Arnold* (1980), *Crying & Pleading* (1980, reissue).

Arnold, James 'Kokomo'

b. 15 February 1901, Lovejoy's Station, Georgia, USA. d. 8 November 1968, Chicago, Illinois, USA. 'Kokomo' Arnold was a left-handed slide blues guitarist who learned the basics of his style from his cousin, James Wigges. After working in steel mills in Illinois and Pennsylvania he became a dedicated fisherman and moonshiner who looked upon his musical success as an adjunct to 'real life.' Arnold developed an unorthodox method of playing guitar, based on a style that had originally been popular in a few states in the deep south. He held the instrument flat, using a slide to create an eerie, ringing sound. Unlike the relaxed and often casual approach of many of his contemporaries, Arnold's was an urgent, aggressive style, and he achieved remarkable results with his unusual method of guitar playing and the curiously high-pitched, often unintelligible singing that went with it. Interspersed in these wailings would be sudden bursts of vocal clarity that gave his statements great authority. He gained a reputation which followed him in his travels throughout the northern states in the years after the end of World War I. Arnold did not record until 1930 when he released 'Paddlin' Blues' (a breakneck blues personalization of 'Paddling Madeline Home') and 'Rainy Night Blues' under the sobriquet 'Gitfiddle Jim' for Victor in Memphis. He continued to record throughout the 30s, all his further work appearing on the Decca label. His biggest hit was the double-a-side 'Old Original Kokomo Blues' (named after a brand of coffee) and 'Milk Cow Blues' the latter of which he recorded in no less than five numbered versions. It was picked up by other bluesmen and enjoyed a second vogue when it was recorded by rock 'n' rollers such as Elvis Presley and Eddie Cochran in the 50s. With notable exceptions, Arnold's work tended to follow a pattern, but was always enlivened by his powerful slide work and original lyrics. He also added his guitarist talents to recordings by Roosevelt Sykes, Mary Johnson and Peetie Wheatstraw. Arnold ceased recording in 1938 following disagreements with Mayo Williams of Decca Records In the early 60s he made a few appearances in Chicago, during the revival of interest in his brand of folk blues. For all his rather fleeting moments in the limelight, Arnold was an influence on Robert Johnson, who was, in his turn, one of the most seminal of the second-generation blues singers whose legacy

helped to shape rock music. Arnold died in Chicago in November 1968.
Selected albums: *Master Of The Bottleneck Guitar* (1987), *Kokomo Arnold 1930-38* (1990), *Down And Out Blue* (1990). Compilations: *Kokomo Arnold And Peetie Wheatstraw* (c.1933), *Kokomo Arnold And Casey Bill* (c.1933).

August, Joe 'Mr. Google Eyes'

b. Joseph Augustus, 13 September 1931, New Orleans, Louisiana, USA. A soulful R&B singer in the Roy Brown tradition, August began performing as a novelty act - The Nation's Youngest Blues Singer - in his early teens, performing with the likes of Paul Gayten and Annie Laurie. In 1949 he was signed to Coleman Records who brought him north to record with Billy Ford And His Musical V-8s and although none of the tracks charted, the mighty Columbia Records was interested enough to buy his contract and re-record the Coleman tracks with Billy Ford's band. August stayed in the New York area for the next few years recording one-off deals for various record labels including Domino, Lee and Regal and in the early 50s settled for a short while in Los Angeles, recording for Duke (with Johnny Otis) and Flip. In the late 50s he returned to New Orleans and made his last recordings for Dot and Instant. He continues to perform and is active in management and politics
Album: *Rock My Soul* (1986).

Austin, Lovie

b. Cora Calhoun, 19 September 1887, Chattanooga, Tennessee, USA, d. 10 July 1972. A formally-trained pianist and arranger, Austin worked in vaudeville for a number of years. She also led her own band and in the early and mid-20s, while house pianist for Paramount Records, she accompanied many leading blues singers. Tired of touring on the TOBA circuit, she settled in Chicago, where she remained for the rest of her life, working as musical director at a number of theatres. Despite, or perhaps because of, her formal training, Austin was not a good jazz player, either as a soloist or in ensembles, but she displayed a good ear for the needs of singers and always provided a sensitive accompaniment to leading exponents of the blues such as Ida Cox, Alberta Hunter and Ma Rainey.

Selected albums: *Alberta Hunter With Lovie Austin And Her Blues Serenaders* (1961), *Blue Serenaders*

B

Bailey, Kid

One of the most elusive of Mississippi blues singers, Bailey made one record in 1929, singing in forceful but melancholy fashion, and playing guitar in a style recalling Charlie Patton and Willie Brown, with whom he is known to have worked. 'Rowdy Blues', on which Bailey is joined by a second guitarist, bases its accompaniment on Brown's 'M&O Blues'. Remembered as having appeared in many small Delta towns, he also played with Tommy Johnson, and is believed to have died in the 60s.
Compilation: *Son House And The Great Delta Blues Singers* (1990).

Baker, LaVern

b. Delores Williams, 11 November 1928, Chicago, Illinois, USA. LaVern Baker was discovered in a Chicago nightclub by bandleader Fletcher Henderson. Although still in her teens, the singer won a recording deal with the influential OKeh Records, where she was nicknamed 'Little Miss Sharecropper' and 'Bea Baker'. Having toured extensively with the Todd Rhodes Orchestra, Baker secured a prestigious contract with Atlantic Records, with whom she enjoyed a fruitful relationship. 'Tweedle Dee' reached both the US R&B and pop charts in 1955, selling in excess of one million copies, and the artist was awarded a second gold disc two years later for 'Jim Dandy'. In 1959, she enjoyed a number 6 pop hit with 'I Cried A Tear' and throughout the decade Baker remained one of black music's leading performers. Although eclipsed by newer acts during the 60s, the singer scored further success with 'Saved', written and produced by Leiber And Stoller, and 'See See Rider', both of which inspired subsequent versions, notably by the Band and the Animals. Baker's final chart entry came with 'Think Twice' a 1966 duet with Jackie Wilson as her 'classic' R&B intonation grew increasingly out of step with the prevalent soul/Motown boom. After leaving Atlantic, Baker is probably best known for 'One Monkey Don't Stop The Show'. In the late 60s, while entertaining US troops in Vietnam, she became ill, and went to the Philippines to recuperate. She stayed there in self-imposed exile for 22 years. In 1992, she undertook a short UK tour, but audience numbers were disappointing for the only lady, along with Aretha Franklin, who had, at that time, been elected to the US Rock 'n' Roll Hall Of Fame.
Albums: *LaVern* (1956), *LaVern Baker* (1957), *LaVern Baker Sings Bessie Smith* (1958), *Blues Ballads* (1959), *Precious Memories* (1959), *Saved* (1961), *See See Rider* (1963), *I'm Gonna Get You* (1966). Compilations: *The Best Of LaVern Baker* (1963), *Real Gone Gal* (1984).

Baker, Mickey

b. McHouston Baker, 15 October 1925, Louisville, Kentucky, USA. After spells in reform school and a children's home, he moved to New York in 1941. He lived on the fringes of the criminal world but took up the guitar and quickly became a virtuoso, equally adept at jazz and blues styles. From the late 40s, Mickey 'Guitar' Baker played on hundreds of recording sessions, accompanying such artists as Ray Charles, the Coasters, Ivory Joe Hunter, Ruth Brown and Screaming Jay Hawkins. Baker recorded occasionally under his own name and in 1956 teamed up with guitarist/vocalist Sylvia Vanderpool. After an unsuccessful version of 'Walking In The Rain', the atmospheric 'Love Is Strange' (co-written by Bo Diddley) by Mickey And Sylvia was a US Top 20 hit on RCA/Groove in 1956. Later singles on Vik and RCA were only minor hits, although the duo contributed to Ike And Tina Turner's 'It's Gonna Work Out Fine' (1961), where Baker's is the male voice answering Tina's. Some of Baker's solo recordings were collected on a 1959 album for Atlantic. In the early 60s, he emigrated to Paris and joined the expatriate community of jazz musicians in the French capital. He toured Europe with such artists as Memphis Slim and Champion Jack Dupree, and performed at the 1973 Montreux Jazz Festival. Baker also arranged the strings for Fleetwood Mac's version of 'Need Your Love So Bad' (1968). During the 70s, he cut several albums in Europe, including a pair for Stefan Grossman's guitar-instructional label, Kicking Mule.
Albums: *The Wildest Guitar* (1959), *But Wild* (1963), *The Blues And Me* (1974), *Take A Look*

LaVern Baker

Inside (1975), *Up On The Hill* (1975), *Blues And Jazz Guitar* (1977), *Jazz-Rock Guitar* (1978).

Baker, Willie

Baker's singing and 12-string blues guitar work on his 1929 recordings are heavily influenced by the Atlanta musicians Robert Hicks ('Barbecue Bob'), Charley Lincoln ('Laughing Charley') and Curley Weaver, sharing with them nasal singing, bassy guitar work played in open G, and the use of a bottleneck on the treble strings. Baker also shares repertoire with this group, making it the more surprising that none of their associates remembered him. He is reported to have lived in Patterson, in southeast Georgia, and is thought to have derived his style from records, and personal contact with Hicks, who was known to have visited the area with a medicine show. Some of Baker's recordings are in an older, non-bottleneck style, with a strong ragtime influence. He was last heard of in Miami, Florida in the mid-60s.
Album: *Georgia Blues Guitars* (80s).

Bakerloo

Originally the Bakerloo Blues Line, this late 60s power-blues trio from Tamworth, Staffordshire, England were briefly compared to Cream. Ironically the band's leader Dave 'Clem' Clempson later found himself singing Cream numbers many years later as a member of Jack Bruce's band. The original Bakerloo comprised Clempson (guitarist/vocalist), Terry Poole (bass) and Keith Baker (drums). Their self-titled album is a collector's item, both as one of the initial Harvest fold-out sleeves and for the music therein. The extended 'Moonshine' gave each member the opportunity to show his musical dexterity. Clempson was soon tempted away to join Jon Hiseman's Colosseum, and Bakerloo was terminated. Keith Baker re-emerged in one of early line-ups of Uriah Heep, later teaming up again with Terry Poole in May Blitz.
Album: *Bakerloo* (1969).

Ballen, Ivin

Ballen formed his 20th Century Records label in Philadelphia during World War II, specializing in a diverse range of music from Jewish humour to gospel. In January 1948, he purchased Sam Goody's Gotham Records and S-G Music Publishing, adding a strong R&B and jazz label to its roster, with artists such as Tiny Grimes, Leo Parker, Jimmy Preston, Johnny Sparrow, Jimmy Rushing and David 'Panama' Francis. In the early 50s leasing deals were arranged with a network of various independent labels throughout the country; from Washington DC, to New York City, Los Angeles, Chicago and Tulsa. The range of styles was enlarged to encompass hillbilly, vocal group R&B and even the down-home blues of Dan Pickett, John Lee Hooker and Eddie Burns. Ballen entered the rock 'n' roll and rockabilly market of the mid-50s, and like many of the small independents found that he could not compete with the big-selling majors such as RCA and Decca. He wound down the label in the late 50s.

Banashak, Joe

b. 15 February 1923, Baltimore, Maryland, USA, d. 1985. A jazz fan as a teenager, Banashak entered record distribution after serving in World War II. After marrying a Texan, he moved to Houston and in the mid-50s took charge of a distribution network based in New Orleans. There he founded Minit Records with local disc jockey Larry McKinley in 1959. With Allen Toussaint as house producer and songwriter, Minit and its sister label Instant were responsible for many hits of the early 60s from New Orleans artists such as Ernie K-Doe ('Mother-In-Law'), Chris Kenner ('I Like It Like That'), Jessie Hill ('Oo Poo Pah Doo') and the Showmen ('It Will Stand'). National distribution was handled by Imperial and when Toussaint left for army service in 1963, the creative dynamic was gone and Banashak sold the Minit catalogue to Lew Chudd of Imperial. Banashak persevered with Instant Records and a new partner, Irving Smith. The label's most successful artist was Kenner who continued to record for Instant until 1969, while Toussaint's studio band backed other local artists like Art Neville, Eskew Reeder (aka Esquerita) and Lee Dorsey. On the subsidiary label, Alon, Toussaint's group the Stokes recorded 'Whipped Cream' later a big hit for Herb Alpert's Tijuana Brass. Shortly afterwards, Toussaint left the company. Banashak continued with new A&R men Sax Kari and Eddie Bo who produced blues and soul tracks for Instant until the late 60s. The company became inactive in the 70s.

Barbecue Bob

b. Robert Hicks, 11 September 1902, Walton County, Georgia, USA, d. 21 October 1931, Lithonia, Georgia, USA. His older brother Charley (later known as Charley Lincoln), learned guitar first, but Robert seems to have followed soon after, also learning from Curley Weaver's mother Savannah. Both brothers played a 12-string. Bob moved to Atlanta in 1924, where he worked at a barbecue, which gave him his pseudonym. Here he was heard by a talent scout and made his first records in 1927. This began a successful recording career that lasted just four years but produced over 50 tracks of fine blues. His music is characterized by a heavy, percussive style, often using a bottleneck. His voice is rather rough but carries a slow blues as well as more up-tempo dance numbers. In 1930, he recorded as part of the Georgia Cotton Pickers, with Curley Weaver and Buddy Moss, and he also appeared as accompanist on Nellie Florence's single 1929 session. Well established as one of the principal figures on the Atlanta blues scene of the time, his career was tragically cut short by his death from pneumonia at the age of 29.
Albums: *Brown Skin Gal* (1978), *Chocolate To The Bone* (1992).

Barbee, John Henry

b. 14 November 1905, Henning, Tenessee, USA. d. 3 November 1964, Chicago Illinios. Born William George Tucker, Barbee worked with John Lee 'Sonny Boy' Williamson and Sunnyland Slim before assuming his new name when he left the south after a shooting incident. Barbee moved to Chicago, where he recorded a session for Vocalion Records on 8 September 1938. Only one coupling was released and made no impact on the record-buying public. Barbee continued to work on the streets in the company of such men as Moody Jones until drafted into the army in the early 40s. 'Rediscovered', he recorded for Victoria Spivey in 1964 before joining the American Folk Blues Festival for its tour of Europe. This jaunt was cut short by illness and he returned to the USA only to be involved in a car crash. He was in jail as a result of this accident when he died of a heart attack.
Album: *Storyville 171* (1964).

Barker, Louis 'Blue Lu'

b. 13 November 1913, New Orleans, Louisiana, USA. Barker began her career as a dancer and singer in New Orleans but did not record until 1938 after her move to New York. She is almost certainly the 'Lu Blue' who recorded with Erskine Hawkins in July of that year. Under her own name she continued to record for Decca until 1939. She enjoyed a second period of recording activity between 1947-49 with her work appearing mainly on Apollo and Capitol. A band singer of note, she has been cited as an influence to Billie Holliday and Eartha Kitt. Barker's blues were often slyly humorous and marked by a wonderful sense of timing. Married to New Orleans jazz guitarist Danny Barker, she usually worked in his company, as well as with many of the great names in jazz and was still performing in 1977.
Albums: *Red White And Blues*, (1980), *Sorry But I Can't Take You - Woman's Railroad Blues* (1980).

Barnes, Roosevelt 'Booba'

b. 25 September 1936, Longwood, Mississippi, USA. A self-taught singer, guitarist and harmonica player, Barnes plays 'unvarnished gut level blues', strongly influenced by Howlin' Wolf. His first instrument was the harmonica, which he began to play at the age of eight, and he sat in with many of the local blues musicians around Greenville, Mississippi in the 50s. He formed the first band under his own leadership in 1956 or 1957 and started playing guitar in 1960. In 1964 he moved to Chicago, Illinois and stayed there until 1971 when he returned to Greenville, where he has remained until the present day. In 1973, he travelled to Chicago to record as a backing musician with the Jones Brothers: these recordings remain unissued. In 1990 Barnes became the first Mississippi-based performer to record an album for the Rooster Blues label.
Album: *The Heartbroken Man* (1990).

Barrelhouse Buck

b. Thomas McFarland, 16 September 1903, Alton, Illinois, USA, d. April 1962. On his 1929 debut recording, Barrelhouse Buck sang reflectively, like many St. Louis pianists, but his playing was more percussive than that of his contemporaries. This resulted partly from his experience as a drummer, and partly from a conscious decision to make his style different. By 1934, he had adopted a fierce, growling vocal to match his swinging piano, and perhaps also to compete with his accompanists, drawn from among a rasping fiddler, a clarinettist, and Peetie Wheatstraw's guitar. Together they made exciting dance music, and it is regrettable that Barrelhouse Buck did not record again until shortly before his death, at a hurried session which produced a brief album, marred by an out-of-tune piano.

Albums: *Backcountry Barrelhouse* (1962), *St. Louis Piano Styles* (1989).

Bartholomew, Dave

b. 24 December 1920, Edgard, Louisiana, USA. Dave Bartholomew was one of the most important shapers of New Orleans R&B and rock 'n' roll during the 50s. A producer, arranger, songwriter, bandleader and artist, Bartholomew produced and co-wrote most of Fats Domino's major hits for Imperial Records. Bartholomew started playing the trumpet as a child, encouraged by his father, a dixieland jazz tuba player. He performed in marching bands throughout the 30s and then on a Mississippi riverboat led by Fats Pichon beginning in 1939, and learned songwriting basics during a spell in the US Army. Upon his return to New Orleans in the late 40s he formed his first band, which became one of the city's most popular. He also backed Little Richard on some early recordings. Bartholomew worked for several labels, including Specialty, Aladdin and De Luxe, for whom he had a big hit in 1949 with 'Country Boy'. In the same year he started a long-term association with Imperial as a producer and arranger. The previous year Bartholomew had discovered Domino in New Orleans's Hideaway Club and he introduced him to Imperial. They collaborated on 'The Fat Man', which, in 1950, became the first of over a dozen hits co-authored by the pair and produced by Bartholomew. Others included 'Blue Monday', 'Walking To New Orleans', 'Let The Four Winds Blow', 'I'm In Love Again', 'Whole Lotta Loving', 'My Girl Josephine' and 'I'm Walkin'', the latter also becoming a hit for Ricky Nelson.

Dave Bartholomew

Bartholomew's other credits included Smiley Lewis's 'I Hear You Knocking' (later a hit for Dave Edmunds) and 'One Night' (later a hit for Elvis Presley, with its lyrics tamed), Lloyd Price's 'Lawdy Miss Clawdy', and records for Shirley And Lee, Earl King, Roy Brown, Huey 'Piano' Smith, Bobby Mitchell, Chris Kenner, Robert Parker, Frankie Ford and Snooks Eaglin. In 1963, Imperial was sold to Liberty Records, and Bartholomew declined an invitation to move to their Hollywood base, preferring to stay in New Orleans. In 1972, Chuck Berry reworked 'My Ding-A-Ling', a song Bartholomew had penned in 1952, into his only USA number 1 single.

Although Bartholomew, who claims to have written over 4,000 songs, recorded under his own name, his contribution was primarily as a behind-the-scenes figure. He recorded a dixieland album in 1981 and in the early 90s was still leading a big band at occasional special events such as the New Orleans Jazz & Heritage Festival.

Albums: *Jump Children* (1984), *The Monkey* (1985), *Heritage* (1986), *Graciously* (1987). Compilation: *The Best Of Dave Bartholomew: The Classic New Orleans R&B Band Sound* (1989).

Battiste, Harold

b. New Orleans, Louisiana, USA. A former jazz pianist, Battiste turned to production on joining the staff at Specialty Records. Initially based in Los Angeles, he returned to his hometown in 1956 to administer a newly-founded wing, but the venture floundered on head-office intransigence. In 1960 Battiste switched to Ric, where he produced Joe Jones's US Top 3 hit, 'You Talk Too Much' and arranged several sessions for Lee Dorsey, including the singer's debut hit 'Ya Ya'. Harold also established the ambitious musicians' collective, AFO (All For One). The houseband included pianist Allen Toussaint, but although the label enjoyed chart entries with Prince La La and Barbara George, recurring arguments with distributors brought about its downfall. Having returned to Los Angeles, Battiste secured work as an arranger with Phil Spector, and became re-acquainted with Sonny Bono. A former colleague at Specialty, Bono later formed a singing duo with his wife and invited Battiste to assist with production. Initial releases by Sonny And Cher, as well as attendant solo singles, proved highly-

popular, but a rift developed when Harold's contributions were largely uncredited. However a new partnership with fellow New Orleans-exile Mac Rebennack resulted in the creation of the monicker Dr. John. Battiste matched the singer's husky inflections with a skillful blend of voodoo incantations and classic 'Crescent City' rhythms, exemplified on the highly-popular *Gris Gris* (1968).

Batts, Will

b. 24 January 1904, Michigan, Mississippi, USA, d. 18 Feb 1956, Memphis, Tennessee, USA. Batts played violin in his father's string band from the age of nine, and was also proficient on guitar and mandolin. Moving to Memphis in 1919, he was a part-time musician, playing in the jug band led by Jack Kelly. His distinctive fiddle playing, equally capable of a punchy muscularity and a languid sensuousness, may be heard behind Frank Stokes on some 1929 recordings, and on a more extensive series made by Jack Kelly's South Memphis Jug Band in the 30s. From 1934, Batts led his own band, and two private recordings from 1954 survive; 'Kansas City' and 'Lady Be Good' testify both to Batts's own versatility and to the continuity of the musical tradition from which he came.

Baxter, Andrew And Jim

b. Calhoun, Georgia, USA. A father and son duo, playing violin and guitar respectively, the Baxters recorded at four sessions between 1927 and 1929. Their records offer a rare example of an older, more rural, black music tradition in Georgia. While some were blues, notably the gentle and melancholy 'KC Railroad Blues', others such as 'Georgia Stomp' were country dance tunes, similar in many ways to some of the white traditional music recorded around the same time. The latter even included spoken dance calls of the type more usually associated with white country music. Emphasizing this connection, Andrew, the elder of the two (who is said to have been half Cherokee Indian) made one record with the white old-time group the Georgia Yellow Hammers, at the 1927 session.
Album: *The East Coast States, Vol. 2* (1968).

Beaman, Lottie

b. c.1900, possibly in Kansas City, Missouri, USA. Beaman was one of the first generation of female blues singers to record. Details of her life are sparse although it is known that her maiden name was Lottie Kimbrough before her marriage to William Beaman in the early 20s. She was billed as 'The Kansas City Butterball', having worked in its bars and taverns as a teenager. Between 1924 and 1929, she recorded in Kansas, Chicago and Richmond Indiana, sometimes in the company of her brother Sylvester Kimbrough or whistler/singer Winston Holmes. Although not possessing one of the greatest voices she was known and appreciated as a 'moaner' for the quality of despair that she could bring to her blues. Her work was also issued under the names Jennie Brooks, Lottie Brown, Clara Cary, Lottie Everson, Martha Johnson, Lena Kimbrough, Lottie Kimbrough and Mae Moran.

Album: *Lottie Beaman (Kimborough) 1924/26 And Louella Miller 1928* (1983).

Bell, Carey

b. Carey Bell Harrington, 14 November 1936, Macon, Mississippi, USA. Bell began to play harmonica after being inspired by the records of Muddy Waters, Little Walter, and Sonny Boy 'Rice Miller' Williams. Carey played with a white C&W band and with his 'stepfather', Lovie Lee. He moved to Chicago with Lee in the mid-50s, and besides picking up harmonica tips from Little Walter and Walter Horton, he also learned guitar from David 'Honeyboy' Edwards, although his main instrument throughout the 60s was bass guitar. He was recorded on Maxwell Street with Robert Nighthawk in 1964, and appeared on a Earl Hooker album in 1968. He quickly recorded his debut album for Delmark, and has appeared on record regularly since, both as leader and accompanist. He has lengthy spells with Muddy Waters and Willie Dixon, and in 1988 recorded what is claimed to be the world's first ever CD-only issue of a blues album. Bell is regarded as one of the leading blues harmonica players, and is also an underrated singer. He has encouraged many of his children to become blues musicians, with the best-known being Lurrie Bell.

Albums: *Carey Bell's Blues Harp* (1969), *Last Night* (1973), with Lurrie Bell *Son Of A Gun* (1984), *Straight Shoot* (1987), *Harpslinger* (1988), *Mellow Down Easy* (1991), with Lurrie Bell *Dynasty* (1990).

Bell, Edward 'Ed'

b. May, 1905, Forest Deposit, Alabama, USA. d. 1965. A guitarist who, it has recently been confirmed, also recorded as 'Barefoot Bill' and 'Sluefoot Joe' between 1927 and 1930. Bell stands as the most influential Alabama artist in pre-war blues recordings. With well over three-quarters of his material issued, Bell's 'Mamlish Blues' and 'Hambone Blues' were to define the style of the region and his contemporaries. His influences could still be detected in the 70s' recordings of fellow Alabamian, John Lee. The circumstances of Bell's death are shrouded in mystery but it is thought he died in the 60s during a civil right's march.

Albums: *Ed Bell's Mamlish Moan* (1983), *Barefoot Bill's Hard Luck Blues* (1984).

Bell, Jimmy

b. 29 August 1910, Peoria, Illinois, USA. d. 31 December 1987, Chicago, Illinois, USA. In high school, Bell learned guitar and piano, and boxed semi-professionally, before becoming a full-time musician in 1930. He worked as a jazz and swing band pianist in the midwest, picking up repertoire and stylistic influences from Roosevelt Sykes, Albert Ammons, Pete Johnson, Art Tatum and Earl Hines. After the war, Bell played sophisticated jump blues, influenced by the Nat 'King' Cole Trio, and made a few recordings. Gambling led to financial problems, and thence to crime, including dealing in heroin, for which he served prison terms in the 50s and 60s. In 1979 he received a six-year sentence for possession of forged food stamps. If not as original as he claimed, Bell remained a forceful and versatile musician in the 70s, playing cocktail music for a living, but still well in command of an eclectic blues, boogie and swing repertoire.

Album: *Stranger In Your Town* (1979).

Bell, Lurrie

b. 13 December 1958, Chicago, Illinois, USA. The second son of Carey Bell, Lurrie's musical interests were encouraged from an early age by his father and guitarist Roy Johnson. By the age of eight Bell was regularly called onstage for guest appearances. In his teens he joined Ko Ko Taylor's band as guitarist. In the 80s he established himself as both a respected bandleader and an in-demand session player, and he toured Europe frequently. He gave up music in 1986, but marked his return three years later with two well-received recordings for the JSP label. Lurrie's soulful, Little Milton-influenced singing and agile guitar playing mark him as a promising prospect.

Albums: *Everybody Wants To Win* (1989), with Carey Bell *Dynasty!* (1989).

Bell, T.D.

b. 26 December 1922, Lee County, Texas, USA. Bell did not take up blues guitar until his early twenties, after military service. Not surprisingly, the major influence on his style was 'T-Bone' Walker. His band was one of the major attractions of the Austin scene, and backed visiting artists at the Victory Grill, and on tour through west Texas, Arizona and New Mexico. Bell gave up playing in the early 70s when disco made live musicians uneconomic, but resumed in the late 80s in partnership with his longtime associate Erbie Bowser; they were still an impressive team.

Album: *It's About Time* (1992).

Bender, D C

b. 19 June 1919, Arbana, Texas, USA. Like JB Lenoir, D.C.'s initials held no other significance. Raised on a farm in Polk County, Texas, Bender was taught to play the guitar by local musician, Hardy Gibson. As a teenager, he took to the itinerant musician's life, working throughout East Texas and Louisiana. Later, in the 40s, he used Houston as his base, playing alongside his first cousin, Lightnin' Hopkins, Smokey Hogg, Wright Holmes and Luther Stoneham. He recorded for Bill Quinn's Gold Star label as D.C. Washington in 1948, and, five years later, accompanied Big Son Tillis on a session recorded in Los Angeles for J R Fullbright's Elko label. He didn't record again until he backed Mabel Franklin's Ritzy single in 1964. By then he'd joined drummer Ivory Lee Semien's band, with whom he recorded a version of 'Boogie Chillen' in 1967. His party piece was to drink a bottle of beer while singing and playing guitar. It is not known whether this was a factor in his reported death during the 80s.

Selected album: *Mr. Fullbright's Blues Vol. 2* (1990).

Bennett, Duster

b. Anthony Bennett, he was a British one-man-band blues performer, in the style of Jesse Fuller and Dr Ross. He played the London R&B club circuit from the mid-60s and was signed by Mike Vernon to Blue Horizon in 1967, releasing 'It's A Man Down There' as his first single. On his first album he was backed by Peter Green and John McVie of Fleetwood Mac. Bennett also played harmonica on sessions for Fleetwood Mac, Champion Jack Dupree, Memphis Slim, Shusha and Martha Velez. He was briefly a member of John Mayall's Bluesbreakers, and in 1974 recorded for Mickie Most's RAK label, releasing a single, 'Comin Home'. He was killed in a road accident in the 70s.

Albums: *Smiling Like I'm Happy* (1968), *Bright Lights* (1969), *12 DBs* (1970), *Fingertips* (1974).

Bennett, Wayne

A skillful blues guitarist, Bennett came to prominence in the mid-50s as a member of Otis Rush's Chicago-based band. From there he was picked by Joe Scott to join the touring and recording orchestra of Bobby 'Blue' Bland. With arrangements by Scott and scintillating solos by Bennett, Bland became the leading live attraction on the chitlin' circuit in the late 50s and early 60s. Bennett's playing also contributed to Bland's numerous hits of the era, such as 'I Pity The Fool' (1961) and 'Stormy Monday Blues' (1962). During this period, Bennett was also a session player for other Duke/Peacock artists such as Junior Parker and Gatemouth Brown. He left Bland's group in the late 60s and subsequently appeared on records by such blues artists as Buddy Guy, Fenton Robinson, Jimmy Reed and Jimmy Rogers. In 1981, Bennett was named Blues Guitarist of the Year by the National Blues Foundation and in the early 90s he was based in Louisiana performing with Willie Lockett and the Blues Krewe.

Bentley, Gladys Alberta

(aka: Fatso Bentley) b. 12 August 1907, Pennsylvania, USA; d. 18 January 1960, Los Angeles, California, USA. Blues singer, pianist and male impersonator, Bentley moved to New York City in her late teens to work at various Harlem nightspots, and was soon recording solo for OKeh Records and with the Washboard

Serenaders for RCA Victor. In the early 30s, she opened a nightspot, the Exclusive Club, and began arranging and directing her own shows, including the successful Ubangi Club Revue. In the early 40s, Bentley moved to California and started a fresh career as a blues shouter, recording in the style for small independents like, Excelsior, Flame, Top Hat and Swingtime. She was much in demand throughout the 50s until her death at home of pneumonia.

Albums: *Boogie Blues - Women Sing And Play Boogie Woogie* (1983, one track only), *Tough Mamas* (1989, one track only).

Benton, Buster

b. Arley Benton, 19 July 1932, Texarkana, Arkansas, USA. Benton sang in a gospel choir as a youngster, before moving in 1952 to Toledo, Ohio, where he began playing guitar and turned to the blues, influenced by Sam Cooke and B.B. King. Around the end of the 50s he settled in Chicago, where he led his own band and recorded for the Melloway, Twinight and Alteen labels. He owned the Stardust Lounge for some time in the early 70s but spent several years as guitarist with Willie Dixon. Benton had a hit for Jewel Records with 'Spider In My Stew' in the mid-70s, and recordings he made later for Ralph Bass were issued on several labels worldwide. In the 80s he recorded for Blue Phoenix, and despite some serious health problems he continues to perform, with his latest recordings available on Ichiban.

Album: *Bluesbuster* (1980).

Bernhardt, Clyde

(aka Ed Barron) b. 11 July 1905, Gold Hill, North Carolina, USA; d. 20 May 1986, Newark, New Jersey, USA. Trombonist Bernhardt paid the usual dues of the jazzman by playing in myriad small territory bands in the mid-west, before moving to New York City in 1928. In 1930, he hit the big time when he was hired by Joe 'King' Oliver to play and sing with his Harlem Syncopators; later with Vernon Andrade, Edgar Hayes (with whom he made his recording debut for Decca), Horace Henderson, Oran 'Hot Lips' Page, Stuff Smith, Fats Waller, Jay McShann, Cecil Scott, Luis Russell, Claude Hopkins and Dud Bascomb. After World War II, Bernhardt formed his own R&B jump combo. Bernhardt's strong feeling for the blues

made him a natural for the R&B scene and he led his own band the Blue Blazers, with whom he recorded in his own right for several small specialist labels between 1946-53, and also backed Wynonie Harris on his debut session for King Records. On these recordings, Bernhardt proved himself to be a talented blues singer in the Jimmy Rushing/Big Joe Turner mould (he once claimed he had been shouting the blues in this style since playing with King Oliver in 1930). From the mid-50s, apart from the occasional gig, Bernhardt worked mainly outside music but was rediscovered in 1968 when he was brought out of retirement to record for Saydisc Matchbox's Blues Series. He formed his own label in 1975 and began touring with his Harlem Blues & Jazz Band which remained hugely popular in Europe, even after Bernhardt's death.

Albums: *Blowin' My Top* (1968), *Blues And Jazz From Harlem* (1972), *More Blues And Jazz From Harlem, Sittin' On Top Of The World!* (1975), *Clyde Bernhardt And The Harlem Blues And Jazz Band* (1975), *Clyde Bernhardt And The Harlem Blues And Jazz Band At The 7th International Jazz Festival, Breda* (1977), *Clyde Bernhardt & The Harlem Blues Jazz Band* (1978), *More Blues & Jazz From Harlem* (1979).

Further reading: *I Remember: Eighty Years Of Black Entertainment, Big Bands And Blues*, Clyde E. B. Bernhardt, Sheldon Harris.

Berry, Richard

b. 11 April 1935, Extension, Louisiana, USA. Berry was brought to Los Angeles as an infant, where he learned piano, playing along with the records of Joe Liggins and his Honeydrippers. In high school he formed a vocal group and began recording in 1953 under various group names (the Hollywood Blue Jays/the Flairs/the Crowns/the Dreamers/the Pharaohs) as well as making solo sessions for Modern's Flair subsidiary. His most famous moments on wax are his earthy contributions to the Robins' 'Riot In Cell Block No.9' and as 'Henry', Etta James's boyfriend, on her early classic 'Roll With Me Henry (The Wallflower)'. Although his main claim to fame is as the composing credit for rock 'n' roll's famous standard 'Louie Louie' which he recorded in 1956 on Flip, but had to wait seven years for its acceptance with the Kingsmen's hit. The song spawned over 300 cover versions. During the 60s and 70s, Berry, inspired by Bobby 'Blue' Bland and his wife Dorothy (herself a recording artist), became a soul singer. He recorded for myriad west coast labels (including his debut album for Johnny Otis's Blues Spectrum label) and continues performing into the 90s.

Albums: Richard Berry & The Dreamers (1963), *Live At The Century Club* (60s), *Wild Berry* (60s), *Great Rhythm & Blues Oldies* (1977), *Get Out Of The Car* (1982), *Louie, Louie* (1986).

Bigeou, Esther

b. c. 1895, New Orleans, Louisiana, USA, d. c. 1935, New Orleans, Louisiana, USA. The light-voiced Esther Bigeou performed and danced in black revues from 1917 to 1930, recording 17 songs for OKeh Records between 1921-23. They are all blues, composed by black Tin Pan Alley writers such as W.C. Handy, Richard M. Jones and Clarence Williams, backed by piano or small jazz bands, and typical of the material offered to black theatre audiences of the day. It has not been possible to reconcile a report that she recorded after 1943 with her alleged date of death being 1935.

Compilation: *Esther Bigeau* (c.90).

Big Maceo

b. Major Meriweather, 31 March 1905, Atlanta, Georgia, USA, d. 26 February 1953, Chicago, Illinois, USA. Big Maceo learned piano while living in a suburb of Atlanta, in his early teens. In 1924 he moved to Detroit where he made his name on the local blues scene. In the early 40s, he made a series of classic recordings with the Chicago guitarist Tampa Red. Maceo's piano lends a distinctive toughness and weight to Tampa's records, while the guitarist complements the other's superb sides with his supple and beautifully expressive slide lines. Maceo's 'Worried Life' was a big hit, and has become one of the most covered of all blues songs, while most of the other tracks he recorded for the Bluebird/Victor company are of comparable quality. These include the achingly plaintive 'Poor Kelly Blues' to powerful instrumental pieces such as 'Chicago Breakdown'. In 1946, he suffered a stroke, and while he made several more records, few of them recaptured the glories of his earlier work.

Compilations: *King Of Chicago Blues Piano, Vols 1 & 2* (1984 - both volumes reissued together on cassette, *Big Maceo*).

Big Maybelle

b. Mabel Louise Smith, 1 May c.1920, Jackson, Tennessee, USA, d. 23 January 1972. Maybelle was discovered singing in church by Memphis bandleader Dave Clark in 1935. When Clark disbanded his orchestra to concentrate on record promotion, Smith moved to Christine Chatman's orchestra with whom she first recorded for Decca in 1944. Three years later, Smith made solo records for King and in 1952 she recorded as Big Maybelle when producer Fred Mendelsohn signed her to OKeh, a subsidiary of CBS. Her blues shouting style (a female counterpart to Big Joe Turner) brought an R&B hit the next year with 'Gabbin' Blues' (a cleaned-up version of the 'dirty dozens' on which she was partnered by songwriter Rose Marie McCoy). 'Way Back Home' and 'My Country Man' were also best sellers. In 1955, she made the first recording of 'Whole Lotta Shakin' Goin' On', which later became a major hit for Jerry Lee Lewis. Big Maybelle was also a star attraction on the chitlin' circuit of black clubs, with an act that included risque comedy as well as emotive ballads and brisk boogies. Leaving OKeh, she next recorded for Savoy where in 1956 'Candy' brought more success. Two years later she appeared in *Jazz On A Summer's Day*, the film of that year's Newport Jazz Festival. Despite her acknowledged influence on the soul styles of the 60s, later records for Brunswick, Scepter and Chess made little impact until she signed to the Rojac label in 1966. There she was persuaded to cut some recent pop hits by the Beatles and Donovan and had some minor chart success of her own with versions of 'Don't Pass Me By' and '96 Tears'. The latter was composed by Rudy Martinez who also recorded it with his band ? & the Mysterians. Maybelle's career was marred by frequent drug problems which contributed to her early death in Cleveland Ohio in January 1972.

Albums: *Big Maybelle Sings* (1958), *Blues, Candy And Big Maybelle* (1958), *What More Can A Woman Do?* (1962), *The Soul Of Big Maybelle* (1964), *Great Soul Hits* (1964), *Got A Brand New Bag* (1967), *The Gospel Soul Of Big Maybelle* (1968), *The Last Of* (1973). Compilations: *The*

OKeh Sessions (1983), *Roots Of R&R And Early Soul* (1985).

Big Town Playboys

Often cited as 'the best R&B revival band in Britain', the Playboys were inspired by the increasing interest in R&B which occurred in the late 70s. Originally from the west Midlands, their popularity has survived personnel changes, although pianist/vocalist Mike Sanchez, whose style is clearly based on that of Amos Milburn, is the obvious frontman. Ex-Savoy Brown and Chicken Shack bassist Andy Sylvester and former leader Ricky Cool are also important figures in the band's history, though the latter left in the 80s. With a large repertoire of 50s R&B songs, a swinging rhythm section and excellent horns, the band are often called on to back visiting Americans, including Little Willie Littlefield, Jimmy Nelson, and Champion Jack Dupree (they recorded with the latter in 1989).
Albums: *Playboy Boogie* (1985), *Now Appearing* (1990).

Big Twist And The Mellow Fellow

Big Twist (b. Larry Nolan, 1937, Terra Haute, Indiana, USA, d. 14 March 1990, Broadview, Illinois, USA) was the lead singer and leader of this R&B big band. He began singing in church in southern Illinois when he was six years old, and in the 50s was drummer and vocalist with the Mellow Fellows, an R&B group. In the early 70s he teamed up with guitarist Pete Special and tenor saxophonist Terry Ogolini, and the group has albums released by Flying Fish and Alligator. Their work revealed an approach and breadth of repertoire (including blues, R&B and soul) that was ahead of its time. Big Twist died of a heart attack in March 1990, but the group continued, fronted by singer Martin Allbritton from Carbondale, Illinois, and saxophonist producer Gene Barge also on vocals.
Albums: *Big Twist And The Mellow Fellows* (1980), *One Track Mind* (1982), *Live From Chicago - Bigger Than Life* (1987), with Big Twist, *Playing For Keeps* (1983), with Martin Allbritton *Street Party* (1990).

Bihari, Lester, Jules, Saul And Joe

The Bihari family moved in 1941 from Oklahoma to Los Angeles where eldest brother Jules went into business as a supplier and operator of juke-boxes to the black community. The next step was to ensure the supply of suitable blues and R&B recordings to feed the juke-boxes and with Joe and Saul, he founded the Modern Music Company in 1945. As well as recording west coast artists such as Jimmy Witherspoon and Johnny Moore's Three Blazers, the brothers worked with local producers in Houston, Detroit and Memphis who supplied Modern with more rough-hewn blues material by such artists as Lightnin' Hopkins, John Lee Hooker and B.B. King. In 1951, the fourth brother, Lester, set up the Meteor label in Memphis. Meteor was responsible for some of Elmore James' earliest records as well as rockabilly by Charlie Feathers. Other Modern group labels included RPM, (for which Ike Turner produced Howlin' Wolf), Blues & Rhythm and Flair. During the early 50s, the Bihari brothers released a wide range of material, even aiming at the pop charts by covering R&B titles from other labels. Among its successes were Etta James' 'Wallflower', 'Stranded In The Jungle' by the Cadets, 'Eddie My Love' by the Teen Queens and Jessie Belvin's 'Goodnight My Love'. The arranger/producer of many Modern tracks was Maxwell Davis.

However, by the late 50s, the Modern group turned its attention towards reissuing material on the Crown budget-price label which also included a series of big-band tribute albums masterminded by Davis. After the company got into financial difficulties the Biharis released recordings by Z.Z. Hill, Lowell Fulson and B.B. King on the Kent label. But the death of Saul Bihari in 1975 and Joe's departure from the company led to a virtual cessation of recording as the remaining brothers concentrated on custom pressing at their vinyl record plant. In 1984, the year of Jules Bihari's death, the family sold the catalogues of Modern, Flair, Kent, Crown and RPM. Seven years later, the labels passed into the hands of a consortium of Virgin Records (US), Ace (Europe) and Blues Interactions (Japan). These companies continued an extensive reissue programme which the Ace label had initiated as licensee of the Modern group in the early 80s.

Bishop, Elvin

b. 21 October 1942, Tulsa, Oklahoma, USA.

Bishop moved to Chicago in his teens to study at university. An aspiring guitarist, he became one of several young, white musicians to frequent the city's blues clubs and in 1965 he joined the houseband at one such establishment, Big John's. This group subsequently became known as the Paul Butterfield Blues Band, and although initially overshadowed by guitarist Michael Bloomfield, it was here Bishop evolved a distinctive, if composite style. Elvin was featured on four Butterfield albums, but he left the group in 1968 following the release of *In My Own Dream*. By the following year he was domiciled in San Francisco, where his own group became a popular live fixture. Bishop was initially signed to Bill Graham's Fillmore label, but these and other early recordings achieved only local success.

In 1974, Dickie Betts of the Allman Brothers Band introduced the guitarist to Capricorn Records which favoured the hippie/hillbilly image Elvin had fostered and understood his melange of R&B, soul and country influences. Six albums followed, including *Let It Flow, Juke Joint Jump* and a live album set, *Live! Raisin' Hell*, but it was a 1975 release, *Struttin' My Stuff*, which proved most popular. It included the memorable 'Fooled Around And Fell In Love' which, when issued as a single, reached number 3 in the US chart. The featured voice was that of Mickey Thomas, who later left the group for a solo career and subsequently became frontman of Jefferson Starship. The loss of this powerful singer undermined Bishop's momentum and his new-found ascendancy proved short-lived. Elvin's career suffered a further setback in 1979 when Capricorn filed for bankruptcy. Although he remains a much-loved figure in the Bay Area live circuit, the guitarist's recorded output has been thin on the ground during the last ten years, most recently on the Alligator label, with Dr. John on *Big Fun*.

Albums: *The Elvin Bishop Group* (1969), *Feel It* (1970), *Rock My Soul* (1972), *Let It Flow* (1974), *Juke Joint Jump* (1975), *Struttin' My Stuff* (1975), *Hometown Boy Makes Good!* (1976), *Live! Raisin' Hell* (1977), *Hog Heaven* (1978), *Is You Is Or Is You Ain't My Baby* (1982), *Big Fun* (1988).

Black, James

b. 1 February 1940, New Orleans, Louisiana, USA, d. 30 August 1988. Born into a musical family, Black studied music at Southern University, Baton Rouge, and also drummed in the quintessential training ground for New Orleans rhythm, a marching band. His first professional break came with an R&B outfit in 1958. He replaced Ed Blackwell in Ellis Marsalis's band when Blackwell left to join Ornette Coleman in California. In the early 60s he relocated to New York with R&B singer Joe Jones and toured with Lionel Hampton. It is him playing drums on the Dixie Cups' 'Chapel Of Love'. He played and recorded with Cannonball Adderley, Yusef Lateef and Horace Silver. If Black had not subsequently returned to New Orleans (working with artists including Professor Longhair, the Meters, Fats Domino and Lee Dorsey) his unerring beat - funky but free - would have made him a big name in jazz.

Albums: *The Adderley Brothers In New Orleans* (1962), with Yusef Lateef *Live At Pep's* (1964).

Black Ace

b. Babe Kyro Lemon Turner, 21 December 1907, Hughes Springs, Texas, USA, d. 7 November 1972, Fort Worth, Texas, USA. Black Ace was a blues guitarist from childhood, but his mature style developed after he moved to Shreveport in the mid-30s and met Oscar Woods. In 1937 he recorded six superb blues for Decca, singing in his deep voice and playing fluent, complex slide guitar, his steel bodied instrument held across his lap and fretted with a small bottle. Ace was a frequent broadcaster on local radio, and made an appearance in the 1941 film *Blood Of Jesus,* but after Army service from 1943, he largely abandoned music; when found in 1960, however, he had retained all his abilities, and recorded a splendid album.

Album: *Black Ace* (1961). Compilation: *Texas In The Thirties* (1988).

Black Bob

This pianist was an accompanist on hundreds of blues records in the 30s, mainly for Bluebird, backing Big Bill Broonzy, Jazz Gillum, Tampa Red, Lil Johnson, Washboard Sam and many others. His identity was the subject of years of speculation, for it seemed absurd that the possessor of a prodigious stride and blues technique should be completely anonymous. Circumstantial evidence suggested that his true name as Bob Alexander, but his immediately

Elvin Bishop

recognizable style, percussive yet sparkling and melodious, is very similar to that on an unissued test by Bob Hudson, and Memphis Slim, asked if he had known a Bob Hudson, replied, 'Yeah. We called him Black Bob.'

Black Boy Shine

b. Harold Holiday, he was one of what has come to be known as the 'Santa Fe' school of pianists, a loose group of blues artists who played the barrelhouses of south-east Texas in the pre-war years. He recorded in the mid-30s, for the Vocalion label, demonstrating a warm singing voice, complemented by a light, rolling, but nevertheless highly skillful piano style, and the lyrics of his songs, like 'Brown House Blues', described very evocatively the places he travelled to and played in. As well as recording on his own, he shared one session with fellow Texans Howlin' Smith and Moanin' Bernice Edwards, although only a few tracks featuring their combined talents were issued.
Album: *Black Shine Boy* (1989).

Black Cat Bones

The original line-up of this London-based blues band included Paul Kossoff (guitar), Stuart Brooks (bass) and Simon Kirke (drums). Producer Mike Vernon invited the group to back pianist Champion Jack Dupree on his 1968 release, *When You Feel The Feeling*, and attendant live appearances, but momentum faltered when Kossoff and Kirke left to form Free. A restructured Black Cat Bones - Brian Short (vocals), Derek Brooks (guitar), Rod Price (guitar, vocals) and Phil Lenoir (drums) - joined Stuart Brooks for *Barbed Wire Sandwich*, but the revised unit failed to capture the fire of its predecessor.
Album: *Barbed Wire Sandwich* (1970).

Black Ivory King

b. David Alexander. A four track recording session in Dallas, Texas in 1937 revealed a reflective pianist and singer, with a simple, direct style related to that of the 'Santa Fe' school which included Conish 'Pinetop' Burkes and Black Boy Shine. His version appears to be the original of the classic Texas train blues 'Flying Crow', which turns into poetry the timetable of a journey from Port Arthur to Kansas City. Even a topical updating of 'Red Cross Store

Blues' into 'Working For The PWA' has a wistful lyricism.
Albums: *The Piano Blues Vol. 11*, *Texas Santa Fe* (1979), *Texas Piano Styles* (1989).

Blackwell, Francis Hillman 'Scrapper'

b. 21 February 1903, North Carolina, USA, d. 7 October 1962, Indianapolis, Indiana. Blackwell was one of the most brilliantly innovative guitarists to work in the blues idiom and his unique style defies categorization, being of a quality close to jazz. He was of Cherokee Indian descent and one of 16 children born to Payton and Elizabeth Blackwell. The details of his childhood are confused but it is known that he was taken to Indianapolis sometime in 1906, where he grew up inheriting his father's interest in music (Payton was a fiddler). Self-taught on guitar and piano he began to work as a part-time musician during his teenage years, sometimes straying as far as Chicago but always returning to Indianapolis. In the course of his career he recorded many satisfying and impressive blues guitar solos under his own name, but gained his greatest fame in the company of Leroy Carr. Their piano/guitar duets in support of Carr's warm vocals set the standard for all such combinations throughout the 30s. Scrapper is reported to have been a somewhat difficult and withdrawn man, and his partnership with Carr was sometimes rocky. However, on Carr's death from alcoholism in 1935, Blackwell recorded a tribute to his 'old pal' and largely dropped out of sight. Rediscovered in the late 50s, he recorded again and it was discovered that his mastery of the guitar had not totally diminished, while his blues had become more personal and intense. He was shot by an unknown assassin in 1962.
Compilation: *The Virtuoso Guitar Of Scrapper Blackwell* (1971).

Blackwell, Willie '61'

b. c.1898. Blackwell spent much of his life in Memphis, where he still resided as late as the 70s. Among his early associates were Calvin Frazier (who was reputedly his nephew), stepson Robert Jnr. Lockwood and Robert Johnson. Another musician with whom Blackwell worked in Detroit was Baby Boy Warren. Blackwell was not a particularly inventive musician, but his circle paid keen attention to his original lyrics, and the eight songs he

recorded for Bluebird in 1941, (together with two cut for the Library of Congress the following year), are the work of one of the most inventive lyricists in blues. No other singer reflects that hitching a ride would be easier if he knew Masonic hailing signs, or sees World War II as a chance to send his baby son 'a Jap's tooth' to help ease the process of teething! Blackwell was a truly eccentric, a one-of-a-kind artist.
Albums: *Walking Blues* (1979), *Mississippi Country Blues Vol. 2* (1987).

Blanchard, Edgar

A guitarist and bandleader, Blanchard was a permanent feature of the New Orleans music scene from the 40s to the 60s. By 1947 he was in charge of the resident band at the Down Beat Club on Rampart Street with Roy Brown as one of the vocalists. Blanchard's most well-known band was the Gondoliers. An early version had a two-guitar line-up with Ernest McLean, while in the 60s, the group included Dimes Dupont (alto saxophone), Alonzo Stewart (drums), Frank Fields (bass) and Lawrence Cotton (piano). The band was renowned for its stylistic versatility. Although he frequently played on sessions, Blanchard seldom recorded under his own name. There were singles for Peacock in 1949 and instrumentals for Specialty in the late 50s, including 'Mr Bumps', a tribute to the label's head of A&R, Robert 'Bumps' Blackwell, on which Blanchard duetted with guitarist Roy Montrell. In 1959 he recorded 'Knocked Out' for Johnny Vincent's Ric label, of which he was briefly musical director. His final records were somewhat uncharacteristic raucous blues tracks like 'Tight Like That'. Made for Joe Banashak's Minit label in the late 60s, they remained unissued until after Blanchard's death in September 1972.

Bland, Billy

b. 5 April 1932, Wilmington, North Carolina, USA. Billy Bland was an R&B singer whose best-known recording was the 1960 US Top 10 hit 'Let The Little Girl Dance'. Bland, the youngest of 19 children, began his career in 1947 in New York City, where he performed in the bands of Lionel Hampton and Buddy Johnson before starting his own group, the Four Bees. He was brought to New Orleans by producer Dave Bartholomew in 1954 and sang

on a single for Imperial Records, 'Toy Bell'. Bland signed to Old Town Records in 1955 and recorded singles that were hits regionally, such as 'Chicken In The Basket' and 'Chicken Hop'. He recorded the bouncy 'Let The Little Girl Dance' in late 1959, also for Old Town, and it reached the charts in early 1960, eventually climbing to number 7. Bland put three further singles in the pop charts but never repeated that record's success. He retired in the 70s. No albums were recorded.

Bland, Bobby 'Blue'

b. Robert Calvin Bland, 27 January 1930, Rosemark, Tennessee, USA. Having moved to Memphis with his mother, Bland started singing with local gospel groups there, including amongst others the Miniatures. Eager to expand his interests, he began frequenting the city's infamous Beale Street where he became associated with an *ad hoc* circle of aspiring musicians named, not unnaturally, the Beale Streeters. Bobby's recordings from the early 50s show him striving for individuality, but any progress was halted by a spell in the US Army. When the singer returned to Memphis in 1954 he found several of his former associates, including Johnny Ace, enjoying considerable success, while Bland's recording label, Duke, had been sold to Houston entrepreneur Don Robey. In 1956 Bland began touring with 'Little' Junior Parker. Initially he doubled as valet and driver, a role he reportedly fulfilled for B.B. King, but simultaneously began asserting his characteristic vocal style. Melodic big-band blues singles, including 'Farther Up The Road' (1957) and 'Little Boy Blue' (1958) reached the US R&B Top 10, but Bobby's craft was most clearly heard on a series of superb early 60s releases including 'Cry Cry Cry', 'I Pity The Fool' and the sparkling 'Turn On Your Lovelight', which was destined to become a much-covered standard. Despite credits to the contrary, many such classic works were written by Joe Scott, the artist's bandleader and arranger. Bland continued to enjoy a consistent run of R&B chart entries throughout the mid-60s but his recorded work was nonetheless eclipsed by a younger generation of performers. Financial pressures forced the singer to cut his touring band and in 1968 the group broke up altogether. His relationship with Scott, who died

Bobby 'Blue' Bland

in 1979, was irrevocably severed. Nonetheless, depressed and increasingly dependent on alcohol, Bland weathered this unhappy period. He stopped drinking in 1971; his record company, Duke, was sold to the larger ABC Records group, resulting in several contemporary blues/soul albums including *His California Album* and *Dreamer*. Subsequent attempts at pushing the artist towards the disco market were unsuccessful but a 1983 release, *Here We Go Again*, provided a commercial life-line. Two years later Bland was signed by Malaco Records, specialists in traditional southern black music, who provided an empathetic environment. One of the finest singers in post-war blues, Bobby Bland has sadly failed to reach the popular acclaim his influence and craft perhaps deserves.

Albums: with 'Little' Junior Parker *Blues Consolidated* (1958), with Parker *Barefoot Rock And You Got Me* (1960), *Two Steps From The Blues* (1961), *Here's The Man* (1962), *Call On Me* (1963), *Ain't Nothin' You Can Do* (1964), *The Soul Of The Man* (1966), *Touch Of The Blues* (1967), *Spotlighting The Man* (1968), *His California Album* (1973), *Dreamer* (1974), with B.B. King *Together For The First Time - Live* (1974), with King *Together Again - Live* (1976), *Get On Down* (1975), *Reflections In Blue* (1977), *Come Fly With Me* (1978), *I Feel Good I Feel Fine* (1979), *Sweet Vibrations* (1980), *You Got Me Loving You* (1981), *Try Me, I'm Real* (1981), *Here We Go Again* (1982), *Tell Mr. Bland* (1983), *Members Only* (1985), *After All* (1986), *Blues You Can Use* (1987), *Portrait Of The Blues* (1992). Compilations: *Woke Up Screaming* (1981), *The Best Of Bobby Bland* (1982), *Foolin' With The Blues* (1983), *Blues In The Night* (1985), *The Soulful Side Of Bobby Bland* (1986), *Soul With A Flavour 1959-1984* (1988).

Blasters

Formed in Los Angeles, California, USA, in 1979, the Blasters were one of the leading proponents of the so-called US 'roots-rock' revival of the 80s. Originally comprised of Phil Alvin (vocals), his songwriter brother Dave (guitar), John Bazz (bass) and Bill Bateman (drums), the group's first album in 1980 was *American Music* on the small Rollin' Rock label. Incorporating rockabilly, R&B, country and blues, the album was critically applauded for

both Dave Alvin's songwriting and the band's ability to update the age-old styles without slavishly re-creating them. With a switch to the higher-profile Slash label in 1981, the group released a self-titled album which was also well-received. Pianist Gene Taylor was added to the group and 50s saxophonist Lee Allen guested (and later toured with the group). With Slash picking up distribution from Warner Brothers the album reached the Top 40, due largely to positive press reports. (Three later albums would chart at lower positions.) A live EP recorded in London followed in 1982 but it was the following year's *Non Fiction*, a thematic study of the working class that critics likened to Bruce Springsteen and Tom T. Hall, which earned the band its greatest acclaim so far. By this time saxophonist Steve Berlin had also joined the fold.

Berlin had joined Los Lobos when *Hard Line*, was issued in 1985. The album included a song by John Cougar Mellencamp and guest backing vocals by the Jordanaires. Dave Alvin departed the group upon its completion to join X and was replaced by Michael 'Hollywood Fats' Mann, who died of a heart attack at the age of 32 while a member of the band. Phil Alvin and Steve Berlin kept a version of the group together until 1987 at which point it folded. Both Alvin brothers have recorded solo albums and worked on other projects.

Albums: *American Music* (1980), *The Blasters* (1981), *Non Fiction* (1983), *Hard Line* (1985). Solo albums: Phil Alvin *Unsung Stories* (1986); Dave Alvin *Romeo's Escape* (UK title *Every Night About This Time*) (1987).

Blind Blake

b. Arthur Blake (or possibly Phelps), 1890s, Jacksonville Florida, USA d. c.1933. One of the very finest of pre-war blues guitarists, Blind Blake is nevertheless a very obscure figure. Almost nothing is known of his early years, but it is reputed that he moved around the east coast states of the USA, as various musicians have recalled meeting him in a number of different locations. It seems likely, however, that he settled in Chicago sometime in the 20s, and it was there that he first recorded for Paramount Records in 1926. Along with Blind Lemon Jefferson he was one of the first black guitarist to make a commercially successful record.

Blues Brothers

Following his first hit, the ragtime guitar solo 'West Coast Blues' he recorded regularly, producing about 80 issued tracks.

It has been argued that Blake should not be described as a blues artist, and indeed his songs range from straight blues, through older traditional-style items like 'Georgia Bound' to vaudeville numbers like 'He's In The Jailhouse Now'. Whatever the idiom, his accompaniment was always a model of taste, skill and creative imagination - his notes cleanly picked and ringing: his rhythms steady. His musical talents are perhaps given fullest rein on the stunningly dextrous ragtime solos such as 'Southern Rag' and 'Blind Arthur's Breakdown'. Further superb Blake accompaniments can be heard on the records of other artists such as Ma Rainey and Irene Scruggs, and there is one very memorable duet with Charlie Spand, 'Hastings Street'. As well as his many solo records, he occasionally appeared with a small band. It is likely that he died soon after the demise of Paramount Records in the early 30s, but his influence lived on in the work of eastern artists such as Blind Boy Fuller and others.

Albums: *Ragtime Guitar's Foremost Fingerpicker* (1984), *1926-1929 - The Remaining Titles* (1985).

Bloomfield, Mike

b. 28 July 1944, Chicago, Illinois, USA, d. 15 February 1981. For many, both critics and fans, Bloomfield was the finest white blues guitarist America has so far produced. He first picked up the instrument at the age of 13, developing an interest in the blues from records by John Lee Hooker and Lightnin' Hopkins. After attending Chicago blues and R&B clubs, by the late 50s he had begun to sit in on sessions. Among his most frequent collaborators was Big Joe Williams, while venues included the small coffee house, the Fickle Pickle, which he owned. This allowed him to spend much of the early 60s honing his technique as back up to artists including Bob Dylan, John Hammond Jnr. and Peter, Paul And Mary.

Although signed to Columbia Records in 1964 as the Group (with Charlie Musslewhite and Nick Gravenites) it was his emergence in 1965 as the young, shy guitarist in the Paul Butterfield Blues Band that bought him to public attention.

He astonished those viewers who had watched black blues guitarists spend a lifetime, and still not play with as much fluidity and feeling as Bloomfield. That same year he was an important part of musical history, when folk purists accused Dylan of committing artistic suicide at the Newport Folk Festival. It was Bloomfield who was his electric lead guitarist, and it would be Bloomfield behind the electric guitar on Dylan's 60s masterpieces, *Highway 61 Revisited* and 'Like A Rolling Stone'.

On leaving Butterfield in 1967 he immediately formed the seminal Electric Flag, although he had departed by the time the first album had begun to slide down the US charts. His 1968 album *Super Session* with Stephen Stills and Al Kooper became his biggest selling record. It led to a short but financially lucrative career with Kooper. The track 'Stop' on the album epitomized Bloomfield's style; clean, crisp, sparse and emotional. The long sustained notes were produced by bending the string with his fingers underneath the other strings so as not to affect the tuning.

It was five years before his next satisfying work appeared, *Triumvirate,* with John Paul Hammond and Dr. John (Mac Rebennack). And so the pattern of Bloomfield's career began, no sooner had he become a star; than he became a recluse. Subsequent albums were distributed on small labels and did not gain national distribution. Plagued with a long-standing drug habit he occasionally supplemented his income by scoring music for pornographic movies. He also wrote three film music soundtracks, *The Trip* (1967), *Medium Cool* (1969) and *Steelyard Blues* (1973). Additionally he taught music at Stanford University in San Francisco, wrote advertising jingles and was an adviser to *Guitar Player* magazine.

Bloomfield avoided the limelight, possibly because of his away-from-home insomnia, which hampered his touring, but mainly because of his intelligent perception of what he felt an audience wanted from him; 'Playing in front of strangers leads to idolatry, and idolatry is dangerous because the audience has a preconception of you, even though you cannot get a conception of them'. In 1975 he was cajoled into forming the 'supergroup' KGB with Rick Grech, Barry Goldberg and Carmine

Mike Bloomfield

Appice. Predictably the whole affair was anathema to him and the album was an unmitigated disaster. Bloomfield then resorted to playing mostly acoustic music and had an extraordinarily prolific year when in 1977 he released five albums, the most notable being the critically acclaimed *If You Love These Blues, Play 'Em As You Please*, released through *Guitar Player* magazine. A second burst of activity occurred shortly before his tragic death when another three album's worth of material was recorded. Bloomfield was found dead in his car from a suspected accidental drug overdose, a sad end to a 'star' who had constantly avoided stardom in order to maintain his own integrity.
Albums: *Super Session* (1968), *The Live Adventures Of Mike Bloomfield And Al Kooper* (1969), *Fathers And Sons* (1969), with Barry Goldberg *Two Jews Blues* (1969), *It's Not Killing Me* (1969), with others *Live At Bill Graham's Fillmore West* (1969), *Triumvirate* (1973), *Try It Before You Buy It* (1975), *Bloomfield/Naftalin* (1976), *Mill Valley Session* (1976), *There's Always Another Record* (1976), *I'm Always With You* (1977), *If You Love These Blues, Play 'Em As You Please* (1977), *Analine* (1977), *Michael Bloomfield* (1977), *Count Talent And The Originals* (1977), *Mike Bloomfield And Woody Harris* (1979), *Between The Hard Place And The Ground* (1980), *Livin' In The Fast Lane* (1980), *Gosport Duets* (1981), *Red Hot And Blues* (1981), *Cruisin' For A Bruisin'* (1981), *Retrospective* (1984), *Junco Partners* (1984), as KGB *KGB* (1976).
Further reading: *The Rise And Fall Of An American Guitar Hero*, Ed Ward.

Blue, 'Little' Joe

b. Joseph Valery, 23 September 1934, Vicksburg, Mississippi, USA, d. 22 April 1990. Brought up in Tallulah, Louisiana, Joe moved to Detroit in 1951, obtaining work in the car plants. He was drafted into the army in 1954 and served two-and-a-half years in Korea. On his return, having always been attentive to the blues, Joe moved into the music business. He had many singles released on a variety of labels but made his first real impression when 'Dirty Work Going On' was released on Chess in 1966. Subsequently he had albums issued on the Jewel and Space labels before his final two albums appeared on Evejim. 'Dirty Work Going On' was particularly well received. Often judged, unfairly, to be a B.B. King imitator Joe Blue stuck closer to the basics than did his model, and many felt that he pointed out the way B.B. should have gone. Throughout his career on record he made a habit of re-recording certain numbers as if convinced that he could always improve them. He toured constantly, until just days before his death from cancer.
Albums: *Blue's Blues* (1987), *Dirty Work Going On* (1987).

Blue Horizon Records

Britain's most important independent R&B company, Blue Horizon was founded by Mike Vernon, who issued 100 albums during its five-year history.
From 1964-66, Vernon ran the magazine *R&B Monthly* while working at Decca Records, where he produced records by John Mayall and Champion Jack Dupree. His first independent releases were limited-edition singles on Purdah by Savoy Brown, T.S. McPhee (see Groundhogs), Jo-Ann Kelly and Mayall with Eric Clapton. Vernon also set up Outasite to release singles by mainly American artists. Blue Horizon was launched in 1967, with distribution through CBS. As well as issuing US blues material (Otis Rush, Elmore James and B.B. King), Vernon signed the best of the British R&B scene. There were releases by Chicken Shack, Duster Bennett, Top Topham and Jellybread but by far the most successful was Fleetwood Mac, whose 'Albatross' reached number 1 in Britain. After Fleetwood Mac switched labels, Vernon moved Blue Horizon to Polydor where the most successful act was Dutch rock group Focus. After the Polydor agreement had expired, Vernon closed down the label to concentrate on a career as a producer, creating hits with Focus, Olympic Runners, Bloodstone and Dexy's Midnight Runners. Blue Horizon was revived in 1988 for releases by De Luxe Blues Band, Dana Gillespie, Lazy Lester and Ray Gelato's Giants Of Jive.

Blues Band

This vastly experienced British blues-rock outfit was put together - initially 'just for fun' - in 1979 by former Manfred Mann band colleagues Paul Jones (b. Paul Pond, 24 February 1942, Portsmouth, England; vocals/harmonica) and Tom McGuinness (b. 2 December 1941,

Blues Band

London, England; guitar). They brought in slide guitarist and singer Dave Kelly (ex-John Dummer Band, Rocksalt) (b. 1948, London, England), who suggested the bass player from his then-current band Wildcats, Gary Fletcher (b. London, England). On drums was McGuinness's hit-making partner from the early 70s, Hughie Flint (b. 15 March 1942, Manchester, England). Such a confluence of name players brought immediate success on the pub/club/college circuit and, despite the group's humble intentions, recordings followed. *The Official Blues Band Bootleg Album* was literally just that; inability to pay studio bills had forced them to press copies privately from a second copy tape. It sold extremely well, however, and Arista soon stepped in, releasing the master recording and putting out four further albums by 1983. The band had split in 1982, but reformed three years later after a one-off charity performance. Recent releases have placed far more emphasis on original material and auger well for the future. Ex-Family drummer Rob Townsend (b. 7 July 1947, Leicester, England) replaced Flint in 1981. Albums: *The Official Blues Band Bootleg Album* (1980), *Ready* (1980), *Itchy Feet* (1981), *Brand Loyalty* (1982), *Bye Bye Blues* (1983), *These Kind Of Blues* (1986), *Back For More* (1990), *Fat City* (1991).

Blues Brothers

Formed in 1978, this US group was centred on comedians John Belushi (b. 24 January 1949, Chicago, Illinois, USA. d. 5 March 1982, Los Angeles, California, USA) and Dan Aykroyd (1 July 1952, Ottawa, Ontario, Canada). Renowned for contributions to the satirical *National Lampoon* team and television's *Saturday Night Live*, the duo formed this 60s-soul styled revue as a riposte to disco. Taking the epithets Joliet 'Jake' Blues (Belushi) and Elwood Blues (Aykroyd), they embarked on live appearances with the assistance of a crack backing group, which included Steve Cropper (guitar), Donald 'Duck' Dunn (bass) and Tom Scott (saxophone). *Briefcase Full Of Blues* topped the US charts, a success which in turn inspired the film *The Blues Brothers* (1980). Although reviled by several music critics, there was no denying the refreshing enthusiasm the participants brought to R&B and the venture has since acquired a cult status. An affectionate, if anarchic, tribute to soul and R&B, it featured cameo appearances by Aretha Franklin, Ray Charles, John Lee Hooker and James Brown. Belushi's death from a drug overdose in 1982 brought the original concept to a premature end, since when Aykroyd has continued a successful acting career, notably in *Ghostbusters*. However, several of the musicians, including Cropper and Dunn, later toured and recorded as the Blues Brothers Band. The original Blues Brothers have also inspired numerous copy-cat/tribute groups who still attract sizeable audiences, over 10 years after the film's release. In August 1991, interest in the concept was again boosted with a revival theatre production in London's West End.

Albums: *Briefcase Full Of Blues* (1978), *The Blues Brothers* (1980, film soundtrack), *Made In America* (1980), as the Blues Brothers Band *The Blues Brothers Band Live* (1990). Compilation: *The Best Of The Blues Brothers* (1981).

Blues Project

The Blues Project was formed in New York City in the mid-60s by guitarist Danny Kalb and took its name from a compendium of acoustic musicians on which he participated. Tommy Flanders (vocals), Steve Katz (guitar), Andy Kulberg (bass, flute), Roy Blumenfeld (drums), plus Kalb, were latterly joined by Al Kooper, fresh from adding the distinctive organ on Bob Dylan's 'Like A Rolling Stone'. The quintet was quickly established as the city's leading electric blues band, a prowess heard on their debut album *Live At the Cafe Au Go Go*. Flanders then left for a solo career and the resultant four-piece embarked on the definitive *Projections* album. Jazz, pop and soul styles were added to their basic grasp of R&B to create an absorbing, rewarding collection, but inner tensions undermined an obvious potential. By the time *Live At The Town Hall* was issued, Kooper had left the group to form Blood, Sweat And Tears, where he was subsequently joined by Katz. An unhappy Kalb also quit the group, but Kulberg and Blumenfeld added Richard Greene (violin), John Gregory (guitar/vocals) and Don Kretmar (bass/saxophone) for a fourth collection, *Planned Obselescence*. The line-up owed little to the old group, and in deference to this new direction, changed their name to Sea Train.

In 1971, Kalb reclaimed the erstwhile moniker and recorded two further albums with former members Flanders, Blumenfeld and Kretmar. This particular version was supplanted by a reunion of the *Projections* line-up for a show in Central Park, after which the Blues Project name was abandoned. Despite their fractured history, the group is recognised as one of the leading white R&B bands of the 60s.

Albums: *Live At The Cafe Au Go-Go* (1966), *Projections* (1967), *Live At The Town Hall* (1967), *Planned Obselescence* (1968), *Lazarus* (1971), *Blues Project* (1972), *Reunion In Central Park* (1973).

Blythe, Jimmy

b. c.1901, Louisville, Kentucky, USA, d. 21 June 1931. Growing up in Chicago, Blythe was taught to play piano and made his first records in 1924. He recorded extensively, if often anonymously, being first-call accompanist for numerous record dates by singers. He also formed and led many pick-up bands for record dates, using such names as the State Street Ramblers, the Chicago Footwarmers and the Washboard Ragamuffins. Along the way Blythe worked with many fine jazzmen of the 20s, amongst them Johnny Dodds and Freddie Keppard. By the end of the 20s he was in less demand and he died in 1931.

Compilations: *Cutting The Boogie: Piano Blues And Boogie Woogie* (1924-41 recordings).

Bogan, Lucille

b. Lucille Anderson, 1 April 1897, Amory, Mississippi, USA, d. 10 August 1948. Bogan was one of the toughest female blues singers of the pre-war era. Although not as sophisticated as Bessie Smith, she started to record as early as 1923 and never worked in a true jazz band context. Instead to utilise a string of gifted pianists including 'Cow Cow' Davenport, Will Ezell and, particularly, Walter Roland; or a more 'countrified' group including guitars or even banjos. After a wobbly first session, her voice deepened and by 1927 she was really into her stride singing blues exclusively, often from the point of view of a street-walker. She seemed preoccupied with the life, expressing herself fluently, uncompromisingly and - during one famous session in 1936 - obscenely. Raised as Lucille Anderson in Birmingham, Alabama, she recorded after 1933 as Bessie Jackson, producing some of her best work between then and 1935 in the company of Roland. She was married at least once, to one Nazareth Bogan, and was the mother of two children. After her own career ended she managed Bogan's Birmingham Busters, a group organized by her son. In later life she moved to the west coast where she died of coronary sclerosis in August 1948.

Compilations: with Roland *Jook it, Jook It* (1970), *Women Won't Need No Men* (1986).

Bollin, A.D. (Zuzu)

b. 1922, Frisco, Texas, USA, d. 19 October 1990, Dallas, Texas, USA. One of the legion of guitarists who embraced the innovatory style of T-Bone Walker, for decades, Bollin's reputation rested on two records made in Dallas for Bob Sutton's Torch label in 1951/2. He didn't take up music until 1947, after service in the US Navy. He got help in his guitar technique from T-Bone himself, while singing with the E.X. Brooks Band in Omaha, Nebraska. His first band, formed in 1949, included jazzmen Booker Ervin and David 'Fathead' Newman. He also worked with Ernie Fields, Milton (Brother Bear) Thomas and Percy Mayfield. His first record, 'Why Don't You Eat Where You Slept Last Night'/ 'Matchbox Blues', featured Newman and Leroy Cooper, both later to work with Ray Charles. The second single, 'Stavin' Chain'/ 'Cry, Cry, Cry', used members of Jimmy McCracklin's band. Both records were later reissued. Apart from two untraced 1954 titles, Bollin didn't record again until his rediscovery in 1988. During the 50s, Bollin worked with Joe Morris and Jimmy Reed before retiring from music at the end of the decade. Rediscovered by Chuck Nevitt, he recorded the album *Texas Bluesman,* sponsored by the Dallas Blues Society. He toured Europe in 1989 and was in the process of recording a second album at the time of his death. Two titles from these sessions were added to a reissue of the first album.

Album: *Texas Bluesman* (1991).

Bond, Graham

b. 28 October 1937, Romford, Essex, England, d. 8 May 1974, London, England. The young orphan was adopted from the Dr Barnardo's home and given musical tuition at school. The 'legendary' Graham Bond has latterly become recognised as one of the main instigators of British R&B along with Cyril Davies and Alexis Korner. His musical career began with Don Rendell's quintet in 1961 as a jazz saxophonist, followed by a stint with Korner's famous ensemble Blues Incorporated. By the time he formed his first band in 1963 he had made the Hammond organ his main instrument, although he showcased his talent at gigs by playing both alto saxophone and organ simultaneously. The seminal Graham Bond Organisation became one of the most respected units during 1964. The impressive line-up of Ginger Baker (drums), Jack Bruce (bass) and Dick Heckstall-Smith (saxophone - replacing John McLaughlin on guitar), played a hybrid of jazz, blues and rock that was musically and visually stunning. Bond was the first person in Britain to play a Hammond organ through a Leslie speaker cabinet and the first to use a Mellotron. The original Organisation made two superlative and formative albums *Sound Of '65* and *There's A Bond Between Us*. Both featured original songs mixed with standards. The band interpreted 'Walk On The Wild Side', 'Wade In The Water' and 'Got My Mojo Working'. Bond's own, 'Have You Ever Loved A Woman' and 'Walkin' In The Park' demonstrated his songwriting ability. Ironically such musicianship was unable to find a commercially acceptable niche. The jazz fraternity regarded Bond's band as too noisy and rock-based, while the pop audience found his music complicated and too jazzy. The small but loyal R&B club scene cognoscenti however, loved them. Ironically 30 years later the Tommy Chase Band are pursuing an uncannily similar road, now under the banner of jazz. As the British music scene changed, so the Organisation were penalized for staying close to their musical roots and refusing to adapt. Along the way, Bond had lost Baker and Bruce who had departed to form Cream, although the addition of Jon Hiseman on drums reinforced their musical pedigree. When Hiseman and Heckstall-Smith left to form Colosseum they showed their debt to Bond by featuring 'Walkin' In The Park' on their debut album. Disenchanted with the musical tide, Bond moved to the USA where he made two albums for the Pulsar label. Both records showed a veering away from jazz and R&B although the slightly more contemporary songs were an odd coupling with the Hammond organ. Neither album fared well and Graham returned to England in 1969. The music press welcomed his re-appearance, but a poorly attended Royal

Graham Bond

Albert Hall homecoming concert must have bitterly disheartened its subject. The new band; the Graham Bond Initiation, featured his wife Diane Stewart. The unlikely combination of astrological themes, R&B and public apathy doomed this promising unit. By now Graham had started on a slow decline into drugs, depression, mental disorder and dabblings with the occult. Following a reunion with Ginger Baker in his ill-fated Airforce project, and a brief spell with the Jack Bruce Band, Bond formed a musical partnership with Pete Brown; this resulted in one album and for a short time had a stabilizing effect on Bond's life. By 1974, following a nervous breakdown, drug addiction and two further unsuccessful conglomerations, Holy Magick and Magus, the cruellest of ironies happened on 8 May 1974; he was killed when he fell under the wheels of a London underground train at Finsbury Park station. Whether or not Graham Bond could ever have reached the musical heights of his 1964 band is open to endless debate. What has been acknowledged, is that he was an innovator, a catalyst and a major influence on British R&B.
Albums: *The Sound Of '65* (1965), *There's A Bond Between Us* (1966), *Mighty Grahame Bond* (1968), *Love Is The Law* (1968 - the latter two albums were re-packaged as *Bond In America* in 1971), *Solid Bond* (1970), *We Put The Majick On You* (1971), *Holy Magick* (1971), *Bond And Brown: Two Heads Are Better Than One* (1972), *This Is Graham Bond* (1978 - an edited version of *Bond In America*), *The Beginnings Of Jazz-Rock* (1977), *The Graham Bond Organisation* (1984), *Live At Klook's Kleek* (1988).
Further reading: *The Smallest Place In The World*, Dick Heckstall-Smith, *Graham Bond*; *The Mighty Shadow*, Harry Shapiro.

Bonds, Son

b. 16 March 1906, Brownsville, Tennessee, USA, d. 31 August 1947, Dyersburg, Tennessee, USA. Unlike many of his contemporaries in the blues field, Bonds lived his whole life in the area in which he was born. By his twenties he had learned guitar, and was playing with other musicians from the same area such as Hammie Nixon and Sleepy John Estes. Between 1934-41, he made several records, first for Decca and later for Bluebird, in which his downhome musical roots were tempered by the commercial blues sound of the period. At his first sessions he was accompanied by Nixon on either harmonica or jug, while at his later ones Estes supported him. He also repaid the compliment with the latter. From his last session, some tracks on which he sang appeared as the Delta Boys. He died some years later from an accidental gunshot wound.
Compilation: *Complete Recordings* (1988).

Bonner, Weldon 'Juke Boy'

b. 2 March 1932, Bellville, Texas, USA, d. 29 June 1978, Houston, Texas, USA. Like many blues singers, Bonner's first musical experiences were in singing spirituals as a child. He took up guitar when he was about 13-years-old and began to build up his experience following a move to Houston a few years later. In the mid-50s he was based on the west coast and made his first record for Bob Geddin's Irma label (issued as Juke Boy Barner), playing a driving rhythm guitar and punctuating the vocals with harmonica phrases, a combination that was to become his trademark. On his second record, for Goldband in 1960, he was billed as the One Man Trio. Following this, his musical activity was based entirely around Houston for a few years, until other titles from the Goldband sessions were issued on an album on the Storyville label in Europe. The interest this generated led to further recordings and albums on Flyright in the UK and Arhoolie in the USA consolidated his reputation. In 1969 Bonner visited Europe. His ability to compose topical blues with thoughtful and imaginative lyrics, coupled with an expressive vocal style and self-contained instrumental accompaniments, made him highly popular with his new audience, and many tours and new recordings resulted. Unfortunately, his success was to be short-lived, and he died of cirrhosis of the liver in 1978.
Album: *I'm Going Back To The Country* (1968). Compilations: *They Call Me Juke Boy* (1989), *1960-1967* (1991).

Bookbinder, Roy

b. 5 October 1941, New York City, New York, USA. Bookbinder began playing guitar in the early 60s and was initially inspired by Dave Van Ronk. He met Rev. Gary Davis in 1968, ostensibly for guitar lessons, but was travelling with him within a month. Davis regarded

Bookbinder as one of his best students. Towards the end of the 60s he recorded for a Blue Goose Records anthology, and in 1970 he made his first full album for Adelphi, dedicated to Pink Anderson, whom Bookbinder brought back into the public eye. The album was extremely well-received, with most reviewers commenting on the honesty and individuality of his country blues interpretations. He continues to tour and record (currently for Rounder Records), playing what his press releases call 'old time country and hillbilly blues'.

Albums: *Travellin' Man* (1971), *Bookeroo* (1988).

Booker, Charley

b. 3 September 1925, Quiver Valley, near Sunflower, Mississippi, USA, d. 20 September 1989, South Bend, Indiana, USA. While some singers left Mississippi to seek wider recognition, others like Charley Booker remained, their music retaining traditions that urban sophistication expunged. Booker learned the guitar from his father, Lucius, and uncle, Andrew Shaw. Boyd Gilmore, q.v., was a childhood friend. He moved to Greenville in 1947, playing in drummer Jesse 'Cleanhead' Love's band, and broadcasting over WGVM radio. In January 1952, along with Gilmore and harmonica player Houston Boines, he recorded four titles with Ike Turner, released on the Modern and Blues & Rhythm labels. 'Rabbit Blues', 'Moonrise Blues', 'No Ridin' Blues' and 'Charley's Boogie Woogie', sung in a distinctive voice with natural vibrato, revealed the influence of Charley Patton. Within a year, he recorded in Memphis for Sam Phillips, but the trenchantly rhythmic 'Walked All Night' and 'Baby I'm Coming Home' were not released until 1977. Booker moved to South Bend, Indiana in 1953, where he remained, rarely performing, until his death in 1989.

Booze, Beatrice 'Bea'

b. 23 May 1920, Baltimore, USA, d. c.70s. One of the few female blues guitarists Bea Booze, was thought to have been the discovery of pianist and talent scout Sammy Price who introduced her to Decca records in 1942. Despite recording topical numbers like 'Uncle Sam Come And Get Him' and 'War Rationin' Papa', it was her rendition of the standard 'See See Rider' with which she found fame. Her recording career was short-lived, though she did tour with the Andy Kirk Band in the mid-40s, make one 78 rpm record as Muriel (Bea Booze) Nicholas And Her Dixielanders for 20th Century in 1946, and recorded four tracks for Apollo in 1950. Her last known recordings were with Sammy Price in the early 60s for the Stardust label.

Borum, Willie

b. 4 November 1911, Memphis, Tennessee, USA, d. c.60s. Borum learned guitar as a child from his father and Jim Jackson later adding harmonica, on which he learned much from Noah Lewis. He played in the streets in jug bands, and worked in Mississippi with Garfield Akers, Willie Brown and Robert Johnson. In 1934, he accompanied his fellow Memphians Hattie Hart and Allen Shaw on record for Vocalion, four tracks of his own that were not released. After serving in the US Army during World War II he continued to play occasionally, but had largely retired from music until a brief return as a result of discovery by blues historian/producer Sam Charters in 1961. This resulted in two good albums, an appearance in a documentary film, and a few concerts. He is reported to have died towards the end of the decade.

Albums: *Introducing Memphis Willie B* (1961), *Hard Working Man* (1961).

Boy, Andy

b. c.1906, Galveston, Texas, USA, d. USA. One of a group of Texas blues piano players that included Rob Cooper and Robert Shaw, Boy worked the seaport towns of the southern coast including Houston and Galveston. His playing has touches of older ragtime styles as well as blues, as can be heard from his excellent accompaniments for the smooth vocals of Houston singer Joe Pullum, but his best work is the set of eight recordings he made for Bluebird in San Antonio in 1937, notably the beautiful 'Church Street Blues'. He also accompanied Walter Cowboy Washington at the same session. He was last heard of in the 50s, in Kansas City where he relocated around the time of World War II.

Compilation: *Texas Seaport 1934-1937* (1978).

Boyd, Eddie

b. Edward Riley Boyd, 25 November 1914, Stovall, Mississippi, USA. Boyd is a half brother of Memphis Slim and a cousin of Muddy Waters. He spent his early years on Stovall's Plantation but ran away after a dispute with an overseer. Self-taught on guitar and piano he worked around the south during the 30s, as both 'Little Eddie' and 'Ernie' Boyd, from a base in Memphis, before settling in Chicago where he worked in a steel mill. He was active in music, performing with Waters, Johnny Shines and John Lee 'Sonny Boy' Williamson before he had his first big hit under his own name with 'Five Long Years' on the Job label in 1952. He recorded extensively for Chess, having successes with '24 Hours' and '3rd Degree'. He journeyed to Europe during the 'Blues Boom' of the 60s and, considering himself too assertive to live comfortably in the USA, took up residence first in Paris and later in Finland. During this period he appeared with artists as diverse as Buddy Guy and John Mayall and recorded in England, Sweden, Switzerland, Germany, France and Finland. His piano-playing is steadily functional rather than spectacular and his main strength is his ability to put together lyrics which are pithy and acidic. 'Five Long Years' has become a blues standard and features in the repertoires of many singers including Waters and B.B. King.
Albums: *Rattin' And Running Around* (1982), *No More Of This Third Degree* (1982).

Boze, Calvin

Remembered as being a senior - and the school band leader - by Charles Brown at Prairie View College in Texas, trumpeter Boze (or Boaz as his name appears early on) first came to the public's attention on recordings with the west coast band's of Russell Jacquet (Globe) and Marvin Johnson (G&G). In 1949, he began recording as a vocalist in a strong Louis Jordan vein for Aladdin Records with Maxwell Davis and his band. Although he never made a huge impression on the R&B charts, his recordings were all solid, earthy R&B jive advocating 'Working With My Baby' (who made his lolly pop, and his peanut brittle), and 'Waiting And Drinking'. He is best known for the classic 'Safronia B' and the b-side - Boze's celebration of his adopted home - 'Angel City Blues', as well as a couple of songs he wrote for old homeboy Charles Brown - 'Texas Blues' and 'Hot Lips And Seven Kisses' - also recorded for Aladdin.
Albums: *Havin' A Ball* (1988), *Choo Choo's Bringing My Baby Home* (1989).

Bracey, Ishmon

b. 9 January 1901, Byram, Mississippi, USA, d. 12 February 1970, Jackson, Mississippi, USA. Bracey's blues had the uncompromising directness both of the aggressive youngster, and of the preacher he eventually became, with little of the melodic decoration and conscious artistry of his associate Tommy Johnson. He learned guitar from the Rev. Rubin Lacey, with whom he played. Bracey was also accompanied by Johnson and others, while performing at black social events around Jackson. It was in company with Johnson that he recorded for Victor in 1928. Bracey taking second opposition to Charley McCoy, whose mandolin-like guitar is a perfect foil to Bracey's nasal singing and unadorned guitar playing. A subsequent session for Paramount in 1930 was marred by the unsympathetic clarinet of Ernest Michall. In 1951, Bracey embraced religion and was ordained in the Baptist church, he thereafter refused to play blues.
Album: *Ishman Bracey* (1983).

Bradford, Perry 'Mule'

b. 14 February 1893, Montgomery, Alabama, USA, d. 20 April 1970. Although Bradford began his professional career as a performer, playing piano in tent shows, it was as a songwriter that he made his greatest impact. In 1920 he was managing blues singer Mamie Smith when she was invited by OKeh Records to record two of his vaudeville songs, (Bradford had originally written the songs for Sophie Tucker, but at the last minute she was unable to make the date). The records were sufficiently successful for OKeh's boss, Fred Hager, to want more; and so on her subsequent session of 20 August 1920, Mamie Smith became the first singer to record the blues when she sang Bradford's 'Crazy Blues'. Bradford enjoyed considerable success in the blues boom that followed and during the 20s he also assembled some fine all-star bands to make records. Perry Bradford's Jazz Phools included Louis Armstrong, Buster Bailey, James P. Johnson and

Don Redman. After the 20s, however, Bradford seemed incapable of keeping abreast of changes in musical taste and he drifted into obscurity. He published his autobiography five years before his death.

Compilations: *Perry Bradford, Pioneer Of The Blues* (1920-27 recordings), with Louis Armstrong *Young Louis: The Sideman* (1924-27 recordings).

Further reading: *Born With The Blues*, Perry Bradford.

Branch, Billy

b 3 October 1952 , Chicago, Illinois, USA. In the late 60s Branch played with Jimmy Walker but he first came to the public notice at a widely-reported and highly controversial 'Battle Of The Harmonicas' hosted and won by Little Mac Simmons (though public opinion was that Branch was the real winner). His initial recording was backing McKinley Mitchell, and the first tracks under his own name were made for Barrelhouse Records in 1975. Branch is now widely regarded as one of the best young harmonica blues players (and a fine singer). In addition to leading the Sons Of The Blues, he is an experienced session musician (with Lou Rawls, Saffire, and Johnny Winter, among others) and was part of Alligator Records' 1990 *Harp Attack!* session. Branch is also committed to teaching young people about the blues and frequently plays in schools.

Albums: with Lurrie Bell *Chicago's Young Blues Generation* (1982), *Mississippi Flashback* (1992).

Braun Brothers

Jules and Dave Braun formed Deluxe Records in early 1944 in Linden, New Jersey, recording such top acts as the Billy Eckstine and Benny Carter Orchestras and the Four Blues. The label became arguably the first to tap the wealth of talent in New Orleans and in 1947 recorded Paul Gayten ('True'), Annie Laurie ('Since I Fell For You'), Roy Brown ('Good Rockin' Tonight'), and Dave Bartholomew. The DeLuxe record plant and warehouse was razed by a fire in late 1947 and was sold to King Records. The Brauns, retaining a 49 per cent interest in DeLuxe, went on to incorporate Regal Records in July 1949 with the help of Fred Mendelsohn. Paul Gayten and Annie Laurie ('I'll Never Be Free') continued to be

successful Regal artists along with new stars like Larry Darnell ('I'll Get Along Somehow', 'For You, My Love') and Doc Sausage ('Rag Mop'), and in 1950 established stars such as Alberta Hunter, Cab Calloway, Ernie Fields and Savannah Churchill began recording for the new label. However, the Brauns were again in financial difficulties and their stars were wooed away by the major labels. The end of Regal and the Brauns' involvement in the record business came in November 1951, when the company was liquidated.

Brewer, 'Blind' James

b. 3 October 1921, Brookhaven, Mississippi, USA. In the early 60s much of the interest generated by the blues in Chicago was focused on the Maxwell Street open-air market, where musicians could be found playing on the sidewalk with their electric guitars plugged into extensions hired out by local home owners. 'Blind' James Brewer was, by this time, a religious singer who went on to form the Church Of God In Christ, a convocation of local preachers dedicated to work in the Maxwell Street area. Born blind, he had worked as a blues singer since his teenage years, moving from Mississippi to St. Louis before joining Arvella Gray, another well-known street singer, in Chicago. During the 'boom' years of the 60s Brewer found work on the college circuit, appeared on television and saw his recorded work issued on such labels as Heritage, Flyright and Testament.

Brim, Grace

b. c.1924. One of the few female musicians active on the post-war Chicago blues scene, Brim appeared with her husband John Brim's group, the Gary Kings. At her first recording session in 1950, she played harmonica and sang, demonstrating a pleasant though not especially expressive, vocal style. Later she took to the drums, although on at least one record she managed to sing and play harmonica too. Some records appeared under her own name, some as Mrs John Brim, but mostly she played a subordinate role on John's records, and can be heard lending very solid support on his fine topical blues 'Tough Times', with Eddie Taylor and Jimmy Reed. She continued to play for many years, both with her husband and with

other groups, and they appeared together on a single in the 70s.
Album: *Chicago Slickers* (1981).

Brim, John

b. 10 April 1922, Hopkinsville, Kentucky, USA. Born on a farm, Brim played blues guitar from an early age. In the mid-40s, he relocated to Chicago, where he joined the burgeoning post-war blues scene, playing with artists such as John Lee 'Sonny Boy' Williamson, Muddy Waters and later Jimmy Reed. The tough sound of his music placed him firmly in the Chicago style of the day, his vocals were raw and convincing and his guitar-playing rough yet effective. His records, some of which featured his wife Grace Brim singing and playing drums, appeared on a variety of labels, but the best were probably the later 50s tracks, such as 'Rattlesnake' (which was based on Big Mama Thornton's 'Hound Dog' and featured the superb harmonica work of Little Walter), 'Lifetime Blues' and the topical 'Tough Times'. Brim has continued to play, issuing an interesting if rather rough single in the 70s, and a fine half-album of tough Chicago blues in the late 80s.
Albums: *Whose Muddy Shoes* (1970), *Chicago Blues Sessions* (1989).

Brock, 'Big' George

b. Mississippi, USA. Brock's father gave him a harmonica as a Christmas present when he was aged eight. At the age of 12, he sang at a 'fish fry' and later worked in many clubs in his native state. He settled in St. Louis, Missouri, in 1953, and after playing in a club for some time, he took it over. He subsequently closed the club and became a bandleader again, working with Ike Turner and employed Albert King as his lead guitarist. Brock refused an opportunity to record in 1963, and eventually made his first single in 1990, followed by an album on his own label later the same year. Brock describes himself as 'a low down pure blues singer', strongly influenced by Howlin' Wolf, B.B. King, Muddy Waters, Elmore James and Jimmy Reed. He is the proud possessor of a gold belt, successfully defended in numerous harmonica championships.
Album: *Should Have Been There* (1990).

Brooks, 'Big' Leon

b. 19 November 1933, Rabbit Foot Farm, near Sunflower, Mississippi, USA, d. 22 January 1982, Chicago, Illinois, USA. Brooks began playing blues harmonica when he was six years old. His original inspiration was Sonny Boy 'Rice Miller' Williamson, but after moving to Chicago in the 40s he met Little Walter Jacobs, described by Brooks as 'my coach' - a fact obvious to anyone who has heard both men's music. In the 50s, brooks led his own band on a sporadic basis, and supplied accompaniment to Jimmy Rogers, Otis Rush, Robert Nighthawk, and others. He was disillusioned by the changes in the blues in the early 60s and left music until 1976, when he once again began to sing and play in Chicago's blues clubs, despite serious ill health. He died of a heart attack in 1982.
Compilation: *Living Chicago Blues, Volume 5* (1980, four tracks only).

Brooks, Hadda

b. Hadda Hopgood, 29 October 1916, Los Angeles, California, USA. Brooks began taking piano lessons as a young child, later studying classical music in Los Angeles and Chicago. In 1945 record executive Jules Bihari, just starting Modern Records, heard Hadda's playing and signed her. Her first single, 'Swinging The Boogie', was issued in 1945. billed as 'Queen Of The Boogie' (a film of the same name was made in 1947). The follow-up 'Rockin' The Boogie' set the style for the rest of her career, although the many boogies she recorded - often modern arrangements of classical music like 'Humoresque' or 'Hungarian Rhapsody No. 2' - were usually backed with fine vocal blues or ballads. Although not trained in the blues, she became somewhat typecast as a boogie-woogie pianist, and counted Count Basie (who backed her on a single) and actor Humphrey Bogart (who cast her in a film) among her admirers. In 1951 she became the first black woman to host her own television show in California., as well as recording for London and OKeh Records. She toured with the Harlem Globetrotters in her spare time before moving to Australia for most of the 60s. In semi-retirement, she still retains a few choice engagements each year at certain Los Angeles restaurants and hotels and has released the occasional single on the small Rob Ray, Alwin and Kim labels.

Lonnie Brooks

'Big' Bill Broonzy

Albums: with Pete Johnson *Boogie Battle* (1977), *Queen Of The Boogie* (1984), *Romance In The Dark* (1988).

Brooks, Lonnie

b. Lee Baker Junior, 18 December 1933, Dubuisson, Louisiana, USA. Brooks took up the electric guitar while living in Port Arthur, Texas, playing as Guitar Junior with Clifton Chenier and Lonesome Sundown. His first solo record was the local hit 'Family Rules', made for Eddie Shuler's Goldband label in 1957. At this time, he also wrote and recorded 'Pick Me Up On Your Way Down' (with Barbara Lynn on backing vocals) and 'The Crawl' which was revived 30 years later by the Fabulous Thunderbirds. These tracks were reissued on a Charly album in 1984. Guitar Junior moved to Chicago in 1959, recording and touring with Jimmy Reed. He made an unsuccessful single for Mercury ('The Horse') before changing his stage name again, to Lonnie Brooks. During the 60s, Brooks performed in the Chicago area, making singles for Midas, Palos, USA and Chess, where 'Let It All Hang Out' was a local hit. In 1969, he made an album for Capitol but his career only began to develop when he toured Europe with Willie Mabon in 1975. There he recorded in France for Black And White and in 1978 he signed to Chicago blues label, Alligator. During the 80s, Lonnie Brooks made five Alligator albums and built up a large following on the Midwest college and club circuit and made several trips to Europe.

Albums: *Broke And Hungry* (1969), *Sweet Home Chicago* (1975), *Bayou Lightning* (1979), *Turn On The Night* (1981), *Hot Shot* (1983), *The Crawl* (1984), *Live At Pepper's* (1985), *Wound Up Tight* (1987), *Live From Chicago - Bayou Lightning Strikes* (1988), *Satisfaction Guaranteed* (1991).

Broonzy, 'Big' Bill

b. William Lee Conley Broonzy, 26 June 1893 (or 1898), Scott, Mississippi, USA, d. 15 August 1958, Chicago, Illinois, USA. Broonzy worked as a field hand, and it was behind the mule that he first developed his unmistakable, hollering voice, with its remarkable range and flexibility. As a child he made himself a violin, and learned to play under the guidance of an uncle. For a time, he worked as a preacher, before settling finally to the secular life of the blues singer; after service in the army at the end of World War I, he moved to Chicago, where he learned to play guitar from Papa Charlie Jackson.

Despite his late start as a guitarist, Broonzy quickly became proficient on the instrument, and when he first recorded in the late 20s, he was a fluent and assured accompanist in both ragtime and blues idioms. His voice retained a flavour of the countryside, in addition to his clear diction, but his playing had the up-to-date sophistication and assurance of the city dweller. The subjects of his blues, too, were those that appealed to blacks who, like him, had recently migrated to the urban north, but retained family and cultural links with the south. As such, Broonzy's music exemplifies the movement made by the blues from locally made folk music to nationally distributed, mass media entertainment. He was sometimes used as a talent scout by record companies; and was also favoured as an accompanist, and up to 1942 recorded hundreds of tracks in this capacity, as well as over 200 issued, and many unissued, titles in his own right. His own records followed trends in black taste; by the mid-30s they were almost always in a small-group format, with piano, and often brass or woodwind and a rhythm section, but his mellow, sustained guitar tones were always well to the fore. Despite his undoubted 'star' status - not until 1949 was it necessary to put his full name on a race record; just 'Big Bill' was enough - the questionable financial practices of the record industry meant that his income from music did not permit a full-time career as a musician until late in his life. When recording resumed after World War II, Broonzy had lost some of his appeal for black audiences, but by this time he had shrewdly moved his focus to the burgeoning white audience, drawn from jazz fans and the incipient folksong revival movement. He had played Carnegie Hall in 1938 (introduced as a Mississippi ploughhand!), and in 1951 was one the blues' first visitors to Europe. He recorded frequently, if from a narrowed musical base, changing his repertoire radically to emphasize well-known, older blues like 'Trouble In Mind', blues-ballads like 'John Henry', popular songs such as 'Glory Of Love' and even protest numbers including the witty 'When Do I Get To Be Called A Man'.

He became a polished raconteur, and further

developed his swinging, fluent guitar playing, although on slow numbers he sometimes became rather mannered, after the fashion of Josh White. Broonzy was greatly loved by his new audience, and revered by the younger Chicago blues singers. In 1955 he published an engaging, anecdotal autobiography, compiled by Yannick Bruynoghe from his letters. It should be noted that Broonzy had learned to write only in 1950, from students at Iowa State University, where he worked as a janitor. Broonzy was a proud, determined man, and a pivotal figure in blues, both when it was the music of black Americans, and as it became available to whites the world over. His reputation suffered after his death, as his later recordings were deemed as pandering to white tastes. The importance of his earlier contribution to black music was not fully understood. Broonzy was an intelligent and versatile entertainer, his immense talent was always at the service of his audience and their expectations.

Selected albums: *Big Bill And Sonny Boy* (1964), *Trouble In Mind* (1965), *Big Bill's Blues* (1968), *The Young Big Bill Broonzy* (1969), *Bluebird No. 6* (c.1977) *Midnight Steppers* (1986), *Big Bill Broonzy Vol. 1* (1986), *Vol. 2* (1988), *Vol. 3* (1989), *Sings Folk Songs* (1989), *The 1955 London Sessions* (1990), *Remembering Big Bill Broonzy* (1990), *Good Time Tonight* (1990), *Big Bill Broonzy And Washboard Sam* (1991, rec. 1953), *Do That Guitar Rag 1928-35* (1992), *1934-47* (1992).

Brown, Andrew

b. 25 February 1937, Jackson, Mississippi, USA, d. 11 December 1985. A very versatile musician, Brown began playing guitar as a youngster and after moving with his mother to Chicago in 1946, was influenced by Earl Hooker. In the 50s he was associated with Freddie King and Magic Sam, but he also played jazz. He was drafted into the armed services in 1956, and on his discharge settled just outside Chicago. In the mid-60s he recorded for the Four Brothers label; his singles usually coupled an excellent blues with a more commercial side, and he also wrote material for G.L. Crockett. He released a single on Brave in the early 70s, and despite health problems recorded for Alligator, Black Magic and Double Trouble in the years preceding his death from lung cancer.

Albums: *Living Chicago Blues Volume Five* (1980, three tracks only), *Big Brown's Chicage Blues* (1982), *On The Case* (1985).

Brown, Angela

b. 1953, Chicago, Illinois, USA. Brown began her musical career by singing gospel music in church and although she was aware of the blues she did not sing them until around 1980, when she played the role of 'Ma' Rainey in the stage musical. Following this, she worked in the numerous Chicago blues clubs, often accompanied by pianists Little Brother Montgomery or Erwin Helfer. Her debut recordings were released by the Red Beans label in 1983, and the first album under her own name was made in 1987 for the German label Schubert. Although she was dubbed 'the Bessie Smith of the 80s' a deserved title given her strong renditions of vaudeville blues material, her powerful voice is also well-suited to more modern blues styles.

Album: *The Voice of Blues* (1987), *The 2nd Burnley National Blues Festival* (1990).

Brown, Bessie

There were two blues singers operating during the 20s using the name Bessie Brown and biographical details are slim for both. One, known to have worked as a male impersonator and speculated to have been born around 1895 in Cleveland, Ohio, began her career on record in 1925 billed as 'The Original' Bessie Brown - probably indicating a conflict with her namesake who had had records issued a year previously. Just to confuse things further she also used the names Caroline Lee and Sadie Green, the last also being used by popular singer Vaughn De Leath. Brown was married to Clarence Shaw and appears to have retired from show business in the early 30s. Her rival worked on the TOBA circuit with her husband George W. Williams in an act that at one time included a young Fats Waller. Her career on record seems to have been restricted to the brief period on the Columbia label during 1924.

Compilations: *Mean Mothers* (1980), *Female Blues Singers Vol. 4* (1990).

Brown, Buster

b. 15 August 1911, Cordele Georgia, USA, d. 31 January 1976. Brown played harmonica at local clubs and made a few recordings including 'I'm Gonna Make You Happy' in 1943. Brown moved to New York in 1956 where he was discovered by Fire Records owner Bobby Robinson while working in a chicken and barbecue joint. In 1959, he recorded the archaic sounding blues 'Fannie Mae', whose tough harmonica riffs took it into the US Top 40. His similar-sounding 'Sugar Babe' (1961) was covered in the UK by Jimmy Powell. In later years he recorded for Checker and for numerous small labels including Serock, Gwenn and Astroscope. Brown died in Brooklyn, New York City in January 1976.

Albums: *New King Of The Blues* (1959), *Get Down With Buster Brown* (1962), *Raise A Ruckus Tonite* (reissue 1976).

Brown, Charles

b. 1920, Texas City, Texas, USA. Despite learning piano while a child, Brown became a teacher of chemistry. In 1943, living in Los Angeles, he realized that he could earn more money working as a pianist-singer. At that time, the top small group in Los Angeles was the Nat 'King' Cole Trio, but when Cole moved on, the Three Blazers, led by Johnny Moore (guitarist brother of Oscar Moore) and whom Brown had just joined, moved into the top spot.

By 1946 the band was a national favourite, with hit records and appearances at New York's Apollo Theatre. In 1948 the group broke up although Moore continued to lead a band with the same name. Brown was now on his own and virtually unknown as a solo performer. In the early 50s a string of successful records, many featuring his own compositions, boosted his career. Additionally, his work was recorded by such artists as B.B. King, Ray Charles, Sam Cooke, Amos Milburn and Fats Domino, with whom Brown recorded 'I'll Always Be In Love With You' and 'Please Believe Me'. He was heavily influenced by Robert Johnson, Louis Jordan, and especially by Pha Terrell, the singer with the Andy Kirk band. Brown's singing evolved into a highly melodic ballad style which still showed signs of his blues roots. He aptly defined himself as a 'blue ballad singer'. In a sense he has the velevty sound of Cole, encrusted with the tough cynicism of Leroy Carr and Lonnie Johnson. Unlike Cole, Brown's star waned, although he had successful records with songs such as 'Christmas Comes But Once A Year'. One follower was Ray Charles, who, early in his career, modelled his singing on an amalgam of Brown and Cole's style. By the end of the 60s Brown was working in comparative obscurity at Los Angeles

Charles Brown

nightspots. An appearance at the 1976 San Francisco Blues Festival boosted his reputation, but his working pattern remained pretty much unaltered into the 80s.

Albums: *Race Track Blues* (50s), *Music, Maestro, Please* (60s), *Someone To Love* (1992). Compilations: *Charles Brown And Johnny Moore's Three Blazers* (40s recordings), with others *Great Rhythm And·Blues Oldies Vol. 1* (50s recordings).

Brown, Clarence 'Gatemouth'

b. 18 April 1924,Vinton, Louisiana, USA (some sources give Orange Texas, where he was raised from the age of three weeks). Brown's father was a musician who taught him to play guitar and fiddle, and during his youth he heard the music of Tampa Red, Bob Wills, Count Basie, and others. He toured the south as a drummer with a travelling show before being drafted into the army. On his discharge he worked as a musician in San Antonio, Texas, where he honed his guitar skills sufficiently enough to impress Don Robey, who offered him a spot at his club in Houston. It was here that Gatemouth's big break came, when he took over a show from 'T-Bone' Walker, after Walker was taken ill. He was so well-received that Robey took him to Los Angeles to record for the Aladdin Label on 21 August 1947. In 1948 he set up his own Peacock label, for which Brown recorded until 1961. Many of these records are classics of Texas guitar blues, and were enormously influential. During the 60s Gatemouth broadened his stylistic base to include jazz and country, best exemplified by his 1965 Chess recordings made in Nashville. These were pointers to the way Brown's music was to develop later. In the 70s he recorded a mixed bag of albums for the French Black And Blue label (including a Louis Jordon tribute set), a couple of cajun/country/rock hybrids and a good blues album for Barclay Records. In the 80s, Rounder showcased Gatesmouth's versatile approach successfully by matching him with a big, brassy band, and he has also recorded for Alligator. In recent years Brown has tended to showcase his fiddle-playing to the detriment of his still excellent blues guitar picking, but he remains a fine singer and extremely talented instrumentalist, whatever genre of music he turns his attention to.

Selected albums: *Alright Again* (1982), *San Antonio Ballbuster* (1982), *One More Mile* (1983), *Atomic Energy* (1984), *The Original Peacock Recordings* (1984), *Texas Guitarman - Duke Peacock Story, Vol. 1* (1986), *Pressure Cooker* (1987, rec. 70s), *Texas Swing* (1988, early 80s recordings), *The Nashville Session 1965* (1989).

Brown, Dusty

b. 11 March 1929, Tralake, Mississippi, USA. A self-taught blues harmonica player, Brown enjoyed a certain amount of success after moving to Chicago in the 40s. He started by sitting in with artists such as Muddy Waters, but soon formed his own band. In 1955, he had a record issued on the local Parrot label (and there were also another couple of tracks, unissued until over 30 years later), his accompanists featuring, among others, the pianist Henry Gray. Later in the decade, he recorded for Bandera, but again there can have been little commercial success (although, again, a couple of unissued sides have appeared in subsequent years). He gave up attempting to make a living from music until the 70s, when he made a comeback, taking advantage of the renewed interest in the music, in particular from the European market.

Album: *Hand Me Down Blues* (1990).

Brown, Gabriel

b. unknown date, probably Florida, USA; d. early 70s, Florida, USA. Apart from the fact that he was the first country blues artist (and one of only very few) to have been recorded in the state of Florida - and this by the Library of Congress, not a commercial record company - virtually nothing is known of the early biography of this singer and guitarist. The Library of Congress sessions were carried out by Alan Lomax and black folklorist and writer Zora Neale Hurston, and produced enough material for a very worthwhile album to be compiled in the 70s. By 1943, Brown had moved north, and was living in Asbury Park, New Jersey. From this base, he seems to have been active on the blues scene in New York and began recording in that year for Joe Davis's record company, chalking up another record by being the first country bluesman to make records in New York after the beginning of World War II. Over the next nine years, he recorded many tracks for Davis, all of which were in a down-home country blues vein, and featuring only Brown

Clarence 'Gatemouth' Brown

and his guitar. His sound is distinctive, even idiosyncratic, and the material is mostly original. Sometimes, for example, 'The Jinx Is On Me', with its superstitious lyrics and bottleneck guitar accompaniment, the style points back to his southern roots, while at other times it displays an urban sophistication. Brown later returned to Florida, where he drowned in a boating accident.

Compilations: *Out In The Cold Again* (1975), *1943-1945* (1981), *1944-1952* (1984).

Brown, Henry

b. 1906, Troy, Tennessee, USA, d. 28 June 1981. Brown moved to St. Louis about 1918, and apart from army service (as a musician) in World War II, he spent his entire musical life there. His economical but highly inventive piano playing usually featured a bouncy, four to the bar chordal bass, and was heard on record both solo and behind a number of St. Louis artists in the 20s and 30s, including Mary Johnson, Alice Moore and the 'gutbucket' trombonist Ike Rodgers. He recorded a superb album in 1960 for Paul Oliver. Thereafter he was recorded sporadically, but less successfully, until 1974. He had been in declining health for some time before his death in June 1981.

Albums: *Henry Brown Blues* (1960), *The Blues In St. Louis* (1984).

Brown, Lee

Brown was an associate of the Tennessee musicians who accompanied Sleepy John Estes, and whose guitar is heard on Brown's first record. Jimmy Rogers recalled him as an irascible paranoid, and Hammie Nixon, who last saw him in the late 60s, recalls that when they first met as hobos, Brown was on the run from a murder charge. Brown recorded sporadically from 1937-40, and also had two records issued in 1946, making several versions of his theme song 'Little Girl, Little Girl'. He was a limited pianist - his best records are those on which Sam Price plays piano as part of a small jazz band - and his laconic, unemotional singing is perhaps an attempt to emulate the success of Curtis Jones.

Album: *Lee Brown* (1987).

Brown, Lillyn

b. 24 April 1885, Atlanta, Georgia, USA, d. 8 June 1969, New York City, New York, USA. Brown was in show business from 1894-1934 (at one time billed as 'the Kate Smith of Harlem'), returning for a period in the 50s. A singer, dancer and male impersonator, she added blues to her act in 1908. In 1921 she recorded four titles with her Jazz-bo Syncopators. The music, as her background and the group's name imply, is a hybrid of blues, jazz, and the ragtime influenced pop of a decade earlier, with 'If That's What You Want Here It Is' being a particularly impressive, spirited performance. In the 50s, she operated an acting and singing school, and from 1956 was secretary to the Negro Actors' Guild, also writing and directing plays for her church as late as 1965.

Album: *Female Blues Singers B/C* (1990).

Brown, Nappy

b. Napoleon Brown Culp 12 October 1929, Charlotte, North Carolina, USA. Brown began his career as a gospel singer, but moved to R&B when an appearance in Newark, New Jersey led to a recording contract with Savoy in 1954. A deep-voiced, highly individual R&B singer, he had a number of hits during the 50s, including 'Don't Be Angry' (1955), the Rose Marie McCoy/Charlie Singleton song 'Pitter Patter' (a pop hit in Patti Page's cover version), 'It Don't Hurt No More' (1958) and 'I Cried Like A Baby' (1959). He also made two original version of 'The Night Time Is The Right Time' a 1958 hit for Ray Charles. A prison term kept Brown inactive for much of the 60s. He returned to music with an album for Elephant V in 1969 and recorded gospel music in the 70s with the Bell Jubilee Singers for Jewel and as Brother Napoleon Brown for Savoy. In the 80s, Brown was rediscovered by a later generation of blues enthusiasts. He performed at festivals and recorded for Black Top and Alligator, with guitarist Tinsley Ellis accompanying him on *Tore Up*. Brown also appeared on a live album recorded at Tipitina's in New Orleans in 1988. He recorded in 1990 for Ichiban.

Albums: *Nappy Brown Sings* (1955), *The Right Time* (1958), *Thanks For Nothing* (1969), *Something Gonna Jump Out The Bushes* (1988), *Tore Up* (1989), *Apples & Lemons* (1990).

Brown, Olive

b. 30 August 1922, St. Louis, Missouri, USA.

The family moved to Detroit, Michigan when Olive was three months old, though they often returned to visit St. Louis, where she began singing in church. In the 30s and 40s she sang with many well-known bands (including Todd Rhodes) and recorded for Our World Records in 1948. In the 50s she made a demonstration tape for Don Robey which was released by Ace in 1988; it presented Olive as a typical R&B singer for the time. The following decade Brown appeared on the Spivey and Blues spectacle labels, and in 1973 she recorded as a vaudeville-blues styled singer for JTP Records. She continues to work in this area.

Album: *The New Empress Of The Blues* (1973), with various artists *Peacock Chicks & Duchesses Sing The Blues* (1988, three tracks).

Brown, Richard 'Rabbit'

b. c.1880, New Orleans, Louisiana, USA, d. 1937, New Orleans, Louisiana, USA. Nicknamed for his small stature, 'Rabbit' Brown made a living in the streets and brothels of New Orleans, singing in a gritty voice and playing fluent guitar that incorporated flamenco runs, string snapping and high speed bass runs; he also took tourists for rowboat rides on Lake Ponchartrain. He recorded in 1927, singing black pop songs from before World War I, two long and remarkable ballads about the 'Titanic' and a local kidnapping, and the poignant 'James Alley Blues', named for the slum birthplace he shared with Louis Armstrong.

Compilation: *The Greatest Songsters* (1990).

Brown, Robert

b. 15 July 1910. Walnut Ridge, Arkansas, USA, d. 13 November 1966, Chicago, Illinois, USA. Aka 'Washboard Sam', 'Ham Gravy', 'Shuflin Sam'. In the increasingly sophisticated world of urban blues in the late 30s, when clarinets, trumpets and saxophones were becoming more popular as the music edged towards R&B, Robert Brown was something of an oddball. He played the washboard, an instrument described as 'semi-legitimate' at best. His strength was his deep, strong voice and his ability to deliver lyrics that were both pertinent to the times and often than not, humorous. He was a close friend of Big Bill Broonzy, who often joked that Brown was his half-brother, a claim that cannot be affirmed although, they did both come to

Chicago from the same rural area of Arkansas. Brown's popularity is emphasized by the fact that he was recorded constantly between 1935 and 1949 by Victor Records and that almost everything was issued. He was a mainstay of a shifting group of musicians centred on A&R man Lester Melrose which included Broonzy, Tampa Red, Jazz Gillum and Memphis Slim. They often played on each others sessions and joined together in groups like the Hokum Boys and the State Street Swingers, thus giving rise to what writer Sam Charters described as 'the Bluebird Beat'. Brown's popularity declined sharply as the 50s arrived and he recorded under his own name for only one more label, Chess in 1953, and one of these records was issued as being by Little Walter. He played on the Spivey recordings made by John Henry Barbee in 1964 but died before he could take advantage of the revived interest in blues.

Albums: *Washboard Sam* (1965), *Feeling Lowdown* (1972).

Brown, Roy James

b. 10 September 1925, New Orleans, Louisiana, USA, d. 25 May 1981, Los Angeles, California, USA. Brown formed his own gospel quartet, the Rookie Four, and frequently sang in the local church before moving to California in 1942. After two years as a professional boxer, he began entering and winning amateur talent contests with his renditions of the pop songs of his idol, Bing Crosby. He returned to Louisiana in 1945 and formed his first jump band, the Mellodeers, for a long-term residency at the Club Granada in Galveston, Texas. There he worked for some time with Clarence Samuels as a double act, the Blues Twins, and was recorded illegitimately by the local Gold Star label. By this time, Brown had eschewed Tin Pan Alley pop for jump blues, and was singing in a highly original style for the time, utilizing his gospel background and his extremely soulful voice. Returning to New Orleans penniless in 1947, Brown tried in vain to sell a song he had written to the great blues shouter Wynonie Harris. When Harris turned the song down, Brown sang the number with Harris's band and, legend has it, tore up the house. The song, 'Good Rockin' Tonight', was soon recorded by Brown for DeLuxe and sold so well throughout the south that, ironically, Wynonie Harris covered it for King Records. A

Roy Brown

popular phrase from the song persuaded Brown to rename his combo the Mighty Mighty Men, and he recorded extensively for DeLuxe and, later, King Records between 1947-55 during which time he had further success with such songs as 'Boogie At Midnight', 'Hard Luck Blues', 'Love Don't Love Nobody', 'Long About Sundown' and 'Trouble At Midnight'. During this phase of his career, the gospel-soul singer wailed about earthy secular subjects (some of them too ribald to be released for thirty years or more) and inspired such devotees including B.B. King, Bobby 'Blue' Bland, Jackie Wilson, Little Richard and James Brown.

In 1956, Dave Bartholomew signed Brown to Imperial Records where he spent his time split successfully between making mediocre Fats Domino-styled records or covering pop-rockabilly hits. And he slid further into pop during 1959 at King Records. Things improved in the soul era with a handful of good Willie Mitchell-arranged singles in Memphis for Home Of The Blues. A decade of label hopping followed with Brown working often with Johnny Otis's band, until 1977 when a great deal of interest was generated with the release of *Laughing But Crying*, a collection of vintage

tracks issued on Jonas Bernholm's Route 66 label. The following year Brown toured Europe to packed houses and rave reviews and returned to the USA to a similar reception. A string of successful nationwide appearances culminated in Brown's storming return to the New Orleans's Jazz & Heritage Festival in April 1981. He died peacefully the following month.

Albums: *Hard Times* (1968), *Hard Luck Blues* (1976), *Laughing But Crying* (1977), *Great Rhythm & Blues Oldies* (1977), *Good Rocking Tonight* (1978), *Cheapest Price In Town* (1979), *Saturday Nite* (1982), *Good Rockin' Tonight* (1984), *I Feel That Young Man's Rhythm* (1985), *Boogie At Midnight* (1985), *The Bluesway Sessions* (1988), *Blues DeLuxe* (1992).

Brown, Tommy

Discovered by the Griffin Brothers while touring in Atlanta, Georgia in 1950, Brown recorded for Savoy Records in Atlanta under his own name - with the Griffin's band in support - before moving north to Washington, DC to join the brothers in their touring and recording unit. His first Dot recording with the Griffin Brothers was a cover of Dave Bartholomew's 'Tra-La-La', and it was a huge success peaking at

Beulah Bryant

number 7 in the R&B charts in August 1951. This was followed by an even bigger hit in December when Brown's emotional 'Weepin' & Cryin'' reached number 3, and heralded a succession of such histrionic records. Leaving the Griffins Brothers in 1952, Brown returned to Savoy for one session billed as 'Tommy 'Weepin' & Cryin'' Brown'. He then recorded in a variety of blues and R&B styles for various labels; King Records (including a vocal version of 'Honky Tonk' with Bill Doggett), United (with Walter Horton), Groove, Imperial and ABC. He remained a nightclub singer and comedian in Atlanta throughout the 60s and 70s and is currently reported to be working in a nursing home.

Albums: with the Griffin Brothers *Riffin' With The Griffin Brothers Orchestra* (1985), with Walter Horton arid Alfred Harris *Harmonica Blues Kings* (1986).

Brown, Walter

b. August 1916, Dallas, Texas, USA, d. June 1956, Lawton, Oklahoma, USA. Discovered by bandleader Jay McShann just a few days before his band's debut recording session for Decca Records in Dallas in April 1941, Brown became the band's biggest selling point, with his laid-back blues style on such successful titles as 'Hootie Blues', 'Lonely Boy Blues', and the million-selling 'Confessin' The Blues'. In 1945, owing to a drug problem, Brown left the band to work and record as a soloist, although he often used McShann and/or old colleagues on his later recordings for King (1945/6), Signature (1947), Mercury (1947), Capitol (1949) and Peacock (1951). He is reported to have retired to Lawton, Oklahoma, during the early 50s where he opened his own nightclub. He died in June 1956 from drug-related disorders. In spite of his personal life, Walter 'Confessin' The Blues' Brown recorded over 50 individual blues in his unique lazy drawl during his 10 year recording career and seldom produced a less than outstanding performance. He has been named as a major influence by artists as diverse as Chuck Berry and Clarence 'Big' Miller.

Albums: *Confessin' The Blues* (1981), with Jay McShann *The Early Bird Charlie Parker* (1982), with McShann *Hootie's KC Blues* (1983).

Bryant, Beulah

b. Blooma Walton, 20 February 1918, Dayton, Alabama, USA, d. 31 January 1988, New York City, New York, USA. Bryant frequently sang with local church groups before moving to California in 1936 where she heard, and was influenced by, Ella Fitzgerald. After winning a networked radio show amateur contest the following year, she formed her own trio and began making regular appearances on the west coast. In 1945 she moved to New York and began working as a solo artist. Her recording career began in the late 40s on the tiny Do-Kay-Lo label, switching to MGM (many of the masters being provided by Joe Davis), and making a final session for Excello in 1955. Throughout the 50s, 60s and 70s Bryant was used extensively in radio, films and television. She also maintained an exhaustive touring schedule. In 1979 she resumed her recording career with a fine session for Victoria Spivey's label.

Album: with Irene Redfield, Millie Bosman *Blues Women* (1985).

Buchanan, Roy

b. 23 September 1939, Ozark, Alabama, USA, d. August 1988. The son of a preacher, Buchanan discovered gospel music through the influence of travelling revivalists. This interest engendered his love of R&B and having served an apprenticeship playing guitar in scores of minor groups, he secured fame on joining Dale Hawkins in 1958. Although Buchanan is often erroneously credited with the break on the singer's much-lauded 'Suzie Q', contributions on 'My Babe' and 'Grandma's House', confirmed his remarkable talent. Roy also recorded with Freddie Cannon, Bob Luman and the Hawks, and completed several low-key singles in his own right before retiring in 1962. However, he re-emerged the following decade with *Roy Buchanan*, an accomplished, versatile set which included a slow, hypnotic rendition of the C&W standard 'Sweet Dreams'. *Loading Zone* was an accomplished album and contained two of his finest (and longest) outings; the pulsating 'Green Onions' featured shared solos with the song's co-composer Steve Cropper and the extraordinary 'Ramon's Blues'(again with Cropper). His trademark was a battered Fender Telecaster guitar, which gave a distinctive

Roy Buchanan

treble-sounding tone to his work. A series of similarly crafted albums were released, before the guitarist again drifted out of the limelight. His career was rekindled in 1986 with the promising *When A Guitar Plays The Blues*, but despite enjoying the accolades of many contemporaries, including Robbie Robertson, Buchanan was never comfortable with the role of virtuoso. A shy, reticent individual, he made several unsuccessful suicide attempts before hanging himself in a police cell in 1988, following his arrest on a drunk-driving charge.

Albums: *Roy Buchanan* (1972), *Second Album* (1973), *That's What I'm Here For* (1974), *In The Beginning* (1974), *Rescue Me* (1975), *Live Stock* (1975), *A Street Called Straight* (1976), *Loading Zone* (1977), *You're Not Alone* (1978), *My Babe* (1981), *When A Guitar Plays The Blues* (1986), *Dancing On The Edge* (1987), *Hot Wire* (1987). Compilation: *Early Roy Buchanan* (1989, compiled from his work as a backing musician).

Buckwheat Zydeco

b. Stanley Dural, 1947, Lafayette, Louisiana, USA. Dural started his musical career playing piano and organ in local bands around southeast Louisiana. As Buckwheat Zydeco emerged as one of the leaders of zydeco music, the accordion-led dance music of southern Louisiana's French-speaking Creoles, in the late 80s and early 90s. Dural, taking the nickname 'Buckwheat', worked with R&B singers Joe Tex, Barbara Lynn and Clarence 'Gatemouth' Brown during the 60s. Following a period playing keyboards in Clifton Chenier's band, he took up accordion and moved to the indigenous sound of zydeco. He formed his own funk band, the Hitchhikers, in the 70s, followed by the Ils Sont Partis Band in 1979. That outfit recorded eight albums for Blues Unlimited, Black Top and Rounder Records before accordionist Dural formed Buckwheat Zydeco. Signed to Island Records in 1987, the group had recorded three albums for the label by 1990, the latter produced by David Hidalgo of Los Lobos.

Albums: *One For The Road* (1979), *100% Fortified Zydeco* (1985), *Buckwheat Zydeco* (1986), *Waitin' For My Ya Ya* (1987), *On A Night Like This* (1987), *Taking It Home* (1988), *Turning Point* (1988), *Buckwheat Zydeco And The Ils Sont Partis Band* (1988), *Where There's Smoke There's Fire* (1990).

Buford, 'Mojo' George

b. 10 November 1929, Hernando, Mississippi, USA. Buford began to dabble with the harmonica at the age of 12, while living in Memphis but he started playing seriously after hearing Little Walter's 'Juke'. He moved to Chicago in 1952 and formed the Savage Boys, a band 'adopted' by Muddy Waters to retain his club residency while he was on tour. Buford recorded behind Jojo Williams in 1959 and in the same year joined Muddy's band for the first of several spells. In 1962, Buford left and moved to Minneapolis where he acquired his nickname by fulfilling requests for 'Got My Mojo Working'. While there, he recorded sporadically under his own name until the late 70s. In 1967 he recorded with several of Muddy Waters's sidemen and later played on several of Waters's recording sessions. Buford returned to Chicago in 1978, making an album for Rooster Blues, and in the 80s moved back to Memphis. He has also recorded sessions in Europe for Isabel and JSP Records. Buford's vocals and his approach to blues still remain close to the Waters sound. Album: *State Of The Blues Harp* (1989).

Bumble Bee Slim

b. Amos Easton, 7 May 1905, Brunswick, Georgia, USA, d. 1968, Los Angeles, California, USA. Bumble Bee Slim was a blues guitarist, although he seldom played on record; it was as a singer that he recorded prolifically from 1931-37. Leaving home around 1920, he led a wandering life for eight years before settling in Indianapolis, and later Chicago. As a singer, he was influenced by Naptown's Leroy Carr, and his songs convey a modified version of Carr's bittersweet aesthetic. Easton appears friendly, confiding and philosophical, sometimes bruised by life's adversities, but never crushed by its tragedies. In part, no doubt, this is a reflection of his own personality, but it also typifies the switch from personal expression to performance art of recorded blues in the 30s. His records were very popular; songs such as 'B&O Blues' and 'Sail On, Little Girl, Sail On' fed back into folk tradition, and several were big enough hits to be remade with fresh lyrics, and 'New' prefixed to their titles. Slim's pleasant personality, the distinguished calibre of many of his accompanists, and the way his blues mirrored black life in the 30s all contributed to his star

Buckwheat

status. Nevertheless, lack of reward seems to have prompted him temporarily to stop recording in 1937, and to move to Los Angeles, where he had three records issued for black consumption, and released an unsuccessful album for the new white audience, accompanied by cool jazz musicians.

Albums: *Bee's Back In Town* (1962), *City Blues* (1973), *Vintage Country Blues* (1976), *Bumble Bee Slim* (1987).

Bunn, Teddy

b. c.1909, Freeport, Long Island, New York, USA, d. 20 July 1978. A remarkably gifted self-taught guitarist, Bunn freelanced for most of his life. Perhaps as a result of his never being long in one place, his achievements are often overlooked. He was an inventive soloist, skilfully weaving intriguing patterns from deceptively simple single lines. In this respect, he pre-dated Charlie Christian, whose arrival on the jazz scene effectively obliterated the efforts of every other guitarist. In Bunn's case this was unfortunate and his subsequent neglect is unfair. He switched from acoustic to electric guitar around 1940. Bunn was also a vocalist (he started out as a calypso singer) and this led him into an important musical collaboration with Leo Watson. Their group, the Spirits Of Rhythm, were one of the most original vocal outfits of the 30s and 40s. During this same period, Bunn played guitar with several leading blues and jazzmen, including Duke Ellington, John Kirby, Jimmy Noone, Bob Howard, Johnny Dodds, Oran 'Hot Lips' Page, Peetie Wheatstraw, Mezz Mezzrow, Sidney Bechet and Lionel Hampton. Bunn was able to move comfortably into R&B in the 50s, working with Jack McVea and Louis Jordan. By the end of the decade he had taken the extra step into rock 'n' roll. During the last decade of his life Bunn was in very poor health and worked only rarely.

Compilations: *Teddy Bunn* (1930-39 recordings), *The Spirits Of Rhythm* (1932-34 recordings), with Mezz Mezzrow and Tommy Ladnier *The Panassie Sessions* (1938-39 recordings).

Burkes, Conish 'Pinetop'

Connie Burkes was one of the extensive school of blues pianists operating in jukes, lumber camps, and tank towns along the course of the Santa Fe Railroad network in Texas, USA. This sparse information is virtually all that is known about Burke, and comes from the the the memories of surviving contemporaries. He recorded only once; a six track session made for Vocalion in San Antonio, Texas, during 1937.

Compilation: *The Piano Blues Volume II* (1979).

Burleson, Hattie

Burleson was an important figure on the Texas, USA blues scene; she made a few records, including a tribute to her lover, 'Jim Nappy', but was most significant as an entrepreneur. Dallas based, she ran a stable of singers, dancers and musicians which was the mainstay of shows at Ella B. Moore's Park Theater. Along with lesser known artists, Burleson managed Lillian Glinn, and was instrumental in getting her, and a good many other Texas musicians, on to records, where she made sure they cut her compositions. Burleson also ran a dancehall and a Marathon dancing rink in Dallas, and her road shows toured throughout the south-west under Jim Nappy's management; even in the mid-50s she was touring in south Texas with a small show.

Albums: *Texas Blues - Dallas* (1980), *Female Blues Singers B/C* (1990).

Burnett, 'T-Bone'

b. John Henry Burnett, 1945, St. Louis, Missouri, USA. Burnett was a member of Bob Dylan's Rolling Thunder Revue who became a highly regarded producer and songwriter during the 80s. He grew up in Texas playing guitar in local bands before travelling to Los Angeles to produce Delbert And Glen and recorded a solo album for Uni. After touring with Delaney And Bonnie and the B-52's he joined Dylan's touring troupe. When the Rolling Thunder concerts were over, Burnett founded the Alpha Band with ex-Dylan accompanist Steve Soles (guitar) and David Mansfield (guitar/mandolin). The group made three albums between 1976-79. After the demise of the Alpha Band, Burnett made a solo album for Takoma and his growing reputation was evidenced by the presence of guitarists Ry Cooder and Richard Thompson on *Proof Through The Night*. He later toured with Thompson and Elvis Costello, releasing a 1985 single with the latter as the Coward Brothers. He also co-wrote with Bono of U2. Among the artists Burnett has produced are Leo Kottke, Los

Lobos and Bruce Cockburn.

Albums: *J. Henry Burnett* (1972), *Truth Decay* (1980), *Proof Through the Night* (1983), *Behind The Trap Door* (1984), *'T-Bone' Burnett* (1986), *The Talking Animals* (1988).

Burns, Eddie

b. 8 February, 1928, Mississippi, USA Inspired by John Lee 'Sonny Boy' Williamson and self-taught, Burns was a stalwart of the immediate post-war Detroit blues scene, being first recorded in 1948 by Bernie Bessman. He was the man responsible for giving John Lee Hooker his break and used Burns as a session musician for Hooker in 1949. This session produced four tracks including the fast shuffle, 'Burnin'Hell', which was notable for Burn's powerful harmonica playing. Throughout the 50s and 60s he periodically recorded for Joseph Van Battle, who either released the material on his own JVB and Von labels or else sold the masters to concerns like Gotham and Checker. Rarely straying from his home state of Michigan, Burns briefly visited Europe in 1972 under the billing Eddie 'Guitar' Burns, recording an album in London for Action. He returned three years later for a more intensive tour under the 'American Blues Legends '75' banner. Since then Eddie Burns has stayed mostly in Detroit working day-jobs, playing clubs in the evening and occasionally appearing at festivals.

Albums: *Detroit Black Bottom* (1975) *Treat Me Like I Treat You* (1985), *Detroit* (1990).

Burrage, Harold

b. 30 March 1931, Chicago, Illinois, USA, d. 26 November 1966, Chicago, Illinois, USA. A great singer and pianist in the city blues tradition, Burrage was a well-known face on Chicago's west side R&B scene by his late teens. In 1950 he made his first recordings for Decca backed by Horace Henderson's septet, resulting in Claude Trenier's suggestive 'Hi Yo Silver' which spawned several cover versions. He made one-off sessions for Aladdin (1951) and States (1954) before hitting his stride between 1956-58 with Cobra Records, with whom he recorded in his own right in a soul-blues vein as well as backing artists such as Magic Sam, Otis Rush and Ike Turner. He continued in the same style in his brief associations for VeeJay Records Paso and Foxy, but in 1962 he joined One-Der-Ful's

M-Pac subsidiary and over the following four years laid down his prime work, including his only real hit, 'Got To Find A Way', which reached number 31 in the August 1965 R&B charts. He died tragically young at the age of 35, at the home of his friend Tyrone Davis.

Compilation: *She Knocks Me Out* (1981 rec. 1956-1958).

Burris, J.C.

b. 1928, Selby, North Carolina, USA, d. 15 May 1988, Greensboro, North Carolina, USA. Burris learned harmonica from his uncle Sonny Terry. He left his farm work in his early 20s and moved to New York, where between 1955 and 1960 he made some recordings with Granville 'Sticks' McGhee, Brownie McGhee and Terry. At the turn of that decade, he moved out to the west coast, settling eventually in San Francisco, where he began to make a name for himself on the local folk-blues scene. A stroke disabled him for some years, but he eventually returned to music, performing regularly and making an album in 1975. His style owed much to Terry's, but he added his own distinctive touches, performing solo, playing bones as well as his harmonica, and sometimes appearing with a wooden dancing doll.

Album: *One Of These Mornings* (1975).

Burse, Charlie

b. 25 August 1901, Decatur, Alabama, USA, d. 20 December 1965, Memphis, Tennessee, USA. A banjoist from childhood, Burse moved to Memphis in 1928, and joined the Memphis Jug Band on guitar. He quickly imposed his extrovert personality on their music, and seems to have effectively become co-leader with Will Shade. The band's last recordings in 1934 owed much to his scat singing and Fats Waller inspired vocal interjections. The jazz influence is even more marked on the 1939 recordings by Charlie Burse And His Memphis Mudcats, which featured an alto saxophone. Relocated in 1956, he recorded occasionally until 1963, usually in association with Will Shade.

Albums: *American Skiffle Bands* (1958), *Beale Street Mess Around* (1976), *Charlie Burse & James De Berry* (1989). *The Memphis Jug Vol. 2* (1991), *Vol. 3* (1991), *1932-34* (1991).

Paul Butterfield

Butler, George 'Wild Child'

b. 1 October 1936, Autaugville, Alabama, USA. Butler was one of the last of the wandering bluesmen. He suffered from the general lack of interest in older musical forms shown by the black record-buying public, yet still managed to make his most prized recordings, during the mid to late 60s. His introduction to the blues came via his elder brother Edward (he was one of twelve children) but his imagination was really sparked by the recordings of Sonny Boy 'Rice Miller' Williamson, and with a harmonica in his pocket he took to the road. He recorded a single for Shaw Records in Montgomery, Alabama in 1964 but his real break came when Willie Dixon introduced him to Stan Lewis's Jewel label which, operating out of Shreveport, Louisiana, was the only label of any size still producing records for the southern juke-box trade. Since that time his output on record has remained limited although his tough harmonic style has continued to earn him a living.

Selected albums: *Open Up Baby* (1984), *Keep On Doin' What You're Doin'* (1991).

Butterbeans And Susie

Butterbeans (b. Jody Edwards Butterbeans, 19 July 1895, Georgia, USA, d. 28 October 1967) and Susie (b. Susie Hawthorn, 1896, Pensacola, Florida, USA, d. 5 December 1963, Chicago, Illinois, USA) were one of the most durable teams in black vaudeville. They appeared together from before their marriage in 1916 until just before Susie's death nearly 50 years later. They supported Trixie Smith in 1920 and James Brown in 1959, and headlined their own revues in the late 20s. Their recordings were miniature comic sketches in song and speech, with Butterbeans always cast as the henpecked, put-upon husband and Susie as the dominant wife, making both sexual ('I Wanna Hot Dog For My Roll') and financial ('Papa Ain't No Santa Claus, Mama Ain't No Christmas Tree') demands. Sometimes backed by top jazz musicians, their performances, though seldom explicitly blues, usually had blues inflections.

Albums: *Butterbeans And Susie* (1960), *Daddy's Got The Mojo* (1989).

Butterfield, Paul

b. 17 December 1942, Chicago, Illinois, USA, d. 3 May 1987. As a catalyst, Butterfield helped shape the development of blues music played by white musicians in the same way that John Mayall and Cyril Davis were doing in Britain. Butterfield had the advantage of standing in with Howlin' Wolf, Muddy Waters and his mentor Little Walter. Butterfield sang, composed and led a series of seminal bands throughout the 60s, but it was his earthy Chicago-style harmonica playing that gained him attention. He was arguably the first white man to play blues with the intensity and emotion of the great black blues harmonica players. Mike Bloomfield, Mark Naftalin, Elvin Bishop, David Sanborn and Nick Gravenites were some of the outstanding musicians that passed through his bands. His now infamous performance at the 1965 Newport Folk Festival gave him the distinction of being the man who supported Bob Dylan's musical heresy, by going electric. In 1973 his new venture *Better Days* went on the road to average response, and during subsequent years he struggled to find success. Ill health plagued him for some time, much of it caused by aggravating stomach hernias caused by his powerful harmonica playing. Butterfield's legacy stays, his influence untinged and much of his catalogue is still available. *East-West* remains his best-selling and most acclaimed work, although the rawness of the debut album also has many critical admirers.

Albums: *Paul Butterfield Blues Band* (1966), *East-West* (1966), *The Resurrection Of Pigboy Crabshaw* (1968), *In My Own Dream* (1968), *Keep On Movin'* (1969), *Live* (1971), *Sometimes I Just Feel Like Smilin'* (1971), *Offer You Can't Refuse* (1972), *Better Days* (1973), *It All Comes Back* (1973), *Better Days* (1973), *It All Comes Back* (1974), *Put It In Your Ear* (1976), *North South For Bearsville* (1981), *The Legendary Paul Butterfield Rides Again* (1986). Compilation: *Golden Butter - Best Of The Paul Butterfield Blues Band* (1972).

Cage, James 'Butch'

b. 16 March 1894, Hamburg, Mississippi, USA, d. 1975, Zachary, Louisiana, USA. Butch Cage moved to Louisiana following the great 1927 floods, and worked at various menial jobs, entertaining his neighbours at weekend parties and, if they were musicians, playing alongside them. After being recorded in 1959, Cage and his partner Willie B. Thomas were a sensation at the 1960 Newport Folk Festival. Cage had begun his musical career on fife, and was also a respectable guitar player, but his main instrument was the fiddle. He had learned to play the instrument in 1911 from two elderly musicians, and his playing preserved the rasping dissonances of African fiddle music. His repertoire encompassed religious music, blues and popular song, and was an integral part of the life of his community.
Albums: *Country Negro Jam Session* (1960), *I Have To Paint My Face* (1969), *Raise A Ruckus Tonight* (1979).

Call, Bob

Bob Call was a blues pianist, active in Chicago and best known for his accompaniments. He recorded in the late 20s with a number of artists, including Thomas A. Dorsey, Elzadie Robinson and James 'Boodle It' Wiggins. Robinson's 'St. Louis Cyclone Blues' was a particularly outstanding recording. He also recorded one single track under his own name at this time, '31 Blues'. In 1948, he appeared on record again, one side a piano-led instrumental, the other featuring the vocals of Grant Jones.
Compilation: *The Piano Blues, Volume 2* (1977).

Callicott, Joe

b. 1901, Nesbit, Mississippi, USA, d. 1969, Mississippi, USA. Joe Callicott spent his whole life in the area south of Memphis, and his music has affinities with that of his neighbour Jim Jackson and especially Frank Stokes, with whom he sometimes worked in Memphis. His chief musical associate, however, was Garfield Akers, and it was as Akers' second guitarist that he first

recorded in 1929. Callicott's solitary 78 rpm single was recorded the following year, pairing 'Fare Thee Well Blues', from the songster tradition, with 'Travelling Mama Blues', an amalgam of contemporary verses, both sung in a high, forceful voice to a rhythmic accompaniment. Callicott virtually ceased playing in 1959 when Akers died; although he had slowed down somewhat, his guitar rhythms were still metronomic. His voice became gentler, making the sound of his music more akin to that of Frank Stokes (minus the melodic embellishments usually provided by Stokes' second guitar or violin accompanists). Callicott favoured extended performances, but his ability to play in a variety of keys and tunings saves his work from the monotony that might be expected from the steady rhythmic tread, so that the overall effect is gently hypnotic.
Selected albums: *Deal Gone Down* (1968), *Mississippi Delta Blues, Volume 2* (1968), *Presenting The Country Blues* (1969), *Son House And The Great Delta Blues Singers* (1990).

Campbell, Eddie

b. 6 May 1939, Duncan, Mississippi, USA. Campbell began playing music on a one-string guitar, and later moved to Chicago with his family at the age of seven. He was inspired by Muddy Waters to learn to play seriously, and in the late 50s he was part of the coterie of young, exciting blues guitarists on the city's west side (acquaintances included Magic Sam, Otis Rush, Luther Allison and Willie James Lyons). He made a few recordings for small, local labels but his debut album in the 70s suffered from poor distribution. He did, however, gain international acclaim in 1979 as a member of the American Blues Legends tour. He returned to Chicago, but settled in Europe in 1984 and has since acquired a large following for his style of blues.
Albums: *King Of The Jungle* (1977, remixed 1985), *Let's Pick It* (1985), *The Baddest Cat On The Block* (1985), *Mind Trouble* (1988).

Campbell, John

b. 1952, Shreveport, Louisiana, USA. Campbell, a white man, became an authentic sounding blues singer/guitarist after a serious drag racing accident in 1967, which left him without one of his eyes and several thousand stitches in his face. Prior to this crash, he had been curious about

John Campbell

music – his grandmother played lap steel guitar – but he was more interested in becoming a tearaway. During his lengthy period of recuperation, much of it spent in solitude, he taught himself to play guitar and became devoted to the work of the black bluesmen who had recorded for the local Jewel label in Shreveport; in particular John Lee Hooker and Lightnin' Hopkins, who became his major influence. Leaving school in the late 60s, he became a travelling troubadour, working as opening act for 'Gatemouth' Brown and Hubert Smith, ultimately relocating to New York where he played local clubs for many years. His recording debut came in 1988, when guitarist Ronnie Earl sent a tape of Campbell to the specialist Crosscut label in Germany. Earl produced his first album *A Man And His Blues*, but it was hardly distributed in the USA, and he remained an obscure cult figure until he began working with guitarist Alexander Kennedy. He and Kennedy were opening for Albert King in New York when he was signed by Elektra, and in 1991 released *One Believer*, produced by Dennis Walker (also Robert Gray's producer) backed by members of both Gray's band and Joe Ely's group. Campbell plays solely amplified acoustic guitar, and his songwriting partnership with Walker and Kennedy has produced several modern blues classics like 'Devil In My Closet', 'Tiny Coffin' and 'Take Me Down'.

Albums: *A Man And His Blues* (1988), *One Believer* (1991).

Canned Heat

This popular, but ill-fated blues/rock group was formed in 1965 by two Los Angeles-based blues aficionados: Alan Wilson (b. 4 July 1943, Boston, Massachusetts, USA; vocals, harmonica, guitar) and Bob 'The Bear' Hite (b. 26 February 1943, Torrance, California, USA; vocals). Wilson, nicknamed 'Blind Owl' in deference to his thick-lensed spectacles, was already renowned for his distinctive harmonica work and had accompanied Son House on the veteran bluesman's post 'rediscovery' album, *Father Of Folk Blues*. Wilson's obsession with the blues enabled him to have a massive archive blues collection by his early twenties. The duo was joined by Frank Cook (drums) and Henry Vestine (b. 25 December 1944, Washington, DC, USA; guitar), a former member of the Mothers Of Invention. They took the name Canned Heat from a 1928 recording by Tommy Johnson and employed several bassists prior to the arrival of Larry Taylor, an experienced session musician who had worked with Jerry Lee Lewis and the Monkees.

Canned Heat's debut album was promising rather than inspired, offering diligent readings of such 12-bar standards as 'Rollin' And Tumblin'', 'Dust My Broom' and 'Bullfrog Blues'. However, the arrival of new drummer Alfredo Fito (b. Adolfo De La Parra, 8 February 1946, Mexico City, Mexico) coincided with a newfound confidence displayed almost immediately on *Boogie With Canned Heat*. This impressive selection introduced the extended 'Fried Hookey Boogie', a piece destined to become an in-concert favourite, and the hypnotic remake of Jim Oden's 'On The Road Again', which gave the group a UK Top 10 and US Top 20 hit single in 1968. Wilson's distinctive frail high voice, sitar-like guitar introduction and accompanying harmonica has enabled this version to become a classic. A double set, *Livin' The Blues*, featured some of the group's finest moments, including an enthralling version of Charlie Patton's 'Pony Blues' and a 19-minute *tour de force* 'Parthenogenesis', which captured the quintet at their most experimental. However, it was Wilson's adaptation of a Henry Thomas song, 'Bulldoze Blues', which proved most popular. The singer retained the tune of the original, rewrote the lyric and emerged with 'Goin' Up The Country', whose simple message caught the prevalent back-to-nature attitude of the late 60s,. This evocative performance charted in the US and UK Top 20, and was one of the highlights of the successful Woodstock movie.

Between 1969-70 Canned Heat recorded four more albums, including a spirited collaboration with blues boogie mentor John Lee Hooker, and an enthralling documentary of their 1970 European tour. *Hallelujah* boasted one of artist George Hunters's finest album covers. It also featured 'Get Off My Back', which in its day was used by hi-fi buffs to check their systems were in phase, as the cross-channel switching in the mix was outrageously overdone. *Future Blues* marked the arrival of guitarist Harvey Mandel, replacing Henry Vestine, who could no longer tolerate working with Larry Taylor. The

Canned Heat

reshaped band enjoyed two further UK hits with a cover of Wilbert Harrison's 'Let's Work Together', which reached number 2, and the cajun-inspired 'Sugar Bee', but were rocked by the suicide of Alan Wilson, whose body was found in Hite's backyard on 3 September 1970. His death sparked a major reconstruction within the group. Taylor and Mandel left to join John Mayall, the former's departure prompting Vestine's return, while Antonio De La Barreda became Canned Heat's new bassist. The new quartet completed *Historical Figures And Ancient Heads*, before Bob Hite's brother Richard replaced Barreda for the band's 1973 release, *The New Age*. The changes continued throughout the decade, undermining the band's strength of purpose. Bob Hite, the sole remaining original member, attempted to keep the group afloat, but was unable to secure a permanent recording deal. Spirits lifted with the release of *Human Condition*, but the years of struggle had taken their toll. On 5 April 1981, following a gig at the Palomino Club, the gargantuan vocalist collapsed and died of a heart attack. Despite the loss of many key members, the Canned Heat name has survived. Inheritors Larry Taylor and Fito De La Parra completed 1989's *Re-heated* album with two new guitarists, James Thornbury and Junior Watson. They now pursue the lucrative nostalgia circuit.

Albums: *Canned Heat* (1967), *Boogie With Canned Heat* (1968), *Livin' The Blues* (1968), *Hallelujah* (1969), *Vintage - Canned Heat* (1969, early recordings), *Future Blues* (1970), *Live At The Topanga Canyon* (1970), with John Lee Hooker *Hooker 'N' Heat* (1971), *Canned Heat Concert (Recorded Live In Europe)* (1971), *Memphis Heat* (1971), *Historical Figures And Ancient Heads* (1972), *The New Age* (1973), *Rollin' And Tumblin'* (1973), *One More River To Cross* (1974), *Human Condition* (1978), *Boogie Assault - Live In Australia* (1981), *Captured Live* (1981), with Hooker *Hooker 'N' Heat - Live* (1981), *Kings Of The Boogie* (1982), *Dog House Blues* (1983), *Re-Heated* (1989). Compilations: *Canned Heat Cook Book (The Best Of Canned Heat)* (1969), *The Very Best Of Canned Heat* (1973), *Greatest Hits* (1988), *The Best Of Hooker 'N' Heat* (1989), *Let's Work Together - The Best Of Canned Heat* (1989).

Cannon, Gus

b. 12 September 1883, Red Banks, Mississippi, USA, d. 15 October 1979, Memphis, Tennessee, USA. As a youth, Cannon was a proficient fiddler, as well as a guitarist and pianist, but his main instrument was the banjo. Cannon, whose parents had been slaves, made his first banjo at the age of 12 from a guitar neck and a bread pan. He was taught to play in Clarksdale, Mississippi by a musician named Bud Jackson and studied other local players, such as W.C. Handy. It was as 'Banjo Joe' that Cannon appeared on the 'medicine shows' every summer from 1914-29, working as a farm labourer during the winter months While in Chicago with a medicine show he recorded for Paramount in 1927, with Blind Blake on guitar. Spurred on by the 1927 success on Victor of the Memphis Jug Band, Cannon added a coal-oil can on a neck harness to his equipment, and was signed when Victor came to Memphis in 1928. Cannon's Jug Stompers recorded annually from 1928-30, producing some of the finest and most bluesy jug band 78s. As fashions changed, Cannon ceased playing the streets for money in 1950, but he kept in practice, and made some recordings for folklorists in 1956 and 1961. In 1963 came an unlikely moment of fame, when the Rooftop Singers had a number 1 hit with 'Walk Right In', which the Stompers had recorded in 1929. He continued to make occasional recordings for friends in the 70s, though naturally they are of diminishing liveliness. Cannon has since been considered by music historians as one of the links between pre-blues Negro folk music and the blues.

Albums: *American Skiffle Bands* (1958), *Walk Right In* (1962). Compilations: *Old Country Blues* (1979), *Gus Cannon 1963* (1988), *Will Shade And Gus Cannon 1961* (1989), *The Complete Works* (1989), *Gus Cannon* (1991), *Gus Cannon & Noah Lewis* (1991).

Cannon's Jug Stompers

Led by Gus Cannon, the Jug Stompers were the finest and most blues orientated of the Memphis jug bands, recording for Victor from 1928 to 1930. Guitarists Ashley Thompson and Elijah Avery passed through the group's trio format in 1928 before vocalist Hosea Woods became the third member. The permanent fixtures were Cannon himself, (playing rushing, syncopated banjo and a fruity, ribald jug) and harmonica player Noah Lewis. The group blended the light hearted novelties of the medicine shows with strutting ragtime pieces and deeply emotional blues, particularly when Lewis took the vocal duties; Cannon's booming singing was more suited to the extrovert side of their repertoire. Of the group's members other than Cannon and Lewis, Woods died in the 30s, and Avery's subsequent history is unknown; Thompson was still playing in 1971 but died during the mid-70s.

Albums: *Cannon's Jug Stompers* (1974), *Old Country Blues* (1979), *The Complete Works* (1989), *Gus Cannon* (1991), *Gus Cannon & Noah Lewis* (1991).

Carolina Slim

b. Edward P. Harris, 22 August 1923, Leasburg, North Carolina, USA, d. 22 October 1953, Newark, New Jersey, USA. Little is known about Harris, but it seems that he started his musical career in North Carolina and moved to Newark about the time of his first recordings in 1950. Records followed on three different labels, under four different pseudonyms; Carolina Slim, Jammin' Jim, Country Paul and Lazy Slim Jim. These records are unusual for their time in that many of them feature solo country blues, either in the Carolina style of Blind Boy Fuller, or blatant copies of Lightnin' Hopkins, although all are skilful and convincing performances. At his best, Slim could synthesize his influences to produce a satisfyingly distinctive sound, but unfortunately he did not live long enough to develop a real style of his own.

Compilation: *Carolina Blues And Boogie* (1985).

Carr, Leroy

b. 27 March 1905, Nashville, Tennessee, USA, d. 29 April 1935. A self-taught pianist, Carr grew up in Kentucky and Indiana but was on the road working with a travelling circus when still in his teens. In the early 20s he was playing piano, often as an accompanist to singers, mostly in and around Covington, Kentucky. In the mid-20s he partnered 'Scrapper' Blackwell, touring and recording with him. Carr's singing style, a bitter-sweet, poetic way of interpreting the blues, brought a patina of urban refinement to the earthy, rough-cut intensity of the earlier country blues singers. Even though he rarely worked far afield, his recordings of his own compositions, which included 'Midnight Hour Blues', 'Hurry Down Sunshine', 'Blues Before Sunrise' and, especially, 'How Long, How Long Blues', proved enormously influential. Although he died young, Carr's work substantially altered approaches to blues singing and powerful echoes of his innovatory methods can be heard in the work of artists such as Champion Jack Dupree, Cecil Gant, Jimmy Rushing, Otis Spann, Eddie 'Cleanhead' Vinson and T-Bone Walker, who, in their turn, influenced countless R&B and rock 'n' roll singers of later generations. An acute alcoholic, Carr died on 29 April 1935.

Selected albums: *Leroy Carr (1928)* (1983), *Blues Before Sunrise* (1988), *Leroy Carr: 1929-1934* (1989), *Naptown Blues* (1988).

Carter, Bo

b. Armenter Chatmon, 21 March 1893, Bolton, Mississippi, USA, d. 21 September 1964, Memphis, Tennessee, USA. One of Henderson Chatmon's many musical sons, Bo Carter was a performing, and occasionally a recording, member of the family band, the Mississippi Sheiks. He played on guitar and violin, but it was as a solo singer and guitarist that he was best known on record. A talented and original player whose steel guitar provided him with an instantly recognizable sound, he was the first to record 'Corrine Corrina', and could compose sensitive, introspective songs like 'Sorry Feeling Blues'. However, both his guitar talents and his sensitivity were under-employed on record, where he recorded many tracks with titles like 'Banana In Your Fruit Basket' and 'Please Warm My Weiner' with stereotyped accompaniments. Blindness and changing fashions ended his career in the early 40s, and he died in poverty.

Compilations: *Greatest Hits* (1970), *Twist It Babe* (1974), *Banana In Your Fruit Basket* (1978), *Bo Carter* (1982).

Carter, Joe

b. 6 November 1927, Midland, Georgia, USA. In 1952 Carter settled in Chicago and is chiefly known as an Elmore James-styled slide guitarist and singer, although he can also play in a more modern vein. Carter made his only full album for the Barrelhouse label in 1976, though he has had numerous tracks released by JSP, MCM and

Leroy Carr

Red Lightnin , he also appeared in the BBC television documentary series *The Devils's Music*. In the late 70s he toured Europe, billed on some appearances as 'Elmore James Junior' and continues to play the clubs around Chicago as one of the city's few remaining slide guitarists in the traditional style.

Album: *Mean And Evil Blues* (1976). Compilations: *The Devil's Music* (1976), *Original Chicago Blues* (1982, 1976 recordings), *I Didn't Give A Damn If Whites Bought It! Volume One* (1984, rec 1977).

Carter, Vivian, And James Bracken

In 1948, Jim Bracken (b. 1909, Kansas City, Missouri, USA, d. 1972), set up Vivian's Record Shop in Gary Indiana, named after his radio announcer wife, Vivian Carter (b. 1920, Tunica, Mississippi. USA, d. 12 June 1989). Five years later, the duo started the VeeJay label to record Chicago's blues and R&B talent. Their first artists were blues singer Jimmy Reed and doo-wop group the Spaniels whose 'Goodnight Sweetheart Goodnight' was VeeJay's first R&B hit in 1954. Subsequently, Reed provided a series of 13 chart records between 1955 and 1961. The musical directors of the company were Calvin Carter (Vivian's brother) and Ewart Abner who signed artists such as Dee Clark and the Impressions. During the 50s, VeeJay also recorded gospel music (Swan Silvertones, Staple Singers) and licensed in R&B material from all over the USA. Pop success followed in the 60s with 'Duke Of Earl' by Gene Chandler and 'Sherry' by the Four Seasons. Then, in 1963, VeeJay was offered tracks by a new British group who had been turned down by Capitol, the US sister company to their UK label. At first, singles by the Beatles made little impact but after the onset of Beatlemania, Bracken and Carter had Top 10 hits with 'Please Please Me' and 'Twist And Shout'. The headquarters were briefly moved to Los Angeles but like many other small, locally-based labels, VeeJay could not compete on a national level and its financial affairs were insufficiently supervised by the owners. By 1966 the company was bankrupt. After the collapse, Abner joined Motown while Bracken and Carter ran small labels like J.V. and Ra-Bra. Bracken died in 1972 while Vivian Carter died in Gary in June 1989.

Caston, Leonard 'Baby Doo'

b. 2 June 1917, Sumrall, near Hattisburg, Mississippi, USA, d. 22 August 1987, Minneapolis, Minnesota, USA. More than just a blues pianist, Baby Doo Caston was a musician whose range included popular and light classical music. His early influence and mentor was his cousin Alan Weathersby who taught him to play guitar at an early age. After a couple of moves they began playing around the Nachez area and were managed by Leonard's mother Minda. Baby Doo took up the piano around 1936 and moved to Chicago where he heard people like Earl Hines, Big Bill Broonzy and T-Bone Walker, but was most influenced by Leroy Carr. He played with the Five Breezes and his own group, the Rhythm Rascals Trio, before the war found him on a United States Overseas entertainment tour with Alberta Hunter. He worked through China, Burma, India, Egypt, Africa and Europe, a high spot being a command performance for General's Eisenhower, Montgomery and Zhukov in Frankfurt on Main in 1945. Returning to Chicago he formed the Big Three Trio with Willie Dixon and Ollie Crawford, with whom he recorded for Bullet, Columbia and OKeh as well as working as a soloist (recording an album on his own Hot Shot label) and supporting many blues artists. His final job was a long-standing engagement in Minneapolis where he died of heart failure. His autobiography *From Blues To Pop* (1974) was written with the aid of Jeff Todd Titon.

Albums: *Hot Shot* (1986), *I Feel Like Steppin' Out* (1986), *Willie Dixon And The Big Three Trio* (1990).

Cat Iron

b. William Carradine, c.1896, Garden City, Louisiana, USA, d. c.1958, Natchez, Mississippi, USA. A folklorist's mishearing of his surname resulted in the evocative billing given this singer and guitarist's only album. Recorded on a single day in 1958, at first he would play only stirring versions of old hymns with slide accompaniment, but later consented to record a number of fine blues, including the important blues-ballad 'Jimmy Bell'. Cat Iron made a television appearance that year, but is believed to have died soon afterwards.

Album: *Cat Iron Sings Blues & Hymns* (1960).

Cephas, John

b. 4 September 1930, Washington, DC, USA. Cephas was raised in Bowling Green, Kentucky, and learned guitar from local musicians and from records. His music is indebted to Blind Boy Fuller and Eugene 'Buddy' Moss, and his dexterous, slightly anonymous playing shares with them a ragtime-influenced complexity. His singing voice is deep and rather unvaried, and his repertoire eclectic, drawing on both tradition and recordings (including, surprisingly, those of Skip James). Cephas has led a settled life as a civil service carpenter, with music a sideline; only in the 70s did his talent come to wider notice, when he began to play festivals and to record, at first with Wilbert 'Big Chief' Ellis and, since Ellis's death, with the young harmonica player Phil Wiggins.
Albums: *Living Country Blues, Volume 1* (1981), *Dog Days Of August* (1986).

Charles, Bobby

b. Robert Charles Guidry, 1938, Abbeville, Louisiana, USA. Charles became well-known in the 50s when three of his songs - 'See You Later Alligator', 'Walkin' To New Orleans' and 'But I Do' - were successfully covered by Bill Haley, Fats Domino and Clarence 'Frogman' Henry. The composer also recorded in his own right for Chicago's Chess label, but returned to the south the following decade for a series of low-key, largely unsuccessful, releases. The singer's career was relaunched in 1972 upon signing with Albert Grossman's Bearsville label. *Bobby Charles* featured support from several members of the Band, and this excellent album combined the artist's R&B and cajun roots to create a warm, mature collection. The set offered several excellent compositions, the highlight of which was the much-covered 'Small Town Talk'. Charles then guested on both of the albums by Paul Butterfield's Better Days, but he has since maintained a relatively low profile. However a new recording, *Clean Water*, was released in Europe in 1987.
Albums: *Bobby Charles* (1972, later reissued as *Small Town Talk* in 1988), *Clean Water* (1987). Compilations of Chess recordings: *Bobby Charles* (1983), *Chess Masters* (1986).

Charles, Ray

b. Ray Charles Robinson, 23 September 1930, Albany, Georgia, USA. Few epithets sit less comfortably than that of genius; Ray Charles has

Bobby Charles

borne this title for over thirty years. As a singer, composer, arranger and pianist, his prolific work deserves no other praise. Born in extreme poverty, Ray was slowly blinded by glaucoma until, by the age of seven, he had lost his sight completely. He learned to read and write music in braille and was accomplished on several instruments by the time he left school. Orphaned at age 15, Charles drifted around the Florida circuit, picking up work where he could, before moving across the country to Seattle. Here he continued his itinerant career, playing piano at several nightclubs in a style reminiscent of Nat 'King' Cole.

Ray began recording in 1949 and this early, imitative approach was captured on several sessions. Three years later Atlantic Records acquired his contract, but initially the singer continued his 'cool' direction, baring only an occasional hint of the passions later unleashed. 'It Should've Been Me', 'Mess Around' and 'Losing Hand' best represent this early R&B era, but Ray's individual style emerged as a result of his work with Guitar Slim. This impassioned, almost crude blues performer sang with a gospel-based fervour that greatly influenced Charles' thinking. He arranged Slim's million-selling single, 'Things That I Used To Do', of which the riffing horns and unrestrained voice set the tone for Ray's own subsequent direction. This effect was fully realized in 'I Got A Woman' (1954), a song soaked in the fervour of the Baptist Church, but rendered salacious by the singer's abandoned, unrefined delivery. Its extraordinary success, commercially and artistically, inspired similarly compulsive recordings including 'This Little Girl Of Mine' (1955), 'Talkin' 'Bout You' (1957) and the lush and evocative 'Don't Let The Sun Catch You Crying' (1959), a style culminating in the thrilling call and response of 'What'd I Say' (1959). This acknowledged classic is one of the all-time great encore numbers to be found being performed by countless singers and bands in stadiums, clubs and bars all over the world. However, Charles was equally adept at slow ballads, as his heartbreaking interpretations of 'Drown In My Own Tears' and 'I Believe To My Soul' (both 1959) clearly show. Proficient in numerous styles, Ray's recordings embraced blues, jazz, standards and even country, as his muscular reading of 'I'm Movin' On' attested.

In November 1959, Charles left the Atlantic label for ABC Records, where he secured both musical and financial freedom. Commentators often note this as the point at which the singer lost his fire, but early releases for this new outlet simply continued his groundbreaking style. 'Georgia On My Mind' (1960) and 'Hit The Road Jack' (1961) were, respectively, poignant and ebullient, and established the artist as an international name. This stature was enhanced further in 1962 with the release of the massive selling album, *Modern Sounds In Country And Western*, a landmark collection which produced the million-selling single 'I Can't Stop Loving You'. Its success defined the pattern for Ray's later career; the edges were blunted, the vibrancy was stilled as Charles' repertoire grew increasingly inoffensive. There were still moments of inspiration, 'Let's Go Get Stoned' and 'I Don't Need No Doctor' brought a glimpse of a passion now too often muted, while *Crying Time*, Ray's first album since kicking his heroin habit, compared favourably with any Atlantic release. This respite was, however, temporary and as the 60s progressed so the singer's work became less compulsive and increasingly MOR. Like most artists, he attempted cover versions of Beatles' songs and had substantial hits with versions of 'Yesterday' and 'Eleanor Rigby'. Two 70s' releases, *A Message From The People* and *Renaissance*, did include contemporary material in Stevie Wonder's 'Living In The City' and Randy Newman's 'Sail Away', but subsequent releases reneged on this promise. Charles' 80s' work included more country-flavoured collections and a cameo appearance in the film *The Blues Brothers*, but the period is better marked by the singer's powerful appearance on the USA For Africa release, 'We Are The World' (1985). It brought to mind a talent too often dormant, a performer whose marriage of gospel and R&B prepared the basis for soul music. His influence is inestimable, his talent widely acknowledged and imitated by formidable white artists such as Steve Winwood, Joe Cocker, Van Morrison and Eric Burdon. Charles has been honoured with countless awards during his career including the Lifetime Achievement Award. He has performed rock, jazz, blues and country with spectacular ease but it is as 'father of soul music' that remains his greatest title.

Ray Charles

Selected albums: *Hallelujah, I Love Her So* aka *Ray Charles* (1957), *The Great Ray Charles* (1957), with Milt Jackson *Soul Meeting* (1958), *Ray Charles At Newport* (1958), *Yes Indeed* (1958), *What'd I Say* (1959), *The Genius Of Ray Charles* (1959), *Ray Charles In Person* (1960), *Genius Hits The Road* (1960), *The Genius After Hours* (1961), *The Genius Sings The Blues* (1961), *Dedicated To You* (1961), *Genius + Soul = Jazz* (1961), with Betty Carter *Ray Charles And Betty Carter* (1961), *Modern Sounds In Country And Western Music* (1962), *Modern Sounds In Country And Western Music, Volume 2* (1962), *Ingredients In A Recipe For Soul* (1963), *Sweet And Sour Tears* (1964), *Have A Smile With Me* (1964), *Live In Concert* (1965), *Country And Western Meets Rhythm And Blues* aka *Together Again* (1965), *Crying Time* (1966), *Ray's Moods* (1966), *Ray Charles Invites You To Listen* (1967), *A Portrait Of Ray* (1968), *I'm All Yours, Baby!* (1969), *Doing His Thing* (1969), *My Kind Of Jazz* (1970), *Love Country Style* (1970), *Volcanic Action Of My Soul* (1971), *A Message From The People* (1972), *Through The Eyes Of Love* (1972), *Come Live With me* (1974), *Renaissance* (1975), *Live In Japan* (1975), with Cleo Laine *Porgy And Bess* (1976), *True To Life* (1977), *Love And Peace* (1978), *Ain't It So* (1979), *Brother Ray Is At It Again* (1980), *Wish You Were Here Tonight* (1983), *Do I Ever Cross Your Mind* (1984), *Friendship* (1985), *Just Between Us* (1988). Compilations: *The Ray Charles Story* (1962), *A Man And His Soul* (1967), *25th Anniversary In Show Business Salute To Ray Charles* (1971), *The Right Time* (1987), *The Collection* (1990 - ABC recordings). In addition to these releases Charles' big band recorded the following: *My Kind Of Jazz* (1970), *Jazz Number II* (1973), *My Kind Of Jazz, Part 3* (1975).

Further reading: *Brother Ray*, Ray Charles and David Ritz.

Chatmon, Sam

b. 10 January 1897, Bolton, Mississippi, USA, d. 2 February 1983, Hollandale, Mississippi, USA. Guitarist Sam Chatmon was one of the many children of ex-slave fiddler Henderson Chatmon, all of whom were musicians. Besides Sam, Lonnie (as the fiddling half of the Mississippi Sheiks), Bo (as Bo Carter) and pianist Harry all made recordings in the 30s In addition Sam's own son, Singing' Sam, is a bass guitarist.

Sam Snr.'s 1936 recordings with Lonnie, as the Chatmon Brothers are, not surprisingly, similar to those of the Mississippi Sheiks, who were the one black string band to become major stars on record. When white interest in the blues was aroused in the 60s, Sam proved to be the only member of the family to have survived with his musical faculties intact, and came out of almost 20 years of musical retirement to perform for the new audience until his death. A strong, somewhat inflexible vocalist, and a fluent, though rather anonymous, pattern picker, Chatmon in his later career played mostly blues, emphasizing the risqué when he was not covering the recorded hits of others. Perhaps more interesting than this side of his repertoire were the minstrel and popular songs of his youth like 'I Get The Blues When It Rains' and 'Turnip Greens'. He claimed, with some plausibility, to have composed 'Cross Cut Saw', twice made famous by Tommy McClennan and later by Albert King.

Albums: *The Mississippi Sheik* (1970), *The New Mississippi Sheiks* (1972), *Hollandale Blues* (1977), *Sam Chatmon's Advice* (1979), *Mississippi String Bands* (1989).

Chenier, C.J.

b. 28 September 1957, Port Arthur, Texas, USA. C.J. is the son of 'King Of Zydeco' Clifton Chenier. He began playing saxophone whilst in school but grew up knowing little about Louisiana zydeco music, and he spoke English at home. However, he learned quickly when he became a member of his father's band, replacing saxophonist John Hart. He recorded with his father and around 1984 he began to play accordion, graduating to opening shows as his father's health deteriorated. When his father died, he left his accordion to C.J., who has since recorded under his own name and rapidly established himself as a force to be reckoned with in the blues and zydeco market.

Albums: *Let Me In Your Heart* (1989), *Hot Rod* (1990).

Chenier, Clifton

b. 25 June 1925, Opelousas, Louisiana, USA, d. 12 December 1987. This singer, guitarist, accordion and harmonica player is regarded by many as the 'King' of zydeco music. Chenier was given lessons on the accordion by his father, and started performing at dances. He also had the advantage of being able to sing in French patois, English and Creole. In 1945, Chenier was working as a cane cutter in New Iberia. In 1946, he followed his older brother, Cleveland, to Lake Charles. He absorbed a wealth of tunes from musicians such as Zozo Reynolds, Izeb Laza, and Sidney Babineaux, who, despite their talent, had not recorded. The following year, Chenier travelled to Port Arthur, along with his wife Margaret, where he worked for the Gulf and Texaco oil refineries until 1954. Still playing music at weekends, Chenier was discovered by J.R. Fulbright, who recorded Clifton at radio station KAOK, and issued records of these and subsequent sessions. In 1955, 'Ay Tee Tee' became his best selling record, and he became established as a R&B guitarist. By 1956, having toured with R&B bands, he had turned to music full-time. In 1958, Chenier moved to Houston, Texas, and from this base played all over the South. Although ostensibly a cajun musician, he had also absorbed zydeco, and R&B styles influenced by Lowell Fulson. Chenier's first ventures into recording, saw his name mistakenly spelt, Cliston. During the 60s, Chenier, played one concert in San Francisco, backed by Blue Cheer. Chenier recorded for a number of notable labels, including, Argo and Arhoolie, in a bid to reach a wider audience. 'Squeeze Box Boogie' became a hit in Jamaica in the 50s. The style of music he played is now termed 'World Music', but was by no means widely heard before the 60s. In later life, apart from suffering from diabetes, he had part of his right foot removed due to a kidney infection in 1979. Although this prevented him from touring as frequently, his influence was already established. *Sings The Blues* was compiled from material previously released on the Prophecy and Home Cooking labels.

Albums: *Louisiana Blues And Zydeco* (1965), *Black Snake Blues* (1966), with Lightnin' Hopkins, Mance Lipscomb *Blues Festival* (1966), *Bon Ton Roulet* (1967), *King Of The Bayous* (1970), *Live At A French Creole Dance* (1972), *Out West* (1974), *Bad Luck And Trouble* (1975), *Bogalusa Boogie* (1975), *In New Orleans* (1979), *Frenchin' The Boogie* (1979), *Red Hot Louisiana Band* (mid-70s), *Boogie 'N' Zydeco* (1980), *Live At The 1982 San Francisco Blues Festival* (1982), *I'm Here* (1982), with Rob Bernard *Boogie In*

Black And White (mid-80s), *Live At St. Mark's* (late 80s, CD release), *The King Of Zydeco, Live At Montreux* (late 80s, CD release). Compilations: *Classic Clifton* (1980), *Sixty Minutes With The King Of Zydeco* (1986), *Sings The Blues* (1987).

Chess Records

Polish-born brothers Leonard and Philip Chess were already proprietors of several Chicago nightclubs when they established the Aristocrat label in 1947. Its early repertoire consisted of jazz and jump-blues combos, but these acts were eclipsed by the arrival of Muddy Waters. This seminal R&B performer made his debut with 'I Can't Be Satisfied', the first of many superb releases which helped establish the fledgling company. Having then secured the services of Sunnyland Slim and Robert Nighthawk, the brothers confidently bought out a third partner, renaming their enterprise Chess in 1950. Initial releases consisted of material from former Aristocrat artists, but the new venture quickly expanded its roster with local signings Jimmy Rogers and Eddie Boyd, as well as others drawn from the southern states, including Howlin' Wolf. Their recordings established Chess as a leading outlet for urban blues, a position emphasized by the founding of the Checker subsidiary and attendant releases by Little Walter, Sonny Boy Williamson (Rice Miller) and Elmore James. Other outlets, including Argo and Specialist were also established and during the mid-50s the Chess empire successfully embraced rock 'n' roll with Chuck Berry and Bo Diddley. White acts, including Bobby Charles and Dale Hawkins also provided hits, while the label's peerless reputation was sufficient to attract a new generation of virtuoso blues performers, led by Otis Rush and Buddy Guy. The R&B boom of the 60s, spearheaded by the Rolling Stones and later emphasized by John Mayall and Fleetwood Mac, brought renewed interest in the company's catalogue, but the rise of soul in turn deemed it anachronistic. Although recordings at the Fame studio by Etta James, Irma Thomas and Laura Lee matched the artistic achievements of Motown and Atlantic, ill-advised attempts at aiming Waters and Wolf at the contemporary market with *Electric Mud* and *The New Howlin' Wolf Album*, were the nadir of their respective careers. The death of Leonard Chess on 16 October 1969 signalled the end of an era and Chess was then purchased by the GRT corporation. Phil left the company to run the WVON radio station, while Leonard's son, Marshall, became managing director of Rolling Stones Records. Producer Ralph Bass remained in Chicago, cataloguing master tapes and supervising a studio reduced to recording backing tracks, but he too would vacate the now-moribund empire. Chess was later acquired by the All Platinum/Sugarhill companies, then MCA who, in tandem with European licensees Charly, have undertaken a major reissue programme.

Compilations: *Chess: The Rhythm And The Blues* (1988), *The Chess Story: Chess Records 1954-1969* (1989), *First Time I Met The Blues* (1989), *Second Time I Met The Blues* (1989).

Chicken Shack

Chicken Shack was the product of eccentric guitarist Stan Webb, veteran of several R&B groups including the Blue 4, Sound Five and the Sounds Of Blue. The latter, active between 1964 and 1965, included Webb, Christine Perfect (b. 12 July 1943, Birmingham, England; piano/vocals) and Andy Sylvester (bass), as well as future Traffic saxophonist Chris Wood. Webb and Sylvester then formed the core of the original Chicken Shack who enjoyed a long residency at Hamburg's famed Star Club before returning to England in 1967. Christine Perfect then rejoined the line-up which was augmented by several drummers until the arrival of Londoner, Dave Bidwell. Producer Mike Vernon then signed the quartet to his Blue Horizon label. *Forty Blue Fingers Freshly Packed And Ready To Serve* was finely balanced between original songs and material by John Lee Hooker and Freddie King, to whom Webb was stylistically indebted. *OK Ken?* emphasized the guitarist's own compositions, as well as his irreverence, as he introduces each track by impersonating well-known personalities, including John Peel, Harold Wilson and Kenneth Williams. The quartet also enjoyed two minor hit singles with 'I'd Rather Go Blind' and 'Tears In The Wind', the former of which featured a particularly moving vocal from Perfect, who then left for a solo career (later as Christine McVie). Her replacement was Paul Raymond from Plastic Penny. Ensuing releases, *100 Ton Chicken* and *Accept*, lacked the appeal of their predecessors and their heavier perspective caused a rift with Vernon, who dropped the band from his blues label. Friction within the line-up resulted in the departure of Raymond and Bidwell for Savoy Brown, a group Sylvester later joined.

Webb reassembled Chicken Shack with John Glassock (bass, ex-Jethro Tull) and Paul Hancox (drums) and embarked on a period of frenetic live work. They completed the disappointing *Imagination Lady* before Bob Daisley replaced Glassock, but the trio broke up, exhausted, in May 1973 having completed *Unlucky Boy*. The guitarist established a completely new unit for *Goodbye Chicken Shack*, before dissolving the band in order to join the ubiquitous Savoy Brown for a USA tour and the *Boogie Brothers* album. Webb then formed Broken Glass and the Stan Webb Band, but he has also resurrected Chicken Shack on several occasions, notably between 1977 and 1979 and 1980 and 1982, in order to take advantage of a continued popularity on the European continent which, if not translated into record sales, assures this instinctive virtuoso a lasting career. In the 90s, Stan 'The Man' Webb was once again delighting small club audiences with his latest version of Chicken Shack.

Albums: *Forty Blue Fingers Freshly Packed And Ready To Serve* (1968), *OK Ken?* (1969), *100 Ton Chicken* (1969), *Accept! Chicken Shack* (1970), *Imagination Lady* (1972), *Unlucky Boy* (1973), *Goodbye Chicken Shack* (1974), *The Creeper* (1978), *The Way We Are* (1979), *Chicken Shack* (1979), *Roadie's Concerto* (1981). Compilations: *Stan The Man* (1977), *The Golden Era Of Pop Music* (1977), *In The Can* (1980), *Collection: Chicken Shack* (1988).

Christian, Little Johnny

b. 19 August c.30s, Mississippi, USA. He sang in a church choir as a youngster, and continued singing gospel music after moving to Chicago in 1951, working and recording with the Highway QCs from 1957-61. In the 60s he worked as a bass player with Otis Rush, Elmore James and others, before joining Jimmy Dawkins as both bassist and singer. He formed his own band in the 70s working exclusively as a singer, and recorded several singles in the 80s. Renowned for his soulful vocals, Christian made his debut album for the Chicago-based Big Boy label at the end of the decade.

Album: *Somebody Call My Baby* (1989).

Chudd, Lew

Chudd was a US radio producer during the 30s, creating the *Let's Dance* show which featured Benny Goodman and Xavier Cugat. He later became the head of the Los Angeles bureau of the NBC network. During the early 40s Chudd worked for the Office of War Information and set up Crown Records to record jazz. After selling Crown, he founded Imperial Records in 1946 to cater for the growing black and Hispanic population of southern California. Chudd maintained a roster of Mexican artists like Los Madrugadores and Herman Padilla until 1953. In the R&B field, Imperial initially recorded west coast jump blues by artists including Charlie Davis, King Porter and Poison Gardner. But after meeting New Orleans bandleader Dave Bartholomew in Houston in 1949, Chudd moved into the newer R&B style. He came to New Orleans in December of the same year and almost immediately he and Bartholomew discovered Fats Domino. Domino's 'The Fat Man' and '3 x 7 = 21' by Jewel King were the label's first hits, in 1950. Leaving Bartholomew to record further R&B artists, Chudd signed performers in the gospel, blues (Smokey Hogg) and country fields, though of these only Slim Whitman was commercially successful. Consequently, Imperial focussed exclusively on R&B for the next few years. In New Orleans, Bartholomew provided hits by Chris Kenner and Roy Brown in addition to Domino while Los Angeles bandleader Ernie Freeman had a pop hit with 'Raunchy'. By 1957, Chudd was ready to plunge into the white teenage market, signing boyish television star Ricky Nelson who had over a dozen Top 20 hits in the following five years. Imperial also released rock material by Sandy Nelson and Frankie Ford. In 1961, Chudd purchased New Orleans label Minit from Joe Banashak but two years later Imperial itself was bought out by Al Bennett's Liberty/United Artists company, based in Los Angeles. Chudd himself retired from the music business.

Clapton, Eric

b. Eric Patrick Clapp, 30 March 1945, Ripley, Surrey, England. The world's premier living rock guitarist will be forever grateful to his grandparents, for it was they who bought him his first guitar. The young Eric was raised by his grandparents Rose and Jack Clapp after his natural mother could not face bringing up an illegitimate child at the age of 16. Eric received the £14 acoustic guitar for his 14th birthday, then proceeded to copy the great blues guitarists, note for note. His first band was the Roosters, a local R&B group whose members included Tom McGuinness, a future member of Manfred Mann, and latterly part of the Blues Band. Clapton stayed for eight months until he and McGuinness left to join Casey Jones And The Engineers. This brief sojourn ended in 1963 when Clapton was sought out by the Yardbirds, an aspiring R&B band, who needed a replacement for their guitarist Tony Topham. The reputation the Yardbirds then built was largely centred around Eric, who had already attained his nickname 'Slowhand' by the partisan crowd at Richmond's Crawdaddy club. Clapton stayed for 18 months until musical differences interfered. The Yardbirds were taking a more pop-orientated direction and Eric just wanted to play the blues. The perfect vehicle for his frustrations was John Mayall's Bluesbreakers, one of Britain's top blues bands. It was with Mayall that Clapton would earn a second nickname; 'God'! Rarely had there been such a meteoric rise to such an exalted position. Clapton only made one album with Mayall but the record is now a classic. *Bluesbreakers* shows Clapton on the now famous cover behind a copy of the *Beano* comic.

He was elevated to superstar status with the formation of Cream in 1966 and together with ex-Graham Bond Organisation members, Jack Bruce and Ginger Baker he created one of the most influential rock bands of our time. Additionally, as L'Angelo Mysterioso he played the beautiful lead solo on George Harrison's 'While My Guitar Gently Weeps' for the Beatles *The Beatles* ('The White Album'). Cream lasted just over two years, and shortly after their demise he was back again with Ginger Baker, this time as Blind Faith. The line-up was completed by Steve Winwood and Rick Grech. This 'supergroup' was unable to stay together for more than one self-titled album, although their financially lucrative American tour made the impending break-up easier to bear. During the tour Clapton befriended Delaney And Bonnie and decided he wanted to be their guitarist. He joined them before the sweat had dried, following his last Blind Faith gig in January 1970. He played on one album, *Delaney And Bonnie On Tour*, and three months later he had absconded with three of the former band to make the disappointing *Eric Clapton*. The band then metamorphosed into Derek And The Dominos. This memorable unit, together with Duane Allman, recorded one of his most famous compositions: the perennial 'Layla'. This clandestine love song was directed at George Harrison's wife Pattie, with whom Clapton had become besotted. George, unaware of this, invited Eric to play at his historic Bangla Desh Concert in August 1971. Clapton then struggled to overcome a heroin habit that had grown out of control, since being introduced to the drug during the recording of *Layla And Other Assorted Love Songs*. During the worst moments of his addiction he began to pawn some of his precious guitars and spent up to £1,500 a week to feed his habit.

Pete Townshend of the Who was appalled to discover that Eric was selling his guitars and proceeded to try to rescue Clapton and his girlfriend Alice Ormsby-Gore from certain death. Townshend organized the famous Eric Clapton At The Rainbow concert as part of his rehabilitation crusade, along with Steve Winwood, Rick Grech, Ron Wood and Jim Capaldi. His appearance broke two years of silence, and wearing the same suit he had worn at the Bangla Desh concert he played a majestic and emotional set. Although still addicted, this was to be the turning point in his life and following pleas from his girlfriend's father, Lord Harlech, he entered the famous Harley Street clinic home of Dr Meg Patterson for the initial treatment.

A rejuvenated Clapton began to record again and released the buoyant *461 Ocean Boulevard* in August 1974. The future pattern was set on this album; gone were the long guitar solos, replaced instead by relaxed vocals over shorter, more compact songs. The record was an incredible success, a number 1 hit in the US and number 3 in the UK. The singles drawn from it were also hits, notably his number 1 US hit with Bob Marley's 'I Shot The Sheriff'. Also included was the autobiographical message to himself, 'Give Me Strength' and the beautifully mantric 'Let It Flow'. Clapton ended 1974 on a high note, not only had he returned from the grave, but he had finally succeeded in winning the heart of Pattie Harrison.

During 1975 he maintained his drug-free existence, although he became dependant on alcohol. That same year he had further hits with *There's One In Every Crowd* and the live *E.C. Was Here*. Both maintained his reputation. Since then Clapton has continued to grow in stature. During 1977 and 1978 he released two further big selling albums, *Slowhand* and *Backless*. Further single success came with the gentle 'Lay Down Sally' (co-written with Marcella Detroit, later of Shakespear's Sister) and 'Promises', while other notable tracks were 'Wonderful Tonight', J.J. Cale's 'Cocaine', and John Martyn's 'May You Never'. Clapton had completely shrugged off his guitar hero persona and had now become an assured vocalist/songwriter, who, by chance, played guitar. A whole new audience, many of whom had never heard of the Yardbirds or Cream, saw Clapton as a clean, healthy individual with few vices, and no cobwebs in his attic. Clapton found additional time to play at the Band's historic *Last Waltz* concert.

The 80s have been even kinder to Clapton with every album selling vast quantities and being critically well-received. *Another Ticket* and *Money And Cigarettes*, which featured Ry Cooder, were particularly successful during the beginning of the 80s. *Behind The Sun* benefited from the firm production hand of Clapton's close friend Phil Collins. Collins played drums on his next album, *August*, which showed no sign of tiredness or lack of ideas. This particularly strong album contained the excellent hit 'Behind The Mask' and an exciting duet with Tina Turner on 'Tearing Us Apart'. Throughout the record Clapton's voice was in particularly fine form. *Journeyman* in 1989 went one better, not only were his voice and songs creditable but 'Slowhand' had discovered the guitar again. The album contains some of his finest playing. Not surprisingly it was a major success. Clapton has contributed to numerous artists' albums over many years, including; John Martyn, Phil Collins, Duane Allman, Marc Benno, Gary

Eric Clapton

Brooker, Joe Cocker, Roger Daltrey, Jesse Davis, Dr. John (Mac Rebannack), Bob Dylan, Aretha Franklin, Rick Danko, Champion Jack Dupree, Howlin' Wolf, Sonny Boy Williamson, Freddie King, Alexis Korner, Ronnie Laine, Jackie Lomax, Christine McVie, the Mothers Of Invention, the Plastic Ono Band, Otis Spann, Vivian Stanshall, Stephen Stills, Ringo Starr, Leon Russell, Doris Troy, Roger Waters and many, many more. He also appeared as the Preacher in Ken Russell's film of Pete Townshend's rock-opera *Tommy*.

Clapton has enjoyed a high-profile during the past few years with his touring, the Live Aid appearance, television documentaries, two biographies, and the now annual season of concerts at London's Royal Albert Hall. His 24 nights there in 1991 was a record. Such is his popularity that he could fill the Albert Hall every night for a year. As a final bonus to his many fans he plays three kinds of concerts, dividing the season with a series of blues nights, orchestral nights and regular nights. In the 90s Clapton's career went from strength to strength, although the tragic death of his son Conor in 1991 halted his career for some months. During December 1991 he toured Japan with George Harrison, giving Harrison the moral support that he had received more than a decade earlier. He has already earned the title of the greatest white blues guitarist of our time, but he is now on the way to becoming one of the greatest rock artists of the era too. An encouraging thought for a man whose life had all but ended in 1973.

Albums: *What's Shakin'?* (1966, three tracks as the Powerhouse with Steve Winwood, Jack Bruce, Pete York and Paul Jones). *Eric Clapton* (1970), *Eric Clapton's Rainbow Concert* (1973), *461 Ocean Boulevard* (1974), *There's One In Every Crowd* (1975), *E.C. Was Here* (1975), *No Reason To Cry* (1976), *Slowhand* (1977), *Backless* (1978), *Just One Night* (1980), *Another Ticket* (1981), *Money And Cigarettes* (1983), *Backtrackin'* (1984), *Behind The Sun* (1985), *August* (1986), with Michael Kamen *Homeboy* (1989, television soundtrack), *Journeyman* (1989), *24 Nights* (1991), *Rush* (1992, film soundtrack). Compilations: *Time Pieces - The Best Of Eric Clapton* (1982), *History Of Eric Clapton* (1972), *Crossroads* (1988), *The Cream Of Eric Clapton* (1989), *MTV Unplugged* (1992).

Further reading: *Survivor*, Ray Coleman. *Eric Clapton: Lost In The Blues*, Harry Shapiro.

Clarke, William

b. 29 March 1951, Inglewood, California, USA. Clarke began playing harmonica at the age of 16, inspired by the records of Junior Wells and Walter Horton. He turned professional two years later, and by the late 70s had become a well-respected harmonica player and singer on the Los Angeles blues scene. He associated with Smokey Wilson, Shakey Jake Harris, and George 'Harmonica' Smith, with the latter in particular being a great influence. Clarke has recorded in his own right for the Good Time, Rivera, and Alligator labels, and in 1991 he also paid homage to his roots by playing on some tracks of an acclaimed Los Angeles blues anthology *Hard Times*, which he compiled and produced for Black Magic Records.

Albums: *Hittin' Heavy* (1978), *Can't You Hear Me Calling* (1983), *Blowin' Like Hell* (1990), *Serious Intentions* (1992).

Clay, W.C.

b. 1927, Jonestown, Mississippi, USA. Along with a number of Mississippi and Arkansas based blues artists, Clay played with the *King Biscuit* radio show entertainers, including Sonny Boy 'Rice Miller' Williamson. After 1950, and following the death of Williamson in 1965, Clay regularly featured on the show playing Williamson favourites like 'Keep It To Yourself'. In 1976 he was living in Elaine, near Helena, Arkansas.

Album: with various artists *Keep It To Yourself - Arkansas Blues, Volume 1* (1983).

Clayton, Peter J. 'Doctor'

b. 19 April 1898, Georgia, USA, d. 7 January 1947, Chicago, Illinois, USA. Although he recorded a little over a dozen records in as many years (1930-46), his compositions influenced many blues singers, most notably Sunnyland Slim and B.B. King. His distinctive vocals, which usually ended in falsetto 'whoops', have been greatly imitated, but it is as songwriter that he is best remembered. Of his handful of recordings about half-a-dozen have become blues standards, including 'Hold That Train Conductor', 'Gotta Find My Baby' and 'I Need My Baby', courtesy of B.B. King. Those musicians who knew Clayton recall that he was

William Clarke

a bizarre character prone to outlandish dressing, performing in bare feet and verging on being alcoholic. However, recordings like '41 Blues', castigating Hitler and threatening him with a razor, and 'Pearl Harbour Blues', a scathing attack on the 'dirty Japanese', belie this apparent frivolity. In the autumn of 1946, Clayton developed tuberculosis and died in hospital the following year.

Selected albums: *Gotta Find My Baby 1941-46* (1987), with Sunnyland Slim *Dr. Clayton And His Buddy 1935-47* (1989).

Clearwater, Eddy

b. Eddy Harrington, 10 January 1935, Macon, Mississippi, USA. Clearwater grew up hearing C&W records and began playing guitar in church after moving to Birmingham, Alabama when he was 13 years old. He settled in Chicago in 1950 and was playing blues within a few years. Although primarily a powerful west-side Chicago-style blues singer and guitarist, he has also displayed, both on record and stage, a penchant for Chuck Berry-influenced rock 'n' roll, soul, and country. He is a popular performer, both in the USA and Europe, and has made numerous recordings for a variety of labels, although versatility often means that he fails to satisfy any listener completely despite the fact that he can perform in almost any musical genre.

Album: *The Chief* (1980), *Two Times Nine* (1992), *Help Yourself* (1992).

Climax Blues Band

Originally known as the Climax Chicago Blues Band, this long-enduring group comprised of Colin Cooper (b. 7 October 1939, Stafford, England; vocals/saxophone), Peter Haycock (b. 4 April 1952, Stafford, England; vocals/guitar), Richard Jones (keyboards), Arthur Wood (keyboards), Derek Holt (b. 26 January 1949, Stafford, England; bass) and George Newsome (b. 14 August 1947, Stafford, England; drums). They made their recording debut in 1969 with *The Climax Chicago Blues Band* which evoked the early work of John Mayall and Savoy Brown. Its somewhat anachronistic approach gave little indication of a potentially long career. Jones departed for university prior to the release of *Plays On*, which displayed a new-found, and indeed sudden, sense of maturity. A restrictive

adherence to 12-bar tempos was replaced by a freer, flowing pulse, while the use of wind instruments, in particular on 'Flight', inferred an affiliation with jazz-rock groups like Colosseum and Blodwyn Pig.

In 1970 CCBB switched labels to Harvest. Conscious of stereotyping in the wake of the blues' receding popularity, the group began emphasizing rock-based elements in their work. *A Lot Of Bottle* and *Tightly Knit* reflected a transitional period where the group began wooing the affections of an American audience responsive to the unfettered styles of Foghat or ZZ Top. Climax then embarked on a fruitful relationship with producer Richard Gottehrer who honed the group's live sound into an economic, but purposeful, studio counterpart. *Rich Man*, their final album for Harvest, and *Sense Of Direction* were the best examples of their collaboration. Richard Jones rejoined the band in 1975 having been a member of the Principal Edwards Magic Theatre since leaving university. The band enjoyed a surprise UK hit single when 'Couldn't Get It Right' reached number 10 in 1976, but the success proved temporary. Although they have pursued a career into the 90s, the Climax Blues Band have engendered a sense of predictability and consequently lost their eminent position as a fixture of America's lucrative FM rock circuit.

Albums: *Climax Chicago Blues Band* (1969), *Plays On* (1969), *A Lot Of Bottle* (1970), *Tightly Knit* (1971), *Rich Man* (1972), *FM/Live* (1973), *Sense Of Direction* (1974), *Stamp Album* (1975), *Gold Plated* (1976), *Shine On* (1978), *Real To Reel* (1979), *Flying The Flag* (1980), *Lucky For Some* (1981), *Sample And Hold* (1983), *Total Climax* (1985), *Drastic Steps* (1988). Compilations: *1969-1972* (1975), *Best Of The Climax Blues Band* (1983), *Loosen Up (1974-1976)* (1984), *Couldn't Get It Right* (1987).

Cobbs, Willie

b. 15 July 1940, Monroe, Arkansas, USA. As a youngster, Cobbs was deeply involved in gospel music in his local area. He moved to Chicago in 1951, where he received tuition in the blues harmonica from Little Walter. After his national service from 1953-57 he returned to Chicago and recorded (as a singer only) in 1958. In 1961 he made 'You Don't Love Me', now a much covered standard which has overshadowed

Eddy Clearwater

Cobbs' musical career. Since the 60s he has been based in the south, recording downhome blues singles (sometimes with backing vocals as a nod to the soul market) for a plethora of small labels, although in 1991 he did record for collector label Rooster Records.
Compilation: *Hey Little Girl* (1991).

Cole, Ann

b. Cynthia Coleman, 24 January 1934, Newark, New Jersey, USA. Her father sang with the family gospel group, the Coleman Brothers, and young Cynthia began singing in her grandfather's church as a child. In 1949, after absorbing the diverse influences of Billie Holiday and Mahalia Jackson, she formed the gospel group, the Colemanaires, with her cousins, which recorded for Timely Records between 1953 and 1954. However, in 1954 she started a secular career under the name Ann Cole, recording obscure sides for Timely and Mor-Play before switching to Baton Records in 1956, where she had success with the original versions of 'Easy, Easy, Baby' and 'Got My Mo-Jo Working (But It Just Won't Work On You)'. After leaving Baton in 1959, a subsequent re-recording of her biggest Baton hit 'In The Chapel' was unsuccessful, and Ann Cole was further hampered by a serious accident which eventually resulted in her being confined to a wheelchair. Her final record, released on Roulette in 1962, charted for one week at number 99, and Ann Cole returned to performing the spirituals and hymns that were her first inspiration.
Album: *Got My Mojo Working* (1984).

Coleman, Burl C. 'Jaybird'

b. 20 May 1896, Gainsville, Alabama, USA, d. 28 June 1950, Tuskegee, Alabama, USA. A blues harmonica player who recorded 15 titles between 1927 and 1930, Coleman drew his material from sources as varied as children's playground songs and spirituals. Whatever the source of his nickname, it was unlikely that was for his voice being similar to that of the bird - his singing and playing were rooted in that of the field-holler. His technique was best exemplified by 'No More Good Water', a call-and-response blues, where the harmonica's wailing quality is used as a second voice. It is thought he spent the last two decades of his life

as a street musician in Bessemer, Alabama, finally succumbing to cancer at the age of 54. He, and George 'Bullet' Williams, are the only known harmonica players from Alabama recorded in their own right.
Compilation: with George 'Bullet' Williams *Alabama Harmonica Kings* (1988).

Coleman, Gary 'BB'

b. 1 January 1947, Paris, Texas, USA. Coleman remembers hearing blues on record and radio as a child, and recalls his favourites as Jimmy Reed, Muddy Waters, Lightnin' Hopkins, Chuck Berry and Freddie King. He taught himself to play guitar around the age of 11; it remains his main instrument, although he is now a multi-instrumentalist. He has always worked as a professional musician; in 1986 he recorded an album for his own Mr B.'s Records label, which was leased to Ichiban Records who made it a very successful seller. Coleman has since become a major figure at Ichiban, not only with his own contemporary blues records, but also for his work as producer and musician with such artists as Barbara Lynn, Blues Boy Willie, Little Johnny Taylor, and Chick Willis.
Album: *Nothing But The Blues* (1987), *You Can't Beat Me Rockin'* (1988), *One Night Stand* (1989), *Dancin' My Blues Away* (1990), *Romance Without Finance Is A Nuisance* (1991). Compilation: *The Best Of Gary 'BB' Coleman* (1991).

Coleman, Jesse 'Monkey Joe'

b. c.1906. Little is known about this vocalist/pianist other than that he recorded his first tracks for the Bluebird label in New Orleans in 1935 at a session which he shared with Little Brother Montgomery. Thereafter his work appeared on Vocalion and OKeh, having being recorded in Chicago. He is rumoured to have recorded again in 1961. His somewhat loose piano style and choice of material has given rise to speculation that he may have been from Mississippi.
Album: *Crescent City Blues (Little Brother Montgomery)* (1975).

Collins, Albert

b. 3 October 1932, Leona, Texas, USA. Collins is the embodiment of the Texas blues guitar sytle, slashing out blocked chords and sharp flurries of treble notes (played without a

88

plectrum) to produce an 'ice-cold' sound from his Telecaster. He uses non-standard tuning on his guitar and a capo to locate a songs' key up and down the neck. As a youth he developed his style by listening to fellow-Texan Clarence 'Gatemouth' Brown and to his own cousin Willow Young. His first singles, released from 1958 onwards on small local labels, were exciting shuffle instrumentals, of which 'Frosty' became a blues standard, and it was not until the late 60s that he was confident enough to use his laconic, understated singing voice with any regularity. A series of splendid studio and live albums over the past 15 years, extending his basic Texas style over the boundaries of jazz and funk, has established him as a major international blues attraction. His stage shows, which often include a walk through the audience as he plays his guitar on its 100-foot lead, are memorable events.

Albums: *The Cool Sound Of* (1965), *Trash Talkin* (1969), *Love Can Be Found Anywhere, Even In A Guitar* (1969), *The Complete* (1970), *Alive And Cool* (1971), *There's Gotta Be A Change* (1971), *Ice Pickin'* (1978), *Frostbite* (1980), *Frozen Alive* (1981), *Don't Lose Your Cool* (1983), *Live In Japan* (1984), *Cold Snap* (1986), with Johnny Copeland and Robert Cray *Showdown* (1987), *The Ice Man* (1991), *Molten Ice* (1992).

Collins, Sam 'Crying'

b. 11 August 1887, Louisiana, USA, d. 20 October 1949, Chicago, Illinois, USA. Sam Collins was raised in McComb, Mississippi, just over the border from his native state, and by 1924 was performing in local barrelhouses at weekends. He was an intermittent partner of King Solomon Hill (Joe Holmes), and shared with him the use of falsetto singing and slide guitar. Holmes was an associate of Willard Thomas, and elements of Thomas's style influenced Collins. Collins was extensively recorded by both Gennett in 1927 and ARC in 1931, but many titles unfortunately remained unissued; it is clear, though, that he played blues, spirituals, medicine show numbers and pop songs; the repertoire of a songster, in fact. As a blues guitarist, Collins was not a virtuoso, and by conventional standards he was often out of tune, but he provided a steady beat for dancing, and his bottleneck playing, ranging freely through the treble and bass registers, was

an effective foil to his eerie singing, for which one record company billed him as 'Cryin' Sam Collins And His Git-Fiddle' in its advertising. He migrated to Chicago in the late 30s, and died there of heart disease.

Selected album: *The Jailhouse Blues* (1990).

Cooder, Ry

b. Ryland Peter Cooder, 15 March 1947, Los Angeles, California, USA. One of rock's premier talents, Cooder mastered the rudiments of guitar while still a child. He learned the techniques of traditional music from Rev. Gary Davis and by the age of 17 was part of a blues act with singer Jackie DeShannon. In 1965 he formed the Rising Sons with Taj Mahal and veteran Spirit drummer Ed Cassidy, but this promising group broke up when the release of a completed album was cancelled. However the sessions brought Ry into contact with producer Terry Melcher, who in turn employed the guitarist on several sessions, notably with Paul Revere And The Raiders. Cooder enjoyed a brief, but fruitful, association with Captain Beefheart And His Magic Band. His distinctive slide work is apparent on the group's debut album, *Safe As Milk*, but the artist declined an offer to join on a permanent basis. Instead he continued his studio work, guesting on sessions for Randy Newman, Little Feat and Van Dyke Parks, as well as to the soundtracks of *Candy* and *Performance*. Cooder also contributed to the Rolling Stones' album *Let It Bleed*, and was tipped as a likely replacement for Brian Jones until clashes with Keith Richard, primarily over authorship of the riff to 'Honky Tonk Woman', precluded further involvement.

Cooder's impressive debut album included material by Leadbelly, Sleepy John Estes and Blind Willie Johnson, and offered a patchwork of Americana which became his trademark. A second collection, *Into The Purple Valley*, established his vision more fully and introduced a tight but sympathetic band, which included long-standing collaborators, Jim Keltner and Jim Dickinson. By contrast, several selections employed the barest instrumentation, resulting in one of the artist's finest releases. The rather desolate *Boomer's Story* completed Cooder's early trilogy and in 1974 he released the buoyant *Paradise And Lunch*. His confidence is immediately apparent on the reggae interpretation of 'It's All Over Now' and the silky 'Ditty Wa Ditty', and it was this acclaimed collection that established him as a major talent. A fascination with 30s topical songs was now muted in favour of a greater eclecticism, which in turn anticipated Cooder's subsequent direction. *Chicken Skin Music* was marked by two distinct preoccupations. Contributions from Flaco Jiminez and Gabby Pahuini enhanced its mixture of Tex-Mex and Hawaiian styles, while Cooder's seamless playing and inspired arrangements created a sympathetic setting. The guitarist's relationship with Jiminez was maintained on a fine in-concert set, *Showtime*, but Cooder then abandoned this direction with the reverential *Jazz*. This curiously unsatisfying album paid homage to the dixieland era, but a crafted-meticulousness denied the project life and its creator has since disowned it.

Cooder then embraced a more mainstream approach with *Bop Till You Drop*, an ebullient, rhythmic, yet rock-based collection, reminiscent of Little Feat. The album, which included cameo-performances from soul singer Chaka Khan, comprised of several urban R&B standards, including 'Little Sister', 'Go Home Girl' and 'Don't Mess Up A Good Thing'. Its successor, *Borderline*, offered similar fare, but when the style was continued on a third release, *The Slide Area*, a sense of weariness became apparent. Such overtly commercial selections contrasted with Cooder's soundtrack work. *The Long Riders*, plus *Paris, Texas* and *Crossroads* owed much to the spirit of adventure prevalent in his early work, while the expansive tapestry of these films allowed a greater scope for his undoubted imagination. It was five years before Cooder released an official follow-up to *The Slide Area* and although *Get Rhythm* offered little not already displayed, it re-established purpose to his rock-based work. This inventive, thoughtful individual has embraced both commercial and ethnic styles with equal dexterity, but has yet to achieve the widespread success that his undoubted talent deserves. In 1992, Cooder had joined up with Nick Lowe, Jim Keltner and John Hiatt to record and perform under the name of Little Village.

Albums: *Ry Cooder* (1970), *Into The Purple Valley* (1971), *Boomer's Story* (1972), *Paradise And Lunch* (1974), *Chicken Skin Music* (1976), *Showtime* (1976), *Jazz* (1978), *Bop Till You Drop* (1979),

Borderline (1980), *The Long Riders* (1980, film soundtrack), *The Border* (1980, film soundtrack), *Ry Cooder Live* (1982), *The Slide Area* (1982), *Paris, Texas* (1985, film soundtrack), *Bay* (1985, film soundtrack), *Blue City* (1987, film soundtrack), *Crossroads* (1987, film soundtrack), *Get Rhythm* (1987), *Johnny Handsome* (1989, film soundtrack), with Little Village *Little Village* (1992). Compilation: *Why Don't You Try Me Tonight* (1985).

Cooper, Mike
b. c.1940. A strong singer and guitarist based for many years in Reading, Berkshire, England, Cooper was one of the leading lights of the country blues movement in Britain in the 60s. He also ran a popular folk/blues club in Reading and was one of the instigators of the Matchbox label, for which he recorded. Between 1968 and 1974 he appeared on the Pye, Dawn, and Fresh Air labels, and he also contributed his guitar work to records by Ian A. Anderson (now editor of *Folk Roots*), John Dummer, Stefan Grossman, and Heron. However, by the end of the 60s he was moving away from the blues towards a wider 'world music' approach and he appears very rarely in England these days, although he did team up with Anderson again in the mid-80s.
Selected albums: *Oh Really* (1969), *Trout Steel* (1970), with Ian A. Anderson *The Continuous Preaching Blues* (1986).

Cooper, Trenton
b. 1923, Hope, Arkansas, USA. This talented blues pianist, played in his college orchestra before joining an R&B band led by Jay Franks. The band also contained Nelson Carson on guitar. Cooper also co-wrote Frank's 'Fish Tail'. After 1950 Cooper played in the popular R&B combo led by Jimmy Liggins, the Drops Of Joy. When he was recorded by blues historian Jim O'Neal in 1976, he was the director of the Cooperative Education office at the University of Arkansas in Pine Bluff.
Album: with various artists *Keep It To Yourself - Arkansas Blues, Volume 1* (1983).

Copeland, Johnny
b. 27 March 1937, Haynesville, Louisiana, USA. A former boxer, Johnny 'Clyde' Copeland was active as a guitarist and singer on the Houston

Johnny Copeland

blues scene during the late 50s and 60s. He made numerous singles for such labels as Mercury ('All Boy' 1958), Paradise, Golden Eagle ('Down On Bending Knees') and Crazy Cajun. His version of Bob Dylan's 'Blowin' In The Wind' was issued by New York-based Wand in 1965 and there were later records for Atlantic. The renewed interest in the blues during the 70s brought a recording deal with Rounder and Copeland's Nappy Brown-influenced vocals were heard to good effect on a 1977 album with Arthur Blythe (saxophone). He joined the festival circuit and a rousing performance at Chicago in 1984 with fellow Texan guitarists Albert Collins and Gatemouth Brown led to the Grammy-winning *Showdown!* (1985). This collaboration with Collins and Robert Cray included the Copeland originals 'Lion's Den' and 'Bring Your Fine Self On Home'. Later albums were released by Rounder and included *Bringin' It All Back Home*, recorded in Africa.

Albums: *Copeland Special* (1977), *Make My Home Wherever I Hang My Hat* (1982), *Texas Twister* (1983), *Bringin' It All Back Home* (1986), *Ain't Nothin' But A Party* (1988), *When The Rain Starts Fallin'* (1988), *Boom Boom* (1990).

Copeland, Martha

'An exclusive Columbia recording artist' despite also recording for Victor and OKeh, Copeland was one of the legion of second-string female blues singers of the 'classic' period. She recorded 34 tracks between 1923 and 1928 and demonstrated a good 'moaning' style on occasions with considerable humour. Despite some promotion by Columbia who billed her as 'everybody's mama' she never achieved the popularity of stable mates Bessie and Clara Smith.

Corley, Dewey

b. 18 June 1898, Halley, Arkansas, USA, d. 15 April 1974, Memphis, Tennessee, USA. An interest in music inherited from his father led Corley to a career playing a variety of instruments - including harmonica, wash-tub bass and kazoo - in jug bands in Memphis, from the 20s to the 50s. He played with the famous Memphis Jug Band, and also Jack Kelly's South Memphis Jug Band, although he does not seem to have appeared on any of either group's records. In the 60s and into the early 70s, he was able to take advantage of the revival of interest in blues and related music, making a number of recordings and appearing at several folk festivals, both as accompanist to other artists and in his own right.

Album: *Mississippi Delta Blues, Volume 1* (1969).

Cotten, Elizabeth 'Libba'

b. 1893, USA, and raised in Chapel Hill, North Carolina, d. 29 July 1987. Cotten had wanted a guitar from a very early age. As a result, she saved enough to buy a $3.75 Stella Demonstrator guitar. Without recourse to formal lessons, she taught herself to play in her now eccentric style using just two fingers. To complicate matters, she played a guitar strung for a right-handed player, but played it upside down, as she was left-handed. 'Freight Train' was written by Cotten when she was still just 12 years old. Being so young, and coming from a God-fearing family, she was told that it was her duty to serve the Lord and so put aside the guitar until the late 40s. Married at 15, she was later divorced and moved to Washington, D.C. to look for work. She worked as a domestic in Maryland for Ruth Crawford Seeger, the wife of ethnomusicologist Charles Seeger. One day she played 'Freight Train' in the house to Mike and Peggy Seeger. Despite the fact that Cotten had written the song many years earlier, it was not until 1957, and after numerous court cases, that she secured the copyright to the song. Her blues rag and traditional style became familiar. Her second album was recorded and edited by Mike Seeger. In 1972, Cotten received the Burl Ives Award for her role in folk music. She appeared at a number of east coast folk festivals, such as Newport and Philadelphia, and on the west coast at the UCLA festival. This was in addition to playing occasional coffee houses and concerts. In 1975 she was a guest performer at the Kennedy Centre in Washington on a programme of native American music. 'Freight Train' recorded by Chas McDevitt and Nancy Whiskey, reached number 5 in the UK charts in 1957, but was less successful in the USA where it only reached the Top 40. Cotten received a Grammy award for her third, and final, album *Elizabeth Cotten Live*, and continued performing until just a few months before her death on 29 July 1987, in Syracuse, New York, USA.

Selected albums: *Elizabeth Cotten* (1957), *Elizabeth Cotten Volume 2: Shake Sugaree* (1965), *Elizabeth Cotten Volume 3: When I'm Gone* (1965), *Elizabeth Cotten Live* (1984).

Cotton, James

b. 1 July 1925, Tunica, Mississippi, USA. A guitarist and harmonica player, he learned his blues harp style from Sonny Boy 'Rice Miller' Williamson in Arkansas before returning to Memphis to lead his own group with guitarist Pat Hare. There he recorded 'Cotton Crop Blues' (Sun 1954) with its tough guitar solo by Hare and backed Willie Nix. Moving to Chicago, Cotton replaced Junior Wells in the Muddy Waters group in 1955. He stayed for five years, contributing harmonica solos to Waters' tracks such as 'Got My Mojo Workin'' and 'I Feel So Good'. After performing with Waters at the Newport Jazz Festival in 1960, Cotton began to develop a solo career. He later toured Europe, and recorded for Vanguard, Verve-Forecast, Capitol (where a 1970 album was produced by Todd Rundgren) Buddah (the soul-flavoured *100% Cotton* and *High Energy*, produced by Allen Toussaint), Alligator and Antone's. Although he developed a versatile approach, incorporating jazz and soul elements, Cotton retained his Mississippi blues roots, re-recording an old Sun tune 'Straighten Up Baby' on his 1991 album for Antone's.

Albums: *From Cotton With Verve* (1964), *Chicago - The Blues - Today!, Vol 2* (1964), *Super Harp - Live And On The Move* (1966), *Cut You Loose* (1967), *Taking Care Of Business* (1970), *100% Cotton* (1974), *High Energy* (1975), *High Compression* (1984), *Live From Chicago* (1986), *Live At Antone's* (1988), *My Foundation* (1988), *Take Me Back* (1988), *Mighty Long Time* (1991), *Live At Electric Lady* (1992).

Cotton, Sylvester

Nothing is known about Cotton except what can be gleaned from 18 tracks that he recorded in Detroit in 1948-49 for Bernie Besman's Pan American Record Company. Only three of these were issued at the time (although all have now appeared on album), and one of those was credited to John Lee Hooker when leased to Modern. The other two appeared, properly credited, on a Sensation label 78 rpm release. All of Cotton's recordings featured solo guitar and

vocal country blues and were very basic and primitive for the period. It is apparent that he extemporized some songs in the studio, most notably the very personal lyrics of 'I Tried'.
Album: *I Tried* (1984).

Council, Floyd

b. 2 September 1911, Chapel Hill, North Carolina, USA, d. June 1976, Sanford, North Carolina, USA. Sometimes known as Dipper Boy or The Devil's Daddy-In-Law, Council learned to play blues guitar (and also mandolin) in his youth and played on the streets of his home town in a small band. In 1937, he was spotted in this location by a talent scout, which led to his making records. Following two sessions in New York, three discs were released, and a later session produced a further two sides that remain unissued. On a number of other records, he played second guitar to Blind Boy Fuller, and his style was in the popular east coast vein associated with that artist. Indeed, some of his records were sub-credited to Blind Boy Fuller's Buddy. He continued to play for many years, although he did not record again.
Album: *Bull City Blues* (1972).

Country Jim

b. Jim Bledsoe, c.1925, near Shreveport, Louisiana, USA. A somewhat obscure character, Bledsoe made several records in Shreveport, in 1949-50. As the pseudonym suggests, they were of down-home country blues, accompanied only by his guitar, a string bass, and occasionally drums. The first was issued on the local Pacemaker label, under the name Hot Rod Happy, but the later ones appeared on Imperial and saw wider distribution. A year or so later he made a couple of long sessions for the Specialty company, but nothing was issued at the time, although a few sides were to appear on albums in the 70s.
Albums: *Down South Blues* (1977), *Country Blues* (1973).

Cousin Joe

b. Pleasant Joseph (aka Brother Joshua and Smilin' Joe), 20 December 1907, Wallace, Louisiana, USA, d. 2 October 1989, New Orleans, Louisiana, USA. Joe began singing at an early age, playing the ukulele for trips at sporting events and around the gambling joints

Cream

and brothels of the Crescent City. His professional career started around 1930 with the formation of his band, the Jazz Jesters. After teaching himself to play the piano, he was associated with several local orchestras (with A.J. Piron, Harold DeJean and Joseph Robichaux) as well as leading his own Smilin' Joe's Blues Trio. In 1942 Joe decided to try his luck in New York. His recording career began in 1945 with Mezz Mezzrow's King Jazz label, and he went on to record for Philo/Aladdin, Savoy, Gotham, DeLuxe, Signature, Decca, Flip and Imperial between 1945-54. In the 60s and 70s, Joe became a favourite at US and European jazz and blues concerts, making a number of appearances on British television. He resumed his recording career with albums a variety of labels such as Black & Blue (1972), Bluesway (1973), Big Bear (1974) and Great Southern Records (1985). He had left New York City in 1948 to avoid the heavy drug scene and this was obviously a sensible move as he lived to the respectable age of 81, dying of the rare complaint (at least for a blues or jazz musician) of 'natural causes'.

Albums: *Bad Luck Blues* (1972), *Cousin Joe Of New Orleans* (1973), *Gospel-Wailing, Jazz-Playing, Rock 'N' Rolling, Soul-Shouting, Tap-Dancing Bluesman from New Orleans* (1974), *Cousin Joe From New Orleans: In His Prime* (1984), *Relaxin' In New Orleans* (1985).

Covington, Blind Bogus Ben

Covington had played banjo and rack harmonica in the streets of Birmingham, Alabama, USA, singing blues and hokum and, as his 1928 record labels indicate, pretending to be blind, though evidently with no great conviction. His most startling number began 'I heard the voice of a porkchop say, come unto me and rest'. He was a member of a jug band which included Joe Lee 'Big Joe' Williams, though it seems unlikely that this was the Birmingham Jug Band which recorded in 1930. Covington was probably the same man as Ben Curry, who recorded four tracks in 1932.

Compilation: *Alabama Jug And String Bands* (1988).

Cray, Robert

b. 1 August 1953, Columbus, Georgia, USA. The popularity of guitar-based blues during the 80s had much to do with the unassuming brilliance of Cray. Although he formed his first band in 1974, it was not until *Bad Influence* in 1983 that his name became widely known. His debut *Who's Been Talking*, failed because the record label folded (it has since been re-issued on Charly). Cray's music is a mixture of pure blues, soul and rock and his fluid, clean style owes much to Albert Collins and Peter Green, while on faster numbers a distinct Jimi Hendrix influence is heard. The Robert Cray Band features long-time bassist Richard Cousins, Dave Olson (drums) and Peter Boe (keyboards). *Strong Persuader* in 1987 became the most successful blues album for over two decades and Cray has taken this popularity with calm modesty. He is highly regarded by experienced stars like Eric Clapton, who in addition to recording Cray's 'Bad Influence', invited him to play at his 1989 marathon series of concerts at London's Royal Albert Hall and record with him. In 1988 Cray consolidated his reputation with the superb *Don't Be Afraid Of The Dark*, which featured some raucous saxophone playing from David Sanborn. *Midnight Stroll* featured a new line-up which gave Cray a tougher sounding unit and moved him out of mainstream blues. Cray represents the best of the new generation of blues guitarists.

Albums: *Who's Been Talkin'* (1979), *Bad Influence* (1983), *False Accusations* (1985), with Albert Collins and Johnny Copeland *Showtime* (1985), *Strong Persuader* (1986), *Don't Be Afraid Of The Dark* (1988), *Midnight Stroll* (1990), *I Was Warned* (1992).

Crayton, Pee Wee

b. Connie Curtis, 18 December 1914, Liberty Hill, Texas, USA, d. 25 June 1985, Los Angeles, California, USA. After learning to play ukulele and banjo as a child, Crayton took up the guitar in his mid-20s. He was inspired by Charlie Christian and T-Bone Walker, the latter of whom taught Crayton the basics of electric guitar playing. His tutelage was completed at the side of another legendary guitarist, John Collins, and he began playing with local bands before graduating to Ivory Joe Hunter's bay area band in 1946. After making his recording debut with Hunter for Pacific Records, he recorded his first efforts under his own name and these were later issued on 4 Star Records after his success with Modern. In 1947 Crayton formed a trio, and

Robert Cray

after an obscure release on the tiny Gru-V-Tone label, began recording for Modern Records between 1948 and 1951, finding success with 'Blues After Hours', 'Texas Hop', and his biggest hit 'I Love You So', soon after he switched to Aladdin and Recorded In Hollywood for one-off sessions. Imperial Records took Crayton to New Orleans in 1954-55 to record with Dave Bartholomew's band, and the following year he moved to Detroit to record for Fox and VeeJay in nearby Chicago. During this period he was admired by and became the inspiration for a local young guitarist called Kenny Burrell. Moving back to Los Angeles in 1960, he recorded an unissued session for Kent Records (Modern) and subsequently recorded single sessions for the Jamie/Guyden, Smash and Edco labels, before leaving the music business in 1964 for five years, after recording the obscure *Sunset Blues Band* for Liberty's Sunset subsidiary. Rediscovered in the blues boom of the late 60s, he recommenced his recording career with an unissued session for Blue Horizon, a well-received album for Vanguard entitled *Things I Used To Do*, and an explosive appearance with Johnny Otis' band at the 1970 *Monterey Festival*. The five years or so before his death coincided with another resurgence of interest in blues and R&B, and this saw Crayton reaching an even wider audience with albums recorded for his friend Johnny Otis, solo albums and albums with Big Joe Turner on Pablo, new blues projects for the Murray Brothers, and Ace Records initiating a large-scale reissue programme of his Modern Records classics from the late 40s and early 50s.

Albums: *Pee Wee Crayton* (1959), *After Hours* (1960), *Sunset Blues Band* (1965), *Things I Used To Do* (1970), *Monterey Festival* (1970), *Blues Guitar Genius* (1980), *Great R&B Oldies* (1982), with Big Joe Turner *Every Day I Have The Blues* (1982), *Peace Of Mind* (1982), *Rocking Down Central Avenue* (1982), *Blues Before Dawn* (1986), *Memorial Album* (1986), *Make Room For Pee Wee* (1987), *Early Hours* (1987), *After Hours Boogie* (1988), *Blues After Dark* (1988), *Blues After Hours* (1988).

Cream

Arguably the most famous trio in rock music, Cream comprised: Jack Bruce (b. John Symon Asher Bruce, 14 May 1943, Glasgow, Lanarkshire, Scotland; bass/vocals), Eric Clapton (b. Eric Patrick Clapp, 30 March 1945, Ripley, Surrey, England; guitar) and Ginger Baker (b. Peter Baker, 19 August 1940, Lewisham, London, England; drums). In their two-and-a-half years together, Cream made such an impression on fans, critics and musicians as to make them one of the most influential bands since the Beatles. They formed in the height of swinging London during the 60s and were soon thrust into a non-stop turbulent arena, hungry for new and interesting music after the Merseybeat boom had quelled. Cream were announced in the music press as a pop group, Clapton from John Mayall's Bluesbreakers, Bruce from Manfred Mann and Baker from the Graham Bond Organisation. Their debut single 'Wrapping Paper' was a comparatively weird pop song, and made the lower reaches of the charts on the strength of its insistent appeal. Their follow-up single, 'I Feel Free' unleashed such energy that it could only be matched by Jimi Hendrix. The debut *Fresh Cream* confirmed the promise: this band are not what they seem. With a mixture of blues standards and exciting originals, the album became one of the records for any credible music fan to own. It reached number 6 in the UK charts. That same crucial year, *Disraeli Gears* with its distinctive day-glo cover went even higher, and firmly established Cream in the USA, where they would spend most of their touring life. This superb album showed a marked progression from their first, in particular the songwriting of Jack Bruce and his lyricist, former beat poet, Pete Brown. Landmark songs like 'Sunshine Of Your Love', 'Strange Brew' and 'SWLABR' (She Was Like A Bearded Rainbow), were performed with precision. Already rumours of a split prevailed as news filtered back from America of fights and arguments between Baker and Bruce. Meanwhile their live performances were nothing like they had thus far committed to vinyl. The long improvisational pieces, based around fairly simple blues structures were awesome. Each member had a least one party piece during concerts, Bruce with his frantic harmonica solo on 'Traintime', Baker with his trademark drum solo on 'Toad' and Clapton with his strident vocal and fantastic solo on 'Crossroads'. One disc of the superb two-record set *Wheels Of Fire* captured Cream live, at their inventive and exploratory best. Just a month after its release, while it sat on top of the US charts they announced they would disband at the end of the year following two final concerts. The famous Royal Albert Hall farewell concerts were fortunately captured on film, the posthumous *Goodbye* repeated the success of its predecessors, as did to a lesser degree the remaining live scrapings from the bottom of the churn. Cream came and went in one very long blink of an eye, leaving an indelible mark on rock music.

Albums: *Fresh Cream* (1966), *Disraeli Gears* (1967), *Wheels Of Fire* (1968), *Goodbye* (1969), *Live Cream* (1970), *Live Cream, Volume 2* (1972). Compilations: *The Best Of Cream* (1969), *Heavy Cream* (1973), *Strange Brew - The Very Best Of Cream* (1986).

Crockett, G.L.

b. c.1929, Carrollton, Mississippi, USA. In the late 50s George L. Crockett was living on Chicago's west side and sitting in as a singer with Magic Sam, Freddie King and others. He made his first record for the Chief label in 1958, later reissued by USA and Checker: 'Look Out Mabel' was a much sought item in the late 70s, often cited as the black rockabilly record. In 1965 he recorded the Jimmy Reed soundalike 'It's A Man Down There' for Four Brothers Records and it was the company's biggest hit (a US R&B Top 10 and pop Top 100). There were two less successful singles before Crockett died of a cerebral haemorrhage on 14 February 1967.

Compilation: *Chess Rockabillies* (1978, one track only).

Crudup, Arthur 'Big Boy'

b. 24 August 1905, Forest, Mississippi, USA, d. 28 March 1974 Nassawadox, Virginia, USA. During the 40s and early 50s Arthur Crudup was an important name in the blues field, his records selling particularly well in the south. For much of his early life Crudup worked in various rural occupations, not learning to play the guitar until he was 32. His teacher being one 'Papa Harvey' a local bluesman. Crudup's guitar style never became adventurous but it formed an effective backdrop for his high, expressive voice. The story is that Crudup was playing on the sidewalk in Chicago when he was spotted by

music publisher, and general 'Mr Fixit' for the blues in the Windy City, Lester Melrose. Like many others from his background, Big Boy's first recordings were his most countryfied; 'If I Get Lucky' and 'Black Pony Blues' were recorded in September 1941 and must have sold largely to the same group of resident and ex-patriot southerners who were buying records by Tommy McClennan and Sleepy John Estes. During the next 12 years he recorded approximately 80 tracks for Victor including songs that became blues standards. 'Mean Old Frisco' was later picked up by artists as diverse as Brownie McGhee (1946) and B.B. King (1959) and was one of the first blues recordings to feature an electric guitar. He recorded 'Dust My Broom' in 1949 and the following year moonlighted for the Jackson, Mississippi label Trumpet under the name 'Elmer James'. Despite attempts to update his sound by the introduction of piano, harmonicas and saxophones, by 1954 Big Boy's heyday was over. When Bobby Robinson contracted him from Chicago to record an album of his hits for Fire in 1962 the project had to be delayed until the picking season was over, Crudup having given up music and gone back to working on the land. Robinson's interest may have been sparked by two of Crudup's compositions, 'That's All Right' and 'My Baby Left Me' having been recorded by Elvis Presley. Presley also cut Crudup's 'I'm So Glad You're Mine' but there is no reason to suspect that Crudup benefited much from this. A second career bloomed for Big Boy with the interest taken in blues by a white audience in the mid-60s beginning with an album for Bob Koester's Delmark label. From then on he appeared at campuses and clubs in the USA and even journeyed to Europe - always encouraged to perform in a country style. It appears likely that, with his superior lyrics and wide cross-racial popularity, Big Boy Crudup gave more to the blues than he ever received in return.

Selected albums: *Mean Ol' Frisco* (1962, reissued 1989), *The Father Of Rock And Roll* (1972).

Crump, Jesse

b. 1906, Paris, Texas, USA. A pianist and organist, Crump was touring on the TOBA circuit in his early teens as a singer, dancer, instrumentalist and comedian. His duet recordings with Billy McKenzie are in a vaudeville vein, but he was an excellent blues accompanist, as best shown by his many recordings with Ida Cox, to whom he was married for some years. From the late 30s he gave up touring in favour of nightclub residencies, settling first in Muncie, Indiana, later on the west coast, where he recorded with Bob Scobey's Frisco Band in 1956. By the early 60s, he had effectively retired.

Crutchfield, James

b. 25 May 1912, Baton Rouge, Louisiana, USA. A self-taught pianist, Crutchfield left home when young and found work in the saw mills and lumber camps of Louisiana and Texas. In a logging camp in Bogalusa he met pianist Little Brother Montgomery who taught him to play '44 Blues'. In the late 40s Crutchfield moved to St. Louis where he worked in clubs, coming into contact with many of the city's celebrated pianists like Henry Brown and Roosevelt Sykes. Around 1955, Charlie O'Brien, blues fan and policeman, introduced Crutchfield to John Bentley, who included four of his songs in a series of albums devoted to St. Louis jazz and blues pianists. Crutchfield resurfaced in the early 80s, toured parts of Europe and recorded an album for the Swingmaster label in Holland.
Album: *Original Barrelhouse Blues* (1985).

Cuby And The Blizzards

The Netherland's premier blues band, Cuby And The Blizzards originated in the town of Grolloo and was founded when Harry 'Cuby' Muskee (vocals/harmonica) joined forces with Eelco Gelling (lead guitar). The group, also known as C+B, was later completed by Hans Kinds (guitar), Willy Middel (bass) and Dick Beekman (drums). Their debut single, 'Stumble And Fall' (1965), bore a debt to the Pretty Things, but successive releases, including 'Your Body Is Not Your Soul' and 'Back Home A Man', revealed a startling individuality. Gelling's incisive style, which drew praise from John Mayall, was already evident on *Desolation*, while the group also completed the excellent *Praise The Blues* with veteran US pianist Eddie Boyd. Their kudos was further enhanced on accompanying Van Morrison during a tour of Holland undertaken following the singer's departure from Them. Although Muskee and

Gelling remained at the helm, changes in personnel undermined the unit's progress. Pianist Herman Brood was one of many musicians passing through the Blizzards' ranks as they fused their blues-based style to progressive rock. However, by 1976 the duo had tired of their creation and while Muskee formed the Harry Muskee Band, Gelling opted to join Golden Earring. The long career of Cuby And The Blizzards was then maintained by Herman Deinum (bass), Hans Lafaille (drums) - both of whom had joined in 1969 - Rudy van Dijk (vocals), Paul Smeenk (guitar) and Jeff Reynolds (trumpet). This line-up remained active into the 80s.
Albums: *Desolation* (1966), with Eddie Boyd *Praise The Blues* (1967), *Groeten Uit Grolloo* (1967), *Trippin' Thru' A Midnight Blues* (1968), *Live!* (1968), *On The Road (Boek En Plaat)* (1968), *Cuby's Blues* (1969), *Appleknockers Flophouse* (1969), *Too Blind To See* (1970), *King Of The World* (1970), *Simple Man* (1971), *Sometimes* (1972), *Ballads* (1973), *Afscheidsconsert* (1974), *Kid Blue* (1976), *The Forgotten Tapes* (1979, unreleased recordings), *Cuby And The Blizzards, Featuring Herman Brood - Live* (1979). Compilations: *The Best Of Cuby And The Blizzards* (1974), *Old Times Good times* (1977).

Cully, Frank 'Floorshow'

b. 7 August 1918, Salisbury, Maryland, USA. Began playing with local bands in Richmond, Virginia and Cully led his own unit from the age of 15. He later moved to New York City where his fiery saxophone playing, both alto and tenor, dominated many jazz combos. He formed his own R&B group in the mid-40s, recording for Lenox and Continental and backing Wynonie Harris on King. In 1948, he was signed by the fledgling Atlantic label and led its first house band, backing the early stars of R&B as well as recording around 30 tracks under his own name - including the hit 'Coleslaw' - mainly with his band's superb pianist, Van Walls. He later recorded for RCA Victor, Parrot, Chess, and Baton. Known for being an histrionic showman (hence the nickname 'Floorshow'), as well as a good musician, he retired from music in 1975 and today lives in Newark, New Jersey.
Selected albums: *Rock 'N' Roll* (1955), *Rock & Roll* (1989).

Curtis, James 'Peck'

b. 7 March 1912, Benoit, Mississippi, USA, d. 1 November 1970, Helena, Arkansas, USA. Peck Curtis was a blues drummer, whose musical roots lay in playing washboard for medicine shows, with which he travelled throughout the American southern states in the 30s. He also played with the South Memphis Jug Band and later accompanied a young Howlin' Wolf. He is particularly associated, however, with Sonny Boy Williamson (Rice Miller), with whom he played for many years on the famous *King Biscuit Time* radio show, which broadcast from Helena. In 1952, he made some recordings, but these were not issued at the time (one appeared many years later). In the 60s, he began to work with Houston Stackhouse, and a number of their recordings appeared on albums, including one in which he told the story of Miller's death.

Albums: *Arkansas Blues* (1970), *Mississippi Delta Blues Volume 1* (1969).

D

Daddy Stovepipe

b. Johnny Watson, 12 April 1867, Mobile, Alabama, USA, d. 1 November 1963, Chicago, Illinois, USA. Johnny Watson, called Daddy Stovepipe because of his top hat, was an itinerant street musician for most of his long life. He was recorded playing guitar and rack harmonica as early as 1924 and, with Whistlin' Pete, in 1927. A longer series of records with his wife, Mississippi Sarah, singing and playing jug, were recorded in 1931 and 1935, and included a lively 'Greenville Strut', referring to the Mississippi town where they lived. After Sarah's death in 1937, Watson went to Texas playing there with zydeco bands and Mexican musicians (from whom he learned 'South Of The Border'). From 1948, he resided in Chicago, playing both secular music (mostly pop and old-time songs) and gospel on Maxwell Street until just before his death.

Albums: *Blues From Maxwell Street* (1961), *Harmonicas Unlimited* (1986).

Dallas, Leroy

b. 12 December 1920, Mobile, Alabama, USA. Dallas travelled the south in the 30s and 40s, teaming up for some time with Frank Edwards, and sang in the Chicago streets for a while before settling in New York from 1943. His 1949 recordings for Sittin' In With, are in a small group format with Brownie McGhee (with whom Dallas had played guitar and washboard in the 30s) and Big Chief Ellis; they bear little sign of urbanization (indeed his springy guitar rhythms positively countrify 'Jump Little Children, Jump', usually a preserve of blues shouters.) By 1962, he had ceased to play professionally, but was still a capable guitarist and a convincing singer. His subsequent whereabouts is unknown.

Albums: *Country Blues Classics Vol. 4* (c.1966), *Blues All Around My Bed* (c.1967).

Daniels, Julius

b. 1902, Denmark, South Carolina, USA, d. 18 October 1947, Charlotte, North Carolina, USA. Daniels was a guitarist and singer and one of the first black artists in the south-eastern states to record. He effectively represented an older and more localized musical tradition. Although he only made a few records, the music he left behind embraced blues, sacred music and even songs similar to the white country music of the day, all accompanied with light, melodic picking. At his first session, in Atlanta in 1927, he was supported by guitarist Bubba Lee Torrence, and although the latter's contribution was rather low-key, they shared the billing on the resulting records. During his second session, later that same year, he used another guitarist, Wilbert Andrews. Both Torrence and Andrews probably came from Pineville, North Carolina, where Daniels lived, but nothing more is known about them.

Compilation: with Lil McClintock *Atlanta Blues, 1927-30 (Complete Recordings in Chronological Order)* (1986).

Darby, 'Blind' Teddy

b. 2 March 1906, Henderson, Kentucky, USA. Born sighted, Darby lost his eyesight in the 20s, after moving to St. Louis, where he was to stay the rest of his life. Later in that decade, he learned to play guitar and established himself on the local blues scene. In 1929, he made his first records, and over the next few years made several more for four different labels, including three which were issued under the pseudonym Blind Squire Turner. His plaintive vocals and melodic blues style had the capacity to be quite distinctive, but more often he reflected other popular contemporaries, sounding on occasions like Leroy Carr, or fellow citizen Peetie Wheatstraw. In the 50s, he was ordained a deacon, and although he made some recordings in 1964, these have not been issued.

Album: *St. Louis Country Blues* (1985).

Darby And Tarlton

b. John James Rimbert Tarlton, 1892, Chesterfield County, South Carolina, USA. When a small child, he learned to play banjo and harmonica but at the age of eight, he changed to guitar. He soon took to playing, using a knife blade or bottle neck to fret the strings and became very efficient in the playing of negro blues and Hawaiian music, as well as the old time songs he learned from his mother. He left home in 1912 and travelled extensively from Texas and California to New York, working in cotton mills and oilfields and on occasions playing as a street musician in Chicago and New York, or touring with medicine shows. In 1923, he became friendly with Frank Ferera, who did much to popularize the Hawaiian guitar in America and from him learned the use of a steel bar, in lieu of the knife blade. He finally changed to an automobile wrist-pin in the late 20s and used it until his death. In 1926, he formed a partnership with Tom Darby, a guitarist and singer from Columbus, Georgia. Early in 1927, they auditioned for Columbia and in November that year, at their second session, they recorded 'Columbus Stockade Blues' and 'Birmingham Jail'. When offered the choice of a flat fee or royalties for the recordings, they accepted a fee of $75, which proved an ill-chosen decision, since both songs went on to become country standards. Tarlton arranged 'Birmingham Jail' when he was actually in gaol, as a result of an involvement in illicit moonshine. Art Satherley was quoted as saying that their version of the song was the greatest hillbilly record that he ever recorded because

both, as former convicts, could feel their material so deeply. Between 1927 and 1933, Tarlton recorded about 80 songs for Columbia, Victor or ARC; some were solos and others with Darby. On their duet recordings, Darby (a fine player who picked guitar in a style often described as 'black derived') mainly sang the lead vocal with Tarlton playing the steel guitar and adding harmony work, which at times included a yodel. During the early 30s, Tarlton toured in the south and in 1931, when not recording with Darby, he once worked in a cotton mill in Rockingham, South Carolina, with the Dixon Brothers. The Dixons, Dorsey and Howard, learned much from Tarlton's steel and ordinary guitar-playing ability and his influence was to show when they in turn became recording artists. Ironically, Tarlton and Darby never really got on together and in 1933, they parted and Darby returned to farming. Tarlton continued to play and worked with various bands and medicine shows until the mid-40s, when he semi-retired. Around 1963, he was persuaded to return to more active participation and played at several festivals and even recorded an album. Tarlton died in 1973 and it is believed that Darby died in the late 60s. John Morthland commented that 'If any one musician could be said to have laid the groundwork for future generations of steel players from western swing right up to today's pedal steel, it would probably be Tarlton'.

Albums: *Steel Guitar Rag* (1963), *Darby And Tarlton* i (1973), *Darby And Tarlton* ii (1974).

Darnell, Larry

b. Leo Edward Donald, 1929, Columbus, Ohio, USA, d. 3 July 1983, Columbus, Ohio, USA. Darnell began singing in Columbus gospel choirs and started sneaking into local clubs in the early 40s to sing for cash. At the age of 15 he joined the travelling show, Irwin C. Miller's Brownskin Models, which he quit in New Orleans after being offered a residency at the famous Dew Drop Inn. Something of a heart-throb, he became known as 'Mr Heart & Soul' and secured a recording contract with Regal in 1949, with whom he scored big hits with 'For You My Love' and the two-part 'I'll Get Along Somehow', backed by Paul Gayten's band. Moving to New York in 1950, Darnell's later tracks for Regal, OKeh, Savoy and DeLuxe

Larry Darnell

failed to live up to the early successes. Having made the odd recording in the 60s for Warwick, Argo and Instant, he retired from popular music in 1969, although he continued to sing for the church and contribute to the occasional benefit until two years before his death from cancer in 1983.

Album: *I'll Get Along Somehow* (1982).

Davenport, Charles Edward 'Cow Cow'

b. 23 April 1894, Anniston, Alabama, USA, d. 3 December 1955, Chicago, Illinois, USA. One of the most distinctive themes utilized in boogie-woogie is the train imitation 'Cow Cow Blues' from which this consummate performer derived his nickname. Charles Davenport's father, a preacher, wanted to see his son follow him to a career in the church but it was not to be. Instead the piano laid claim to Charles at an early age and he took up the insecure life of the medicine show musician. He joined Barhoot's Travelling Carnival working the backwaters of Alabama. Here his basically rag-time piano style was subjected to the influence of Bob Davis and the lusty, rolling result was to be the basis of Charles' success on record throughout the 20s. He moved into vaudeville with blues singer Dora Carr as 'Davenport And Co'. Davenport made his first recordings for Gennett (unissued) and Paramount in 1927. Thereafter he linked up with Vocalion both as performer and talent scout. As well as recording under his own name (and as George Hamilton, the Georgia Grinder and Bat The Hummingbird) he supported many other artists, forming a particularly successful liaison with singer Ivy Smith. During this period he tried several ventures outside music, failing as a record shop owner and opening his own café. He also fell foul of southern law and spent six months in jail. In 1938 he suffered an attack of apoplexy which left him deficient in his right hand. He continued to perform as a singer but a move to New York found him eventually washing dishes in the Onyx Club, from where he was rescued by pianist Art Hodes. He recovered sufficiently to record again as a pianist, for the Comet and Circle labels, in 1945 and 1946. Davenport worked towns as far apart as Atlanta, Cleveland and Nashville. He has composer credit for two much-played standbys of the traditional jazz scene, 'Mama Don't Allow' and '(I'll Be Glad When You're Dead) You Rascal You' and was sole composer of the 40s hit, 'Cow Cow Boogie'.

Albums: *Cow Cow Blues* (1978), *Alabama Strut* (1979).

Davenport, Jed

b. Mississippi, USA. Davenport settled in Memphis, where he performed when not touring with medicine shows. He played guitar, trumpet and jug, but it was on harmonica that he recorded, beginning in 1929 with exciting, highly vocalized versions of 'How Long How Long Blues' and 'Cow Cow Blues'. In 1930, he recorded with his Beale Street Jug Band, which included Kansas Joe and Memphis Minnie, producing in 'Beale Street Breakdown' a tour-de-force both of harmonica pyrotechnics and of ensemble work. A later recording by substantially the same ensemble was credited to Memphis Minnie And Her Jug Band, probably as a marketing ploy. Davenport was last seen in Memphis in the 60s.
Album: *Memphis Harmonica Kings* (1983).

Davies, Cyril

b. 1932, Buckinghamshire, England, d. 7 January 1964. Along with Alexis Korner and Graham Bond, the uncompromising Davies was a seminal influence in the development of British R&B during the beat boom of the early 60s. His superb wailing and distorted harmonica shook the walls of many clubs up and down Britain. Initially he played with Alexis Korner's Blues Incorporated and then formed his own band, the All-Stars, featuring Long John Baldry, renowned session pianist Nicky Hopkins and drummer Mickey Waller. Their Chicago-based blues was raw, loud and exciting. Like Bond he died at a tragically young age, after losing his battle with leukaemia.
Album: *The Legendary Cyril Davies* (1970).

Davis, Blind John

b. 7 December 1913, Hattiesburg, Mississippi, USA, d. 12 October 1985, Chicago, Illinois, USA. Davis taught himself piano after being blinded in 1923, and led his own six-piece band for 15 years from 1938. He professed not to care for blues, but his fame rests on the hundreds of blues accompaniments he recorded during the late 30s and early 40s. Among those who used him were Big Bill Broonzy, Tampa Red and 'Doctor' Peter Clayton. Usually he worked in a small band setting where his generally unspectacular playing would sometimes show a quiet inventiveness. His self-accompanied 1938 vocal recordings are mediocre, but his backup work, with its rolling right hand figures, was both immediately recognizable and creatively varied. In the postwar years, Davis was an early visitor to Europe, recording two albums in Paris in 1952, revealing a personal taste for song such as 'O Sole Mio' and 'Lady Be Good'. Despite his declared preferences they, and subsequent, albums emphasized blues and boogie, with a smattering of jazz and popular music. Seldom profound (although his song 'No Mail Today' is a beautiful piece of controlled melancholy), Davis was always proficient and professional.
Albums: *Live In Hamburg* (1974), *The Incomparable Blind John Davis* (1974), *Stomping On A Saturday Night* (1978), *In Memoriam* (1986), with Lonnie Johnson *Blues For Everybody* (1979).

Davis, CeDell 'Big G'

b. 1926, Halena, Arkansas, USA. An excellent slide guitar and harmonica player Davis performed briefly as a member of the King Biscuits Time entertainers in the early 50s with Sonny Boy 'Rice Miller' Williamson before joining guitarist, Robert Nighthawk's band. In 1961 he moved to Pine Bluff, Arkansas and continued to work locally and occasionally with Nighthawk, who along with Tampa Red, influenced his slide guitar playing. Because of the effects of childhood polio which denied him the full use of his hands, Davis played the guitar upside down and used a butter knife for a slide. He is now reported to be living in a nursing home in Pine Bluff.
Compilation: *Keep It To Yourself, Arkansas Blues Volume 1* (1983).

Davis, Gary, 'Blind' Rev.

b. 30 April 1896, Laurens, South Carolina, USA, d. 5 May 1972, Hammonton, New Jersey, USA. This highly accomplished guitarist was self-taught from the age of six. Partially blind from an early age, he lost his sight during his late twenties. During the Depression years, he worked as a street singer in North Carolina, playing a formidable repertoire of spirituals, rags, marches and square dance tunes. In 1933, he was ordained a Baptist minister and continued to tour as a gospel preacher. During the mid-30s,

Cyril Davies

he recorded some spiritual and blues songs for ARC. After moving to New York in 1940, he achieved some fame on the folk circuit and subsequently recorded for a number of labels, including Stinson, Riverside, Prestige-Bluesville and Folkways. *Harlem Street Singer*, released in 1960, was an impressive work, which emphasized his importance to a new generation of listeners. Davis taught guitar and greatly inspired Stefan Grossman. Among Davis's devotees were Bob Dylan, Taj Mahal, Ry Cooder and Donovan. Davis visited the UK in 1964, and returned as a soloist on several other occasions. He appeared at many music festivals, including Newport in 1968, and was the subject of two television documentaries in 1967 and 1970. He also appeared in the film *Black Roots*. His importance in the history of black rural music cannot be overestimated.
Compiliaton: *Pure Religion And Bad Company* (1991).

Davis, Jimmy 'Maxwell Street'

b. Charles Thomas, 1925, Clarksdale, Mississippi, USA. After spells as a singer and dancer with touring minstrel shows, and an unissued 1952 recording session for Sun, Davis moved to Chicago, playing for tips on Maxwell Street (sometimes outside a small restaurant which he operated there). His guitar playing is dark, complex and vigorous; in its emphasis on bass lines, it is much influenced by his Mississippi neighbour Tony Hollins, and by John Lee Hooker, from whom Davis learned much during a late 40s stay in Detroit. His singing, too, has the brooding, introspective manner of Hooker and other Delta-born blues singers. As well as traditionally based material, Davis incorporates a number of recorded hits into his repertoire, but makes them his own by his personal, committed peformances.
Albums: *Maxwell Street Jimmy Davis* (1965), *Chicago Blues Sessions Volume 11* (1989).

Davis, Larry

b. 4 December 1936, Kansas City, Missouri, USA. One of many blues artists to be solely remembered for one early record, despite an ongoing career, Larry Davis continues to make distinctive albums for the contemporary market. Moving to Little Rock, Arkansas, with his father in 1944, he learned to play drums in the school

band. His first gig was with harmonica player Sunny Blair, though he wasn't present on Blair's sessions for RPM and Meteor in 1952. He also played with guitarist Sammy Lawhorn and Gilbert Cables. Fenton Robinson and Charles McGowan came to Little Rock in 1955 and Davis joined their band before moving on to St. Louis. In 1957, Davis, McGowan, Billy Gayles and pianist Ernest Lane travelled to California, working there for a year. The following year Davis recorded with Robinson for Duke Records in Houston. 'Texas Flood' was his first and best-known recording, followed by 'Angels In Houston' and 'Will She Come Home'. Davis didn't record again until the late 60s, cutting Robinson's 'The Years Go Passing By' for B.B. King's Virgo label and then sessions from which tracks were issued on Kent and Pieces. Further recordings for Hub City and True Soul in the 70s, on which Davis played guitar, went unnoticed. He was recorded live at J.B. Hutto's St. Louis club in 1980 but the album was only issued in Japan. Davis' first studio album, *I Ain't Beggin' Nobody*, was made for the St. Louis Pulsar label in 1988. In 1992 he recorded *Sooner Or Later* for Ron Levy's Bullseye Blues label, an album which mixes Southern Soul in the Bobby Bland manner with more straighforward guitar blues.
Albums: *I Ain't Beggin' Nobody* (1988), *Sooner Or Later* (1992).

Davis, Walter

b. 1 March 1912, Grenada, Mississippi, USA, d. 22 October 1963, St. Louis, Missouri, USA. Based in St. Louis for most of his life, Davis learned piano at an early age. Between 1930 and 1941 he made many records, mainly issued on the Bluebird label, establishing himself as one of the most popular blues artists of the era. At first he was accompanied by another pianist, Roosevelt Sykes, but from 1935 onwards he developed a very distinctive style based around his own straightforward, but instantly recognizable, piano playing, a melancholy vocal and thoughtful, well-developed lyrics. Many of these records featured accompanying guitarists such as Big Joe Williams and Henry Townsend, the latter in particular demonstrating considerable musical empathy with Davis. After World War II, the Victor company released a further two records by Davis, but without recapturing his former commercial success. Nevertheless, in the late 40s he made several records for the Nashville-based Bullet label, and another two for Victor in 1952, which included some of his finest and most affecting performances.

Albums: *Let Me In Your Saddle* (1987), *The Bullet Sides* (1986), *First Recordings 1920-1932* (1993).

Dawkins, Jimmy

b. 24 October 1936, Tchula, Mississippi, USA. Dawkins taught himself to play blues guitar in the early 50s and moved to chicago in 1955, forming his own band two years later, while also working club dates with bluesmen such as Jimmy Rogers and Magic Sam. Dawkins is an expressive singer and a strong, inventive guitarist, and in the latter capacity he has been called on for recording sessions by many artists from the 60s onwards. Luther Allison, Wild Child Butler, Phil Guy and Johnny Young are only a few in a long list. He has recorded under his own name for many labels, including Delmark, Black And Blue, MCM, Excello, Isabel, JSP and Rumble Records. Dawkins is a quiet man who takes his blues very seriously; in the early 70s he was contributor to *Blues Unlimited* magazine, and in the 80s he ran his own Leric label, recording artists like Little Johnny Christian rather than promoting his own career.

Album: *All For Business* (1973).

Dee, David

b. David Eckford, c.1942, Greenwood, Mississippi, USA. Dee's family moved to East St. Louis when he was a baby. He sang gospel music when he was 12-years-old and after a spell in the services he formed the short-lived vocal group David And The Temptations. In 1968 he began playing bass guitar in his own band, switching to guitar in 1972 - influenced by Little Milton, Albert King, B.B. King, and Eddie 'Guitar Slim' Jones. In 1982 he enjoyed a big local hit with the uptempo blues 'Going Fishing' on Oliver Sain's Venessa label, which established him as a major figure on the St. Louis blues scene, and Edge Records and Ichiban have also issued Dee's material.

Albums: *Sheer Pleasure* (1987), *Portrait Of The Blues* (1988, reissue of Vanessa material).

Delafose, John

b. 16 April 1939, Eunice, Louisiana, USA. Starting on violin as a child, Delafose moved to harmonica and eventually accordion, the instrument on which he is best known, leading his zydeco band the Eunice Playboys. He played for local dances in his younger days, but retired from music after his marriage. At the age of 30 Delafose began playing again, quickly establishing his music as some of the most distinctive in the black French idiom, firmly based in the older traditions but also with contemporary ingredients. One characteristic aspect of his bands has been the presence of his own sons on a variety of instruments. He has made a number of records, the most successful being 'Joe Pitre A Deux Femmes', a local hit for him in the early 80s.

Albums: *Zydeco Man* (1980), *Uncle Bud Zydeco* (1982).

Delmark Records

Formed 1953 in St. Louis, Missouri, USA as Delmar Records, by Bob Koester. Delmark became a key blues label and was still in operation in the 90s. It was among the first record companies to record entire albums as opposed to the dominant singles of the 50s. After releasing dixieland jazz records, Delmark delved into the blues in 1956 with an album by pianist Rufus Perryman. Big Joe Williams' *Piney Woods Blues* was an early release and helped establish the label. Moving to Chicago in 1958, Koester added modern jazz to his roster, while recording albums by bluesmen, including Sleepy John Estes and Roosevelt Sykes. In 1965, *Hoodoo Man Blues* by Junior Wells was a big seller for the company. In the 70s the label concentrated on Chicago blues by such artists as Magic Sam, Otis Rush and J.B. Hutto. During that decade Delmark also purchased reissue rights for the United and States labels and released classic 50s material by Memphis Slim, Robert Nighthawk and others. More recently they have expanded to record new artists in addition to acquiring Apollo Records.

Detroit Junior

b. Emery H. Williams Junior, 26 October 1931, Haynes, Arkansas, USA. Junior became interested in music in the mid-40s. In the early 50s, as a pianist and bandleader, he had a

residency in a Detroit club where he backed artists such as Rosco Gordon and Amos Milburn-the latter influenced his songwriting. Eddie Boyd took Junior to Chicago, where he teamed up with J.T. Brown and then later with Mac Simmons. From 1960 onwards, Junior recorded singles for many local labels. His best-known songs were the much-covered 'Money Tree' and 'Call My Job'. In the late 60s and 70s he toured and recorded with Howlin' Wolf and besides recording albums for The Blues On Blues and Wolf labels, he was also part of Alligator's *Living Chicago* series. However, this talented blues entertainer remains under-recorded.
Album: *Chicago Urban Blues* (1972).

Dicey, Bill

b. 25 May 1936, Annapolis, Maryland, USA. Dicey began playing harmonica at three-years-old, and turned his attention to blues about five years later. In his teens he was the drummer with an otherwise all-black band playing popular R&B hits of the day. In 1953 he was drafted, and after his discharge his interest in music waned. In the mid-60s Dicey was based in Atlanta, Georgia, where he was enticed into playing harmonica again, and worked (and recorded some unissued material) with Buddy Moss. In the late 60s he settled in New York, where he was associated with Charles Walker. Dicey also became a prolific session musician with Spivey Records. He has recorded under his own name for the P&P, Spivey, and JSP labels and while his vocals are rudimentary, his blues harmonica playing can be outstanding.
Album: *Fool In Love* (1987).

Diddley, Bo

b. Elias Bates (later known as Elias McDaniel), 30 December 1928, McComb, Mississippi, USA. After beginning his career as a boxer, where he received the soubriquet 'Bo Diddley', the singer worked the blues clubs of Chicago with a repertoire influenced by Louis Jordan, John Lee Hooker and Muddy Waters. In late 1954, he teamed up with Billy Boy Arnold and recorded demos of 'I'm A Man' and 'Bo Diddley'. Re-recorded at Chess Studios with a backing ensemble comprising Otis Spann (piano), Lester Davenport (harmonica), Frank Kirkland (drums) and Jerome Green (maracas),

the a-side 'Bo Diddley' became an R&B hit in 1955. Before long, Diddley's distorted, amplified, custom-made guitar, with its rectangular shape and pumping rhythm style became a familiar, much-imitated trademark, as did his self-referential songs with such titles as 'Bo Diddley's A Gunslinger', 'Diddley Daddy' and 'Bo's A Lumberjack'. His jive-talking routine with 'Say Man' (a US Top 20 hit in 1959) and 'Pretty Thing' and 'Hey Good Lookin'', which reached the lower regions of the UK charts in 1963. By then, Diddley was regarded as something of an R&B legend and found a new lease of life courtesy of the UK beat boom. The Pretty Things named themselves after one of his songs while his work was covered by such artists as the Rolling Stones, Animals, Manfred Mann, Kinks, Yardbirds, Downliner's Sect and the Zephyrs. Diddley subsequently jammed on albums by Chuck Berry and Muddy Waters, and appeared infrequently at rock festivals. His classic version of 'Who Do You Love' became a staple cover for a new generation of USA acts ranging from Quicksilver Messenger Service to the Doors, Tom Rush and Bob Seger, while the UK's Juicy Lucy took the song into the UK Top 20.
Like many of his generation, Diddley attempted to update his image and in the mid-70s released *The Black Gladiator* in the uncomfortable guise of an ageing funkster. *Where It All Begins*, produced by Johnny Otis (whose hit 'Willie And The Hand Jive' owed much to Diddley's style), was probably the most interesting of his post 60s albums. In 1979, Diddley toured with the Clash and in 1984 took a cameo roll in the film *Trading Places*. A familiar face on the revival circuit, Diddley is rightly regarded as a seminal figure in the history of rock 'n' roll. His continued appeal to younger performers was emphasized by Craig McLachlan's hit recording of 'Mona' in 1990.
Albums: *Bo Diddley* (1962), *Go Bo Diddley* (1962), *Bo Diddley Is A Gunslinger* (1963), *Hey Bo Diddley* (1963), *Bo Diddley* (c.60s), *Bo Diddley Rides Again* (1963), *Bo Diddley's Beach Party* (1963), *Bo Diddley Goes Surfing* (1963), *Bo Diddley In The Spotlight* (c.60s), *Hey Good Looking* (1964), *Let Me Pass* (1965), *The Originator* (c.60s), *Superblues* (c.60s), *The Super Super Blues Band* (1968), *Big Bad Bo* (1974), *Another Dimension* (1971), *The Bo Diddley London*

Bo Diddley

Sessions (1973), *Two Guitar Greats* (1974), *The Black Gladiator* (1975), *Where It All Begins* (c.70s), *The 20th Anniversary Of Rock 'N' Roll* (1976), *Hey Bo Diddley* (1986). Compilations: *Chess Masters* (1988), *EP Collection* (1991).

Dillard, Varetta

b. 3 February 1933, Harlem, New York City, USA. Dillard spent most of her childhood years in hospital as a result of a bone deficiency. Where she discovered singing as a therapy. Encouraged and inspired by Carl Feaster, lead singer with the Chords, Varetta began entering talent shows, which led to two consecutive wins at the Apollo's infamous Amateur Hour. Signed to Savoy Records in 1951, she made her own records and duetted with H-Bomb Ferguson, and found success with 'Mercy Mr Percy', 'Easy, Easy Baby', 'Promise Mr Thomas' and, after Johnny Ace's untimely demise, 'Johnny Has Gone'. In 1956 she switched to RCA Victor/Groove where, much to her distaste, she was made to capitalize on James Dean's death with 'I Miss You Jimmy'. Later recordings for Triumph and MGM's Cub subsidiary failed to match her Savoy successes, and she ended her solo recording career in 1961, although she carried on into the late 60s by joining her husband's group, the Tri-Odds, which were active in the Civil Rights Movement, performing jazz, a cappella and Black poetry.
Albums: *Double Crossing Daddy* (1984), *Mercy Mr Percy* (1988), *Got You On My Mind* (1989), *The Lovin' Bird* (1989).

Dixon, Floyd

b. 8 February 1929, Marshall, Texas, USA. Aka J Riggins Jnr., Dixon began playing piano and singing as a child, absorbing every influence from gospel and blues, to jazz, and even hillbilly. In 1942 his family moved to Los Angeles and he came into contact with fellow ex-Texan Charles Brown who took a shine to young Floyd and turned the boy on to his brand of cool, jazzy night club blues as singer and pianist with Johnny Moore's Three Blazers. When the Blazers split up, Dixon was a natural choice for a substitute Charles Brown, and he made early recordings in the Brown style with both Eddie Williams (the Blazers' bassist) for Supreme and with Johnny Moore's new Blazers for Aladdin and Combo. His own trio recorded extensively

for Modern, Peacock and Aladdin labels between 1947 and 1952; then later, in a harder R&B style, for Specialty, Cat and Checker; and in the late 50s and 60s for a host of tiny west coast and Texas independent labels. In 1975 Dixon made a comeback, beginning with a tour of Sweden and became the first artist to be featured on Jonas Bernholm's celebrated Route 66 reissue label. Dixon was commissioned to write a blues, 'Olympic Blues' for the 1984 Los Angeles games.
Albums: *Opportunity Blues* (1976), *Houston Jump* (1979), *Empty Stocking Blues* (1985), *Hitsville Look Out, Here's Mr. Magnificent* (1986).

Dixon, Mary

A native of Texas, Dixon is otherwise a biographical blank. Her five records, made in New York in 1929, include a pop coupling 'Dusky Stevedore' and 'I Can't Give You Anything But Love', but otherwise are exclusively blues, with interesting lyrics about sex, violence and superstition. They are distinguished by first class jazz accompaniments. Her powerful singing voice has a distinctive nasal tones of many women from her native state, and her imitation of Bubber Miley's growling trumpet is an arresting gimmick.
Album: *The Complete Blues Sessions Of Gladys Bentley & Mary Dixon* (c.1975).

Dixon, Willie

b. 1 July 1915, Vicksburg, Mississippi, USA, d. 29 January 1992. At an early age Dixon was early interested in both words and music, writing lyrics and admiring the playing of Little Brother Montgomery. As an adolescent, Dixon sang bass with local gospel groups, had some confrontation with the law, and hoboed his way to Chicago, where he became a boxer. He entered music professionally after meeting Baby Doo Caston, and together they formed the Five Breezes, whose 1940 recordings blend blues, jazz, pop and the vocal group harmonies of the Inkspots and the Mills Brothers. During World War II, Dixon resisted the draft, and was imprisoned for 10 months. After the war, he formed the Four Jumps Of Jive before reuniting with Caston in the Big Three Trio, who toured the Midwest, and recorded for Columbia. The trio featured vocal harmonies, and the jazz-influenced guitar work of Ollie Crawford.

Floyd Dixon

Dixon's performing activities lessened as his involvement with Chess Records increased. By 1951 he was a full-time employee, as producer, A&R representative, session musician, talent scout, songwriter, and occasionally name artist. Apart from an interlude when he worked for Cobra in a similar capacity, Dixon was to be with Chess until 1971. The relationship with Chess was ultimately complex; he was forced to regain control of his copyrights by legal action. Meanwhile, Dixon was largely responsible for the sound of Chicago blues on Chess and Cobra, and of the black rock 'n' roll of Chuck Berry and Bo Diddley. He was also used on gospel sessions by Duke/Peacock; and his bass playing was excellent behind Rev. Robert Ballinger. Dixon's productions of his own songs included Muddy Waters' 'I'm Your Hoochie Coochie Man', Howlin' Wolf's 'Spoonful', Diddley's 'You Can't Judge A Book By Its Cover', Otis Rush's 'I Can't Quit You Baby' (a triumph for Dixon's and Rush's taste for minor chords), and Koko Taylor's 'Wang Dang Doodle', among many others. In the early 60s, Dixon teamed up with Memphis Slim to play the folk revival's notion of blues, and operated as a booking agent and manager, in which role he was crucial to the American Folk Blues Festival Tours of Europe. Many British R&B bands recorded his songs, including the Rolling Stones and Led Zeppelin, who adapted 'You Need Love'. After leaving Chess, Dixon went into independent production with his own labels, Yambo and Spoonful, and resumed a recording and performing career. He also administered the Blues Heaven Foundation, a charity which aimed to promote awareness of the blues, and to rectify the financial injustices of the past. Willie Dixon claimed 'I am the blues'; and he was, certainly, hugely important in its history, not only as a great songwriter, but also as a producer, performer and mediator between artists and record companies.

Albums: *Willie's Blues* (1959), *Memphis Slim & Willie Dixon At The Village Gate* (1960), *I Am The Blues* (1970), *Peace* (1971), *Catalyst* (1973), *Mighty Earthquake And Hurricane* (1983), *I Feel Like Steppin'Out* (1986), *Gene Gilmore & The Five Breezes* (1989), *Hidden Charms* (1988), *The Chess Box* (1989), *Willie Dixon & The Big Three Trio* (1990).

Domino, Fats

b. Antoine Domino, February 26 1928, New Orleans, Louisiana, USA. From a large family, he learned piano from local musician Harrison Verrett who was also his brother-in-law. A factory worker after leaving school, Domino played in local clubs such as the Hideaway. It was there in 1949 that bandleader Dave Bartholomew and Lew Chudd of Imperial Records heard him. His first recording, 'The Fat Man', became a Top 10 R&B hit the next year and launched his unique partnership with Bartholomew who co-wrote and arranged dozens of Domino tracks over the next two decades. Like that of Professor Longhair, Domino's playing was derived from the rich mixture of musical styles to be found in New Orleans. These included traditional jazz, Latin rhythms, boogie-woogie, Cajun and blues. Domino's personal synthesis of these influences involved lazy, rich vocals supported by rolling piano rhythms. On occasion his relaxed approach was at odds with the urgency of other R&B and rock artists and the Imperial engineers would frequently speed up the tapes before Domino's singles were released. During the early 50s, Domino gradually became one of the most successful R&B artists in America. Songs like 'Goin' Home' and 'Going To The River', 'Please Don't Leave Me' and 'Don't You Know' were best-sellers and he also toured throughout the country. The touring group included the nucleus of the band assembled by Dave Bartholomew for recordings at Cosimo Matassa's studio. Among the musicians were Lee Allen (saxophone), Frank Field (bass) and Waltet 'Papoose' Nelson (guitar).

By 1955, rock 'n' roll had arrived and young white audiences were ready for Domino's music. His first pop success came with 'Ain't That A Shame' in 1955, though Pat Boone's cover version sold more copies. 'Bo Weevil' was also covered, by Teresa Brewer but the catchy 'I'm In Love Again' with its incisive saxophone phrases from Allen took Domino into the pop Top 10. The b-side was the 20s standard 'My Blue Heaven', which Verrett had sung with Papa Celestin's New Orleans jazz band, given an up-tempo treatment. Domino's next big success also came with a pre-rock 'n' roll song, 'Blueberry Hill'. Inspired by Louis Armstrong's 1949 version, Domino used his creole drawl to

Willie Dixon

Fats Domino

perfection. Altogether, Fats Domino had nearly 20 US Top 20 singles in the six years between 1955 and 1960. Among the last of them was the majestic 'Walking To New Orleans', a Bobby Charles composition which became a string-laden tribute to the sources of his musical inspiration. His track record in the *Billboard R&B* lists however is impressive, with 63 records making the charts. He continued to record prolifically for Imperial until 1963, maintaining a consistently high level of performance. There were original compositions like the jumping 'My Girl Josephine' and 'Let the Four Winds Blow' and covers of country songs (Hank Williams' 'Jambalaya') as well as standard ballads like 'Red Sails In The Sunset', his final hit single in 1963. The complex off-beat of 'Be My Guest' was a clear precursor of the ska rhythms of Jamaica, where Domino was popular and toured in 1961. The only unimpressive moments came when he was persuaded to jump on the twist bandwagon, recording a number titled 'Dance With Mr Domino'.

By now, Lew Chudd had sold the Imperial company and Domino had switched labels to ABC Paramount. There he recorded several albums with producers Felton Jarvis and Bill Justis, but his continuing importance was in his tours of North America and Europe which re-created the sound of the 50s for new generations of listeners. The quality of Domino's touring band was well captured on a 1965 live album for Mercury from Las Vegas with Roy Montrell, (guitar), Cornelius Coleman (drums) and the saxophones of Herb Hardesty and Lee Allen. Domino continued this pattern of work into the 70s, breaking the pattern slightly when he gave the Beatles' 'Lady Madonna' a New Orleans treatment. He made further albums for Reprise (1968) and Sonet (1979), the Reprise sides being the results of a reunion session with Dave Bartholomew. In 1991, EMI which now owns the Imperial catalogue, released a scholarly box-set of Domino's remarkable recordings. He remains a giant figure of R&B musically and physically.

Selected albums: *Carry On Rockin'* (1955), *Fats Domino - Rock and Rollin'* (1956), *This Is Fats Domino!* (1957), *Here Stands Fats Domino* (1958), *Fabulous Mr D* (1958), *Let's Play Fats Domino* (1959), *Fats Domino Sings* (1960), *I Miss You So* (1961), *Twistin' The Stomp* (1962), *Just Domino* (1963), *Here Comes Fats Domino* (1963), *Fats On Fire* (1964), *Fats Domino '65* (1965), *Getaway With Fats Domino* (1966), *Fats Is Back* (1968), *Sleeping On The Job* (1979). Numerous compilations are always available.

Dorsey, Thomas A.

b. 1 July 1899, Villa Rica, Georgia, USA. Born into a religious family, Dorsey nevertheless shunned sacred music for many years, although it is in that idiom that he was to make the biggest impact. He learned to play piano in his youth, and when he settled in Chicago in 1916 began to carve out a career for himself on the blues scene there. In the early 20s, he toured as a musician in the Ma Rainey show. Between 1928 and 1932 he recorded extensively as a blues artist, under his pseudonym Georgia Tom, as partner to Tampa Red, as part of groups such as the Hokum Boys, and as accompanist to a great many artists, from obscure figures such as Auntie Mary Bradford and Stovepipe Johnson to big names like Big Bill Broonzy, Memphis Minnie and Victoria Spivey. Despite the comparative brevity of this period of his career, he was very influential, for the quality and variety of his piano accompaniments, and also for one of his best known records, with Tampa Red, 'It's Tight Like That' a smutty, double meaning song that was enormously popular and led to a vast number of cover versions, copies and variants. In 1930, he began to compose and publish religious songs, and two years later, at the height of his success as a blues musician, Dorsey renounced this idiom and moved to gospel music, with which he was to stay for the rest of his long career. He joined singer Sallie Martin, and developed a new career with the Gospel Choral Union. His successful blues recording career led him straight into recording gospel songs, dropping the pseudonym Georgia Tom in favour of his own full name. One of his biggest successes, however, has been as songwriter and it was when the Heavenly Gospel Singers recorded his song 'Precious Lord' that he really began to make his name in this respect; the song has become one of the best known, and most prolifically recorded, of all black gospel songs. He has remained active into a remarkably old age, appearing in a television film as late as the 80s, still preaching and singing.

Album: *Georgia Tom* (1989).

Dotson, Big Bill

An obscure figure, Big Bill Dotson is known only for one record, made around 1952, possibly in Houston, Texas, and issued on the Black & White label. Singing accompanied only by his guitar, his style on this very limited evidence was reminiscent of Lightnin' Hopkins, and indeed, his two tracks have appeared on a Hopkins album, credited to that artist. His vocals were rather lighter and his guitar work more rudimentary than those of the more famous artist, but he deserves his own small place in blues history.
Album: *Blues From The Deep South* (1969).

Dotson, Jimmy

b. 19 October 1934, Ethel, Louisiana, USA. Dotson began his musical career singing blues at a local juke joint, but later developed his skills to encompass drums and guitar. He played in a band with Lazy Lester, and later with Silas Hogan in a group called the Rhythm Ramblers. Although Hogan was the leader of this group, their first record was made with Dotson on vocals. Two singles were issued on Jay Miller's own Rocko and Zynn labels, under Dotson's name, both in an upbeat R&B vein, quite different from Hogan's downhome blues sound. Dotson lived in Memphis for several years and had another single issued on the Home Of The Blues label, but moved back to Baton Rouge in the early 80s and resumed his career at Tabby Thomas' Blues Box club.
Albums: *Baton Rouge Blues* (1985), *Baton Rouge Harmonica* (1988).

Douglas, K.C.

b. 21 November 1913, Sharon, Mississippi, USA, d. 18 October 1975, Berkeley, California, USA. Baptised with initials only, Douglas came from a strict Baptist family, father John a minister who disapproved of blues. Though interested in the guitar, he didn't get one until 1936, taking instruction from uncle Scott Douglas and cousin Isadore Scott. Moving to Jackson, Mississippi in 1940, he met Tommy Johnson, having previously copied his style from records. In 1945, he moved to Vallejo, California as a government recruit to work in the Kaiser shipyard. He then moved north to

Richmond and met harmonica player Sidney Maiden. The pair recorded for Bob Geddins' Down Town label in 1948, Douglas singing 'Mercury Boogie' using a guitar loaned by Lowell Fulson, and Maiden, 'Eclipse Of The Sun', songs for which each man was subsequently lauded. In 1954, Douglas moved to Oakland and recorded 'K.C. Boogie' for Rhythm, another Geddins label. Two years later, he was recorded at a house party, the resulting performance released as an album on Cook, a New York label. In 1960-1 he was recorded several times by Arhoolie owner Chris Strachwitz, who leased two albums to Bluesville. He also backed Maiden and Mercy Dee Walton on albums recorded at the same time and released on both labels. In the late 60s, he made singles for Galaxy and Blues Connoisseur. His last album featured him with a band that included harmonica player Richard Riggins.
Selected albums: *K.C. Blues* (1962), *The Country Boy* (1974).

Doyle, Charlie 'Little Buddy'

No biographical details are available for Doyle, an obscure, impoverished, blind American street blues singer who, as his name implies, was also a dwarf. He was thought to have been born in Memphis, perhaps at the turn of the century and recorded 10 tracks there for Columbia in July 1939, which were to be a major influence on Detroit bluesman, Baby Boy Warren. Other Memphis musicians like Walter Horton, Will Shade and Furry Lewis claim to have worked with him; Shade and Horton both profess to be the harmonica player on his recordings. Informants report that Doyle probably died in early 1940 but this has never been confirmed.

Dranes, Arizona Juanita

b. c.1905, Dallas, Texas, USA. A member of the Church Of God In Christ and possibly of Mexican extraction, Arizona Dranes combined a high, forceful voice with the rocking barrel-house piano style associated with the 'South Eastern School' to create joyful, ground-breaking gospel records that were an inspiration to many later performers. Richard M. Jones, who as well as being a pianist acted as a talent scout, discovered the blind singer performing in the church of Reverend Samuel Crouch in Fort Worth, Texas and took her to Chicago to record for the OKeh label in 1926. In the ensuing two years she recorded 16 tracks under her own name, including some in the company of Sara Martin and two piano solos, as well as possibly accompanying other singers. She was also instrumental in introducing the famous Rev. F.W. McGee to record, his first outings being in support of her third session. Dranes' opportunities to record were often restricted by the severe bouts of influenza to which she was prone. After her correspondence with the record company ceased, she disappeared back into the depression-bound south.

Album: *Barrel House Piano With Sanctified Singing* (1976).

Drifting Slim

b. Elmon Mickle, 24 February 1919, Keo, Arkansas, USA, d. 17 September 1977. He was inspired to sing and play harmonica by John Lee 'Sonny Boy' Williamson, whose style he emulated successfully on local radio stations in the 40s. Mickle formed his first band in 1951 and recorded for the Modern/RPM company; he learned to play guitar and drums and worked occasionally as a one-man band. In 1957 he moved to Los Angeles, where he recorded for several small labels (including Elko, E.M., J Gems, Wonder, Magnum and Styletone, using the pseudonym Model T. Slim for the latter), and in 1966 he made an album for Milestone Records. Poor health prevented him playing many club dates in the 70s; he died of cancer in September 1977.

Album: as Model T. Slim *Somebody Done Voodoo The Hoodoo Man* (1980).

Dr. John

b. Malcolm John Rebennack, 12 November 1940, New Orleans, Louisiana, USA. Dr. John has built a career since the 60s as a consummate New Orleans musician, incorporating funk, rock 'n' roll, jazz and R&B into his sound. Rebennack's distinctive vocal growl and virtuoso piano playing brought him acclaim among critics and fellow artists, although his commercial successes have not equalled that recognition. Rebennack's musical education began in the 40s when he accompanied his father to blues clubs. At the age of 14 he began frequenting recording studios, and wrote his first songs at that time. By 1957 he was working as a

session musician, playing guitar, keyboards and other instruments on recordings issued on such labels as Ace, Ric, Rex and Ebb. He made his first recording under his own name, 'Storm Warning', for Rex during that same year. His first album was recorded for Rex in 1958, and others followed on Ace and AFO Records with little success. In 1958 he also co-wrote 'Lights Out', recorded by Jerry Byrne, and toured with Byrne and Frankie Ford.

By 1962 Rebennack had already played on countless sessions for such renowned producers as Phil Spector, Harold Battiste, H.B. Barnum and Sonny Bono (later of Sonny And Cher). Rebennack formed his own bands during the early 60s but they did not take off. By the mid-60s Rebennack had moved to Los Angeles, where he fused his New Orleans roots with the emerging west coast psychedelic sound, and he developed the persona Dr. John Creux, The Night Tripper. The character was based on one established by singer Prince La La, but Rebennack made it his own through the intoxicating brew of voodoo incantations and New Orleans heritage. An album, *Zu Zu Man*, for A&M Records, did not catch on when released in 1965.

In 1968 Dr. John was signed to Atco Records and released *Gris Gris*, which received critical acclaim but did not chart. This exceptional collection included the classic 'Walk On Gilded Splinters' and inspired several similarly styled successors, winning respect from fellow musicians, resulting in Eric Clapton and Mick Jagger guesting on a later album. The same musical formula and exotic image were pursued on follow-up albums *Babylon* and *Remedies*. Meanwhile, he toured on the rock festival and ballroom circuit and continued to do session work. In 1971, Dr. John charted for the first time with *Dr. John, The Night Tripper (The Sun, Moon And Herbs)*. The 1972 *Gumbo* album, produced by Jerry Wexler, charted, as did the single, 'Iko Iko'. His biggest US hit came in 1973 with the single 'Right Place, Wrong Time', which reached number 9; the accompanying album, *In The Right Place*, was also his best-selling, hitting number 24. These crafted, colourful albums featured the instrumental muscle of the Meters, but despite a newfound popularity, the artist parted from his record label, Atlantic, and subsequent work

Dr. John

failed to achieve a similar status.

During that year he toured with the New Orleans band the Meters, and recorded *Triumvirate* with Michael Bloomfield and John Hammond. The single 'Such A Night' also charted in 1973. Dr. John continued to record throughout the 70s and 80s, for numerous labels, among them United Artists, Horizon and Clean Cuts, the latter releasing *Dr. John Plays Mac Rebennack*, a solo piano album, in 1981. In the meantime, he continued to draw sizeable audiences as a concert act across the USA, and added radio jingle work to his live and recording work (he continued to play on many sessions). He recorded *Bluesiana Triangle* with jazz musicians Art Blakey and David 'Fathead' Newman and released *In A Sentimental Mood*, a collection of interpretations of standards, on Warner Brothers Records. Despite employing a low-key approach to recording, Dr. John has remained a respected figure, re-emerging in 1989 with *In A Sentimental Mood*, a collection of standards which included a moody duet with Rickie Lee Jones. His live appearances are now less frequent, but this irrepressible artist continues his role as a tireless champion of Crescent City music.

Albums: *Gris Gris* (1968), *Babylon* (1969), *Remedies* (1970), *Dr. John, The Night Tripper (The Sun, Moon And Herbs)* (1971), *Dr. John's Gumbo* (1972), *In The Right Place* (1973), with John Hammond, Mike Bloomfield *Triumvirate* (1973), *Desitively Bonnaroo* (1974), *Hollywood Be Thy Name* (1975), *Cut Me While I'm Hot* (1975), *City Lights* (1978), *Tango Palace* (1979), *Love Potion* (1981), *Dr. John Plays Mac Rebennack* (1981), *The Brightest Smile In Town* (1983), with Chris Barber *Take Me Back To New Orleans* (1983), *Such A Night - Live In London* (1984), *In A Sentimental Mood* (1989). Compilations: *I Been Hoodood* (1984), *In The Night* (1985), *Zu Zu Man* (1987), *Bluesiana Triangle* (1990).

Dukes, 'Little' Laura

b. 10 June 1907, Memphis, Tennessee, USA. An early start in music led Little Laura Dukes to a lifetime of involvement with entertainment in Memphis. Her father had been a drummer with W.C. Handy's band, but it was a less sophisticated idiom that Dukes chose, playing blues with the jug bands for which that city is so well known. She sang and played banjo and ukelele with the Will Batts' Novelty Band, and although they made two recordings in the early 50s, these were not issued until 20 years later. She made some more records with the revival of interest in blues and related music in the 70s, and also appeared in a BBC television series. As late as the 80s, she was still performing in Memphis, at the Blues Alley club, set up to showcase the city's blues talent.

Album: *South Memphis Jug Band* (1975).

Dummer, John, Blues Band

This UK band came into being in 1965, evolving from the Muskrats and the Grebbells, and lasted until the early 70s, surviving numerous personnel changes. The line-up included prominent British blues artists such as pianist Bob Hall, guitarist Dave Kelly and his sister Jo Ann, Mike Cooper, and Tony McPhee. The band backed touring American artists John Lee Hooker and Howlin' Wolf, and recorded albums for Mercury and Vertigo between 1969 and 1973. Drummer John Dummer went on to work with English pop vocal group Darts in the mid-70s.

Albums: *Cabal* (1969), *John Dummer's Blues Band* (1969).

Dunbar, Scott

b. 1904, Deer Park Plantation, Mississippi, USA. Dunbar taught himself guitar as a child, and despite some involvement with a local string band, his music was idiosyncratic and unpredictable, combining seemingly spontaneous guitar playing with a singing style that veers abruptly between normal and falsetto registers; the total performance often seems almost a free form exploration of the song. Dunbar never travelled more than 100 miles from his rural home, and was further isolated by his illiteracy, which meant that his lyrics were memorized, and often startlingly fragmented. He seldom - and by the 60s, never - played for black audiences, owing to his wife's fear of possible violence. He combined work as a fisherman and guide with playing for tourists, and his repertoire reflected this, with popular tunes outnumbering blues substantially.

Album: *From Lake Mary* (1970).

Dunn, Roy

b. 13 April 1922, Eatonton, Georgia, USA, d. 2

March 1988, Atlanta, Georgia, USA. Dunn was a blues guitarist and singer, who had learned from and played with Georgia artists such as Curley Weaver, Buddy Moss and Blind Willie McTell in the 30s, although he was of a younger generation. This meant that he missed out on recording at a time when his style of music was at its most commercially popular. In his younger days, he sang in a family gospel quartet, the Dunn Brothers, then between the late 30s and early 40s he toured with a series of other gospel groups. In the early 70s, he recorded an album, and appeared at a number of blues festivals. He is also credited as a major source of information and contacts by researchers in the blues of the east coast states.

Album: *Know'd Them All* (1974).

Dupree, 'Champion' Jack

b. William Thomas Dupree, 4 July 1910, New Orleans, Louisiana, USA, d. 21 January 1992. Orphaned in infancy, Dupree was raised in the Colored Waifs Home for Boys until the age of 14. After leaving, he led a marginal existence, singing for tips, and after learning piano from musicians such as Willie 'Drive-'em-down' Hall. Dupree also became a professional boxer, and blended fighting with hoboing through the 30s, before retiring from the ring in 1940, and heading for New York. Initially, he travelled only as far as Indianapolis, where he fell in with musicians who had been associates of Leroy Carr. Dupree rapidly became a star of the local black entertainment scene, as a comedian and dancer as well as a musician. He acquired a residency at the local Cotton Club, and partnered comedienne Ophelia Hoy. In 1940, Dupree made his recording debut, with music that blended the forceful, barrelhouse playing and rich, Creole-accented singing of New Orleans with the more suave style of Leroy Carr. Not surprisingly, a number of titles were piano/guitar duets, although on some Jesse Ellery's use of amplification pointed the way forward. A few songs covered unusual topics, such as the distribution of grapefruit juice by relief agencies, or the effects of drugs. Dupree's musical career was interrupted when he was drafted into the US Navy as a cook; even so he managed to become one of the first blues singers to record for the folk revival market while on leave in New York in 1943. Dupree's first wife died while he was in the navy, and he took his discharge in New York, where he worked as a club pianist, and formed a close musical association with Sonny Terry and Brownie McGhee. His own post-war recording career commenced, with a splendid series of solo recordings for Joe Davis, on some of which the influence of Peetie Wheatstraw is very evident. More typical were the many tracks with small groups recorded thereafter for a number of labels from 1946-53, and for King between April 1953 and late 1955. As ever, these recordings blend the serious with the comic, the latter somewhat tastelessly on songs like 'Tongue Tied Blues' and 'Harelip Blues'. 'Walking The Blues', a comic dialogue with Teddy 'Mr Bear' McRae, was a hit on King, and the format was repeated on a number of titles recorded for RCA's Vik and Groove.

In 1958, Dupree made his last American recordings until 1990; 'Blues From The Gutter' appears to have been aimed at white audiences, as was Dupree's career thereafter. In 1959, he moved to Europe, and has since lived in Switzerland, England, Sweden, and Germany, touring extensively and recording prolifically, with results that vary from the excellent to the mediocre and serving as both stamp of authenticity and licensed jester to the European blues scene.

Albums: *Blues From The Gutter* (1958), *The Blues Of Champion Jack Dupree* (1963), *From New Orleans To Chicago* (1966), featuring Mickey Baker *Champion Jack Dupree And His Blues Band* (1967), *Scoobydoobydoo* (1969), *Rub A Little Boogie* (1982), *Junker Blues* (1985), *Shake Baby Shake* (1987), *Live At Burnley* (1990), *Blues For Everybody* (1990), *The Joe Davis Sessions* (1990), *Back Home In New Orleans* (1990).

Duskin, 'Big' Joe

b. 10 February 1921, Birmingham, Alabama, USA. In the 30s Joe moved with his family to Cincinnati, Ohio, where he began playing piano, inspired by the records of Roosevelt Sykes, Albert Ammons, and Pete Johnson. During World War II he was drafted into the Army and met Ammons, Johnson, and Meade 'Lux' Lewis on USO shows. After demobilization Joe promised his preacher father that he would not play 'the devil's music' while the old man (in his 80s) was still alive; however,

'Champion' Jack Dupree

he lived to be 104! Duskin's debut album was finally released by Arhoolie Records in 1979 and revealed him as a worthy bearer of the boogie-woogie tradition. Later albums have appeared on the Special Delivery and Wolf labels, and Duskin has also recorded behind Dave Peabody and The Blues Band.

Albums: *Cincinnati Stomp* (1979), *Don't Mess With The Boogie Man* (1988), *Live* (1990).

Dyer, Johnny

b. 1938, Rolling Fork, Mississippi, USA. This singer/harmonica player knew guitarist Smokey Wilson in Mississippi, and the two have often teamed up now that they are both based in Los Angeles. Dyer has sat in with many blues notables, including Jimmy Reed, Jimmy Roger and George Smith. He recorded for Shakey Jake (Harris)'s Good Time label in the late 70s, revealing, as do his other recordings, a strong Little Walter influence. Some tracks appeared in the early 80s on a undistinguished album issued in Japan by Mina Records. In 1983 he recorded for Murray Brothers, with a band including members of the Mighty Flyers, and in 1991 his best recorded track was issued on a Los Angeles blues anthology compiled by longtime associate William Clarke. Album: *Johnny Dyer And The LA Jukes* (1983), one track only *Hard Times* (1991).

E

Ealey, Robert

b. 1924, probably Texas, USA. Ealey began singing with a gospel quartet but switched to blues at the age of 15. He eventually settled in Fort Worth and worked as a drummer with Up Wilson, Zuzu Bollin, and Frankie Lee Sims in the 50s. He has been associated with the Bluebird Lounge in Fort Worth for more than 30 years and is now its owner. The club itself is a local institution, and Ealey appears there as a

singer. Like the club, his music is rough and ready, and has been captured on record by the Blue Royal and Amazing companies. Albums: *Live At The New Bird Nite Club* (1977), *Bluebird Open* (1984).

Earl, King

b. Ronnie Earl 1953, New York City, New York, USA. Earl was inspired to play blues guitar after seeing Muddy Waters at a club in Boston, Massachusetts. He lists his influences as Robert Junior Lockwood, B.B. King, Magic Sam, and T-Bone Walker, among others. Earl quickly graduated to playing clubs around the Boston area, and he also spent some time in Chicago and Texas, backing many touring blues artists. He replaced Duke Robillard in Roomful Of Blues and stayed with them for almost eight years, leaving in the mid-80s to pursue a successful solo career. He has also become an in-demand session guitarist, particularly with Black Top Records. Often called 'Mr Intensity', Earl is rated as one of the finest blues guitarists alive.

Albums: *I Like It When It Rains* (1990), *Peace Of Mind* (1990).

Easy Baby

b. Alex Randall, 3 August 1934, Memphis, Tennessee, USA. Easy Baby is an accomplished blues singer/harmonica player who was already involved in the west Memphis blues scene before he moved to Chicago in 1956, where he worked with local groups and led his own band for a time. He gave up music for many years, then began singing and playing again in the mid-70s, when he recorded for the Barrelhouse and Mr. Blues labels (with further material recorded for these companies issued by Rooster and JSP). He rarely plays in Chicago clubs nowadays.

Album: *Sweet Home Chicago Blues* (1977).

Edwards, Archie

b. 1918, Rocky Mount, Virginia, USA. From a musical family Edwards, desire to be a guitar player developed out of the Saturday night gatherings his father held at their home during his childhood. As a teenager he learned to sing and play by mimicking the 78s of Blind Lemon Jefferson, Mississippi John Hurt and hillbilly artist, Frank Hutchinson. Most of his life he has held down day jobs, only performing at

weekends or evenings at clubs in Washington, D.C. Recently, Edwards has become a great favourite on the festival circuit having visited Europe in the 80s and recorded for the German L&R label. Together with John Jackson and John Cephas, Archie Edwards is the continuation of the east coast blues tradition begun in the 30s by Blind Boy Fuller.
Album: *My Road Is Rough And Rocky* (1980).

Edwards, Clarence

b. 1933, Linsey, Louisiana, USA. Edwards began playing blues guitar at around the age of 12, when he moved into Baton Rouge. In the 50s and 60s, he was working the same local blues circuit as men like Lightnin' Slim, in bands with names such as the Boogie Beats and the Bluebird Kings. His first experience of recording was in a traditional setting, in sessions for folklorist Harry Oster between 1959 and 1961, with his brother Cornelius and violinist James 'Butch' Cage. Nine years later, he recorded again, this time with a more contemporary sound, and since the mid-80s, when the blues scene revived with the help of Tabby Thomas's Blues Box club, he has been playing regularly again. In 1990, he made his first album, a powerful mixture of acoustic and electric sounds in the swamp blues style.
Album: *Swamp's The Word* (1990).

Edwards, David 'Honeyboy'

b. 28 June 1915, Shaw, Mississippi, USA. Born and raised in the Mississippi Delta country, Edwards played with and learned from such important blues figures as Charley Patton, Robert Johnson and Big Joe Williams. His first recordings were made for the Library of Congress in 1941, a set of typical Mississippi country blues, demonstrating a tense, emotional vocal delivery and considerable skills on harmonica and, particularly, guitar. Ten years later, his first commercial recording appeared on the obscure Texas label ARC, and in the next couple of years he also recorded for Sun Records in Memphis and Chess in Chicago, although nothing was issued at the time. Rediscovered in the 60s in Chicago, Edwards has made several fine albums, encompassing traditional country blues as well as more urban stylings. He has also toured widely, playing in Europe several times in recent years.
Albums: *I've Been Around* (1979), *White Windows* (1989), *Mississippi Blues: Library Of Congress Recordings* (1991), *Delta Bluesman* (1992).

Edwards, Frank

b. 20 March 1909, Washington, Georgia, USA. Raised in St. Petersburg, Florida, Edwards took up guitar at an early age, adding rack harmonica in 1934. He became an itinerant musician, with his home base in Atlanta, where he played with the Star Band, whose members included Leroy Dallas, a longtime associate. In 1941, Edwards recorded for OKeh Records, a session which was set up by *Lester Melrose*, manager of Tommy McClennan, with whom he was travelling at the time. Settling in Atlanta after World War II, he recorded for Savoy in 1949, but the titles were unissued until the 60s, by which time Edwards himself had stopped playing; rediscovered in the 70s, however, he proved able to re-create his old sound with little difficulty.
Albums: *Living With The Blues* (1964), *Sugar Mama Blues* (1969), *Done Some Travelin'* (1973), *Chicago Blues* (c.1987), *Georgia Blues* (1990).

Edwards, Moanin' Bernice

b. c.1910, Houston, Texas, USA. Bernice Edwards was described by Sippie Wallace as being 'one of the family'; the family in question was Sippie's own renowned Thomas Family of Houston, Bernice being the same age as its most gifted member, the child prodigy, Hersal. From another member of the family, Hociel, she learned to play the piano and sing the blues. She remained in Houston when the family moved north and was often in the company of Black Boy Shine (Harold Holliday). When she recorded for Paramount in 1928 these influences were evident in her introspective 'moanin' blues and her piano style. When she attended her third and last session (for ARC in 1935) she was in the company of Holliday and one record was issued by her, Holliday and Howling Smith together. Apart from the fact that she later married and joined the church, little more is known.
Album: *The Thomas Family* (1977).

Electric Flag

The brief career of the much vaunted Electric Flag was begun in 1967 by the late Mike Bloomfield, following his departure from the influential Paul Butterfield Blues Band. The

original group comprised of Bloomfield (b. 28 July 1944, Chicago, Illinois, USA, d. 15 February 1981; guitar), Buddy Miles (drums/vocals), Nick Gravenites (b. Chicago, Illinois, USA; vocals), Barry Goldberg (keyboards), Harvey Brooks (bass), Peter Strazza (tenor saxophone), Marcus Doubleday (trumpet) and Herbie Rich (baritone saxophone). All members were well-seasoned professionals coming from a variety of musical backgrounds. Their debut at the 1967 Monterey Pop Festival was a noble start. Their excellent *A Long Time Comin'* was released in 1968 with additional members Stemziel (Stemsy) Hunter and Mike Fonfara and was a significant hit in the USA. The tight brassy-tinged blues numbers were laced with Bloomfield's sparse but bitingly crisp Fender Stratocaster guitar. Tracks such as 'Killing Floor' were perfect examples of vintage Flag. The band was unable to follow this release, and immediately began to fall apart, with founder Bloomfield being the first to go. Buddy Miles attempted to hold the band together but the second album was a pale shadow of their debut, with only 'See To Your Neighbour' showing signs of a unified performance. Miles then left to form the Buddy Miles Express, while Gravenites became a songwriting legend in San Francisco. Harvey Brooks, following years of session work, including the Bloomfield/Kooper/Stills *Super Session*, turned up as a member of Sky. An abortive Flag reunion produced the lacklustre and inappropriately titled *The Band Kept Playing*.
Albums: *The Trip* (1967, film soundtrack), *A Long Time Comin'* (1968), *The Electric Flag* (1969), *The Band Kept Playing* (1974).

Ellis, Wilbert 'Big Chief'
b. 10 November 1914, Birmingham, Alabama, USA, d. 20 December 1977, Birmingham, Alabama, USA. A part-time musician, Ellis also worked as a taxi driver, bartender and gambler. His blues piano was rooted in the rolling, hard hitting styles of Birmingham, to which was added a strong influence from Walter Davis. Resident in New York from 1936, he made a few splendid records under his own name in the 50s, and accompanied Tarheel Slim, Brownie McGhee, Jack Dupree and others. Rediscovered in Washington in the 70s, he returned to performing, enthusiastically and with

unimpaired skills, until his death.
Albums: *Big Chief Ellis* (1976), *Let's Have A Ball* (1978).

Embry, 'Queen' Sylvia
b. 1941, Wabbaseka, Arkansas, USA. Embry began playing piano as a child and sang in church choirs, moving to Memphis at the age of 19. In the 60s she settled in Chicago, where she met and married blues guitarist Johnny Embry, who taught her to play bass guitar. In the 70s she worked for several years with Lefty Dizz and she can be seen playing bass and singing one song with his band in the film *Mississippi Delta Blues*. She shared the credit with her husband on an album for Razor Records, was part of Alligator's *Living Chicago Blues* project, and had an album released as by Blues Queen Sylvia on the German L&R label. A strong singer and fine bass player, *Living Blues* magazine reported in 1985 that she had turned her back on blues and was playing gospel music.
Albums: Johnny And Sylvia Embry *After Work* (1980), four titles only *Living Chicago Blues Volume Six* (1980), as Blues Queen Sylvia *Midnight Baby* (1983).

Emerson, Billy 'The Kid'
b. William Robert Emerson, 21 December 1929, Tarpon Springs, Florida, USA. Emerson's father was a blues singer and the young Emerson played piano with the Billy Battle Band and other local groups before serving in the forces in 1952-54. On his return, he joined Ike Turner's band in Memphis. Here Emerson made his first records for Sun which displayed his talent for wordplay and included 'No Teasing Around', the jive-talking 'The Woodchuck' and 'Red Hot', a song later taken up by rockabilly singer Billy Lee Riley and by Bob Luman. He moved to Chicago soon afterwards, playing piano or organ on numerous recording sessions and releasing singles under his own name in 1955-57 for VeeJay ('Every Woman I Know Is Crazy About An Automobile', later revived by Ry Cooder) and in 1958-59 for Chess ('I'll Get You Too'). There were later records for Mad (1960), M-Pac (the dance craze song 'The Whip',1963) and USA (1963) before Emerson formed his own Tarpon label in the mid-60s. Among his Tarpon singles was 'I Dig The Funky Broadway'.

Billy 'The Kid' Emerson

Albums: (reissues) *Little Fine Healthy Thing* (1980), *Crazy 'Bout Automobiles* (1982).

Estes, Sleepy John

b. John Adams Estes, 25 January 1899, Ripley, Tennessee, USA, d. 5 June 1977, Brownsville, Tennessee, USA. This influential blues singer first performed at local house-parties while in his early teens. In 1916 he began working with mandolinist James 'Yank' Rachell, a partnership that was revived several times throughout their respective careers. It was also during this formative period that Estes met Hammie Nixon (harmonica), another individual with whom he shared a long-standing empathy. Estes made his recording debut in September 1929. He eventually completed eight masters for the RCA company, including the original versions of 'Diving Duck Blues', 'Poor John Blues' and the seminal often-covered 'Milk Cow Blues'. These assured compositions inspired interpretations from artists as diverse as Taj Mahal, Tom Rush and the Kinks. However, despite remaining an active performer throughout the 30s, Estes retired from music in 1941. A childhood accident impaired Estes' eyesight and by 1950 he had become completely blind. The singer resumed performing with several low-key sessions for Hammie Nixon, before re-asserting his own recording career in 1962. Several

excellent albums for Chicago's Delmark label followed, one of which, *Broke And Hungry*, featured a young Michael Bloomfield on guitar. Estes, Nixon and Rachell also made a successful appearance at the 1964 Newport Folk Festival and the three veterans continued to work together until 1976 when Estes suffered a stroke. Selected albums: *The Legend Of Sleepy John Estes* (1962), *Broke And Hungry, Ragged And Hungry Too* (1963), *Portraits In Blues, Volume 10* (1964), *Brownsville Blues* (1965), *Down South Blues* (1974), *1929-30 Sessions* (1978), *The Blues Of Sleepy John Estes '34-'40* (1982), *The Blues Of Sleepy John Estes '34-'40, Volume Two* (1983), *First Recordings* (1992).

Evans, Joe, And Arthur McLain

'The Two Poor Boys' were black, and are reported to have come from Fairmount, in east Tennessee, where whites outnumbered blacks by 12 to one. This goes some way to explaining the eclecticism of, and the large white influence on, their music. Recorded in 1927 and 1931, they performed blues, but this only made up about half of their issued titles; they also cut medicine show material, coon songs, 20s pop, white fiddle pieces like 'Sourwood Mountain' (transferred to mandolin and guitar), black ballads like 'John Henry', and a parody of Darby And Tarlton's 'Birmingham Jail'. As well as

Sleepy John Estes with Hammie Nixon and Yank Rachell

ranging widely in styles, they featured a remarkable variety of instruments: guitar, kazoo, piano, mandolin, and violin. It is thought that both men played guitar and kazoo, and Evans the other instruments.

Evans, Lucky

b. 1 May 1937, Estabuchie, Mississippi, USA. Also known as 'Lucky Lopez', Evans was inspired by the singing and playing of his father and began to play the guitar at the age of eight. As a teenager he worked with a band in Milwaukee and then travelled throughout the southern states until 1964 when he settled in Chicago, having joined Howlin' Wolf's band. He worked with many of the city's leading bluesmen in the 60s and made his debut recording in 1967 (only one track was released). He next recorded in 1973, financing the session himself, In 1988, he visited Britain, touring incessantly and slowly establishing a reputation as one of the great underrated blues singers. He recorded in England for the JSP and Borderline labels.

Evans, Marjorie Ann 'Margie'

b. 17 July 1940, Shreveport, Louisiana, USA.

Evans was largely inspired by Billie Holiday and Bessie Smith. After moving to Los Angeles in her late teens, she began working with Billy Ward's Sextet between 1958 and 1964. She made some unissued recordings for Dore Records in Hollywood in the early 60s and began touring with Ron Marshall's orchestra from the mid-to-late 60s. In 1969 she joined the Johnny Otis band, recorded for Epic and extensively toured the USA and the Far East. In 1972 she began touring with Willie Dixon's Chicago All-Stars, and made her first solo recordings for Yambo (1972), United Artists (1973), and Buddah (1974). She was particularly renowned for her powerful live performances at clubs and jazz festivals in the USA and Europe. In recent years she has released two fine albums on L&R Records.
Albums: *Mistreated Woman* (c.80s), *Another Blues Day* (c.80s).

Even Dozen Jug Band

Formed in 1963 by Peter Siegel and Stefan Grossman. Renowned in their respective fields, namely bluegrass and blues, the two musicians brought several colleagues into the line-up to create a mutually satisfying style once punningly referred to as 'jug-grass'. *The Even Dozen Jug Band*, released in January 1964, was their sole recorded legacy, but the ensemble is better recalled as an important meeting point for several influential figures. Grossman and Siegel aside, the line-up also included John Benson, better known as John Sebastian, Maria D'Amato (later Maria Muldaur), Steve Katz, a future member of the Blues Project and Blood Sweat And Tears, and Joshua Rifkin, who subsequently acquired fame for his interpretations of Scott Joplin's piano rags. It should be noted, however, that not all of these artists appear on all of the songs. The Jug Band's brief tenure ended in disagreement between those who wished to maintain the group's 'fun' status and those who wished to assume a more professional approach. The split allowed the above individuals to pursue a more independent path.

Album: *The Even Dozen Jug Band* (1964).

Ezell, Will

b. 1896, Shreveport, Louisiana, USA. Ezell had a recording career under his own name, that lasted from September 1927 to September 1929, and produced a total of 17 tracks including alternative takes. His fame rests not only on his outstanding piano work but on being one of the originators of boogie-woogie. His 'Pitchin' Boogie' was one of the earliest known uses of the term. In his role as 'house pianist' for Paramount Records he supplied musical support for artists such as Lucille Bogan, Blind Roosevelt Graves, Side-Wheel Sallie Duffie and Bertha Henderson and he is also rumoured to have worked for Bessie Smith. Although Ezell was well respected by contemporaries such as Little Brother Montgomery and Cripple Clarence Lofton, he seems to have fallen foul of the great Depression as nothing is known of him after his last appearance in a recording studio in 1931.

Album: *Pitchin' Boogie* (1986).

F

Fabulous Thunderbirds

Formed in Texas, USA in 1977, the Thunderbirds comprised, Jimmy Vaughan (b. 20 March 1951, Dallas, Texas, USA; guitar), Kim Wilson (b. 6 January 1951, Detroit, Michigan, USA; vocals/harmonica), Keith Ferguson (b. 23 July 1946, Houston, Texas, USA; bass) and Mike Buck (b. 17 June 1952; drums). They emerged from the post-punk vacuum with a solid, unpretentious brand of R&B. Their debut album, *The Fabulous Thunderbirds* aka *Girls Go Wild* offered a series of powerful original songs as well as sympathetic cover versions, including a vibrant reading of Slim Harpo's 'Scratch My Back'. This mixture has sustained the group throughout its career, although it took a move from Chrysalis to the Epic label to provide the success which their exciting music deserved. The Thunderbirds' line-up has undergone some changes, with former Roomful Of Blues drummer Fran Christiana (b. 1 February 1951, Westerly, Rhode Island, USA) replacing Mike Buck in 1980, and Preston Hubbard (b. 15 March 1953, Providence, Rhode Island, USA) joining after Ferguson departed. Throughout these changes, Wilson and Vaughan, the brother of the late blues guitarist Stevie Ray Vaughan, have remained at the helm. Drummer Buck formed the Leroi Brothers in 1980, while Ferguson went on to forge a new career with the Tail Gators. Although both of these groups offer a similar bar band fare, the Thunderbirds remain, unquestionably, the masters.
Albums: *The Fabulous Thunderbirds* aka *Girls Go Wild* (1979), *What's The Word* (1980), *Butt Rockin'* (1981), *T-Bird Rhythm* (1982), *Tuff Enuff* (1986), *Hot Number* (1987), *Powerful Stuff* (1989). *Portfolio* (1987, contains a cross-section of early recordings).

Fahey, John

b. 28 February 1939. Fahey grew up in Takoma Park, Maryland, USA and learned to play country-style guitar in the footsteps of Hank Williams and Eddie Arnold at the age of 13, inspired by the recordings of Blind Willie Johnson, and other blues greats. He toured during his teens with Henry Vestine (later of Canned Heat), in addition to gaining a BA in Philosophy and Religion. Fahey's style is based on an original folk blues theme, encompassing blues, jazz, country and gospel music, and at times incorporating classical pieces, although he still retains an almost traditional edge in his arrangements. His 12-string work often features open tunings. He has now become an influence to other American acoustic guitarists. Having set up his own Takoma Records label, with a $300 loan, he released *The Transfiguration Of Blind Joe Death*. This perplexing album subsequently became a cult record during the late 60s. It was a record to be seen with rather than actually play. He later signed with Vanguard Records, in 1967, and released virtually one album a year until quitting the company. Later still, after a brief sojourn with Reprise Records, he was dropped due to insufficient sales. Fahey was also quick to spot other talent and was the first to record Leo Kottke. His work was heard in the film *Zabriskie Point*, but generally his influence is greater than his own success. Having come through drug problems, Fahey retains a cult following. His recorded output is prolific and he continues to perform, although only occasionally. He wrote a thesis on Charlie Patton which has been published.
Selected albums: *The Transfiguration Of Blind Joe Death* (1959), *Guitar* (c.60s), *John Fahey i* (1966), *Days Are Gone By* (1967), *Requia* (1967), *John Fahey ii* (1968), *The Yellow Princess* (1969), *The Voice Of The Turtle* (1968), *Death Chants And Breakdowns* (1968), *The New Possibility: Christmas Album* (c.60s), *Of Rivers And Religion* (1972), *After The Ball* (1973), *Fare Forward Voyagers* (1974), *Old Fashioned Love* (1975), *Yes Jesus Loves You* (1980), *John Fahey Visits Washington, D.C.* (1980), *Live In Tasmania* (1981), *Let Go* (1984), *Rain Forests, Oceans And Other Themes* (1985). Compilations: *The Best Of John Fahey 1959-1977* (1977), *The Essential John Fahey* (1979).

Farka, Ali Toure

From Mali, vocalist-guitarist Farka plays in a style uncannily close to the original Delta blues of Robert Johnson and his successors. This coincidence, picked up on by adventurous British world music critics and broadcasters in the late 80s, gave him a brief flush of popularity in Europe and the USA.

Albums: *Bandolobourou* (1985), *Special* (1987), *Yer Sabou Yerkoy* (1989).

Fieldstones

A Memphis-based electric band, the Fieldstones play an eclectic repertoire, mixing versions of traditional blues like 'Dirt Road' and 'Sweet Home Chicago' with more modern material like Little Milton's 'Little Bluebird' and Albert King's 'Angel Of Mercy'. Vocals are shared by guitarist Willie Roy Sanders, formerly of the Binghampton Blues Boys and drummer Joe Hicks, and vary between the older, brooding, Delta style and an intense, soul-cum-west side Chicago vein. Their enjoyable live performances talents, do not always stand up to exposure on albums. However their music reflects a Memphis State University's need to release material illustrative of academic research.

Album: *Memphis Blues Today* (1982).

Fleetwood Mac

The original Fleetwood Mac was formed in July 1967 by Peter Green (b. Peter Greenbaum, 29 October 1946, Bethnel Green, London, England; guitar) and Mick Fleetwood (b. 24 June 1947, London, England; drums), both of whom had recently left John Mayall's Bluesbreakers. They secured a recording deal with Blue Horizon Records on the strength of Green's reputation as a blues guitarist before the label's overtures uncovered a second guitarist, Jeremy Spencer (b. 4 July 1948, Hartlepool, Cleveland, England), in a semi-professional group, the Levi Set. A temporary bassist, Bob Brunning, was recruited into the line-up, until a further Mayall acolyte, John McVie (b. 26 November 1945, London, England), was finally persuaded to join the new unit. Peter Green's Fleetwood Mac, as the group was initially billed, made its debut on August 12, 1967 at Windsor's National Jazz And Blues Festival. Their first album, *Fleetwood Mac*, released on Blue Horizon in February the following year, reached the UK Top 5 and established a distinctive balance between Green's introspective compositions and Spencer's debt to Elmore James. A handful of excellent cover versions completed an album that was seminal in the development of the British blues boom of the late 60s.

The group also enjoyed two minor hit singles with 'Black Magic Woman', a hypnotic Green composition later popularized by Santana, and a delicate reading of 'Need Your Love So Bad', first recorded by Little Willie John. Fleetwood Mac's second album, *Mr. Wonderful*, was another triumph, but while Spencer was content to repeat his established style, Green, the group's leader, extended his compositional boundaries with several haunting contributions, including the heartfelt 'Love That Burns'. His guitar playing, clean and sparse but always telling, was rarely better, while McVie and Fleetwood were already an instinctive rhythm section. *Mr. Wonderful* also featured contributions from Christine Perfect (b. 12 July 1943, Birmingham, England), pianist from Chicken Shack, and a four-piece horn section, as the group began to leave traditional blues behind. A third guitarist, Danny Kirwan, (b. 13 May 1950, London, England), was added to the line-up in September 1968. The quintet scored an immediate hit when 'Albatross', a moody instrumental reminiscent of 'Sleep Walk' by Santo And Johnny, topped the UK charts. The single, which reached number 2 when it was reissued in 1973, was the group's first million seller.

Fleetwood Mac then left Blue Horizon, although the company subsequently issued *Blues Jam At Chess*, on which the band jammed with several mentors, including Buddy Guy, Otis Spann and Shakey Horton. Following a brief interlude on Immediate Records, which furnished the hypnotic 'Man Of The World', the quintet made their debut on Reprise with 'Oh Well', their most ambitious single to date, and the superb *Then Play On*. This crafted album unveiled Kirwan's songwriting talents and his romantic leanings offset the more worldly Green. Although pictured, Jeremy Spencer was notably absent from most of the sessions, although his eccentric vision was showcased on a self-titled solo album.

Fleetwood Mac now enjoyed an international reputation, but it was a mantle too great for its leader to bear. Peter Green left the band in May 1970 as his parting single, the awesome 'The Green Manalishi', became another Top 10 hit. He was replaced by Christine Perfect, now married to John McVie, and while his loss was an obvious blow, Kirwan's songwriting talent

Fleetwood Mac

and Spencer's sheer exuberance maintained a measure of continuity on a fourth album, *Kiln House*. However in 1971 the group was rocked for a second time when Spencer disappeared mid-way through an American tour. It transpired he had joined a religious sect, the Children Of God and while Green deputized for the remainder of the tour, a permanent replacement was found in a Californian musician, Bob Welch (b. 31 July 1946, California, USA).

The new line-up was consolidated on two melodic albums, *Future Games* and *Bare Trees*. Neither release made much impression with UK audiences who continued to mourn the passing of the Green-led era, but in America the group began to assemble a strong following for their new-found transatlantic sound. However, further changes occurred when Kirwan's chronic stage-fright led to his dismissal. Bob Weston, a guitarist from Long John Baldry's backing band, was his immediate replacement, while the line-up was also bolstered by former Savoy Brown vocalist, Dave Walker. The group, however, was unhappy with a defined

frontman and the singer left after only eight months, having barely completed work on their *Penguin* album. Although not one of the band's strongest collections, it does contain an excellent Welch composition, 'Night Watch'.

The remaining quintet completed another album, *Mystery To Me*, which was released at the time of a personal nadir within the group. Weston, who had been having an affair with Fleetwood's wife, was fired midway through a prolonged US tour and the remaining dates were cancelled. Their manager, Clifford Davis, assembled a bogus Mac to fulfil contractual obligations, thus denying the 'real' group work during the inevitable lawsuits. Yet despite the inordinate pressure, Perfect, Welch, McVie and Fleetwood returned with *Heroes Are Hard To Find*, a positive release which belied the wrangles surrounding its appearance. Nonetheless the controversy proved too strong for Welch, who left the group in December 1974. His departure robbed Fleetwood Mac of an inventive songwriter whose American perspective helped redefine the group's approach.

It was while seeking prospective recording studios that Fleetwood was introduced to Stevie Nicks and Lindsey Buckingham via the duo's self-named album. Now bereft of a guitarist, he recalled Buckingham's expertise and invited him to replace Welch. Lindsey accepted on condition that Nicks also join, thus cementing Fleetwood Mac's most successful line-up. *Fleetwood Mac*, released in 1975, was a promise fulfilled. The newcomers provided easy, yet memorable compositions with smooth harmonies while the British contingent gave the group its edge and power. A succession of stellar compositions, including 'Over My Head', 'Say You Love Me' and the dramatic 'Rhiannon', confirmed a perfect balance had been struck giving the group their first in a long line of US Top 20 singles. The quintet's next release, *Rumours*, proved more remarkable still. Despite the collapse of two relationships - the McVies were divorced, Buckingham and Nicks split up - the group completed a remarkable collection which laid bare the traumas within, but in a manner neither maudlin nor pitiful. Instead the ongoing drama was charted by several exquisite songs; 'Go Your Own Way', 'Don't Stop', 'Second Hand News' and 'Dreams', which retained both melody and purpose. An enduring release, *Rumours* has sold upwards of 25 million copies and is second to Michael Jackson's *Thriller* as the best-selling album of all time.

Having survived their emotional anguish, Fleetwood Mac was faced with the problem of following-up a phenomenon. Their response was *Tusk*, an ambitious double-set which showed a group unafraid to experiment, although many critics damned the collection as self-indulgent. The title track, a fascinating instrumental, was an international hit, although its follow-up, 'Sara', a composition recalling the style of *Rumours*, was better received in the USA than the UK. An in-concert selection, *Fleetwood Mac: Live*, was released as a stop-gap in 1980 as rumours of a complete break-up flourished. It was a further two years before a new collection, *Mirage*, appeared by which point several members were pursuing independent ventures. Buckingham and Nicks, in particular, viewed their own careers with equal importance and *Mirage*, a somewhat self-conscious attempt at creating another *Rumours*, lacked the sparkle of its illustrious predecessor. It nonetheless yielded

three successful singles in 'Hold Me', 'Gypsy' and Buckingham's irrepressible 'Oh Diane'.

Five years then passed before a new Fleetwood Mac album was issued. *Tango In The Night* was a dramatic return to form, recapturing all the group's flair and invention with a succession of heartwarming performances in 'Little Lies', 'Family Man' and 'You And I (Part 2)'. Christine McVie contributed a further highpoint with the rhythmic sing-a-long 'Anyway'. The collection was, however, Lindsey Buckingham's swan-song, although his departure from the band was not officially confirmed until June 1988. By that point two replacement singer/guitarists, ex-Thunderbyrd Rick Vito (b. 1950) and Billy Burnette (b. 7 May 1953), had joined the remaining quartet. The new line-up's debut, *Behind The Mask*, ushered in a new decade and era for this tempestuous group, that gained strength from adversity and simply refused to die. Its success confirmed their status as one of the major groups in the history of popular music.

Albums: *Fleetwood Mac* (1968), *Mr. Wonderful* (1968), *English Rose* (1969), *Then Play On* (1969), *Blues Jam At Chess* aka *Fleetwood Mac In Chicago* (1969), *Kiln House* (1970), *Future Games* (1971), *Bare Trees* (1972), *Penguin* (1973), *Mystery To Me* (1973), *Heroes Are Hard To Find* (1974), *Fleetwood Mac* (1975), *Rumours* (1977), *Tusk* (1979), *Fleetwood Mac Live* (1980), *Mirage* (1982), *Live In Boston* (1985), *London Live '68* (1986), *Tango In The Night* (1988), *Behind The Mask* (1989). Compilations: *The Pious Bird Of Good Omen* (1969), *The Original Fleetwood Mac* (1971), *Fleetwood Mac's Greatest Hits* (1971), *The Vintage Years* (1975), *Albatross* (1977), *Man Of The World* (1978), *Best Of* (1978), *Cerurlean* (1985), *Greatest Hits: Fleetwood Mac* (1988). Further reading: *Fleetwood: My Life And Adventures With Fleetwood Mac*, Mick Fleetwood with Stephen Davis.

Floyd, Frank

b. 11 October 1908, Toccopola, Mississippi, USA, d. 7 August 1984, Memphis, Tennessee, USA. Having spent much of his earlier years travelling the southern states of the USA, playing in carnivals and street shows, Floyd, aka Harmonica Frank, developed a solo guitar and harmonica style much influenced by black country blues. This led to his first recordings -

made by Sam Phillips in Memphis in 1951 - being issued on the Chess label, at that time oriented entirely towards a black audience. These, along with later recordings which Phillips issued in 1954 on his own Sun label, in particular 'Rocking Chair Daddy' stand as direct precursors to the first Elvis Presley records, also on Sun, in their mixture of white and black styles, although Floyd was to see no such commercial success. In the late 50s, he recorded again for a self-owned label, and there was an album for Barrelhouse in 1975.

Album: *Harmonica Frank Floyd* (1975).

Ford, Robben

b. Robben Lee Ford, 16 December 1951, Woodlake, California, USA. A jazz, blues and rock guitarist, Robben is the most celebrated member of the musical Ford family. His father Charles was a country musician, his brothers Patrick and Mark are bluesmen, playing drums and harmonica respectively. Inspired initially by Mike Bloomfield and Eric Clapton, Ford's first professional engagement was with Charlie Musslewhite in 1970. He formed the Charles Ford Band with his brothers in 1971, then backed Jimmy Witherspoon from 1972-74. He toured and recorded with both Joni Mitchell (as part of L.A. Express) and George Harrison in 1974, the resulting exposure bringing him a considerable amount of session work. In 1978, he formed the Yellowjackets with keyboards player Russell Ferrante and also found time to record a patchy solo debut *Inside Story*. The early 80s saw him performing with Michael McDonald and saxophonist Sadao Watanabe; in 1986 he joined the Miles Davis band on its tour of the USA and Europe. *Talk To Your Daughter* was a triumphant return to his blues roots, and picked up a Grammy nomination in the 'Contemporary Blues' category. Ford plays cleanly in an uncluttered style (like Mike Bloomfiled), but occasionally with the frantic energy of Larry Carlton. He is an outstanding guitarist, and one who is often overlooked when discussing brilliant virtuosity.

Albums: with the Charles Ford Band *The Charles Ford Band* (1972), *Inside Story* (1978), with the Charles Ford Band *Reunion* (1982), solo *Talk To Your Daughter* (1988), with Mark Ford *Mark Ford With The Robben Ford Band* (1991), *Robben Ford And The Blue Line* (1992).

Foster, Leroy 'Baby Face'

b. 1 February 1923, Algoma, Mississippi, USA, d 26 May 1958, Chicago, Illinois, USA. A guitarist and drummer, Foster followed the black migration north in the 40s, and worked Maxwell Street and the clubs. Foster's singing was indebted to John Lee 'Sonny Boy' Williamson, and like Williamson he was equally impressive on both uptempo and slow, intense blues. In 1948, he made his debut on record, singing a riotous 'Locked Out Boogie' and a reflective 'Shady Grove Blues', with Muddy Waters providing guitar. Foster also made fine recordings for JOB with Snooky Pryor, Sunnyland Slim and Robert Lockwood in support; for Parkway Records, he participated in a magnificent session with Little Walter and a contract-jumping Muddy Waters, which constitutes, above all on the two part 'Rollin' And Tumblin'' a manifesto for the transformation of Mississippi Delta blues in the Chicago ghetto.

Albums: *Genesis The Beginnings Of Rock* (1972), *Blues Is Killing Me* (1983), *The Blues World Of Little Walter* (1985).

Foster, Little Willie

b. 5 April 1922, Clarksdale, Mississippi, USA. Foster came to Chicago in 1941, already playing guitar, piano and harmonica. Tutored on the latter instrument by Walter Horton, he played on Maxwell Street, and in a band with Homesick James, Floyd Jones and Moody Jones. Foster recorded two singles in the mid-50s, and 'Crying The Blues', one of the titles, sums up both his emotional singing and his wailing, swooping harmonica. Shortly thereafter, he was shot and semi-paralysed; he improved slowly, and remained able to play and sing, but only rarely in public. Floyd Jones stated that Foster fatally shot a man, and was placed in a mental hospital early in 1974, but since he was photographed in the Chicago streets in September of that year, this information must be treated with caution.

Albums: *Chicago Blues - The Early 1950s* (1965), *King Cobras* (1980).

Franklin, Guitar Pete

b. Edward Lamonte Franklin, 16 January 1928, Indianapolis, Indiana, USA, d. 31 July 1975, Indianapolis, Indiana, USA. Franklin's mother

wrote many songs for her lodger Leroy Carr, and Pete's interest in music developed early, beginning with piano, on which he was as adept as on guitar. His guitar playing was influenced by local musicians Scrapper Blackwell and Jesse Ellery (who recorded as accompanist to Jack 'Champion' Dupree), but he could change his playing completely to fit with an amplified Chicago ensemble. As a pianist, Franklin was, not surprisingly, indebted to Leroy Carr, but on both instruments he was an original and remarkably accomplished musician, who was not recorded to the extent his talent merited.

Albums: *Guitar Pete's Blues* (1963), *Windy City Blues* (1975), *Indianapolis Jump* (1977).

Frazier, Calvin

b. 16 February 1915, Osceola, Arkansas, USA, d. 23 September 1972, Detroit, Michigan, USA. The Frazier family was large and musical, and used their skill to praise God; father Van played fiddle, guitar and banjo, mother Bell played bass, Lonnie, Rebecca and Johnny all played guitar and mandolin, as did Calvin. By 1922, they lived in South Hobart Place in Memphis, along with cousin Johnny Shines. Nine years later, Shines linked up with Calvin and Johnny, and played for handouts on the Memphis streets. During the early 30s, Calvin also worked with Robert Johnson and James 'Peck' Curtis. In April 1935, Frazier was involved in a shooting incident that forced him to leave town, in company with Johnson and Shines. The trio fled to Canada and found work in religious broadcasting, playing on *The Elder Moten Hour*. Shortly after returning to Detroit, Shines and Johnson moved on, but Frazier stayed, teaming up with guitarist, Sampson Pittman. They were recorded in October 1938 for the Library of Congress by Alan Lomax, Frazier revealing a guitar style whose boogie patterns and falsetto vocals echoed Johnson's. During the 40s, he played with Big Maceo, Baby Boy Warren and Eddie Kirkland but didn't record again until 1952 for Savoy, with pianist T.J. Fowler's band. He also played on sessions by Baby Boy Warren and Washboard Willie. He recorded infrequently during the 50s; 'Lilly Mae', first cut for the Library of Congress, and 'Have Blues, Must Travel' were recorded for Fortune and JVB, the latter also issued by Checker.

Selected album: *I'm In The Highway Man* (1980).

Frost, Frank

b. 15 April 1936, Auvergne, Arkansas, USA. Frost's skills encompass keyboards and guitar, but like many other blues artists, he started with the harmonica. He learned much from Sonny Boy 'Rice Miller' Williamson in the mid-50s and appeared regularly with him on the famous radio show *King Biscuit Time*. In 1962 he recorded for Sam Phillips with a band that included guitarist Big Jack Johnson, with whom Frost still plays and records. One single and an album resulted, featuring a very tough and raw, but tight, down-home blues sound, unusual on record at this time. A similar sound emerged from his next sessions in Nashville in 1966, which produced three fine singles and, later, an album on Jewel Records. Frost went back to mainly local performing after this, in the juke joints around his home area in the Mississippi Delta, but has also continued to make records and tour. He has undertaken some highly-acclaimed appearances in Europe, and also appeared in the feature film *Crossroads*.

Albums: *Jelly Roll King* (1990), *Midnight Prowler* (1989).

Fuller, Blind Boy

b. Fulton Allen, 1908, Wadesboro, North Carolina, USA, d. 13 February 1941. One of a large family, Fuller learned to play the guitar as a child and had begun a life as a transient singer when he was blinded, either through disease or when lye water was thrown in his face. By the late 20s he was well-known throughout North Carolina and Virginia, playing and singing at county fairs, tobacco farms and on street corners. At one time he worked with two other blind singers, Sonny Terry and Gary Davis. Amongst his most popular numbers were 'Rattlesnakin' Daddy', 'Jitterbug Rag' (on which he demonstrated his guitar technique) and the bawdy 'What's That Smells Like Fish?' (later adapted by Hot Tuna as 'Keep On Truckin'') and 'Get Your Yas Yas Out'. At one point in his career he was teamed with Brownie McGhee. In 1940, in Chicago, Fuller's style had become gloomy as can be heard on 'When You Are Gone'. Hospitalized for a kidney operation, Fuller contracted blood poisoning and died on 13 February 1941. One of the foremost exponents of the Piedmont blues style, there was a strong folk element in Fuller's work. The manner in which he absorbed and re-created stylistic patterns of other blues forms made him an important link between the earlier classic country blues and the later urbanized forms. Among the singers he influenced were Buddy Moss, Floyd Council, Ralph Willis and Richard 'Little Boy Fuller' Trice. (Shortly after Fuller's death Brownie McGhee was recorded under the name Blind Boy Fuller No 2.)

Compilations: *East Coast Piedmont Style* (1935-39 recordings), *Blind Boy Fuller* (1935-40 recordings), *Blind Boy Fuller And Brownie McGhee* (1936-41 recordings), *On Down* (1937-40 recordings), *Truckin' My Blues Away* (1991).

Fuller, Jesse 'Lone Cat'

b. 12 March 1896, Jonesboro, Georgia, USA. d. 29 January 1976, Oakland, California, USA. A veteran of the tent shows, Fuller fashioned himself a unique one-man-band of six-string bass (played with his right foot), a combination of kazoo, harmonica, microphone fixed to a harness around his neck, a hi-hat cymbal (played with the left foot) and a 12-string guitar. His success came in the late 50s as a result of appearances on USA television following Ramblin' Jack Elliot's lionization via his recording of 'San Francisco Bay Blues'. In the 50s he made three albums of original and traditional material and by the mid-60s became the darling of the 'coffee house circuit' after Bob Dylan cited him as one of his influences. Similar success was to follow in Britain resulting from Donovan's performance of 'San Francisco Bay Blues' on UK Independent Television's *Ready Steady Go* music programme in 1965.

Albums: *'Frisco Bound* (1968), *San Francisco Bay Blues* (1988).

Fuller, Johnny

b. 20 April 1929, Edwards, Mississippi, USA. Major Fuller moved his family west to Vallejo, California in 1935, perhaps drawn by work in the shipyards. Although he played guitar, son Johnny was a largely self-taught musician, his first interest being C&W music, the songs of Ernest Tubb and Gene Autry. At 15, he was singing in church, later forming the Teenage Gospel Singers, which became the Golden West Gospel Singers. About 1948 he made solo gospel records for Jackson, and for several years performed every Sunday on stations KWBR in

Oakland, and KRE in Berkeley. In the early 50s, he learned piano and organ and played blues in a style that suggested Charles Brown without the sophistication. This was evident on his first record, 'Train, Train Blues', for Bob Geddins' Rhythm label. Subsequent sessions were sold to Flair and Hollywood. His tribute, 'Johnny Ace's Last Letter', leased to Aladdin, became his first success and put him on the package tour circuit for several years. His 1956 single for Imperial, 'Don't Slam That Door', was later covered by Snooks Eaglin. Later records for Irma and Specialty strayed into rock 'n' roll and rockabilly. He spent much of the 60s outside music, returning to the clubs of Oakland and Richmond at the end of the decade. In 1973 he recorded an album, released in Australia, combining new material with older songs such as 'Fools Paradise', 'Bad Luck Overtook Me' and 'Strange Land', with a band that also featured Philip Walker. Further club and festival work continued through the 70s, since when nothing has been reported.

Selected album: *Fuller's Blues* (1974).

Fulson, Lowell

b. 31 March 1921, Tulsa, Oklahoma, USA. Blues guitarist Lowell Fulson (whose surname is often mistakenly misspelled Fulsom) recorded steadily from 1946 until the late 70s and still performs regularly on the USA and European club circuits. He began his career in his native Oklahoma performing with string bands and backing country blues vocalist Alger 'Texas' Alexander in the late 30s. During World War II he was stationed in Oakland, California, where he met record producer Bob Geddins. Following his discharge from the US Navy, Fulson recorded for several labels under the direction of Geddins, including Big Town, Down Beat, Gilt Edge and Trilon. His first hit occurred in 1950 on the Swing Time label when he reworked Memphis Slim's 'Nobody Loves Me' into 'Every Day I Have The Blues'. At that time his 12-piece orchestra included Ray Charles on piano. Also playing with Fulson around this time was tenor saxophonist Stanley Turrentine. Fulson recorded for Aladdin Records in 1953 and then switched to Checker Records, a subsidiary of Chess Records the following year. His first side for that company, 'Reconsider Baby', was covered by Elvis

Presley. Fulson stayed with that company into the early 60s and then moved to Kent Records, which changed the spelling of his name. Among his biggest hits for Kent were 'Black Nights' in 1965 and 'Tramp' the next year. The latter song, co-written with Jimmy McCracklin, was later a hit for Otis Redding and Carla Thomas. In 1968 Fulson went over to Jewel Records and then for a succession of small labels including Crazy Cajun and Granite. By the early 90s his early work often appeared on reissues, but Fulson's new material was only being released on minor labels, such as France's Blue Phoenix Records.

Albums: *Lowell Fulson* (1965), *Soul* (1966), *Tramp* (1967), *Lowell Fulsom Now!* (1968), *In A Heavy Bag* (1970), *Let's Go Get Stoned* (1971), *I've Got The Blues* (1973), *Lovemaker* (1978), *Think Twice Before You Speak* (1984), *The Ol' Blues Singer* (1975), *Blue Days, Black Nights* (1986), *I Don't Know My Mind* (1987), *Back Home Blues* (1992). Compilations: *Man Of Motion* (1981), *Everyday I Have The Blues* (1984), *Baby Won't You Jump With Me* (1987), *Lowell Fulson 1946/57* (1987).

Fundeburgh, Anson

b. Dallas, Texas, USA. Fundeburgh played blues guitar with local bands and in 1981 recorded with the Fabulous Thunderbirds. He later formed his own band, the Rockets and signed to blues revivalist label Black Top in 1984. Fundeburgh's guitar pyrotechnics made the group a favourite at blues festivals, where they often performed with veteran harmonica player Sam Myers (b. Mississippi 1936). Myers is also featured on *My Love Is Here To Stay* and *Sins*. In 1990, the group recorded with Snooks Eaglin.

Albums: *Talk To You By Hand* (1984), *She Knocks Me Out* (1985), *My Love Is Here To Stay* (1986), *Sins* (1987), *Rack 'Em Up* (1989).

G

Gaines, Roy

b. 12 August 1934, Houston, Texas, USA. The brother of Grady Gaines, Roy became interested in the electric guitar at an early age and began fraternizing with other local young blues guitarists such as Clarence Holloman and Johnny Copeland. Gaines made his debut with an obscure release on the Miami-based Chart label before coming to the attention of local Houston bandleader and head of Duke Records' house band, Bill Harvey. Gaines was featured with Harvey's band on various releases by Big Mama Thornton and Bobby 'Blue' Bland in 1955 for the Duke and Peacock labels before being enticed away by an impressed Chuck Willis. After moving to New York City, Gaines recorded with Willis for Atlantic as well as signing to RCA Victor's Groove subsidiary under his own name. This resulted in two releases in 1956. The following year he signed to DeLuxe, returned to Victor in 1958 and experienced a lean decade in the 60s with only two releases on the small Del-Fi and Uni labels. In the 70s, Gaines was again in demand, both in public appearances and as guitarist with the celebrated Crusaders. In 1981, Red Lightnin Records cut into his busy touring schedule and recorded a fine album, *Gainelining*, which demonstrated Gaines' four decades of musical influence.
Album: *Gainelining* (1981).

Gaither, Bill

Gaither's first issued recordings were made in 1935. This session included an unissued tribute to Leroy Carr, who had died the same year, and Gaither, billed on many of his records as 'Leroy's Buddy', recorded a 'Life Of Leroy Carr' as late as 1940. Gaither's guitar playing was, not surprisingly, in the manner of Carr's partner Scrapper Blackwell, while his regular pianist Honey Hill imitated Carr. Gaither's light, wistful voice continues the imitative process, as do his bittersweet lyrics, which sometimes contain interesting topical material. Evidently popular with contemporary black record buyers,

and more of an original than his avowed indebtedness to his inspirations might suggest, Gaither nevertheless lacks both the musical variety and the poetic depth of Carr and Blackwell.
Albums: *Leroy's Buddy* (1977), *Volume 1* (1986), *Leroy's Buddy* (1990).

Gallagher, Rory

b. 2 March 1949, Ballyshannon, Co. Donegal, Eire. Having served his musical apprenticeship in the Fontana and Impact Showbands, Gallagher put together the original Taste in 1965. This exciting blues-based rock trio rose from regional obscurity to the verge of international fame, but broke up, acrimoniously, five years later. Gallagher was by then a guitar hero and embarked on a solo voyage supported by Gerry McAvoy (bass) and Wilgar Campbell (drums). He introduced an unpretentious approach, which has marked a career that has deftly retained all the purpose of the blues without erring on the side of reverence. Gallagher's early influences were Lonnie Donegan, Woody Guthrie, Chuck Berry and Muddy Waters and he has strayed very little from that path of influence.
The artist's refreshing blues guitar work which featured his confident bottleneck playing was always of interest and by 1972 Gallagher was a major live attraction. Campbell was replaced by Rod De'ath following the release of *Live In Europe*, while Lou Marrin was added on keyboards. This line-up remained constant for the next six years and was responsible for Gallagher's major commercial triumphs *Blueprint* and *Irish Tour '74*. De'ath and Martin left the group in 1978. Former Sensational Alex Harvey Band drummer Ted McKenna joined the ever-present McAvoy but was in turn replaced by Brendan O'Neill, who has retained the drum spot to date. Former Nine Below Zero member and blues harmonica virtuoso Mark Feltham is now a full time 'guest'. Gallagher has quietly got on with his career. Shunning the glitzy aspect of the music business, he has toured America over 25 times in addition to touring the globe. twice. His record sales have reached several millions and he retains a fiercely loyal following. He has now had the opportunity to record with his heroes like Donegan, Waters, Jerry Lee Lewis and Albert King and his love of his homeland

has resulted in contributions to the work of the Fureys, Davy Spillane and Joe O'Donnell. Gallagher has retained his perennial love for the blues, his original Stratocaster guitar (now badly battered) and the respect of many for his uncompromising approach.

Albums: *Rory Gallagher* (1971), *Deuce* (1971), *Live! In Europe* (1972), *Blueprint* (1973), *Tattoo* (1973), *Irish Tour '74* (1974), *Saint . . . And Sinner* (1975), *Against The Grain* (1975), *Calling Card* (1976), *Photo Finish* (1978), *Top Priority* (1979), *Stage Struck* (1980), *Jinx* (1982), *Defender* (1987), *Fresh Evidence* (1990). Compilations: *In The Beginning* (1974), *The Story So Far* (1976), *The Best Years* (1976), *Edged In Blue* (1992), *Rory Gallagher Boxed* (4CD set 1992).

Garlow, Clarence

b. 27 February 1911, Welsh, Louisiana, USA, d. 24 July 1986, Beaumont, Texas, USA. Brought up in the black community in South Louisiana and East Texas. Garlow learned guitar and accordian. On the former, his principal influence was T-Bone Walker, and the smooth, jazzy Walker sound is to be heard on many of his records, particularly the early ones which appeared in the late 40s and early 50s on locally-distributed record labels such as Macy's, Lyric and Feature. Other records show a more rocking R&B tendency, and one single on Flair Records, that pairs 'Route 90' and 'Crawfishin'' is a classic of its kind. Later, there was a fine zydeco pairing on Folk Star Records, while recording for Jay Miller he moved towards the swamp blues sound. Garlow retired from playing in the early 60s, but worked for some years as a postman and a disc jockey in Beaumont, Texas. Compilation: *1951-1958* (1983).

Garrett, Robert 'Bud'

b. 1916, Free Hill Tennessee, USA. A jack of all trades when not playing music, Garrett has resided for most of his life in Free Hill, an isolated community founded by freed slaves around 1830. He cut a splendid electric blues single for Excello in 1962, and played occasional festivals from the 80s, by which time he was the only performer in Free Hill of the live music which had been otherwise supplanted by disco and cable TV. His music included a few originals, which often employed a talking blues structure, but consisted largely of blues standards by the likes of Little Milton and T-Bone Walker, and country music by such as Don Williams and Merle Haggard, adapted to blues formats.

Albums: *The Excello Story* (1972), *Free Hill* (1985).

Geddins, Bob

b. 1913, Marlin, Texas, USA, d. 16 February 1991, Oakland, California, USA. A black entrepreneur, Geddins operated a series of labels from the late 40s, recording blues and gospel in the Bay Area. Lacking capital and distribution, he had to lease his recordings to larger labels; if a hit resulted, the artists were lured away. In this way, Geddins, lost **Lowell Fulson**, **Jimmy McCracklin**, **Roy Hawkins,** Ray Agee and **Koko Taylor**. Among other hits, Geddins composed '**Johnny Ace**'s Last Letter' and 'Haunted House' for Johnny Fuller (the latter also was a hit for **Gene Simmons** and the Compton Brothers.) Geddins also wrote the classic 'My Time After Awhile', and reworked a pre-war **Curtis Jones** song into 'Tin Pan Alley'. Geddins was a prime mover behind the Oakland blues scene of the 40s and 50s, but his business abilities were not the equal of his composing and producing talents.

Gibson, Clifford

b. 17 April 1901, Louisville, Kentucky, USA, d. 21 December 1963, St. Louis, Missouri, USA. The bulk of Gibson's recordings (20 titles) were made in 1929, by which time Gibson was one of the most respected blues guitarists in St. Louis. Influenced by Lonnie Johnson, Gibson had a similar clear diction and a penchant for original, moralizing lyrics. His guitar work, characterized by extended treble runs, was outstanding: clean, precise, inventive, and at times astonishingly fast. Away from the studios, he worked as a street musician, assisted by a performing dog. He recorded (in a small band format) as Grandpappy Gibson for Bobbin in 1960.

Album: *Beat You Doing It* (c.1972).

Gibson, Lacy

b. 1 May 1936, Salisbury, North Carolina, USA. Gibson's family settled in Chicago in 1949 and he quickly became involved in the city's blues scene, receiving tips on blues guitar playing from musicians such as Muddy Waters and T-Bone

Walker. Besides working with innumerable blues artists, he was also involved in the jazz scene. He recorded with Buddy Guy in 1963 and worked on many sessions. Gibson had two singles of his own on the Repeto label, and had material released on album by the Alligator, Red Lightnin', El Saturn, and Black Magic labels. He is a strong vocalist and very talented blues guitarist who seems to be equally at home in small west-side Chicago bars or European concert halls.

Albums: four tracks only *Living Chicago Blues Volume Five* (1980), *Switchy Titchy* (1983).

Gillum, William McKinley 'Jazz'

b. 11 September, 1904, Indianola, Mississippi, USA. d. 29 March 1966, Chicago, Illinois, USA. Gillum had a tough childhood which began when his parents died during his infancy. He was farmed out to an uncle who, as well as a deacon, seems to have been a bully. This harrowing period was rendered bearable only by the boy's interest in music; he learned to play the organ and the harmonica. Gillum ran away at the age of seven and found work in fields and stores, augmenting his income by playing harmonica on street corners' until 1923 when he travelled north to Chicago to try his luck in the music business. He formed a long association with Big Bill Broonzy and started his recording career with him in 1934. The blues harmonica came into its own in 1937 when John Lee 'Sonny Boy' Williamson began his immensely successful career. Although second only to Williamson in popularity, Gillum was nowhere near as inventive a musician or as exciting a singer. His strength lay in his ability as a song-writer. Despite this his work as a performer and sideman was much in demand throughout the 30s and 40s when he was a stalwart of the Bluebird/Victor labels. In 1961 he recorded an album for Folkways Records but participated only marginally in the 'blues boom' before he was shot dead during an argument in 1966. Despite his limitations, at his best Gillum recorded some very satisfactory performances and was popular both with his black audience and white collectors.

Albums: *You Got To Reap what You Sow* (1970), *Jazz Gillum* (1985).

Gilmore, Boyd

b. 12 June 1910, Belzoni, Mississippi, USA, d. 23 December 1976, Fresno, California, USA. A guitarist, though seemingly not recorded as such, and an exuberant singer, Gilmore recorded for Modern in 1952 with Ike Turner on piano and James Scott Jnr. on guitar; Scott was an early victim of technology when an introduction and guitar break by Elmore James were spliced into 'Ramblin' On My Mind' The following year, Gilmore recorded for Sun, backed by Earl Hooker's band, but the results were not issued until later. Gilmore performed in Delta juke joints for a while, also playing in St. Louis and Pine Bluff, Arkansas, before settling in California for the remainder of his life.

Albums: *Memphis & The Delta* (c.1969), *Mississippi Blues* (c.1972), *Sun Records The Blues Years* (1985).

Glinn, Lillian

b. c.1902, near Dallas, Texas, USA. Glinn's career as a blues-singing recording artist, and vaudeville performer was brief but successful. She was the protege of Hattie Burleson, a Texas blues singer who first heard Glinn sing in a Dallas church. Although religious, Glinn allowed herself to pursue the worldly course that led to R.T. Ashford securing her a recording contract with Columbia in 1927. During the following two years she recorded 22 titles for that label. Her blues were notable for their apposite lyrics sung in a warm mature manner. She was still young when she gave up her career to return to the 'other world' of the church and when interviewed by Paul Oliver in 1970 she was reluctant to recall her long-gone temporal fame.

Album: *Lillian Glinn* (1978).

Good Rockin' Charles

b. Charles Edwards, 4 March 1933, Pratt City, Alabama, USA, d.18 May 1989, Chicago, Illinois, USA. One of the journeyman musicians of the Chicago blues scene, Charles Edwards was engaged to play harmonica on a Jimmy Rogers session in the 50s, but failed to turn up; an attempt by Eli Toscano to record him failed for similar reasons, and it was not until 1975 that he recorded an album. This, and a trip to Europe, revealed him to be, if not a innovative performer, then an outgoing and entertaining one, and a harmonica player of considerable authority, influenced by both Sonny Boy 'Rice Miller' and John Lee 'Sonny Boy' Williamson. Album: *Good Rockin' Charles* (1976).

Gordon, Archie 'Stomp'

Singer and pianist Gordon led a fine, jump quintet throughout the 50s which included Billy Brooks on trumpet and 'Little' Hiawatha Edmundson on tenor saxophone. Beginning with Decca's 48000 R&B series in 1952, with whom the band recorded the insulting 'Damp Rag', the Gordon band recorded excellent tracks for Mercury in 1953 - including an uproarious celebration of the then recent Kinsey Sex Report in 'What's Her Whimsey Dr Kinsey?' - and later recorded for Chess and Savoy in the mid-50s.

Gordon, Jimmie

Blues artist Gordon was St. Louis, USA-based, and billed on one record as 'Peetie Wheatstraw's brother; on another, 'Black Gal', he appeared as 'Joe Bullum', an attempt by Decca to pass him off as Joe Pullum. Like 'Black Gal', many of his recordings were covers of then-popular blues. Gordon was a slightly anonymous figure, and has excited little attention from researchers. Nevertheless, his records are often worthwhile, for he combines the ingratiating approach of Bumble Bee Slim with some of Wheatstraw's forcefulness, and was often backed by enjoyable small jazz bands. He was also a more than competent pianist, although he seldom played on his own records.
Albums: *Jimmie Gordon* (1987), *Jimmie Gordon* (1989).

Gordon, Rosco(e)

b. 1934, Memphis, Tennessee, USA. A self-taught pianist with no acknowledged influences other than a presumed awareness of the work of Amos Milburn and Little Willie Littlefield. Gordon was part of the Beale Streeters group in the late 40s, alongside Johnny Ace, B.B. King and later, Bobby 'Blue' Bland. Ike Turner, then a freelance producer and talent scout, recognised Gordon's powerful singing and recorded him for Modern. He was still a teenager when he first recorded at Sam Phillips' Memphis Recording Service in January 1951. Phillips sold masters to both Chess in Chicago and RPM in Los

Angeles. Thus, Gordon's 'Booted' appeared on both labels, a possible factor in its becoming the number 1 R&B hit in the spring of 1952. The follow-up, 'No More Doggin'', was another Top 10 R&B hit and typified what became known as 'Rosco's Rhythm', a loping boogie shuffle rhythm that predated and perhaps influenced Jamaican ska and blue-heat music. Gordon signed to Phillips' own Sun label in 1955, recording a regional hit, 'The Chicken', which led to his appearance in the film *Rock Baby, Rock It,* two years later. Moving to New York, he formed the duo, Rosco and Barbara, making singles for Old Town. Many tracks recorded during this time remained unissued until the 70s and 80s. His most well-known song reached number 2 in the R&B charts and was recorded in 1960 for the Chicago-based label, Vee Jay. With its catchy sax-driven riff, 'Just A Little Bit' captured the imagination of British R&B groups as well as black record buyers. A version by Merseybeat band the Undertakers was a minor hit in 1964. Further records for ABC, Old Town, Jomada, Rae-Cox and Calla made little impression and in 1970, Gordon created his own label, Bab-Roc, issuing records by himself and his wife Barbara. An album of new compositions plus remakes of his hits was recorded for Organic Productions in 1971 but never released. A brief visit to England in 1982 brought a reunion with B.B. King, onstage at London's 100 club. At that time he was financing recordings from his own cleaning business but nothing has appeared in the intervening decade.
Selected albums: *The Legendary Sun Performers: Rosco Gordon* (1978), *Best Of* (1980), *Rosco Gordon Vol. 1* (1981) *Rosco Gordon Vol.2* (1982), *Keep On Doggin'* (1982), *Memphis Masters* (1982), *Rosco Rocks Again* (1983), *Bootin' Boogie* (1990), *Lets Get High* (1990).

Graham, Davey

b. 22 November 1940, Leicester, England, of Scottish and Guyanese parents. An influential guitarist in British folk circles, Graham's itinerant travels throughout Europe and North Africa resulted in a cosmopolitan and unorthodox repertoire. By the early 60s he was a fixture of the London fraternity and his 1961 recording with Alexis Korner, *3/4 A.D.,* showcased his exceptional talent. The EP

included the much-feted 'Angie', an evocative instrumental which Paul Simon and Bert Jansch would later cover. *Folk, Blues & Beyond* showcased Graham's eclectic talent, with material drawn from Charles Mingus, Leadbelly, Bob Dylan and Blind Willie Johnson. The expressive instrumental, 'Maajun (A Taste Of Tangier)', emphasized the modal element of Graham's playing and although never more than adequate as a singer, his inspired guitar work was a revelation. *Folk Roots New Routes* was an unlikely collaboration with traditional vocalist Shirley Collins, and while the latter's purity was sometimes at odds with Graham's earthier approach, the album is rightly lauded as a milestone in British folk music. Graham maintained his idiosyncratic style throughout the 60s, experimenting with western and eastern musical styles, but although the respect of his peers was assured, commercial success proved elusive. Drug problems and ill health undermined the artist's progress, but he later re-emerged with two excellent albums for the specialist Kicking Mule outlet. During his latter years, he has resided in west Scotland where he has taught guitar, whilst continuing to perform on the folk club circuit, often performing on double bills with Bert Jansch, and demonstrating his credentials as one of Britain's finest folk-blues guitarists.
Albums: *Guitar Player* (1963), *Folk, Blues & Beyond* (1964), with Shirley Collins *Folk Roots New Routes* (1965), *Midnight Man* (1966), *Large As Life And Twice As Natural* (1968), *Hat* (1969), *Holly Kaleidoscope* (1970), *Godington Boundary* (1970), *Complete Guitarist* (1978), *Dance For Two People* (1979). Compilation: *Folk Blues And All Points In Between* (1990).

Grand, Otis
b. Fred Bishti 14 February 1950, Beirut Lebanon. Otis spent most of his life in the USA, with a few years in France. He began playing guitar at the age of 13 and names his influences as B.B. King, T-Bone Walker, Otis Rush, and Johnny Otis. He played with many San Francisco Bay area blues artists. Otis Grand And The Dance Kings created a sensation when they burst onto the British blues scene in the late 80s; enhanced on the first album (a W.C. Handy award nomination) by the presence of Joe Louis Walker. The second album includes guests

Jimmy Nelson, Pee Wee Ellis, and Walker again. A great live attraction, Grand was voted 'UK Blues Guitarist Of The Year' in 1990. Much is expected from this exceptional talent.
Albums: *Always Hot* (1988), *He Knows The Blues* (1991), with Philip Walker *Big Blues From Texas* (1992).

Granderson, John Lee
b. 11 April 1913, Ellendale Tennessee, USA, d. 22 August 1979, Chicago, Illinois, USA. Granderson left home when he was in his teens, moving to Chicago, Illinois in 1928. Although not a professional musician, he did work with John Lee 'Sonny Boy' Williamson, among others. He turned to music full-time in the 60s and he was featured as a sideman and a leader on many anthologies, although he never had a full album in his own right. Granderson sang and played guitar close to the style of the Memphis musicians of his youth. He stopped performing in public in 1975 and died of cancer in 1979.
Compilation: *Chicago Breakdown* (contains two tracks from 1963).

Grant, Leola B. 'Coot'
b. Leola B. Pettigrew, 17 June 1893, Birmingham, Alabama, USA. Aka Patsy Hunter and Leola B. Wilson. The daughter of a black tavern owner and Indian mother, the good-looking Leola B. was directed to a life as an entertainer at a very early age. Between the ages of eight and 17 she was part of Mayme Remington's Pickaninnies and toured Europe and South Africa. Around 1912 she met - and later married 'Kid' Wesley Wilson with whom she formed a vaudeville duo. Both their act and marriage were lasting and successful. Their career on record began in 1925 and continued until 1946. Coot gave up performing in 1955 and Kid Socks died in 1958. Their recordings together reflected their stage personae of squabbling husband and wife, but Grant also recorded serious blues numbers under her own name, some in the company of the celebrates guitarist Blind Blake (1926) and others with the Sidney Bechet/Mezz Mezzrow quintet (1946)
Album: *The Complete Blind Blake* (1991).

Gray, Arvella
b. Walter Dixon, 28 January 1906, Somerville, Texas, USA, d. 7 September 1980, Chicago,

Illinois, USA. Brought up to farm work, Gray left home early and travelled, eventually moving north. In 1930, he lost his sight and two fingers of his left hand in a fight, and took to making music for a living. He played blues, with a rudimentary bottleneck guitar style, on the streets of Chicago for many years, and became well-known for his regular appearances at the Maxwell Street outdoor market and other locations around the city. He attracted the attention of younger blues fans and, in the 60s and 70s, appeared in concerts, festivals and even a couple of short films. His repertoire was limited, but he made a number of records, including some singles, which he sold on the streets.
Album: *The Singing Drifter* (1972).

Gray, Henry
b. 19 January 1925, Kenner, Louisiana, USA. Having grown up in rural Louisiana, where he taught himself piano at an early age, Gray moved to Chicago in the 40s. He soon built a solid reputation as a band pianist in the city's blues clubs, and as accompanist on records by artists such as Junior Wells and Billy Boy Arnold. His own recordings in the early 50s featured strong, rocking blues, but they remained unissued for many years. Following a long period with the Howlin' Wolf band, he moved back to Louisiana in 1969. He has continued to work in music, including stints at Tabby Thomas's Blues Box club, and has made several fine records, most notably singles on Jay Miller's Blues Unlimited label and Sunland, and an album made during a European tour in 1977.
Albums: *They Call Me Little Henry* (1977), *Lucky Man* (1988).

Green, Clarence
b. 15 March 1929, Galveston, Texas, USA. A self-taught blues piano player, Clarence 'Candy' Green performed on radio and in the numerous clubs of Galveston, a naval town known as the 'Playground Of The South'. His first record was 'Green's Bounce', made in Houston for Eddie's in 1948. His brother Cal Green was a guitarist who also recorded. Candy recorded 'Hard Headed Woman' (Peacock) before starting army service in 1951. Returning to Texas two years later, he remained a familiar figure in local clubs throughout the 50s, sometimes recording as

Galveston Green and working with Clarence 'Gatemouth' Brown. In 1966 he cut the soulful 'I Saw You Last Night' (Duke).
Album: *Lady in Red* (1982, reissue date).

Green, L.C.
b. L.C. Green, 23 October 1921, Minter City, Mississippi, USA, d. 24 August 1985, Pontiac, Michigan, USA. Vocally and for repertoire, Greene, whose records were issued without the final 'e' to his name, was indebted to John Lee 'Sonny Boy' Williamson. His amplified guitar playing is clearly Mississippi Delta-derived, but probably owes something to the popularity of fellow Detroit blues singer John Lee Hooker. Greene recorded in the early 50s (often with his cousin Walter Mitchell on harmonica) for Joe Von Battle's shoestring operation, which leased a few sides to Dot Records, but he never got the breaks accorded to Hooker, whom he equalled for guitar talent and power, though not for songwriting ability.
Album: *Detroit Blues Guitar Killers!* (1977).

Green, Leothus 'Pork Chops'
Biographical detail is scanty for this remarkable blues pianist and is largely based on the memories of Roosevelt Sykes and Little Brother Montgomery. It is likely that Green originated from, Mississippi but he made his name working in St. Louis, Missouri. He is believed to have died around 1944. His recordings spanned the years 1929-37 and show him to have been a distinctive and versatile performer who deserves greater recognition than he has received to date. His most famous role was in his influencing Sykes, for whom he acted to a degree as of a blues catalyst. He also he taught Sykes to play Montgomery's most famous and difficult composition known as 'The Forty-fours'.
Compilation: *The Piano Blues, Volume 18* (1983).

Green, Lil
b. 22 December 1919, Mississippi, USA, d. 14 April 1954. Growing up in Chicago, Green began to sing in clubs in the mid-30s. By the end of the decade she was appearing regularly at some of the city's best-known nightspots and was recording with artists such as Big Bill Broonzy, who wrote several songs for her, including 'Country Boy Blues' and 'My Mellow Man'. Green composed some well-known songs

herself, among them 'Romance In The Dark', later covered by Mary Ann McCall, Jeri Southern and Billie Holiday. In the early 40s she toured with Tiny Bradshaw and Luis Russell but never really broke away from the black theatre circuit and those areas of the record business that catered specifically for black audiences. The limitations this placed upon her career were severe, even in the case of one of Green's most popular recordings, of Joe McCoy's 'Why Don't You Do Right'. The record was heard by Peggy Lee, who was then with Benny Goodman and his orchestra. Their cover version was an enormous hit, thus further shading Green's fortunes. Although signed by Atlantic Records in 1951, she was in poor health and died in 1954.

Compilation: *Romance In The Dark* (1940-46 recordings).

Green, Peter

b. Peter Greenbaum, 29 October 1946, Bethnel Green, London, England. Having served an apprenticeship in various semi-professional groups, including the Muskrats and the Tridents, Peter Green became one of several guitarists who joined John Mayall's Bluesbreakers as a temporary substitute for Eric Clapton during the latter's late 1965 sabbatical. When Mayall's preferred choice returned to the fold, Green joined Peter Bardens (organ), Dave Ambrose (bass) and Mick Fleetwood (drums) in a short-lived club band, the Peter B's. The entire unit subsequently formed the instrumental core to the Shotgun Express, backing singers Rod Stewart and Beryl Marsden, but the guitarist found this role too restrictive and left after a matter of weeks. Green rejoined Mayall in July 1966 when Clapton left to form Cream. Over the next 12 months Peter made several telling contributions to the Bluesbreakers' recordings, most notably on the group's third album, *A Hard Road*. This powerful release featured two of the guitarist's compositions, of which 'The Supernatural', a riveting instrumental, anticipated the style he would forge later in the decade. The seeds of Green's own group were sown during several sessions without Mayall and a Bluesbreakers 'solo' single, 'Curly', was released in March 1967. Two months later Peter left to form his own group with drummer Mick Fleetwood. The two musicians added a second

guitarist, Jeremy Spencer, to form Fleetwood Mac, whose line-up was eventually completed by another former Mayall sideman, John McVie. Fleetwood Mac became one of the most popular groups of the era, developing blues-based origins into an exciting, experimental unit. Green's personality, however, grew increasingly unstable and he became estranged from his colleagues. 'Pete should never have taken acid,' Fleetwood later recalled. 'He was charming, amusing, just a wonderful person (but) off he went and never came back.'

Green has followed an erratic course since leaving the group in May 1970. His solo debut, *The End Of The Game*, was a perplexing collection, consisting of six instrumentals, each of which were little more than jams. An atmospheric single, 'Heavy Heart', followed in June 1971, while a collaboration with one Nigel Watson, 'Beasts Of Burden', was issued the following year. Peter also made sporadic session appearances but following a cameo role on Fleetwood Mac's *Penguin* album, the guitarist dropped out of music altogether. The mid-70s proved particularly harrowing; this tormented individual was committed to two mental institutions in the wake of his unsettled behaviour. Green returned to active recording in 1979 with *In The Skies*, a light but optimistic collection which showed traces of his erstwhile fire and included a version of 'A Fool No More', first recorded by Fleetwood Mac. A second album, *Little Dreamer*, offered a more blues-based perspective while two further releases attempted to consolidate the artist's position.

In 1982 Green, now calling himself Greenbaum, began touring with a group named Kolors, but the results were unsatisfactory. A hastily concocted album consisting of outtakes and unfinished demos was issued, the last to bear the guitarist's name as leader. A collaboration with former Mungo Jerry singer Ray Dorset aside, this once-skilful musician has again abandoned music. Nicknamed the 'Wizard' by local children, Green lives a hermit-like existence at present, shunning any links with his past.

Albums: *The End Of The Game* (1970), *In The Skies* (1979), *Little Dreamer* (1980), *Whatcha Gonna Do* (1981), *Blue Guitar* (1981), *White Sky* (1982), *Kolors* (1983).

Greer, 'Big' John

After recording some obscure tracks for Bob Shad's Sittin' In With label, tenor saxophonist and vocalist Greer came to prominence with Lucky Millinder's Orchestra during 1948-50, with whom he recorded for RCA-Victor and King including 'Sweet Slumber', 'Let It Roll Again'. He concurrently pursued his solo recording career, albeit using small units from Millinder's band, billed as his Rhythm Rockers, on RCA-Victor between 1949 and 1955. While there, he notched up his only chart hit in 1951 with the Howard Biggs and Joe Thomas-penned 'Got You On My Mind'. Greer's last tracks were made in 1956 for King Records, and included a remake of his big Millinder hit 'Sweet Slumber'. Like his old Millinder bandmate, Bullmoose Jackson, John Greer recorded some of the most exciting R&B of the 50s, always utilizing the finest New York musicians available, but his main claim to fame was with syrupy ballads which, although well-received by his contemporary audience, are held in less regard by modern R&B collectors.
Album: *R&B In New York City* (1988).

Grey Ghost

b. Roosevelt Thomas Williams, 7 December 1903, Bastrop, Texas, USA. For blues researchers, Williams lived up to his nickname for most of his life, known only as a reported influence on Mercy Dee. Williams hoboed around the southwest performing from the 20s to the late 40s, until he settled in Austin. He was recorded by a folklorist in 1940 ('Hitler Blues') and was also recorded after his retirement in 1965. None of these recordings was issued until 1987. Despite an out-of-tune piano, he was clearly a major player in the tradition of the 'Santa Fe' group that included Robert Shaw, Buster Pickens and Pinetop Burks. Grey also had a working pianist's repertoire of ballads and pop songs. Recorded again in 1988, he played a remarkably strident version of 'Somebody Stole My Gal', which, though slower, was still very impressive
Albums: *Grey Ghost* (1987), *Texas Piano Professors* (1989).

Griffin Brothers

Jimmy and Ernest 'Buddy' Griffin From Norfolk, Virginia, but based in Washington, DC, the Griffin Brothers Orchestra comprised Jimmy on trombone, Buddy on piano, Wilbur Dyer and Virgil Wilson on saxophone with Jimmy Reeves and Emmett 'Nab' Shields on bass and drums. Introduced to Randy Wood in 1950, the band began recording for his label Dot Records; their biggest hits were the songs of their vocalists Margie Day - 'Street Walkin' Daddy' and 'Little Red Rooster' amongst others - and Tommy Brown - 'Tra-La-La' and 'Weepin' And Cryin''. During a southern tour in April 1950, Jimmy and Buddy were asked to participate in the Roy Brown session for DeLuxe which resulted in his biggest hit, 'Hard Luck Blues'. However, they returned to their own band, which now included Noble 'Thin Man' Watts on tenor saxophone, and recorded with Dot Records until they split up in 1954. The brothers each made their own solo recordings for Dot after the split and subsequently Jimmy went to Atco Records in New York, while Buddy had some success in Chicago on the Chess label with vocalist Claudia Swann.
Albums: *Riffin' With The Griffin Brothers Orchestra* (1985), with Margie Day *I'll Get A Deal* (1986).

Griffith, Shirley

b. 26 April 1908, Brandon, Mississippi, USA, d. 18 June 1974, Indianapolis, Indiana, USA. Griffith (a male blues singer despite his given name) learned guitar at age 10, and gained further instruction from Tommy Johnson, his greatest influence, in the mid-20s. By the end of the decade he was settled in Indianapolis, his home for the rest of his life. He worked with Scrapper Blackwell, but his closest associate was J.T. Adams, with whom he recorded in the early 60s. Griffith was little heard of thereafter, though he recorded a capable solo album in the 70s.
Albums: *Indiana Avenue Blues* (1963), *Saturday Blues* (1963), *Mississippi Blues* (1973), *Indianapolis Jump* (1976).

Grimes, Carol

Vocalist Grimes came to prominence in 1969 after joining Delivery. The band began life as a blues group, but gradually adopted a more experimental path. They completed one album before disbanding, following which Carol embarked on a solo career. She formed Uncle Dog in 1972, but this promising group failed to match early expectations and the singer then resumed her independent path. Grimes' powerful intonation was shown to great effect on *Warm Blood*, but despite stellar support from members of Area Code 615 and the Average White Band, the set failed to highlight her talent. Subsequent sporadic releases were punctuated by the short-lived Sweet F.A. and appearances on sessions ranged from Chilli Willi And The Red Hot Peppers to the Tom Robinson Band. An underrated artist, Grimes continues to perform and enjoys considerable popularity on the Continent.

Albums: *Warm Blood* (1974), *Carol Grimes* (1976), *Carol Grimes* (1977), *Eyes Wide Open* (1986), *Why Don't They Dance* (1989).

Grossman, Stefan

b. 16 April 1945, Brooklyn, New York, USA. Grossman discovered traditional music during his forays into Manhattan's Greenwich Village. He studied under Rev. Gary Davis and absorbed the country-blues technique of Son House, Mississippi John Hurt and Skip James before forming the influential Even Dozen Jug Band in 1963. Three years later Grossman recorded and annotated the instruction record, *How To Play Blues Guitar*, and was working with the Fugs, a radical East Side poet/bohemian group. Stefan also played with the Chicago Loop, which featured pianist Barry Goldberg, prior to leaving for Europe in 1967. He remained in Italy and Britain for many years, recording a succession of impressive, if clinical country blues albums. A superb guitarist, his work is best heard on *Yazoo Basin Boogie* and *Hot Dogs*, while further tuition albums provided valuable insights into the rudiments of different techniques. In the late 70s Grossman helped establish the Kicking Mule label which acted as a channel for his own releases and those working in a similar vein.

Albums: *How To Play Blues Guitar* (1966), *Aunt Molly's Murray Farm* (1969), *Grammercy Park Sheik* (1969), with Danny Kalb *Crosscurrents* (1969), *Yazoo Basin Boogie* (1970), *Ragtime Cowboy Jew* (1970), *Those Pleasant Days* (1971), *Hot Dogs* (1972), *Stefan Grossman Live* (1973), *Memphis Jellyroll* (1974), *Bottleneck Seranade* (1975), *How To Play Ragtime Guitar* (1975), *My Creole Belle* (1976), *Country Blues Guitar* (1977),

Fingerpicking Guitar Techniques (1977), *How To Play Blues Guitar, Volume 2* (1978), *Stefan Grossman And John Renbourn* (1978), with John Renbourn *Under The Volcano* (1980), *Thunder On The Run* (1980), *Shining Shadows* (1988).

Groundhogs

The original Groundhogs emerged in 1963 when struggling UK beat group the Dollarbills opted for a more stylish name; Tony 'T.S.' McPhee (b. 22 March 1944, Humberstone, Lincolnshire, England; guitar), John Cruickshank (vocals/harp), Bob Hall (piano), Pete Cruickshank (b. 2 July 1945, Calcutta, India; bass) and Dave Boorman (drums) also adopted a 'John Lee' prefix in honour of mentor John Lee Hooker, whom the quintet subsequently backed in concert and on record. John Lee's Groundhogs recorded two singles before breaking up in 1966. McPhee completed several solo tracks with producer Mike Vernon before rejoining Pete Cruickshank in Herbal Mixture, a short-lived, pseudo-psychedelic group. In 1968 the two musicians formed the core of a reformed Groundhogs alongside Steve Rye (vocals/harmonica) and Ken Pustelnik (drums). The new unit made its debut with the rudimentary *Scratching The Surface*, but were then cut to a trio by Rye's departure. A second set, *Blues Obituary*, contained two tracks, 'Mistreated' and 'Express Man', which became in-concert favourites as the group embarked on a more progressive direction. This was confirmed with *Thank Christ For The Bomb*, the Groundhogs' powerful 1970 release which cemented a growing popularity. McPhee composed the entire set and his enthusiasm for concept albums was maintained with its successor, *Split*, which examined schizophrenia. Arguably the group's definitive work, this uncompromising selection included the classic 'Cherry Red'. Pustelnik left the group following the release of *Who Will Save The World?* in 1972. Former **Egg** drummer Clive Brooks (b. 28 December 1949, London, England) was an able replacement, but although the Groundhogs continued to enjoy a fervent popularity, their subsequent recordings lacked the fire of those early releases. The trio was also beset by managerial problems and broke up in 1975, although McPhee maintained the name for two releases, *Crosscut Saw* and *Black Diamond*.

The guitarist resurrected the Groundhogs' sobriquet in 1984 in the wake of interest in an archive release, *Hoggin' The Stage*. Although Pustelnik was one of several musicians McPhee used for touring purposes, the most effective line-up was completed by Dave Anderson (bass), formerly of Hawkwind, and drummer Mike Jones. McPhee has in recent years appeared as a solo performer as part of a 70s nostalgia tour.

Albums: *Scratching The Surface* (1968), *Blues Obituary* (1969), *Thank Christ For The Bomb* (1970), *Split* (1971), *Who Will Save The World?* (1972), *Hogwash* (1972), *Solid* (1974), *Crosscut Saw* (1976), *Black Diamond* (1976), *Razor's Edge* (1985), *Back Against The Wall* (1987), *Hogs On The Road* (1988). Compilations: *Groundhogs Best 1969-1972* (1974), *Hoggin' The Stage* (1984).

Guesnon, Creole George

b. 25 May 1907, New Orleans, Louisiana, USA, d. 5 May 1968, New Orleans, Louisiana, USA. A jazz banjoist and guitarist, Guesnon worked in many 'Crescent City' bands from 1927 to 1965, often recording as a sideman from 1951. He also toured with Little Brother Montgomery's Jackson-based Southland Troubadours in the mid-30s, and it may have been this experience that prompted 'Mississippi Town', a blues tribute to Jackson recorded in 1940. ('Iberville And Franklin' did the same for New Orleans.) Guesnon did not play on these recordings, which show him to have been a likeable, clear-voiced singer, as adept at ballads as with the blues.

Albums: *Jazz Crusade* album (title not known) (1960), *Blues Bands* (1990).

Guitar Gable

b. Gabriel Perrodin, 17 August 1937, Bellvue, Louisiana, USA. Learning guitar in his teens Gable was influenced by the ringing, melodic style of Guitar Slim. He recorded for Jay Miller with his band the Musical Kings in 1956-57, and several successful singles were issued on Excello Records. The music was very much in the South Louisiana R&B mould, with a touch of New Orleans rock 'n' roll, Gable's distinctive guitar provides a very effective complement to the lead vocals of King Karl. Guitar Gable's band retained its popularity in local clubs throughout the rest of the 50s, but it appears he retired from performing when he joined the army around 1959.

Album: *Cool, Calm, Collected* (1984).

Guitar Nubbit

b. Alvin Hankerson, 1923, Fort Lauderdale, Florida, USA. Nicknamed 'Nubbit' following the loss of the tip of his right thumb at the age of three in a hurricane. Hankerson grew up in Georgia, relocating to Boston, Massachusets in 1945. Taking up guitar in 1948, he was unable to teach himself, and abandoned the instrument after a year, only resuming in 1954 when he took some lessons. In the early 60s, he recorded for the local Bluestown label and, being a young, original blues singer, caused some excitement among the attentive, white audiences. His isolation from the mainstream of blues led to some remarkable lyrics 'I whistled to my shotgun, and it crawled down off the wall', but heard at length, his music lacks variety. After a brief exposure on the local folk scene, Nubbit returned to obscurity. In 1990 he released a 12-inch single 'Reliving The Legend'.

Guitar Shorty

b. John Henry Fortescue, 24 January 1923, Belhaven, North Carolina, USA, d. 26 May 1976, Rocky Mount, North Carolina, USA. Discovered in 1970, Guitar Shorty beguiled researchers with tales of teaching guitar to the Beatles and playing with the New York Philharmonic; it thus came as a surprise that he really had, as he claimed, recorded in New York (two unissued titles, for Savoy in 1952). A street singer and farm labourer, he lived in squalid and desperate poverty, with alcohol a temporary, and eventually a permanent, release. Unusual for the Carolinas in its frequent use of the bottleneck, his guitar playing was however not truly regional at all, but rather like his singing, a unique, free-form construction of Shorty's own devising, obeying no rules but his own sense of what sounded good.

Albums: *Carolina Slide Guitar* (1972), *Alone In His Field* (1975).

Gunter, Arthur

b. 23 May 1926, Nashville, Tennessee, USA, d. 16 March 1976, Port Huron, Michigan, USA. Arthur Gunter wrote and recorded 'Baby Let's Play House' for Excello in the summer of 1954. That December, The Thunderbirds vocal group recorded their version, issued on DeLuxe, in Miami. Three months later, it was one side of Elvis Presley's fourth Sun single. That's when Arthur Gunter discovered that he had no ambition to write another hit. His father was a preacher; he and his brothers, Jimmy and Junior, and cousin Julian, sang spirituals as The Gunter Brothers Quartet. He learned guitar from another brother, Larry, and absorbed blues old and new - Blind Boy Fuller and Big Boy Crudup, Jimmy Reed and Blind Lemon Jefferson. He hung around the record store run by Ernie Young, founder of Excello and Nashboro. There he met pianist Skippy Brooks, and played gigs with Brooks' band, the Kid King Combo. Most of the time he performed with just cousin Julian on drums. 'Baby Let's Play House' was his first record, and a hit in the Nashville area. None of his succeeding 11 singles did as well, and Excello dropped him in 1961. His brother Little Al also made two singles for the company. Al Gunter moved to Port Huron, Michigan in 1966 and lost touch with music. In 1973 he won $50,000 in the Michigan State Lottery, and played as part of the Ann Arbor Blues Festival's 'Music Of Detroit' afternoon.

Guy, Buddy

b. George Guy, 30 July 1936, Lettsworth, Louisiana, USA. An impassioned and influential guitarist, Buddy Guy learned to play the blues on a rudimentary, home-made instrument, copying records heard on the radio. By the mid-50s he was sitting in with several of the region's leading performers, including Slim Harpo and Lightnin' Slim. In 1957 Guy moved north to Chicago. He initially joined the Rufus Foreman Band but was quickly established as an artist in his own right. The guitarist's first single was released the following year, but his career prospered on meeting Willie Dixon. This renowned composer/bassist brought the young musician to Chess Records where, as part of the company's houseband, he appeared on sessions by Muddy Waters and Howlin' Wolf. Guy also made several recordings in his own right, of which the frenzied 'First Time I Met The Blues' and the gutsy 'Stone Crazy' are particularly memorable.

As well as pursuing his own direction, Guy also established a fruitful partnership with Junior

Wells. Having completed telling contributions to the harpist's early releases, *Hoodoo Man Blues* and *It's My Life Baby*, the guitarist recorded a series of excellent albums for the Vanguard label which combined classic 'Chicago' blues with contemporary soul styles. His fiery playing was rarely better and Guy won attention from the rock audience through appearances at the Fillmore auditorium and his support slot on the Rolling Stones 1970 tour. The artist's career lost momentum during the 70s as the passion which marked his early work receded. Guy has nonetheless retained a considerable following on the international circuit. In 1990 he was one of the guests during Eric Clapton's memorable blues night at London's Royal Albert Hall. The following he released the magnificent *Damn Right I Got The Blues* which was recorded with the assistance of Clapton, Jeff Beck and Mark Knopfler. The critical acclaim put Guy firmly back in the echelon's as one of the outstanding blues guitarists currently performing.
Albums: *A Man And The Blues* (1968), *This Is Buddy Guy* (1968), *Buddy And The Juniors* (1970), *Hold That Plane!* (1972), *Buddy Guy And Junior Wells Play The Blues* (1972), *I Was Walking Through The Woods* (1974), *Hot And Cool* (1978), *Got To Use Your House* (1979), *Dollar Done Fell* (1980), *DJ Play My Blues* (1982), *Drinking' TNT And Smokin' Dynamite* (1982), *The Original Blues Brothers - Live* (1983), *Ten Blue Fingers* (1985), *Live At The Checkerboard, Chicago, 1979* (1988), *Breaking Out* (1988), *Damn Right I Got The Blues* (1991). Compilations: *I Left My Blues In San Francisco* (1967), *In The Beginning* (1971), *Buddy Guy* (1983), *Chess Masters* (1987), *Stone Crazy* (1988), *I Ain't Got No Money* (1989), *The Complete Chess Studio Sessions* (1992).

Guy, Phil

b. 28 April 1940, Lettsworth, Louisiana, USA. Phil, the younger brother of Buddy Guy, learned to play guitar as a child. He followed in Buddy's footsteps, playing after him with local artists Big Poppa and Raful Neal. He recorded as accompanist for his brother in 1957, for Neal around 1958, and for Slim Harpo (James Moore) in the mid-60s. He joined his brother's band in Chicago in 1969, and has been based there ever since. He has worked and recorded with many of the city's leading artists, such as his brother

Buddy Guy

146

Buddy, Junior Wells, Byther Smith, and Jimmy Dawkins. Phil spent most of the 80s consolidating his own musical career, showing himself to be a tough electric Chicago bluesman, with a raw guitar style influenced by artists including Guitar Slim. He has recorded several fine sets for JSP; albums have also appeared on Isabel and Red Lightning.

Albums: *The Red Hot Blues Of Phil Guy* (1982), *Bad Luck Boy* (1983), *It's A Real Mutha Fucker* (1985), *I Was Once A Gambler* (1987), *Tina Nu* (1989), *Tough Guy* (1989).

Hall, Vera

b. c.1906, Livingstone, Alabama, USA, d. 29 January 1964, Tuscaloosa, Alabama, USA. Primarily a gospel singer whose speciality was the unaccompanied spiritual, Vera Hall was discovered by author Ruby Tarrt, who introduced her to John and Alan Lomax. Between the years 1937 and 1940 the Lomaxes recorded in excess of 50 a cappella spirituals, blues and children's songs by Hall, together with a further 60 duetting with her cousin, Dock Reed. She resurfaced in the late 40s when folklorist Harold Courlander found her working as a housekeeper in Tuscaloosa and recorded her as part of his 'Negro Folk Music Of Alabama' project for Folkways Records. Alan Lomax returned to Alabama in 1959 and included her in his 'Southern Folk Heritage' series for Atlantic records, the most memorable of which was her haunting field holler, 'Wild Ox Moan'.

Hammond, John (Jnr.)

b. John Paul Hammond, 13 November 1943, he is the son of jazz and rock producer John Hammond. The younger Hammond took up blues guitar and harmonica while at college and joined the New York coffeehouse scene in 1963. In the same year he recorded the first of

five albums for Vanguard. On *So Many Roads*, he was backed by the Hawks, the group who later became the Band. Even after the folk/blues boom had died away, Hammond continued with his Chicago-blues based music, playing at small clubs and campuses. He continued to record frequently, for Atlantic (1968-70) where Robbie Robertson and Bill Wyman were among the accompanists and Columbia (1971-73) where he took part in a so-called 'supersession' in 1973 with Dr John and Mike Bloomfield. Hammond's work was also heard on the soundtrack of the film *Little Big Man* in 1970. Oblivious to musical fashion, Hammond maintained his commitment to blues over the next two decades, releasing albums on a range of labels including Capricorn, Sonet, Rounder, Demon and Pointblank, the Virgin subsidiary for which his 1992 album was recorded.

Albums: *John Hammond* (1963), *Big City Blues* (1964), *Country Blues* (1964), *So Many Roads* (1965), *Mirrors* (1967), *I Can Tell* (1967), *Sooner Or Later* (1968), *Southern Fried* (1969), *Source Point* (1970), *Little Big Man* (soundtrack) (1971), *I'm Satisfied* (1972), *Triumvirate* (1973), *Can't Beat The Kid* (1975), *My Spanish Album* (1975), *Solo* (1976), *Footwork* (1978), *Hot Tracks* (1978), *Mileage* (1980), *Frogs For Snakes* (1982), *Live In Greece* (1984), *Nobody But You* (1988), *Prophet And Higher Ground* (1988), *Got Love If You Want It* (1992).

Hancock, Hunter

A San Antonio, Texan, disc jockey on station KMAC, Hancock moved to California and got a job as a jazz presenter on radio station KFVD (latterly KPOP) in Los Angeles in 1943. Switching exclusively to what later developed as R&B, Hancock launched his *Harlem Matinee* radio show in June 1948, and became known for his wild hollering and screaming. His playing the new music predated Alan Freed by several years. Hancock was soon a popular figure at the many black clubs on Central Avenue. He became fast friends with Johnny Otis and presided over many shows at Otis' Barrelhouse club. In 1951, Hancock presented two concert shows, *The Blues & Rhythm Midnight Matinee,* from the Olympic Auditorium, showcasing local black artists like Floyd Dixon, Big Jay McNeely, Maxwell Davis and Peppermint Harris. The results have recently been issued for the first

time on Sweden's Route 66 label. Hancock remained an advocate for R&B throughout the 50s, moving to KGFJ and KFOX and back to KPOP, and in February 1959 he formed his own Swingin' label, based just off Sunset Boulevard. His first release was 'There Is Something On Your Mind' by Big Jay McNeely which had been recorded two years earlier, but nevertheless reached number 5 on the R&B charts. Swingin', and its sister label Magnum, ceased business in late 1964 after several dozen R&B and vocal group releases by such artists as of Marvin & Johnny, Joe Houston and Rochell & the Candles. At this time Hancock was still a disc jockey on KGFJ until he retired from the music business in 1968.
Album: *Hunter Hancock Presents 'Blues & Rhythm Midnight Matinee'* (1985).

Hare, Auburn 'Pat'

b. 20 December 1930, Parkin, Arkansas, USA, d. 26 September 1980, St. Paul Minnesota, USA. Pat Hare is best known for his excellent work as an accompanying guitarist, with Little Junior Parker's Blue Flames, then with the Muddy Waters band in Chicago, Illinois. He appeared on several records by both, during the 50s and early 60s. Prior to that he had played with Howlin' Wolf, and done session work in Memphis, at the Sam Phillips studio, where he accompanied James Cotton on his earliest recordings. While there, he recorded a few tracks under his own name (not issued until many years later), including one titled 'I'm Gonna Murder My Baby'. This title proved to be prophetic, as he was convicted in 1964 for murdering a girlfriend, as well as a policeman; he died of cancer while still serving his sentence in prison.
Album: *The Sun Box* (1985).

Harlem Hamfats

Despite their name, the Hamfats were Chicago, Illinois based, and perhaps the first group created (by J. Mayo Williams) solely to make records. With some variation, the personnel was New Orleans trumpeter Herb Morand, the brothers Joe and Charlie McCoy on guitar and mandolin, clarinettist Odell Rand, pianist Horace Malcolm, John Lindsay or Ransom Knowling on bass, and Pearlis Williams or Fred Flynn, drums. Morand and Joe McCoy (as 'Hamfoot Ham') handled the vocals. The Hamfats blended New Orleans jazz with blues, the primary aim being to provide entertaining, danceable music. Their first release, 'Oh! Red', was a considerable hit in 1936, and was frequently reworked, both by the Hamfats themselves and by others. They recorded extensively, and were also used as studio accompanists, until 1939, by which time Morand had returned to New Orleans, and changing fashions had made their sound no longer commercially attractive.
Albums: *Hot Chicago Jazz, Blues & Jive* (1981), *Harlem Hamfats* (1988), *Harlem Hamfats* (1989), *Frankie 'Half-Pint' Jaxon* (1989), with Rosetta Howard *Harlem Hamfats* (1990).

Harman, James

b. 1946, Anniston, Alabama, USA. One of the leading white harmonica players on America's west coast, Harman's love of the instrument was instilled in him by his father. As a youngster in Alabama, James played with a local blues musician called Radio Johnson, and bought R&B discs. By the age of 16 he led his own band. In 1970 he moved to California and had to abandon music for some years due to health problems. However, he was unable to stop playing music for very long. In the 80s he made acclaimed recordings for the Rivera and Rhino labels. Harman is a fine singer and harmonica player whose approach to the blues is one of having fun.
Albums: *Those Dangerous Gentlemens* (1987), *Extra Napkins* (1988), *Strictly Live...In '85 Volume One* (issued 1990).

Harmonica, Fats

b. Harvey Blackston, 8 September 1927, McDade, Louisiana, USA. Fats taught himself to play harmonica while growing up on his grandfather's farm. He subsequently moved to Los Angeles during World War II and became a professional musician in 1956. In the early 60s his debut recording, a raunchy cover of Hank Ballards's 'Tore Up', was a hit and remains a popular item. For some years Fats worked on tours with major artists, but in the 70s he returned to club work, and has recorded for many labels. His gruff vocals and downhome harmonica are often backed by soul bands. In 1986 Fats teamed up with local disc jockey and bandleader Bernie Pearl whose music is much more in sympathy with Fats' straightforward, rocking blues approach.

Albums: with Bernie Pearl *Live At Café Lido* (1990), with Bernie Pearl *I Had To Get Nasty* (1991).

Harpo, Slim

b. James Moore, 11 January 1924, Lobdel, Louisiana, USA, d. 31 January 1970. The eldest of an orphaned family, Harpo worked as a longshoreman and building worker during the late 30s and early 40s. One of the foremost proponents of post-war rural blues, Moore began performing in Baton Rouge bars under the name Harmonica Slim. He later accompanied Lightnin' Slim, his brother-in-law, both live and in the studio, before commencing his own recording career in 1957. Christened 'Slim Harpo' by producer Jay Miller, the artist's solo debut coupled 'I'm A King Bee' with 'I Got Love If You Want It'. Influenced by Jimmy Reed, he began recording for Excello and enjoyed a string of popular R&B singles which combined a drawling vocal with incisive hamonica passages. Among them were 'Raining In My Heart' (1961), 'I Love The Life I Live', 'Buzzin'' (instrumental) and 'Little Queen Bee' (1964). These relaxed, almost lazy, performances, which featured an understated electric backing, set the tone for Moore's subsequent work. His warm, languid voice enhanced the sexual metaphor of 'I'm A King Bee', which was later recorded by the Rolling Stones. The same group also covered the pulsating 'Shake Your Hips', which Harpo first issued in 1966, while the Pretty Things, the Yardbirds and Them featured versions of his songs in their early repertoires.

Harpo scored a notable US Top 20 pop hit in 1966 with 'Baby Scratch My Back' (also a number 1 R&B hit), which revitalized his career. Never a full-time musician, Harpo had his own trucking business during the 60s although he was a popular figure during the late 60s blues revival, with appearances at several renowned venues including the Electric Circus and the Fillmore East, but suffered from a fatal heart attack on 31 January 1970.

Albums: *Rainin' In My Heart* (1961), *Baby Scratch My Back* (1966), *Tip On In* (1968). Compilations: *The Best Of Slim Harpo* (1969), *He Knew The Blues* (1970), *Blues Hangover* (1976), *Got Love If You Want It* (1980), *Shake Your Hips* (1986), *I'm A King Bee* (1989).

Harris, Alfred

b. possibly Mississippi, USA. An obscure harmonica player and singer, Alfred Harris (aka Blues King Harris or Johnny Harris) recorded on three separate occasions in the 50s, each time under a different name. The first, in 1950 or 1951 was during a field trip by the Bihari brothers, in Mississippi, Arkansas or Tennessee, and featured Harris with a second guitarist, playing acoustic, in a very downhome style. A few years later there was a session in Chicago, with James Bannister and Earl Dranes, in a more electric, urban style. Neither of these two sessions was issued until many years later. Finally, there was a single, also recorded in Chicago, in 1956.

Album: *Harmonica Blues Kings* (1986).

Harris, Don 'Sugarcane'

b. 8 June 1938, Pasadena, California, USA. A multi-instrumentalist, trained in the classics by his mother, Sugarcane Harris came to the blues late, citing Little Walter and Jimmy Reed as inspirations. From 1957 to 1963 he and school-friend Dewey Terry led a group called the Squires. They also performed as a vocal duo, Don And Dewey, recording breathless rock 'n' roll with the same explosive energy as Specialty label-mate Little Richard. White cover artists did well out of their material. Dale And Grace sold over a million copies of their classic 'Leavin' It All Up To You' and the Righteous Brothers adopted their stage act. Gradually, Harris started applying his knowledge of classical violin to improvising. Frank Zappa, long a fan (and product himself of the west coast 50s blues scene), encouraged him on the instrument, leading to the gargantuan Harris solos on *Hot Rats* and *Burnt Weenie Sandwich*. Harris had started listening to jazz - John Coltrane, Horace Silver - and he injected a raw, blues tonality into ambitious outings that were like a violinist's response to Coltrane's new intensity. 1970's *Sugarcane* included R&B, proto-funk and an astonishing classical pastiche 'Funk & Wagner'. Later work with John Mayall was less gripping, but important albums appeared under his own name and that of Pure Food & Drug Act, a group he ran with guitarist Harvey Mandel.

Described by Joachim Berendt in the mid-70s as 'the dominant violinist of the contemporary world', Sugarcane's laidback attitude did not help his career. Last heard of preparing an album called *Midnight DJ* with old associate Dewey Terry (1985), it seems that of late Sugarcane has been keeping his inspired answer to blues/classical/jazz divisions to himself.

Albums: *Don & Dewey* (1957-60), with Johnny Otis *Cuttin' Up* (1969), with John Mayall *USA Union* (1970), *Sugarcane* (1970), *Fiddler On The Rock* (1971), with Jean Luc Ponty, Michael Urbaniak *The Summit* (1971), *Flashin' Time* (1973), with Pure Food & Drug Act *Choice Cuts* (c.1970s).

Harris, Edward P.

b. 22 August 1923, Leasburg, North Carolina, USA, d. 22 October 1953, Newark, New Jersey, USA. Harris learned guitar from his father, and is said to have been an itinerant musician before settling in Newark, but his background is otherwise obscure. None of the records he made between 1950 and 1952 was ever released under Harris's real name; he was variously known as Carolina Slim, Lazy Slim Jim, Jammin' Jim, Paul Howard and Country Paul. His music is a blend, probably acquired mainly from records, of the contemporary Texas styles of Lightnin' Hopkins and the 30s North Carolina/Georgia music of Buddy Moss and Blind Boy Fuller.

Albums: *Faded·Picture Blues* (c. 1970), *Carolina Blues & Boogie* (1985).

Harris, Hi Tide

b 26 March 1946, San Francisco, California, USA, d. 1990 Japan. His real name was reportedly Willie Boyd or Willie Gitry. He was brought up in Richmond, California, and sang in vocal groups as a youngster; he also learned to play guitar in the early 60s, going on to play with Big Mama Thornton, Jimmy McCracklin, and others (he also recorded with McCracklin). Following a spell in Los Angeles (1969-71), he formed his own band around 1972. In 1973 he joined Charlie Musselwhite's band, and the following year he toured and recorded with John Mayall. Harris was also involved in film work: he wrote the theme song for *Mandingo* (sung by Muddy Waters) and sang on the soundtrack of *Leadbelly*. Harris was 'an excellent guitarist in both the slide and regular fingerstyles' (*Blues Unlimited*).

Album: *Celebrating With Hi-Tide Harris* (1980).

Harris, Peppermint

b. Harrison D. Nelson Jnr., 17 July 1925, Texarkana, Texas, USA. This blues singer acquired his monicker in the 40s when Bob Shad, proprietor of Sittin' In With Records, simply could not remember his new signing's real name. Harris chose to hold onto the name as a means of keeping his religious family from knowing that he engaged in the practice of singing that form of music. Harris's major recordings were recorded for Aladdin Records in the early 50s, the best known being his 1951 number 1 R&B waxing 'I Get Loaded' (more recently covered by Elvis Costello and Los Lobos). Harris later recorded for many different labels including Modern Records, X, Cash & Money, Combo, Checker Records, Duke Records, Jewel Records and other labels. He continued to record into the 70s.

Albums: *Sittin' In With Historical Recordings* (1979), *I Get Loaded* (1987), *Shout And Rock* (1988). Compilation: *Houston Can't Be Heaven* (1989).

Harris, William

Born around the turn of the 20th century, Harris was a blues singer and guitarist from the Mississippi Delta who made recordings in 1927 and 1928 (although not all of them have survived). This makes him one of the very earliest musicians from that hugely influential area to make a record, and he is also of considerable interest in his own right. His vocals had a plaintive, crying effect which lent great emotional power to his songs, which varied from rocking dance tunes to intense slow blues, punctuated by flashing single string runs, wedded to lyrics notable for their memorable if rather bizarre imagery (eg 'Have you ever woke up with bullfrogs on your mind?') This all adds up to a very distinctive and compelling musical legacy.

Album: *William Harris And Buddy Boy Hawkins* (1978).

Harrison, Vernon 'Boogie Woogie Red'

b. 18 October 1925, Bayville, Louisiana, USA. Though born in Louisiana, pianist Vernon

Harrison was taken to Detroit when he was two years old and, like his contemporaries Eddie Burns and Eddie Kirkland, became a stalwart of the Detroit blues scene using the billing of 'Boogie Woogie Red'. He is best known for his session work with John Lee Hooker and, although a very active club performer for three decades, the first album in his own right did not materialize until the early 70s. In 1973 he toured Europe as part of the 'American Blues Legends' package and suffered the misfortune of breaking his wrist during the tour which somewhat marred his European debut. His overall recording output has been small and he prefers to work as an accompanist.

Hart, Hattie

b. c.1900, USA. One of the finest of the women blues singers in Memphis, Hart was a strong-voiced, darkly sensuous singer, whose lyrics celebrated sex and drugs. She made a largely unissued session with the guitarists Allen Shaw and Willie Borum in 1934, and previous to this had recorded with the Memphis Jug Band. It is thought that she recorded in Chicago in 1938 as Hattie Bolten, which may have been her married or her maiden name. She had left Memphis by 1946, and her subsequent whereabouts are unknown.

Albums: *Memphis Girls* (1988), *Blue Ladies Vol. 2* (1989), *Memphis Jug Band Associates And Alternate Takes* (1991).

Hartley, Keef

b. 8 March 1944, Preston, Lancashire, England. Together with Colosseum, the Keef Hartley Band of the late 60s, forged jazz and rock music sympathetically to appeal to the UK progressive music scene. Drummer Hartley had already seen vast experience in live performances as Ringo Starr's replacement in Rory Storm And The Hurricanes. When Merseybeat died, Hartley was enlisted by the London based R&B band the Artwoods, whose line-up included future Deep Purple leader Jon Lord. Hartley was present on their only album *Art Gallery* (now a much sought-after collectors item). He joined John Mayall's Bluesbreakers and was present during one of Mayall's vintage periods. Both *Crusade* and *Diary Of A Band* highlighted Hartley's economical drumming and faultless timing. The brass-laden instrumental track on John Mayall's *Bare Wires* is titled 'Hartley Quits'. The good natured banter between Hartley and his ex-boss

Keef Hartley Band

continued onto Hartley's strong debut *Half Breed*. The opening track 'Hearts And Flowers' has the voice of Mayall on the telephone officially sacking Hartley, albeit tongue-in-cheek, while the closing track 'Sacked' has Hartley dismissing Mayall! The music in-between features some of the best ever late 60s jazz-influenced blues, and the album remains an undiscovered classic. The band for the first album comprised: Miller Anderson, guitar and vocals, the late Gary Thain (b. New Zealand d. 19 March 1976; bass), Peter Dines (organ) and Spit James (guitar). Later members to join Hartley's fluid line-up included Mick Weaver (aka Wynder K. Frog) organ, Henry Lowther (b. 11 July 1941, Leicester, England; trumpet/violin), Jimmy Jewell (saxophone), Johnny Almond (flute), Jon Hiseman and Harry Beckett. Hartley, often dressed as an American Indian, sometimes soberly, sometimes in full head-dress and war-paint, was a popular attraction on the small club scene. His was one of the few British bands to play the Woodstock Festival, where his critics compared him favourably with Blood Sweat And Tears. *The Battle Of NW6* in 1969 further enhanced his club reputation, although chart success still eluded him. By the time of the third album both Lowther and Jewell had departed, although Hartley always maintained that his band was like a jazz band, in that musicians would come and go and be free to play with other aggregations.

Dave Caswell and Lyle Jenkins came in and made *The Time Is Near*. This album demonstrated Miller Anderson's fine songwriting ability, and long-time producer Neil Slaven's excellent production. They were justly rewarded when the album briefly nudged its way into the UK and US charts. Subsequent albums lost the fire that Hartley kindled on the first three, although the formation of his Little Big Band and the subsequent live album had some fine moments. The recording at London's Marquee club saw the largest ever band assembled on the tiny stage, almost the entire British jazz/rock fraternity seemed to be present,including Chris Mercer, Lynn Dobson, Ray Warleigh, Barbara Thompson, and Derek Wadsworth. Regrettably Hartley has been largely inactive for many years apart from the occasional tour with John Mayall and sessions with Michael Chapman.

Albums: *Halfbreed* (1969), *Battle Of NW6* (1970), *The Time Is Near* (1970), *Overdog* (1971), *Little Big Band* (1971), *Seventy Second Brave* (1972), *Lancashire Hustler* (1973), *Dog Soldier* (1975). Compilation: *The Best Of Keef Hartley* (1972).

Hawkins, Roy

Based in Richmond, California, Hawkins was an early discovery of label-owner Bob Geddins who found him playing piano and singing in an Oakland club in 1946. With a band that included William Staples on tenor saxophone and Ulysses James on guitar, Hawkins had his first recordings released on Geddins' Cavatone and Down Town labels in 1948. Some of the tracks raised sufficient interest for Modern Records to purchase Hawkins contract and some of the Down Town masters. This new label began recording him seriously over the next three years with some of Los Angeles' finest musicians including Maxwell Davis, T-Bone Walker and Johnny Moore. Hawkins' biggest hits were the visionary 'Why Do Everything Happen To Me', reaching number 3 in the USA charts in 1950, and the ironical 'The Thrill Is Gone' reaching number 6 in the US in 1951. Subsequent Modern/RPM sessions and those for Rhythm (1958) and Kent (1961) had Hawkins only singing, backed by a guest pianist (a car accident had left him paralyzed in one arm). Nowadays a shadowy figure, known only to west coast blues fans, Hawkins and his recordings were very influential in their day and have been covered by the likes of Ray Charles, B.B. King and James Brown. It is believed Hawkins died in poverty in 1973.

Albums: *Why Do Everything Happen To Me* (1979), *Highway 59* (1984).

Hawkins, Ted

b. Theodore Hawkins Jnr, 28 October 1937, Biloxi, Mississippi, USA. More a modern-day 'songster' than a bluesman, Hawkins' repertoire encompasses pop hits, country and folk standards, soul numbers and originals. He grew up with gospel music, learned to play guitar at the age of 12, taught in the bluesy 'Vestapol' (or Open C) style by local musicians. He plays with such force that he protects his left hand with a glove. As a boy, he was sent to a reformatory, and spent several terms behind bars. He left home in the 50s, hoboing first to Chicago, Illinois, then to New York, Pennsylvania and New Jersey, ending up in California. He recorded 'Baby'/'Whole Lot Of Women' for the Hollywood-based Money label in 1966; in 1971 he was spotted busking by producer Bruce Bromberg with whom he made an album in 1972. He has continued to perform on street corners and California's Ocean Front Walk; this aspect of Hawkins' career is documented on the *Venice Beach Tapes* recorded, ironically, in Tennessee in 1985. *Happy Hour* consolidated his reputation, particularly in Britain where he has a sizeable following. Despite retaining an undoubtedly 'rural' feel in performance, Hawkins owes much vocally to his hero Sam Cooke and to the great soul stylists of the 60s. Above all, he remains one of the finest contemporary interpreters of melancholic material.

Albums: *Watch Your Step* (1972), *On The Boardwalk: The Venice Beach Tapes* (1986), *Happy Hour* (1987), *Dock Of The Bay: The Venice Beach Tapes II* (1987), *I Love You Too* (1989). Compilation: *The Best Of Venice Beach Tapes* (1989).

Hawkins, Walter 'Buddy Boy'

Hawkins represents one of the most fascinating lacunae in the history of the blues. It is rumoured that he was raised around Blythville, Mississippi but what minimal research has been done has never produced anything conclusive. What is certain is that he was a unique performer who used a guitar style and vocal delivery that have defied categorization. He recorded 12 tracks for Paramount between 1927 (Chicago) and 1929 (Richmond, Indiana), much prized by collectors, which included his oddly constructed blues, rag tunes and the peculiar 'Voice Throwing Blues' which gave rise to speculation that he may have been a medicine show ventriloquist. Evidence from his songs certainly seems to indicate that he was a rambler or hobo.

Album: *Complete Recordings* (1981).

Jeff Healey

Healey, Jeff

b. 25 March 1966, Toronto, Ontario, Canada. Blind since developing eye cancer when one year old, Healey is a white blues-rock guitarist and singer who plays in an unusual, instinctive lap-held style. He received his first guitar at the age of three and has been a proficient multi-instrumentalist since childhood. At 15, he formed Blue Direcon and gigged regularly in the Toronto area. In 1985, Healey was invited to play alongside Texas bluesman Albert Collins who, much impressed, in turn introduced him to Stevie Ray Vaughan. The Jeff Healey Band (Joe Rockman, b. 1 January 1957, Toronto, Canada; bass/vocals and Tom Stephen, b. 2 February 1955, St. John, New Brunswick, Canada; drums) was formed the same year and began playing all over Canada. They released singles on their own Forte label - and produced accompanying videos - before signing to Arista in 1988. *See the Light* was released in 1989 and came wrapped in a sash bearing tributes from guitar giants like Vaughan and B.B. King. It sold nearly two million copies; a world tour followed later in the year. A film, *Roadhouse* (1989), starring Patrick Swayze and Ben Gazzara was released; it featured Healey in an acting/singing role as a blind blues guitarist. *Hell To Pay* tended more towards hard rock and featured Mark Knopfler, George Harrison, Jeff Lynne and Bobby Whitlock in addition to Healey's regular band.
Albums: *See The Light* (1989), *Hell To Pay* (1990), with various artists *Roadhouse* (1989, includes four Jeff Healey tracks), *Feel This* (1992).

Heartsman, Johnny

b. 9 February 1937, San Fernando, California, USA. Heartsman grew up in Oakland and is now renowned as 'one of the blues' most accomplished instrumentalists' (Dick Shurman). As a youngster he was inspired to play guitar by the music of T-Bone Walker, Pee Wee Crayton, and Lafayette Thomas. He quickly developed into a sought-after bandleader and studio musician. He has recorded on guitar, bass, organ, and flute, (he made his own first recordings in 1957 for the Music City label) and has played with a long list of west coast blues, R&B, and soul artists including Jimmy McCracklin, Joe Simon, Johnny Fuller, Jimmy

Wilson, and Tiny Powell. Buddy Guy borrowed much of Heartsman's playing on his version of 'My Time After Awhile'. In 1976 Heartman settled in Sacramento, California, and has recorded only infrequently since then.
Selected albums: *Sacramento* (1987), *The Touch* (1991).

Hegamin, Lucille

b. 29 November 1894, Macon, Georgia, USA, d. 1 March 1970, New York, New York, USA. Hegamin was recorded from 1920 onwards, in the wake of Mamie Smith's breakthrough for black singers. Her background was in vaudeville, which required versatility and the ability to respond to popular taste. Her repertoire on record is more blues-inflected black pop than pure blues, but the songs often have great charm, and Hegamin's delivery, forceful but melodious and flexible with precise, clear diction, is very appealing. She stopped recording in 1926, excluding one 1932 record, but continued stage and club work (including stardom with the touring company of *Shuffle Along* in the role played on Broadway by Florence Mills) until 1934, when she became a nurse. Coaxed out of retirement, she made some fine recordings in 1961 and 1962 before returning to the church work that occupied her last years.
Albums: *Songs We Taught Your Mother* (1962), *Blue Flame* (1973).

Hemphill, Jessie Mae

b. c.1940, Mississippi, USA. From a family whose musical activities can be traced back a number of generations (her grandfather Sid Hemphill and aunt Rosa Lee Hill both made recordings), Hemphill has been playing and singing since she was a young girl in the 50s. She sings blues, most of which she writes herself, based on her own experiences and plays guitar in a local style, using droning chords and beating time on a tambourine with her foot. She also plays drums in a fife and drum band, one of the last active examples of an old Mississippi tradition. She has made a number of recordings, including a couple of singles issued by a venture owned by Memphis State University, and has frequently played at concerts and festivals as far afield as Europe.
Album: *She Wolf* (1983).

Henderson, Rosa

b. Rosa Deschamps, 24 November 1896, Henderson, Kentucky, USA, d. 6 April 1968, New York, New York, USA. Henderson was a person of many aliases, her most well-known stage name was the one she took from her husband and vaudeville partner Douglas 'Slim' Henderson, but others were more arbitrarily chosen. She had records issued under the titles Flora Dale, Rosa Green Mae/Mamie Harris, Sara Johnsson, Sally Ritz, Josephine Thomas, Gladys White and Bessie Williams. Her large record output and continuing success on the stage indicate the popularity of her big voice and engaging persona. Her blues was largely divorced from any country influence but sometimes showed considerable awareness of current musical trends. Her career appears to have ended in the early 30s.

Albums: *Mean Mothers* (1980), *Big Mamas* (1982).

Hendrix, Jimi

b. Johnny Allen Hendrix, 27 November 1942, Seattle, Washington, USA, d. 18 September, 1970. His father subsequently changed his son's name to James Marshall Hendrix. More superlatives have been bestowed upon Hendrix than almost any other rock star. Unquestionably one of music's most influential figures, Jimi Hendrix brought an unparalleled vision to the art of playing electric guitar. Self-taught and with the burden of being left-handed with a right-handed guitar he spent hours absorbing the recorded legacy of southern-blues practitioners, from Robert Johnson to Muddy Waters, Howlin' Wolf to B.B. King. The aspiring musician joined several local R&B bands while still at school, before enlisting as a paratrooper in the 101st Airborne Division. It was during this period that Hendrix met Billy Cox, a bass player upon whom he would call at several stages in his career. Together they formed the King Kasuals, an in-service attraction later resurrected when both men returned to civilian life. Hendrix was discharged in July 1962 after breaking his right ankle. He began working with various touring revues backing, among others, the Impressions, Sam Cooke and the Valentinos. He enjoyed lengthier spells with the Isley Brothers, Little Richard and King Curtis, recording with each of these acts, but was unable to adapt to the discipline their performances required. Despite such individuality, the experience and stagecraft gained during this formative period proved essential to the artist's subsequent development. By 1965, Jimi was living in New York. In October he joined struggling soul singer Curtis Knight, signing a punitive contract with the latter's manager, Ed Chaplin. This ill-advised decision would return to haunt the guitarist. In June the following year Hendrix, now calling himself Jimmy James, formed a group initially dubbed the Rainflowers, then Jimmy James And The Blue Flames. The quartet, which also featured future Spirit member Randy California, was appearing at the Cafe Wha? in Greenwich Village when Chas Chandler was advised to see them. The Animals' bassist immediately recognized the guitarist's extraordinary talent and persuaded him to come to London in search of a more receptive audience. Hendrix arrived in England in September 1966. Chandler became his co-manager, in partnership with Mike Jeffries (aka Jeffreys), and immediately began auditions for a suitable backing group. Noel Redding (b. 25 December 1945, Folkstone, Kent, England) was selected on bass, having recently failed to join the New Animals, while John 'Mitch' Mitchell (b. 9 July 1947, Ealing, Middlesex, England), a veteran of the Riot Squad and Georgie Fame's Blue Flames, became the trio's drummer.

The new group, dubbed the Jimi Hendrix Experience, made its debut the following month at Evereux in France. On returning to England they began a string of club engagements which attracted pop's aristocracy, including Pete Townshend and Eric Clapton. In December the trio released its first single, the brilliantly understated 'Hey Joe', but its UK Top 10 placing encouraged a truly dynamic follow-up in 'Purple Haze'. The latter was memorable for its pyrotechic guitar work and psychedelic-influenced lyrics, such as the famous line: ''Scuse me while I kiss the sky'.

His trademark Fender Stratocaster and Marshall Amplifier were punished night after night. Having fulfilled pop's requirements, the group enhanced its reputation with exceptional live appearances. Here Hendrix drew on black music's cultural heritage to produce a startling visual and audio bombardment. Framed by a halo of long, wiry hair, his slight figure was clad

Jimi Hendrix

in colourful, *de rigueur* psychedelic garb, and although never a demonstrative vocalist, his delivery was curiously effective. Hendrix's playing technique drew its roots from the blues artists, but it encompassed an emotional palette far greater than any contemporary guitarist. Eric Clapton, Jeff Beck and Pete Townshend all tried: but Hendrix *did it*, while they stood aghast. Rapier-like runs vied with measured solos, matching energy with ingenuity, while a plethora of technical possibilities - distortion, feedback and even sheer volume - brought texture to his overall approach. His technique was so impressive it was irrational. This assault was enhanced by a flamboyant stage persona in which Hendrix used the guitar as a physical appendage. He played his instrument behind his back, between his legs or, in simulated sexual ecstasy, on the floor. Such practices brought criticism from radical quarters, who claimed the artist had become an 'Uncle Tom', employing tricks to carry favour with a white audience. These accusations had denied a similar showmanship from generations of black performers, from Charley Patton to 'T-Bone' Walker, but Hendrix prevailed and in doing so created a climate to allow future stars such as Michael Jackson and Prince to express themselves fully.

Redding's clean, uncluttered bass lines provided the backbone to Hendrix's improvisations, while Mitchell's anarchic drumming, as unfettered as his leader's guitar work, was an innovatory foil. Their concessions to the pop world now receding, the Experience completed an astonishing debut album which ranged from the apocalyptical vision of 'I Don't Live Today', the blues of 'Red House' to the funk of 'Fire' and 'Foxy Lady'. Jimi Hendrix returned to America in June 1967 to appear, sensationally, at the Monterey Pop Festival. During one number (Dylan's 'Like A Rolling Stone') he paused and informed the crowd that he was re-tuning his guitar, later in the same song he admits forgetting the words. Such cheek, humour and unparalleled confidence endeared him to the crowd. His performance was a sensation, best remembered for his largesse in picking the guitar with his teeth and then burning it with lighter fuel.

He was now fêted in his homeland, and following an ill-advised tour supporting the Monkees, the Experience enjoyed reverential audiences in the country's nascent concert circuit. *Axis: Bold As Love*, revealed a lyrical capability, notably the title track, the jazz-influenced 'Up From The Skies', and 'Little Wing', a delicate love song bathed in emotion through the delicate tones of his guitar, which offered a gentle perspective closer to that of the artist's shy, offstage demeanour. Released in December 1967, the collection completed a triumphant year, artistically and commercially, but within months the fragile peace began to fragment. In January 1968, the Experience embarked on a gruelling American tour encompassing 54 concerts in 47 days. Hendrix was now tiring of the wild man image which had brought initial attention, but his desire for a more eloquent art was perceived as diffident by spectators anticipating gimmickry. An impulsive artist, he was unable to disguise below-par performances, while his relationship with Redding grew increasingly fraught as the bassist rebelled against the set patterns he was expected to play.

Electric Ladyland, the last official Experience album, was released in October. This extravagant double set was initially deemed 'self-indulgent', but is now recognized as a major work. It revealed the guitarist's desire to expand the increasingly limiting trio format, and contributions from members of Traffic (Chris Wood and Steve Winwood) and Jefferson Airplane (Jack Casady) embellished several selections. The collection featured a succession of classic-styled performances - 'Gypsy Eyes', 'Crosstown Traffic' - while the astonishing 'Voodoo Chile (Slight Return)', a posthumous number 1 single, showed how Hendrix had brought rhythm, purpose and mastery to the recently invented wah-wah pedal. *Electric Ladyland* included two UK hits, 'The Burning Of The Midnight Lamp' and 'All Along The Watchtower'. The former dared to tell us in the plausible lyric that 'traffic lights turn blue' before the listener realises. The latter, an urgent restatement of a Bob Dylan song, was particularly impressive, and received the ultimate accolade when the composer adopted Hendrix's interpretation when performing it live on his 1974 tour.

Despite such creativity, the guitarist's private and professional life was becoming problematic. He was arrested in Toronto for possessing heroin, but although the charges were later dismissed, the proceedings clouded much of 1969. Chas Chandler had meanwhile withdrawn from the managerial partnership and although Redding sought solace with a concurrent group, Fat Mattress, his differences with Hendrix were now irreconcilable. The Experience played its final concert on June 29 1969; Jimi subsequently formed the Gypsies Sons And Rainbows with Mitchell, Billy Cox (bass), Larry Lee (rhythm guitar), Juma Sultan and Jerry Velez (both percussion). This short-lived unit closed the Woodstock Festival, during which Hendrix performed his famed rendition of the 'Star Spangled Banner'. Perceived by some critics as a political statement, it came as the guitarist was increasingly subjected to pressures from different radical quarters. In October he formed an all-black group, Band Of Gypsies, with Cox and drummer Buddy Miles, intending to accentuate the African-American dimension in his music. The trio made its debut on 31 December 1969, but its potential was marred by Miles' comparatively flat, pedestrian drumming and unimaginative compositions. Part of the set was issued as *Band Of Gypsies*, but despite the inclusion of the exceptional 'Machine Gun', this inconsistent album was only released to appease former manager Chaplin, who acquired the rights in part-settlement of a miserly early contract.

The Band Of Gypsies broke up after a mere three concerts and initially Hendrix confined his efforts to completing his Electric Ladyland recording studio. He then started work on another double set, the unreleased *First Rays Of The New Rising Sun*, and later resumed performing with Cox and Mitchell. His final concerts were largely frustrating, as the aims of the artist and the expectations of his audience grew increasingly divergent. His final UK appearance, at the Isle Of Wight festival, encapsulated this dilemma, yet at times the music produced at this concert was truly mesmerizing.

The guitarist returned to London following a short European tour. On 18 September 1970, his girlfriend, Monika Danneman, became alarmed when she was unable to rouse him from sleep. An ambulance was called, but Hendrix was pronounced dead on arrival at a nearby hospital. The inquest recorded an open verdict, death caused by suffocation due to inhalation of vomit. Eric Burdon claimed at the time to possess a suicide note but this has never been confirmed.

Two posthumous releases, *Cry Of Love* and *Rainbow Bridge*, mixed portions of the artist's final recordings with masters from earlier sources. These were fitting tributes, but many others were tawdry cash-ins, recorded in dubious circumstances, mispackaged, mistitled and serving only to dilute his outstanding career. This imbalance has been redressed of late with the release of fitting archive recordings, but the Hendrix legacy also rests in his prevailing influence on fellow musicians. Many, notably white, guitarists, have adopted superficially his trademarks, but Jimi's influence on black performers, from Miles Davis to George Clinton and Prince, has in turn inspired new and compulsive music. Hendrix has influenced and appears likely to influence rock music more than any other individual, and remains a colossal legend.

Albums: *Are You Experienced?* (1967), *Axis: Bold As Love* (1967), *Electric Ladyland* (1968), *Band Of Gypsies* (1970). The rest of the extensive Hendrix catalogue was compiled after his death. *Cry Of Love* (1971), *Experience* (1971), *Isle Of Wight* (1971), *Rainbow Bridge* (1971), *Hendrix In The West* (1971), *More Experience* (1972), *War Heroes* (1972), *Soundtrack Recordings From The Film Jimi Hendrix* (1973), *Loose Ends* (1974), *Crash Landing* (1975), *Midnight Lightnin'* (1975), *Nine To The Universe* (1980), *The Jimi Hendrix Concerts* (1982), *Jimi Plays Monterey* (1986), *Band Of Gypsies 2* (1986), *Live At Winterland* (1987), *Radio One* (1988), *Live And Unreleased* (1989). Compilations: *Smash Hits* (1968), *The Essential Jimi Hendrix* (1978), *The Essential Jimi Hendrix Volume Two* (1979), *The Singles Album* (1983), *Kiss The Sky* (1984), *Cornerstones* (1990).

Further reading: *Hendrix - A Biography*, Chris Welch. *Jimi - An Intimate Biography Of Jimi Hendrix*, Curtis Knight. *Jimi Hendrix - Voodoo Child Of The Aquarian Age*, David Henderson. *Crosstown Traffic/Jimi Hendrix And Post-War Pop*, Charles Shaar Murray. *Jimi Hendrix - Electric Gypsy*, Harry Shapiro and Caesar Glebbeek. *The Hendrix Experience*, Mitch Mitchell and John Platt. *Are You Experienced*, Noel Redding and Carol Appleby.

Henley, John Lee

b. 13 February 1919, Canton, Mississippi, USA. Henley learned harmonica as a child and played for country dances. Moving to Chicago in 1943, he spent time with John Lee 'Sonny Boy' Williamson and picked up a good deal of technique, although his only record, recorded in 1958, owes more to the other Sonny Boy 'Rice Miller' Williamson, whom Henley had heard in Mississippi. He claimed to have accompanied Big Boy Spires, his regular partner at the time, on a 1953 recording session, but never regarded himself as a professional musician. Mid-60s recordings for Testament explored his early repertoire, with titles like 'Slidin' Devil,' 'Old Mule' and 'Two Step', but nothing was issued. Album: *World Of Trouble* (1982).

Henry, Clarence 'Frogman'

b. 19 March 1937, Algiers, Louisiana, USA. Henry began performing during the 50s with a New Orleans-based R&B group led by Bobby Mitchell. The singer later began work with bandleader Paul Gayten who accompanied him on his 1957 smash 'Ain't Got No Home'. However it was not until 1961 that 'But I Do' provided a follow-up to this novelty song, earning Henry a US number 4 and UK number 3 hit. Co-written by Bobby Charles, the song featured several seasoned New Orleans musicians, including the young Allen Toussaint, and relaunched Henry's career. The same year a further international success, 'You Always Hurt The One You Love' - previously a hit for the Mills Brothers in 1944 - echoed the same effortless style. The following single fared better in the UK, with 'Lonely Street'/'Why Can't You' just missing out the Top 40, but it was the artist's last substantial hit. He continued to record for a variety of companies, and a 1969 collection, *Is Alive And Well*, was acclaimed as a fine example of the 'Crescent City' style. Since then Henry has remained a popular live attraction in his adopted city.

Albums: *You Always Hurt The One You Love* (1961), *Is Alive And Well And Living In New Orleans* (1969), *New Recordings* (1979), *Little Green Frog* (1987). Compilation: *Legendary Clarence 'Frogman' Henry* (1983).

Hicks, Edna

b. 14 October 1895, New Orleans, Louisiana, USA, d. 16 August 1925, Chicago, Illinois, USA. Sister of Herb Morand, and step-sister of

Clarence 'Frogman' Henry

Lizzie Miles, Hicks was a light-voiced singer reminiscent of Esther Bigeou. In musical comedy from 1916, she recorded vaudeville blues for no fewer than eight companies in 1923-24. Her death, the result of burns after a domestic accident with gasoline, robbed the blues of a promising artist.

Hill, Bertha 'Chippie'

b. 15 March 1905, Charleston, South Carolina, USA, d. 7 May 1950, New York City, New York, USA. Bertha Hill was in show business as a singer and dancer aged 14, when she claimed to have stolen the show from Ethel Waters. Nicknamed for her youth and smallness, she settled in Chicago in the 20s. Her dark, hard voice was especially suited to blues, and good trumpeters seemed to inspire her; her finest recordings are those with Joe 'King' Oliver and Louis Armstrong. She retired in the late 20s on her marriage, but was persuaded to return to singing and recording for the growing white jazz audience in the mid-40s. Still a fine singer, she was a hit at the 1948 Paris Jazz Festival, but a promising second career was ended by a hit and run driver.
Albums: *Sounds Of The Twenties Vol. 4* (c.1965), *The Great Blues Singers* (c.1965), *Ida Cox/Chippie Hill* (c.1975), *When Women Sang The Blues* (1976), *Montana Taylor* (1991).

Hill, King Solomon

b. Joe Holmes, 1897, McComb, Mississippi, USA, d. 1949, Sibley, Louisiana, USA. Controversy long surrounded the identity of this itinerant blues singer. He fused the styles of his friends Sam Collins and Ramblin' Thomas (respectively south Mississippi and east Texas/Louisiana musicians), and elements from Blind Lemon Jefferson, into the eerie bottleneck guitar sound that accompanied his eerie falsetto on his 1932 recordings. His stage-name was derived from his address in Louisiana King Solomon Hill Baptist Church having given its name to the community of Yellow Pines. Holmes's masterpieces are 'The Gone Dead Train', and 'Whoopee Blues', the former a hobo's lament made the more impressive by his near impenetrable diction. 'Whoopee Blues' transforms an anodyne Lonnie Johnson song, imbuing it with the brimstone reek of Hell with which the singer threatens his erring girlfriend.

Album: *Backwoods Blues* (1991).

Hill, Rosa Lee

b. 25 September 1910, Como, Mississippi, USA, d. 22 October, 1968, Senatobia, Mississippi, USA. The daughter of Sid Hemphill, Rosa Lee Hill grew up in a musical family, playing a broad repertoire for both whites and blacks. Her recordings are confined to blues, which she sang 'from my mouth, and not from the heart', feeling them to be incompatible with her religious faith. Her blues are typical of Panola County, where she spent her whole life: accompanied by a droning guitar, her songs have an inward-looking, brooding feel, comparable to those of Fred McDowell. Hill and her husband were sharecroppers, and lived in dire poverty, particularly towards the end of their lives, when their house burned down and they had to move to a tumbledown shack.
Albums: *Blues Roll On* (1961), *Mississippi Delta Blues Vol. 2* (c.1970), *Roots Of The Blues* (1977).

Hines, Earl 'Fatha'

b. 28 December 1903, Dusquene, Pennsylvania, USA, d. 22 April 1983. An outstanding musician and a major figure in the evolution of jazz piano playing, Hines began his professional career in 1918. By that time he had already played cornet in brass bands in his home town. By 1923, the year in which he moved to Chicago, Hines had played in several bands around Pittsburgh and had been musical director for singer Lois Deppe. He performed in bands in Chicago and also toured theatre circuits based on the city. Among the bands with which he played were those led by Carroll Dickerson and Erskine Tate. In 1927 he teamed up with Louis Armstrong, playing piano, acting as musical director and, briefly, as Armstrong's partner in a nightclub (the third partner was Zutty Singleton). With Armstrong, Hines made a series of recordings in the late 20s which became and have remained classics: these were principally Hot Five, Hot Seven or Savoy Ballroom Five tracks but also included the acclaimed duet 'Weather Bird', one of the peaks of early jazz. Also in 1927 he was with Jimmy Noone's band and the following year was invited to form a band for a residency at Chicago's Grand Terrace. Although enormously popular at this engagement, the long residency, which lasted throughout the 30s, had an adverse

Earl 'Fatha' Hines

effect upon the band's standing in big band history. Less well-known than the bands that toured the USA during the swing era, it was only through records and occasional radio broadcasts from live venues that the majority of big band fans could hear what Hines was doing. With outstanding arrangers such as Jimmy Mundy and top-flight sectionmen including Trummy Young, Darnell Howard and Omer Simeon, the band was in fact advancing musically at a speed which outstripped many of its better-known contemporaries. This was particularly so after 1937 when arranger Budd Johnson arrived, bringing an advanced approach to big band styling which foreshadowed later developments in bebop. The reason why Hines stayed at the Grand Terrace for so long is open to question, but some who were there have suggested that he had little choice: the Grand Terrace was run by mobsters and, as Jo Jones remarked, 'Earl had to play with a knife at his throat and a gun at his back the whole time he was in Chicago'.

In the early 40s Hines hired several musicians who modernized the band's sound still further, including Dizzy Gillespie, Charlie Parker and Wardell Gray, which led to Duke Ellington dubbing the band 'the incubator of bebop'. Hines also hired singers Billy Eckstine and Sarah Vaughan; but he eventually folded the big band in 1947 and the following year joined Louis Armstrong's All Stars, where he remained until 1951. He then led his own small groups, holding a long residency at the Club Hangover in San Francisco. In 1957 he toured Europe as co-leader, with Jack Teagarden, of an all-star band modelled on the Armstrong All Stars. For all this activity, however, Hines's career in the 50s and early 60s was decidedly low-profile and many thought his great days were over. A series of concerts in New York in 1964, organized by writer Stanley Dance, changed all that. A succession of fine recording dates capitalized upon the enormous success of the concerts and from that point until his death Hines toured and recorded extensively.

Despite the heavy schedule he set himself the standard of his performances was seldom less than excellent and was often beyond praise. If, in later years, his accompanying musicians were of a very different calibre to their leader, his own inventiveness and command were at their peak and some of his performances from the 70s rank with his groundbreaking work from half a century before. A brilliant and dynamic player, Hines had an astonishing technique which employed a dramatic tremolo. As indicated, as a soloist his powers of invention were phenomenal. However, he was initially an ensemble player who later developed into a great solo artist, unlike many pianists who began as soloists and had to adapt their style to suit a role within a band. Hines adopted an innovative style for the piano in jazz in which he clearly articulated the melody, used single note lines played in octaves, and employed his distinctive tremolo in a manner that resembled that of a wind player's vibrato. All this helped to land his technique with the potentially misleading term, 'trumpet style'. The number of pianists Hines influenced is impossible to determine: it is not too extravagant to suggest that everyone who played jazz piano after 1927 was in some way following the paths he signposted. Certainly his playing was influential upon Nat 'King' Cole, Mary Lou Williams, Billy Kyle and even the much less flamboyant Teddy Wilson, who were themselves important innovators of the 30s. During this period, perhaps only Art Tatum can be cited as following his own star.

Albums: *Earl Hines And His New Sound Orchestra* (1954), *The Earl Hines Trio* i (1954), *Earl Hines At Club Hangover* (1955), *Earl 'Fatha' Hines Plays Fats Waller* (1956), *Earl 'Fatha' Hines And His All Stars Vols 1 & 2* (1956), *After You've Gone* (1956), *Here Is Earl Hines* (1957), *The Earl Hines Trio* ii (1957), *The Earl Hines Trio* iii (1957), *The Jack Teagarden-Earl Hines All Stars In England* (1957), *The Earl Hines Quartet* i (1958), *The Earl Hines Quartet* ii (1960), *A Monday Date* (1961), *Earl Hines And His All Stars* i (1961), *Earl Hines And His All Stars* ii (1961), *Earl Hines With Ralph Carmichael And His Orchestra* (1963), *Spontaneous Explorations* (1964), *The Earl Hines Trio At The Little Theatre, New York* (1964), *Fatha* (1964), *The Earl Hines Quartet* iii (1964), *The Earl Hines Trio* iv (1964), *The Earl Hines Trio With Roy Eldridge And Coleman Hawkins Live At The Village Vanguard* (1965), *Earl Hines & Roy Eldridge At The Village Vanguard* (1965), *Hines '65/Tea For Two* (1965), *Blues In Thirds* (1965), *Paris Session* (1965), *Father's Freeway* (1965), *Once Upon A Time* (1966), *Hines' Tune* (1965), *The Earl Hines Trio* v (1966), *Earl Hines At The Scandiano di Reggio, Emilia* (1966), *Blues So Low (For Fats)* (1966), *Dinah* (1966), *The Earl Hines Trio* vi (1966), *Blues And Things* (1967), *Fatha Blows Best* (1968), *A Night At Johnnie's* (1968), *Master Jazz Piano Vols 1 & 2* (1969), *Earl Hines At Home* (1969), *Boogie Woogie On St Louis Blues* i (1969), *Quintessential Recording Session* (1970), *Fatha And His Flock On Tour* (1970), *Earl Hines And Maxine Sullivan Live At The Overseas Press Club, New York* (1970), *Earl Hines In Paris* (1970), *It Don't Mean A Thing If It Ain't Got That Swing* (1970), *Master Jazz Piano Vols 3 & 4* (1971), with Jaki Byard *Duet* (1972), *Earl Hines* i (1972), *Solo Walk In Tokyo* (1972), *Tour De Force* (1972), *Earl Hines Plays Duke Ellington Vols 1-3* (1972), *My Tribute To Louis* (c.1972-73), *Hines Does Hoagy* (c.1972-73), *Hines Comes In Handy* (c.1972-73), *Back On The Street* (1973), *Live At The New School* (1973), *Quintessential Recording Session Continued* (1973), *An Evening With Earl Hines And His Quartet* (1973), *Earl Hines Plays George Gershwin* (1973), *The Earl Hines Quartet* iv (1973), *Swingin' Away* (1973), *Quintessential 1974* (c.1973-74), *Earl Hines* ii (1974), *One For My Baby* (1974), *Master Of Jazz Vol. 2* (1974), *Earl Hines At The New School Vol. 2* (1974), *West Side Story* (1974), *Live!* (1974), *Fireworks* (1974), *Hines '74* (1974), *At Sundown* (1974), *The Dirty Old Men* (1974), *Jazz Giants In Nice* (1974), *Piano Portraits Of Australia* (1974), *Concert In Argentina* (1974), *Earl Hines In New Orleans With Wallace Davenport And Orange Kellin Vols 1 & 2* (1975), *Earl Hines Plays Duke Ellington Vol. 4* (1975), *Earl Hines At Saralee's* (1976), *Live At Buffalo* (1976), *Jazz Is His Old Lady And My Old Man* (c.1977), *Lionel Hampton Presents Earl 'Fatha' Hines* (1977), *Giants Of Jazz Vol. 2* (1977), *Earl Hines In New Orleans* (1977), *Father Of Modern Jazz Piano/Boogie Woogie On St Louis Blues* ii (1977), *East Of The Sun* (1977), *Texas Ruby Red* (1977), *Deep Forest* i (1977), with Harry 'Sweets' Edison *Earl Meets Harry* (1978), with Edison, Eddie 'Lockjaw' Davis *Earl Meets Sweets And Jaws* (1978), *Fatha's Birthday* (1981), *Deep Forest* ii (1982), *Earl Hines Live At The New School* (1983). Compilations: *Louis Armstrong Classics Vol. 3* (1928 recordings), *Swingin' Down* (1932-33 recordings), *Fatha Jumps* (1940-42 recordings), *The Indispensable Earl Hines* (1944-66 recordings), *Earl Hines Big Band* (1945-46 recordings).

Further reading: *The World of Earl Hines*, Stanley Dance.

Hinton, Joe

b. 15 November 1929, Evansville, Indiana, USA, d. 13 August 1968, Boston, USA. Hinton recorded a string of R&B singles for the Texas-based Back Beat label in the late 50s and 60s, the best known of which, a cover of Willie Nelson's 'Funny', reached the Top 20 in the USA. Hinton first applied his falsetto to gospel music with the Blair Singers and the Spirit Of Memphis Quartet. He moved to Memphis, Tennessee to work with the latter group, which recorded for the Peacock label. In 1958 Peacock president Don Robey convinced Hinton to switch to secular music and in 1958 signed him to the Back Beat subsidiary. Hinton's first single for the label was 'Ladder of Love', which did not sell well. It was not until the 1963 'You Know It Ain't Right' that Hinton reached the charts, at number 20. After one other minor chart single, 'Better To Give Than Receive', Hinton had his greatest success with the Nelson ballad, which rose to number 13 in 1964. There was one further single in the charts that year, 'I Want A Little Girl', but Hinton's career declined after that. He recorded for Back Beat until 1968, when he died of skin cancer.
Albums: *Funny (How Time Slips Away)* (1964), *Joe Hinton* (1973).

Hogan, Silas

b. 15 September 1911, Louisiana, USA. Hogan learned guitar from his uncles, but also from records by artists such as Kokomo Arnold and Blind Lemon Jefferson. He moved to Baton Rouge during his late 20s and over the years established himself on the city's blues scene. His band first recorded in 1959, with a record issued under the name of drummer Jimmy Dotson. From 1962-65 Hogan made a series of fine blues singles with producer Jay Miller, issued on Excello Records. These included upbeat R&B as well as doomy downhome blues, but their quality is consistently high - the band always tight, and Hogan singing with power and conviction. The influence of Jimmy Reed and Lightnin' Slim is occasionally evident, but Hogan always retains his own distinctive sound. During the blues revival of the late 60s and early 70s, a few recordings were made by Hogan in Baton Rouge and released on Arhoolie and Blue Horizon. Later, in the 80s he became one of the resident artists at Tabby Thomas's Blues Box,

and has recently recorded an album issued by Blues South West in the UK.
Albums: *Free Hearted Man* (1961-65), *Trouble At Home* (1962-65), *The Godfather* (1989).

Hogg, Andrew 'Smokey'

b. 27 January 1914, Westconnie, Texas, USA, d. 1 May 1960, McKinney, Texas. USA. Born in northeast Texas Smokey came from a clan that included blues singers Lightnin' Hopkins, and John Hogg. He learned to play the guitar, and piano early in life under the instruction of his father, Frank. One of seven children he looked upon music as a means of escape from labour in the fields. He sang around Dallas and Greenville and was popular enough to be known as Little Peetie Wheatstraw after his idol. He worked joints with men like B.K. Turner (Black Aces) and D.C. Bender. In 1937 he recorded two tracks for Decca, which, though much valued by collectors, made no impression on the blues buying public of the time. Sometime during the war he was drafted and served in the US Army but by 1947 he was in Los Angeles, where he recorded for the Exclusive label, again without much success. His breakthrough came after he had moved back to Texas where he recorded 'Too Many Drivers'; released under the Modern label in 1947. Back in Los Angeles, but still for Modern, he recorded his biggest hit 'Little School Girl'. Now established, he began, like many of his contemporaries, to hop from label to label, recording for Specialty, Imperial, SIW, Mercury and many smaller concerns. He enjoyed a good deal of popularity, especially with older fans, and this allowed him to survive the initial impact of rock 'n' roll. Smokey's work seems to be something of an acquired taste and collectors are divided quite violently when judging its worth. He had no such problems with his black audience when his rural blues were sung to a small (often saxophone led) band accompaniment and were appearing on labels from Texas to the coast.
Albums: *Smokey Hogg* (1962), *I'm So Lonely* (1964), *Original Folk Blues* (1967), *Sing The Blues* (1971), with Earl Hooker, Lightnin' Hopkins *Hooker, Hopkins And Hogg* (1973), *U Better Watch That Jive* (1974), *Going Back Home* (1984), *Everybody Needs Help* (1986).

Hogg, John

b. 1912, Westconnie, Texas, USA. Hogg was the reason that his cousin Smokey Hogg went to try his luck in Los Angeles in 1947. John had been there since 1942, after several years of roaming which took him as far from his Texas home of Greenville as Denver, Colorado and Oklahoma - where he worked as a rodeo performer. He was never a committed blues man but did have the advantage of being taught some guitar by the Los Angeles based Pee Wee Crayton. Hogg worked occasional gigs, retaining his day job. He recorded for Mercury and Octive in 1951, probably on the strength of his relationship with Smokey, and proved himself a performer of some ability. The pattern of treating music as a side-line continued although he did record again for Advent Records in 1974, appearing that year at the San Diego Blues Festival.
Compilation: *Texas Blues* (1965).

Hogg, Willie 'Smokey'

b. 19 November 1908, Centerville, Texas, USA. Poor recording, and the record company's half-hearted attempt to pass him off as the real (and long dead) Smokey Hogg, obscured the genuine abilities of this New York based blues singer, who played good electric guitar in duet with Benny Jefferson, and sang traditionally based blues in a high voice. Stylistically, he was in the southwestern mainstream, his music more reminiscent of Lowell Fulson than of the man he claimed to be, though as might be expected, there are echoes of the real Smokey Hogg.
Compilation: *The All Star Blues World Of Spivey Records* (1970).

Hokum Boys

'Hokum', with its connotations of verbal cleverness, was first applied to black music on record in the billing of 'Tampa Red's Hokum Jug Band' (performing 'It's Tight Like That', hokum's archetypal song). Tampa and his partner Georgia Tom were prominent in the hokum craze of the late 20s and early 30s. The Hokum Boys were varied in personnel, and appeared on various labels; besides Tampa and Tom, participants included Big Bill Broonzy, Ikey Robinson, Jimmy Blythe, Blind Blake, Teddy Edwards, Casey Bill Weldon, Black Bob, Washboard Sam and 'hokum girl' Jane Lucas.

Also in the spirit of hokum were Frankie Jaxon (vocalist with the Hokum Jug Band) and Kansas City Kitty. Hokum groups favoured danceable rhythms and skilful musicianship, but the 'hokum' part of the billing seems chiefly to refer to the verbal content, heavily reliant on *double entendres* which are often ingenious and sometimes witty, and which probably seemed less tedious in the pre-album era. It has been plausibly suggested that the appeal of the Hokum Boys, apart from their obvious entertainment value, was to a black audience newly migrated from the south, and wanting to confirm its newly urbanized sophistication.
Albums: *You Can't Get Enough Of That Stuff* (1976), *The Remaining Titles* (1988), *The Famous Hokum Boys* (1989).

Holiday, Billie 'Lady Day'

b. Eleanora Fagan, 7 April 1915, Philadelphia, Pennsylvania, USA. d. 17 July 1959. Billie taught herself to sing during her early teens in Baltimore, Maryland, where she was brought up until moving to New York in 1928 or 1929, (accounts vary). Factual inaccuracies and elements of myth and exaggeration have clouded the picture of her formative years despite the best efforts of researchers to present her career story in a properly ordered manner. Until quite recently (c.1990) it was generally accepted that Holiday had been born in Baltimore, as the singer herself asserted in her 1956 autobiography, *Lady Sings The Blues*. But in view of the tortuous nature of her childhood and the fact that her mother, Sadie Fagan, and father, Clarence Holiday, took her to Baltimore while she was still very young - and they were both teenagers at the time of her birth - it is hardly surprising that memories of her first years should be less than reliable. Holidays's parents probably never married, and it seems unlikely that they lived together for any length of time. Clarence Holiday, a banjo and guitar player is remembered principally for his work with Fletcher Henderson's band in the early 30s. He remains a somewhat shadowy figure who left his daughter in the care of Fagan or other relatives. As a musician with touring bands in the later 20s Holiday *père* would often be away from home. According to Billie, life 'on the road' meant that Baltimore came to be 'just another one-night stand' on his itinerary.

Billie Holiday

During the stay with Henderson, which lasted until 1932, the guitarist severed connections with the Fagans and in Billie's words 'married a West Indian woman named Fanny'. However Billie proved hard to shake off after joining her mother in New York's Harlem district, and when rent on their apartment was overdue, she confronted Clarence at the Roseland Ballroom – where Henderson's orchestra enjoyed a lengthy 'residency' – and extorted money by threatening to show him up publicly. These fragments of information about Holiday's deprived, cruelly exploited and extravagantly ill-fated early history have significance for several reasons. They prove she had learned how to survive extreme poverty, race prejudice and the injustice of black ghetto life by the time she was 15 or 16, and lend credence to claims that she was 'big for her age' and could pass for a girl of 18 or so (the reason Clarence yielded to her demands when she threatened to call him 'Daddy' in front of his young female admirers). Also, they hint at a more influential relationship between father and daughter (no matter how tenuous it might have been) than Holiday revealed in print. This enigmatic association is typical of the Holiday family. Clarence, a more than competent guitarist with a reputation for 'good time' in a rhythm section, seemed surrounded by paradox. Through the 30s, even after his barely noted death early in 1937, compilers of books which included record reviews and personnel listings employed the spellings Haliday or Halliday, and there is evidence that Billie used that name occasionally until persuaded to sing professionally as Billie Holiday. Her father might have had reasons for playing his identity cards close to his chest – Billie discovered at Clarence's funeral a half-brother and half-sister she didn't know she had, present with their mother, a wealthy white woman – but for jazz historians the interest lies in tracking down a link between her father's fine, relaxed sense of rhythm and her own astonishing command of time and swing: *laid-back* swing of a type not previously heard on records by singers. Not that rhythmic expertise was the most potent feature of Holiday's revolutionary style. Her use of tonal variation and vibrato, skill at phrasing after the manner of a jazz instrumentalist, of re-shaping a melody line to make it her own and also fitting in the jazz context; her approach to the lyric of a popular song so as to enhance its meaning in the light of her unique personality – all these qualities, and many more, were elements in the work of a truly original artist.

Since Holiday had very little schooling and no formal musical training, her extraordinary creative gifts were intuitive in the first place. However, her clear diction, methods of manipulating pitch, improvising on a theme, establishing with uncanny accuracy a variety of emotional moods ranging from the joyous, optimistic, flirtatious even, to the tough, defiant, proud, disillusioned and buoyantly barrelhouse, were not plucked out of the air, acquired without practice. In other words, Holiday 'paid her dues', to use a jazz musicians' cliché; and this she did in a most demanding milieu, that of obscure New York speakeasies and Harlem nightclubs such as Pods' and Jerry's Log Cabin, the Yeah Man, Monette Moore's Supper Club, the Hot-Cha, Alabama Grill and Dickie Wells's place. She even sang at the local Elks club in order to pick up a few dollars in tips. Throughout adolescence she had considered singing to be a natural accomplishment, unlikely to become a source of income. As soon as she found there was money in it, she decided to sing for a living. Poverty was the spur, the initial incentive, but the dedication she then displayed to the mastering of jazz-craft is not easy to explain. No amount of theorizing will help to a real understanding of her seemingly instinctive gift for music-making. Mildred Bailey, a talented and already established jazz vocalist, heard swiftly of the appearance of a new 'voice' on 133rd Street – described by Holiday as 'the real swing street' during the early 30s – and visited the Harlem club to judge for herself. Bailey, hardly likely to deliver a charitable assessment of any potential rival, admitted to her husband, vibraphonist and xylophonist Red Norvo: 'That girl's got it.' The 'it' would be difficult to define, as a streak of genius always has been, but what Holiday possessed nobody could teach her. She was a perfectionist in her fashion, depending upon her excellent ear, innate taste and honesty of purpose to make up artistically for her small voice and range. This integrity, so far as vocal sound and style went, is the more baffling because of the insecurity and brutal ugliness of her childhood. Family separations were no fault of Sadie Fagan's; being black and impoverished, with little financial support from Clarence Holiday, she had no choice but to take 'domestic' work where she could find it. She felt protective of Billie, anxious about her moral welfare, but was seldom in a position to supervise her; and Billie could have done with a restraining hand. Jazz critic Whitney Balliett has written that 'she was a wild one' during the early years in Baltimore, sent to a Catholic reformatory at the age of ten and introduced to prostitution two years later. Holiday was consistent in claiming that she had been committed to the Catholic institution on false charges made by a would-be rapist, also that she had been raped at a very early age and while still a virgin. Doubtless there is truth in these protestations, and none that knew her as an adolescent dispute her independent spirit and stubborn refusal to compromise over principles held dear. She summed up her capacity for survival in the somewhat sardonic yet self-satisfied lyric of her own creation, 'Billie's Blues'. On later versions - but not on the first recording, cut in 1936 - she employs (and to great effect) the lines: 'I ain't good looking, and my hair ain't curled/but my mother she give me something, it's goin' to carry me through this world'.

Holiday might have inherited, apart from looks and colouring and such physical attributes as tone of voice, some characteristics of behaviour and temperament: resiliency, determination, combativeness, a warm and generous nature, an enthusiasm for cooking and eating food, and, we can assume, a liking for the company of jazz musicians. Sadie Fagan exerted a benign influence on her wayward daughter, in so far as that was possible, bringing to her lifestyle the nearest thing to stability it had known. However, the real marvel is not that Holiday overcame the vicissitudes and traumas of those early years to blossom into a healthy, attractive young woman with natural dignity, insidious charm, pride in her ability, and a kind of sensuous charge which elicited a powerful response from the majority of men in her audience. That is wonder enough; the miracle is how she came from nowhere onto the music scene with a distinctive style of jazz singing which sounded wholly original and marked her at once as a major new star, for those with the ears and judgement to perceive it.

One such was Benny Goodman, others included Norvo and Bailey and the well-connected record producer and talent spotter John Hammond. It has frequently been stated that fame and success depend largely on an artist or performer being in the right place at the right time. In Holiday's case, the lucky break came when she found herself by sheer chance singing in front of Hammond in Monette's joint. In early 1933 Hammond was 22 and already in the habit of making the rounds of Harlem places where jazz and blues entertainment might be found. On the night in question he stopped off at the 133rd Street club with the intention of listening to Monette. Instead of the blues singer, a performer who had been recording since 1923, he heard the unknown girl deputizing for Monette (absent, playing in a Broadway show) and was immediately impressed. 'She sang popular songs in a manner that made them completely her own', Hammond wrote later in his autobiography, praising her excellent memory for lyrics and sense of phrasing. He also gave Holiday the first press notice of her career. In April 1933 it appeared in the *Melody Maker*, and Hammond wrote: 'This month there has been a real find in the person of a singer called Billie Halliday'; again, the confusion about Billie's name. In addition, she never felt comfortable with her given first name, Eleanora - although her mother continued to use it - and adopted that of film actress Billie Dove, a childhood favourite whom she regarded as the epitome of glamour. 'I was crazy for her', Billie recalled. 'I tried to do my hair like her and eventually I borrowed her name'. If the movie star had a beneficial influence as role model - and with hindsight it is clear that a more fitting adopted name would be hard to find - two prime musical influences, Bessie Smith, and Louis Armstrong, were the key inspirational figures in her jazz development. Remembering how she used to run errands in Baltimore for 'a woman on the corner' because the woman (in fact the madam of a brothel) let her play records by Smith, finest of the classic blues singers of the 20s, and trumpet king Armstrong, Holiday said: 'Many's the whipping I got for listening to their records when I was a child. Guess I was nine years old then. Been listening to Pops and Bessie ever since that time. Sure, I copied Bessie and Louis but not note for note. Their music inspired me'. Holiday's earlier recordings prove the point.

Although subtle influences of Armstrong's trumpet and vocal style can be detected in her singing, the overall effect is entirely personal. Her way of putting a lyric over is shared by no other vocalist of that era. When she has finished, a song sounds vividly new, filled with transcendental meaning and transformed by a hundred and one elaborations of tone, tune and accent. What Holiday learned from the example of her twin mentors was the desirability of finding out *your* best way of expressing what you wish to say and then sticking to it with the conviction that it is as good a style as any that preceded or followed it. Broadcaster and writer Benny Green (in a liner note for the album *A Billie Holiday Memorial*) refers to her refusal to conform to the accepted commercial formulas and her insistence upon being unable to change her way of singing. 'She couldn't or wouldn't sing a song strictly as written because she was simply not equipped to do so', he observes, adding perceptively: 'Or rather, she was too richly equipped to do so, and it is because of this artistic obstinacy of hers that we have been bequeathed a recorded legacy of singing that is startling in its freshness, its animation, its unblemished jazz taste, and above all in its unashamed sincerity'. This is where Hammond came into the picture as a decisive influence on her future. He represented a real break in Holiday's long run of bad luck because he had the power and willingness to forward the careers of those he thought worthy of special aid. The enthusiasm of his initial reaction to the promising youngster was shown in his description, 'She is incredibly beautiful and sings as well as anybody I ever heard', printed in the 1933 *Melody Maker*. Living up to his reputation, Hammond 'got into the habit of bringing people uptown to hear Billie'. Benny Goodman shared his opinion of Holiday and agreed to record with her. In the course of three sessions during November and December 1933, two songs were recorded with Goodman in charge of a nine-man studio group, most of whom were strangers to the already nervous Holiday. 'Your Mother's Son-in-Law' was the first record she ever made; 'Riffin' The Scotch', a lightweight novelty concoction, was the second.

Neither was successful as a showcase for her -

nor, in truth, designed to be - because her role in the proceedings presented Holiday as band vocalist in a setting which stressed the instrumental prowess of Goodman, trombonist Jack Teagarden and other soloists. However, the singer managed to stamp her imprint on the vocal refrains and, for a young black performer with no experience of recording and, in her words, 'afraid to sing in the mike', came across as reasonably confident. For Hammond, the disc debut was a disappointment, the record sold poorly and made little impression at the time. In retrospect, though, its importance emerges. Holiday was on her way, and as Hammond noted in his autobiography, those unregarded items 'are now collectors' classics', adding that Holiday and Goodman had both 'taken a giant step forward'. As for the Lady (she had already earned that nickname on the Harlem club circuit for her regal sense of dignity), expecting little she was not disappointed. Holiday's nickname was amended by Lester Young who added a typically personal touch, calling her Lady Day. Billie responded in kind: 'I named him the President, and actually I was the Vice President . . . of the Vipers Society. We were the Royal Family of Harlem'. Royalties were not routinely paid to recording artists in those days, and Holiday remembered receiving a flat fee of about 35 dollars for her work. Having a record on the market was no great deal; she placed little value on either song, not bothering to include them in her club or stage programmes or future recording repertoire.

Looking back, during a 1956 radio interview, she told Willis Conover her voice sounded 'so high and funny' that 'Your Mother's Son-in-Law' could have been a comedy performance. Possibly Holiday under-valued this number which, with its cheerful and ingenious lyric, became a big feature for songstress Valaida Snow in *Blackbirds Of 1934*. Holiday continued her round of club dates and, early in 1935, her career was given a boost when she won a week's engagement at the Apollo Theatre, Harlem's most famous and, for up-and-coming artists, formidable entertainment centre. Holiday, then just 20 years old, felt so scared of the notorious audience that she had to be pushed on stage from the wings. Regaining some composure after the first number, she battled on to enjoy wholehearted acclaim at the end of her third choice, 'The Man I Love'. The Apollo rewarded her with a further booking. 'Billie returned to the theatre for the week of 2 August 1935', writes John Chilton in his *Billie's Blues* biography, 'only this time she changed her billing: instead of Halliday she called herself Holiday'.

By this time too, the singer had returned to the record studio (2 July 1935) and used her real name on a session organized by Hammond and directed by Teddy Wilson. In Wilson, an accomplished musician and sensitive pianist, Holiday had found the sympathetic partner she needed to reveal the full range of her talents. The four songs picked for this groundbreaking record date were above average - 'I Wished On The Moon' and 'Miss Brown To You' were film numbers - and the easygoing jam-session atmosphere suited Holiday admirably. She responded to Wilson's masterly accompaniments and solo playing, and to the brilliance of Goodman, Roy Eldridge and Ben Webster, and similar jazz aces on subsequent recordings. They in turn seemed to be spurred by the rhythmic thrust and innovative magic of her singing. Hammond, who booked the pick-up bands from the best musicians available in New York City at the relevant time, was in charge of the strategy which enabled these sessions to retain the relaxed mood he was after, and did so much to win the series of Wilson-Holiday records a reputation as some of the finest small-group-with-vocal jazz put on wax during the 30s. He worked closely with Wilson in the selection of material and personnel, did what he could to influence the type of arrangement used, and the two men agreed on informal get-togethers by Holiday and the pianist in order to spare her (and the band) the slog of lengthy rehearsals. This format was adhered to for various reasons, not least of which was the relatively low cost of the product coupled with the fact that it turned out to be ideal for the burgeoning jukebox trade. The musicians worked out simple routines for each number on the spot, depending largely on 'head arrangements' (thus precluding the need for paid orchestrations), and three or four usable titles emerged from most of the sessions. The records paid off sufficiently well to satisfy the market men.

To those of Holiday's generation, including jazz collectors in Europe, coming fresh to these wondrous sounds as manifested through a gramophone horn or speaker, the matter of sales figures and profitability would not have merited consideration. Here was a rising star who could invest ordinary popular songs with the emotional kick of a first-rate blues or ballad composition. Whether the 78s were released under Wilson's name or Holiday's - and since 10 July 1936 she had achieved own-name status on the Vocalion label - the right stuff was still there. Often the musical mixture had a different feel, Wilson being replaced by various pianists from time to time - but almost every record was an exciting discovery and proved to be a lasting pleasure. Young enthusiasts liked her work inordinately without knowing precisely why, but this hardly mattered until she began to alter, and she thought improve, her expressive technique. Then, a section of her hard-core jazz following felt she had taken a downward path.

Following appearances at a few slightly more prestigious venues than hitherto, Holiday sang with the bands of Count Basie (1937-38) and Artie Shaw (1938). She enjoyed the company of the bandsmen; the majority of them enjoyed her spirit as 'one of the guys', and greatly admired her as a vocalist. (Her opposite number on the bandstand was blues singer Jimmy Rushing.) In spite of this rapport, the period with Basie was not a consistently happy one for Holiday, who encountered setbacks on the road and rejection by management people who disliked her 'way-out' style, or criticism from friends advising her to tailor her singing to the perceived requirements of the orchestra. As usual, Lady Day refused to compromise. On top of these problems, she had been much affected by learning on 1 March 1937 - by a long-distance call from Dallas, Texas - of her father's death. She quit the Basie band, or was fired, in February of 1938 and, reservations about the touring life notwithstanding, joined Shaw almost at once and was on the road again, this time with a white band. She ran into trouble with racists, especially in the 'Jim Crow' Southern states, and before the end of the year had left Shaw. It was to be her final farewell as a band member: from now on she would be presented as a solo artist. It is worth noting that with Shaw Holiday recorded only a single title, 'Any Old Time' (24 July 1938), and this caused ill-feeling between them, although much blame can be laid at the doors of music publishers and record producers who preferred to hear their 'properties' sung more or less as written. Also, contractual obligations clashed, Holiday having signed with a company which prohibited her recording for any other label; and inevitably disputes arose over money. In defence of her artistry, it has to be said that Billie endowed the refrain of 'Any Old Time' with her own vocal texture and message. A warmth of sentiment was always vital to Holiday if any musical collaboration was to be successful in her estimation; her association with Shaw was reputedly well on the warm side, which made the split more regrettable.

She explained her viewpoint on sympathetic accompaniment to a *Melody Maker* reporter on her visit to England in February 1954. 'I prefer to work with musicians who can play something pretty while I'm singing without getting in my way. I was always crazy about Lester's tenor playing. He blew music I liked, didn't try to drown the singer. Teddy was the same, trumpeter Buck Clayton too. And Hodges has always been my boy.' The love of singing and playing came through from the start. But how was it achieved? Hammond made this point: 'It astonishes me at how casually we were able to assemble such all-star groups. It wasn't that we didn't know how great they were. We did. It was simply a Golden Age . . . an abundance of superbly skilled exponents on every instrument. And yet business wasn't that good. And they all came for union scale'. Astonishing also was the way the new girl equalled in heat and fire power the best efforts of these seasoned professionals. Wilson confirms the element of job satisfaction present. 'Those sessions were sheer joy. Since everyone knew he was playing with the best there was, everyone on the date stimulated everybody else. That's why those records stand up so well 40 years later.' We could add 10 or 20 years to that figure, while realising that such conditions - ideal for the creation of brief jazz masterworks - cannot and should not be replicated today.

All probabilities suggest that the records closest to her heart were those recorded in association with Wilson, her beloved Lester Young and trumpet favourite Buck Clayton. And there is an emerging consensus that the inspirational partnership of Holiday and Young - musical and emotional - led to a batch of the finest vocal interpretations of her life. Undeniably, these discs and others made between 1935 and 1942 are among 'the crown jewels of jazz', to use the phrase of Dan Morgenstern (Director, Institute of Jazz Studies, Rutgers University), and will repay and reward careful study and regular replays. Some songs and performances are better than just good, and some comparatively poor - a consequence of the spontaneous approach - but Billie's gift for transforming lyrics enabled her to turn 'drivel into poetry', as Morgenstern put it.

Early in 1939, Holiday's career took a giant step upwards. Again Hammond proffered a helping hand, as did Barney Josephson who dreamed of running a racially integrated nightclub in New York's Greenwich Village. Hammond was the one who invested in the project and, asked to advise on appropriate attractions for liberal patrons, recommended Holiday. Thus, she opened at Café Society with Frankie Newton's band that January, scored at once with the multi-racial audience and had her first taste of stardom at the Café whose slogan read 'The wrong place for the right people'. Holiday stayed there for nearly nine months, during which time she was given a song-poem, 'Strange Fruit', Lewis Allen's anti-lynching protest, which led her to a real hit record and new and international fame as a purveyor of socially significant ballads. Those who knew the singer well swear she suspected the author's motives at first, and was reluctant to perform 'Strange Fruit' in public in spite of Josephson's special pleading. When she agreed, she still considered it an unwise choice - until impressed by its spellbinding impact on the customers. The song continued to be identified with Holiday who, on 20 April 1939, made a record of this controversial title for the Commodore label, her own having refused to release it. Opinion divided sharply on the merits of 'Strange Fruit' as a jazz vehicle, and the effect it had upon her instinctive taste and artistry. Critics feared it could lead to a self-consciousness which would destroy the strangely innocent qualities of earlier days. Billie, some decreed, was an interpreter of popular song, not *serious* music but music to be taken seriously. After 'Strange Fruit' brought acclaim as an exponent of protest song, the danger lay in her taking herself seriously as a dramatic heavyweight. Hammond's verdict on the 'Strange Fruit' story? 'The shock value helped her career (but) in many ways I think the song hurt Billie as an artist.'

A distinction needs to be made between live and recorded performance; the visual appeal, the stillness and beauty of her bearing, exerted an almost hypnotic influence on audiences, and her live recitation of the anti-lynching lyric seldom failed to convince crowds, whether large or small, black or white, with its sincerity. On the Commodore 78, likewise, the integrity of the performance as a whole is patently clear (after a slightly dubious instrumental opening sets the mood) as Holiday sees how to put the sombre message across without sensational stresses or flourishes, trusting as ever to her own way of doing it. The record sold well in the USA and enjoyed a *succès d'estime* in Europe where copies were understandably scarce. Three more titles were cut for Commodore on that session, all taken at leisurely speeds and emphasizing the vocalist's role. Ironically, a blues called 'Fine And mellow', casually made up the night before by Holiday and Commodore's Milt Gabler, who insisted on recording a blues, became Holiday's 'biggest-selling record' and a staple item in her repertoire. Originally released on the reverse side of 'Strange Fruit,' the blues might have assisted the sales of the 78, since the protest song was thought by numbers of radio stations to be too inflammatory to broadcast. Although Holiday's name was regarded by the general public as being virtually synonymous with blues ('Billie's Blues', 'Lady Sings . . . ', etc) she did not specialize in that idiom and did not consider herself a blues singer, for all her devotion to 'the Empress', Bessie Smith.

Scottish author Iain Lang once wrote that Holiday's voice was to the swing era what Smith's was to the jazz of the 20s, and as the sound of jazz progressed into the 40s and 50s Holiday responded positively if unwisely to some changes in the musical and social climate. Already an eager drinker, smoker (of tobacco as well as marijuana), eater, dresser and shopper with a sexual appetite described as 'healthy-plus', she embraced the hard-drug culture of the 40s as to the manner born. She was having troublesome love affairs, nothing new to her, but on 25 August 1941 married Jimmy Monroe. It was a union that did nothing to ease her situation, and before long the marriage broke

up. Nobody now can say when exactly, and by whom, but Holiday was turned on to opium and then heroin. The details are unimportant; the addiction hardly affected her singing at first, although her behaviour grew increasingly unpredictable, and she gained a reputation for unreliability. At last she was earning real money, as much as $1,000 weekly, it was reported, and about half that sum was going to pay for her 'habit'. Nevertheless, she had got the public recognition she craved. In the first *Esquire* magazine poll (1943) the critics voted her best vocalist, topping Mildred Bailey and Ella Fitzgerald in second and third places respectively.

In the mid-40s Holiday was a stellar act, in spite of drug problems, and one accompanist spoke years later of her 'phenomenal musicianship.' The series of 78s - 36 titles made for Decca Records with a wide variety of more commercially acceptable accompaniments, including strings on a dozen or so sides and a vocal group on two - rank with the mature Holiday's most accomplished performances, technically speaking, although the revolutionary approach had become more calculating and mannered. To compensate, she turned up the emotional heat, depending on her imagination to deliver the right touch. Among these 78s, recorded between October 1944 and March 1950, are a number of gems of jazz singing - among them 'Lover Man', 'Porgy', 'Good Morning Heartache', 'You Better Go Now' and, as a welcome example of Lady Day back to top form as a commanding, exuberant, mistress of swing phrasing, the mid-tempo blues-drenched 'Now Or Never'. Holiday and band are really preaching here, the former giving her expressive enunciation a real outing on, for instance, the word 'consideration'. To round off this set, assembled on three *The Lady Sings* albums, she exhibits another facet of her craft by duetting comfortably with Armstrong on 'My Sweet Hunk O' Trash' and sharing space on a second Armstrong track. At this stage of her life Holiday experienced regular bouts of depression, pain and ill-health, not all of them brought about by over-indulgence in booze, drugs and 'bad-news' husbands or lovers.

In 1947 she was sentenced to a long term in the Federal Reformatory, West Virginia. The attendant publicity disastrously affected her confidence while drugs slowly weakened her physique. Running her own big band with husband Joe Guy in 1945 had cost Holiday a sum reckoned to be $35,000, and that blow was followed by the death of her mother, Sadie. According to John Chilton, for long afterwards Holiday would lament to friends 'Duchess is gone now you know', Duchess being the name Lester Young bestowed on Sadie Fagan in younger days. Another disappointment to Holiday's professional aspirations was her failure to secure a film break. She made brief appearances in the 1935 *Symphony In Black* and one or two shorts, but pinned her hopes to a part she was offered in the jazz film, *New Orleans* (1946). Both Holiday and her idol, Armstrong, had roles involving a great deal of music-making - much of it left in the cutting room - but the purported jazz story turned out to be a nonsensical fantasy; and worse, Holiday and Armstrong were cast as servants. She was quoted later as saying: 'I fought my whole life to keep from being somebody's damn maid. It was a real drag . . . to end up as a make-believe maid'. The picture failed but gave her valuable international exposure, and jazz fanciers were pleased to see and hear sequences featuring Holiday Armstrong, Kid Ory, Woody Herman and other musicians. For Holiday it was goodbye to themovies.

From the 50s on, Billie and trouble seemed often to be inseparable, and to recount a list of her brushes with police, managers, agents, club owners, drug-dealing lovers and assorted musicians would serve no useful purpose here. The changes in her music reflected the realities of her existence. 'Her way with a song', observed Henry Pleasants in *The Great American Popular Singers*, 'was to take it apart and put it together again in her own image'. As a consequence of her criminal record on drugs, Holiday's cabaret card was withdrawn by the New York Police Department. This prevented her appearance at any venue where liquor was on sale, and effectively ruled out New York nightclubs. In her eyes it amounted to an absolute injustice and one, she made clear on her first day in London, she bitterly resented. 'I'm trying to get my police card back', she told *Melody Maker,* 'I'm not the only one: some kids have been in trouble two, three times and are still working. So why pick on me? Somebody's

got a hand in it somewhere; some kind of politics'. Many would agree she was being picked on, perhaps on account of her intransigent nature. An old friend of hers, the singer-guitarist Josh White (one of very few who dared to encroach on her 'property' with a recording of 'Strange Fruit') later expressed this opinion: 'She'd had to fight all her life, and most people hate fighters, I can tell you'. Holiday had hoped to escape from her trials and torments in Europe, and it is likely she took solace from the gratifying appreciation, awareness of her work, and unquestioning friendship she found away from her homeland. This opinion is given credence by the upward lift noticeable in her performance. In the *New Yorker* of 4 November 1991 Whitney Balliett wrote that the old lightsome Holiday continued to surface occasionally. 'She sang, startlingly, like the bluebird of 1937 on a European tour she made in 1954. She also sang well', he went on, 'on the CBS television show *The Sound Of Jazz* in 1957'.

In England she spoke with assurance of being able to do things with a song she could never have achieved in girlish days. The concert at London's Royal Albert Hall, at which she delivered 15 songs, ending with 'Strange Fruit', gave substance to her boast. Afterwards, pianist Dill Jones said: 'Billie is one of the most poised women I've ever seen, and unquestionably the greatest jazz singer I have heard since Louis'. In 1956, her outspoken autobiography (written with William Dufty) brought increased fame, or notoriety. In 1957, Holiday was still making good money but by the following year the drink and drugs crucially influenced her vocal control, and the 'hoarsely eloquent voice', to borrow a description from Pleasants, had increased in hoarseness at the expense of the eloquence. Sandy Brown once remarked; 'In a certain sense, Billies's "bad" records are sometimes better than her good ones'. Pleasants, also tackled the subject of her decline with a sympathetic analysis. 'What little voice Billie ever had deteriorated towards the end of her life. In her progress along the dividing line between speech and sustained melody she wandered more often, and even farther, in the direction of speech. She also tended to wander farther and farther from pitch', he wrote. Adding that she had learned more about life and her own singing, he concluded: 'She was more resourceful. Her ornamentation was richer and more varied. The voice, formerly weak at the bottom, now had lovely dark tones down to the low G and F and even below'. Discerning listeners can hear all the recordings now and, having paid the money, will take their choice. One further segment of the Holiday discography deserves attention: it is the body of work on the Clef-Verve label (produced or master-minded by Norman Granz) which placed her in a jazz setting and encouraged her to shine when she and the small-group accompaniment felt right. These recordings (1952-57) include a number of satisfying performances, and several worthy of high praise. As for the final albums with the Ray Ellis Orchestra, they are, for the majority of jazz fanciers, a painfully acquired taste, although certain tracks, most notably 'You've Changed' on *Lady In Satin* are immensely moving on their own somewhat theatrical terms.

Billie Holiday paid a second and last visit to Europe late in 1958, and came to London to make a television appearance on Granada's *Chelsea At Nine* show in February 1959. By then she was looking frail, was unhappy about the departure of her final husband Louis McKay (if they were legally married then), but not prepared to give in. After the consumption of most of a bottle of vodka, and the careful application of her stage make-up, she looked strikingly good and managed a short set which communicated in a sufficiently raw fashion to leave a lasting impression on those witnessing it then, or seeing a video of the programme now. She spoke again of the Albert Hall concert, where the crowd of 6,000 gave her one of the greatest receptions of her life, and said she wished to settle in Britain. At the time she probably meant it, believing she would benefit from the genuine approval she needed so much. Once back home she might have thought differently, but her pianist Mal Waldron, asked about her wanting to emigrate to England, said: 'I knew Billie loved the Europeans, and if she had remained in Europe I believe she would be alive today'. The opportunity to move never came; her condition worsened and at the end of May she was taken to hospital suffering from heart and liver disease. Harried still by the police, and placed under arrest in her private room, she was charged with 'possession' and put

under police guard - the final cruelty the system could inflict upon her. Thus the greatest of jazz singers died in humiliating circumstances at 3.10 am on 17 July 1959 with $750 in notes taped to one leg - an advance on a series of promised articles.

She was, by her reckoning, only 44 years old and did not live to rejoice in the flood of books, biographical features, critical studies, magazine essays, album booklets, discographies, reference-book entries, chapters in innumerable jazz volumes, films and television video 'biopics' which far exceed any form of recognition she experienced in her lifetime. The 1972 filmed version of *Lady Sings The Blues*, considerably less honest and revealing than the much maligned original story, starred Diana Ross who did her best against long odds. This picture, despite its manifold shortcomings, introduced millions around the globe to the art of Holiday, reviving a then-flagging interest in her recordings. In the opinion of English journalist Jim Godbolt the continuous retelling of her story - and this includes a growing number of club, concert and stage tributes to Lady Day - has made Holiday 'unquestionably the most famous of all jazz singers'. If true, it would have confirmed her sour view of the methods by which the entertainment world allots its glittering prizes. 'There's no damn business like show business', she wrote. 'You had to smile to keep from throwing up'.

Selected albums: *The Billie Holiday Story* (1973), *Lady And The Legend Vols 1, 2* and *3.* (1984), *Billie Holiday At Monterey 1958* (1986), *The Legendary Masters* (1988), *Quintessential Vols 1, 2, 3, 4* and *5.* (1988), *Billie Holiday: The Voice Of Jazz* (1992, 8 CD set)

Further reading: *Billie's Blues*, John Chilton.

Holley, 'Lyin' Joe

Holley was recorded in April 1977 by George Paulus of Barrelhouse Records, who estimated his age as 'early sixties'. Holley had travelled throughout the southern USA and played in St. Louis and Detroit before settling in Chicago. He reputedly played blues piano at house parties and at the Provident Barber Shop on Saturdays for many years, and his recordings reveal a traditionally-based pianist with a large repertoire and an ability to improvise memorable lyrics over a tough piano accompaniment. Holley is

important as 'one of the last of the house party entertainers' but remains a very obscure figure, although he is reportedly still around the Chicago area.
Albums: *So Cold In The USA* (1982, rec. 1977), four tracks only *Piano Blues Legends* (1983).

Holmes, Winston, And Charlie Turner

Turner played rack harmonica and guitar, and was an accomplished player of blues and ragtime (and, on unissued titles, of Sousa marches); Holmes sang, but played no instrument, although he appears to play clarinet in a photograph promoting a record by Lottie Kimbrough on his Merritt label. Neither the clarinettist nor Kimbrough, who was sick, showed up for the session, so Holmes and Kimbrough's sister Estella sat in. As might be inferred, Holmes was an energetic and resourceful music promoter in Kansas City, arranging concerts, and recording sessions on his own and other labels, and being responsible for the debut (on Merritt) of Rev. J.C. Burnett. Holmes's own recordings, both with Turner and with Kimbrough, reveal a surreal sense of humour, and possibly a medicine show background; along with the blues, he parodied sentimental ballads and black church services, throwing in yodelling, whistling and bird calls.
Album: *Lottie Kimbrough and Winston Holmes* (c.1988).

Holmes, Wright

b. 4 July 1905, Hightower, Texas, USA. Apart from a spell of wartime defence work in the north, Holmes was based in Houston from 1930, by which time he was already a blues singer and guitarist, working in clubs on Dowling Street. His first recordings in 1947 were not issued because the producer felt he sounded too much like Lightnin' Hopkins, a judgment belied by three titles recorded the same year, and issued by Miltone and Gotham. Some of Holmes's lyrics come from Texas Alexander ('Alley Special' is based on two Alexander recordings), but both words and music (including vocal melodies) sound completely improvised; his guitar playing determinedly obscures its basic pulse with syncopations, changes of tempo, and explosive, random-sounding runs. Holmes gave up blues by 1950, and was last seen in 1967, by which

time he had lost a leg and turned to religion.
Album: *Alley Special* (1988).

Holts, Roosevelt

b. 15 January 1905, Tylertown, Mississippi, USA. Although he had been singing and playing blues guitar since his 20s, Holts was over 60 before he became known outside of his home area of southern Mississippi and Louisiana. A friend and companion of Tommy Johnson during the 30s, Holts learned to play many of that artist's pieces. In the 50s, he settled in Louisiana, and it was there he was discovered in the 60s. The Johnson connection seems to have rather preoccupied those who produced his records, but his repertoire was much wider and more substantial, and both his instrumental and vocal skills were remarkable for a performer of his age. For a short time around the end of the 60s, he issued some singles on his own label, Bluesman.
Album: *Presenting The Country Blues* (1968).

Homesick James

b. James Williamson 3 May 1914, Somerville, Tennessee, USA. Williamson's father was a drummer and by the age of 14, he was playing guitar at local dances and taverns. Williamson developed a 'bottle-neck' style by sliding a pocket-knife up and down the strings. In 1932 he moved north to Chicago and by the end of the decade had formed a small band which toured the southern states during the 40s. Among its members were Snooky Pryor and Baby Face Leroy Foster. His first recording was 'Lonesome Ole Train' (Chance 1952). From the mid-50s, Williamson worked regularly with his cousin Elmore James, playing second guitar on many of Elmore's most famous records. Now known as Homesick James, he recorded his own most famous track for USA in 1962. An updated version of Robert Johnson's 'Crossroads', its pounding rhythms and heavily amplified bottleneck made it a landmark in city blues. After the death of Elmore James in 1963, Homesick James saw himself as the standard-bearer of his cousin's powerful guitar style. He recorded for Prestige and toured Europe in 1973, where he made an album with Pryor for Jim Simpson's Birmingham, England label, Big Bear.
Albums: *Blues From The Southside* (1964),

174

Homesick James & Snooky Pryor (1973), *Ain't Sick No More* (1973), *Home Sweet Homesick* (1976).

Hooker, Earl

b. Earl Zebedee Hooker, 15 January 1930, Clarksdale, Mississippi, USA, d. 21 April 1970. Hooker's interest in music was kindled at an early age. A self-taught guitarist, he began his itinerant career as a teenager, and having toured America's southern states in the company of Robert Nighthawk, Ike Turner and many others, Earl made his first, rudimentary recordings in 1952. The artist followed a sporadic release schedule throughout the 50s, but by the end of the decade Hooker had settled in Chicago where he began a more consistent output. However his early work was spread over several of the city's independent outlets, and although undeniably talented, the search for elusive success saw Hooker aping the styles of contemporaries rather than forging one of his own. The guitarist asserted his gifts more fully in the wake of the blues revival and became one of the city's most highly-regarded talents. He made a rare UK television appearance on the pioneering music programme *Ready Steady Go*, performed in-concert at London's Royal Albert Hall and toured Europe with the American Folk-Blues festival. Hooker also completed albums for several specialist labels, and led his own band, Electric Dust, but the tuberculosis which he had battled against throughout his life finally took its toll. Earl Hooker died in a Chicago sanitarium in April 1970.

Albums: *Don't Have To Worry* (1969), *Sweet Black Angel* (1970), with Lightnin' Hopkins and Smokey Hogg *Hooker, Hopkins And Hogg* (1973), *Do You Remember* (1973), *Hooker And Steve* (1975), *First And Last* (1975), *Two Bugs And A Roach* (1976), *Play Your Guitar, Mr. Hooker* (1985). Compilations: *There's A Fungus Amung Us* (1972), *The Leading Brand* (1978), *Calling All Blues* (1986).

Hooker, John Lee

b. 22 August 1917, Clarksdale, Mississippi, USA. Born into a large family of agricultural workers, Hooker's first musical experiences, like those of so many other blues singers, were in church. A contrivance made from an inner tube attached to a barn door represented his first makeshift attempts at playing an instrument, but he subsequently learned some guitar from his stepfather William Moore, and they played together at local dances. At the age of 14, he ran away to Memphis, Tennessee, where he met and played with Robert Lockwood. A couple of years later he moved to Cincinnatti, where he stayed for about 10 years and sang with a number of gospel quartets. In 1943, he moved to Detroit, which was to be his home for many years, and began playing in the blues clubs and bars around Hastings Street, at the heart of that city's black section. Over the years he had developed the unique guitar style that was to make his music so distinctive and compelling. In 1948 he was finally given the chance to record. Accompanied only by his own electric guitar and constantly tapping foot, 'Boogie Chillen' with its driving rhythm and hypnotic drone of an accompaniment, was a surprise commercial success for Modern Records.

Over the next several years, they leased a large amount of his material first from Bernie Besman and later from legendary Detroit entrepreneur Joe Von Battle (both of whom also tried a few Hooker issues, respectively on their own Sensation and JVB labels). Most of these early recordings feature Hooker performing entirely solo; only a few are duets with Eddie Kirkland or another guitarist, and there are one or two with a band. It seems that this solo setting was not typical of his live work at the time, which would have used a small band, probably including piano, second guitar and drums, but his idiosyncratic sense of timing has always made him a difficult musician to accompany and it may be that recording him solo was the most reliable way of ensuring a clean take. Nevertheless, his solo sound on these early records was remarkably self-sufficient. His unique open-tuned guitar enabled him to combine a steady rhythm with inspired lead picking, thereby making full use of his rich, very bluesy baritone vocals. Although this one-man-band format might suggest a throwback to a more downhome ambience, there is a certain hipness and urbane sophistication about these performances that represent a significant departure from the rural background of Hooker's music and contribute very strongly to his characteristic sound. While a solo blues singer was something of an anachronism by this time, the records nonetheless sold consistently.

John Lee Hooker

From the late 40s to the early 50s, Hooker recorded prolifically and enjoyed an enormously successful run with Modern, producing such classic records as 'Crawling King Snake', 'In The Mood', 'Rock House Boogie' and 'Shake Holler & Run'. As well as these successes under his own name, he saw records released on a wide variety of labels, under a deliberately bewildering array of different pseudonyms: Johnny Williams on Gotham, Birmingham Sam And His Magic Guitar on Savoy, John Lee Booker on Chess, Delta John on Regent, The Boogie Man on Acorn, Johnny Lee on DeLuxe and Texas Slim or John Lee Cooker on King. Most of these were also leased from Joe Von Battle. His recording success led to tours. He played the R&B circuit across the country and this further developed his popularity with the black American public. In 1955, he severed his connection with Modern and began a long association with VeeJay Records of Chicago.

By this time, the solo format was finally deemed too old-fashioned for the contemporary R&B market and all of these recordings used a tight little band, often including Eddie Taylor on guitar, as well as piano and various combinations of horns. The association with VeeJay proved very satisfactory, both artistically and commercially, producing a string of hits such as 'Dimples', 'Maudie' and 'Boom Boom' and promoting further extensive tours. In the late 50s, as the market for R&B was beginning to contract, a new direction opened up for Hooker and he began to appear regularly at folk clubs and folk festivals. He found himself lionized by a new audience consisting mainly of young, white listeners. The folk connection also resulted in new recordings, issued on album by Riverside. These reverted to the solo format, with an acoustic guitar. While these recordings lacked the hard edge of the best of his earlier commercial sides, they were fascinating for the fact that the producers encouraged him to dig back into his older repertoire. Several songs reflecting his rural Mississippi background, such as 'Bundle Up And Go' and 'Pea Vine Special' were given his distinctive treatment. These records spread his name more widely, when they were released overseas. In the early 60s his reputation grew as he was often cited by younger pop and rock musicians, in particular the Rolling Stones, as a major influence. As a result international tours soon followed. Throughout this period, he continued to release singles and albums on VeeJay, but records also appeared on other labels. Later in the 60s, he made a number of records for Bluesway, aimed at this younger market. The connection with a new generation of musicians led to various 'super sessions', predictably of varying quality, but it perhaps bore fruit most successfully in the early 70s with the release of *Hooker 'N' Heat*, in which he played with the American rock blues band Canned Heat. Their famous long improvised boogies clearly owed a great deal to the influence of the older man. Although the popular enthusiasm for blues waned for a while in the late 70s and early 80s, Hooker's standing has rarely faltered and he has continued to tour, latterly with the Coast To Coast Blues Band. His early recordings have been repackaged and re-released over and over again, with those companies who used him pseudonymously in the early days now proudly taking the opportunity to capitalize on his real name. He has also made many new records but few of these have been of outstanding quality. A remarkable transformation came in 1989 when he recorded *The Healer*. This superb album featured guests on most tracks including Bonnie Raitt, Los Lobos and arguably the finest track, a duet with Carlos Santana on the title track. If such a thing as 'latin blues' existed , this was it. This album has since become one of the biggest selling blues albums of all time and has helped fuel a blues revival in prompting older statesmen to record again. *Mr Lucky* reached number .3 in the UK album charts, setting a record for

Hooker, at 74, as the oldest artist to achieve that position. On this second guest album he was paired with Ry Cooder, Van Morrison, Albert Collins and a gamut of other superstars. In his old age, Hooker has begun to fulfil the role of elder statesman of the blues, even appearing in an advertisement for a multi-national chemical corporation, but this has not prevented him from touring and he continues to perform widely and often. John Lee is genuinely loved by fellow musicians. Bonnie Raitt stated in 1992 that his guitar sound was one of the most erotic things she had ever heard. For a man in his 70s he still has humour and ability, most of all he has incredible 'style'.
Selected albums: *The Folk Blues Of John Lee Hooker* (1959), *Hooker 'N' Heat* (1971), *The Healer* (1989), *The Detroit Lion* (1990), *Boogie Awhile* (1990), *More Real Folk Blues: The Missing Album* (1991), *Mr. Lucky* (1991), *Free Beer And Chicken* (1992), *Simply The Truth* (1992), *Boom Boom* (1992). Compilation: *Collection: John Lee Hooker - 20 Blues Greats* (1985), *The Ultimate Collection 1948-1990* (1992), *The Best Of John Lee Hooker 1965-1974* (1992), *Blues Brother* (1992).

Hopkins, Joel

b. 3 January 1904, Centreville, Texas, USA, d. 15 February 1975, Galveston, Texas, USA. An elder brother of Lightnin' Hopkins, guitarist Joe learned his trade from Blind Lemon Jefferson when they travelled together during the 20s. Joel Hopkins spent most of his life working outside of music, but in 1947 he accompanied brother Lightin' on his famous Gold Star recording of 'Short Haired Woman'. He resurfaced in 1959 to record a handful of archaic Texas blues for historian and folklorist, Mack McCormick. The latter part of his life was spent in ill heath, and he died from a heart attack in 1975.
Selected album: with Lightnin' Hopkins *Joel & Lightnin' Hopkins 1959* (1990), *Lightnin' Joel & John Henry* (1992).

Hopkins, Lightnin'

b. Sam Hopkins, 15 March 1912, Centreville, Texas, USA, d. 30 January 1982. One of the last great country blues singers, Hopkins' lengthy career began in the Texas bars and juke joints of the 20s. Towards the end of the decade he

Lightnin' Hopkins

formed a duo with a cousin, Texas Alexander, while his Lightnin' epithet was derived from a subsequent partnership with barrelhouse pianist Thunder Smith, with whom he made his first recordings. Hopkins' early work unveiled a masterly performer. His work first came to prominence when, after being discovered by Sam Charters at the age of 47, *The Roots Of Lightnin' Hopkins* was released in 1959 and numerous sessions followed. His sparse acoustic guitar and narrated prose quickly made him an important discovery, appealing to the audience of the American folk boom of the early 60s. His harsh, emotive voice and compulsive, if irregular guitar work, carried an intensity enhanced by the often personal nature of his lyrics. He became one of post-war blues most prolific talents, completing hundreds of sessions for scores of major and independent labels. This inevitably diluted his initial power but although Hopkins' popularity slumped in the face of Chicago's electric combos, by the early 60s he was re-established as a major force on the college and concert-hall circuit. In 1967 the artist was the subject of an autobiographical film, *The Blues Of Lightnin' Hopkins*, which subsequently won the Gold Hugo award at the Chicago Film Festival. Like many other bluesmen finding great success in the 60s (Muddy Waters and John Lee Hooker), he too recorded a 'progressive' electric album: *The Great Electric Show And Dance*. He maintained a compulsive work-rate during the 70s, touring the USA, Canada and, in 1977, Europe, until ill-health forced him to reduce such commitments. Hopkins was a true folk poet, embracing social comments into pure blues. Lightnin' died in 1982, his status as one of the major voices of the blues assured.

Selected albums: *The Roots Of Lightnin' Hopkins* (1959), *Down South Summit Meeting* (1960), *The Great Electric Show And Dance* (1968), *Lightnin' Hopkins* (1991), *The Complete Prestige/Bluesville Recordings* (1992), *The Complete Aladdin Recordings* (1992), *Lightnin' Joel & John Henry* (1992), *Sittin' In With Lightnin' Hopkins* (1992).

Horton, Walter 'Shakey'

b. 6 April 1918, Horn Lake, Mississippi, USA, d. 8 December 1981, Chicago, Illinois, USA. Horton, also aka 'Mumbles', claimed to have taught himself harmonica by the time he was five years old, and certainly the extraordinary skill he achieved speaks of a very special affinity with the instrument. By his teens, he was in Memphis and beginning to make a living from music. He later claimed to have been on recordings by the Memphis Jug Band in 1927, but as he would have been only nine years old, this seems unlikely. More plausibly, he may have been the harmonica accompanist on Buddy Doyle's 1939 records. Throughout the 40s, he continued to develop his skills on the instrument, but it was not until 1951 that he recorded in his own right, back in Memphis. Over the next two years he made a series of recordings, many of which were not to be issued until many years later, but which show a remarkable talent, singing and playing his harmonica with great skill and imagination. One of the finest was 'Easy' a slow instrumental solo, accompanied only by Jimmy DeBerry's guitar, issued on Sun in 1953. Later that year, he was again in Chicago and issued two sides under Johnny Shines's name. With Horton's brilliant, soaring and swooping harmonica work and Shines's uniquely powerful, impassioned vocals, 'Evening Sun' with its flip side 'Brutal Hearted Woman' was widely regarded as one of the finest blues records from post-war Chicago.

Throughout the decade, he was playing regularly in Chicago, sometimes with Shines, or with Muddy Waters. He appeared on some of the latter's recordings, as well as others by Jimmy Rogers, Arbee Stidham and Sunnyland Slim. In the 60s, he reached a new audience, travelled widely in the USA and toured Europe with blues packages. As time went on, he demonstrated his versatility by adding pop and jazz themes to his repertoire, as well as showing a fondness for Latin tunes such as 'La Cucaracha' and 'La Paloma'. He was always primarily a blues player and the tough, electric sounds of Memphis and Chicago remained the essence of his music through many fine recordings in the 60s and 70s.

Albums: *Mouth Harp Maestro* (1988), *Fine Cuts* (1978), with Joe Hill Louis, Mose Vinson *The Be-Bop Boy* (1993).

House, Son

b. Eddie James House Jnr, 21 March 1902, Riverton, Mississippi, USA, d. 19 October 1988, Detroit, Michigan, USA. Brought up in a religious home, Son House was drawn to the ministry in his youth, and only took up the

Son House

guitar, and the blues, as late as 1927. Throughout his life there was to be a tension between his religious feelings and his secular way of life (including the playing of blues). In 1928 he served a year in jail for manslaughter (in self-defence). In 1930, he met Charley Patton at Lula, where he was spotted by a Paramount talent scout. House, Patton, Willie Brown and Louise Johnson travelled north to a memorable recording session, at which House recorded three two-part blues (together with one untraced record, and a test located in 1985). All were the work of an extraordinary musician. House was no virtuoso, but he brought total conviction to his performances: his ferocious, barking voice, driving bass ostinato, and stabbing bottleneck phrases blended into an overwhelming totality that, for all its impact on the listener, was fundamentally introspective. In the 30s, House and Brown played widely through Mississippi, Arkansas and Tennessee, and House taught both Muddy Waters and Robert Johnson some guitar technique and the 'Walking Blues' theme.

In 1941, following a tip from Waters, Alan Lomax of the Library of Congress located House at Lake Cormorant and made a number of recordings, including some hollers and three pieces which invaluably preserve House and Brown playing in a band with Fiddlin' Joe Martin (mandolin) and Leroy Williams (harmonica). Lomax returned the following year to supplement the single House solo recorded in 1941; the results document the breadth of House's repertoire, and catch him at the peak of his powers. In 1943, he moved to Rochester, New York, and had retired from music by 1948. When re-discovered in 1964, House was infirm, alcoholic, and barely able to play, but was fired by the admiration of his young white fans, and regained most of his abilities, recording a splendid album for Columbia, and providing an unforgettable experience for all who saw him in concert. All the intensity of his early recordings remained, and even when he was clearly in renewed physical and mental decline, it was a privilege to witness his music. He retired from performing in 1974, and lived quietly in Detroit until his death.

Selected albums: *The Real Delta Blues* (1974), *Son House & The Great Delta Blues Singers* (1990), *The Complete Library Of Congress Sessions* (1990), *Death Letter Blues* (1991).

Houston, Edward 'Bee'

b. 19 April 1938, San Antonio, Texas, USA, d. 19 March 1991, Los Angeles, California, USA. Houston ran a band in San Antonio and did back-up work for visiting artists such as Brook Benton, Little Willie John, Junior Parker and Bobby 'Blue' Bland. In 1961 he moved to the west coast, and played with McKinley Mitchell, Little Johnny Taylor and (his most enduring association) Big Mama Thornton. His playing was influenced by Clarence 'Gatemouth' Brown and B.B. King, but his album was both lacking in individuality and was too soul-influenced for the white blues audience at whom it was aimed. As a result he failed to become a name artist. Little was heard of Houston thereafter until it was reported that he had died from alcoholism in 1991.

Album: *Bee Houston* (1970).

Houston, Joe

b. 1927, Austin, Texas, USA. Joe Houston was inspired to take up the saxophone after seeing Count Hastings playing with Tiny Bradshaw's Orchestra, and lists Joe Thomas, Charlie Parker and Arnett Cobb among his other influences. By 1949 he became associated with Big Joe Turner, and made his recording debut on Turner's sole release on the Rouge label and probably played on Turner's first Freedom session. Houston's own recording career began in 1949 with Freedom Records, although his biggest successes were with 'Worry-Worry-Worry' (recorded by Bob Shad for his Sittin In With label but actually issued on Mercury in 1951), 'Cornbread And Cabbage Greens' and 'Blow, Joe, Blow' (both for Macy's Records also in 1951), and with 'All Night Long' (recorded for both the Money and Caddy labels, after Houston relocated to Los Angeles in 1955). Other recordings were issued on a gamut of labels; Modern/RPM/Crown, Imperial/Bay'ou, Combo, Lucky, Recorded In Hollywood, Cas, Dooto and other independent Los Angeles labels. In recent years, Houston has made a comeback with personal appearances.

Albums: *Kicking Back* (c.1983), *Rockin' At The Drive In* (1984), *Earthquake* (1985), *Rockin' 'N' Boppin'* (1988).

Hovington, Frank

b. 9 January 1919, Reading, Pensylvania, USA, d. 21 June 1982, Felton, Delaware, USA. Raised in Frederica, Delaware, Hovington was playing banjo and guitar by 1934, learning from Adam Greenfield and William Walker. From 1939 to 1971, he played intermittently with Gene Young. Hovington's music and repertoire were influenced by the omnipresent Blind Boy Fuller, but he played with a firm thumb beat, and sometimes took considerable rhythmic liberties. Moving to Washington, DC in 1948, Hovington occasionally went to Philadelphia, where he worked with Doug Quattlebaum and Washboard Slim (Robert Young); in Philadelphia. He also played with Blind Connie Williams, and this, together with his occasional work in jazz and gospel groups, probably accounts for the relative sophistication of his harmonies.
Album: *Lonesome Road Blues* (1975), *Lonesome Home Blues* (1982).

Howard, Camille

b. 29 March 1914, Galveston, Texas, USA. Howard took over the stool from Betty Hall Jones as pianist with Roy Milton's Solid Senders in the early 40s. She recorded with Milton on all his prime recordings for Specialty Records and his own Roy Milton/Miltone labels of the 40s and early 50s, and was occasionally featured singing her 'Groovy Blues', 'Mr Fine', 'Thrill Me' and 'Pack Your Sack, Jack' among others. Remaining with Milton, Howard simultaneously pursued her own recording career from 1946 when she recorded for the small Pan American label with James Clifford's band and, more notably, with her own sessions for Specialty which resulted in her successful instrumental boogies (including her biggest hit 'X-temperaneous Boogie') and small band R&B vocals (like the similarly successful 'Money Blues'). In 1953 Howard was signed to Federal for two west coast sessions and she went to Chicago and VeeJay for her final single in 1956. Camille Howard still lives in Los Angeles, where her voice and keyboard skills are reserved only for spiritual performances.
Albums: with Edith Mackey, Priscilla Bowman, Christine Kittrell *Rock 'N' Roll Mamas* (1985), with Lil Armstrong And Dorothy Donegan *Brown Gal* (1987), *X-Temperaneous Boogie* (1989).

Howard, Rosetta

b. c.1914, Chicago, Illinois, USA, d. 1974, Chicago, Illinois, USA. Initially a dancer, Rosetta Howard moved into singing by joining in with jukebox selections at the club where she worked, graduating to live work in Chicago with Jimmie Noone, Eddie Smith and Sonny Thompson. Her warm tones are heard on a distinguished series of lighthearted, jazz-tinged blues recordings made with the Harlem Hamfats between 1937 and 1939, and she also recorded with Henry 'Red' Allen. In 1947 Howard recorded with Willie Dixon's Big Three Trio, including a fine version of 'Ebony Rhapsody', but from the early 50s she devoted her time to church work at Thomas A. Dorsey's Pilgrim Baptist Church.
Albums: *Rosetta Howard* (1989), *Harlem Hamfats (with Rosetta Howard)* (c.1989).

Howell, Peg Leg

b. Joshua Barnes Howel, 5 March 1888, Eatonton, Georgia, USA, d. 11 August 1966, Atlanta, Georgia, USA. Howell's music is a complex mixture of blues, street vendors' cries, gamblers' argot, fragments of narrative ballads and, in the company of his 'Gang' (usually guitarist Henry Williams and fiddler Eddie Anthony), white fiddle pieces, ragtime, and other dance music. As a soloist, he sang introspective pieces, with a plaintive delivery, accompanied by short melodic fragments on guitar. His work with his group was very different, the lyrics delivered in a low growl as part of perhaps the liveliest, and rowdiest, party music on record. Also a bootlegger (for which he served time), Howell abandoned music in 1934 when Anthony died, and was very ill when found in 1963. An album was released that year, primarily to generate royalties, but it is hard listening.
Albums: *The Legendary Peg Leg Howell* (1963), *Volume 1* (1986), *Volume 2* (1982).

Howlin' Wolf

b. Chester Arthur Burnett, 10 June 1910, West Point, Mississippi, USA, d. 10 January 1976, Hines, Illinois, USA. Howlin' Wolf was one of the most important of the southern expatriates who created the post war blues out of their rural past and moulded it into the tough 'Chicago sound' of the 50s. He was one of six children

Howlin' Wolf

born to farmer Dock Burnett and his wife Gertrude and spent his earliest years around Aberdeen, Mississippi, where he sang in the local baptist church. In 1923 he relocated to Ruleville, Mississippi, and 10 years later moved again to work on Nat Phillips' Plantation at Twist, Arkansas. By this time he was working in music, appearing at local parties and juke joints. He had been inspired by performers like Charley Patton and Tommy Johnson, both of whom he had met, and he took much of the showmanship of his act from them, although his hoarse, powerful voice and eerie 'howling' were peculiarly his own. Other seminal Mississippi figures, Robert Johnson and Son House, also proved influential.

During this period he enjoyed many nicknames such as 'Big Foot' and 'Bull Cow' but it was as Howlin' Wolf that his fame grew. He was a huge man of commanding presence and threatening aspect who contemporary Johnny Shines once likened to a wild animal, saying that he (Shines) was scared to lay his hand on him.

Throughout the 30s Wolf combined farming with working in music, sometimes travelling in the company of people like Shines, Robert Johnson, and Sonny Boy 'Rice Miller' Williamson. Sonny Boy, who courted and married Wolf's half-sister Mary, taught his new brother-in-law to play some harmonica and Wolf also fooled around with the guitar. Wolf's first marriage had been to a sister of singer Willie Brown and it was during this time that he married his second wife, Lillie Handley. It was a union that lasted until his death. During 1941-44 Wolf was drafted into the army but once he got out he formed his own group and gained sufficient fame to be approached by KWEM, a west Memphis radio station, which was involved in competition for the local black audience and saw Wolf's potential. For KWEM, Wolf worked as a disc jockey as well as performing himself and this brought him to the attention of Sam Phillips, who was recording material in Memphis and leasing it to others for sale in the black communities of the north and western areas of the USA. Phillips, who considered Wolf to be one of the greatest talents he knew, originally made separate deals with the Bihari Brothers in California and the Chess Brothers of Chicago to issue Wolf's recordings. The success of Wolf's early recordings led to something of a war between these two camps, with each trying to attract him under their own aegis. On the evidence of some of the songs that he recorded at the time, it seems that Wolf was tempted to take a 'stroll out west', but in the event he went to Chicago 'the onliest one who drove out of the south like a gentleman'.

In Memphis, Wolf, whose recording sessions were often under the command of Ike Turner, had been lucky to employ the talents of guitarist Willie Johnson, who refused to move north, and in Chicago that good fortune held as he worked first with Jody Williams and then the unique Hubert Sumlin. The raw delta sound of Wolf's earlier records assured him of a ready made audience once he reached Chicago and he quickly built a powerful reputation on the club circuit and extended it with such classic records as 'Smokestack Lightning' and 'Killing Floor'. Like his great rival Muddy Waters he maintained that audience, and a Chess recording contract, through the lean times of rock 'n' roll and into the blues boom of the 60s. He came to Europe with the AFBF in 1964 and continued to return over the next ten years. The Rolling Stones and the Yardbirds did much to publicize Wolf's (and Muddy's) music, both in ·Europe and white America and as the 60s progressed, the newer artists at Chess saw their audience as the emerging, white, 'love and peace' culture and tried to influence their material to suit it. Wolf's music was a significant influence on rock and many of his best-known songs - 'Sitting On Top Of The World', 'I Ain't Superstitious', 'Killin' Floor', 'Back Door Man' and 'Little Red Rooster' - were recorded by acts as diverse as the Doors, Cream, the Rolling Stones, the Yardbirds and Manfred Mann. Few, however, rivalled the power or sexual bravura displayed on the originals and only Don Van Vliet (Captain Beefheart) came close to recapturing his aggressive, raucous voice. A compelling appearance on the teen-oriented **Shindig** television show (at the behest of the Rolling Stones) was a rare concession to commerciality. His label's desire for success, akin to the white acts he influenced, resulted in the lamentable *The Howlin' Wolf Album*, which the artist described as 'dog shit'. This ill-conceived attempt to update earlier songs was outshone by *The London Howlin' Wolf Sessions*, on which Wolf and long-serving guitarist Hubert Sumlin were joined by an array of guests including Eric Clapton, Steve Winwood, and Rolling Stones

members Bill Wyman and Charlie Watts.

Wolf, along with others like Muddy Waters, resisted this move but were powerless to control it. They were, of course, men in their 50s; set in their ways but needing to maintain an audience outside the dwindling Chicago clubs. Fortunately Wolf outlived this trend, along with those for piling well known artists together into 'super bands'. Wolf continued to tour but his health was declining. After a protracted period of illness Howlin' Wolf died of cancer in the Veterans Administration Hospital in 1976. His influence has survived the excesses of the 'swinging 60s' and is to be seen today in the work of many of the emerging black blues men such as Roosevelt 'Booba' Barnes.

Selected albums: *Moaning In The Moonlight* (1959), *Howlin' Wolf* (aka *The Rocking Chair Album*) (1962), *The Real Folk Blues* (1963), *Big City Blues* (1966), *The Super Blues Band* (1967), *More Real Folk Blues* (1967), *The Howlin' Wolf Album* (aka *The Dog Shit Album*) (1969), *Message To The Young* (1971), *The London Sessions* (1971), *Alive And Cookin' At Alice's Revisited* (1972), *The Back Door Wolf* (1973), *Change My Way* (1975), *Ridin' In The Moonlight* (1982), *Live In Europe 1964* (1988), *Memphis Days Vol 1* (1989), *Memphis Days Vol 2* (1990), *Howlin' Wolf Rides Again* (1991). Compilations: *Real Folk Blues* (1966), *More Real Folk Blues* (1967), *Going Back Home* (1970), *The Back Door Wolf* (1974), *Chess Blues Masters* (1976), *The Legendary Sun Performers* (1977), *Chess Masters* (1981), *Chess Masters 2* (1982), *Chess Masters 3* (1983), *The Wolf* (1984), *Golden Classics* (1984), *The Howlin' Wolf Collection* (1985), *His Greatest Hits* (1986), *Howlin' For My Baby* (1987), *Shake For Me - The Red Rooster* (1988), *Smokestack Lightnin'* (1988), *Red Rooster* (1988), *Moanin' And Howlin'* (1988), *Cadillac Daddy* (1989).

Howlin' Wilf

b. early 60s. As a youngster in Essex, England. Wilf was interested in 50s rock 'n' roll, leading to a later appreciation of Chicago blues, particularly the music of Little Walter, and he received his first electric guitar in 1977, when he was 15 years old. His first band, the DMFs, played at Colchester Labour Club in 1983. He initially recorded with a rockabilly band for a compilation issued by Lost Moment Records in 1984. Two years later he moved to London,

where he was touted as one of England's best young blues singers, and with his band the Vee-Jays he quickly established himself as one of the mainstays of the capital's blues scene. In 1989 he disbanded the Vee-Jays and took his music in more of an R&B direction. His scattered recordings bear witness to the fact that he is regarded primarily as a live entertainer.
Video: *Live Wilf* (1987).

Huff, Luther

b. 5 December 1910, Fannin, Mississippi, USA, d. 18 November 1973, Detroit, Michigan, USA. Luther and younger brother Percy, made only two records in 1951 but they cleaved so startlingly and entertainingly to the old traditions that they have been prized ever since. They learned guitar from older brother Willie and cousin Donnee Howard and, like them, played at fish fries and country picnics. One picnic, held at a plantation in Belzoni, lasted 13 days. Luther bought a mandolin in 1936 and taught himself to play. Drafted into the army in 1942, Luther saw service in England, France and Belgium, where, in 1944, he recorded two acetates, now lost. In 1947, he moved to Detroit and started what would be a large family of 12 children. Percy stayed in Jackson, Mississippi, driving a taxicab. On a visit in 1950, Luther bumped into Sonny Boy Williamson (Rice Miller), who suggested that he and Percy record for Trumpet. Needing train fare home to Detroit, Huff contacted Lillian McMurry and, in January and February 1951, the pair recorded 'Dirty Disposition', '1951 Blues', 'Bull Dog Blues' and 'Rosalee', the latter pair featuring Luther's mandolin. Luther returned north to work at the Chrysler factory, and later, for Plymouth, making little effort to continue as a musician. In 1968, along with brothers Willie and Percy, he was recorded by Adelphi Records, but the results were never issued.
Album: *Delta Blues - 1951* (1990).

Hughes, Joe 'Guitar'

b.1937, Texas. A product of Houston's third ward, Joe Hughes turned to music at an early age under the influence of the work of T-Bone Walker. He claims to have used money earned washing dishes to buy his first electric guitar at the age of 14 and to have been appearing professionally by the time he was 16. His first band was the Dukes Of Rhythm which included in its line-up Hughes' neighbour and friend Johnny Copeland. When this group disbanded in 1964 Hughes joined Grady Gaines working for Little Richard's old group the Upsetters. His next job was working as a member of Bobby 'Blue' Bland's band which he left in the wake of Bland's supporting star Al 'TNT' Braggs. After three years with Braggs, Hughes moved on to playing lead with Julius Jones and the Rivieras and from there to various groups operating around the Houston area. An upsurge of interest in the post-war Texas blues brought Joe to some prominence during the early 80s since which he has toured in Europe and recorded for Double Trouble Records of Holland.
Album: *Craftsman* (1988).

Hull, Papa Harvey, And Long Cleve Reed

Probably from northern Mississippi, Hull and Reed, together with guitarist Sunny Wilson, formed a little group of black songsters. Reed and Wilson's two-guitar accompaniment was a blend of parlour guitar and ragtime. They sang blues, but much of their repertoire was from the turn of the century, when blues was not yet the dominant black music, and included ballads, medicine show material, and coon songs; their harmony singing, too, was of an earlier age. Long Cleve Reed may also have been Big Boy Cleveland, who recorded shortly after Hull and Reed, playing a slide guitar blues and 'Quill Blues', a fife solo unparalleled on commercial race records.
Album: *The Songster Tradition* (1991).

Hunter, Alberta

b. 1 April 1895, Memphis, Tennessee, USA, d. 17 October 1984. Growing up in Chicago, Hunter began her remarkable career singing at Dago Frank's, one of the city's least salubrious whorehouses. There she sang for the girls, the pimps and the customers, earning both their admiration and good money from tips. Later, she moved on and marginally upwards to a job singing in Hugh Hoskins's saloon. She continued to move through Chicago's saloons and bars, gradually developing a following. She entered the bigtime with an engagement at the Dreamland Cafe, where she sang with Joe 'King' Oliver's band. Amongst the songs she sang was

'Down Hearted Blues', which she composed in collaboration with Lovie Austin and which was recorded in 1923 by Bessie Smith. During the 20s and early 30s Hunter often worked in New York, singing and recording with many leading jazzmen of the day, amongst them Louis Armstrong, Sidney Bechet, Eubie Blake, Fletcher Henderson and Fats Waller. She also appeared in various shows on and off Broadway. A visit to London prompted so much interest that she was offered the role of Queenie in *Showboat* at the Drury Lane Theatre, playing opposite Paul Robeson. This was in the 1928/9 season and during the 30s she returned frequently to London to appear at hotels and restaurants, including an engagement at the Dorchester Hotel with Jack Jackson's popular band. She also appeared in the UK musical film, *Radio Parade Of 1935*. The 30s saw her in Paris and Copenhagen too, always meeting with enormous success. In the 40s she continued to appear at New York clubs and to make records, notably with Eddie Heywood. Amongst these recordings are two of her own compositions, 'My Castle's Rockin'' and 'The Love I Have For You'. In the war years she toured extensively to perform for US troops. In the early 50s she visited the UK with Snub Mosley and again toured with the USO, this time to Korea. She played a number of club dates but these were increasingly hard times and in 1954 she retired from showbusiness. Now aged 60, she began a new career as a nurse. In 1961 writer and record producer Chris Alberston persuaded her to record two albums, but she remained at her new profession. Then, in 1977, her employers caught onto the fact that diminutive Nurse Hunter was 82 and insisted that she should retire. Having already lived a remarkably full life she could have been forgiven for calling it a day, but she was a tough and spirited lady. She supplied the score for the film, *Remember My Name* (1978) and, invited to sing at Barney Josephson's club, The Cookery in Greenwich Village, New York, she was a smash hit and began her singing career all over again. She made numerous club and concert appearances, made more records and appeared on several television shows. Early in her career she sometimes performed and occasionally recorded under different names, including May Alix and Josephine Beaty. She sang with power

and conviction, her contralto voice having a distinct but attractive vibrato. Inimitably interpreting every nuance of lyrics, especially when they were her own, she made many fine recordings. Even late in her career, she controlled her audiences with a delicately iron hand, all the while displaying a sparkling wit and a subtle way with a risqué lyric. It is hard to think of any singer who has improved upon her performances of certain songs, notably 'The Love I Have For You' and 'Someday, Sweetheart'.

Selected albums: *Classic Alberta Hunter: The Thirties* (1935-40 recordings), *Alberta Hunter With Lovie Austin And Her Blues Serenaders* (1961), *Amtrak Blues* (c.1980), *The Glory Of Alberta Hunter* (c.1980).

Hunter, John Thurman (Long John)

b. 13 July 1931, Ringold, Louisiana, USA. The son of a sharecropper, Hunter was raised on a farm in Magnolia, Arkansas. Until his mid-20s, he heard little else but country music, only hearing blues after moving to Beaumont, Texas, to work in a box factory. Attending a B.B. King gig, he was inspired to try his own hand at playing the guiitar after witnessing its effect on women. From 1955, he spent three years in Houston, having one record, 'Crazy Girl', released on Duke. On August 7 1957, he moved with his band, The Hollywood Bearcats, to El Paso. Soon after his arrival, he was engaged to play the Lobby Club, a gig he held for more than a decade. Between 1961 and 1971, he made four rock-oriented singles, including 'El Paso Rock' and 'The Scratch', for Yucca Records in Alamogordo, New Mexico. These and other titles were issued on album in 1986. A year earlier, he'd cut his first album, *Smooth Magic,* for the Boss label. His second album, *Ride With Me*, was recorded in Austin in 1992 with Texas veterans, T.D. Bell and Erbie Bowser, and the Antones rhythm section. Hunter's lean guitar style and characterful voice indicate there's more to Texas blues than Albert Collins. Album: *Texas Border Town Blues* (1986), *Ride With Me* (1992).

Hurt, Mississippi John

b. John Smith Hurt, 3 July 1893, Teoc, Mississippi, USA, d. 2 November 1966. One of the major 'rediscoveries' during the 60s' folk

blues revival, Mississippi John Hurt began playing at informal gatherings and parties at the turn of the century, when guitars were still relatively uncommon. Although he worked within the idiom, Hurt did not regard himself as a blues singer and his relaxed, almost sweet, intonation contrasted with the aggressive approach of many contemporaries. In 1928 he recorded two sessions for the OKeh label. These early masters included 'Candy Man Blues', 'Louis Collins' and 'Ain't No Tellin' (aka 'A Pallet On The Floor'), songs which were equally redolent of the ragtime tradition. For the ensuing three decades, Hurt worked as a farm-hand, reserving music for social occasions. His seclusion ended in 1963. Armed with those seminal OKeh recordings, a blues aficionado, Tom Hoskins, followed the autobiographical lyric of 'Avalon Blues' and travelled to the singer's hometown. He persuaded Hurt to undertake a series of concerts which in turn resulted in several new recordings. Appearances at the Newport Folk Festival ensued, before the artist completed several sessions for the Vanguard label, supervised by folksinger Patrick Sky. These included masterly reinterpretations of early compositions, as well as new, equally compelling pieces. Hurt's re-emergence was sadly brief. He died at Grenada County Hospital on 2 November 1966 following a heart attack, having inspired a new generation of country-blues performers.
Albums: *Mississippi John Hurt - Folk Songs And Blues* (1963), *Worried Blues* (1964), *Blues At Newport* (1965), *Best Of Mississippi John Hurt* (1965, live recording), *Last Sessions* (1966), *Mississippi John Hurt - Today* (1967), *Last Sessions* (1973). Compilations: *The Immortal Mississippi John Hurt* (1967), *Avalon Blues* (1982), *Shake That Thing* (1986), *Monday Morning Blues* (1987), *Mississippi John Hurt 1963* (1988).

Hutto, J.B.

b. Joseph Benjamin Hutto, 26 April 1926, Elko, near Blackville, South Carolina, USA, d. 12 June 1983, Chicago, Illinois, USA. Hutto's family moved to Augusta, Georgia when he was three years old, and he later sang in the Golden Crowns Gospel Singers, before moving to Chicago in 1949. While in Chicago he began to play drums and sing blues with Johnny Ferguson's Twisters, and during the intervals he taught himself to play Ferguson's guitar. In 1954 he recorded for the Chance label and these tracks are now considered to be classics of post-war blues. Hutto's slide guitar demonstrated that he was influenced by Elmore James but had utilized his style to create a unique, personal sound; however, at the time of release, the records met with little success. In 1965 J.B. and his unit the Hawks were the resident band at Turner's Blue Lounge (he worked there for over ten years), when they recorded for the influential Vanguard series *Chicago/The Blues/Today*. Following this, Hutto recorded for many collector labels including Testament, Delmark, JSP, Amigo, Wolf, Baron, Black And Blue, and Varrick, with much of the later material, in particular, being licensed to different companies, and appearing on numerous anthologies. Hutto's music was raunchy, electric slide guitar blues that found great favour among young white blues enthusiasts. During live sets he would walk out into the audience and climb over tables in clubs, while continuing to play; 'party blues' was how one critic so aptly described it. Hutto died of cancer in June 1983. He was a major influence on his nephew Lil' Ed Williams who still performs some of Hutto's songs.
Albums: *Slideslinger* (1982), *Slippin' And Slidin'* (1983).

I

Ironing Board Sam

b. Sammie Moore, 1939, Rockfield, South Carolina, USA. Sam learned to play the organ as a youngster, concentrating on boogie-woogie and gospel music before turning to blues while playing in Miami, Florida. He formed his first band in 1959 and acquired his stage name when based in Memphis; he mounted his keyboard on an ironing board. Initially he loathed the name but turned it to his advantage by giving away ironing boards at his shows! *Blues Unlimited* described Sam as having 'a really great voice and his songs have strong lyrics'. His music has appeared on several labels including Holiday Inn, Atlantic, Styletone and Board, and his live sets include 'very fine, intense blues and jazz' (*Living Blues*). His onstage antics include playing in a tank of water! He is now based in New Orleans.
Compilation: 2 tracks only *Blues Is Here To Stay* (1973).

J

Jackson, Armand 'Jump'

b. 25 March 1917, New Orleans, Louisiana, USA, d. 31 January 1985, Chicago, Illinois, USA. Jackson's forceful 'sock' rhythm was heard on many of the blues records made in Chicago in the late 40s and 50s. In 1946-47, he appeared as bandleader on sessions for Columbia, Specialty and Aristocrat; vocalists included St. Louis Jimmy, Roosevelt Sykes, Sunnyland Slim and Baby Doo Caston. As well as performing, Jackson was active as a booking agent, and in 1959 founded La Salle Records, recording himself, Eddie Boyd, Eddy Clearwater, Little

Mack Simmons and Sunnyland Slim among others. In 1962 he was the drummer for the inaugural American Folk Blues Festival tour of Europe, although by this date his swing era sound had largely been supplanted in Chicago blues by the 'back beat' of Fred Below.
Album: *Chicago Rock With Jump Jackson And Friends* (c.1980).

Jackson, Arthur (Peg Leg Sam)

b. 18 December 1911, Jonesville, South Carolina, USA, d. October 27 1977, Jonesville, South Carolina USA. Also known as Peg Pete, Jackson learned to play the harmonica when he was ten years old, listening to local men, Butler Jennings and Biggar Mapps, who played in an older style known as 'accordion'. He'd already learned many secular and spiritual songs from his mother, Emily. He left home about this time and spent much of his adult life travelling, and learned his blues style in the late Twenties from Elmon 'Keg Shorty' Bell. He lost the lower part of his right leg under a freight train in Durham, N.C. in 1930. Seven years later, he teamed up with Pink Anderson on the medicine show circuit, which he worked for the next 30 years, mostly in partnership with Chief Thundercloud. He also played regularly in Rocky Mount, N.C. at Fenner's Warehouse, a focal point for musicians like Tarheel Slim, Willie Trice and Brownie McGhee. In later years, the right side of his face was scarred while trying to break up a domestic argument. He was first recorded by Pete Lowry in August 1970, in the company of Baby Tate and Pink Anderson. Jackson became a favourite at folk festivals and also recorded in New York with Louisiana Red. He died on the family homestead he'd left as a child.
Selected albums: *Medicine Show Man* (1973), *Joshua* (1975).

Jackson, Bo Weavil

Bo Weavil Jackson presents another of those conundrums that are sent to try researchers of early blues recordings. Virtually nothing is known of his life apart from the fact that he was discovered playing for tips on the streets of Birmingham, Alabama, USA and on two occasions in 1926, he made recordings in Chicago. The first of these was for Paramount under the name Jackson and the second for Vocalion as Sam Butler. Just what his real name

was remains a mystery, as does his place of origin. Paramount publicity referred to his being from the Carolinas, although all references in his songs seem to point to a long familiarity with Alabama. Whoever he was, he was an outstanding performer whose high-pitched, expressive voice and chilling slide guitar can be enjoyed as much today as when first recorded. Thirteen known tracks are attributed to Jackson; four are religious numbers and the remainder are early blues made up from individual traditional verses subjected to the singers personal interpretation.
Albums: *Complete Recordings* (1982), *1926* (1983).

Jackson, 'Bullmoose'

b. Benjamin Clarence Jackson, 1919, Cleveland, Ohio, USA, d. 31 July 1989, Cleveland, Ohio, USA. Jackson become interested in music at an early age, and received singing and violin lessons by the age of four. In high school he learned to play the saxophone, and upon his graduation in the late 30s was hired by legendary trumpeter Freddie Webster to play alto and tenor with his Harlem Hotshots. Moving briefly to Buffalo, New York in the early 40s, Jackson returned to Cleveland to a job at the Cedar Gardens where he was discovered by bandleader Lucky Millinder in 1944, who needed a musician to replace tenor saxophonist Lucky Thompson. Recording initially as simply a talented accompanist with Millinder's orchestra on Decca and as a guest musician with Big Sid Catlett's band on Capitol, Jackson astounded his colleagues by substituting for blues shouter Wynonie Harris one night in Lubbock, Texas. He remained a part of the Millinder aggregation until June 1948 with the huge success of his R&B hit 'I Love You, Yes I Do'. He began making records under his own name from 1945 with King/Queen and Superdisc as well as appearing on Millinder's Decca tracks. In the 1948 musical film *Boarding House Blues*.
Jackson enjoyed great success on King Records between 1947 and 1954 with ballads like 'I Love You, Yes I Do' (which spawned innumerable cover versions for every conceivable market), 'All My Love Belongs To You', and 'Little Girl Don't Cry'. Bullmoose was also responsible for some of the hottest, most suggestive R&B ever recorded and it is these titles - 'Big Ten-Inch (Record)', 'I Want A Bow-Legged Woman', 'Nosey Joe' and 'Oh John' - that have found favour with the current crop of jump and R&B revival bands. Jackson moved to Chess' short-lived Marterry subsidiary in 1955, moved to the tiny Encino label in 1956, and was reduced to making recuts of his old hits in the early 60s for Warwick and 7 Arts. By that time he had taken a job with a catering firm during the week and simply played the occasional weekend gig. In 1974 he had a cameo appearance in the dramatic film *Sincerely The Blues*, led a jazz band at the Smithsonian Institute in 1976, and went on to tour France and North Africa with Buck Clayton's Quartet. In 1983 Bullmoose was tracked down by the Pittsburgh-based band, the Flashcats, who had been covering his risque R&B songs, and after 35 years he was big news again with a sell-out tour, a new recording contract with Bogus Records, a celebrated show at Carnegie Hall and a European tour with the Johnny Otis Show in 1985.
Albums: *Big Fat Mamas Are Back In Style Again* (1980), *Moosemania!* (1985), *Moose On The Loose* (1985).

Jackson, Jim

b. c.1890, Hernando, Mississippi, USA, d. 1937, Hernando, Mississippi, USA. Emerging from the minstrel and medicine show circuit, Jackson was a well-known figure around the Memphis area where he worked with artists such as Robert Wilkins, Furry Lewis and Gus Cannon. His first record, 'Jim Jackson's Kansas City Blues, Parts 1 & 2' recorded for Vocalion in October 1927, became one of the first, and biggest, 'race' hits. He later recorded 'Parts 3 & 4' and many variations on its basic theme. He continued to record for various labels up until 1930, and some 40 tracks of his work are extant. Jackson was never an outstanding guitarist and his success was based on his humour; although it has not dated well, occasional numbers such as 'I Heard The Voice Of A Pork Chop' can still raise a smile.
Album: *Kansas City Blues* (1980).

Jackson, John

b. 25 February 1924, Woodville, Virginia, USA. Born into a musical family, Jackson began to play guitar at around five years old, learning also from a convict who worked on a chain gang.

Jackson's music, at least some of which was learned from records, covers a wide range of traditional southern material, including blues, rags, country dance tunes and ballads (which have earned him the description of songster rather than blues singer), and he plays in a style related to other black guitarists from the eastern states, such as Blind Blake and Blind Boy Fuller. Since the 60s Jackson has made many records, including one where he played second guitar to Buddy Moss, as well as concert and festival appearances, both in the USA and overseas.

Selected albums: *Blues And Country Dance Tunes from Virginia* (1965), *In Europe* (1969).

Jackson, Melvin 'Lil' Son

b. 16 (or 17) August 1915, Barry, Texas, USA, d. 30 May 1976, Dallas, Texas, USA. Friends persuaded Melvin Jackson to send in a fairground recording to Bill Quinn, the owner of Gold Star Records, in the hope that it might lead to a recording contract. It did, and between 1948 and 1954 Jackson, who had moved on to the more prestigious Imperial label, made records in a style that combined his rural roots with currently acceptable R&B sounds. These sold well, particularly in his home state, Texas, and on the west coast, where many black Texans had emigrated. He toured extensively, but after a road accident retired from music to work in an automobile scrap yard. Having been raised in a sharecropping environment and taught to play guitar by his father, Johnny, Lil' Son ran away from home during the 30s. He has been described as a sincere man and religion seems to have played an important part in his life. He worked with the Blue Eagle Four Spiritual group before being drafted into the army. He served in the UK, France and Germany before returning to take up a career as a blues singer. After leaving the music scene he worked as a mechanic and was also employed by his local church. Fortunately Chris Strachwitz of Arhoolie Records traced and recorded him again, in 1960, in a more simple setting. Jackson died of cancer in 1976.

Albums: *Lil Son Jackson* (1960), *Rockin' An' Rollin'* (1983).

Jackson, 'New Orleans' Willie

Jackson sang comic renditions of opera tunes in blackface at a New Orleans ice cream parlour. His mid-20s recordings are versatile and vaudevillian, strong dance numbers, *double entendres*, and humorous vignettes of Darktown life, ranging from the church to politics and the judiciary. He also sang a number of traditionally-based blues, covered contemporary hits like 'Kansas City Blues', and made the first recording of 'T.B. Blues', generally associated with Victoria Spivey.

Album: *New Orleans Willie Jackson* (1989).

Jackson, Papa Charlie

b. c.1885, New Orleans, Louisiana, USA, d. 1938, Chicago, Illinois, USA. Papa Charlie Jackson belonged to the first generation of rural black singers to record. He was a banjo player who had toured the South in medicine shows and worked anywhere else where he thought he might make money. He became popular after his first records were issued by Paramount in 1924, by which time he seems to have already moved to Chicago where he often performed for tips in the Maxwell Street market. Like numerous banjoists from the minstrel tradition, Jackson was something of a humorist and many of his 70 or more recordings were sanitized versions of bawdy songs. He recorded with Freddie Keppard's Jazz Cardinals in 1926, taking the vocal on 'Salty Dog', a number he had already recorded under his own name with marked success. Despite providing support for artists such as Ma Rainey, Lucille Bogan and Ida Cox Jackson's recording activities suffered a hiatus between 1930 and 1934 owing to the onset of the Depression and the demise of Paramount. He recorded for Vocalion in 1934 and recorded an unreleased session with Big Bill Broonzy in 1935. He scuffled on Chicago's west side until his death in 1938.

Album: *Fat Mouth* (1970).

Jacobs, Matthew (Boogie Jake)

b, c.1929, Marksville, Louisiansa, USA. Like many blues artists with a small discography, Matthew Jacobs was a reluctant performer, even at the height of his (limited) popularity. Learning guitar from a neighbour, Ernest Barrow, Jake's first public performance was with second cousin, Little Walter Jacobs, at the Golden Lantern Club in Marksville. Soon afterwards, he moved to Baton Rouge, met drummer Joe Hudson, and played clubs like the

Elmore James

Apex & Rhythm. He came to the notice of Jay Miller and was invited to play on a Slim Harpo session, supposedly playing the distinctive guitar riff on 'King Bee'. Miller recorded Jake sometime later, in company with Lazy Lester and Katie Webster; of several titles, only 'Early Morning Blues' and 'I Don't Know Why' were issued decades later on Flyright. In 1959, he was approached by New Orleans record distributor Joe Banashak, who proposed that Jake launch his Minit label. 'Early Morning Blues and 'Bad Luck And Trouble' ('I Don't Know Why' in disguise) were recorded sometime in June. About a month later, a second single was recorded, 'Loaded Down' and the swamp-pop 'Chance For Your Love'. Jake's music had the flavour of the juke joint and his first single was picked up for national distribution by Chess Records. For a while, he toured with other Minit artists and alongside Lightnin' Slim, but disillusionment caused him to take his family west to California, remaining outside music throughout the 60s. His appearance at the 1974 San Francisco Blues Festival led to more regular work and a session for the Blues Connoisseur label in 1977. At this time, he had formed a partnership with another Louisiana migrant, Schoolboy Cleve White.
Selected album: *Loaded Down With The Blues* (1987).

James, Elmore

b. 27 January 1918, Richland, Mississippi, USA, d. 23 May 1963. Although his recording career spanned 10 years, Elmore James is chiefly recalled for his debut release, 'Dust My Broom'. This impassioned, exciting performance, based on a virulent composition by country blues singer Robert Johnson, was marked by the artist's unfettered vocals and his searing, electric slide guitar. James formative years were spent in Mississippi juke joints where he befriended Rice Miller (Sonny Boy Williamson), a regular performer on the US radio station KFFA's *King Biscuit Time* show. Elmore accompanied Miller for several years, and through his influence secured his initial recording deal in 1951. James then moved to Chicago where he formed the first of several groups bearing the name 'the Broomdusters'. Subsequent recordings included different variations on that initial success - 'I Believe', 'Dust My Blues' - as well as a series of

compositions which proved equally influential. 'Bleeding Heart' and 'Shake Your Moneymaker' were later adopted, respectively, by Jimi Hendrix and Fleetwood Mac, while the guitarist's distinctive 'bottleneck' style resurfaced in countless British blues bands. James style was accurately copied by Fleetwood Mac's Jeremy Spencer, who would often have 'Elmore James' segments in their act during the late-60s. Another James devotee was Brian Jones of the Rolling Stones, whose early stage name of Elmo Lewis, and bottleneck guitar work paid tribute to James. John Mayall's 'Mr. James' was a thoughtful tribute to this significant performer who sadly did not live to reap such acclaim. In May 1963, James suffered a fatal heart attack at the home of his cousin, Homesick James who, along with J.B. Hutto, then assumed the late musician's mantle.
Selected albums: *Blues After Hours* (1961), *Original Folk Blues* (1964), *Something Inside Of Me* (1968), *To Know A Man* (1969), *Whose Muddy Shoes* (1969), *Blues In My Heart, Rhythm In My Soul* (1969), *The Legend Of Elmore James* (1970), *Cotton Patch Hotfoots* (1974), *All Them Blues* (1976), *One Way Out* (1980), *The Best Of Elmore James* (1981), *Got To Move* (1981), *King Of The Slide Guitar* (1983), *Red Hot Blues* (1983), *The Original Meteor And Flair Sides* (1984), *The Elmore James Collection* (1985), *Let's Cut It* (1986), *King Of The Bottleneck Blues* (1986), *Shake Your Moneymaker* (1986), *Pickin' The Blues* (1986), *Greatest Hits* (1987), *Chicago Golden Years* (1988), *Dust My Broom* (1990).

James, Etta

b. Jamesetta Hawkins, 25 January 1938, Los Angeles, California, USA. James introduction to performing followed an impromptu audition for Johnny Otis, backstage at San Francisco's Fillmore Auditorium. 'Roll With Me Henry', her 'answer' to the Hank Ballard hit, 'Work With Me Annie', was re-titled 'The Wallflower' in an effort to disguise its risqué lyric and became an R&B number 1. 'Good Rockin' Daddy' provided another hit, but the singer's later releases failed to chart. Having secured a deal with the Chess group of labels, James unleashed a series of powerful songs including 'All I Could Do Was Cry' (1960), 'Stop The Wedding' (1962) and 'Pushover' (1963). She also recorded several duets with Harvey Fuqua.

Etta James

Heroin addiction sadly blighted both her personal and professional life, but in 1968 Chess took her to the Fame studios. The resultant *Tell Mama*, was a triumph, and pitted James abrasive voice with the exemplary Muscle Shoals houseband. Its highlights included the proclamatory title track, a pounding version of Otis Redding's 'Security' (both of which reached the R&B Top 20) and the despairing 'I'd Rather Go Blind', which was later a Top 20 UK hit for Chicken Shack. The 1973 album *Etta James* earned her a US Grammy nomination, despite her continued drug problems, something she would not overcome until the mid-80s. A 1977 album, *Etta Is Betta Than Evah*, completed her Chess contract, and she moved to Warner Brothers. *Deep In The Night*, was a critics' favourite. A live album, *Late Show*, released in 1986, featured Shuggie Otis and Eddie 'Cleanhead' Vinson. A renewed public profile followed her appearance at the opening ceremony of the Los Angeles Olympics in 1988 and was followed by *Seven Year Itch*, her first album for Island Records in 1989. This, and the subsequent release, *Stickin' To My Guns*, found her back on form, aided and abetted once more by the Muscle Shoals team.

Albums: *At Last!* (1961), *Second Time Around* (1961), *Etta James* (1962), *Etta James Sings For Lovers* (1962), *Etta James Rocks The House* (1964), *Queen Of Soul* (1965), *Tell Mama* (1968), *Etta James Sings Funk* (1970), *Losers Weepers* (1971), *Etta James* (1973), *Come A Little Closer* (1974), *Etta Is Betta Than Evah!* (1978), *Deep In The Night* (1978), *Changes* (1980), *Good Rockin' Mama* (1981), *Tuff Lover* (1983), *Blues In The Night* (1986), *Late Show* (1986), *Seven Year Itch* (1989), *Stickin' To My Guns* (1990), *The Right Time* (1992). Compilations: *Etta James Top Ten* (1963), *Peaches* (1973), *Good Rockin' Mama* (1981), *Chess Masters* (1981), *Tuff Lover* (1983), *R&B Queen* (1986), *Her Greatest Sides, Volume One* (1987), *R&B Dynamite* (1987), *Chicago Golden Years* (1988), *On Chess* (1988).

James, Frank 'Springback'

James recorded his piano blues between 1934 and 1937. The first tracks released in the depths of the Depression, sold in miserable quantities; they show a strong affinity to the styles of St. Louis. Later recordings mostly included Willie Bee James on guitar, and are influenced by the popular recording team of Leroy Carr and Scrapper Blackwell. James wrote strong, original lyrics, but was often a monotonous performer. Sometimes, however, he struck a more compelling stance, as on the erotic 'Snake Hip Blues' and the seemingly autobiographical 'Poor Coal Loader' and 'Will My Bad Luck Ever Change?'

Album: *Frank 'Springback' James* (1988).

James, Jesse

It was once believed that James was a convict, brought to the studio under guard to make his four recordings in 1936, and that he broke down before they were completed. This romantic extrapolation from the lyrics of 'Lonesome Day Blues', 'I'm goin' to the Big House, an' I don't even care . . . I might get four or five years, lord, an' I might get the chair', seems to be untrue; James was probably Cincinnati based, for he accompanied titles by Walter Coleman. James was a rough, two-fisted barrelhouse pianist, with a hoarse, declamatory vocal delivery, equally suited to the anguished 'Lonesome Day Blues', to a robust version of 'Casey Jones' and the earthily obscene 'Sweet Patuni', which was issued much later on a bootleg 'party' single.

Album: *Piano Blues Vol. 2 - The Thirties* (1987).

James, Skip

b. Nehemiah Curtis James, 9 June 1902, Bentonia, Mississippi, USA, d. 3 October 1969, Philadelphia, Pennsylvania, USA. A solitary figure, James was an emotional, lyrical performer whose talent as a guitar player and arranger enhanced an already impressive body of work. His early career included employment as a pianist in a Memphis whore-house, as well as the customary appearances at local gatherings and road houses. In 1931 he successfully auditioned for the Paramount recording company, for whom he completed an estimated 26 masters. These exceptional performances included 'Devil Got My Woman', written when his brief marriage broke down, as well as 'Hard Time Killin' Floor Blues' and 'I'm So Glad', which was subsequently recorded by Cream. James abandoned music during the late 30s in favour of the church and was ordained as a Baptist minister in 1942. He briefly resumed more secular pursuits during the 50s, and was

Skip James

brought back to public attention by guitarists John Fahey, Bill Barth and Canned Heat's Henry Vestine, who discovered the dispirited singer in a Mississippi hospital. James remained a reserved individual, but his accomplished talents were welcomed on the thriving folk and college circuit where he joined contemporaries such as Mississippi John Hurt and Sleepy John Estes. Two superb collections for the Vanguard label, *Skip James Today* and *Devil Got My Woman*, showcased James' remarkable skills. His high, poignant voice brought an air of vulnerability to an often declamatory genre and his albums remain among the finest of the country-blues canon. Recurring illness sadly forced James to retire and he died in 1969 following a prolonged battle with cancer.

Albums: *The Greatest Of The Delta Blues Singers* (1964), *Skip James Today!* (1965), *Devil Got My Woman* (1968), *I'm So Glad* (1978), *Live At The 2nd Fret, Philadelphia, 1966* (1988).

Compilations: *I'm So Glad* (1978), *The Complete 1931 Session* (1986).

James, Willie Bee

Chicago-based James could sing blues to good effect - he issued a fine 78 on Vocalion Records - but the bulk of his recording was done as a studio guitarist for Bluebird Records during the 30s. James light, swinging guitar was reminiscent of Big Bill Broonzy, but he was equally at home backing relatively unemotional northern singers such as Bumble Bee Slim, Merline Johnson and Curtis Jones, as well as dueting with Tennessee guitarist John Henry Barbee or the pianist Frank James, and as a member of Tampa Red's pop-inflected Chicago Five.

Selected albums: *Chicago Blues* (1985), *Mississippi Country Blues Vol. 2* (1987), *The Yas Yas Girl* (1989).

Jefferson, Blind Lemon

b. July 1897, Wortham, (Couchman) Texas, USA, d. December 1929, Chicago, Illinois, USA. Jefferson was one of the earliest and most influential rural blues singers to record. He was one of seven children born to Alex Jefferson and Classie Banks (or Bates) and was either blind or partially blind from early childhood. As his handicap precluded his employment as a farm hand he turned to music and sang at rural parties, on the streets of small towns, in cafes, juke joints and brothels. This mode of life turned him into a wanderer and he travelled far, though he always maintained his links with Texas. Like many 'blind' singers stories are told of his ability to find his way around and read situations. He was usually armed and was even said to have been involved in shooting incidents. In late 1925, or early 1926, he was taken to Chicago by a Dallas record retailer to record for Paramount Records. His first offerings were two religious tracks which were issued under the pseudonym Reverend. L.J. Bates. Soon after this, in he was to begin the long series of blues recordings which made him famous throughout black America and even affected the work of rural white musicians. Between 1926 and 1929 he had more than 90 tracks issued, all bar two appearing on Paramount. His only known photograph, taken from a Paramount publicity shot, shows a portly man of indeterminate age wearing clear glasses over closed eyes set in a 'baby' face. He was accorded the distinction (shared with Ma Rainey) of having a record issued with his picture on the label and described as 'Blind Lemon Jefferson's Birthday Record'. He had a good vocal range, honed by use in widely different venues, and a complicated, dense, free-form guitar style that became a nightmare for future analysts and copyists because of its disregard for time and bar structure, but suited his music perfectly and spoke directly to his black audience, both in the city and in the country. His success can be measured by the fact that he once owned two cars and could afford to hire a chauffeur to drive them. He is also said to have employed boys to lead him. Leadbelly, and T-Bone Walker both claimed to have worked for him in this capacity during their youth. His later recordings seemed to lose some of the originality and impact of his earlier work but he remained popular until his sudden and somewhat mysterious death. Legend has it that he froze to death on the streets of Chicago, although a more likely story is that he died of a heart attack while in his car, possibly during a snow storm, and was abandoned by his driver. At this date it is unlikely that the truth will ever be established. His records continue to be issued after his death and some recorded tributes have been made. His body was transported back to Texas for burial.

Selected albums: *King Of The Country Blues* (1985), *The Complete* (1991).

Jeffery, Robert

b. 14 January 1915, Tulsa, Oklahoma, USA, d. 20 July 1976, San Diego, California, USA. A blues guitarist, influenced by Blind Lemon Jefferson, as well as a pianist, Jeffery worked with a carnival as a young man, snake charming and boxing against all comers. He moved to California 'with the rest of the Okies' in the Depression, working as a car mechanic and playing piano on weekends, often at a club owned by Thomas Shaw. After his retirement, he made some festival appearances and recordings on piano in the 70s, and was still a good guitarist, although he insisted he had given it up.

Album: *San Diego Blues Jam* (1974).

Jenkins, Bobo

b. John Pickens Jenkins, 7 January 1916, Forkland, Alabama, USA, d. 14 August, 1984, Detroit, Michigan, USA. After hoboing from 1928, and wartime army service, Jenkins settled in Detroit from 1944. In 1954, he recorded for Chess, singing and playing guitar on a classic record, with both sides notable for the swooping, amplified harmonica of Robert Richard; 'Democrat Blues' was unusual in being politically explicit. In the 50s Jenkins also recorded for Boxer and Fortune (the latter session again featuring Richard on excellent versions of 'Baby Don't You Want To Go' and '10 Below Zero'). At this time, Jenkins worked as a photographer in the ghetto bars, and his pictures are a valuable and fascinating record of the musicians and their audience. In the 70s, he founded the Big Star label, and issued three albums.

Albums: *Detroit Blues - The Early 1950s* (1966), *The Life Of Bobo Jenkins*, (1972), *Here I Am A*

Fool In Love Again (1975), *Detroit All Purpose Blues* (c.1978), *Blues For Big Town* (1989).

John, Little Willie

b. William Edgar John, 15 November 1937, Cullendale, Arkansas, USA, d. 26 May 1968. The brother of singer Mable John, Willie was one of the most popular 50s R&B. His first hit, 'All Around The World', also known as 'Grits Ain't Groceries', was followed by a spectacular double-sided smash, 'Need Your Love So Bad'/'Home At Last'. The a-side of this successful coupling was later recorded by Fleetwood Mac. It was followed by 'Fever'/'Letter From My Darling', both sides of which also reached the US R&B Top 10. 'Fever', written by Otis Blackwell (as 'Davenport') and Eddie Cooley, was a million-selling single in its own right, topping that particular chart in May 1956. However, the song is more closely associated with Peggy Lee, who took the song into the US and UK charts in 1958. 'Talk To Me, Talk To Me' gave Little Willie John another gold disc that year, while in 1959 he scored further success with 'Leave My Kitten Alone', a favoured song of British beat groups. The singer's professional career faltered during the 60s while his private life ended in tragedy. Convicted of manslaughter in 1966, John died of a heart attack in Washington State Prison in 1968.

Albums: *Fever* (1956), *Talk To Me* (1958), *Mister Little Willie John* (1958), *Action* (1960), *Sure Things* (1961), *The Sweet, The Hot, The Teen Age Beat* (1961), *Come On And Join* (1962), *These Are My Favourite Songs* (1964), *Little Willie John Sings All Originals* (1966). Compilations: *Free At Last* (1970), *Grits And Soul* (1985), *Fever* (1990).

John, Mable

b. 3 November 1930, Bastrop, Louisiana, USA. The elder sister of Little Willie John, author of 'Leave My Kitten Alone', Mable John was an early signing to Berry Gordy's Tamla-Motown label. She appeared on the first Motortown Revue (1959) and recorded four singles for the company. After an interlude running a small Chicago outlet, she signed to Stax in 1966. Here Mable specialized in 'deep' ballads, pitting her emotive pleas against a complementary Booker T. And The MGs/Mar-Keys backing. 1966's 'Your Good Thing (Is About To End)', a tale of

infidelity and the consequences thereof which Lou Rawls later took into the pop chart, was the first of seven releases. In 1968 she joined Ray Charles' Raelettes, and ceased performing as a solo artist. Her distinctive voice is nonetheless audible on several of the group's Tangerine recordings. Mable John subsequently worked as an advisor on *Lady Sings The Blues*, Berry Gordy's film biography of Billie Holiday.

Johnson, Bessie

A gospel singer from one of the Sanctified sects, Johnson was from Columbus, Mississippi, and was last heard of in Arkansas in 1964. Remembered by Lonnie McIntorsh as 'the singingest woman I've ever known,' Johnson possessed a huge contralto voice, with a rasping vibrato as wide as a church door. She was at her best when accompanied by McIntorsh's metronomic guitar, or that of Will Shade; her own Sanctified Singers were endearingly ragged, and she had to order them to 'Come on' or 'Get the beat'. The fact that recordings including such *ad libs* were released speaks for their raw authenticity. Two tracks by the Memphis Sanctified Singers (on which Shade played guitar) beautifully contrast her rough style with Melinda Taylor's sweeter voice.

Album: *Bessie Johnson* (c.1965).

Johnson, 'Big' Jack

b. 30 July 1940, Lambert, Mississippi, USA. Johnson's father led a local band and at the age of 13 Jack was sitting in on acoustic guitar. He was inspired by B.B. King's records to switch to electric guitar five years later, and in 1962 he sat in with Frank Frost and Sam Carr, with whom he continues to work sporadically. This group recorded an album for Sam Phillips in 1963 (credited to Frank Frost And The Nighthawks) and another for Jewel in 1966, again under Frost's name. In 1979 they made an album as 'The Jelly Roll Kings', featuring Johnson's first vocals on record, and his first album under his own name, released in 1987, confirmed that he had very strong traditional Mississippi blues roots. His follow-up album in 1989 was more experimental and musically less successful, but a single for Rooster in 1990 found him back on form.

Album: *The Oil Man*

Johnson, 'Blind' Willie

b. c.1902, Marlin, Texas, USA, d. c.1949, Beaumont, Texas, USA. Blind Willie Johnson was arguably the greatest and most popular 'sanctified' singer to record in the pre-World War II era. His forceful singing and stunning guitar work ensured that he continued to sell records even into the Depression. His blindness has been attributed to many causes, the most likely being that his step-mother threw lye-water in his face during a jealous fit when he was about seven. That he should turn to music after this is a recurring motif in the stories of many blind black singers, but even earlier Johnson had admitted to a desire to preach. Now he combined the two talents to produce outstandingly powerful religious music as he played for tips on the streets. Despite this commitment to the church there seems to have been a secular side to his music and it remains probable that he recorded two unissued blues under the pseudonym of Blind Texas Marlin at his second session for Columbia. Johnson began recording for the label in December 1927, by which time he had moved to Dallas, and his first release became an instant success selling in excess of 15,000 copies. Between then and April 1930 he recorded a total of 30 issued tracks (all for the same company), maintaining a level of quality that is amazing even by today's standards. Early research on Johnson's life was done by Sam Charters when he interviewed Johnson's wife Angeline in the late 50s. The picture was fleshed out, 20 years later, by the work of Dan Williams who reported on Johnson's travelling habits, including a spell in the company of Blind Willie McTell. Charters also noted the influence exerted on his singing style by an obscure, older singer Madkin Butler, and his early commitment to the Church Of God In Christ. Many of Johnson's recordings feature a second, female vocalist and it was long assumed that one of these was Angeline. Now it seems more likely that this is an early girlfriend (possibly wife) of Johnson's named Willie B. Harris whose affiliations were with the 'Sanctified' church. Willie Johnson had returned to the Baptist fold by the time he married Angeline in June of 1930. When using a second vocalist Johnson favoured a ragged antiphonal approach to his singing, in which he usually employed a marked false bass, and when performing alone he used his guitar as the second voice, often leaving it to complete his own vocal lines. He could finger-pick but is most famous for his outstanding slide technique. Possibly his most well-known piece today is the free-form guitar impersonation of a congregation moaning 'Dark Was The Night And Cold The Ground', which was used in its original form in Pasolini's film *The Gospel According To Saint Mark* and adapted by Ry Cooder as the theme music to *Paris, Texas*. Johnson lived his later years in Beaumont, Texas and it was there that his house caught fire some time in the 40s. Johnson survived the fire but returned to the house and slept on a wet mattress covered by newspapers. This resulted in the pneumonia which killed him.

Selected albums: *Praise God I'm Satisfied* (1989), *Sweeter As The Years Go By* (1990).

Johnson, Edith

b. Edith North, 2 January 1903, St. Louis, Missouri, USA, d. 28 February 1988, St. Louis, Missouri, USA. In 1925, Edith married Jesse Johnson, who was OKeh Records' 'race' talent scout in St. Louis, and went to work in his record shop. In 1929, she recorded 18 splendid blues tracks playing good piano on 'Nickel's Worth Of Liver Blues', and having a hit with 'Honey Dripper Blues'. Her voice was light but tough, sometimes hinting at violence, and making the threat explicit on 'Good Chib Blues'. Her husband's disapproval ended her singing career until 1961, when she made a few recordings that showed her to be still an expressive vocalist, with some interesting compositions. By this time, she had been for many years a successful operator of small businesses, and her elegant appearance belied the toughness of her repertoire.

Albums: *The Blues In St. Louis* (1984). *Honey Dripper Blues* (1991).

Johnson, Ella

b. 22 June 1923, Darlington, North Carolina, USA. Johnson moved to New York City at the age of 17 to be with her brother, bandleader Buddy Johnson, who began featuring her unique voice on the most successful of his many fine songs on Decca Records. Beginning with 'Please, Mr Johnson' in 1940, she continued with blues and jazz standards-to-be 'That's The Stuff You Gotta Watch', 'Since I Fell For You'

and 'I Still Love You' among dozens of others. She had a solitary release on the small Harlem label in 1946, and moved to Mercury with Buddy's band in 1953, where she recorded her first album *Swing Me*. She continued having strong sellers like 'I Don't Want Nobody (To Have My Love But You)', and moved on to Roulette in 1958; her final few releases in the early 60s were on Old Town and Mercury. By the mid-60s, Buddy Johnson had disbanded and Ella, still a relatively young woman, retired to be with him in his last few years until his death in 1977. She still lives in New York City, but has not resumed her musical career.
Albums: *Swing Me* (1956, reissued 1988), *Say Ella* (1983).

Johnson, Henry

b. 8 December 1908, Union, South Carolina, USA, d. February 1974, Union, South Carolina, USA. Johnson was an elderly man before he became known as a blues singer outside his immediate home area, but he had learned guitar in childhood from his brother, and later taught himself piano. Henry sang religious material in church in his younger days, and later in quartets, appearing on radio with the West Spring Friendly Four and the Silver Star Quartet in the 30s. His musical career was only ever part-time, but on his retirement, he was discovered by blues enthusiasts and made a number of recordings, as well as personal appearances in South Carolina. He appeared on two albums exhibiting a strong, distinctive singing voice and a powerful guitar style, especially when playing bottleneck. Oddly, a single was issued in the UK, featuring two fine solo performances.
Album: *Union County Flash* (1973).

Johnson, James

Johnson was a bass and lead guitarist based in Baton Rouge, Louisiana, USA. He taught himself to play bass from records while at high school and played with a local band called Big Poppa And The Canecutters. It was Big Poppa who introduced him to Slim Harpo (James Moore) and Johnson worked with him during the 60s, initially on bass but later replacing Rudi Richard as lead guitarist; Johnson is best-known for playing the lead on Harpo's big hit 'Baby Scratch My Back'. After Harpo's death in 1970, Johnson virtually stopped playing and has a full-

time job outside music. However, at the beginning of the 90s he was playing bass with Raful Neal in Baton Rouge on a part-time basis.

Johnson, James 'Stump'

b. 17 January 1902, Clarksville, Tennessee, USA, d. 5 December 1969, St. Louis, Missouri, USA. Called 'Stump' for his short stature, Johnson was the brother of Jesse Johnson, and was raised in St. Louis from 1909. He learned piano in pool rooms, his brother's record shop, and Boots' club on the levee. In 1928, he made his first records, had a hit with 'The Duck's Yas-Yas-Yas'. Johnson continued to record until 1933, although gambling seems to have been more important to him than music. He employed a typical St. Louis four-to-the-bar chordal bass, with economical right hand decoration, and sang in a wistful voice that sometimes delivered remarkably forthright sexual material. He recorded again in 1964, but was in sad decline.
Album: *The Duck's Yas-Yas-Yas* (1981).

Johnson, Jimmy

b. James Thompson, 25 November 1928, Holly Springs, Mississippi, USA. Jimmy came from a musical family and was a singer and guitarist with several gospel groups until 1959, nine years after he moved to Chicago. At that time he sat in with Magic Sam and Freddie King, following the lead of his blues playing brothers Syl Johnson and Mac Thompson aka Mac Johnson, but in the 60s Jimmy was much more involved in the soul scene. He returned to the blues in the 70s and played second guitar with Jimmy Dawkins and Otis Rush, but after recording for MCM in 1975, he has enjoyed a moderately successful solo career. His beautiful, gospel-tinged songs and performances put him in the premier rank of modern blues artists.
Selected albums: *Johnson's Whacks* (1979), *Bar Room Preacher* (1983).

Johnson, Johnnie

b. 1924, Fairmont, West Virginia, USA. Johnson's name may not be well-known but his sound has been heard by millions: he was the piano player on most of Chuck Berry's classic Chess Records tracks. Johnson began learning to play piano at the age of seven without the benefit of lessons, influenced by jazz and

198

Lonnie Johnson

boogie-woogie musicians such as Earl Hines, Meade 'Lux' Lewis and Clarence 'Pinetop' Smith. After a spell in the US Army Johnson began performing professionally in 1946 and in 1952, leading the Sir John Trio, hired the young Berry as his guitarist. Berry soon began writing the group's songs and became its leader. Chess artist Muddy Waters suggested the group audition for that label and Berry was signed in 1955. Johnson can be heard on Berry hits such as 'Maybellene', 'Roll Over Beethoven' and 'Johnny B. Goode', which Berry has stated was written for Johnson. Johnson also played in Berry's road band but in the 60s left, working with blues guitarist Albert King, among others. Johnson led his own band in the 70s but still worked with Berry on occasion. He was featured in the 1986 Berry concert film *Hail! Hail! Rock And Roll* and later appeared as a guest on Keith Richards' debut solo album, *Talk Is Cheap*. Johnson has recorded sparingly under his own name, releasing his first solo album in 1987. Album: *Blue Hand Johnnie* (1987), *Rockin' Eighty-Eights* (1991).

Johnson, Lonnie

b. Alonzo Johnson, 8 February 1889, New Orleans, Louisiana, USA, d. 16 June 1970. One of the most influential and original blues musicians. In the early 1900s he played guitar and violin in saloons in his home town. He performed around the red light district Storyville. Shortly before the outbreak of war he visited Europe, returning to New Orleans in 1919. During his absence most of his closest relatives had died in an influenza epidemic and Johnson soon took to the road. He played guitar and banjo in bands in St Louis and then Chicago where he established his reputation as one of the USA's most popular blues singers. For two years the OKeh Record Company issued one of his records every six weeks. During this period he became a member of the house band at OKeh, recording with many leading jazz and blues artists, sometimes as accompanist, other times as duettist. Among the blues singers with whom he recorded were Texas Alexander and Victoria Spivey. The jazz musicians with whom he played on 20s sessions included Duke Ellington, Eddie Lang, McKinney's Cotton Pickers, King Oliver and, most notably, Louis Armstrong. During the 30s Johnson divided his time

between record sessions, club dates and radio shows. This was not all; like many of his New Orleans compatriots, he seems to have had a deep suspicion that the bubble would one day burst and he worked regularly outside music, usually at menial and physically demanding jobs. In the 40s Johnson began to gain in popularity, adopting the amplified guitar and singing programmes of blues intermingled with many of his own compositions, one of which, 'Tomorrow Night', was a successful record. In the 50s he played in the UK but performed mostly in the USA, living and playing in Chicago and, later, Cincinnati before settling in Philadelphia. In the 60s he again visited Europe and also appeared in New York and in Canada, where he became resident owning his own club in Toronto, for the last few years before his death in 1970. Johnson's ability to cross over from blues to jazz and back again was unusual amongst bluesmen of his generation. He brought to his blues guitar playing a level of sophistication that contrasted vividly with the often bitter directness of the lyrics he sang. His mellow singing voice, allied to his excellent diction, helped to make him one of the first rhythm balladeers. He influenced numerous blues and jazz guitarists, amongst them T-Bone Walker, Lowell Fulson, B.B. King, Teddy Bunn, Eddie Durham and Charlie Christian. Albums: *Lonnie Johnson Vol. 1* (1926-28), *Lonnie Johnson* (1926-42), *Historical Recordings* (1927-32), with Eddie Lang *Blue Guitars Vols 1/2* (1927-29).

Johnson, Luther 'Georgia Snake Boy'

b. Lucius Brinson Johnson, 30 August 1934, Davidsboro, Georgia, USA, d. 18 March 1976. Johnson was a guitarist/bassist/vocalist who formed his first band in Chicago at the age of 19. His boyhood ambition was to play with Muddy Waters; he achieved this in the 60s. Johnson played in the raw, urban style of Waters, and was also proficient at older country blues styles. His first recording (as 'Little Luther') was for Chess and he also recorded with Waters' sideman for the Spivey and Douglas labels. In the 70s he made two albums for the Black And Blue company while touring Europe. Johnson lived in Boston Massachusetts from 1970 until his death from cancer in 1976. Album: *Born In Georgia* (1972), *On The Road*

Again (1991, rec. 1972). Compilation: *Chicken Shack* (1967/68).

Johnson, Luther 'Guitar Junior'

b. 11 April 1939, Itta Bena, Mississippi, USA. Johnson's early musical experience was in gospel and he taught himself guitar around 1954, switching to blues before he moved with his family to Chicago's west side in 1955. he played local clubs, teamed up with Magic Sam in the early 60s; Johnson is now regarded as one of the foremost exponents of the guitar-based west side blues style. He spent most of the 70s as a member of Muddy Waters' band, with whom he recorded and also had his own recordings issued on the Big Beat, MCM, Black And Blue, Alligator, Blue Phoenix (the latter also available on Rooster Blues) and Bullseye Blues labels, and was featured on three albums by the Nighthawks.
Selected albums: *Luther's Blues* (1976), *I Changed* (1979), *Doin' The Sugar Too* (1984), *I Want To Groove With You* (1990), *It's Good To Me* (1992).

Johnson, Luther 'Houserocker'

Johnson was an Atlanta, Georgia, USA-based blues singer and guitarist who learned a few rudiments of music from his father but was largely self-taught. His career began around the mid-60s when he worked as a backing musician for major blues artists appearing in Altanta's clubs, and in the early 80s he began establishing a reputation with his band the Houserockers. He works regularly at Blind Willie's, Atlanta's best-known blues club, both as a bandleader (his group is now known as the Shadows) in his own right and as backing guitarist for bigger names. He achieved a measure of international prominence in 1990 with the release of a well-received album on Ichiban; the mixture of blues standards and original material revealed a talented modern blues musician with his roots deep in the tradition.
Album: *Takin' A Bite Outta The Blues* (1990).

Johnson, Mary

b. c.1900, Eden Station, Mississippi, USA. Johnson had six children by Lonnie Johnson during their marriage (1925-32). She began her own recording career in 1929 in the company of Henry Brown's piano and Ike Rodgers' trombone. Mary continued to appear on the St. Louis music scene at least up until her last recordings as a blues singer in 1936, working with stalwarts such as Roosevelt Sykes, Peetie Wheatstraw, Tampa Red and Thomas A. Dorsey. By the 40s she was doing church work and in 1948 she recorded for the Coleman Label with the Mary Johnson Davis Gospel Singers. By the name she employed for these recordings it appears likely that she had remarried. Johnson had been employed as a hospital worker in St. Louis for years before she retired in 1959.
Selected albums: *Ike Rodgers' Gut Bucket Trombone* (1968), *Piano Blues Vol. 19* (1984).

Johnson, Merline

b. c.1912, Mississippi, USA. Information on Johnson's early years is sketchy. She began recording in 1937, and enjoyed a successful recording career for several years, making a large number of records until 1941, accompanied by some of the major blues musicians in Chicago at that time, including Big Bill Broonzy, Lonnie Johnson and Blind John Davis (sometimes credited as Her Rhythm Rascals). Her vocals were tough and confident, occasionally reminiscent of Memphis Minnie, with an inclination to the sensual as well as the witty. Her nickname, 'The Yas Yas Girl' (a rare American instance of rhyming slang) bears out this image. Some of her records, however, had a jazzier orientation. She recorded again at a single session after the war, in 1947, but nothing further is known of her.
Album: *The Yas Yas Girl* (1989).

Johnson, Pete

b. 25 March 1904, Kansas City, Missouri, USA, d. 23 March 1967. After playing drums when a teenager, Johnson switched to piano in 1926 and swiftly became a leading exponent of the blues. He was also an excellent accompanist to blues singers; especially Joe Turner, with whom he established a partnership that lasted for the rest of his life. In 1936 the ubiquitous John Hammond brought Johnson and Turner to New York where they played at the Famous Door. Two years later Johnson played at one of Hammond's Spirituals To Swing concerts at Carnegie Hall and later performed and recorded with Albert Ammons and Meade 'Lux' Lewis as the Boogie Woogie Trio. During the 40s, Johnson continued his solo career, interspersed with engagements with Ammons and, often, Joe Turner. In the 50s Johnson toured the USA and Europe and made several records with Turner and with Jimmy Rushing. As a blues and boogie-woogie pianist, Johnson was superb and his thunderous left hand was always a joy to hear. In the recordings he made with Turner he invariably rose above himself, delivering both forceful solos and lifting the singer to some of his best work. Shortly after playing at the Newport Jazz Festival in 1958 Johnson suffered a stroke which incapacitated him. He did venture back to the recording studios in 1960 but did not appear again in public until 1967, when he was helped onstage to receive an ovation from the audience at the Spirituals To Swing 30th Anniversary concert. He took a bow and was being led off when the band swung into his best-known composition, 'Roll 'Em Pete', and his old companion, Joe Turner, prepared to sing. Johnson sat down at the piano alongside Ray Bryant and began picking uncertainly at the keys. Then, gradually, with Bryant laying down a solid left hand, Johnson showed that there was still music inside him. It was a long way from great piano playing but given the circumstances it was a highly emotional moment. It was made more so when, two months later, in March 1967, Johnson died.

Albums: with others *Spirituals To Swing* (1938-39), *The Essential Jimmy Rushing* (1955), with Joe Turner *The Boss Of The Blues* (1956), with others *Spirituals to Swing 30th Anniversary Concert* (1967). Compilations: *Master Of Blues And Boogie Woogie Vols 1-2* (1939-49), *The Boogie King* (1940-44), *The Rarest Pete Johnson Vols 1, 2* (1947-54).

Johnson, Robert

b. Robert Leroy Johnson, 8 May 1891, Hazlehurst, Mississippi, USA, d. 16 August 1938, Greenwood, Mississippi, USA. For a subject upon which it is dangerous to generalise, it hardly strains credulity to suggest that Johnson was the fulcrum upon which post-war Chicago blues turned. The techniques which he had distilled from others' examples, including Charley Patton, Son House and the unrecorded Ike Zinnerman, in turn became the template for influential musicians such as Muddy Waters, Elmore James and those that followed them. Endowed by some writers with more originality

than was in fact the case, it was as an interpreter that Johnson excelled, raising a simple music form to the level of performance art at a time when others were content to iterate the conventions. He was one of the first of his generation to make creative use of others' recorded efforts, adapting and augmenting their ideas to such extent as to impart originality to the compositions they inspired. Tempering hindsight with perspective, it should be noted that only his first record, 'Terraplane Blues', sold in any quantity; even close friends and family remained unaware of his recorded work until decades later, when researchers such as Gayle Dean Wardlow and Mack McCormick contacted them. In all, Johnson recorded 29 compositions at five sessions held between 23 November 1936 and 20 June 1937; a further 'bawdy' song recorded at the engineers' request is as yet unlocated. It has never been established which, if any, of his recordings were specifically created for the studio and what proportion were regularly performed, although associate Johnny Shines attested to the effect that 'Come On In My Kitchen' had upon audiences. Similarly, the image of shy, retiring genius has been fabricated out of his habit of turning away from the engineers and singing into the corners of the room, which Ry Cooder identifies as 'corner loading', a means of enhancing vocal power. That power and the precision of his guitar playing are evident from the first take of 'Kind-hearted Women Blues', which like 'I Believe I'll Dust My Broom' and 'Sweet Home Chicago', is performed without bottle-neck embellishment. All eight titles from the first session in San Antonis, Texas, exhibit the attenuated rhythm patterns, adapted from a boogie pianist's left-hand 'walking basses', that became synonymous with post-war Chicago blues and Jimmy Reed in particular. Several alternate takes survive and reveal how refined Johnson's performances were, only 'Come On In My Kitchen' being played at two contrasting tempos. Eight more titles were recorded over two days, including 'Walkin Blues', learned from Son House, and 'Cross Road Blues', the song an echo of the legend that Johnson had sold his soul to the Devil to achieve his musical skill. 'Preachin' Blues' and 'If I Had Possessions Over Judgement Day' were both impassioned performances that show his ability was consummate. The balance

Robert Johnson

of his repertoire was recorded over a weekend some seven months later in Dallas. These 11 songs run the gamut of emotions, self-pity, tenderness and frank sexual innuendo giving way to representations of demonic possession, paranoia and despair. Fanciful commentators have taken 'Hellhound On My Trail' and 'Me And The Devil' to be literal statements rather than the dramatic enactment of feeling expressed in the lyrics. Johnson's ability to project emotion, when combined with the considered way in which he lifted melodies and mannerisms from his contemporaries, gainsay a romantic view of his achievements. Nevertheless, the drama in his music surely reflected the drama in his lifestyle, that on an itinerant with a ready facility to impress his female audience. One such dalliance brought about his end a year after his last session, poisoned by a jealous husband while performing in a jook joint at Three Forks, outside Greenwood, Mississippi. At about that time, Columbia A&R man John Hammond was seeking Johnson represent country blues at a concert, entitled 'From Spirituals To Swing', that took place at New York's Carnegie Hall on 23 December 1938, with Big Bill Broonzy taking Johnson's place. Robert Johnson possessed unique abilities, unparalleled in his contemporaries and those that followed him. The importance of his effect on subsequent musical developments cannot be diminished but neither should it be seen in isolation.

Selected album: *Robert Johnson: The Complete Recordings*.

Further reading: *Searching For Robert Johnson*, Peter Guralnick.

Johnson, Syl

b. Sylvester Thompson, 1 July 1936, Holly Springs, Mississippi, USA. Johnson was the youngest of three children and his family moved to Chicago during the late 40s. An elder brother, Mac Thompson, played bass with the Magic Sam Blues Band. Having learned guitar and harmonica, Johnson began frequenting the city's southside blues clubs, playing alongside Howlin' Wolf, Muddy Waters and Junior Wells. His first recordings were made in 1956 accompanying Billy Boy Arnold, after which Syl appeared on sessions for Shakey Jake, Junior Wells and Jimmy Reed. In 1959 Federal released Johnson's first solo single, 'Teardrops',

and he recorded unsuccessfully for several independents until signing with Twilight (later changed to Twinight), in 1967. His debut there, 'Come On Sock It To Me', reached number 12 in the R&B chart. Johnson, however, was not solely confined to performing. He also produced several local acts including Tyrone Davis and Otis Clay while the Deacons, his backing group, featuring brother Jimmy Johnson on guitar, enjoyed a minor hit on the singer's Shama label. Syl was then spotted by Willie Mitchell and 'Dresses Too Short' (1968) was recorded with the Mitchell's Hi Records house band. The remaining Twinight sessions were divided between Memphis and Chicago. Johnson remained with the label until 1971, recording two albums in the process. Free to sign with Hi, he began a series of releases which matched those of labelmate Al Green for excellence. Brash, up-tempo topsides, including 'Back For A Taste Of Your Love' and 'We Did It', contrasted often reflective couplings, of which 'Anyway The Wind Blows' and 'I Hear The Love Chimes' were particularly emotive. The third of his exemplary albums for Hi, *Total Explosion*, produced Syl's only substantial R&B hit when his version of 'Take Me To The River' (1975) reached number 7. However, his final years at Hi were dogged by internal problems and towards the end of the decade he reactivated his Shama label. A contemporary blues/soul collection, *Ms Fine Brown Frame* (1982), was licensed to Boardwalk, while a French album, *Suicide Blues*, followed in 1984. By the mid-80s, he had semi-retired from the music business and opened a string of fast-food fish restaurants.

Albums: *Dresses Too Short* (1968), *Is It Because I'm Black?* i (1970), *Back For A Taste Of Your Love* (1973), *Diamond In The Rough* (1974), *Total Explosion* (1976), *Uptown Shakedown* (1979), *Brings Out The Blues In Me* (1980), *Ms Fine Brown Frame* (1983), *Suicide Blues* (1984), *Foxy Brown* (1988). Compilations: *Brings Out The Blues In Me* (1986), *Is It Because I'm Black?* ii (1986), *The Love Chimes* (1986), *Stuck In Chicago* (1989).

Johnson, Tommy

b. c.1896, Mississippi, USA, d. 1 November 1956. Although his recorded output was contained within a mere four sessions, undertaken in February and August 1928, Johnson remains one of the pivotal figures of delta blues. His work includes 'Cool Drink Of Water Blues', which featured the memorable lyric 'I asked her for water and she brought me gasoline', later adopted by Howlin' Wolf, while a 60s group comprising of enthusiasts took their name from 'Canned Heat Blues'. Johnson's haunting falsetto wrought emotion from his excellent compositions which influenced several artists including the Mississippi Sheiks and Robert Nighthawk. Although Johnson ceased recording prematurely, he remained an active performer until his death from a heart attack in 1956.

Albums: *The Famous 1928 Tommy Johnson/Ishman Bracey Session* (1970), *The Complete Recordings 1928-1930* (1988).

Jones, Birmingham

b. Wright Birmingham, 9 January 1937, Saginaw, Michigan, USA. Moving to Chicago around 1950, Jones was a saxophonist and guitarist with various blues bands throughout the 50s. By the middle of the decade, when he recorded for Ebony, he was a talented Little Walter imitator on harmonica. A 1965 session for Vivid was unissued for many years, and did not live up to the promise of the Ebony 78. Jones returned to club work, but had largely retired from the music business by the mid-70s.

Album: *Chills And Fever* (1985).

Jones, Coley

Jones led the Dallas String Band, the sole recorded exemplars of black Texan string band music, although their line-up on record of two mandolins, guitar and bass omits the violin (and sometimes clarinet and trumpet) which were usually included on live dates. Jones was an indifferent guitarist, but a brilliant mandolinist, at his best on the sparkling 'Dallas Rag'. The band also played pop songs and blues (although, like all their repertoire, the blues were played more as entertainment than for personal expression). As a soloist, Jones performed comic songs such as 'Drunkard's Special' and 'Travelling Man', and humorous monologues. In duet with the female singer Bobbie Cadillac, he pandered to more up-to-date tastes, recording four variants of 'Tight Like That', but it is his, and his band's, songster material that is of more enduring value.

Album: *Coley Jones & the Dallas String Band* (1983).

Jones, Curtis

b. 18 August 1906, Naples, Texas USA, d. 11 September 1971, Munich, Germany. One of a coterie of bluesman who were to make Europe their home, pianist Jones began his recording career in 1947 and his first release, 'Lonesome Bedroom Blues', was a major hit. The song remained in Columbia's catalogue until the demise of the 78, eventually becoming a blues standard in the repertoire of others. On the strength of that success, Jones enjoyed a voluminous recording career until 1941 whereupon he worked outside of music. In 1958 blues enthusiasts located him living in run down conditions in Chicago. In the 60s Jones recorded albums for Bluesville, Delmark, Decca and Blue Horizon. He died in penury, his grave in Germany being sold in 1979 because no one paid for its upkeep.

Albums: *Lonesome Bedroom Blues* (1962), *Blues And Trouble 1937-40* (1983), *In London 1963* (1985).

Jones, Eddie 'Guitar Slim'

b. 10 December, 1926, Greenwood, Mississippi, USA, d. 7 February, 1959, New York City, New York, USA. Jones took the stage styles of his heroes T-Bone Walker and Gatemouth Brown and added his own particular flamboyance to become the first truly outrageous blues performer of the modern era. Along the way he wrote and recorded some blues that remain standards to this day. Raised in Mississippi he combined the intensity associated with singers from that area with the flair of his Texan models. He sang in church choirs in his home state before forming a trio with pianist Huey Smith working around New Orleans. A lean six footer he took on the persona of 'Guitar Slim' as he built a reputation for his extravagant stage-antics and off-stage drinking problem. One of the first performers to turn to the solid bodied electric guitar he began the experimentation with feedback control that reached its apogee with Jimi Hendrix in the late 60s. He combined this with garish stage-wear, that would include matching dyed hair, in fantastic colours and a gymnastic act that would see him leave the stage

and prowl the audience - and even the street outside - with the aid of a guitar cable that might extend to 350 feet and which connected to a PA system rather than to an amplifier. He played loud. The reputation that he built up in the clubs led Imperial Records to record him, as Eddie Jones, in 1951 and though they did not do well at the time, Imperial faired better of them by later re-crediting them to Guitar Slim. Slim's break came when he recorded in 1952 for the Bullet label in Nashville. The hit 'Feelin' Sad' aroused the interest of the Specialty label and sparked off Slim's most productive period. His first release for the new label was to become his anthem; 'The Things That I Used To Do' arranged by his pianist Ray Charles and featuring a distinctive guitar signature that has been reproduced almost as often as the Elmore James 'Dust My Broom' riff. It made Slim a blues force across the nation. In 1956 he left Specialty for Atco which hoped to sell him to the teenage public as Chess had done with Chuck Berry. This did not work out and before Slim could make a come-back he suddenly died from the combined effects of his drinking, fast living, and pneumonia.
Albums: *The Things That I Used To Do Red Cadillacs And Crazy Chicks* (1985), *The Atco Sessions* (1987).

Jones, Floyd

b. 21 July 1917, Marianna, Arkansas, USA, d. 19 December 1989, Chicago, Illinois, USA. Brought up in the Mississippi Delta, Jones had been playing guitar for some years by the time he settled in Chicago around 1945. He soon became part of a seminal group of musicians that had come up from the south and who were in the process of developing the new electric Chicago blues sound. He played with his guitarist cousin Moody Jones and harmonica player Snooky Pryor and their first record together 'Stockyard Blues' and 'Keep What You Got' is a classic of its time and place. Under his own name, he made a number of fine records for JOB, Chess and VeeJay in the early 50s, including the atmospheric 'Dark Road' which owed much to the work of Tommy Johnson. Rediscovered in the 60s' blues boom, he made records again for Testament and Advent.
Album: *Baby Face Leroy & Floyd Jones* (1984).

Jones, Little Hat

b. Dennis Jones. Jones was a taut voiced street singer from San Antonio, Texas, where he recorded 10 blues for ARC Records in 1929 and 1930, also accompanying Texas Alexander on one session. His trademark was a fast, rolling guitar introduction, followed by a marked rallentando as he or Alexander began singing. Only on 'Hurry Blues' did he maintain the pace of his introduction throughout, making the record label mistitle (for 'Worried Blues') inadvertently appropriate. An eclectic guitarist, Jones blended fingerpicking, strumming and boogie basses into a style that, while recognisably within the Texas mainstream, was distinctively his own.
Album: *Texas Blues Guitar* (1987).

Jones, Little Johnny

b. 1 November 1924, Jackson, Mississippi, USA, d. 19 November 1964, Chicago, Illinois, USA. Jones was a key figure in the development of post-war blues piano in Chicago. In the late 40s, he succeeded Big Maceo (a major influence on his own playing) as Tampa Red's partner, and helped move Tampa's music towards the amplified ensemble sound. Besides playing on many sessions, Jones made a few splendid recordings under his own name, two with Muddy Waters and six with the Elmore James band, which he adorned from 1952-60. His extrovert personality is apparent on the rocking 'Sweet Little Woman', but he was also capable of sensitive blues like 'Doin' The Best I Can'. Late in life, he was taped live, solo or with Billy Boy Arnold on harmonica, on titles which admirably display both his ebullient and introspective sides.
Albums: *Chicago Piano Plus* (1972), *Johnny Jones With Billy Boy Arnold* (1979), *Tampa Red* (1982), *King Of The Slide Guitar* (1983), *Midnight Blues* (1987), *Knights Of The Keyboard* (1988).

Jones, Maggie

b. Fae Barnes, c.1900, Hillsboro, Texas, USA. Jones worked in black revue from around 1922, first in New York and later in the Dallas/Fort Worth area until her retirement from show business about 1934. Her history thereafter is unknown. Her Columbia recordings, made between 1924 and 1926, besides including some of the most sensitive recorded playing by Louis

Armstrong and Charlie Green, are the work of one of the finest of the female vaudeville blues singers, with a resonant voice and outstanding technique, powered by a remarkable ability to sustain a note. Never as highly rated as Bessie Smith or Clara Smith, she easily bears comparison with either.

Albums: *Volume 1* (c.1985), *Volume 2* (c.1985).

Jones, Moody

b. 8 April 1908, Earle, Arkansas, USA. From a rural farming background, Jones moved to East St. Louis in the late 20s, by which time he was already making music on home-made instruments. Later, he learned guitar and in 1938, moved to Chicago and joined the blues circuit there. Along with his cousin Floyd Jones and harmonica player Snooky Pryor, he made some records in the late 40s. Their sound combined a powerful downhome Mississippi/Arkansas style with influences from records by artists such as Sonny Boy Williamson – the classic ingredients of post-war Chicago blues. Jones recorded a few tracks under his own name in the early 50s, but these were not issued at the time, despite the emotional quality of his vocals. In later years, he turned away from the blues and became a Christian minister.

Album: *Snooky Pryor* (1990).

Jones, Nyles

b. Robert L. Jones, 12 October 1924, Atlanta, Georgia, USA. At the age of five he moved to Winston-Salem, North Carolina, with his bluesman father and began playing guitar when eight years old, meeting many of the area's leading blues artists, including Rev. Gary Davis and Blind Boy Fuller, both of whom has some influence of his own music. He left home at 16 and travelled throughout the country, meeting Lightnin' Hopkins, who also left his mark on Jones' music. In 1970 he recorded in Pittsburgh for Gemini, and the resulting album and single were acclaimed for their raw blues passion. However, Jones became disillusioned at the lack of financial reward and returned to Winston-Salem in the mid-70s, assuming the name Guitar Gabriel. He was rediscovered and recorded again in 1991.

Albums: *My South/MyBlues* (1970), as Guitar Gabriel *Toot Blues* (1991).

Jones, Paul

b. 24 February 1942, Portsmouth, Hampshire, England. Jones began his singing career while studying at Oxford University. One of several aspirants 'sitting-in' with the trailblazing Blues Incorporated, he subsequently joined the Mann Hugg Blues Brothers, which evolved into Manfred Mann in 1963. This superior R&B act enjoyed several notable hits, including '5-4-3-2-1', 'Do Wah Diddy Diddy' and 'Pretty Flamingo'. The dissatisfied vocalist left the line-up in July 1966, scoring two UK Top 5 hits with the decidedly poppy 'High Time' (1966) and 'I've Been A Bad, Bad Boy' (1967). The latter was drawn from the soundtrack to *Privilege*, a socio-political film set in the near future in which Jones starred with the fashion model Jean Shrimpton. Subsequent singles, including 'Thinking Ain't For Me', 'It's Getting Better' and 'Aquarius', were minor successes as the artist increased his thespian commitments. Numerous appearances on stage and on celluloid followed, although he maintained a singing career through occasional solo recordings. Jones also contributed to the original recording of the Tim Rice/Andrew Lloyd Webber musical *Evita*, but in 1979 he rekindled his first musical love with the formation of the Blues Band. He has continued to lead this popular unit whenever acting commitments allow and Paul hosts a weekly Jazz FM blues/gospel and BBC Radio 2 R&B programme, demonstrating that his enthusiasm is backed up by a sound knowledge of both genres.

Albums: *My Way* (1966), *Privilege* (1967, soundtrack), *Love Me Love My Friends* (1968), *Crucifix On A Horse* (1971). Compilation: *Hits And Blues* (1980).

Joplin, Janis

b. 19 January 1941, Port Arthur, Texas, USA, d. 4 October 1970. Having made her performing debut in December 1961, this expressive singer subsequently enjoyed a tenure at Houston's Purple Onion club. Drawing inspiration from Bessie Smith and Odetta, Joplin developed a brash, uncompromising vocal style quite unlike accustomed folk madonnas Joan Baez and Judy Collins. The following year she joined the Waller Creek Boys, an Austin-based act which also featured Powell St. John, later of Mother Earth. In 1963 Janis moved to San Francisco

Janis Joplin

where she became a regular attraction at the North Beach Coffee Gallery. This initial spell was blighted by her addiction to amphetamines and in 1965 Joplin returned to Texas in an effort to dry out. She resumed her university studies, but on recovery turned again to singing. The following year Janis was invited back to the Bay Area to front Big Brother And The Holding Company. This exceptional improvisational blues act was the ideal foil to her full-throated technique and although marred by poor production, their debut album fully captures an early optimism.

Janis' reputation blossomed following the Monterey Pop Festival, of which she was one of the star attractions. The attendant publicity exacerbated growing tensions within the line-up as critics openly declared that the group was holding the singer's potential in check. *Cheap Thrills*, a joyous celebration of true psychedelic soul, contained two Joplin 'standards', 'Piece Of My Heart' and 'Ball And Chain', but the sessions were fraught with difficulties and Janis left the group in November 1968. Electric Flag members Mike Bloomfield, Harvey Brooks and Nick Gravenites helped assemble a new act, initially known as Janis And The Joplinaires, but later as the Kozmic Blues Band. Former Big Brother Sam Andrew (guitar/vocals), plus Terry Clements (saxophone), Marcus Doubleday (trumpet), Bill King (organ), Brad Campbell (bass) and Roy Markowitz (drums) made up the unit's initial line-up which was then bedeviled by defections. A disastrous debut concert at the Stax/Volt convention in December 1968 was a portent of future problems, but although *I Got Dem Ol' Kozmic Blues Again Mama* was coolly received, the set nonetheless contained several excellent Joplin vocals, notably 'Try', 'Maybe' and 'Little Girl Blue'. However, live shows grew increasingly erratic as her addiction to drugs and alcohol deepened. When a restructured Kozmic Blues Band, also referred to as the Main Squeeze, proved equally uncomfortable, the singer dissolved the unit altogether, and undertook medical advice. A slimmed-down group, the Full Tilt Boogie Band, was unveiled in May 1970. Brad Campbell and late-comer John Till (guitar) were retained from the previous group, while the induction of Richard Bell (piano), Ken Pearson (organ) and Clark Pierson (drums) created a

tighter, more intimate sound. In July they toured Canada with the Grateful Dead, before commencing work on a 'debut' album. The sessions were all but complete when, on 4 October 1970, Joplin died of a heroin overdose at her Hollywood hotel.

The posthumous *Pearl* was thus charged with poignancy, yet it remains her most consistent work. Her love of 'uptown soul' is confirmed by the inclusion of three Jerry Ragavoy compositions, 'My Baby', 'Cry Baby' and the suddenly anthemic 'Get It While You Can', while 'Trust Me' and 'A Woman Left Lonely' shows an empathy with its southern counterpart. The highlight, however, is Kris Kristofferson's 'Me And Bobby McGee', which allowed Janis to be both vulnerable and assertive. The song deservedly topped the US chart when issued as a single and despite a plethora of interpretations, this remains the definitive version. Although a star at the time of her passing, Janis Joplin has not been accorded the retrospective acclaim afforded other deceased contemporaries. She was, like her idol Otis Redding, latterly regarded as one-dimensional, lacking in subtlety or nuance. Yet her impassioned approach was precisely her attraction - Janis knew few boundaries, artistic or personal - and her sadly brief catalogue is marked by bare-nerved honesty.

Albums: *I Got Dem Ol' Kozmic Blues Again Mama!* (1969), *Pearl* (1971), *Janis Joplin In Concert* (1972). Compilations: *Greatest Hits* (1973), film soundtrack including live and rare recordings *Janis* (1975), *Anthology* (1980), *Farewell Song* (1981).

Further reading: *Buried Alive*, Myra Friedman. *Piece Of My Heart*, David Dalton.

Jordan, Charley

b. c.1890, Mabelvale, Arkansas, USA, d. 15 November 1954, St. Louis, Missouri, USA. Jordan arrived in St. Louis in 1925, and became a major figure on the city's blues scene, being closely associated with Peetie Wheatstraw, and acting as a talent scout for record companies. In 1928, he was crippled by a shooting incident connected with his bootlegging activities. Jordan recorded extensively from 1930-37, playing light, clean, but often very complex, ragtime-influenced guitar, and singing his wittily original lyrics in a high, taut voice. He accompanied

Charley Jordan

Louis Jordan

many of his St. Louis contemporaries on disc, notably 'Hi' Henry Brown, for whom his second guitar work is a dazzling display of improvising skills.

Albums: *It Ain't Clean* (c.1980), *The Best Of Charley Jordan* (c.1986), *Charley Jordan* (1987).

Jordan, Louis

b. Louis Thomas Jordan, 8 July 1908, Brinkley, Arkansas, USA, d. 4 February 1975, Los Angeles, California, USA. Saxophonist and singer, Jordan began touring as a teenager with the Rabbit Foot Minstrels, and supported classic blues singers Ma Rainey, Ida Cox and Bessie Smith. In the 30s, after relocating to New York City, he played in the bands of Louis Armstrong, Clarence Williams, Chick Webb and Ella Fitzgerald, appearing with these orchestras on records for RCA Victor, Vocalion and Decca, and making his vocal debut with Webb's band on novelty songs such as 'Gee, But You're Swell' and 'Rusty Hinge'. In 1938 Jordan formed his first combo, the Elks Rendez-Vous Band (after the club at which he had secured a residency), and signed an exclusive deal with Decca. While he had been with Webb, he had often been brought to the front to perform a blues or novelty swing number. These spots had been so well-received that, from the start of his own band, Jordan had decided to promote himself as a wacky musical comedian with a smart line in humorous jive. In early 1939, in line with this image, he changed the band's name to the Tympany Five and enjoyed steady, if unspectacular, success with recordings of 'T-Bone Blues' (1941), 'Knock Me A Kiss' and 'I'm Gonna Move To The Outskirts Of Town' (1942), 'What's The Use Of Gettin' Sober (When You Gonna Get Drunk Again)' and 'Five Guys Named Moe' (1943). After World War II, the Tympany Five really hit their stride with a string of million-selling records, including 'Is You Is Or Is You Ain't My Baby?' (1944), 'Caldonia (Boogie)' (1945), '(Beware, Brother) Beware!', 'Choo Choo Ch'boogie' (1946) and 'Saturday Night Fish Fry' (1949). Other hits which were not so commercially successful, but which are inextricably linked with Jordan's name nevertheless include 'G.I. Jive', 'Buzz Me', 'Ain't Nobody Here But Us Chickens', 'Let The Good Times Roll', 'Reet, Petite And

Gone', 'Open The Door, Richard', 'School Days', and 'Blue Light Boogie'. Jordan remained with Decca until 1954, when he switched briefly to Aladdin (1954), RCA's 'X' subsidiary (1955) and Mercury (1956-57) but, sadly, his reign was coming to an end; the new generation wanted 'fast and loud' not 'smooth and wry', and Jordan, dogged by ill-health, could not compete against rock 'n' roll artists such as Little Richard and Chuck Berry, even though his songs were being recycled by these very performers. Chuck Berry ('Run Joe' and 'Ain't That Just Like A Woman') and B.B. King 'Do You Call That A Buddy?', 'Early In The Morning', 'Just Like A Woman', 'How Blue Can You Get?', 'Buzz Me', 'Let The Good Times Roll' and 'Jordan For President!' in particular, have been successful with Jordan covers. Surprisingly, his performances were taken to the heart of many Chicago blues artists with songs like 'Somebody Done Hoodooed The Hoodoo Man', 'Never Let Your Left Hand Know What Your Right Hand's Doin'' and 'Blue Light Boogie'; even Bill Haley would often admit that his 'revolutionary' musical style was simply a copy of the Tympany Five's shuffles and jumps that had been recorded the previous decade in the same Decca studios.

Owing to his fluctuating health Louis Jordan spent the 60s and 70s working when he could, filling summer season engagements and recording occasionally for small companies owned by old friends including Ray Charles (Tangerine Records), Paul Gayten (Pzazz) and Johnny Otis (Blues Spectrum). His last recordings were as a guest on trumpeter Wallace Davenport's *Sweet Georgia Brown*, after which he suffered eight months of inactivity due to his deteriorating health, and a fatal heart-attack on 4 February 1975. The main factor that set Jordan apart from most of the competition was that he was at once a fine comedian and a superb saxophonist whose novelty value was never allowed to obscure either his musicianship or that of his sidemen, who at one time or another included trumpeters Idrees Sulieman and Freddie Webster (both major influences on boppers like Miles Davis and Dizzy Gillespie), tenor saxophonists Paul Quinichette, Maxwell Davis and Count Hastings, drummer Shadow Wilson, and pianists Wild Bill Davis and Bill Doggett. That Louis Jordan influenced all who came after him, and continues to be a prime source of material for films, theatre, television advertising, R&B bands and bluesmen, 40 or 50 years after his heyday, is a testament to his originality and talent.

Selected albums: *Go! Blow Your Horn* (1957, reissued 1982), *Somebody Up There Digs Me* (1957), *Man, We're Wailin'* (1958), *Let The Good Times Roll* (1958), *Hallelujah...Louis Jordan Is Back* (1964), *One Sided Love* (1969), *Louis Jordan's Greatest Hits* (1969), *Louis Jordan* (1971), *Great R&B Oldies* (1972), *I Believe In Music* (1974), *In Memoriam* (1975), *Louis Jordan's Greatest Hits Volume 2* (1975), *The Best Of Louis Jordan* (1975), *Louis Jordan With The Chris Barber Band* (1976), *Three Hot Big Band Sessions In 1951* (1976), *More Stuff* (1976), *Some Other Stuff* (1977), *Louis Jordan And His Tympany Five* i (1977), *Come On...Get It...*(1978), *Prime Cuts* (1978), *Collates* (1979), *Good Times* (1980), *The Best Of Louis Jordan* (1981), with Oran 'Hot Lips' Page *Jumpin' Stuff* (1981), *Louis Jordan And His Tympany Five* ii (1982), *The Last Swinger, The First Rocker* (1982), *Choo Choo Ch'boogie* (1982), *G.I. Jive* (1983), *Cole Slaw* (1983), *Look Out!...It's Louis Jordan And The Tympany Five* (1983), *Louis Jordan And His Tympany Five, 1944-1945* (1983), *Louis Jordan On Film - Reet, Petite And Gone* (1983), *Louis Jordan On Film - Look Out Sister* (1983), *Go! Blow Your Horn - Part 2* (1983), *Jump 'N' Jive With Louis Jordan* (1984), *Louis Jordan And Friends* (1984), *Jivin' With Jordan* (1985), *Hoodoo Man 1938-1940* (1986), *Knock Me Out 1940-1942* (1986), *Somebody Done Hoodooed The Hoodoo Man* (1986), *Louis Jordan And His Tympany Five, More 1944-1945* (1986), *Rock And Roll Call* (1986), *Rockin' And Jivin', Volume 1* (1986), *Rockin' And Jivin', Volume 2* (1986), *Louis Jordan And His Tympany Five* (1986), *Out Of Print* (1988), *Greatest Hits* (1989), *The V-Discs* (1989), *Hits And Rarities* (1989), *More Hits, More Rarities* (1990), *Rock 'N' Roll* (1990), *The Complete Aladdin Sessions* (1991).

Jordan, Luke

b. c.1890, possibly either Appomattox or Campbell county, Virginia, USA, d. c.1945, Lynchburg, Virginia, USA. The blues scene in pre-war Virginia was poorly documented at the time and few of its members managed to record. Post-war research by Bruce Bastin reveals that Luke Jordan was a prime-mover in the blues enclave centred around Lynchburg. It seems that he did not work outside music but relied on his talent and local fame to see him through. Victor Records discovered him in 1927 and he recorded for them in Charlotte, North Carolina, in August of that year. Jordan's records sold well enough to justify transporting him to New York for a further two sessions in November 1929. Of the total of 10 tracks that he recorded, eight saw release, although only six have been located. The extant sides present a high pitched singer given to a fast delivery backed by a niftily picked Gibson guitar. From the evidence of his records it would seem that a large part of his repertoire was made up from vaudeville songs, though the gambling song 'Pick Poor Robin Clean' may have its roots in the folk tradition. His masterpiece was 'Church Bell Blues', a bravura performance forever associated with him in local tradition, while 'Cocaine Blues' became an early 'crossover' when it was recorded by white bluesman Dick Justice in 1929.

Album: *The Songster Tradition* (1990).

K

Kansas City Red

b. 1926, Drew, Mississippi, USA, d. 6 June 1991, Chicago, Illinois, USA. A drummer and blues singer, in the 40s Red worked for Robert Nighthawk (who recorded Red's song, 'The Moon Is Rising'), and in the 50s for Earl Hooker. He became a club owner in Chicago, and a fixture on the city's blues scene, playing with Johnny Shines, Walter Horton and Sunnyland Slim, and leading his own bands, one of which provided early professional experience for Jimmy Reed. Red claimed to have recorded demos for Chess, JOB and VeeJay Records, but his debut as a name artist came on a 1975 anthology. Thereafter, he continued to do occasional session drumming for various of his Chicago colleagues, and to combine bar management with live gigs.
Album: *Bring Another Half Pint* (1975).

Kelly, Arthur Lee 'Guitar'

b. 14 November 1924, Clinton, Louisiana, USA. Like many blues singers, Kelly learned to play religious songs first, but his main interest was in the blues. In the 40s, he was living near Baton Rouge and beginning to develop his own guitar style, under the influence of local artist Lightning Slim, as well as copying records by artists such as Muddy Waters and Lightnin' Hopkins. Although active on the blues scene through the boom in Baton Rouge blues in the 50s, he never made any records during this time. In the 60s, he formed a small group along with Silas Hogan and at last in 1970, he appeared on a couple of albums of Louisiana blues artists, as well as a single on Excello. He continued his partnership with Hogan for many years, and joined that artist in his residency at Tabby Thomas's Blues Box club, but he has also toured widely, including visits to Europe.
Album: *Louisiana Blues* (1970).

Kelly, Dave

b. 1948, London, England. Kelly's first instrument was trombone, but he became a bottle-neck slide guitar specialist, sitting in with John Lee Hooker and Muddy Waters during a 1966 visit to the USA. On his return, Kelly joined his first R&B band which evolved into the John Dummer Blues Band, with whom he recorded in 1968-69. Leaving the group, he performed as a solo artist on the folk club circuit and played on numerous recording sessions involving a loose-knit circle of London blues musicians which included his sister Jo Ann Kelly (guitar/vocals), Bob Hall (piano) and Bob Brunning (bass). They recorded together as Tramp and as Firefall, while Kelly also played on albums by visiting USA blues singers Son House and Arthur Crudup (*Roebuck Man*, 1974). Around this time Kelly made his first two solo albums for Mercury with accompaniment from Peter Green, Jo Ann, Brunning and Steve Rye (harmonica). Kelly also led an early 70s group called Rocksalt and in 1974 rejoined John Dummer in the Ooblee Dooblee Band. In the late 70s he became a founder member of the Blues Band and when the group temporarily split up, formed his own band with fellow Blues Band members Rob Townshend (drums) and Gary Fletcher (bass), plus Mick Rogers (guitar), Lou Stonebridge (keyboards) and John 'Irish' Earle (saxophone). With numerous personnel changes (including the addition of Peter Filleul on keyboards and Tex Comer on bass), the group continued for several years, touring Europe and recording occasionally for the German label Metronome and Apoloosa, owned by Italian blues fan Franco Ratti. During the 80s, Kelly developed a parallel career in writing jingles and film and television soundtrack music. He rejoined the Blues Band when it reformed in 1989.
Albums: *Keep It In The Family* (1969), *Dave Kelly* (1971), *Survivors* (1979), *Willin'* (1979), *Feels Right* (1981), *Dave Kelly Band Live* (1983), *Heart Of The City* (1987).

Kelly, Jack

b. c.1905, Mississippi, USA. d. c.1960, Memphis, Tennessee, USA. Kelly's first jug band, formed in 1925, included Frank Stokes, Dan Sane and Will Batts. Kelly, Batts, Sane and juggist D.M. Higgs were the South Memphis Jug Band on record in 1933. (Kelly, Batts and a guitarist, possibly Ernest Lawlars, recorded again in 1939.) Their sound was characterized by Kelly's vibrant singing, the broad, bluesy tones of Batts' fiddle and the complex interplay of twin guitars. Kelly's penchant for re-recording the tune of 'Highway No. 61 Blues' is offset by a talent for striking lyrics. After the band broke up in 1934, Kelly worked either solo, with Stokes, or in *ad hoc* bands. In 1953, he recorded for Sun, playing piano with Walter 'Shakey' Horton and Joe Hill Louis. A 78 rpm record was scheduled, but never released; part of one side was issued many years later.

Compilations: *Sun Records The Blues Years* (1985), *Jack Kelly & His South Memphis Jug Band*(1990).

Kelly, Jo Ann

b. 5 January 1944, Streatham, London, England, d. 21 October 1990. This expressive blues singer, sister of Blues Band guitarist Dave Kelly, was renowned as one of the finest of the genre. She made her recording debut in 1964 on a privately-pressed EP and appeared on several specialist labels before contributing a series of excellent performances to guitarist Tony McPhee's Groundhogs recordings, issued under the aegis of United Artists. Her self-titled solo album displayed a hard, gritty vocal delivery evocative of Memphis Minnie and confirmed the arrival of a major talent. In 1969, the singer appeared live with Mississippi Fred McDowell and later made several tours of the USA. Kelly became a constituent part of the British blues circuit, recording with the John Dummer Blues Band, Chilli Willi And The Red Hot Peppers and Stefan Grossman. In 1972, she completed an album with Woody Mann, John Miller and acoustic guitarist John Fahey, before forming a group, Spare Rib, which performed extensively throughout the UK. Kelly recorded a second solo album, *Do It*, in 1976 and maintained her popularity throughout the 70s and 80s with appearances at European blues festivals and judicious live work in Britain. Her last performance was at a festival in Lancashire in August 1990, when she was given the award for Female Singer of the Year by the British Blues Federation. Having apparently recovered from an operation, in 1989, to remove a malignant brain tumour, she died in October 1990.

Albums: *Jo Ann Kelly* (1969), *Jo Ann Kelly, With Fahey, Mann And Miller* (1972), with Pete Emery *Do It* (1976), *It's Whoopie* (1978), with Mississippi Fred McDowell *Standing At The*

Burying Ground (1984), *Just Restless* (1984), *Jo Ann Kelly* (1988). Compilations: with Tony McPhee *Same Thing On Our Minds* (1969), *Retrospect 1964-1972* (1990).

Kennedy, Jesse 'Tiny'

b. 20 December 1925, probably Chattanooga, Tennessee, USA. Blues shouter Kennedy first came to prominence in Kansas City in November 1949, where he recorded a session for Capitol Records with Jay McShann's Quintet. In 1951, he joined Tiny Bradshaw's Orchestra as vocalist, recording two unusual tracks with Bradshaw's band for King Records; unusual in that the two risque blues feature Kennedy duetting with himself as both deep-voiced macho male and shrill female! While touring with the orchestra in the south in 1951-52, Kennedy made some recordings under his own name with local musicians for Trumpet Records at Sam Phillips' Sun studio in Memphis, including the successful 'Strange Kind Of Feelin'' which was later covered by Elmore James. Gotham Records' 20th Century subsidiary leased the hit for the northern market, and Trumpet Records tried unsuccessfully to record another hit by Kennedy in New York City in 1953. Nevertheless, he recorded a fine session for RCA-Victor's Groove subsidiary in April 1955 as the contradictory 'Big Tiny Kennedy' which included a remake of his Trumpet hit, after which he seems to have drifted into obscurity.

Album: with Clayton Love and Jerry 'Boogie' McCain *Strange Kind Of Feelin'* (1990).

Kent, Willie

b. 24 February 1936, Sunflower, Mississippi, USA. Kent was brought up in Shelby, Mississippi, and was influenced by the blues he heard on the radio. He settled in Chicago in 1952 and was soon able to hear the top blues artists live in the clubs, although he was underage. Kent began working as a singer in 1957 and started to play guitar the following year. He quickly switched to bass and formed his own group around 1959. As a bass player, Kent worked in the 60s with Hip Linkchain, Jimmy Dawkins, and Luther 'Guitar Junior' Johnson. In 1975, he shared a live album with Willie James Lyons for the MCM label, and he has subsequently had his intense, powerful vocals and bass playing issued on various labels.

Albums: with Willie James Lyons *Ghetto* (1977), *I'm What You Need* (1989) *Ain't It Nice* (1991).

Key, Troyce

b. 1937, Jordon Plantation, (70m from Monroe), Louisiana, USA. In the early 50s Key became interested in blues after hearing a record by Lightnin' Hopkins and he began playing guitar following a serious illness which resulted in hospitalization . During this time he heard records of Fats Domino, Johnny Otis, Muddy Waters, and others. He was signed by Warner Brothers Records in 1958 and had three singles released. Key teamed up with J.J. Malone in 1961 and they recorded together around three years later; they also had two albums released by Red Lightnin' and enjoyed a British near-hit in 1980 with the single 'I Gotta New Car (I Was Framed)'. He continues to present his good-natured, rocking blues in Oakland, California, at his own club called Eli Mile High, which is also the name of his blues record label.

Albums: both with J.J. Malone *I've Gotta New Car* (1980), *Younger Than Yesterday* (1982).

Kidd, Kenneth

b. 1935, Newton, Mississippi, USA. Aka Prez Kenneth. As a youngster Kidd sang in the church choir but was also attracted to the blues. He settled in Chicago in 1956 and soon tried to learn guitar, switching to bass because he found it easier. In the 60s, Kidd recorded in a Jimmy Reed vein for the Biscayne label. His track 'Devil Dealing' was the prototype for G.L. Crockett's hit 'It's A Man Down There', but he received no credit. Towards the end of the decade he formed his own label, Kenneth Records, and although he recorded on a Hip Linkchain session in 1976, little has been heard of him in recent years. He still works occasionally in west side Chicago clubs.

King, Albert

b. Albert Nelson, 23 April 1923 (although three other dates have also been published), Indianola, Mississippi, USA, d. 21 December 1992. Despite the fact that his work has been overshadowed by that of regal namesake, B.B. King, this exceptional performer was one of the finest in the entire blues/soul canon. King's first solo recording, 'Bad Luck Blues', was released in 1953, but it was not until the end of the decade that he embarked on a full-time career. His early work fused his already distinctive fretwork to big band-influenced arrangements and included

Albert King

his first successful single, 'Don't Throw Your Love On Me Too Strong'. However, his style would not be fully defined until 1966 when, signed to the Stax label, he began working with Booker T. And The MGs. This tightly-knit quartet supplied the perfect rhythmic punch, a facet enhanced by a judicious use of horns. 'Cold Feet', which included wry references to several Stax stablemates, and 'I Love Lucy', a homage to King's distinctive 'Flying V' guitar, stand among his finest recordings. However, this period is best remembered for 'Born Under A Bad Sign' (1967) and 'The Hunter' (1968), two performances which became an essential part of many repertoires including those of Free and Cream. Albert became a central part of the late 60s 'blues boom', touring the college and concert circuit. His classic album, *Live Wire/Blues Power*, recorded at San Francisco's Fillmore Auditorium in 1968 introduced his music to the white rock audience. More excellent albums followed in its wake, including *King Does The King's Thing*, a tribute collection of Elvis Presley material, and *Years Gone By*. His work during the 70s was largely unaffected by prevailing trends. 'That's What The Blues Is All About', borrowed just enough from contemporary styles to provide Albert with a Top 20 R&B single, but the bankruptcy of two outlets dealt a blow to King's career. A five-year recording famine ended in 1983, and an astute programme of new material and careful reissues have kept the master's catalogue alive. King was a commanding live performer and an influential figure. A new generation of musicians, including Robert Cray and the late Stevie Ray Vaughan continue to acknowledge his timeless appeal, a factor reinforced in 1990 when King guested on guitarist Gary Moore's 'back-to-the-roots' collection, *Still Got The Blues*.
Albums: *The Big Blues* (1962), *Born Under A Bad Sign* (1967), *Live Wire/Blues Power* (1968), *King Of The Blues Guitar* (1969), *Years Gone By* (1969), with Steve Cropper and 'Pops' Staples *Jammed Together* (1969), *King, Does The King's Thing* (1970), *Lovejoy* (1971), *The Lost Session* (1971), *I'll Play The Blues For You* (1972), *I Wanna Get Funky* (1974), *Live At Montreux/Blues At Sunrise* (1974), *The Pinch* (1976), *Albert* (1976), *Truckload Of Lovin'* (1976), *Albert Live* (1977), *King Albert* (1977), *New Orleans Heat* (1978), *San Francisco '83* (1983), *I'm*

In A 'Phone Booth, Baby (1984), *Red House* (1991). Compilations: *Travelin' To California* (1967), *Door To Door* (1969, a collection of eight recordings from 1961 coupled with six separate performances by Otis Rush), *Laundromat Blues* (1984), *The Lost Session* (1986), *I'll Play The Blues For You: The Best Of Albert King* (1988), *Wednesday Night In San Francisco* and *Thursday Night In San Francisco* (1990, both are collections of out-takes from the 1968 Fillmore 'Blues Power' performances).

King, B.B.
b. Riley B. King, 16 September 1925, Indianola, Mississippi, USA. The son of a sharecropper, King went to work on the plantation like any other young black in Mississippi, but he had sung in amateur gospel groups from childhood. By the age of 16, he was also playing blues guitar and singing on street corners. At the age 20, he temporarily quit sharecropping and went to Memphis, where he busked, and shared a room for almost a year with his second cousin, Bukka White. However, it was not until 1948 that he managed to pay off his debts to his former plantation boss. After leaving farming, he returned to Memphis, determined to become a star. He secured work with radio station KWEM, and then with WDIA, fronting a show sponsored by the health-tonic Pepticon, which led to disc jockeying on the *Sepia Swing Show*. Here he was billed as 'The Beale Street Blues Boy', later amended to 'Blues Boy King', and then to 'B.B. King'. Radio exposure promoted King's live career, and he performed with a band whose personnel varied according to availability. At this stage, he was still musically untutored, and liable to play against his backing musicians, but it was evident from his first recordings made for Bullet Records in 1949, that his talent was striking.
The Bullet recordings brought King to the attention of Modern Records, with whom he recorded for the next 10 years. As he began to tour beyond the area around Memphis, his first marriage, already under strain, ended in divorce in 1952. By that time, he was a national figure, having held the number 1 spot in the *Billboard* R&B chart for 15 weeks with 'Three O'Clock Blues'. He had embarked on the gruelling trail of one-nighters that has continued ever since. Through the 50s, King toured with a 13-piece

B.B. King

B.B. King

band, adopting a patriarchal attitude to his musicians that has been compared to that of a kindly plantation boss. Briefly, he operated his own Blues Boy's Kingdom label, but had no success. Modern, however, were steadily producing hits for him, although their approach to copyright-standard practice in its day was less ethical, with the label owners taking fictitious credit on many titles. B.B. King's blues singing, was heavily mellifluent, influenced by Peter J. 'Doctor' Clayton and gospel singer Sam McCrary of the Fairfield Four. However, his true revolutionary importance was as an electric guitarist. He admired Charlie Christian and Django Reinhardt as well as Lonnie Johnson, Blind Lemon Jefferson, and also saxophonist Lester Young. He derived ideas about phrasing and harmony from all these musicians. His extensive use of sixths clearly derived from jazz. His sound however, consisted chiefly of a synthesis of the bottleneck styles of the delta-blues (including that of Bukka White) with the jazzy electric guitar of 'T-Bone' Walker. To Walker's flowing, crackling music, King added the finger vibrato that was his substitute for the slide which he had never managed to master. The result was a fluid guitar sound, in which almost every note was bent and/or sustained. This, together with King's penchant for playing off the beat, gave his solos the pattern of speech, and the personification of his beautiful black, gold plated, pearl inlaid Gibson 335 guitar as 'Lucille' seemed highly appropriate.

In 1960, King switched labels, moving to ABC in the hope of emulating Ray Charles' success. The times were against him, however, for black tastes were moving towards soul music and spectacular stage presentation. King had always felt a need to make the blues respectable, removing sexual boasting and reference to violence and drugs. As a result of these endeavours his lyrics were, ironically, closer to those of soul, with their emphasis on love, respect and security in relationships. He remained popular, as his interplay with the audience on a live album recorded in Chicago in 1964 illustrates, but by the mid-60s, his career seemed in decline, with the hits coming from Modern's back catalogue rather than his new company. Revitalization came with the discovery of the blues by young whites; initially musicians, and then the wider audience. In 1968, King played the Fillmore West with Johnny Winter and Mike Bloomfield, who introduced him as 'the greatest living blues guitarist', provoking a standing ovation before he had even played a note. His revival of Roy Hawkins' 'The Thrill Is Gone', which made innovatory use of strings, provided the crucial pop crossover. Consequently, in 1969, King paid his first visit to Europe, where the way had been prepared by Eric Clapton (and where an ignorant reviewer called him an 'up-and-coming guitarist of the Clapton-Peter Green school'). In 1970, he recorded his first collaboration with rock musicians, produced by Leon Russell, who played on and composed some numbers, as did Carole King. King's career has been smooth sailing ever since, and he has been in demand for commercials, movie soundtracks, television show theme tunes, and guest appearances (eg, with U2 on 1989's 'When Love Comes To Town'). His workaholic schedule probably results, in part, from a need to finance his compulsive gambling, but he has also worked unobtrusively to provide entertainment for prisoners (he co-founded the Foundation for the Advancement of Inmate Rehabilitation and Recreation in 1972).

His professional life is marked by a sense of mission, coupled with a desire to give the blues status and acceptability. This he has achieved, bringing the blues into the mainstream of entertainment, although he has done so by removing much of the sense of otherness that first brought many whites to it. Sometimes his live performances can be disappointingly bland, with singalong segments and misplaced attempts to ingratiate, as when he proudly told a Scottish audience of his meeting with Sheena Easton. His recordings since the 70s have been of inconsistent quality. King has deliberately kept in touch with his roots, returning to Mississippi each year to play, but the adulation of rock musicians has been a mixed blessing. Recordings made in London with, among others Alexis Korner, Steve Winwood and Ringo Starr proved particularly disappointing. Equally, his collaboration with jazz-funk band the Crusaders, who produced and played on two albums, stifled his invention, and it has often seemed that King's creativity has run into the sands of MOR pop in a 12-bar format. These are the times when he is most likely to return with a brilliant, vital album that goes back to his roots in jazz, jump and the Delta.

B.B. King has achieved the blues singer's dream; to live in Las Vegas and to have full access to the material benefits which the American way of life still withholds from so many black Americans. Without s doubt, though, things have changed for him; the teenager playing in the 40s streets, became a man with whom the chairman of the Republican Party in the 80s considered it an honour to play guitar. B.B. King was a great influence on the sound of the blues, the sincerity of his singing and the fluency of his guitar spawning a flock of imitators as well as having a more general effect on the music's development, as reflected in the playing of Buddy Guy, his namesakes Freddie and Albert King, 'Little' Joe Blue and innumerable others. Arguably, his most far-reaching effect has been on rock music. King's limitations include an inability to play guitar behind his own singing. This has led him to make strict demarcation between the two, and has encouraged rock guitarists to regard extended solos as the stigmata of authentic blues playing. In lesser hands, this has all too easily become bloated excess or meaningless note-spinning. B.B. King has always aspired to elegance, logic and purpose in his guitar playing; it is ironic that his success has spawned so many imitators possessing so little of those qualities. B.B. King's career, like that of other black musician in America, has been circumscribed by the dictates of the industry. Like Louis Armstrong, he has nevertheless achieved great art through a combination of prodigious technical gifts and the placing of his instinctive improvisatory skills at the service of emotional expression. Also like Armstrong, he stayed firmly within the compass of showbusiness, attempting to give the public what he perceives it to want. His greatest music, however, testifies to his standing as a titanic figure in popular music.

Selected albums: *The Blues* (1960), *B.B. King Wails* (1960), *B.B. King Sings Spirituals* (1960), *King Of The Blues* (1961), *My Kind Of Blues* (1961), *Twist With B.B. King* (1962), *Easy Listening Blues* (1962), *Blues In My Heart* (1962), *Mr. Blues* (1963), *Rock Me Baby* (1964), *Live At The Regal* (1965), *Confessin' The Blues* (1965), *Let Me Love You* (1965), *B.B. King Live On Stage* (1965), *The Soul Of B.B. King* (1966), *The Jungle* (1967), *Blues Is King* (1967), *Lucille* (1968), *Live And Well* (1969), *Completely Well* (1969), *Back In The Alley* (1970), *Indianola Mississippi Seeds* (1970), *Live In Cook County Jail* (1971), *In London* (1971), *L.A. Midnight* (1972), *Guess Who* (1972), *To Know You Is To Love You* (1973), with Bobby 'Blue' Bland *Together For The First Time...Live* (1974), *Friends* (1974), *Lucille Talks Back* (1975), with Bland *Together Again...Live* (1976), *King Size* (1977), *Midnight Believer* (1978), *Take It Home* (1979), *Now Appearing At Ole Miss* (1980), *There Must Be A Better World Somewhere* (1981), *Love Me Tender* (1982), *Blues 'N' Jazz* (1983), *Do The Boogie* (1989), *Lucille Had A Baby* (1989), *Live At The Apollo* (1991), *Singin' The Blues & The Blues* (1991), *There's Always One More Time* (1992). Compilations: *The Incredible Soul Of B.B. King* (1970), *His Best - The Electric B.B. King* (1968), *The Best Of B.B. King* (1973), *The Rarest King* (1980), *The Memphis Master* (1982), *B.B. King - 20 Blues Greats* (1985), *Introducing (1969-85)* (1987), *Across The Tracks* (1988), *My Sweet Little Angel* (1992).

King, Earl

b. Earl Silas Johnson IV, 7 February 1934, New Orleans, Louisiana, USA. The son of a blues pianist, King became an accomplished guitarist and singer with local bands before making his first recordings in 1953 for Savoy ('Have You Gone Crazy') and Specialty ('A Mother's Love'). Strongly influenced by Guitar Slim (Eddie Jones), during the mid-50s he worked with Huey Smith's band and made his biggest hit, 'Those Lonely Lonely Nights' with Smith on piano. This was on Johnny Vincent's Ace label, for whom King was house guitarist.

In 1958, he made a version of 'Everyone Has To Cry Sometime' as Handsome Earl. He went on to record for Rex and Imperial where he made 'Come On' and the R&B hit 'Trick Bag' (1962) which featured King's influential guitar figures. He was also starting to enjoy success as a songwriter, composing the Lee Dorsey hit 'Do Re Mi', 'He's Mine' for Bernadine Washington, 'Big Chief' recorded by Professor Longhair and 'Teasin You', Willie Tee's 1965 R&B hit. Jimmy Clanton, Dr. John and Fats Domino were others who recorded King compositions. During the 60s and early 70s, King himself made recordings for Amy, Wand, Atlantic and

Motown though the Allen Toussaint-produced Atlantic session was not released until 1981 and the Motown tracks remain unissued. King remained active into the 80s, recording with *Room Full Of Blues* for Black Top. His Imperial tracks were reissued by EMI in 1987.
Albums: *New Orleans Rock 'N' Roll* (1977), *Street Parade* (1981), *Soul Bag* (1987), *Room Full Of Blues* (1988), *Glazed* (1988), *Sexual Telepathy* (1990).

King, Eddie

b. c.late 30s/early 40s, Alabama, USA. Eddie was orphaned in 1950 and eventually settled in Chicago, where he played in various blues clubs. He worked as a guitarist with Muddy Waters, Howlin' Wolf, and Willie Dixon in the 50s before he began a long association with 'Little' Mack Simmons at the end of the decade. He recorded with Simmons and Detroit Junior and also released singles under his own name in the early 60s. He worked briefly with Willie Cobbs and he recorded further singles (sometimes in the company of his sister Mae Bee May) and in the 80s he had albums on the Wolf and Double Trouble labels. In the early 90s he was to be found working as lead guitarist for Koko Taylor.
Album: *The Blues Has Got Me* (1987).

King, Freddie

b. Billy Myles, 30 September 1934, Gilmer, Texas, USA, d. 28 December, 1976, Dallas, Texas. Freddie (aka Freddy) was one of the triumvirate of Kings (the others being B.B. and Albert) who ruled the blues throughout the 60s. He was the possessor of a light, laid back, but not unemotional voice and a facile fast-fingered guitar technique that made him the hero of many young disciples. He learned to play guitar at an early age, being influenced by his mother, Ella Mae King and her brother Leon. Although forever associated with Texas and admitting a debt to such artists as 'T-Bone' Walker he moved north to Chicago in his mid-teens. In 1950, he became influenced by local blues guitarists Eddie 'Playboy' Taylor and Robert 'Junior' Lockwood. King absorbed elements from each of their styles, before encompassing the more strident approach of Magic Sam and Otis Rush. Here, he began to sit in with various groups and slowly built up the reputation that was to make him a star. After teaming up with

'Lonesome' Jimmy Lee Robinson to form the Every Hour Blues Boys he worked and recorded with Little Sonny Cooper's band, Earlee Payton's Blues Cats and Smokey Smothers. These last recordings were made in Cincinnati, Ohio, in August 1960 for Sydney Nathan's King/Federal set up and on the same day, King recorded six titles under his own name including the influential instrumental hit, 'Hideaway'. He formed his own band and began touring, bolstering his success with further hits, many of them guitar showpieces, some trivialized by titles like 'The Bossa Nova Watusi Twist', but others showing off his 'crying' vocal delivery. Many, such as '(I'm) Tore Down', 'Have You Ever Loved A Woman' and, particularly 'The Welfare (Turns Its Back On You)' became classics of the (then) modern blues. He continued to record for King Federal up until 1966, his career on record being masterminded by pianist Sonny Thompson. He left King Federal in 1966 and took up a short tenure (1968-69) on the Atlantic subsidiary label Cotillion. Ironically, the subsequent white blues-boom provided a new-found impetus. Eric Clapton was a declared King aficionado, while Chicken Shack's Stan Webb indicated his debt by including three of his mentor's compositions on his group's debut album. The albums which followed failed to capture the artist at his best. This was not a particularly successful move, although the work he did on that label has increased in value with the passage of time. The same could be said for his next musical liaison which saw him working with Leon Russell on his Shelter label. Much of his work for Russell was over-produced, but King made many outstanding recordings during this period and a re-evaluation of that work is overdue. There was no denying the excitement it generated, particularly on *Getting Ready* which was recorded at the famous Chess studio. This excellent set included the original version of the much-covered 'Going Down'. Live recordings made during his last few years indicate that King was still a force to be reckoned with as he continued his good-natured guitar battles with all-comers, and usually left them way behind. *Burglar* featured a duet with Eric Clapton on 'Sugar Sweet', but the potential of this new relationship was tragically cut short in December 1976 when King died of heart failure at the early

Freddie King

age of 43. His last stage appearance had taken place three days earlier in his home town of Dallas.

Albums: *Freddie King Sings The Blues* (1961), *Let's Hideaway And Dance Away* (1961), *Boy-Girl-Boy* (1962), *Bossa Nova And Blues* (1962), *Freddie King Goes Surfing* (1963), *Freddie King Gives You A Bonanza Of Instrumentals* (1965), *24 Vocals And Instrumentals* (1966), *Hide Away* (1969), *Freddie King Is A Blues Master* (1969), *My Feeling For The Blues* (1970), *Getting Ready* (1971), *Texas Cannonball* (1972), *Woman Across The Water* (1973), *Burglar* (1974), *Larger Than Life* (1975). Compilations: *King Of R&B Volume 2* (1969), *The Best Of Freddie King* (1974), *Original Hits* (1977), *1934 - 1976* (1977), *Rockin' The Blues - Live* (1983), *Takin' Care Of Business* (1985), *Live In Antibes, 1974* (1987), *Live In Nancy, 1975 Volume 1* (1988).

King, Saunders

b. 13 March 1909, Staple, Louisiana, USA. Starting out as a singer, and obtaining a job with the NBC network, King took up the electric guitar in 1938 after hearing Charlie Christian. King formed his own band in 1942, which became popular around the San Francisco area, began recording for the small Rhythm Records and his first session produced his biggest hit, 'Saunders Blues'. The song achieved more fame under the title 'S.K. Blues' and became a staple in the repertoires of many blues shouters, such as Jimmy Witherspoon and Big Joe Turner. Later recordings for Modern/RPM/Flair (who bought the Rhythm masters and cheekily reissued 'S.K. Blues' as 'New S.K. Blues'!), Cavatone and Aladdin, failed to emulate the success of 'S.K. Blues', and his final recordings were made in 1961 for Galaxy, after which he retired from professional music, although he was brought back in 1979 when asked to guest on Carlos Devadip Santana's *Oneness* album. Over the years, Saunders King has taken a back seat to the mighty 'T-Bone' Walker, but it is often overlooked that he, in fact, was recorded playing electrified blues guitar before Walker made his recording debut on that instrument.

Albums: *What's Your Story, Morning Glory* (1983), *The First King Of The Blues* (1988).

Kirkland, Eddie

b. 16 August 1928, Kingston, Jamaica, West Indies. The career of guitarist Eddie Kirkland spans 40 years and a variety of musical styles. Soon after his birth the family relocated to the southern states of America and at the age of 15 he took a day job at the Ford Motor Company in Detroit. He met John Lee Hooker and became his regular accompanist both on the club circuit and on record, proving to be one of the few who could follow Hooker's erratic style. Kirkland's first recordings were made in 1952 and throughout the decade he recorded for RPM, King, Cobra, Fortune and Lupine. 1961 saw his first deviation from 'down home' blues when he recorded with King Curtis and Oliver Nelson for Prestige. In the mid-60s he moved to Macon, Georgia where he turned to soul music, eventually signing to Otis Redding's enterprise Volt, in 1965. Redding used Kirkland in his touring band, but Kirkland's role as a soul artist was never more than minor. In the 70s, he returned to his blues roots, recording for Pete Lowery's Trix label, both solo and with small bands, and has since maintained a heavy touring schedule at home and in Europe.

Albums: *The Way It Was* (1983), *Pickin' Up The Pieces* (1985).

Kittrell, Christine

b. 11 August 1929, Nashville, Tennessee, USA. Kittrell made a number of attractive and moderately successful records for local labels during the 50s. A choir member as a child, her voice lacked the distinctive nuance that might have brought her more durable success. Her first record, 'Old Man You're Slipping' (Tennessee 117), was backed by tenor saxman Louis Brooks and his band, with whom she'd made her professional debut six years earlier in 1945. Fats Domino sidemen Buddy Hagans and Wendell Duconge played on her first and biggest hit, 'Sittin' Here Drinking' (Tennessee 128), which brought her a six-week engagement at the Pelican Club in New Orleans. Kittrell had toured with the Joe Turner band in 1951 but she preferred to work around Nashville, at clubs such as the New Era and the Elks. Engaged as singer with Paul 'Hucklebuck' Williams' band in December 1952, *Billboard* noted that the 'five-foot-six chirp' was the 'blues find of the decade'. She made her West Coast debut in 1954 with Earl Bostic and later Johnny Otis. Several releases on the Republic label at this time led to

Eddie Kirkland

only regional success. One session, including 'Lord Have Mercy' (Republic 7096), is reputed to have Little Richard on piano. In August 1954, *Billboard* announced her departure from the R&B field to sing with the Simmons Akers spiritual singers. In the early 60s she recorded for Vee Jay but her original version of 'I'm A Woman' was covered by Peggy Lee. She re-recorded a Republic song, 'Call His Name' (Federal 12540) in 1965, and spent the next few years touring army bases in Southeast Asia. Subsequently, she retired to her Columbus, Ohio home.
Album: *Nashville R&B, Vol 2* (1986).

Knowling, Ransom

b. c.1910. Knowling played bass, and was best known for his extensive work as a session player, used by producer Lester Melrose on hundreds of blues records in Chicago in the 30s and 40s, by artists such as Big Bill Broonzy, Tampa Red and Sonny Boy 'Rice Miller' Williamson. His rock-solid bass work was also used to add a more urban sound to the work of country blues singers like Tommy McClennan. In later years he claimed never to have liked the blues, preferring more sophisticated sounds, but he owes virtually all his fame to that idiom. Although known to have died, details of Ransom's death, as of his birth, are scant.

Koerner, 'Spider' John

b. 31 August 1938, Rochester, New York. USA. A contemporary of Bob Dylan at the University of Minnesota, Koerner subsequently formed an influential country-blues trio with Dave Ray and Tony Glover. Koerner, Ray And Glover completed two albums for Elektra before John recorded his first solo collection, *Spider's Blues*. The three musicians were then reunited at different intervals, although each has pursued an independent path. *Running, Jumping, Standing Still*, Koerner's refreshing collaboration with singer Willie Murphy, was released in 1968, and the artist has since completed two further solo albums.
Albums: with Koerner, Ray And Glover *Blues, Rags And Hollers* (1963), *More Blues, Rags And Hollers* (1964), *The Return Of Koerner, Ray And Glover* (1965), *Live At St. Olaf Festival* (c.60s/70s), *Some American Folk Songs Like They Used To Be* (1974). With Willie Murphy

Running, Jumping, Standing Still (1968). Solo *Spider's Blues* (1965), *Music Is Just A Bunch Of Notes* (1972), *Nobody Knows The Trouble I've Seen* (1986).

Korner, Alexis

b. 19 April 1928, Paris, France, d. January 1984. An inspirational figure in British music circles, Korner was already versed in black music when he met Cyril Davies at the London Skiffle Club. Both musicians were frustrated by the limitations of the genre and transformed the venue into the London Blues And Barrelhouse Club where they not only performed together but also showcased visiting US bluesmen. When jazz trombonist Chris Barber introduced an R&B segment into his live repertoire, he employed Korner (guitar) and Davies (harmonica) to back singer Ottilie Patterson. Inspired, the pair formed Blues Incorporated in 1961 and the following year established the Ealing Rhythm And Blues Club in a basement beneath a local cinema. The group's early personnel included Charlie Watts (drums), Art Wood (vocals) and Keith Scott (piano), but later featured Long John Baldry, Jack Bruce, Graham Bond and Ginger Baker in its ever-changing line-up. Mick Jagger and Paul Jones were also briefly associated with Korner, whose continued advice and encouragement proved crucial to a generation of aspiring musicians. However, disagreements over direction led to Davies's defection following the release of *R&B From The Marquee*, leaving Korner free to pursue a jazz-based path. While former colleagues later found success with the Rolling Stones, Manfred Mann and Cream, Korner's excellent group was largely unnoticed by the general public, although he did enjoy a residency on a children's television show backed by his rhythm section of Danny Thompson (bass) and Terry Cox (drums). The name 'Blues Incorporated' was dropped when Korner embarked on a solo career, punctuated by the formation of several temporary groups, including Free At Last (1967), New Church (1969) and Snape (1972). While the supporting cast on such ventures remained fluid, including for a short time singer Robert Plant, the last two units featured Peter Thorup who also collaborated with Korner on CCS, a pop-based big band which scored notable hits with 'Whole Lotta Love' (1970), 'Walkin'' and 'Tap Turns

Alexis Korner

On The Water' (both 1971). Korner also derived success from his BBC Radio 1 show which extended a highly individual choice of material. He also broadcast on a long-running programme for the BBC World Service. Korner continued to perform live, often accompanied by former Back Door virtuoso bassist Colin Hodgkinson, and remained a highly respected figure in the music fraternity. He joined Charlie Watts, Ian Stewart, Jack Bruce and Dick Heckstall-Smith in the informal Rocket 88 and Korner's 50th birthday party, which featured appearances by Eric Clapton, Chris Farlowe and Zoot Money, was both filmed and recorded. In 1981, Korner began an ambitious 13-part television documentary on the history of rock, but his premature death from cancer in January 1984 left this and many other projects unfulfilled. However, Korner's stature as a vital catalyst in British R&B was already assured.

Albums: by Alexis Korner's Blues Incorporated *R&B From The Marquee* (1962), *Red Hot From Alex* aka *Alexis Korner's All Star Blues Incorporated* (1964), *At The Cavern* (1964), *Alexis Korner's Blues Incorporated* (1964), *Sky High* (1966), *Blues Incorporated (Wednesday Night Prayer Meeting)* (1967); by Alexis Korner *I Wonder Who* (1967), *A New Generation Of Blues* aka *What's That Sound I Hear* (1969), *Both Sides Of Alexis Korner* (1969), *Alexis* (1971), *Mr. Blues* (1974), *Alexis Korner* (1974), *Get Off My Cloud* (1975), *Just Easy* (1978), *Me* (1979), *The Party Album* (1980), *Juvenile Delinquent* (1984), *Live In Paris: Alexis Korner* (1988, archive recordings); by New Church *The New Church* (1970); by Snape *Accidentally Born In New Orleans* (1973), *Snape Live On Tour* (1974). Compilations: *Bootleg Him* (1972), *Profile* (1981), *Alexis 1957* (1984), *Testament* (1985), *Alexis Korner 1961-1972* (1986), *Hammer And Nails* (1987), *The Alexis Korner Collection* (1988).

L

Lacey, Rubin, Rev.
b. 2 January 1901, Pelahatchie, Mississippi, USA, d. c.1972, Bakersfield, California, USA. Learning guitar and mandolin from the unrecorded George Hendrix as a young man, Lacey moved to Jackson, where he contributed to the musical ideas of Tommy Johnson and Ishman Bracey. In 1927, he recorded a solitary, but outstanding 78 rpm record. Lacey's secular career ended when he became a preacher in 1932, but when rediscovered in 1966 he was a mine of information about both his blues and his preaching careers, and became the chief subject of Alfred Rosenberg's book *The Art Of The American Folk Preacher*.
Compilations: *Sorrow Come Pass Me Around* (1975), *Son House And The Great Delta Blues Singers* (1990).

Lamb, Paul
b. 1955, Blyth, Northumberland, England. Lamb's initial interest in blues came from listening to John Mayall's records, he then discovered the music of Sonny Terry, in whose style he thoroughly immersed himself for 12 years. He played in folk clubs and in 1975 was successful in a harmonica championship held in Germany. Around 1980, he began playing amplified harmonica in Walter 'Shakey' Horton's style initially, and as a member of the Blues Burglars he recorded for Red Lightnin' in 1986. Shortly after, Lamb moved to London and formed his own band. In 1990, Paul Lamb And The Kingsnakes were voted UK Blues Band of the Year, and Lamb himself received the Instrumentalist of the Year award. This was a worthy recognition of his position at the forefront of British blues.
Album: *Paul Lamb And The Kingsnakes* (1990).

Lambert, Donald
b. c.1904, Princeton, New Jersey, USA, d. 8 May 1962. Taught initially by his mother, Lambert developed into a leading exponent of the stride piano style. During the late 20s he was much in demand as a solo pianist in clubs and at 'rent parties' in Harlem. From the early 30s he worked mostly in and around New York, spending many years in long residencies at a small number of clubs. Consequently, Lambert's fame was largely localized although he was highly-regarded by fellow pianists. He made a handful of well-received records in the early 40s and a few more in the years just prior to his death in 1962.
Compilations: *Harlem Stride Classics 1960-62* (1979), *Piano Giant - Stride* (1979), *Classics In Stride* (1988).

Landreth, Sonny
Being born in Canton, Mississippi, USA, birthplace or thereabouts of Elmore James, didn't mean that Sonny Landreth had to play slide guitar, but it certainly makes good copy. In fact, after five years in Jackson, Mississippi, the family moved to Lafayette, Louisiana, and Landreth grew up surrounded by cajun music and its lifestyle. At 10, he began studying trumpet in school, and three years later took up the guitar. At 20, he quit college and, with his band Brer Rabbit, moved to Colorado. There, he met Robben Ford, and worked in Michael Murphy's band. He also developed his unique slide technique, chording behind the steel at the 12th fret. Returning to Louisiana, he got involved with several cajun bands, including Zachary Richard, Beausoleil, Red Beans & Rice, and in 1979 became the first white musician in Clifton Chenier's band. His first recordings were made for Huey Meaux in 1973. Then, in 1981, he made, *Blues Attack*, the first of two albums for Jay Miller's Blues Unlimited label. *Way Down In Louisiana* was issued in 1985. When not playing sessions, Landreth toured with his band, Bayou Rhythm. In 1988, he and the band backed John Hiatt on his *Slow Turning* album, touring America and Europe as 'The Goners'. Landreth spent the next two years preparing his *Outward Bound* album, eventually released in 1992. Landreth has been compared to Ry Cooder and David Lindley but his distinctive blend of rock, blues and cajun music gives him prominence in the hierarchy of slide guitarists.
Albums: *Way Down In Louisiana* (1985), with John Hiatt *Slow Turning* (1988), *Outward Bound* (1992).

Laurie, Annie

Rumoured to be Dinah Washington's favourite singer and a big influence on Joe Williams, Annie Laurie sang professionally with the territory bands led by Snookum Russell and Dallas Bartley (the latter with whom she made her recording debut - 'St. Louis Blues' - in 1945), before arriving in New Orleans where she was hired by Paul Gayten. With Gayten's band she had a string of successful records between 1947-50, such as her covers of Buddy Johnson's 'Since I Fell For You' on DeLuxe Records and Lucky Millinder's 'I'll Never Be Free' on Regal - both of which spawned numerous cover versions. Following Regal's demise in 1951, Annie Laurie commenced her solo career on Columbia's reactivated OKeh subsidiary, subsequently recording for Savoy (1956), DeLuxe again (1956-59 - where she had her biggest hit in 1957 with 'It Hurts To Be In Love'), and Ritz (1962). Sometime in the 60s she gave up secular singing and has devoted her voice to the church ever since.
Albums: with Paul Gayten Creole Gal (1979), It Hurts To Be In Love (1988), with Paul Gayten and Dave Bartholomew Regal Records In New Orleans (1991).

Laury, Booker T.

b. c.1918, USA. A Memphis blues pianist, Laury went unrecorded until the late 70s, but even in 1990 was still a vigorous survivor from the barrelhouse tradition. He was dismissed from the intermission spot by the tourist-oriented 'Blues Alley' club as too old fashioned. He learned piano from Mose Vinson and Memphis Slim, whom he claimed to be a cousin. Laury's rough, energetic playing and powerful vocals were much less polished than Slim's. Laury appeared in the Jerry Lee Lewis bio-pic Great Balls Of Fire, and his version of the sexually explicit 'Big Leg Woman' is based on Lewis's adaptation of the original recording by Johnny Temple.
Albums: Nothing But The Blues (1980). Memphis Piano Blues Today (1991).

Lazy Lester

b. Leslie Johnson, 20 June 1933 (or 1923), Torras, Louisiana, USA. Blues harmonica player/vocalist Lazy Lester recorded numerous singles for Excello Records in the late 50s and early 60s. Forming his first band in 1952, the musician's first significant job was as sideman for bluesman Lightnin' Slim. Owing to his slow-moving, laid-back ways, Johnson received his performing name during this period, from record producer J.D. Miller, who was known for his 'swamp pop' sound. Miller recorded Lester and placed him with the Nashville-based Excello in 1958. Lester's first solo single was 'Go Ahead' (1956) and his first local hit 'Sugar Coated Love'/'I'm A Lover Not A Fighter'. The latter was covered in the UK by the Kinks. Lester continued to record as a leader until 1965. He also played harmonica for such artists as the blues-rock guitarist Johnny Winter (an early recording in 1961) and Lonesome Sundown. At the end of the 60s, Lester moved around the country and did not record again until 1987, for the UK Blues 'N' Trouble label. The following year he recorded, Harp & Soul, for Alligator Records, and was back touring the USA in the late 80s and early 90s, enjoying new-found acclaim.
Albums: True Blues (60s, reissued 1987), Lazy Lester Rides Again (1987), Harp & Soul (1988). Compilations: They Call Me Lazy (1977), Poor Boy Blues - Jay Miller Sessions (1987).

Leadbelly

b. Hudson ('Huddie') Leadbetter, 29 January 1889, Mooringsport, Louisiana, USA, d. 6 December 1949, New York City, New York, USA. Leadbelly's music offers an incredible vista of American traditions, white as well as black, through his enormous repertoire of songs and tunes. He learned many of them in his youth when he lived and worked in western Louisiana and eastern Texas, but to which he added material from many different sources, including his own compositions, throughout the rest of his life. He played several instruments, including mandolin, accordion, piano and harmonica, but was best known for his mastery of the 12-string guitar. In his early 20s, he met and played with Blind Lemon Jefferson, but the encounter was to leave little if any lasting impression on his music. His sound remained distinctive and individual, with his powerful, yet deeply expressive vocals, and his 12-string guitar lines, which could be booming and blindingly fast or slow and delicate as appropriate. His style and approach to music developed as he played the red-light districts of towns like Shreveport and

Leadbelly

Dallas - a tough, often violent background that was reflected in songs like 'Fannin Street' and 'Mr Tom Hughes Town'.

Although he built up a substantial local reputation for his music as a young man, he served a number of prison sentences, including two stretches of hard labour, for murder and attempted murder respectively. While serving the last of these sentences, at the Louisiana State Penitentiary at Angola, he was discovered by the folklorist, John A. Lomax, then travelling throughout the south with his son Alan, recording traditional songs and music - frequently in prisons - for the Folk Song Archive of the Library of Congress. On his release (which he claimed was due to his having composed a song pleading with the governor to set him free), Leadbelly worked for Lomax as a chauffeur, assistant and guide, also recording prolifically for the Archive. His complete Library of Congress recordings, made over a period of several years, were issued in 1990 on 12 albums. Through Lomax, he was given the opportunity of a new life, as he moved to New York to continue to work for the folklorist. He also started a new musical career, with a new and very different audience, playing university concerts, clubs and political events, appearing on radio and even on film. He also made many records, mainly aimed at folk music enthusiasts. However, he did get the opportunity to make some 'race' recordings which were marketed to the black listener, but these enjoyed little commercial success, probably because Leadbelly's music would have seemed rather old-fashioned and rural to the increasingly sophisticated black record buyer of the 30s, and although 50 songs were recorded, only six were issued.

The New York folk scene, however, kept him active to some extent, and he played and recorded with people like Josh White, Woody Guthrie, Sonny Terry and Brownie McGhee. There were also a series of recordings in which he was accompanied by the voices of the Golden Gate Quartet, although this was an odd pairing and rather contrived. Some newly composed songs, such as 'New York City' and in particular the pointed 'Bourgeois Blues', which described the racial prejudice he encountered in Washington, DC, show how his perspectives were being altered by his new

circumstances. It was his apparently inexhaustible collection of older songs and tunes, however, that most fascinated the northern audience, embracing as it did everything from versions of old European ballads ('Gallis Pole') through Cajun-influenced dance tunes ('Sukey Jump') and sentimental pop ('Daddy, I'm Coming Home') to dozens of black work songs and field hollers ('Whoa Back Buck'), southern ballads ('John Hardy'), gospel ('Mary Don't You Weep'), prison songs ('Shorty George'), many tough blues ('Pigmeat Papa') and even cowboy songs ('Out On The Western Plains'). His best-known and most frequently covered songs, however, are probably the gentle C&W-influenced 'Goodnight Irene', later to be a hit record for the Weavers (one of whose members was Pete Seeger, who was also to write an instruction book on Leadbelly's unique 12-string guitar style) and 'Rock Island Line' which was a hit for Lonnie Donegan in the UK a few years later. His classic 'Cottonfields' was a major success for the Beach Boys. In 1949, he travelled to Europe, appearing at jazz events in Paris, but the promise of wider appreciation of the man and his music was sadly curtailed when he died later that same year.

Compilations: *Alabama Bound* (1990), *Leadbelly Sings Folk Songs* (1990), *Complete Library Of Congress Sessions* (1990).

Leake, Lafayette

b. c.1920, Wynmie, Mississippi, USA, d. 14 August 1990, Chicago, Illinois, USA. Lafayette Leake was a blues pianist whose prime contribution was collaborating with Chess Records producer, Willie Dixon. After moving to Chicago, Leake first worked with Dixon in 1951, replacing Leonard 'Baby Doo' Caston in Dixon's group the Big Three Trio. Leake performed on many Chess sessions during the 50s and 60s, performing on recordings by Howlin' Wolf, Chuck Berry, Sonny Boy 'Rice Miller' Williamson, Bo Diddley, Junior Wells and Otis Rush. Leake joined Dixon's Chicago Blues All Stars, appearing on the 1969 *I Am The Blues*. He also recorded for the labels Cobra, Ovation and Spivey. Leake died after suffering a diabetic coma.

Leavy, Calvin

b. 1942, Scott, Arkansas, USA. Leavy began his

musical career in the gospel field at the age of 16, but in 1969, he recorded, singing and playing rhythm guitar, a strong southern-blues entitled, 'Cummins Prison Farm'. The song featured an excellent guitar break from Robert Tanner. The recording was released by Calvin C. Brown, owner of Soul Beat Records and became a surprise hit about a year after it was made, subsequently, it was picked up by Shelby Singleton Enterprises. Leavy made several more records for Soul Beat (and associate label Acquarian), often in the company of his bass-playing brother Hosea. Soon after, however, he dropped into obscurity and little has been heard of him, although his hit has become a blues standard. Last reports seem to indicate he was playing bass guitar with a gospel group.
Album: *Cummins Prison Farm* (1977).

Lee, Julia

b. 31 October 1902, Booneville, Missouri, USA, d. 8 December 1958. Beginning her career as a pianist and singer while in her early teens, Lee joined a band led by her brother, George E. Lee (1896-1958), a popular vocalist whose 'Novelty Singing Orchestra' played extensively in and around Kansas City. Despite the musical advances being made by other Kansas City Jazz bands of the time, notably the Lees' great rival, Bennie Moten, they retained their popularity into the mid-30s. After her brother's retirement, Julia Lee continued her career as a solo artist, enjoying a resurgence of popularity during the blues revival of the early and mid-40s. Her recordings of these and the following few years feature leading jazz musicians, including Benny Carter and Red Norvo. An effective if sometimes unprofound performer of the blues, and a disarming singer of popular songs of the day, Lee was well-placed to adapt to the growing public interest in R&B. However, her decision to spend most of her career in Kansas City rather than New York or Los Angeles, where R&B really took off, meant that she was far more unfamiliar to the wider public than many less talented singer-pianists of her generation.
Compilations: *Tonight's The Night (1944-52)* (1982), *Party Time (1946-52)* (1983), *Ugly Papa (1945-52)* (1987), *Snatch And Grab It* (1987), *A Porter's Love Songs* (1988), *Of Lions And Lambs* (1988).

Lee, 'Little' Frankie

b. 29 April 1941, Mart, Texas, USA. Lee began singing as a child, encouraged by his grandmother and, after leaving school, he sang blues around the clubs in Houston, Texas, turning professional at the age of 22. He began recording in 1963 and had singles released on the Houston labels, Great Scott and Peacock. After settling in the San Francisco bay area in 1973, he made singles for Elka and California Gold. Lee had tracks on several anthologies but had to wait until 1984 for the first complete album under his own name, recorded for the Hightone label. Lee admits to varied influences, including Reverend Claude Jeter, Sam Cooke, Roy Acuff and the Everly Brothers, though he has infused these elements into a strong southern soul/blues style.
Album: *Face It!* (1984).

Leecan, Bobby, And Robert Cooksey

Both b. USA. Bobby Leecan was a fine and fluent single string guitarist, banjoist and an occasional kazooist and vocalist. He made most of his recordings in the company of Robert Cooksey, whose rather sweet, warbling harmonica favours clear tone production rather than the slurs and bends of most blues players. Their output lies in the borderland between blues, vaudeville and jazz, ranging from 'Dirty Guitar Blues' to 'Ain't She Sweet', and blending easily with the jazz cornet of Tom Morris. Some sources suggest that they were based in Philadelphia.
Albums: *The Blues Of Bobbie Leecan & Robert Cooksey* (c.1975), *The Remaining Titles* (1986).

Left Hand Frank

b. Frank Craig, 5 October 1935, Greenville, Mississippi, USA. Frank had a rocking good-time approach to the traditional sound of 50s Chicago blues, although his distinctive guitar and vocals were only captured on record for the first time in 1978. At the end of the 70s he enjoyed some international acclaim, but remains one of the blues' lesser-known figures. He received his first guitar for his fourth birthday and quickly learned to play blues and country. He moved to Chicago at the age of 14 and was inspired to play blues by listening to the sounds he could hear coming out of the doors of the clubs. He played behind many of the city's blues

Meade 'Lux' Lewis, Pete Johnson, Albert Ammons and Joe Turner

musicians, including Junior Wells, Theodore 'Hound Dog' Taylor and Willie Cobbs, and recorded a few times as a bass player. He is now based in California.

Albums: *Living Chicago Blues Volume One* (1978, four tracks only), with Jimmy Rogers *The Dirty Dozens* (1985).

Lefty Dizz

b. Walter Williams, 1937, Arkansas, USA. Dizz was taught the rudiments of music by his father, after the family had moved north to Kankakee, Illinois, and he has been a stalwart of the Chicago blues scene since the late 50s, having accompanied numerous blues artists as rhythm or lead guitarist. He reportedly made his first record (credited to the 'Wallets') for the King label in 1960, and he recorded with Junior Wells in the mid-60s. For many years he was based at the Checkerboard Lounge in Chicago. Records under his own name have appeared on the CJ, JSP, Black And Blue, and Isabel labels. He can also be heard on an bootlegged release of the Rolling Stones. His stage name refers to his left-handed playing and his youthful habit of imitating Dizzy Gillespie. Lefty's forté is tough, gritty guitar blues.

Album: *Ain't It Nice To Be Loved* (1989).

Legendary Blues Band

Formed in June 1980, the Legendary Blues Band emerged from the Muddy Waters band of the mid-to-late 70s. The original line-up consisted of Jerry Portnoy (harmonica), Louis Myers (guitar/harmonica), Pinetop Perkins (piano), Calvin Jones (bass) and Willie Smith (drums), with the vocals shared among all the members. There were numerous personnel changes over the intervening years and Smith and Jones are the only remaining original members. The sound remains solidly in the Chicago blues vein. They recorded two albums for the Rounder label in the early 80s and signed with Ichiban in 1989.

Albums: *Life Of Ease* (1981), *Red Hot 'N' Blue* (1983), *Woke Up With The Blues* (1989), *Keeping The Blues Alive* (1990), *U B Da Judge* (1991).

Lenoir, J.B.

b. 5 March 1929, Monticello, Mississippi, USA. d. 29 April 1967, Champaign, Illinois, USA. Christened with initials, Lenoir was taught to

play the guitar by his father, Dewitt. Other acknowledged influences were Blind Lemon Jefferson, Arthur 'Big Boy' Crudup and Lightnin' Hopkins, with the latter's single-string runs and verse tags surviving to become an integral part of the mature Lenoir style. He relocated to Chicago in 1949, and was befriended by Big Bill Broonzy and Memphis Minnie. Having leased his first recordings to Chess in 1952, label owner Joe Brown put out Lenoir's first success, 'The Mojo Boogie' on JOB Records in 1953. A propulsive dance piece sang in a high, keening tenor, it typified one important element in Lenoir's repertoire. The other was exhibited the following year with the release on Parrot of 'Eisenhower Blues', an uncompromising comment upon economic hardship which the singer laid at the President's door. Also released that year, 'Mama Talk To Your Daughter' was another light-hearted boogie that was to become his signature tune, its ebullience mirrored by Lenoir's penchant for wearing zebra-striped jackets on stage. Subsequent records for Chess neglected the serious side of his writing, attempts at emulating previous successes taking preference over more sober themes such as 'We Can't Go On This Way' and 'Laid Off Blues'. Interviewed by Paul Oliver in 1960, Lenoir revealed that seriousness, which in turn was reflected in a series of recordings initiated by Willie Dixon and released to coincide with his appearance with the 1965 American Folk Blues Festival tour of Europe. *Alabama Blues* perfectly reconciled the two extremes of his style, remakes of 'The Mojo Boogie' and 'Talk To Your Daughter' tempering the stark reality of the title song, 'Born Dead' and 'Down In Mississippi', in which Lenoir, with both passion and dignity, evoked America's civil rights struggle of the time. What benefit might have accrued from what, in hindsight, was the masterwork of his career was prevented by his tragic death in a car crash.

Albums: *Alabama Blues* (1965), *Natural Man* (1968), *Chess Blues Masters* (1976), *The Parrot Sessions* (1989), *Alabama Blues* (1991).

Lewis, Meade 'Lux'

b. 4 September 1905, Chicago, Illinois, USA, d. 7 June 1964. Although he was popular in Chicago bars in the 20s, Lewis was little known

Smiley Lewis

elsewhere and made his living running a taxicab firm with fellow-pianist Albert Ammons. A record he made in 1927, 'Honky Tonk Train Blues', but which was not released until 1929, eventually came to the attention of John Hammond some half-dozen years later. Encouraged by Hammond and the enormous success of 'Honky Tonk Train Blues', which he re-recorded in 1936 (and later), Lewis became one of the most popular and successful of the pianists to enjoy fleeting fame during the boogie-woogie craze. With Ammons and Pete Johnson, billed as the 'Boogie Woogie Trio', he played at Hammond's Carnegie Hall 'Spirituals to Swing' concert and at many top New York clubs. Later resident in Los Angeles, Lewis continued to record and tour and make records. From the mid-30s onwards, Lewis often played celeste and such records, together with those he made in the early 40s with Edmond Hall's Celeste Quartet, where the remaining members of the group were Israel Crosby and Charlie Christian, showed him to be much more versatile than his mass audience appeared to assume. Meade died following a road accident in 1964.

Albums: *Yancey's Last Ride* (1954), *Cat House Piano* (1955), *Barrel House Piano* (1956), *The Meade 'Lux' Lewis Trio* (1956), *The Blues Artistry Of Meade 'Lux' Lewis* (1961), *Boogie Woogie House Party* (1962). Compilations: *Honky Tonk Piano* (1988), with others *Meade Lux Lewis Vol. 1 (1927-39)* (1988), with others *Meade Lux Lewis Vol. 2 (1939-54)* (1989), *Tell Your Story* (1989).

Lewis, Noah

b. 3 September 1895, Henning, Tennessee, USA, d. 7 February 1961, Ripley, Tennessee, USA. Lewis's ability to play two harmonicas at once, one with his nose, got him work on the travelling medicine shows, but his recorded music is notable more for its melancholy expressiveness than showmanship - a descriptive train imitation ('Chickasaw Special') apart. He combined technical accomplishment with exceptional breath control and a very subtle, sensitive handling of emotional nuance, whether on his 1927 solos, leading his own jug band in 1930, or as a member of Cannon's Jug Stompers, with whom he recorded from 1928-30. His singing had the same emotional depth as his harmonica playing, most notably on 'Viola Lee Blues' (recorded by the Grateful Dead in the 60s). Lewis lived in poverty, and died of gangrene as a consequence of frostbite.

Album: *Gus Cannon & Noah Lewis* (1991).

Lewis, Smiley

b. Overton Amos Lemons, 5 July 1913, DeQuincy, Louisiana, USA, d. 7 October 1966. While failing to gain the commercial plaudits his work deserved, this New Orleans-based artist was responsible for some of that city's finest music. He made his recording debut, as Smiling Lewis, in 1947 but his strongest work appeared during the 50s. 'The Bells Are Ringing' (1952), took him into the US R&B chart, and his biggest hit came three years later with 'I Hear You Knocking'. This seminal slice of Crescent City blues featured pianist Huey 'Piano' Smith and bandleader Dave Bartholomew, and was revived successfully in 1970 by Dave Edmunds. Smiley's career was dogged by ill-luck. His original version of 'Blue Monday' was a hit in the hands of Fats Domino, while Elvis Presley took another song, 'One Night', and by altering its risque lyric, secured a massive pop hit in the process. A further powerful Lewis performance, 'Shame, Shame, Shame', has subsequently become an R&B standard. This under-rated artist continued recording into the 60s, but died of cancer in 1966.

Album: *I Hear You Knocking* (1961). Compilations: *Shame Shame Shame* (1970), *I Hear You Knocking* (1978), *The Bells Are Ringing* (1978), *Caledonia's Party* (1986), *New Orleans Bounce - 30 Of His Best* (1991).

Lewis, Walter 'Furry'

b. 6 March 1893, Greenwood, Mississippi, USA, d. 14 September 1981, Memphis, Tennessee, USA. Furry Lewis was a songster, a blues musician, a humorist and an all-round entertainer. Raised in the country, he picked up the guitar at an early age and moved into Memphis around 1900 where he busked on the streets. He had experience working on travelling medicine shows under the influence of Jim Jackson after he ran away from home. He worked with W.C. Handy and claimed that Handy presented him with his first good guitar. Hoboing across country in 1916, he had an accident while hopping a train and consequently

Walter 'Furry' Lewis

lost a leg. After this he moved to Memphis and, while performing and recording, he supplemented his income by sweeping the streets. Apart from periods working on riverboats and with medicine shows in the 20s, this remained the style of his life for approximately the next 40 odd years. He recorded 11 titles for Vocalion in 1927, eight for Victor in 1928 and four more for Vocalion in 1929. He had a guitar-style that incorporated aspects of both the Mississippi county style and the lighter more raggy Memphis sound, supplemented by some impressive slide work. His voice was clear and his approach to lyrics often self-mockingly humorous. Several of his recordings were ballads and his treatment of these was equally original. Well-known around the city, he sometimes appeared as part of the Memphis Jug Band. He was one of the first pre-war blues artists to be 're-discovered' and from 1959 he pursued a second successful career on the college circuit and played in several movies including an unlikely appearance with Burt Reynolds in *W.W. And The Dixie Dance Kings*. Still an able performer he made many recordings during this period and was confirmed an Honorary Colonel of the State of Tennessee in 1973. Highly regarded by many performers, he received a touching tribute from Joni Mitchell on 'Furry Sings The Blues', which was featured on her 1976 album *Heijera*.
Albums: *Furry Lewis Blues*, (1959), *Back On My Feet Again* (1961) *Done Changed My Mind* (1962), *Presenting The Country Blues* (1969) *In Memphis* (1970), *On The Road Again* (1970), *Live At The Gaslight* (1971), *When I Lay My Burden Down* (1970). Compilation: *Furry Lewis In His Prime 1927-29* (1988).

Liggins, Jimmy

b. 14 October 1922, Newby, Oklahoma, USA, d. 18 July 1983, Durham, North Carolina, USA. Starting out as a disc jockey and boxer before becoming the driver for his brother Joe's band, the Honeydrippers, Jimmy Liggins taught himself guitar and formed his own band in 1947. Signing for Art Rupe's Specialty label, he immediately had big hits with 'I Can't Stop It', 'Cadillac Boogie' and notably 'Teardrop Blues'. Following a serious accident in 1948, when he was shot in the mouth, he continued with big sellers for Specialty Records, including his

biggest, 1953's 'Drunk'. Like Joe, he left Specialty in 1954, and recorded for Aladdin, before becoming a record distributor and forming his own Duplex Records which survived on few releases from 1958-78, financed from a diverse musical business, ranging from teach-yourself-piano charts to artist management.
Albums: with Joe Liggins *Saturday Night Boogie Woogie Man* (1974), *I Can't Stop It* (1981), *Jimmy Liggins & His Drops Of Joy* (1989).

Liggins, Joe

b. 9 July 1916, Guthrie, Oklahoma, USA, d. 26 July 1987, Los Angeles, California, USA. After attempting various brass instruments, Joe Liggins settled down to study musical composition and piano arrangement. After moving to California, he began writing for and playing with local bands, graduating in the 40s to the respected units of Cee Pee Johnson and Sammy Franklin, the latter of whom he was with when, in 1945 he left to form his own group, the Honeydrippers. He first recorded for Exclusive, with whom Joe Liggins And His Honeydrippers had 10 hits between 1945-49 - including the huge crossover hits 'The Honeydripper' and 'I've Got A Right To Cry' - he followed his brother Jimmy to Specialty in 1950 where the hits continued with 'Rag Mop' and the hugely successful 'Pink Champagne' (*Billboard*'s number 1 blues record of the year). Leaving Specialty in 1954, Liggins went briefly to Mercury (1954) and Aladdin (1956) before returning to Mercury to record an album in 1962. Later singles appeared on tiny independents like his own Honeydripper label and Jimmy Liggins' Duplex Records, and he was enjoying something of a renaissance at the time of his death in 1987.
Albums: *Great R&B Oldies* (1972), with Jimmy Liggins *Saturday Night Boogie Woogie Man* (1974), *Darktown Strutters' Ball* (1981), *Joe Liggins & His Honeydrippers* (1985), *The Honeydripper* (1988), *Joe Liggins & The Honeydrippers* (1989).

Lightfoot, Alexander 'Papa George'

b. 2 March 1924, Natchez, Mississippi, USA, d. 28 November 1971. A self-taught harmonica player, Papa Lightfoot first recorded in 1949 for Peacock Records as part of the Gondoliers vocal group. He had a sporadic recording career in New Orleans in the early 50s (and accompanied

Alexander 'Papa George' Lightfoot

Lil' Ed

Champion Jack Dupree on the King label). The majority of his 50s recordings remained unreleased until Bob Hite, famed blues collector and lead singer with Canned Heat, persuaded Liberty Records to issue them in their 1968 *Legendary Masters* series. This resulted in Lightfoot being rediscovered in 1969 and recording for the Los Angeles-based Vault Records. He was unable to capitalize on this new-found fame because the following year he fell ill and in 1971 died from a heart attack in his home town of Natchez.
Album: *Natchez Trace* (1969).

Lightnin' Slim

b. Otis Hicks, 13 March 1913, St. Louis, Missouri, USA, d. 27 July 1974, Detroit, Michigan, USA. It is as a Louisiana blues stylist that Hicks is best known, having moved to that state in his early teens. He learnt guitar from his father and his brother and made a name for himself on the Baton Rouge blues circuit during the 40s. In 1954, he recorded for J.D. 'Jay' Miller's Feature label, and began that producer's long and fruitful relationship with the blues. These early recordings had a tough, spare sound that helps to place them with the finest downhome blues of the 50s, and the quality was largely maintained over much of the next decade, with many singles leased to Excello Records. His partnership with harmonica player Lazy Lester was particularly effective and releases such as 'Mean Old Lonesome Train', 'Hoodoo Blues' and especially 'Rooster Blues' provided him with commercial success and kept him in demand for tours both locally and farther afield. Many of these demonstrate his particular facility for taking raw material from the work of other popular bluesmen, such as Muddy Waters and Lightnin' Hopkins, and turning it into something entirely his own. The relationship with Miller finally came to an end in 1965, but within a few years, Slim had found a wider forum for his music as he became a regular visitor to Europe.
Albums: *High And Lowdown* (1974), *The Early Years* (1976), *London Gumbo* (1978), *The Feature Sides* (1981), *We Gonna Rock Tonight* (1986), *Rooster Blues* (1987), *Bell Ringer* (1987), *Blue Lightnin'* (1992).

Lil' Ed And The Blues Imperials

b. Ed Williams. Lil' Ed learned slide guitar from his uncle J.B. Hutto. Singing his own compositions, he formed the Blues Imperials in 1975 and built up a reputation on the Chicago club scene. In 1986 Lil' Ed recorded for Alligator with Dave Weld (guitar), James Young (bass) and Louis Henderson (drums). In 1989 Mike Garrett and Kelly Littleton replaced Weld and Henderson.
Albums: *Roughhousin'* (1987), *Chicken, Gravy & Biscuits* (1989), *What You See Is What You Get* (1993).

Lincoln, Charlie

b. Charley Hicks, 11 March 1900, Lithonia, Georgia, USA, d. 28 September 1963, Cairo, Georgia, USA. Like his younger brother Robert 'Barbecue Bob' Hicks, Lincoln learned guitar from Curley Weaver's mother, but was less accomplished than Bob. He recorded from 1927-30, probably thanks to his brother's hit-making status, and his blues are a mix of the sad and the mildly risqué, backed by simple 12-string guitar. Despite being billed as 'Laughing Charley' on a duet with Bob, Lincoln was a man whose mood changed under the influence of drink from introverted to choleric, a trait exacerbated by the alcoholism that followed various family tragedies, notably the premature death of his brother in 1929. On Christmas Day, 1955, he senselessly murdered a man, and spent the rest of his life in prison, repentant and performing only religious songs.
Compilations: *Charley Lincoln* (1983), *Complete Recordings 1927-1930* (1984).

Linkchain, Hip

b. Willie Richard, 10 November 1936, near Jackson, Mississippi, USA, d. 13 February 1989, Chicago, Illinois, USA. As a baby, Linkchain was known as 'Long Linkchain'. Hip heard the blues at home and learned to play acoustic guitar, switching to electric after settling in Chicago in the early 50s. He formed his first band in 1959 and recorded singles in the 60s for the Lola and Sann labels, under the name 'Hip Lanchan'. In the 70s he had a single issued by Blues King, and on the JSP label, an album featuring further titles from this session plus earlier tracks. Albums also appeared on MCM, Rumble (with Jimmy Dawkins), Teardrop (including a collaboration with Jimmy Rogers) and a highly-acclaimed set for Black Magic. Hip died of cancer in 1989. Linkchain's guitar style was unique in the west-side Chicago tradition, and he was a talented songwriter and singer. Album: *Airbuster* (1987).

Linn County

Formed in Chicago, Illinois, USA, this powerful, blues-based quintet - Stephen Miller (organ/vocals), Fred Walk (guitar/sitar), Larry Easter (saxophones/flute), Dino Long (bass) and Jerome 'Snake' McAndrew (drums) - subsequently moved to San Francisco. Their impressive debut *Proud Flesh Soothsayer*, included the lengthy 'Protect And Serve/Bad Things' which showcased the exhilarating interplay between the unit's instrumental protagonists. A more orthodox collection, *Fever Shot*, nonetheless featured several hard-edged, disciplined performances, while a final release, *Till The Break Of Dawn*, offered a vibrant reading of John Lee Hooker's 'Boogie Chillun' as its highlight. By this point McAndrew had been replaced by Clark Pierson, but the group was unable to capitalize upon their cult status and broke up soon afterwards. Miller completed a solo album, which featured the entire Linn County line-up, before joining the Elvin Bishop group. Pierson subsequently drummed in Janis Joplin's Full Tilt Boogie Band.
Albums: *Proud Flesh Soothsayer* (1968), *Fever Shot* (1969), *Till The Break Of Dawn* (1970).

Lipscomb, Mance

b. 9 April 1895, Navasota, Texas, USA, d. 30 January 1976, Navasota, Texas, USA. The son of a former slave and professional fiddle player, Lipscomb initially learned that instrument and later the guitar. For many years he played on a solely local basis, while working as a farmer, and only made his first recordings at the age of 65, in 1960. Over the following 15 years, he made a series of highly regarded albums, mainly for Chris Strachwitz's Arhoolie label. On the strength of these and his frequent live performances, he built up a very strong reputation for his skills as a singer of a wide range of material. His remarkably extensive repertoire encompassed gospel, rags, ballads and other traditional songs, as well as Texas-style blues. He also appeared in several films,

including one bio-pic, entitled, *A Well Spent Life*.
Albums: *You'll Never Find Another Man Like Mance* (1964), *Texas Songster, Volumes 1-6* (c.60s/70s), *Texas Blues* (c.60s/70s). Compilation: *Texas Songster* (1990, CD compilation of the *Texas Songster* series).

Little Milton

b. Milton Campbell Jnr., 7 September 1934, Inverness, Mississippi, USA. Having played guitar from the age of 12, Little Milton made his first public appearances as a teenager in the blues bars and cafes on Greenville's celebrated Nelson Street. He first appeared on record accompanying pianist Willie Love in the early 50s, then under his own name appearing on three singles issued on Sam Phillips's Sun label under the guidance of Ike Turner. Although their working relationship continued throughout the decade, it was on signing to Chicago's Chess/Checker outlet that Milton's career flourished. An R&B-styled vocalist in the mould of Bobby 'Blue' Bland and 'T-Bone' Walker, his work incorporated sufficient soul themes to maintain a success denied less flexible contemporaries. Propelled by an imaginative production, Milton scored a substantial hit in 1965 with the optimistic 'We're Gonna Make It', and followed with other expressive performances, including 'Who's Cheating Who?' (1965) plus the wry 'Grits Ain't Groceries' (1968). Campbell remained with Chess until 1971, whereupon he switched to Stax. 'That's What Love Will Do' returned the singer to the R&B chart after a two-year absence, but despite his appearance in the pivotal *Wattstax* film, Little Milton was unable to maintain a consistent recording career. A series of ill-fitting funk releases from the late 70s reinforced the perception that the artist is at his peak with blues-edged material, something proved by his excellent contemporary work for the Malaco label.
Albums: *We're Gonna Make It* (1965), *Little Milton Sings Big Blues* (1966), *Grits Ain't Groceries* (1969), *If Walls Could Talk* (1970), *Blues 'N' Soul* (1974), *Waiting For Little Milton* (1973), *Montreux Festival* (1974), *Friend Of Mine* (1976), *Me For You, You For Me* (1976), *In Perspective* (1981), *Walkin' The Back Streets* (1981), *I Need Your Love So Bad* (1982), *Age Ain't Nothing But*

A Number (1983), *Playin' For Keeps* (1984), *Annie Mae's Cafe* (1987), *Movin' To The Country* (1987), *I Will Survive* (1988), *Too Much Pain* (1990), *Reality* (1992). Compilations: *Little Milton's Greatest Hits* (1972), *Little Milton* (1976), *Sam's Blues* (1976), *Raise A Little Sand* (1982), *His Greatest Hits* (1987), *Chicago Golden Years* (1988), *Hittin' The Boogie* (1988, Sun recordings), *The Sun Masters* (1990).

Little Son Joe

b. Ernest Lawlars, 18 May 1900, Hughes, Arkansas, USA, d. 14 November 1961, Memphis, Tennessee, USA. Lawlars is best known for his musical partnership with his wife, Memphis Minnie, but he had been playing guitar and singing blues for some years around Memphis before they got together, including a period with Rev. Robert Wilkins, whom he accompanied on record in 1935. He took up with Minnie in the late 30s, replacing her previous husband and partner, Joe McCoy. Like McCoy, Lawlars also made records under his own name, including the well known 'Black Rat Swing', but he mainly appeared in the supporting role, on a large number of sides covering most of the 40s and the early years of the following decade. As their popularity in Chicago waned, they settled back in Memphis and retired from music in the 50s.
Album: *Memphis Minnie* (1964), *Chicago Blues* (1982), *World Of Trouble* (1982).

Little Walter

b. Marion Walter Jacobs, 1 May 1930, Marksville, Louisiana, USA, d. 15 February 1968. A major figure of post-war blues, Little Walter is credited for bringing the harmonica, or 'French harp', out from its rural setting and into an urban context. His career began at the age of 12 when he left home for New Orleans, but by 1946 Jacobs was working in Chicago's famed Maxwell Street. Early recordings for the Ora Nelle label were the prelude to his joining the Muddy Waters band where he helped forge what became the definitive electric Chicago blues group. The harmonica player emerged as a performer in his own right in 1952 when 'Juke', an instrumental recorded at the end of a Waters' session, topped the R&B chart where it remained for eight consecutive weeks. Little Walter And The Night Caps - David Myers

(guitar), Louis Myers (guitar) and Fred Below (drums) - enjoyed further success when 'Sad Hours' and 'Mean Old World' reached the Top 10 in the same chart. The group then became known as Little Walter And The Jukes and although obliged to fulfil recording agreements with Waters, Jacobs actively pursued his own career. He enjoyed further R&B hits with 'Blues With A Feeling' (1953), 'Last Night' (1954) and the infectious 'My Babe' (1955). The last song, patterned on a spiritual tune, 'This Train', was a second number 1 single and became much-covered during later years. Other notable releases included 'Mellow Down Easy' and 'Boom Boom (Out Go The Lights)' which were later recorded, respectively, by Paul Butterfield and the Blues Band. A haunting version of 'Key To The Highway' (1958), previously recorded by Big Bill Broonzy, gave Walter his final Top 10 entry. He nonetheless remained a pivotal figure, undertaking several tours including one of Britain in 1964. His career, however, was undermined by personal problems. A pugnacious man with a quick temper and a reputation for heavy drinking, he died on 15 February 1968 as a result of injuries sustained in a street brawl. This ignominious end should not detract from Little Walter's status as an innovative figure. The first musician to amplify the harmonica, his heavy, swooping style became the lynchpin for all who followed him, including Norton Buffalo, Butterfield and Charlie Musselwhite.
Compilations: *The Best Of Little Walter* (1964), *Hate To See You Go* (1969), *On The Road Again* (1979), *Quarter To Twelve* (1982), *Chess Masters* (1983), *Boss Blues Harmonica* (1986), *Confessin' The Blues* (1986), *Windy City Blues* (1986), *Collection: Little Walter 20 Blues Greats* (1987), *The Blues World Of Little Walter* (1988), *Boss Blues Harmonica* (1988), *The Best Of Little Walter Volume 2* (1989).

Littlefield, 'Little' Willie

b. 16 September 1931, El Campo, Texas, USA. By the age of 16, Littlefield was emulating his hero Amos Milburn, shouting the blues and hammering the pianos of nearby Houston's Dowling Street clubs. He made his recording debut the following year for the local Eddie's Records and for the Freedom label. In August 1949, Littlefield was discovered by the Bihari

Little Walter

brothers, who had flown to Houston to find their own version of Aladdin's Amos Milburn, and signed him to their Los Angeles-based Modern label. Littlefield's first Modern session, recorded in Houston, resulted in the huge hit 'It's Midnight' which featured his school friend, Don Wilkerson, on tenor saxophone. From October 1949, Littlefield was recording in Los Angeles, but subsequent releases did not match the promise of the debut single, in spite of bands which included Jimmy 'Maxwell Street' Davis, Chuck Norris and Johnny Moore. In 1952, Littlefield signed with Federal Records and continued to make fine records in his own right and in duets with Lil Greenwood and Little Esther Phillips. His first Federal session resulted in his best-known recording, 'K.C. Loving' which was later altered slightly by Leiber And Stoller and recorded by Wilbert Harrison as 'Kansas City'. By 1957, Littlefield had moved to northern California, where he recorded for the Rhythm label. He stayed in San José throughout the 60s and 70s, making the occasional club appearance, but in the early 80s he moved with his family to the Netherlands and has since experienced a minor comeback with new material on various European labels and frequent appearances at jazz and blues festivals.
Albums: *K.C. Loving* (1977), *It's Midnight* (1979), *Little Willie Littlefield - Volume One* (1980), *Little Willie Littlefield - Volume Two* (1981), *I'm In The Mood* (1984), *Jump With Little Willie Littlefield* (1984), *Happy Pay Day* (1986), *House Party* (1988), ... *Plays Boogie Woogie* (1988).

Littlejohn, Johnny

b. John Funchess Littlejohn, 16 April 1931, Jackson, Mississippi, USA. Littlejohn taught himself to play guitar, and was inspired by Henry Martin, a blues guitarist friend of his father. In 1946, he left home and was an itinerant worker before settling in Gary, Indiana, in 1951 and taking up the guitar seriously. He quickly became a popular attraction and later relocated to Chicago. A chronically underrated slide guitarist/singer, Littlejohn has recorded for numerous labels, including Ace, Margaret, Bluesway, and Wolf, but his best work is to be found on Arhoolie and Rooster. Although often categorized as an Elmore James influenced player, he can also recall the smooth approach of B.B. King with his picking and singing.
Albums: *John Littlejohn's Chicago Blues Stars* (1968), *So-Called Friends* (1985).

Lockwood, Robert 'Junior'

b. 27 March 1915, Marvell, Arkansas, USA. In his youth, Lockwood learned some guitar from Robert Johnson who was evidently a major influence. Lockwood's earliest recordings emphasize that debt. He worked the Mississippi Delta area throughout the 30s, playing with musicians such as Sonny Boy 'Rice Miller' Williamson and Howlin' Wolf. In 1941, he was in Chicago, Illinois making his first records as a solo artist, as well as some accompaniments to Peter J. 'Doctor' Clayton. Lockwood spent some time as one of the resident musicians on the famous *King Biscuit Time* radio programme, from Helena, Arkansas. In the early 50s he settled in Chicago where he recorded with Sunnyland Slim on piano, and a drummer. Johnson's influence was detectable, but the style was becoming distinctly urban in orientation. Throughout that decade, he played the Chicago blues clubs, and often accompanied Little Walter on record. In 1960, he made some classic recordings with Otis Spann, his delicate runs and big, chunky chords betraying a more sophisticated, jazzy direction. He has continued to be very active in music through the ensuing years, working with Willie Mabon among others. In the late 70s, he formed a touring and recording partnership with John Ed 'Johnny' Shines.
Albums: *Windy City Blues* (1976), *Does 12* (1977).

Lofton, Cripple Clarence

b. 28 March 1887, Kingsport, Tennessee, USA, d. 9 January 1957. Living and playing in Chicago from the age of 20, pianist and vocalist Lofton became a popular accompanist to visiting blues singers, in many instances appearing in this role on record. He worked steadily through the 30s, proving very popular in the Windy City, and enjoyed the fleeting benefits of the boogie-woogie craze. Influenced by Charles 'Cow Cow' Davenport and Jimmy Yancey, he in turn influenced a number of other pianists, notably Meade 'Lux' Lewis.
Compilation: *Clarence's Blues (1930s)* (1988).

Lonesome Sundown

b. Cornelious Green, 12 December 1928, Donaldsonville, Louisiana, USA. Green taught himself piano while growing up, then took guitar lessons in his early 20s. He joined Clifton Chenier's band in 1955, and can be heard on several of that artist's recordings on the Specialty label. The following year he recorded for the first time in his own right and 16 singles were issued over the next nine years under the name given to him by producer Jay Miller - Lonesome Sundown. Many of these, such as 'My Home Is A Prison' and 'Lonesome Lonely Blues', were classic examples of that uniquely Louisiana sound, swamp blues - a resonant production, featuring a strong, booming rhythm section, rippling piano and support from Lazy Lester or John Gradnigo on harmonica and Lionel Prevost on tenor saxophone. Green's vocals and biting lead guitar invariably provide just the right gritty edge. A religious conversion towards the end of this period led to his withdrawal from the music scene, but he returned, if only briefly, to record an excellent album for the Joliet label in the late 70s.

Albums: *Been Gone Too Long* (1977), *Lonesome Whistler* (1983), *If Anybody Asks You* (1988).

Louis, Joe Hill

b. Lester Hill, 23 September 1921, Whitehaven Tennessee, USA, d. 5 August 1957. He learned blues harmonica from Will Shade as a teenager and was given the name Joe Hill Louis after victory in a boxing match. He performed in Memphis in the late 40s, where he became known as 'The Be-Bop Boy' and developed a one-man band act, with guitar, foot-drum and harmonica. Louis's first recordings were made for Columbia in 1949 before he took over B.B. King's radio spot as the Pepticon Boy on WDIA in Memphis. This led to 'Boogie in the Park', a single produced by Sam Phillips for his short-lived Phillips label in 1950. Next, Phillips signed Louis to the Bihari Brothers' Modern label, for which 'I Feel Like A Million' was a local hit. By 1952, Phillips was recording him with a backing group on tracks like 'We All Gotta Go Sometime' and using Louis to accompany such artists as the Prisonaires and Rufus Thomas for whose 'Tiger Man' (1953), he supplied a scintillating guitar solo. There were other tracks for Checker, Meteor and Ace. His final records were made for House Of Sound shortly before his death from tetanus in Memphis in August 1957.

Lonesome Sundown

Joe Hill Louis

Albums: (reissues) *Blues In The Morning* (1972), *The One Man Band 1949-56* (1979).

Love, Clayton

b. 15 November 1927, Mattson, Mississippi, USA. Raised from the age of 12 in Clarksdale, Love studied trombone and band theory in high school, and learned to play the piano while in the army. Returning to Vicksburg, he formed his band, The Shufflers, with schoolfriends Jesse Flowers and Henry Reed, and played the area's nightspots. His first cousin, Earl Reed, had recorded for Trumpet, and recommended Love's group to owner Lillian McMurry. The band first recorded in Jackson, Mississippi. on 3 May 1951, but the titles, 'Susie' and 'Shufflin' With Love', were re-recorded on 10 June and released on Trumpet 138. The following year, in Chicago, he recorded a single for Aladdin.

Back in Clarksdale, Love joined up with Ike Turner with whom he recorded for Modern in 1954, and, as a member of Turner's Kings Of Rhythm, for Federal in April 1957 and reissued in 1991. Despite the band's full gig sheet, Love quit to become a teacher in the St. Louis public school system. After retiring at the end of the 80s, in April 1990 he recorded, in company with Johnnie Johnson and Jimmy Vaughan, *Rockin' Eighty-Eights*, his four songs including a remake of 'The Big Question', first recorded for Federal.
Selected albums: *Trailblazer* (1991), *Rockin' Eighty-Eights* (1991).

Love, Preston

b. 26 April 1921, Omaha, Nebraska, USA. He inherited an alto saxophone from his older brother 'Dude' and obtained his first professional

job in 1940, after which he took lessons from Illinois Jacquet's brother Julius. Inspired further by Count Basie's Earle Warren, Love played with Lloyd Hunter, Nat Towles and Snub Mosely before replacing Warren in Basie's band briefly in 1943. He worked with Lucky Millinder in 1944 and rejoined Basie for a longer spell from 1945-47, after which he played on-and-off in the band of his friend, Johnny Otis. Love also led his own orchestra (recording for his own Spin label and Federal Records) until 1962. Moving to California in 1962, he became a top session-player until he joined Ray Charles' band in 1966, going on to become the west coast house bandleader at Motown. Today, he lectures in African-American music at colleges and writes for local newspapers while maintaining a healthy touring schedule, including frequent trips to Europe.
Albums: *Omaha Barbeque* (c.60s), *Strictly Cash* (1982).

Love, Willie

b. 4 November 1906, Duncan, Mississippi, USA, d. 19 August 1953, Jackson, Mississippi, USA. A musician from an early age, Love's career was spent almost entirely in and around the Mississippi Delta country. In the 40s and 50s, he was a regular performer on the famous radio show, *King Biscuit Time*, but his music is known to us now only because of a handful of records issued on the Trumpet label in the mid-50s. These are tough, downhome blues, on which he demonstrated considerable proficiency on the piano, as well as an effective singing voice. 'Nelson Street Blues', in which he describes the street of that name in Greenville, Mississippi, is particularly notable for its strong and fascinating evocation of the time and place. Among his accompanists were Elmore James, Little Milton and Joe Willie Wilkins.
Compilations: *Clownin' With The World* (1990), *Delta Blues 1951* (1990).

Lubinsky, Herman

b. 30 August 1896, USA, d. 16 March 1974. Lubinsky formed Savoy Records in 1942 in Market Street, Newark, New Jersey after running a record shop on the site for many years. He had previously been responsible for operating New Jersey's first radio station in 1924. Savoy scored a number 1 hit from its first

recording session and, bolstered by this success, went on to build a peerless jazz, gospel and R&B roster in the late 40s with top-selling records by such artists as, on the jazz roster: Charlie Parker, Lester Young, Dexter Gordon, Erroll Garner, J.J. Johnson, Fats Navarro, Miles Davis, Leo Parker, Eddie 'Lockjaw' Davis; gospel: the Kings Of Harmony and the Deep Tones (on the King Solomon subsidiary); and R&B: Dusty Fletcher, Paul Williams, Wild Bill Moore, Hal Singer and Brownie McGhee. In 1948, Savoy opened a successful west coast office under Ralph Bass who continued in Savoy's excellent tradition of recording the finest R&B and bebop, having big hits with Johnny Otis/Little Esther Phillips and Big Jay McNeely. In the 50s, Savoy largely eschewed rock 'n' roll, concentrating on its jazz and ever-expanding gospel catalogue - the latter of which now included Clara Ward, the Drinkard Singers, the Davis Sisters, the Selah Jubilee Singers and, later, Alex Bradford and Jimmy Cleveland. This catalogue would prove to be the company's 'bread and butter' through the 60s and 70s. However, they continued to enjoy R&B success with Nappy Brown, Big Maybelle and Varetta Dillard, as well as making several brilliant territorial forays into the Atlanta and New Orleans musical communities and purchasing important smaller independents labels such as National. Lubinsky remained a strong character, fronting Savoy until just a few months before his death from cancer in March 1974. Savoy Records was purchased by Arista in 1975, and a large-scale reissue programme was commenced.

Lucas, William 'Lazy Bill'

b. 29 May 1918, Wynne, Arkansas, USA. Bill Lucas's first instrument was a guitar, financed by selling a pig, but he really wanted a piano. Living on a farm with five siblings it seemed like a dream when his father actually bought him one in 1932. However, when the family moved to Cape Girardeau, Missouri, the piano was left behind. Lazy Bill had no real contact with the blues until he met Big Joe Williams in St. Louis in 1940. Converted, he moved to Chicago in 1941 and turned back to the piano after playing guitar in support of many of the famous artists of the day. He was one of Little Hudson's Red Devils and recorded with his own Blue Rhythms for the Chance label in 1954.

Experiencing difficulties, due, in part to the nervous condition that had rendered him almost blind since childhood, he moved to Minneapolis, Minnesota, in 1964 where he continued to play, appearing at festivals and recording for his own Lazy label in 1970 and later for the Philo label.

Lutcher, Joe

Brother of Nellie Lutcher, Joe moved from Lake Charles, Louisiana to California where he played his alto saxophone with the Nat 'King' Cole Trio, the Will Mastin Trio and the Mills Brothers. He then signed for Capitol Records in the summer of 1947 (at the same time as Nellie) and had strong sellers with his 'Strato Cruiser', 'No Name Boogie' and the US Top 10 hit 'Shuffle Boogie'. Leaving Capitol in 1948, Lutcher's Jump Band went on to record for Specialty Records, Modern (resulting in a moderate hit with 'Mardi Gras' in 1949, which uncovered his Louisiana connections), London, Peacock and several small obscure independent labels. Meanwhile, Joe undertook some session work, before giving up the 'devil's music' and becoming an evangelist in the mid-50s; he is said to be responsible for converting Little Richard from secular to spiritual music in the late 50s.
Album: *Joe Joe Jump* (1982).

Lyons, Willie James

b. 5 December 1938, Alabama, USA, d. 26 December 1980, Chicago, Illinois, USA. A west side Chicago blues guitarist from the 50s, Lyons worked as a accompanist with many artists, including Luther Allison, Jimmy Dawkins and Bobby Rush. Unaccountably ignored by Chicago record companies, he was taken up by French blues enthusiasts in the 70s. He recorded as an accompanist, made a disappointing half album, and in 1979 visited Europe, where he recorded his only full album. This proved to be the work of a fine singer and guitarist, influenced by B.B. King and Freddie King, 'T-Bone' Walker and Lowell Fulson.
Albums: *Ghetto* (1976), *Chicago Woman* (1980).

M

Mabon, Willie

b. 24 October 1925, Hollywood, Tennessee, USA, d. 19 April 1986. Accompanying himself on piano and secondly on harmonica, Mabon sang an urbane blues style similar to Charles Brown. He moved from Memphis, Tennessee, to Chicago in 1942 and first got on record in 1949 as a member of the Blues Rockers group. After military service he became a popular entertainer in Chicago's Black Belt, and by the early 50s, was well-established as an R&B singer with a number of successful records to his credit. Signed as a solo artist to Chess Records in 1951, Mabon immediately hit with a novelty blues, 'I Don't Know' (R&B number 1, 1952), a remake of a Cripple Clarence Lofton record from 1938. Mabon had other hits with 'I'm Mad' (R&B number 1, 1953), 'Poison Ivy' (R&B Top 10, 1954), and 'Seventh Son' (1955). After leaving Chess in 1956, he continued to record on various small labels, getting his best success on Formal in 1962 with 'Got To Have Some'. During the 70s and 80s, Mabon would flit back and forth between Chicago and Europe, making an occasional album for German and French labels, most of which were poorly received. He found a wider audience in Europe, playing the Montreux Jazz Festival and festivals in Berlin and Holland. A polished performer, with a measure of glossy sophistication to his singing, Mabon retained a strong affinity with the earthier aspects of the blues and was an influence upon Mose Allison.
Albums: *Funky* (1972), *Cold Chilly Woman* (1973), *Come Back* (1973), *The Comeback* (1973), *Live And Well* (1974), *Shake That Thing* (1975), *Sings 'I Don't Know' And Other Chicago Blues Hits* (70s), *Chicago Blues Session* (1980). Compilations: *Chicago 1963* (1974), *I'm The Fixer: Original USA Recordings 1963-64* (1981), *The Seventh Son* (1982), *Blues Roots Volume 16* (1982).

McCain, Jerry

b. 19 June 1930, Gadsden, Alabama, USA. From a musical family, McCain learned harmonica as a

child, and played with local group the Upstarts in the early 50s. He first recorded in Jackson, Mississippi for Lillian McMurry's Trumpet label in 1954 ('Wine-O-Wine', 'Stay Out Of Automobiles', 'East Of The Sun'). A competent singer and fiery harmonica player, McCain next signed to Excello where he recorded a number of songs from 1956-59. After other tracks for Cosimo Mattasa's Rex label and for OKeh, McCain left music in the early 60s. He returned to the studio in 1965, cutting '728 Texas' for Stan Lewis's Jewel label. In the 70s and 80s he worked as a private investigator while continuing to make occasional records and perform at blues festivals. The Atlanta Rhythm Section provided the backing for McCain's cover versions of Slim Harpo's hits, while the 1992 album for Ichiban contained some of his best work including an anti-drug piece, 'Burn The Crackhouse Down'.
Albums: *Sings Slim Harpo* (1973), *Love Desperado* (1992).

McClennan, Tommy

b. 8 April 1908, Yazoo City, Mississippi, USA, d. c.1960 Chicago, Illinois, USA. McClennan's biography is fairly typical of many blues singers of his time and place. He was raised on the J. F. Sligh farm in rural Mississippi and learned to play the guitar at an early age. Working for tips on the streets and at private parties, he became acquainted with other performers such as Honeyboy Edwards and Robert Petway. Petway and McClennan shared a style so close that, later on record, it became difficult to tell them apart, a confusion they sometimes compounded by recording together. McClennan had a limited but effective percussive guitar style, often played by working on a single string. His voice was rough but full of humour, and also capable of expressing poignancy and subtle emotions. Around 1939, he moved to Chicago (as did Petway) and made a name for himself playing at clubs where expatriate southerners gathered to hear the 'down home' sounds of their younger days. McClennan was an uncompromising character, who, according to a famous story told by Big Bill Broonzy, got into trouble by refusing to adapt his songs to conform with northern sensibilities. His refusal to be impressed by the big city found expression in his often used, self-addressed, facetious aside, 'Play it right, you're

in Chicago'. Although his 40-track career on record ended in 1942, he continued to play in the clubs into the post-war boom typified by Muddy Waters and Howlin' Wolf. One of his two known photographs shows him in the company of Sonny Boy Williamson (Rice Miller), Little Walter and Elmore James. His death is unconfirmed, but word of mouth suggests he died, in poverty, around 1960.
Albums: *Travelin' Highway Man* (1990), *I'm A Guitar King* 1990).

McCoy, Joe

b. 11 May 1905, Raymond, Mississippi, USA, d. 28 January 1950, Chicago, Illinois, USA. An early start learning guitar prepared McCoy for a diverse recording career. At first, he partnered his wife, Memphis Minnie, and they made many blues records together in the late 20s and early 30s. McCoy (under the pseudonym Kansas Joe) played beautifully tight, two-guitar arrangements, sometimes one on lead vocals, sometimes the other and occasionally a duet. When the couple split up, McCoy was well-established in Chicago and continued to record as accompanist to other artists, under his own name or a variety of pseudonyms (including religious records as Hallelujah Joe). He adopted a more urbane blues style as time went on and, in 1936, he began a long and successful series of recordings with the jazz-orientated group, the Harlem Hamfats.
Albums: *Memphis Minnie And Kansas Joe, Complete Recordings*, (1991, four vols), *Harlem Hamfats* (1984).

McCoy, Robert

b. 31 March 1912, Aliceville, Alabama, USA, d. 1978, Birmingham, Alabama, USA. Jabbo Williams was a family friend, and Cow Cow Davenport and Pinetop Smith were visitors to the McCoy home. McCoy claimed to have played piano on record behind Jaybird Coleman in 1930 and, in 1937, he accompanied a number of Birmingham artists at a session organised by Lucille Bogan, of whose band he was a member. After war service, McCoy largely retired (though he claimed to have recorded with Jerry McCain). In the early 60s he was extensively recorded by a local enthusiast; attempts to commercialize his sound with R&B musicians and songs failed, but his exploration of the older

repertoire resulted in some valuable performances. Heavily indebted to Race Records for material, and stylistically influenced by Leroy Carr, McCoy nevertheless preserved the rough, percussive piano styles of Birmingham. He had become a church deacon by 1975.
Albums: *Blues And Boogie Woogie Classics* (c.1975), *Birmingham Sessions* (1988).

McCray, Larry

Blues guitarist and singer McCray moved north to Detroit in the late 60s. He worked on assembly lines and played in local clubs throughout the 70s and 80s. In 1990, McCray became the first signing to Virgin's blues subsidiary Pointblank.
Album: *Ambition* (1990).

McDowell, Mississippi Fred

b. 12 January 1904, Rossville, Tennessee, USA, d. 3 July 1972, Memphis, Tennessee, USA. A self-taught guitarist, McDowell garnered his early reputation in the Memphis area by appearances at private parties, picnics and dances. He later moved to Como, Mississippi, and was employed as a farmer until discovered by field researcher Alan Lomax in 1959. Sessions for Atlantic and Prestige confirmed the artist as one of the last great exponents of the traditional bottleneck style and McDowell became a leading light of the 60s blues renaissance. He undertook several recordings with his wife, Annie Mae and, in 1964, appeared at the *Newport Folk Festival* alongside other major 'rediscoveries' Mississippi John Hurt and Sleepy John Estes; a portion of his performance was captured on the attendant film. The following year he completed the first of several releases for the California-based Arhoolie label. These recordings introduced a consistency to his work which deftly combined blues and spiritual material. McDowell also became a frequent visitor to Europe, touring with the American Folk Blues Festival and later appearing in concert in London, where he was supported by Jo Ann Kelly. He appeared on several Dutch television programmes and in two documentary films, *The Blues Maker* (1968) and *Fred McDowell* (1969). The artist was then signed to the Capitol label, for which he recorded *I Don't Play No Rock 'N' Roll*. Arguably one of the finest releases of its genre, its intimate charm belied the intensity the performer still brought to his work. Despite ailing health McDowell continued to follow a punishing schedule with with performances at festivals throughout the USA, but by the end of 1971, such work had lessened dramatically. He died of cancer in July 1972. Although his compositions were not widely covered, the Rolling Stones recorded a haunting version of 'You've Got To Move' on *Sticky Fingers* (1971). McDowell's influence is also apparent in the approach of several artists, notably that of Bonnie Raitt.

Albums: *Mississippi Delta Blues* (1964), *My Home Is In The Delta* (1964), *Amazing Grace* (1964), *Mississippi Delta Blues Volume 2* (1966), *I Don't Play No Rock 'N' Roll* (1969), *Mississippi Fred McDowell And His Blues Boys* (1969), *Mississippi Fred McDowell In London 1* (1970), *Mississippi Fred McDowell In London 2* (1970), *Going Down South* (1970), *Mississippi Fred McDowell* (1971), *Mississippi Fred McDowell 1904-1972* (1974), *Mississippi Fred McDowell And Johnny Woods* (1977), *Miss Delta Blues* (1981), *Miss Delta Blues, Volume Two* (1981), *Keep Your Lamps Trimmed* (1981), *A Double Dose Of Dynamite* (1986), *Fred McDowell 1959* (1988), *When I Lay My Burden Down* (1988), *1962* (1988), with Jo Ann Kelly *Standing At The Burying Ground* (1989).

McGhee, Granville 'Stick'

b. 23 March 1918, Knoxville, Tennessee, USA, d. 15 August 1961, New York City, New York, USA. Like his more famous brother, Brownie McGhee, Granville learned guitar from his father. After seeing action in the World War II, he moved to New York in 1946. The following year, he made his first record, 'Drinkin' Wine Spo-Dee-O-Dee', under his own name. However, it was a later cut of the same song, made for Atlantic in 1949, with a group that included Big Chief Ellis as well as Brownie, that gave him his biggest success. Over the next few years, he made several more records, and appeared as accompanist on others, most notably to Sonny Terry. However, he did not manage to make the move to the new, young, white audience that his brother tapped into so successfully in the late 50s and onwards.

Albums: *Drinkin' Wine Spo-Dee-O-Dee* (1982).

McGhee, Walter Brown 'Brownie'

b. 30 November 1915, Knoxville, Tennessee, USA. McGhee learned guitar from his father, and started early on a musical career, playing in church before he was 10 years old, and on the road with medicine shows, carnivals and minstrel troupes in his early teens. His travels took him into the Carolinas, and his time there proved very influential in moulding his musical style. He met Sonny Terry in 1939, and their partnership was to become one of the most enduring in blues. The following year, he made his first records, reminiscent of those of Blind Boy Fuller; indeed some of them bore the credit 'Blind Boy Fuller No.2'. Also around this time, he settled in New York, where his career took a rather different turn, as he took up with a group of black musicians - including Terry, Leadbelly and Josh White - favoured by the then small white audience for the blues. For a number of years, he catered very successfully both for this audience, playing acoustic blues in an older style, and for an entirely separate one. Through the late 40s and early 50s, he recorded electric blues and R&B aimed at black record buyers. In retrospect, it is this second type that stands up best, and indeed, some of his records from this period rank among the finest blues to come out of New York in the post-war years. He was also very prolific as an accompanist, playing superb lead guitar on records by other artists such as Champion Jack Dupree, Big Chief Ellis and Alonzo Scales, as well as his brother Stick. His partnership with Terry became more firmly established during this period, and, as the original market for blues and R&B faded, they carved a very strong niche for themselves, playing concerts, festivals and clubs, and making albums aimed at the growing audience for folk music. For many years, they travelled the world and made record after record, establishing their names among the best-known of all blues artists. However, critical opinion seems agreed that their music suffered to a large degree during this period, as it was diluted for such a wide, international audience and as successive recordings trod similar ground. McGhee seems to have been inactive since Terry's death in 1986, although in fact their partnership broke up shortly before this.

Selected albums: *1944-1955* (1990), *Home Town Blues* (1990), *The 1958 London Sessions* (1990).

Granville 'Stick' McGhee

Mack, Lonnie

b. 1941, Harrison, Indiana, USA. Lonnie Mack began playing guitar while still a child, drawing early influence from a local blues musician, Ralph Trotts, as well as established figures Merle Travis and Les Paul. He later led a C&W act, Lonnie And The Twilighters, and by 1961 was working regularly with the Troy Seals Band. The following year, Mack recorded his exhilarating instrumental version of Chuck Berry's 'Memphis'. By playing his Gibson 'Flying V' guitar through a Leslie cabinet, the revolving device which gives the Hammond organ its distinctive sound, Mack created a striking, exciting style. 'Memphis' eventually reached the US Top 5, while an equally urgent original, 'Wham', subsequently broached the Top 30. *The Wham Of That Memphis Man* confirmed the artist's vibrant skill, which drew on blues, gospel and country traditions. Several tracks, notably 'I'll Keep You Happy', 'Where There's A Will' and 'Why', also showed Mack's prowess as a soulful vocalist, and later recordings included a rousing rendition of Wilson Pickett's 'I Found A Love'. The guitarist also contributed to several sessions by Freddy King and appeared on James Brown's 'Kansas City' (1967). Mack was signed to Elektra in 1968 following a lengthy appraisal by Al Kooper in **Rolling Stone** magazine. *Glad I'm In The Band* and *Whatever's Right* updated the style of early recordings and included several notable remakes, although the highlight of the latter set was the extended 'Mt. Healthy Blues'. Mack also added bass to the Doors' *Morrison Hotel* (1970) and undertook a national tour prior to recording *The Hills Of Indiana*. This low-key, primarily country album was the prelude to a six-year period of seclusion which ended in 1977 with *Home At Last*. Mack then guested on Michael Nesmith's *From A Radio Engine To The Photon Wing*, before completing *Lonnie Mack And Pismo*, but this regeneration was followed by another sabbatical. He re-emerged in 1985 under the aegis of Texan guitarist Stevie Ray Vaughan, who co-produced the exciting *Strike Like Lightning*. Released on the Alligator label, a specialist in modern blues, the album rekindled this talented artist's career a rebirth that was maintained on the fiery *Second Sight*.
Albums: *The Wham Of That Memphis Man* (1963), *Glad I'm In The Band* (1969), *Whatever's Right* (1969), *The Hills Of Indiana* (1971), *Home At Last* (1977), *Lonnie Mack And Pismo* (1977), *Strike Like Lightning* (1985), *Second Sight* (1987). Compilations: *For Collectors Only* (1970), *The Memphis Sound Of Lonnie Mack* (1974), *Sixteen Rock Guitar Greats* (c.70s).

McKinley, L.C.

b. between 1914 and 1920, Winona, Mississippi, USA, d. 19 January 1970. McKinley is one of the mystery figures of the post-war Chicago blues. He had a much smoother style than most of his contemporaries and was obviously influenced by T-Bone Walker. McKinley was playing in Chicago in the 40s, and recorded as an accompanist to Tampa Red in 1953 and then, under his own name, for States the following year and for Vee-Jay in 1955, and finally for Bea And Baby in 1959, before he dropped out of the music scene. Willie Dixon reputedly attempted to revive his musical career in the 60s, but to little avail.
Compilations: *Chicago Bluesmasters Volume Four* (1985), two Bea And Baby tracks *Meat And Gravy From Cadillac Baby Volume Three: Trying To Make A Living* (1978).

McMahon, Andrew 'Blueblood'

b. 12 April 1926, Delhi, Louisiana, USA, d. 17 February 1984, Monroe, Louisiana, USA. McMahon played blues and hillbilly music in Mississippi and worked with Bukka White in Memphis, Tennessee, before moving to Chicago in 1949. During the 50s he worked with J.B. Hutto and Jimmy Dawkins, and played bass guitar for Howlin' Wolf and recorded during 1960-73. McMahon recorded under his own name for the Bea And Baby label in 1971, and as 'Blueblood' for Dharma Records in 1973. After leaving Wolf, he led a band around the Chicago clubs and recorded a live album for MCM in 1976, following which he returned to his home state and left music. Although he was a limited singer, McMahon always seemed to attract all-star line-ups for his recording sessions.
Albums: *Blueblood* (1973), *Go Get My Baby* (1976).

McMullen, Fred

A shadowy figure, McMullen recorded for ARC in New York in January 1933, playing immaculate bottleneck blues guitar, whether behind his own vocals or with one or other of the Atlanta guitarists, Curley Weaver and Buddy Moss. They also recorded as a trio, with Moss on harmonica. McMullen was listed only once in the 1932 Atlanta City Directory, and Moss maintained that he had returned to his hometown, Macon, Georgia, after the session. The intensity of 'De Kalb Chain Gang' ('They whipped me and they slashed me, forty-five all in my side') suggests that it was autobiographical, and that he may have been on his way home after release from prison when he encountered the Atlanta musicians.

Albums: *Georgia Blues Guitars* (1988), *Buddy Moss* (1990).

Macon, John Wesley 'Shortstuff'

b. 1933, Crawford, Mississippi, USA, d. 28 December 1973, Macon, Mississippi, USA. In the mid-60s, Macon was brought briefly to public attention by his cousin Big Joe Williams. Although 30 years younger than Williams, he performed a remarkably archaic style of blues, featuring simple, insistently rhythmic guitar, often without chord changes, and mode packed vocals which often recalled the field holler. After the trip north with Joe that resulted in his too few recordings, Macon returned home to undeserved obscurity until his death.

Albums: *Mr. Shortstuff & Big Joe Williams* (c.1965), *Hell Bound & Heaven Sent* (1967).

McTell, 'Blind' Willie

b. probably May 1898, McDuffie County, Georgia, USA, d. 19 August 1959, Almon, Georgia, USA. Blind from birth, McTell began to learn guitar in his early years, under the influence of relatives and neighbours in Statesboro, Georgia, where he grew up. In his late teens, he attended a school for the blind. By 1927, when he made his first records, he was already a very accomplished guitarist, with a warm and beautiful vocal style, and his early sessions produced classics such as 'Statesboro Blues', 'Mama Tain't Long Fo Day' and 'Georgia Rag'. During the 20s and 30s, he travelled extensively from a base in Atlanta, making his living from music and recording, on a regular basis, for three different record companies, sometimes using pseudonyms which included Blind Sammie and Georgia Bill. Most of his records feature a 12-string guitar, popular among Atlanta musicians, but particularly useful to McTell for the extra volume it provided for singing on the streets. Few, if any, blues guitarists could equal his mastery of the 12-string. He exploited its resonance and percussive qualities on his dance tunes, yet managed a remarkable delicacy of touch on his slow blues. In 1934, he married, and the following year recorded some duets with his wife, Kate, covering sacred as well as secular material. In 1940, John Lomax recorded McTell for the Folk Song Archive of the Library of Congress, and the sessions, which have since been issued in full, feature him discussing his life and his music, as well as playing a variety of material. These offer an invaluable insight into the art of one of the true blues greats. In the 40s, he moved more in the direction of religious music, and when he recorded again in 1949 and 1950, a significant proportion of his songs were spiritual. Only a few tracks from these sessions were issued at the time, but most have appeared in later years. They reveal McTell as commanding as ever. Indeed, some of these recordings rank amongst his best work. In 1956, he recorded for the last time at a session arranged by a record shop manager, unissued until the 60s. Soon after this, he turned away from the blues to perform exclusively religious material. His importance was eloquently summed up in Bob Dylan's strikingly moving elegy, 'Blind Willie McTell'.

Albums: *Last Session* (1960), *Complete Library Of Congress Recordings* (1969), *Complete Recorded Works 1927-1935* (1990, three CD vols.).

Magic Sam

b. Samuel Maghett, 14 February 1937, Grenada, Mississippi, USA, d. 1 December 1969. Although Sam's immediate family were not musical, he received encouragement from his uncle, 'Shakey Jake' Harris, a popular blues singer on Chicago's west side. Maghett arrived in the city in 1950 and by the age of 20 had secured a recording deal with Cobra Records, an emergent independent label. His debut single, 'All Your Love', a compulsive, assured performance which highlighted Sam's crisp guitar figures, set the pattern for several subsequent releases, but progress faltered upon his induction into the army in 1959. Not a natural soldier, Sam deserted after a couple of weeks' service and was subsequently caught and

'Blind' Willie McTell

sentenced to six months' imprisonment. He was given a dishonourable discharge on release, but the experience had undermined Sam's confidence and his immediate recordings lacked the purpose of their predecessors. However, his debut album, *West Side Soul*, encapsulated an era when Maghett not only re-established his reputation in Chicago clubs, but had become an attraction on the rock circuit with appearances at the Fillmore and Winterland venues in San Francisco. This vibrant record included 'Sweet Home Chicago', later revived by the Blues Brothers. A second collection, *Black Magic*, confirmed his new-found status but its release was overshadowed by Sam's premature death from a heart attack in December 1969. Only days before, Maghett had agreed to sign with the renowned Stax label. His passing robbed the blues genre of a potentially influential figure.

Albums: *West Side Soul* (1968), *Black Magic* (1969). Compilations: *Sweet Home Chicago* (1968), *Magic Sam (1937-1969)* (1969), *Magic Sam Live* (1981, live recordings from 1964), with Earl Hooker *Calling All Blues* (1986), *The Magic Sam Legacy* (1989), *Give Me Time* (1992).

Magic Slim

b. Morris Holt, 7 August 1937, Torrence, Mississippi, USA. Blues guitarist/vocalist Magic Slim became interested in music during childhood. He moved first to nearby Grenada, Mississippi, and then to Chicago in 1955, where he worked as bassist for Magic Sam, who gave Holt his name. He obtained a false identity card so that he was able to play bass with Sam in the bars and clubs. After completing that stay, he switched back to guitar and performed with a Chicago band called Mr. Pitiful And The Teardrops. When that band split up, he moved back to Mississippi, before returning to Chicago once again in 1965, where he reformed the Teardrops with his two brothers (Nick, the bassist, became a permanent member). The band recorded its first single for the local Wes label in 1966, and another for the equally small Mean Mistreater label in 1970. It was not until 1978 that Magic Slim And The Teardrops began recording in earnest, contributing four tracks to an Alligator Records anthology. That was followed by a live album for the small Candy Apple label as well as recordings made in France, which were released in the USA on Alligator as

Raw Magic in 1982. That same year he recorded the highly-praised *Grand Slam* for Rooster Blues Records. A live album recorded in Austria, *Chicago Blues Session*, followed in 1987. *Gravel Road*, released on the small Blind Pig label in the USA, was issued in 1990. His sound is perhaps the tightest of any Chicago blues band working at the present time. This consistently satisfying blues musician recorded singles for numerous labels and, since 1976, he recorded an album for the collector market.

Albums: *Live 'N Blue* (1980), *Raw Magic* (1982), *Grand Slam* (1982), *Chicago Blues Session Volume Three* (1986), *Highway Is My Home* (1978 recordings), *Son Of A Gun* (1988), *Gravel Road* (1990).

Mahal, Taj

b. Henry Saint Clair Fredericks, 17 May 1942, New York City, New York, USA. The son of a jazz arranger, Mahal developed his early interest in black music by studying its origins at university. After graduating, he began performing in Boston clubs, before moving to the west coast in 1965. The artist was a founder member of the legendary Rising Sons, a respected folk-rock group which also included Ry Cooder and Spirit drummer Ed Cassidy. Mahal resumed his solo career when the group's projected debut album was shelved. His first solo album, *Taj Mahal*, released in 1968, was a powerful, yet intimate compendium of electrified country blues which introduced an early backing band of Jesse Davis (guitar), Gary Gilmore (bass) and Chuck Blakwell (drums). A second album, *The Natch'l Blues*, offered similarly excellent fare while extending his palette to include interpretations of two soul songs. This early period reached its apogee with *Giant Steps/The Ole Folks At Home*, a double-album comprising a traditional-styled acoustic album and a vibrant rock selection. Mahal continued to broaden his remarkable canvas. *The Real Thing*, recorded in-concert, featured support from a tuba section, while the singer's pursuit of ethnic styles resulted in the African-American persuasion of *Happy Just To Be Like I Am* and the West Indian influence of *Mo Roots*. He has maintained his chameleon-like quality over a succession of cultured releases, during which the singer has remained a popular live attraction at the head of a fluctuating backing

Taj Mahal

group, known initially as the Intergalactic Soul Messengers, then as the International Rhythm Band.

Albums: *Taj Mahal* (1968), *The Natch'l Blues* (1968), *Giant Steps/The Ole Folks At Home* (1969), *The Real Thing* (1971), *Happy Just To Be Like I Am* (1971), *Recycling The Blues And Other Related Stuff* (1972), *The Sounder* (1973), *Oooh So Good 'N' Blues* (1973), *Mo' Roots* (1974), *Music Keeps Me Together* (1975), *Satisfied 'N Tickled Too* (1976), *Music Fuh Ya'* (1977), *Brothers* (1977), *Evolution* (1977), *Taj Mahal And The International Rhythm Band Live* (1979), *Going Home* (1980), *Live* (1981), *Take A Giant Step* (1983), *Taj* (1987), *Live And Direct* (1987), *Mule Bone* (1991). Compilation: *Going Home* (1980), *The Taj Mahal Collection* (1987).

Maiden, Sidney

b. 1923, Mansfield, Louisiana, USA. A shadowy figure about whom little has been written, Maiden was evidently influenced by John Lee (Sonny Boy) Williamson when learning the harmonica. Sometimes in the Forties, he made the journey west to work in the shipyards around Richmond, California. There he met K.C. Douglas and the pair began to work clubs in the area. In 1948 he and Douglas recorded for Bob Geddins' Down Town, with his 'Eclipse Of The Sun' becoming a notable performance amongst collectors. He next recorded in April 1952 for Imperial, an eight-track session with The Blues Blowers, perhaps including Douglas and Otis Cherry on drums, from which just one single was released. Moving to Los Angeles the following year, he joined up with drummer B. Brown and guitarist Haskell Sadler to inaugurate the Flash label, each man recording one single. 'Hurry Hurry Baby' was an unsteady boogie piece distantly akin to Jimmy Reed's 'You Don't Have To Go'. In 1957, he recorded 'Hand Me Down Baby' for Dig, with guitarist Slim Green. Four years later, he was recruited by Arhoolie boss Chris Strachwitz to participate in sessions with Douglas and Mercy Dee Walton, during which he also recorded an album leased to Bluesville. During the 60s, he formed his own group and worked the Fresno area, since when his whereabouts and fate are unknown.

Album: *Jericho Alley Blues Flash* (1988).

Malone, J.J.

b. 20 August 1935, Pete's Corner, Alabama, USA. Malone was playing guitar and harmonica before his 13th birthday, and he began performing at dances and parties when he was 17. In the mid-50s he spent a year in the Air Force and formed his first band the Rockers, later called Tops In Blues. Once out of the Service in 1957, he formed the Rhythm Rockers in Spokane, Washington, and they worked all over the west coast. In 1966, he settled in Oakland, California, and recorded for the Galaxy label, enjoying a hit with 'Its A Shame' in 1972, and he subsequently had records issued by the Red Lightnin', Cherrie, Paris Album, and Eli Mile High labels. Malone is a soulful vocalist, adept on both piano and guitar and equally convincing at straight blues, rocking R&B, or funk-influenced material.

Albums: *Bottom Line Blues* (1991), with Troyce Key *I've Gotta New Car* (1980).

Mandel, Harvey

b. 11 March 1945, Detroit, Michigan, USA. This fluent, mellifluous guitarist was one of several young aspirants learning their skills in Chicago clubs. A contemporary of Paul Butterfield and Michael Bloomfield, Mandel was a member of both the Charlie Musselwhite and Barry Goldberg blues bands, before moving to the west coast in 1967. His debut album, *Christo Redentor*, was released the following year. This wholly instrumental set, which included contributions from Musslewhite, Graham Bond, and the Nashville musicians later known as Area Code 615, is arguably the guitarist's definitive release, but *Righteous* and *Baby Batter* are equally inventive. Between 1969 and 1971, Mandel was a member of Canned Heat wherein he struck an empathy with bassist Larry Taylor. Both subsequently joined John Mayall for *USA Union* and *Back To The Roots* before the guitarist formed the short-lived Pure Food And Drug Act. He also remained a popular session musician, contributing to albums by Love, the Ventures and Don 'Sugarcane' Harris during this highly prolific period. Mandel continued to record his stylish solo albums throughout the early 70s, and was one of several candidates mooted to replace Mick Taylor in the Rolling Stones. The results of his audition are compiled on the group's 1976 album, *Black And Blue*. This

dalliance with corporate rock was Harvey's last high-profile appearance. In 1985 he signed a recording deal with the newly-founded Nuance label, but no new release has been forthcoming.
Albums: *Christo Redentor* (1968), *Righteous* (1969), *Games Guitars Play* (1970), *Baby Batter* aka *Electric Progress* (1971), with other artists *Get Off In Chicago* (1972), *The Snake* (1972), with Dewey Terry *Chief* (1973), *Shangrenade* (1973), *Feel The Sound Of* (1974). Compilations: *Feel The Sound Of Harvey Mandel* (1974), *Best Of* (1975).

Mars, Johnny

b. 7 December 1942, Laurens, South Carolina, USA. During his youth, his family moved around the southeast, and Mars began playing harmonica before he was in his teens, influenced by older, local players and his sister's collection of blues records. He moved to New Paltz, New York, in 1958 and joined a high school band. In 1961, he was in the Train Riders and a few years later in Burning Bush (as bass guitarist and occasional harmonica player). In 1967, Mars settled in San Francisco, where he led his own band, then moved to England in 1972, working as a singer/harmonica player. He has subsequently recorded for the Big Bear, JSP, Ace, Sundance, President, and Lamborghine labels, sometimes with guitarist Ray Fenwick. Mars is a fine vocalist and a modern, adventurous, blues harmonica player.
Albums: *Oakland Boogie* (1976), *King Of The Blues Harp* (1980).

Martin, Carl

b. 15 April 1906, Big Stone Gap, Virginia, USA, d. 1978. Like his father, the multi-instrumentalist Martin played in a string band, although he is also known for his work in the blues field. In his teens he met Howard Armstrong and, in 1930, the two musicians, along with Martin's brother Roland, recorded under the name of the Tennessee Chocolate Drops. It gives some indication of their sound that the record was also issued in the company's country music series (under a different credit). A couple of years later, Martin moved to Chicago and joined the blues circuit, recording under his own name as well as accompanying diverse artists such as Tampa Red and Freddie Spruell. In the 60s, Martin and Armstrong, with guitarist

Ted Bogan, brought the old string band sound to a new audience.
Album: *Martin, Bogan And Armstrong* (1973).

Martin, Fiddlin' Joe

b. 8 January 1900, Edwards, Mississippi, USA, d. 21 November 1975, Walls, Mississippi, USA. Martin learned guitar and trombone as a boy, later adding mandolin and bass fiddle (hence his nickname). He switched to washboard and drums in the 40s after damaging his hands in a fire. He worked with many Delta blues singers, including Charley Patton, Willie Newbern, Johnnie Temple, Memphis Minnie, Willie Brown and Son House, recording with the last two for the Library of Congress in 1940. Martin played drums for Howlin' Wolf until Wolf went north, but his most enduring association was with Woodrow Adams; he appeared on all Adams' recordings, and they worked Mississippi juke joints together until Martin's death.
Album: *Walking Blues* (1979).

Martin, Sara

b. 18 June 1884, Louisville, Kentucky, USA, d. 24 May 1955, Louisville, Kentucky, USA. A melodious but rather inflexible singer, Martin appears nevertheless to have been a popular success, recording over 120 tracks for OKeh between 1923 and 1928. These include the first recorded blues with guitar accompaniment (by Sylvester Weaver), and the first with a jug band (that of Clifford Hayes, billed as 'Sara Martin's Jug Band'). Although Chicago-based, Martin maintained close connections with Louisville, from where Hayes and Weaver also originated. She worked in vaudeville from 1915-31, thereafter devoting herself to the church and to running a nursing home in Louisville from the 40s until her death.
Albums: *Clifford Hayes Vol. 2* (c.1987), with Sylvester Weaver *The Accompanist* (1988), *Sara Martin* (c.1990).

Mayall, John

b. 29 November 1933, Macclesfield, Cheshire, England. The career of England's premier white blues exponent and father of British blues has now spanned five decades and much of that time has been spent unintentionally acting as a musical catalyst. Mayall formed his first band in 1955 while at college, and as the Powerhouse

John Mayall

Four the group worked mostly locally. Soon after Mayall enlisted for National Service. He then became a commercial artist and finally moved to London to form his Blues Syndicate, the forerunner to his legendary Bluesbreakers. Along with Alexis Korner, Cyril Davis and Graham Bond, Mayall pioneered British R&B. The astonishing number of musicians who have passed through his bands reads like a who's-who. Even more remarkable is the number of names who have gone on to eclipse Mayall with either their own bands or as members of highly successful groups. Pete Frame author of *Rock Family Trees* has produced a detailed Mayall specimen, which is recommended. His roster of musicians included, John McVie, Hughie Flint, Mick Fleetwood, Roger Dean, Davey Graham, Eric Clapton, Jack Bruce, Aynsley Dunbar, Peter Green, Dick Heckstall-Smith, Keef Hartley, Mick Taylor, Henry Lowther, Tony Reeves, Chris Mercer, Jon Hiseman, Steve Thompson, Colin Allen, Jon Mark, Johnny Almond, Harvey Mandel, Larry Taylor, and Don 'Sugercane' Harris.

His 1965 debut, *John Mayall Plays John Mayall*, was a live album which, although badly recorded, captured the tremendous atmosphere of an R&B club. His first single, 'Crawling Up A Hill', is contained on this set and it features Mayall's thin voice attempting to compete with an exciting, distorted harmonica and Hammond organ. *Bluesbreakers With Eric Clapton* is now a classic, and is highly recommended to all students of white blues. Clapton enabled his boss to reach a wider audience, as the crowds filled the clubs to get a glimpse of the guitar hero. *A Hard Road* featured some clean and sparing guitar from Peter Green, while *Crusade* offers a brassier, fuller sound. *The Blues Alone* showed a more relaxed style, and allowed Mayall to demonstrate his musical dexterity. *Diary Of A Band Vol. 1* and *Vol. 2* were released during 1968 and capture their live sound from the previous year; both feature excellent drumming from Keef Hartley, in addition to Mick Taylor on guitar. *Bare Wires*, arguably Mayall's finest work, shows a strong jazz leaning, with the addition of Jon Hiseman on drums and the experienced brass section of Lowther, Mercer and Heckstall-Smith. The album was an introspective journey and contained Mayall's most competent lyrics, notably the beautifully

hymn-like 'I Know Now'. The similarly packaged *Blues From Laurel Canyon* (Mayall often produced his own artwork) was another strong album which was recorded in Los Angeles, where Mayall was domiciled. This marked the end of the Bluesbreakers name and, following the departure of Mick Taylor to the Rolling Stones, Mayall pioneered a drumless acoustic band featuring Jon Mark on acoustic guitar, Johnny Almond on tenor saxophone and flute, and Stephen Thompson on string bass. The subsequent live album, *The Turning Point*, proved to be his biggest-selling album and almost reached the UK Top 10. Notable tracks are the furious 'Room To Move', with Mayall's finest harmonica solo, and 'Thoughts About Roxanne' with some exquisite saxophone from Almond. The same line-up plus Larry Taylor produced *Empty Rooms*, which was more refined and less exciting.

The band that recorded *USA Union* consisted of Americans Harvey Mandel, 'Sugercane' Harris and Larry Taylor. It gave Mayall yet another success, although he struggled lyrically. Following the double reunion, *Back To The Roots*, Mayall's work lost its bite, and over the next few years his output was of poor quality. The halcyon days of name stars in his band had passed and Mayall had to suffer record company apathy. His last album to chart was *New Year, New Band, New Company* in 1975, featuring for the first time a female vocalist, Dee McKinnie, and future Fleetwood Mac guitarist Rick Vito. Following a run of albums which had little or no exposure, Mayall stopped recording, playing only infrequently close to his base in California. He toured Europe in 1988 to small but wildly enthusiastic audiences. That same year he signed to Island Records and released *Chicago Line*. Renewed activity and interest occurred in 1990 following the release of his finest album in many years, *A Sense Of Place*. Mayall was interviewed during a short visit to Britain and sounded positive, happy and unaffected by years in the commercial doldrums. As the sole survivor from the four 60s catalysts, Mayall is too important to be allowed to fade.

Albums: *John Mayall Plays John Mayall* (1965), *Bluesbreakers With Eric Clapton* (1966), *A Hard Road* (1967), *Crusade* (1967), *Blues Alone* (1967), *Diary Of A Band Vol.1* (1968), *Diary Of A Band Vol.2* (1968), *Bare Wires* (1968), *Blues From*

Laurel Canyon (1968), *Looking Back* (1969), *Turning Point* (1969), *World Of John Mayall* (1970), *Empty Rooms* (1970), *USA Union* (1970), *World Of John Mayall Vol.2* (1971), *Back To The Roots* (1971), *Beyond The Turning Point* (1971), *Thru The Years* (1971), *Memories* (1971), *Jazz Blues Fusion* (1972), *Moving On* (1973), *Ten Years Are Gone* (1973), *Down The Line* (1973), *The Latest Edition* (1975), *New Year, New Band, New Company* (1975), *Time Expired, Notice To Appear* (1975), *John Mayall* (1976), *A Banquet Of Blues* (1976), *Lots Of People* (1977), *A Hard Core Package* (1977), *Blues Roots* (1978), *Bottom Line* (1979), *No More Interviews* (1979), *Last Of The British Blues* (1979), *Primal Solos* (1978), *Roadshow Blues* (1982), *The John Mayall Story Vol.1* (1983), *The John Mayall Story Vol.2* (1983), *Last Edition* (1983), *Behind the Iron Curtain* (1986), *Chicago Line* (1988), *A Sense Of Place* (1990).

Mayes, Pete

b. 1938, Houston, Texas, USA. Mayes was being given his first guitar by an uncle after experimenting with string and wire. According to his own story, by the age of 14 he had already worked with Lester Williams, although he did not meet T-Bone Walker, the doyen of all Texas guitarists, until 1954. During the next 20 years, he often worked with Walker and made the acquaintance of many other bluesmen who would later come to fame, most prominently, Joe Hughes. Mayes' first recordings were made in support of Junior Parker and, in 1978, he entered a studio again while in Paris on tour with Bill Doggett. In the meantime, he had three singles issued under his own name on the Ovide label. In 1984, he appeared in the film *Battle Of The Guitars*, the soundtrack of which was issued on album. His own debut album was recorded in Houston during 1984-85 for the Dutch company, Double Trouble.
Album: *I'm Ready* (1986).

Mays, Curley

b. 26 November 1938, Maxie, Louisiana, USA. A nephew of Gatemouth Brown and a cousin of Phillip Walker, Mays was raised in Beaumont, Texas, where he taught himself to play guitar when he was in his early teens. He worked on the streets and in the clubs around Beaumont until his break came in 1959 when he began a three-year stint with the Etta James Revue. Over the years, he also worked with the Five Royales, James Brown and Tina Turner. After a period spent working in hotel bands in Las Vegas, Mays formed his own band in the mid-60s and returned to Texas, where he appeared regularly in clubs from San Antonio to Houston. Veteran Texas bluesman Zuzu Bollin remembered him as a consummate showman blessed with the ability to play the guitar with his bare feet!

Memphis Jug Band

Perhaps the most important and certainly the most popular of the jug bands, the Memphis Jug Band flourished on record, between 1927 and 1934, during which time they recorded some 80 tracks - first for Victor then later for Columbia/OKeh Records. Once they moonlighted for Champion using the name, the Picaninny Jug Band. Their repertoire covered just about any kind of music that anybody wanted to hear, and their personal appearances ran from fish-frys to bar mitzvahs. Recording for their own people, they restricted themselves to ballads, dance tunes (including waltzes), novelty numbers and blues. Normally a knockabout conglomeration, they could produce blues of feeling and beauty when required. The group had an ever-changing personnel that revolved around the nucleus of Charlie Burse and Will Shade. Other members included some of the stars of the Memphis blues scene such as Memphis Minnie, Casey Bill Weldon, Jab Jones, Milton Robey, Vol Stevens, Ben Ramey, Charlie Polk and Hattie Hart. Basically a string band augmented by such 'semi-legitimate' instruments as harmonicas, kazoos, washboards and jugs blown to supply a bass, the MJB had a constantly shifting line-up featuring violins, pianos, mandolins, banjos and guitars in different combinations. This, coupled with ever-changing vocalists, lent their music a freshness, vitality and variety that enables it to charm, entertain or move the listener as much today as it did during the great days of Beale Street. Although they ceased to record in 1934, this loose aggregation of musicians continued to work around Memphis until well into the 40s; some of its members being recorded again by researchers in the 60s.
Albums: *The Memphis Jug Band Vol 1* (1927-28),

Vol 2 (1928-29), Vol 3 (1930), Vol 5 (1932-34), The Memphis Jug Band - Alternate Takes And Associates (1991).

Memphis Minnie

b. Lizzie Douglas, 3 June 1897, Algiers, Louisiana, USA, d. 6 August 1973, Memphis, Tennessee, USA. Raised in Walls, Mississippi, Memphis Minnie learned banjo and guitar as a child, and ran away from home at the age of 13 to play music in Memphis; she worked for a time with Ringling Brothers Circus. When in Mississippi, she played guitar with Willie Brown, and in the 20s made a common-law marriage with Casey Bill Weldon. However, she was with Kansas Joe McCoy by the time of their joint recording debut in 1929. Her guitar playing had a strong rhythm, coupled with the ragtime influence common among the Memphis musicians, and her singing was tough and swaggering. 'Bumble Bee' was a hit, and Joe and Minnie recorded extensively, together and separately; their guitar duets were among the finest in blues. Apart from songs about sex and relationships, Minnie sang about her meningitis (calling it, with gallows humour, 'Memphis Minnie-jitis'), about her father's mule, 'Frankie Jean', and about the guitarist 'Mister Tango'. The McCoys moved to Chicago in the early 30s, but split up in 1935, apparently as a result of Joe's jealousy of his wife's success. By this time, Minnie's music was reflecting changing tastes, usually featuring a piano and string bass, and sometimes trumpet or clarinet and a drummer. She was a star of the Chicago club scene, as she continued to present herself on disc as the tough, independent woman she was in reality. In 1939, she began recording with her third husband, Little Son Joe (Ernest Lawlars) on second guitar. They were early users of amplification, and made swinging music, although it lacked the rich complexity of her early recordings. Her lyrics were of considerable originality, as on a graceful tribute to Ma Rainey, recorded in 1940, six months after Rainey's death. 'Me And My Chauffeur Blues', with its boogieing guitar, also became widely known. In the late 40s, Memphis Minnie ran a touring vaudeville company, and she continued to record after the war, playing tough electric guitar. Her efforts to keep up with trends were proving less successful, however, and in the

mid-50s, she and Joe retired to Memphis. Joe was already unwell, and died in 1961, while Minnie was incapacitated from the late 50s, and lived out her life in nursing homes.

Albums: *Memphis Minnie & Kansas Joe Vols. 1-4* (1991), *Memphis Minnie 1935-41 Vols. 1-5* (1992), *The Postwar Recordings Vols. 1-3* (1992).

Memphis Slim

b. Peter Chatman, 3 September 1915, Memphis, Tennessee, USA, d. 24 February 1988. One of the most popular performers of the blues idiom, Memphis Slim combined the barrelhouse/boogie-woogie piano style of the pre-war era with a sophisticated vocal intonation. A prolific songwriter, his best-known composition, 'Every Day I Have The Blues', has been the subject of numerous interpretations, and versions by Count Basie and B.B. King helped establish the song as a standard of its genre. Although Slim began his career in 1934, deputizing for pianist Roosevelt Sykes, his reputation did not prosper until moving to Chicago at the end of the decade. He supported many of the city's best-known acts, including John Lee 'Sonny Boy' Williamson, and, in 1940, became the regular accompanist to Big Bill Broonzy. The artist made his recording debut for the Bluebird label that year but remained with Broonzy until 1944,, when he formed his own group, the House Rockers. In 1949 Slim enjoyed an R&B number 1 with 'Messin' Around', the first in a series of successful singles, including 'Blue And Lonesome' (1949), 'Mother Earth' (1951) and 'The Come Back' (1953). He remained a popular attraction in Chicago throughout the ensuing decade, but following prestigious appearances at New York's Carnegie Hall and the Newport Jazz Festival, the artist moved to Paris, where he was domiciled from 1961 onwards. Slim toured and recorded extensively throughout Europe, an availability which, perversely, has irritated blues purists who view his work as overtly commercial. His later work certainly lacked the purpose of the young musician, but by the time of his death from kidney failure in 1988, Memphis Slim's role in the development of blues was assured.

Selected albums: *Memphis Slim At The Gate Of The Horn* (1959), *'Frisco Bay Blues* (1960), *Memphis Slim* (1961), *Broken Soul Blues* (1961), *Just Blues* (1961), *Tribute To Big Bill Broonzy*

Memphis Slim

(1961), *Memphis Slim USA* (1962), *No Strain* (1962), *All Kinds Of Blues* (1963), *Alone With My Friends* (1963), *Steady Rolling Blues* (1964), *Memphis Slim* (1964), *The Real Folk Blues* (1966), *Legend Of The Blues* (1967), *Mother Earth* (1969), *Messin' Around With The Blues* (1970), *Born With The Blues* (1971), *Bad Luck And Trouble* (1971), *Blue Memphis* (1971), *South Side Reunion* (1972), *Old Times New Times* (1972), *Soul Blues* (1973), *Classical American Music* (1973), *Legacy Of The Blues, Volume 7* (1973), *Memphis Slim At Lausanne* (1974), *Memphis Slim Live* (1974), *Memphis Slim* (1974), *With Matthew Murphy* (1974), *Blues Man* (1975), *Going Back To Tennessee* (1975), *Rock Me Baby* (1975), *All Them Blues* (1976), *Chicago Boogie* (1976), *Fattening Frogs For Snakes* (1976), *Boogie Woogie* (1978), *Chicago Blues* (1978), *Blues Every Which Way* (1981), *Blues And Women* (1981).

Mercy Dee

b. Mercy Dee Walton, 30 August 1915, Waco, Texas, USA, d. 2 December 1962, Murphy's, California, USA. From an early interest in the piano, stimulated by the many local players of the instrument, Mercy Dee developed an instantly recognizable blues style, with much use of trills and crashing treble chords, complemented by lyrics packed with powerful,

memorable imagery. After moving to California in his 20s, he recorded in a variety of settings between 1949 and 1955, even including rock 'n' roll and pop, but it was in slow blues, such as the much-covered 'One Room Country Shack' and humorous numbers like 'GI Fever', that he could be heard at his best. An album for Arhoolie recorded in the early 60s is particularly worthwhile, as it concentrated on those aspects of his music.
Albums: *Mercy Dee* (1961), *GI Fever* (1985), *Troublesome Mind* (1992).

Mesner Brothers

Leo and Edward Mesner formed Philo Records in 1945 at Santa Monica Boulevard, Hollywood, California, USA, changing the label name to Aladdin the following year. The company had early sales with Helen Humes, Wynonie Harris and Lester Young, but enjoyed its biggest successes after signing Texan musicians Charles Brown and Johnny Moore ('Driftin' Blues'), Amos Milburn ('Chicken Shack Boogie') and Lightnin' Hopkins in 1945 and 1946. Aladdin continued to be one of the major west coast independents throughout the 40s and early 50s with recordings by Floyd Dixon, Gatemouth Brown, Pee Wee Crayton, Lloyd Glenn and Peppermint Harris (five more Texans), Louis

Jordan, Lowell Fulson, Big Jay McNeely, Lynn Hope, and the Five Keys. These artists invariably benefitted from the instrumental and arrangemental expertise of Maxwell Davis. In the mid-50s, Aladdin's biggest sales came with the boy/girl duets of Shirley And Lee ('Let The Good Times Roll') and Gene And Eunice ('Ko Ko Mo'), but sales gradually decreased into the late 50s, despite the brief success of Thurston Harris in 1957, and the following year, the Mesners sold their label to Lew Chudd of Imperial Records.

Mighty Flea
b. Gene Conner, 28 December 1930, Birmingham, Alabama, USA. Flea's family was musical and as a youngster he learned to play trombone and subsequently worked with many jazz legends, including Bunk Johnson, Lionel Hampton, and Count Basie. He enjoyed a very long association with Johnny Otis, and even had a minor R&B hit in 1968 with 'Ode To Billie Joe' on the Eldo label. He has recorded with a long list of jazz, blues, R&B, and soul artists, and came to Europe with Otis in 1972, when he made an album for Big Bear Records which showed that he also has a light, pleasant singing voice. Since then, he has been based in Europe and has recorded and worked in a variety of musical settings; as his calling-card states, he plays 'Rhythm And Blues-Swing-Dixie'.
Albums: *Let The Good Times Roll* (1972), *Sanctified* (1981).

Miles, Lizzie
b. Elizabeth Mary Pajaud, nee Landreaux, 31 March 1895, New Orleans, Louisiana, USA, d. 17 March 1963. As a teenager, Miles sang with outstanding early jazzmen from the age of 16, including Joe 'King' Oliver, Freddie Keppard, Kid Ory and Bunk Johnson. By the early 20s, she had established a reputation in Chicago and New York and she toured Europe in the middle of the decade. The late 20s found her resident in New York, singing in clubs and recording with Oliver and Jelly Roll Morton. Illness kept her out of the business for a few years, but she returned to work in New York and Chicago in the late 30s and early 40s. Miles then abandoned her career, but she returned to nightclub work in the 50s, made records and re-established her reputation in the wake of the dixieland revival,

singing with Bob Scobey, Sharkey Bonano and George Lewis. She retired in 1959, turning her back on music to embrace religion. Often singing in Louisiana Creole patois, Miles had a robust and earthy style which made her a distinctive performer, despite a rather narrow vocal range. Miles was an all-round entertainer, applying her powerful delivery impartially to blues, pop songs, ballads, Creole songs, and improbable Creolized (French language) versions of 'Bill Bailey' and 'A Good Man Is Hard To Find'. She died in March 1963.
Albums: *George Lewis Live At The Hangover Club* (1953-54), *Moans And Blues* (1954), with Red Camp *Torch Lullabies My Mother Sang Me* (1955).

Miller, Clarence 'Big'
b. 18 December 1922, Sioux City, Iowa, USA. Miller moved to Kansas City as a child and his style is in that city's tradition of big-voiced, sophisticated blues singing. In the late 40s and early 50s, he worked with the big bands of Jay Mcshann, Lionel Hampton, Duke Ellington and others. Miller began recording in 1957 for the Savoy label, and continues to record and tour internationally, primarily in a jazz context, up to the present day.

Miller, J.D. 'Jay'
b. c.1922, El Campo, Texas, USA. One of the best-known and most successful record producers from Louisiana, Miller started out as a musician, playing with country and Cajun bands around Lake Charles from the late 30s. After a spell in the services, he started to make records, aimed at a small localised market for Cajun music in southwest Louisiana; these, by obscure artists such as Lee Sonnier and Amidie Breaux, were among the first records in the idiom to appear after the war, and established his position as a pioneer in the field. He continued to record Cajun music and C&W on his Feature and Fais Do-Do labels, including the earliest records by Jimmie C. Newman and Doug Kershaw, and later on Kajun and Cajun Classics, which featured important figures such as Nathan Abshire and Aldus Roger. However, it was when he turned his attention in the mid-50s to black music that Miller began to develop his best-known and most enduring legacy. Between 1954, when he first recorded Lightnin' Slim and the early 60s, he established an extraordinary list

of artists, including Slim, Lonesome Sundown, Slim Harpo, Lazy Lester, Silas Hogan and many others, whose work he leased to the Nashville label, Excello. He also continued to release records on labels of his own, Zynn and Rocko, including rockabilly and local pop by artists such as Johnny Jano and Warren Storm, and in the 70s, on Blues Unlimited. His list of artists is enormous, but just as important was the characteristic sound he achieved in his studio in Crowley, which has become inextricably linked with the indigenous sounds of Louisiana.

Minter, Iverson (Louisiana Red)

b. 23 March 1936, Vicksburg, Mississippi, USA. Although beginning as a sincere imitator of his various heroes, including Muddy Waters, Lightnin' Hopkins and John Lee Hooker, Louisiana Red has gained stature of his own as an instinctual and creative blues singer and guitarist. Red spent his earliest years in a variety of orphanages, his mother having died a week after his birth, his estranged father a victim of Ku Klux Klan violence. Raised in Pittsburg by an aunt, Corrine Driver, he got his first guitar at the age of 11 and instruction from the veteran Crit Walters. At 16, he joined the army and served in Korea. On his return, though claiming to have recorded with Waters and Little Walter, his first known record, 'Gonna Play My Guitar', was released as by Playboy Fuller on his own Fuller label. Another session for Checker as Rocky Fuller yielded a single, 'Soon One Morning'; further titles were reissued during the 80s. Working alongside Hooker and Eddie Kirkland, he gained a reputation as 'a guitar fiend'. Much of the 50s were spent travelling throughout the south. In 1960 he moved to New Jersey and made his first record as Louisiana Red for Atlas; 'I Done Woke Up' was backed by James Wayne & The Nighthawks. After recording an unissued session for Bobby Robinson's Fury label, Red was signed to Roulette in 1962 by veteran producer Henry Glover. His album, The Lowdown Backporch Blues brought him much critical praise. During 1965 he was comprehensively recorded for Festival Records by Herb Abramson, from which the Atco album, Louisiana Red Sings The Blues, was assembled. Further titles appeared on the Red Lightnin' Hot Sauce album. Other sessions took place in 1967, 1971 and 1973. He recorded a

number of sessions in 1975 for Blue Labor, from which two volumes of The Blues Purity Of Louisiana Red were issued; he also participated on albums by Peg Leg Sam, Johnny Shines, Roosevelt Sykes and Brownie McGhee. In 1976 he moved to Germany, where he has remained, touring Europe extensively and recording for several labels, including Black Panther, JSP, L+R, Orchid, MMG and Blues Beacon. He is a dependable if mercurial performer, his spontaneity sometimes a brick wall but often a springboard.
Selected albums: Midnight Rambler (1989), Live At 55 (1991), The Lowdown Backporch Blues (1992).

Mississippi Sheiks

This musical combination flourished between 1930 and 1935, during which time they recorded more than 80 tracks for various 'race' labels. The Sheiks was a string band made up of members and friends of the Chatman family, and included Lonnie Chatman (guitar/violin), Sam Chatman (guitar), Walter Vincson (guitar violin), Bo (Carter) Chatman, (guitar) and Charlie McCoy (banjo/mandolin). Vocal chores were handled by everybody. Most of these individuals pursued independent musical careers either at this time or later. The instrumental abilities of all members were extremely high and their repertoire covered all ground between popular waltzes to salacious party songs, with a fair quantity of high-quality blues thrown in. Their work also appeared under the names the Mississippi Mud Steppers, the Down South Boys and the Carter Brothers.
Albums: Sitting On Top Of The World (1972), Stop And Listen Blues (1973), The Mississippi Sheiks (1984).

Mitchell, Bobby

b. 16 August 1935, Algiers, Louisiana, USA, d. 17 March 1989, New Orleans, Louisiana, USA. After studying music in high school, Mitchell formed a vocal group, the Toppers, in June 1950. The group comprised various high school friends and they entered local talent shows. After being discovered by Dave Bartholomew in 1952, the group began recording for Imperial until they split up in 1955 upon graduation, leading Mitchell to a solo career and his biggest hit the following year, 'Try Rock And Roll'.

This reached number 14 on *Billboard*'s R&B chart - although he is probably better known as the originator of 'I'm Gonna Be A Wheel Someday' which was later covered by Fats Domino. Leaving Imperial in 1958, he recorded infrequently for small local labels like Ronn, Sho-Biz and Rip, and by the late 60s, he was working outside the music business.
Album: *I'm Gonna Be A Wheel Someday* (1979).

Molton, Flora

b. 1908, Virginia, USA, d. 31 May 1990, Washington, DC, USA. Molton began preaching at the age of 17, not taking up guitar until 1943, when she moved to Washington, DC. Virtually blind, she supported herself by playing in the streets. From 1963, she made appearances on the folk circuit, and later signed-up by a European record company, when she visited Europe in 1987. Her slide guitar playing, in 'Vastopol' (open D) was basic, but intense, owing much to the blues whose verbal content she fiercely rejected. Her delivery, mainly, was reminiscent of an unsophisticated Sister Rosetta Tharpe, particularly when Molton was assisted by more skilful musicians.
Albums: *Flora Molton And The Truth Band* (1982), *Gospel Songs* (1988).

Montrell, Roy

b. 27 February 1928, New Orleans, Louisiana, USA. Guitarist Montrell joined Roy Milton's Solid Senders upon his discharge from the US Army in 1951, but soon returned to New Orleans where he formed a trio called the Little Hawkettes, which worked various clubs along Bourbon Street. After touring with Lloyd Price, he began to do session work in New Orleans for Ace and Specialty, recording with artist including Edgar Blanchard and Little Richard. He only had two releases under his own name: one on Specialty in 1956 - the black rock 'n' roll classic 'Ooh Wow That Mellow Saxophone' - and another on Minit in 1960. Virtually the New Orleans session guitarist by 1960, Montrell played with both Allen Toussaint's band and Harold Battiste's AFO combo, and in 1962 he took over from Walter Nelson as Fats Domino's guitarist, becoming Domino's bandleader in the late 60s.

Moore, Alexander (Whistling Alex)

b. 11 November 1899, Dallas, Texas, USA, d. 20 January 1989, Dallas, Texas, USA. A lifelong individualist and eccentric, Moore came in later life to be regarded as a patriarch of Texas piano blues, although his inspirational technique wilfully avoided categorisation. He grew up in Freedman's Town, a section of Dallas where the children of slaves congregated. He became interested in piano while working as a delivery boy for a grocery store, and developed his style in the dives and whorehouses of North Dallas. He recorded six titles for Columbia in December 1929, including the first version of 'Blue Bloomer Blues', and recorded this blues again for Decca in February 1937. With typical initiative, he financed his own session, recording eight titles, of which only two were later issued on album. A session for RPM in 1951 yielded five titles, two issued on a single, a third on album. In July 1960, Chris Strachwitz and Paul Oliver recorded him extensively for Arhoolie and Oliver's 'Conversations With The Blues' project. He was a member of the 1969 American Folk Blues Festival tour of Europe and recorded another album in Stuttgart, Germany. Throughout the 70s he was a feature of the festival circuit. In 1987 he received a Lifetime Achievement Award from the National Endowment for the Arts. Two years later, he recorded his last album for Rounder. Idiosyncratic to the end, he was returning home from a domino game at the Martin Luther King Centre in South Dallas and died on the bus, riding at the front, no doubt.
Selected albums: *Alex Moore* (1960), *Wiggle Tail* (1989).

Moore, Arnold Dwight 'Gatemouth'

b. 8 November 1913, Topeka, Kansas, USA. At the age of 16, Moore went to Kansas City, where he sang with the bands of Bennie Moten, Tommy Douglas and Walter Barnes. Moore was one of the few survivors of the infamous 'Natchez Rhythm Club Fire' tragedy that wiped out most of Barnes' orchestra. His first recordings were made for the small K.C. labels, Chez Paree and Damon, and they caused enough of a stir to interest National Records. They brought Moore to Chicago and New York for four sessions in 1945-46 and were successful with Moore's 'I Ain't Mad At You,

Pretty Baby', 'Did You Ever Love A Woman?' and 'Christmas Blues'. In 1947, Moore joined King Records and re-recorded his national hits along with a lot of new material. By the end of that year he had introduced Wynonie Harris to King and had discarded blues for a new career as the Reverend Moore. He became a gospel disc jockey and recorded gospel music in the early 50s for Chess/Aristocrat, Artists and Coral and recorded gospel albums for Audio Fidelity (1960) and Bluesway (1973). However, Johnny Otis did manage to persuade Moore to recreate some of his blues for a Blues Spectrum album in 1977.

Selected albums: *Gatemouth Moore* (c.50s), *Rev. Dwight 'Gatemouth' Moore & his Gospel Singers* (1960), *After Twenty-One Years* (1973), *Great R&B Oldies* (1977).

Moore, Gary

b. 4 April 1952, Belfast, Northern Ireland. This talented, blues-influenced singer and guitarist formed his first major band, Skid Row, when he was 16 years old - initially with Phil Lynott, who left after a few months for form Thin Lizzy. Skid Row continued as a three-piece, with Brendan Shields (bass) and Noel Bridgeman (drums). They relocated from Belfast to London in 1970 and signed a deal with CBS. After just two albums, they disbanded, leaving Moore to form the Gary Moore Band. Their debut, *Grinding Stone*, appeared in 1973, but their progress was halted the following year while Moore assisted Thin Lizzy after guitarist Eric Bell had left the band. This liaison lasted just four months before Moore was replaced by Scott Gorham and Brian Robertson.

Moore subsequently moved into session work before joining Colosseum II in 1976. He made three albums with them, and also rejoined Thin Lizzy for a 10-week American tour in 1977 after guitarist Brian Robertson suffered a severed artery in his hand. Moore finally became a full-time member of Thin Lizzy, but he subsequently left midway through a US tour and formed a new band called G-Force, though this outfit soon foundered. Moore then resumed his solo career, cutting a series of commercially ignored albums until he scored hit singles in 1985 with 'Empty Rooms' and another collaboration with Phil Lynott, 'Out In The Fields'. Moore's 1989 album *After The War* had

a strong celtic influence, and also featured guest artists such as Ozzy Osbourne and Andrew Eldritch (Sisters Of Mercy). But his breakthrough to mainstream commercial acceptance came in 1990 with the superb, confident guitarwork and vocals of *Still Got The Blues*. Mixing blues standards and originals, Moore was acclaimed as the UK's foremost blues artist, a stature which the subsequent release of *After Hours* - featuring cameo appearances from B.B. King and Albert Collins - has confirmed.

Albums: *Back On The Streets* (1979), *Corridors Of Power* (1982), *Live At The Marquee* (1983), *Rockin' Every Night - Live In Japan* (1983), *Life* (1984, live), *Run For Cover* (1985), *Wild Frontier* (1988), *After The War* (1989), *Still Got The Blues* (1990), *After Hours* (1992). With Skid Row *Skid Row* (1970), *Thirty Four Hours* (1971). With Gary Moore Band *Grinding Stone* (1973). With Colosseum II *Strange New Flesh Bronze* (1976), *Electric Savage* (1977), *War Dance* (1977). With Thin Lizzy *Black Rose* (1979). With G-Force *G-Force* (1979). With Greg Lake Band *Greg Lake* (1981), *Manoeuvers* (1983).

Moore, John Dudley 'Johnny'

b. 20 October 1906, Austin, Texas, USA, d. 6 January 1969, Los Angeles, California, USA. The elder brother of guitarist Oscar Moore, Johnny began playing guitar with his violinist father's string band in 1934 and moved to the west coast, where Oscar joined Nat 'King' Cole's Trio and Moore joined a group called the Blazes. Fired by that group in 1942, Moore decided to form his own group which he christened the Three Blazers. This featured Eddie Williams on bass and, briefly, pianist Garland Finney. When Finney left the trio the following year, Moore hired Charles Brown, a singer and pianist he had seen at an amateur talent show, and the Blazers began recording in 1944 for the small Atlas label. This was followed in 1945-48 by extensive recording for Exclusive, Philo/Aladdin and Modern. During this period the Blazers became a household name with huge hits like 'Driftin' Blues', 'Merry Christmas Baby', 'Sunny Road' and 'More Than You Know'. When Oscar Moore joined the group in 1947, it was the start of several major problems which resulted in a split, and Moore tried to replace Charles Brown with a succession of

soundalikes. The most successful of these was Billy Valentine, who took the Blazers back to the R&B charts with RCA-Victor's 'Walkin' Blues' in 1949. After his 1949-50 association with Victor, Johnny Moore's Blazers recorded for the gamut of Los Angeles labels, but was successful only with 1953's novelty 'Dragnet Blues' on Modern and 1955's morbid 'Johnny Ace's Last Letter' on Hollywood. Johnny Moore and Charles Brown were reconciled in the mid-50s and the real Three Blazers reunited for records on Aladdin, Hollywood and Cenco, however, by that time Moore's cool, sophisticated, melodic blues guitar was out of favour with R&B fans. He was an inspiration to most of the electric blues guitarists of the late 40s and early 50s (he is numbered among B.B. King's Top 10 guitarists of all time), and his solos on recordings by Ivory Joe Hunter, Floyd Dixon and Charles Brown, as well as tracks under his own group, bear witness that he was one of the unsung greats of his instrument.
Albums: with Charles Brown *Sunny Road* (1978), with Brown *Race Track Blues* (1981), with Brown *Sail On Blues* (1989), *This Is One Time, Baby* (1989), *Why Johnny Why?* (1989).

Moore, Johnny B.

b. 24 January 1950, Clarksdale, Mississippi, USA. Moore began playing guitar as a youngster influenced by local musicians. He began playing blues, but later worked with gospel groups as a singer and guitarist, continuing in this direction after he moved to Chicago in 1964. However, he also began working in the clubs as a bluesman and, in 1975, joined the band of Koko Taylor. He stayed with Taylor for five years, recording with her in 1978. He now leads his own group in Chicago and has recorded in his own right for the Wolf and Blues R&B labels. Although Moore is a versatile singer and guitarist, he remains true to the west-side Chicago style of Magic Sam and Otis Rush.
Albums: *Hard Times* (1987), *Chicago Blues Session Volume Five* (1987).

Moore, Monette

b. 19 May 1902, Gainesville, Texas, USA, d. 21 October 1962, Garden Grove, California, USA. Moore was also known as Ethel Mayes, Nettie Potter, Susie Smith and Grace White. Interested in music from an early age, Moore taught herself piano in her early teens and became a fan of Mamie Smith. Among the first wave of classic blues singers, from 1923 onwards she was recording in New York City for Paramount, Vocalion, Columbia and RCA Victor. She also worked with the orchestras of Charlie Johnson, Walter Page and Lucky Millinder in myriad shows and revues. She was briefly married to singer/pianist/songwriter John Erby in the late 20s and in 1933 she opened her own nightclub, Monette's Place, but continued performing and recording. In the early 40s, she moved out to the west coast to record for various specialist labels with Teddy Bunn, Hilton 'Nappy' Lamare and George Lewis, then started a new career in television and films. In 1960 she secured a singing job on the Mark Twain Riverboat at Disneyland theme park in Anaheim, California, where she suffered a critical emphysema attack and died before reaching hospital. Although she did not enjoy an extensive recording career, Moore was a very effective jazz and blues stylist who easily coped with the various styles she encountered during her 40 year career.

Moore, Willie C.

b. 22 April 1913, Kinston, North Carolina, USA, d. 2 May 1971, Albany, New York, USA. Moore began playing guitar about 1930, and in 1934 won a talent contest organised by J.B. Long. It has been speculated that Moore recorded as Boll Weenie Bill for ARC, but this now seems unlikely. When located in 1970, he still possessed a wide repertoire, but died after preliminary recordings had been made.
Album: *Another Man Done Gone* (1978).

Morris, Joseph 'Joe'

b. 1922, Montgomery, Alabama, USA, d. November 1958, Phoenix, Arizona, USA. Morris studied music at Alabama State Teachers' College, and toured with the college band led by the Trenier Twins. Heard by Lionel Hampton in Florida in 1942, Morris joined Hampton's Orchestra, where he became a valued writer/arranger as well as a trumpeter. He remained with Hampton until 1946, when he briefly joined Buddy Rich's band. After forming his own band towards the end of 1946, Morris went on to record for Manor, Atlantic, Decca and Herald, introducing new jazz and R&B stars such as Johnny Griffin, Elmo Hope,

Matthew Gee, Percy Heath, Philly Joe Jones, Laurie Tate and Faye Adams. On the strength of his 'Blues Cavalcade' one of the first self-contained, touring R&B package shows, Morris had several hits including 'Any Time, Any Place, Anywhere' and 'Don't Take Your Love From Me' on Atlantic and, most notably, 'Shake A Hand' and 'I'll Be True' on Herald.

Albums: *Lowdown Baby* (1985), with Johnny Griffin *Fly Mister Fly* (1985).

Moss, Eugene 'Buddy'

b. 26 January 1914, Hancock County, Georgia, USA, d. October 1984, Atlanta, Georgia, USA. It was as a harmonica player that Moss first appeared on record, in 1930, as one of the Georgia Cotton Pickers, with Barbecue Bob and Curley Weaver. Although he apparently learnt guitar from Bob, his playing was distinctly in the ragtime-inflected Eastern blues tradition of artists such as Blind Blake. Moss had his own style, however, a carefully crafted blues sound that was to make his name as one of the most popular Atlanta-based singers of the 30s. He recorded prolifically between 1933 and 1935, sometimes backed by Weaver and occasionally Blind Willie McTell. On later dates he teamed up with Josh White and the two musicians accompanied each other on their respective recordings. Altogether, Moss made over 60 tracks in these three years, but there followed a long hiatus when he was sentenced to a prison term soon after the 1935 session. He was released in 1941 and recorded again, this time with Sonny Terry and Brownie McGhee. The outbreak of war cut short his prospects and he earned his living working outside music until he was rediscovered in the 60s, although this led to only a few new recordings and live appearances.

Selected Albums: *Georgia Blues* (1983), *Red River Blues* (1984).

Motley, Frank

b. 30 December 1923, Cheraw, South Carolina, USA. Motley learned the rudiments of trumpet playing from Dizzy Gillespie and soon developed a novelty technique of playing two trumpets simultaneously, thereafter being known by the nicknames of 'Dual Trumpet' and 'Two Horn' Motley. After navy service, Frank studied music at Chicago and Washington D.C. and formed his own band in 1949. The Motley

Crewe, included drummer T.N.T. Tribble and recorded for Lilian Claiborne who placed masters with Gotham, RCA Victor, Specialty, Gem, DC, Big Town, Hollywood and many other small labels. In the mid-50s, with the advent of rock 'n' roll, Motley married and moved north to Toronto, Canada, where he continued to play and perform until 1984 when he retired to Durham, North Carolina.

Albums: *Frank Motley* (1986), with T.N.T. Tribble *The Best Of Washington D.C. R&B* (1991).

Muldaur, Geoff

b. c.1940, Pelham, New York, USA. Muldaur began performing at the folk haunts of Cambridge, Massachusetts while a student at Boston University. He worked as a soloist at the *Club 47*, as well as becoming a featured member of the Jim Kweskin Jug Band. Muldaur's debut, *Sleepy Man Blues*, boasted support from Dave Van Ronk and Eric Von Schmidt, and offered sterling interpretations of material drawn from country-blues singers Bukka White, Sleepy John Estes and Blind Willie Johnson. Despite this recording, the artist remained with Kweskin until the Jug Band splintered at the end of the 60s. He then completed two albums, *Pottery Pie* (1970) and *Sweet Potatoes* (1972) with his wife, Maria Muldaur, before joining Paul Butterfield's 70s venture, Better Days. The singer resumed his solo career upon the break-up of both the band and his marriage. The Joe Boyd-produced *Geoff Muldaur Is Having A Wonderful Time* showed the artist's unflinching eclecticism, a facet prevailing on all his releases. A longstanding professional relationship with guitarist and fellow Woodstock resident Amos Garrett resulted in *Geoff Muldaur And Amos Garrett*, on which the former's penchant for self-indulgence was pared to a minimum. Despite this trait, Muldaur's entire catalogue is worthy of investigation and deserves respect for its attention to music's ephemera.

Albums: *Sleepy Man Blues* (1963), *Geoff Muldaur Is Having A Wonderful Time* (1975), *Motion* (1976), *Geoff Muldaur And Amos Garrett* (1978), *Blues Boy* (1979).

Murphy, Matt

b. 27 December 1929, Sunflower, Mississippi, USA. He moved to Memphis as a child and learned guitar in the 40s. He joined Tuff Green's band before becoming lead guitarist with Junior Parker's Blue Flames, playing on recording sessions with Parker and Bobby 'Blue' Bland. Murphy's brother Floyd replaced him with Parker when Matt moved to Chicago in 1952. There he spent seven years in Memphis Slim's band, also recording as the Sparks with Sam Chatman (bass/vocals) and John Calvin (saxophone). He toured Europe in 1963 with the Folk Blues package, recording with Sonny Boy 'Rice Miller' Williamson in Denmark. Murphy found a wider audience through his role in the film *The Blues Brothers* as Aretha Franklin's husband and his subsequent tours with the Blues Brothers package. Floyd Murphy joined him for his first solo album, recorded for Antone's in 1990.

Album: *Way Down South* (1990).

Musselwhite, Charlie

b. 31 January 1944, Mississippi, USA. Musselwhite grew up in Memphis where he was inspired to learn harmonica by hearing Sonny Terry on the radio. In 1962, Musselwhite moved to Chicago, performing with Johnny Young, Big Joe Williams and J.B. Hutto. He also linked up with another white blues musician, Mike Bloomfield before the latter went on to join Paul Butterfield's group, Musselwhite emigrated to California, making his first solo recordings for Vanguard. From 1974-75 he made two albums for Chris Strachwitz's Arhoolie label and later cut an instructional record for Stefan Grossman's Kickin' Mule. A growing reputation made Musselwhite a favourite on the festival circuits in the USA and Europe. *Mellow Dee* was recorded during a German tour while *Cambridge Blues* was recorded live at Britain's leading folk festival for Mike Vernon's Blue Horizon label. In 1990, Musselwhite joined Alligator, where John Lee Hooker guested on his 1991 album. Although heavily influenced by Little Walter, Louis Myers and Junior Wells Musslewhite has made his own niche with only the late Paul Butterfield to challenge him as the greatest white blues harmonica player.

Albums: *Stand Back, Here Comes Charlie Musselwhite* (1967), *Charlie Musselwhite* (1968), *Stone Blues* (1968), *Tennessee Woman* (1969), *Memphis, Tennessee* (1969), *Taking My Time* (1974), *Going Back Down South* (1975), *The Harmonica According To Charlie Musselwhite* (1979), *Curtain Call* (1982), *Memphis, Tennessee* (1984), *Mellow Dee* (1986), *Cambridge Blues* (1988), *Tell Me Where Have All The Good Times Gone* (1988), *Ace Of Harps* (1990), *Signature* (1991).

Myers, Dave

b. 30 October 1926, Byhalia, Mississippi, USA. The older brother of Louis Myers, Dave bought a guitar after the family moved to Chicago in 1941. During 1951 he became a member of the Aces, leaving in 1955, a year after Louis. In the late 50s and early 60s he was part of a rock 'n' roll band with Louis, and when the Aces reformed at the end of the 60s, he had the opportunity to record with them and as accompanist to artists, including Carey Bell, Howlin' Wolf, Robert Junior Lockwood, Jimmy Rogers, Homesick, James Williamson and Hubert Sumlin.

Myers, Louis

b. 18 September 1929, Byhalis, Mississippi, USA. Growing up in a musical family, Myers began playing harmonica at the age of eight, and guitar about two years later. He moved to Chicago in 1941 and played with Big Boy Spires for three years. With his brother Dave Myers, Junior Wells and later, drummer Fred Below, he formed the Aces and in the 50s became known for his light, jazzy and swinging guitar blues artists (including some years with the re-formed Aces) and his own material has appeared on the Abco, Advent, and JSP labels. Although he is primarily known for his fluent guitar work, he can also be an impressive harmonica player in the modern amplified style.

Albums: *I'm A Southern Man* (1978), *Wailin' The Blues* (1983).

Myers, Sammy

b. 19 February 1936, Laurel, Mississippi, USA. Originally one of Elmore James' Broomdusters working the Chicago circuit, Sammy Myers' early fame rests on a song he recorded for Johnny Vincent's Jackson, Mississippi based Ace label. 'Sleeping In The Ground', with its Jimmy Reed-like lope supplied by The King Mose Royal Rockers, is one of the classic post-war harmonica blues. It was recorded in Jackson in

Charlie Musselwhite

1957 and the partially blind singer/harmonica player, who also plays drums, went on to produce further singles for the Fury and Soft labels (the latter credited to Little John Myers) before moving back to seek his livelihood in the clubs. He recorded for Vincent again, seeing the results issued as part of an album in 1981. Later he formed an unlikely partnership with the much younger, Texan guitarist Anson Funderburgh performing, with much success, as featured artist with Funderburgh's group the Rockets.

Albums: *Kings Of The Blues, Vol. 2* (anthology) (1979), *Genuine Mississippi Blues* (1981), *My Love Is Here To Stay* (1986), *Sins* (1988), *Talk To You By Hand* (1991).

N

Nathan, Sydney

b. 1904, Cincinnati, Ohio, USA, d. 1968. Nathan learned to play drums and piano in his childhood with the help of local black musicians, but entered the record-selling business in the 30s, although he became a successful songwriter under the pseudonym of 'Lois Mann'. In November 1943 his King Records was launched with releases by local hillbilly acts. These initial releases failed to sell due to the poor pressings; Nathan then decided to learn how to press his own records. In August 1943 King Records was incorporated as an outlet for hillbilly music, and scored early on with hits by the Delmore Brothers and Cowboy Copas. One year later, Syd started his Queen Records subsidiary as a showcase for jazz and R&B acts, making particular use of his friend, Lucky Millinder's Orchestra, with releases by Bullmoose Jackson, Annisteen Allen, David 'Panama' Francis and Sam Taylor - all Millinder alumni. In 1946 Queen Records began recording, issuing some of the finest gospel music by such artists as Swan's Silvertone Singers

and Wings Over Jordan Choir. Nathan's name became synonymous with peerless gospel and exciting R&B thereafter. By August 1947 the Queen label was discontinued and all output - new and old - was issued or reissued on King Records. This switch brought about a change of luck for Nathan; he scored almost immediately with three big hits in Bullmoose Jackson's 'I Love You, Yes I Do', Lonnie Johnson's 'Tomorrow Night' and Wynonie Harris' version of 'Good Rockin' Tonight' and about the same time, Nathan began leasing or acquiring masters from smaller independents like DeLuxe, Miracle and Gotham.

During the 50s and early 60s, King Records went from strength to strength with top-selling R&B artists like Tiny Bradshaw, Earl Bostic, Bill Doggett, Sonny Thompson, Little Willie John and James Brown, and on the new subsidiary label Federal with the Dominoes, Freddie King and others, but by 1964 Nathan's search for innovative recording talent was virtually at an end. King settled down to focus on James Brown's career and to repackage much of its back-catalogue on album. In 1968 Nathan merged with Don Pierce's Starday record company. After Nathan's death, Starday/King and all its off-shoots was sold to Gusto Records of Nashville, Tennessee.

Neal, Raful

b. 6 June 1936, Baton Rouge, Louisiana, USA. That rare thing in the blues, a late developer, Neal wasn't interested in music until seeing Little Walter play at the Temple Room in Baton Rouge in 1958. Buying a harmonica the next day, he was helped by a friend, Ike Brown, to learn its rudiments. Sometime later, he was engaged to join the road band of guitarist Little Eddie Lang. His own first group was called The Clouds, and featured Buddy Guy and drummer Murdock Stillwood. When Guy left, Lazy Lester was one of his replacements. The band toured Louisiana and East Texas, its first residency, the Streamline Club in Port Allen, where Neal took up residence. He recorded 'Sunny Side Of Love' for Peacock in 1968 with little success, and was then refused by Crowley producer, Jay Miller. 'Change My Way Of Living', recorded for La Louisianna in 1969, fared better, and was followed by two records on Whit. During the 70s, he brought his teenage son, Kenny Neal,

into his band and, as time went by, other sons, Noel, Raful Jr., Larry and Darnell, were also recruited. With Kenny now a star in his own right, Raful continues to play in the Baton Rouge area, with forays further afield to play festivals, and record.
Album: *I Been Mistreated* (1991).

Nelson, Jimmy 'T-99'

b. 7 April 1928, Philadelphia, Pennsylvania, USA. Nelson joined his brother (who later became famous as a singer with the Johnny Otis Orchestra under the stage name Redd Lyte) on the west coast in the mid-40s, and began shouting the blues after seeing Big Joe Turner. While singing with the Peter Rabbit Trio in 1951, Jimmy was signed to Modern's RPM subsidiary, with whom he had big R&B hits with his 'T-99 Blues' and 'Meet Me With Your Black Dress On'. In 1955 Nelson moved to Houston, Texas, where he recorded records for Chess and a host of small Texas and California independent labels. From the mid-60s worked outside the music business until he was recorded by Roy Ames in 1971 for Home Cooking Records with Arnett Cobb's band. In recent years he has begun performing again and has toured Europe.
Albums: *Jimmy 'Mr T-99' Nelson* (1981), *Watch That Action!* (1987), with Arnett Cobb And His Mobb *Sweet Sugar Daddy* (1990).

Nelson, Romeo

b. Iromeio Nelson, 12 March 1902, Springfield, Tennessee, USA, d. 17 May 1974, Chicago, Illinois, USA. A Chicago resident from the age of six (apart from a 1915-19 interlude in East St. Louis, where he learned piano) Nelson played rent parties and clubs until the early 40s, otherwise supporting himself by gambling. In 1929 he recorded four titles for Vocalion, among them 'Head Rag Hop' and 'Gettin' Dirty Just Shakin' That Thing', which are two of the finest rent party showpieces on record. Both are complex, endlessly inventive and full of puckish humour, the former track (based on Clarence 'Pine Top' Smiths' 'Pine Top's Boogie Woogie') being taken at breakneck speed. When interviewed in the 60s, Nelson had retired from music altogether.
Compilation: *The Piano Blues Vol. 3 Vocalion* (1977).

Newbern, 'Hambone' Willie

b. c.1899, USA, d. c.1947, USA. Sleepy John Estes, who was taught guitar by Newbern, met him while working on medicine shows in Mississippi. Songs like 'She Could Toodle-Oo' and 'Way Down In Arkansas', made at his sole recording session in 1929, come from his medicine-show repertoire, but Newbern was also a master of the personal blues, composing a remarkable account of his arrest at Marked Tree, Arkansas. His surest claim to fame, however, rests in being the first to record 'Roll And Tumble Blues'. Estes later reported the rumour that Newbern's death was the result of an assault in prison.
Compilation: *The Greatest Songsters* (1990).

Nicholson, J.D.

b. James David Nicholson, 12 April 1917, Monroe, Louisiana, USA, d. 27 July 1991, Los Angeles, California, USA. Nicholson learnt to play the piano from the age of five in church. He later emigrated to the west coast where, influenced by the popular black recording artists of the day, he built up a solo act and travelled and performed all over California. In the mid-40s he teamed up with Jimmy McCracklin and they made their first recordings together; Nicholson played, McCracklin sang and both their styles were very much in the mould of Walter Davis. Over the next decade, Nicholson accompanied a number of well-known artists, such as Lowell Fulson and Ray Agee, and also made some records under his own name. Later in the 50s, he joined Jimmy Reed's band, and also played with Little Walter. He made a few more records in the 60s.
Compilation: *Mr. Fullbright's Blues Vol. 2* (1990).

Nighthawk, Robert

b. Robert McCollum, 30 November 1909, Helena, Arkansas, USA, d. 5 November 1967. Having left home in his early teens, McCollum initially supported himself financially by playing harmonica, but by the 30s had switched to guitar under the tutelage of Houston Stackhouse. The two musicians, together with Robert's brother Percy, formed a string band which was a popular attraction at local parties and gatherings. Robert left the South during the middle of the decade, allegedly after a shooting incident, and settled in St. Louis. He took the name Robert McCoy, after his mother's maiden name, and made contact with several Mississippi-born bluesmen, including Big Joe Williams and John Lee 'Sonny Boy' Williamson. McCoy accompanied both on sessions for the Bluebird label, who then recorded the skilled guitarist in his own right. His releases included 'Tough Luck' and the evocative 'Prowlin' Nighthawk', which in turn engendered the artist's best-known professional surname. Nighthawk then discovered the electric guitar which, when combined with his already dexterous slide technique, created a sound that allegedly influenced Earl Hooker, Elmore James and Muddy Waters. The last musician was instrumental in introducing Nighthawk to the Aristocrat (later Chess) label. It was here the artist completed his most accomplished work, in particular two 1949 masters, 'Sweet Black Angel' and 'Anna Lee Blues'. Both songs were procured from Tampa Red, whose dazzling, clear tone bore an affinity to jazz and was an inspiration on Nighthawk's approach. However, his disciple was unable or unwilling to consolidate the success these recordings secured, and although he continued to record in Chicago, Robert often returned to Helena where he performed with his son, Sam Carr. The guitarist's last substantial session was in 1964 when he completed two tracks, 'Sorry My Angel' and 'Someday', with a backing band that included Buddy Guy and Walter 'Shakey' Horton. Robert Nighthawk died in his hometown on 5 November 1967, leaving behind a small but pivotal body of work.

Albums: *Bricks In My Pillow* (1977), with Elmore James *Blues In D Natural* (1979), *Complete Recordings, Vol. 1 1937* (1985), *Complete Recordings, Vol. 2 1938-40* (1985), *Live On Maxwell Street* (1988), *Black Angel Blues* (1988).

Nix, Willie

b. 6 August 1922, Memphis, Tennessee, USA, d. 8 July 1991, Leland, Mississippi, USA. Starting as a dancer and comedian, Nix switched to drums, and worked in Mississippi, Arkansas and Tennessee from his Memphis base in the 40s and 50s. Recorded in 1951 by Sam Phillips as a blues singing drummer, Nix appeared on albums for Sun, RPM and Checker. Nix moved to Chicago in 1953 where he played the clubs, and recorded four tracks for Chance/Sabre. His

recordings were intense and exuberant, always powered by his propulsive, swinging drumming. Returning to Memphis he supported himself by migrant labour and a little guitar playing. He was largely retired by the end of the 60s, and spent the rest of his life notoriously telling tall tales and behaving eccentrically.

Albums: *Chicago Slickers Vol. 2* (1981), *Sun Records The Blues Years* (1985).

Nixon, Elmore

b. 17 November 1933, Crowley, Louisiana, USA, d. June 1975, Houston, Texas, USA. Little is known of Nixon, although his piano is to be heard on many more records than he made under his own name. His family moved to Houston in 1939, where he would remain until his death. At some stage he trained to join the church, which is presumed to be where he learned to play piano. By his early teens, he was already backing Peppermint Harris on his Gold Star debut. Thereafter he recorded with many Texas artists as a member of alto saxophonist Henry Hayes' Four Kings, including Carl Campbell, Milton Willis, L.C. Williams, Hubert Robinson, Ivory Lee and Hop Wilson. His debut record, 'Foolish Love', was made in 1949 for Sittin In With with the Hayes band. His own music reflected the jump music of the time, having affinities with Little Willie Littlefield. Other sessions followed for Peacock, Mercury, Savoy and Imperial, the latter in 1955. During the mid-60s, he worked with Clifton Chenier, recording on Chenier's sessions for Arhoolie and with Lightnin' Hopkins for Jewel. At other times he led his own band, working around Texas and Louisiana. He underwent serious surgery in 1970 and was largely inactive until his death.

Selected album: *Shout And Rock* (1986).

Nixon, Hammie

b. 22 January 1908, Brownsville, Tennessee, USA, d. 17 August 1984, Brownsville, Tennessee, USA. Nixon was the leading blues harmonica player in Brownsville, and a frequent visitor to Memphis, playing in street bands on jug, kazoo and harmonica. In Brownsville he was an associate of Sleepy John Estes and James 'Yank' Rachell, contributing beautiful, mournful playing to both men's 20s and 30s recordings. He was a major early influence on

John Lee 'Sonny Boy' Williamson, and later on Little Walter. When Estes was located in 1962, Nixon was found also (proving to be a cheery extrovert, despite his sorrowful harmonica sound), and came out of musical retirement to tour and record with Estes until the latter's death. Thereafter, Nixon continued to play concerts and festivals, and made occasional recordings, though these were often disappointing, as they often overemphasized his kazoo and his rudimentary guitar.

Albums: *Hammie Nixon* (1976), *Tappin' That Thing* (1984).

Oden, James Burke

b. 26 June 1903, Nashville, Tennessee, USA, d. 30 December 1977, Chicago, Illinois, USA. He was also known as St. Louis Jimmy, Big Bloke, Poor Boy and Old Man Oden. Although he was quite a capable pianist St. Louis Jimmy Oden's fame rests mainly on his prowess as a blues singer and composer. His most famous song 'Going Down Slow' has been recorded by many famous blues artists, an outstanding version by Howlin' Wolf aided by Willie Dixon, and was something of an anthem with white groups during the 60s. He was born, according to some sources, in 1905, to Henry Oden, a dancer, and Leana West. Both parents died before he was eight years old and his early life remains a blank, largely because he wished it so, until he turned up in St. Louis, Missouri at the age of fourteen working in a barber's shop. St. Louis had a thriving blues community during the 20s and Jimmy Oden found himself a niche in it. He taught himself piano during this period but never played much professionally, believing that there were many better players than himself around who would be able to accompany him. His main influence would seem to be Walter Davis although his most constant companions

were Big Joe Williams and Roosevelt Sykes. It was in the company of Sykes and violinist Curtis Mosby that he made his first foray into a recording studio in 1932. He moved north to Chicago in 1933 and was active in the blues scene of that city from then until the 50s performing, writing, and sometimes managing a band for Eddie Boyd, as well as being involved in the founding of the JOB record label. On one of his later sessions he was backed by the then emerging Muddy Waters and, after his activities were restricted by a serious car accident, he took up lodgings in the basement of Waters' house, paying his rent by supplying the odd song. He benefited briefly from the resurgence of interest in the blues during the 60s, recording albums for such labels as Delmark, Bluesville and Spivey. His death was due to bronchopneumonia.

Album: *Doghouse.*

Odom, Andrew

b.15 December 1936, Denham Springs, Louisiana, USA. Odom occasionally worked under the name of 'BV' or 'Big Voice'. He sang in a church choir as a child; his family moved north in the mid-50s, settling in St. Louis, Missouri. While there Odom sometimes worked with Albert King and reputedly recorded in the late 50s. He moved to Chicago in 1960 where he had long associations with Earl Hooker and Jimmy Dawkins. Singles under Odom's same have appeared on several local labels, and he made his debut album for Bluesway in 1969. Since then he has also recorded for Wasp Music and French labels MCM and Isabel. Odom is an intense, powerful blues singer, influenced by B.B. King and Bobby 'Blue' Bland.

Albums: *Farther On Down The Road* (1969), *Feel So Good* (1982).

Offitt, Lillian

b. 4 November 1938, Nashville, Tennessee, USA. On the evidence of her six releases, Lillian Offit was a plain but lusty blues shouter, of small stature and commensurate talent. She was still attending college when she visited the offices of Nashboro Records in the hope of making a gospel record. Owner Ernie Young suggested that she try secular music, and 'Miss You So' was issued on Excello c.1957. It was successful enough for her to turn professional, and two further singles were issued, with diminishing

success. In 1958 she moved to Chicago to become featured singer with the Earl Hooker band at Robert's Show Lounge. Through Hooker, she met Me London, owner of Chief Records, and cut her first record for the label in February 1960. 'Will My Man Be Home Tonight', heavily featuring Hooker's slide guitar, became a hit in the Chicago area. 'My Man I A Lover', recorded May 1960, and 'Troubles' from a year later, repeated the downward curve of Excello releases. She left music to start a family, preventing her from joining the 1964 American Folk Blues Festival tour, her place taken by Sugar Pie DeSanto. She was last sighted in 1974 as part of the Streakers Rated—X Revue in St. Joseph, Michigan.
Selected album: *Chicago Calling* (1986).

OKeh Records

One of the earliest labels to record black music, OKeh was founded by Otto Heineman in 1920. Its musical director Fred Hagar hired songwriter Perry Bradford to produce 'Crazy Blues' by Mamie Smith, which was a massive hit. To market records to the black audience, the company coined the name race music in its publicity. There was another first in 1923 when Hager's assistant Ralph Peer recorded performances by country music performer Fiddlin' John Carson in Atlanta, Georgia. Although it was sold to Columbia in 1926, OKeh remained the leading blues and jazz label of the 20s, recording tracks by Louis Armstrong, Lonnie Johnson and many others. However, in common with the rest of the record business, its activities were drastically curtailed during the Depression, although Bessie Smith recorded for the label in 1933. OKeh was revived by CBS during the late 30s as a home for R&B music, and in 1950 had a big hit with Johnnie Ray's 'Cry'. Later OKeh artists included Chuck Willis and Screaming Jay Hawkins. In 1962, producer Carl Davis took control of the company, which was now based in Chicago. During this period it became a major soul music label, with hits by artists like Major Lance, Billy Butler and Walter Jackson. After he left to join Brunswick Records, OKeh was gradually phased out by CBS which found a new source of black music in Philadelphia in the 70s.

Owens, Jack

b. 1905, Bentonia, Mississippi, USA. Along with Skip James and the unrecorded Henry Stuckey, Owens was one of the originators of the distinctive blues style developed in Bentonia after World War I, featuring 'deep' lyrics much concerned with death and loneliness, given a high and melismatic delivery. The complex, three finger guitar accompaniment, often in an eerie E minor tuning, blends inextricably with the equally eerie vocal line. Owens was not recorded until 1966, but proved to be a major musician, playing very extended songs with long guitar breaks. He was proud of his guitar prowess and, though fondest of E minor, could play in seven tunings. He has lived in Bentonia all his life, farming and at one time operating a juke joint. His wife's death in 1985 allowed him to play a few concerts further afield; in 1989 he played in Chicago, still a master musician at 84.
Albums: *It Must Have Been The Devil* (1971), *Bentonia Country Blues* (1979), *50 Years - Mississippi Blues In Bentonia* (1991).

P

Page, Cleo

Very much one of the mystery men of the blues, this singer/guitarist caused a minor stir in the 70s with his powerful, raw blue records which were issued on small Los Angeles labels including Goodie Train and Las Vegas. In 1979 JSP Records released enough material for an album which was described by Jim DeKoster in *Living Blues* as 'one of the most striking blues albums of the past year', but Page remains elusive. His music is largely tough, no-nonsense, mostly original blues with sometimes startling lyrics, though JSP also issued a more contemporary sounding risque single entitled 'Hamburger-I Love To Eat It', which was not on the album.
Album: *Leaving Mississippi* (1979).

Palmer, Earl

b. 25 October 1924, New Orleans, Louisiana, USA. Palmer's mother was a vaudeville performer, and from an early age he began entertaining as a singer and dancer. Playing drums in his school band, he started listening to jazz drummers like Big Sid Catlett and Panama Francis, and joined Dave Bartholomew's band in 1947. He recorded with the Bartholomew band and went on to play on many of his productions for Imperial Records, notably Fats Domino's classic records. Palmer is probably featured on virtually every other Crescent City classic, including those Specialty rockers by Little Richard, and Lloyd Price, but in 1956 Aladdin Records hired him as a session arranger to handle their New Orleans sessions. In February 1957, he moved out to Los Angeles to work for Aladdin until the company was liquidated. He remained one of the busiest session drummer on the west coast throughout the 60s and 70s, recording with everyone from Lightnin' Hopkins to Marvin Gaye and subsequently writing movie scores and advertising jingles.

Parker, 'Little' Junior

b. Herman Parker Jnr., 3 March 1927, West Memphis, Arkansas, USA, d. 18 November 1971, Blue Island, Illinois, USA. Despite his later fame some confusion still exists regarding the parents and date and place of birth of Little Junior Parker. Clarksdale, Mississippi and 1932 are sometimes quoted and his parents names are given in combinations of Herman Snr., Willie, Jeanetta or Jeremeter. It is certain is that they were a farming family situated near enough to West Memphis for Little Junior, (who had started singing in church) to involve himself in the local music scene at an early age. His biggest influence in those early days was Sonny Boy 'Rice Miller' Williamson in whose band Junior worked for a while before moving on to work for Howlin' Wolf, before assuming the leadership of the latter's backing band. He was a member of the *ad hoc* group, the Beale Streeters, with Bobby 'Blue' Bland and B.B. King, prior to forming his own band, the Blue Flames in 1951, which included the well regarded guitarist Auburn 'Pat' Hare. His first, fairly primitive, recordings were made for Joe Bihari and Ike Turner in 1952 for the Modern label. This brought him to the attention of Sam Phillips and Sun Records where Junior enjoyed some success with his recordings of 'Feeling Good' although the period is better recalled for the doomy 'Mystery Train', which was later taken up by the young Elvis Presley. His greatest fame on record stemmed from his work on Don Robey's Duke label operating out of Houston, Texas, and it was along with fellow Duke artist Bobby 'Blue' Bland that Little Junior headed the highly successful Blues Consolidated Revue which became a staple part of the southern blues circuit. His tenure with Robey lasted until the mid-60s with his work moving progressively away from his hard blues base. In his later, days Parker appeared on such labels as Mercury, United Artists and Capitol, enjoying intermittent chart success with 'Driving Wheel' (1961), 'Annie Get Your Yo-Yo' (1962) and 'Man Or Mouse' (1966). His premature death in 1971 occurred while he was undergoing surgery for a brain tumour and robbed R&B of one of its most influential figures.
Albums: with Bobby 'Blue' Bland *Blues Consolidated* (1958), with Bland *Barefoot Rock And You Got Me* (1960), *Driving Wheel* (1962), *Like It Is* (1967), *Honey-Drippin' Blues* (1969), *Blues Man* (1969), *The Outside Man* (1970), *Dudes Doing Business* (1971), *I Tell Stories, Sad*

'Little' Junior Parker

And True . . . (1973), *You Don't Have To Be Black To Love The Blues* (1974), *Love Ain't Nothin' But A Business Goin' On* (1974). Compilations: *The Best Of Junior Parker* (1966), *Sometime Tomorrow My Broken Heart Will Die* (1973), *Memorial* (1973), *The ABC Collection* (1976), *The Legendary Sun Performers - Junior Parker And Billy 'Red' Love* (1977), *I Wanna Ramble* (1982).

Parker, Sonny
b. 5 May 1925, Youngstown, Ohio, USA; d. 1957. Raised in Chicago by vaudeville act, Butterbeans And Susie. Parker developed into an all-round entertainer specializing in singing and dancing, and his powerful voice lent itself well to blues shouting. Recording with trumpeter King Kolax for Columbia in 1948, he came to the attention of bandleader Lionel Hampton, and recorded as Hamp's blues vocalist for Decca and MGM over the next three years, covering many of the top US R&B hits of the day ('Drinking Wine, 'Spo-Dee-O-Dee', 'For You My Love', 'Merry Christmas Baby', and 'I Almost Lost My Mind'). During the Hampton years, Sonny recorded sessions in his own name for Aladdin, Spire and Peacock, albeit usually featuring a contingent from the current Hampton orchestra. Later sessions were recorded in the mid-50s for Brunswick, Ultima and Hitts, but Parker continued to tour sporadically with Hampton. In 1957, Hampton brought Parker to Europe, and it was while touring France that Sonny became seriously ill and died.
Selected album: with Wynonie Harris, Jimmy Rushing and Big Joe Turner *The Best Of The Blues Shouters* (c.1970).

Patt, Frank 'Honeyboy'
b. 1 September 1928, Fostoria, Alabama, USA. After singing in church as a child, Patt taught himself guitar soon after emigrating to Los Angeles, California in 1952. There he formed a musical partnership with pianist Gus Jenkins, also from Alabama. Two years later Patt made his first record, with Jenkins, issued on the Specialty label, a powerful blues evoking the scene of a murder, 'Blood Stains On The Wall'. Although years later this came to be regarded as something of a classic, it made little impact at the time, and he had only one more record

issued, in 1957, again with Jenkins. Over the next decade, he worked mostly outside the music business, but his career enjoyed a revival in the 70s, with further recording work and live appearances.
Album: *City Blues* (1973).

Patton, Charley
b. April 1891, Bolton, Mississippi, USA, d. 28 April 1934, Indianola, Mississippi, USA. Charley Patton was small, but in all other ways larger than life; his death from a chronic heart condition at the age of 43 brought to an end a relentless pursuit of the good things then available to a black man in Mississippi - liquor, women, food (courtesy of women), music, and the avoidance of farmwork, which carried with it another *desideratum*, freedom of movement. By 1910, Patton had a repertoire of his own compositions, including 'Pony Blues', 'Banty Rooster Blues', 'Down The Dirt Road', and his version of 'Mississippi Bo Weavil Blues', all of which he was to record at his first session in 1929. He also acquired a number of spirituals, although the degree of his religious conviction is unclear. By the time he recorded, Charley Patton was the foremost blues singer in Mississippi, popular with whites and blacks, and able to live off his music. He was enormously influential on local musicians, including his regular partner Willie Brown, in addition to Tommy Johnson and Son House. Bukka White, Big Joe Williams and Howlin' Wolf were among others whose music was profoundly affected by Patton. His own sound is characteristic from the first: a hoarse, hollering vocal delivery, at times incomprehensible even to those who heard him in person, interrupted by spoken asides, and accompanied by driving guitar played with an unrivalled mastery of rhythm. Patton had a number of tunes and themes that he liked to rework, and he recorded some songs more than once, but never descended to stale repetition. His phrasing and accenting were uniquely inventive, voice and guitar complementing one another, rather than the guitar simply imitating the beat of the vocal line. He was able to hold a sung note to an impressive length, and part of the excitement of his music derives from the way a sung line can thus overlap the guitar phrase introducing the next verse. Patton was equally adept at regular

and bottleneck fretting, and when playing with a slide could make the guitar into a supplementary voice with a proficiency that few could equal.

He was extensively recorded by Paramount in 1929-30, and by Vocalion in 1934, so that the breadth of his repertoire is evident. (It was probably Patton's good sales that persuaded the companies to record the singing of his accompanists, guitarist Willie Brown and fiddler Henry Sims, and Bertha Lee, his last wife.) Naturally, Patton sang personal blues, many of them about his relations with women. He also sang about being arrested for drunkenness, cocaine ('A Spoonful Blues'), good sex ('Shake It And Break It') and, in 'Down The Dirt Road Blues' he highlighted the plight of the black in Mississippi ('Every day, seems like murder here'). He composed an important body of topical songs, including 'Dry Well Blues' about a drought, and the two-part 'High Water Everywhere', an account of the 1927 flooding of the Mississippi that is almost cinematic in its vividness. Besides blues and spirituals, Patton recorded a number of 'songster' pieces, including 'Mississippi Boweavil Blues', 'Frankie And Albert' and the anti-clerical 'Elder Greene Blues'. He also covered hits like 'Kansas City Blues', 'Running Wild', and even Sophie Tucker's 'Some Of These Days'. It is a measure of Patton's accomplishment as a musician and of his personal magnetism that blues scholars debate furiously whether he was a clowning moral degenerate or 'the conscience of the Delta', and whether he was an unthinking entertainer or a serious artist. It is perhaps fair to say that he was a man of his times who yet transcended them, managing to a considerable degree to live the life he chose in a system that strove to deny that option to blacks. A similar verdict applies to his achievements as a musician and lyricist; Patton was not independent of and uninfluenced by his musical environment, but considering how young he was when the blues were becoming the dominant black folk music, around the turn of the century, his achievement consists to a remarkable degree, of taking the given forms and transmuting them by the application of his genius.

Albums: *Volume 1* (1990), *Volume 2* (1990), *Volume 3* (1990), *Founder Of The Delta Blues 1929-1934* (1991).

Perkins, Pinetop

b. Joe Willie Perkins, 7 July 1913, Belzoni, Mississippi, USA. A barrelhouse blues pianist from before his teens, Perkins travelled through Mississippi and Arkansas, and north to St Louis and Chicago, playing piano, and sometimes guitar, behind Big Joe Williams, Robert Nighthawk, John Lee 'Sonny Boy' Williamson and others. He recorded for Sun Records in 1953, although only 'Pinetop's Boogie Woogie' was issued, many years later. He also accompanied Earl Hooker and Boyd Gilmore on Sun, and Nighthawk on Aristocrat. From the early 60s, he settled in Chicago. In 1969, Perkins replaced Otis Spann in the Muddy Waters Band, with which he toured up to and after the leader's death, also working as a solo act.

Selected albums: *Chicago Boogie Blues Piano Man* (c.1986), *Chicago Blues Session, Volume 12* (1989), *Boogie Woogie King* (1986), *The Ultimate Sun Blues Collection* (1991), *With Chicago Beau And The Blue Ice Band* (1992).

Perry, Oliver 'King'

b. 1920, Gary, Indiana, USA. Starting with the violin, Perry learned a variety of instruments in his youth, including bass, trumpet, drums, piano, and clarinet, before the alto saxophone after seeing Johnny Hodges with Duke Ellington's Orchestra. Perry ended up in Los Angeles, in 1945, after a tour with his small band and stayed, recording for Melodisc Records in July of that year. They went on to have records released on Excelsior/United Artists (not the well-known label from recent years) - finding success on the R&B charts with his 'Keep A Dollar In Your Pocket' which was covered by Roy Milton. He also recorded for DeLuxe, Specialty (with whom he had his only other substantial hit, 'Blue And Lonesome'), Dot, RPM, Lucky, Hollywood, Trilyte, Look and Unique through to the late 50s. He turned to selling real estate when work was scarce, but returned to music in 1967 and resumed his recording career on Accent in 1975. He continues to perform around the Bakersfield area and runs his own record company (Octive) and publishing company (Royal Attractions).

Selected album: *King Perry* (1986).

Perryman, Rufus 'Speckled Red'

b. 23 October 1892, Monroe, Louisiana, USA, d. 2 January 1973. Although his singing and piano playing were barely adequate, Perryman's work has about it a rather endearing, basic earthiness. In this respect it is sometimes preferable to the blander styles which developed as the blues became an acceptable part of popular entertainment. He played mostly in the south, achieving wider popularity thanks to recordings, and in the late 50s and early 60s toured Europe. In 1970 he recorded music for the soundtrack of the film *Blues Like Showers Of Rain*. Perryman, who died in 1973, was an elder brother of William 'Piano Red' Perryman.
Album: *The Dirty Dozen* (1961).

Pettis, 'Alabama' Junior

b. Coleman Pettis Jnr., c.1935, Alabama, USA, d. April 1988. Pettis worked under a variety of pseudonyms including Daddy Rabbit, Alabama Junior, and Junior Pettis. He learned to play guitar at the age of eight and moved to Chicago in 1952. He was strongly influenced by Lee Jackson, with whom he worked as rhythm guitarist, and is best known for his year spell working with Magic Slim from 1973-83. He can be heard on several of Slim's records, supplying excellent complementary work to the leader's tough playing, and he also provides occasional lead vocals and compositions. In 1987 he made his only album under his own name for the Wolf label, and he died of cancer at the beginning of April 1988.
Selected album: *Chicago Blues Sessions Volume Four* (1987).

Phillips, Brewer

b. 16 November 1924, Coita, Mississippi, USA. Phillips was on the Chicago blues scene from the mid-50s, when he worked briefly with Memphis Minnie, and from 1957-75 he played rhythm guitar for Hound Dog Taylor, taking occasional solos, and contributing significantly to the Houserockers' brash, energetic sound. After Taylor's death he continued to work the Chicago clubs, making occasional wider forays, and recording tracks that had the unpretentious, funky drive of his former leader, and revealed him to be a capable blues singer.
Albums: *Whole Lotta Blues* (1982), *Ingleside Blues* (1982).

Phillips, Gene

b. Eugene Floyd Phillips, 25 July 1915, St. Louis, Missouri, USA. Phillips learned to play ukulele and switched to guitar at the age of 11, after which he began playing and singing for tips and graduated through several obscure local bands. Between 1941-43, he played guitar behind the Mills Brothers, relocating with them to Los Angeles, and later worked and recorded with Lorenzo Flennoy, Wynonie Harris, Johnny Otis and Jack McVea. Phillips' Charlie Christian-inspired guitar and jump-blues shouting began to be featured on his own recordings for Modern Records from 1945, supported by west coast stalwarts such as Maxwell Davis and Jack McVea. They produced such hits as 'Big Legs', 'Just A Dream' and 'Rock Bottom'. Phillips' later records for RPM, Imperial, Exclusive, Federal (with Preston Love) and Combo, were successful locally and he spent the 50s doing extensive session work with artists such as Percy Mayfield, who played on 'Please Send Me Someone To Love' and Amos Milburn, but retired from the music business with the advent of rock 'n' roll.
Albums: *Gene Phillips & His Rhythm Aces* (1986), *I Like 'Em Fat* (1988).

Phillips, Washington

b. c.1891, Freestone County, Texas, USA, d. 31 December 1938, Austin, Texas, USA. Phillips was unique on records in accompanying his plaintive gospel singing with the ethereal sounds of the dolceola, a zither equipped with a piano-like keyboard, of which only some 100 examples were made following its invention in 1902. Phillips recorded annually for Columbia from 1927-29, and his simple moral homilies were the work of a man who proclaimed his lack of education, preferring to trust in faith. His most famous song is the two-part 'Denomination Blues', an attack on the squabbling of black Christian sects, so titled because it uses the tune of 'Hesitation Blues'.
Album: *Denomination Blues* (1980).

Piano Slim

b. Robert T. Smith, 1 August 1928, La Grange, Texas, USA. Slim began singing and playing saxophone in clubs in the late 40s, but after being shot in the chest he switched to drums, playing behind Lightnin' Hopkins for a spell. He became a pianist when working with a band in Odessa, Texas, and, on moving back to Houston, Henry Hayes taught him about music; he also claims to have recorded around this time. Don Robey recommended Slim to Bobbin Records in St. Louis, and they released a single by him in the late 50s. He remains based in St. Louis, and has played in innumerable bars and clubs. In 1981 he recorded his first album, mostly solo, although with guitarist Amos Sandford on some titles, then two years later he made an album with a band including two horns. Reviewing these two records, both issued by Swingmaster, *Living Blues* stated 'whether you prefer solo piano blues or rocking horn-backed material, Robert T. Smith can deliver the good'.

Selected albums: *Mean Woman Blues* (1981), *Gateway To The Blues* (1983).

Piazza, Rod

b. 1947, Riverside, California, USA. Piazza heard the R&B records his brothers bought in the 50s and formed a blues band when he was around 16 years old. He became friendly with George Smith, a hugh influence on his vocals and harmonica playing. Piazza made two albums with the Dirty Blues Band for ABC-Bluesway, and in the late 60s formed Bacon Fat, who made two albums for Blue Horizon. In the mid-70s he was singer/harmonica player for the Chicago Flying Saucer Band, which became the Mighty Flyers, a good-times blues group very influential in California. In the 80s Piazza also recorded two solo albums in order to showcase his harder blues approach. Additionally, he has recorded on numerous sessions, from Jimmy Rogers and Big Joe Turner to Michelle Shocked.

Albums: *Harpburn* (1986), *So Glad To Have The Blues* (1988), as Rod Piazza And The Mighty Flyers *Blues In The Dark* (1991).

Pichon, Walter 'Fats'

b. 1906, New Orleans, Louisiana, USA, d. 25 February 1967, Chicago, Illinois, USA. Pichon spent his musical career in the area between jazz, blues and pop, leading his own bands occasionally, and working as a pianist for artist including Luis Russell, Fess Williams, Ted Lewis', Mamie Smith, Elmer Snowden and Armand Piron. He recorded a few hokum vocals for Russell under his own name; the

accompanists on the latter included Hawaiian guitarist King Benny Nawahi, for whom Pichon returned the compliment. In the 40s he began a long residency at the Absinthe House, New Orleans, also working in New York and the Caribbean. He was still active in the 60s, although treatment for failing eyesight interrupted his playing for long periods.

Pickens, Buster

b. 3 June 1916, Hempstead, Texas, USA, d. 24 November 1964, Houston, Texas, USA. An early life as an itinerant musician, playing barrelhouses across the southern states, enabled Pickens to develop his downhome blues piano style, although it was firmly in the Texas idiom. Following military service in the World War II, he settled back in Houston, and made his first record, supporting the vocals of Alger 'Texas' Alexander, along with guitarist Leon Benton. He also played regularly with Lightnin' Hopkins, and appeared as accompanist on some of that artist's records for Prestige/Bluesville in the early 60s. He also made a solo album in 1960, which demonstrated his deep knowledge of the Texas blues style. The possibilities of a successful new career in the blues revival, however, were tragically curtailed when he was murdered a few years later.

Selected album: *Texas Barrelhouse Piano* (1960).

Pickett, Dan

b. James Founty. Pickett was a singer and guitarist, whose August 1949 recordings prompted years of speculation. Many noted his stylistic links with the blues of the east coast, and it was through company files that critics discovered his real name. Pickett's repertoire was derived almost exclusively from 30s recordings, and his virtuosity went into the delivery, rather than the composition, of his songs, which sound as if they could have been recorded a decade or so earlier. However, the transformations to which he subjected many songs are the work of a true original. His guitar playing, influenced by Tampa Red, is complex but effortlessly fluent, and perfectly integrated with his intense but extrovert singing, which is often remarkable for the number of words crammed into a single line.

Album: *Dan Pickett & Tarheel Slim* (1991).

Pierce, Billie

b. Wilhemina Goodson, 8 June 1907, Marianna, Florida, USA., d. 29 September 1974. After working for many years as singer or pianist or both in obscure southern clubs (with a brief moment of reflected glory as accompanist to Bessie Smith), Pierce married De De Pierce in 1935 and thereafter played usually in his company. Once again this was out of the spotlight but in the mid-60s their joint careers were revived.
Selected album: *Billie And De De* (1966).

Pierce, De De

b. Joseph De Lacrois, 18 February 1904, New Orleans, Louisiana, USA, d. 23 November 1973. For many years, playing the cornet was only a secondary occupation to Pierce, who played the cornet and occasionally sang. This comment might well be applied to many of the older generation of New Orleans musicians, who traditionally and rightly regarded music as an unreliable business. In Pierce's case, however, he kept up a 'day job' rather longer than most and not until after his marriage in 1935 to singer-pianist Billie Goodson (see Billie Pierce) did he devote himself to a musical career. The husband and wife duo worked regularly, although still within a restricted area, until Pierce retired temporarily in the 50s through ill-health and failing eyesight. The duo made a comeback in the mid-60s achieving international fame with a succession of concert tours and records and, inevitably perhaps, regular appearances at Preservation Hall, where they entertained the tourists of New Orleans.
Albums: *New Orleans Jazz* (1959), *Blues In The Classic Tradition* (1961), *Jazz At Preservation Hall* (1962), *Billie And De De* (1966), *De De Pierce's New Orleans Stompers* (1966).

Powell, Eugene

b. 23 December 1909, Utica, Mississippi, USA. Powell made his first blues records thanks to Bo Carter, who set up a 1936 session for Bluebird. Carter heavily influenced his guitar playing, in sometimes discordant duet with Willie (Bill) Harris. Powell's singing, though warmer than Carter's, had a similar clarity. Powell recorded as 'Sonny Boy Nelson', Nelson being his stepfather's name, and besides his own titles accompanied his then wife, Mississippi Matilda,

and the harmonica player Robert Hill. Powell and Matilda separated in 1952, and he retired from music soon after. In the 70s, he was still a skilful guitarist, and was persuaded by Bo Carter's brother Sam Chatmon to perform for white audiences, although it was not long before he retired again because of his second wife's health problems, and subsequently his own.
Selected albums: *Police In Mississippi Blues* (1978), *Sonny Boy Nelson With Mississippi Matilda And Robert Hill* (1986).

Powell, Jesse

b. 27 February 1924, Fort Worth, Texas, USA. Powell studied music at Hampton University, where he became inspired by Count Basie's Lester Young and Herschel Evans, and played his tenor saxophone with the bands of Oran 'Hot Lips' Page (1942-43), Louis Armstrong (1943-44), and Luis Russell (1944-45). In 1946 he accepted an offer from Count Basie to replace Illinois Jacquet in the reed section. After briefly leading his own band in 1948 and being featured at that year's Paris Jazz Festival, he joined Dizzy Gillespie's Orchestra (1949-50), but the R&B era found him with copious session work and, again, his own unit, which recorded for Federal (the infamous 'Walkin' Blues' sung by Fluffy Hunter) and Jubilee.

Power, Duffy

Power was one of several British vocalists, including Marty Wilde, Billy Fury and Dickie Pride, signed to the Larry Parnes stable. Having completed a series of pop singles, including 'Dream Lover' and 'Ain't She Sweet', the singer embraced R&B in 1963 with a pulsating version of the Beatles' 'I Saw Her Standing There' on which he was backed by the Graham Bond Quartet. Power's later singles included 'Tired, Broke and Busted', which featured support from the Paramounts, but he later supplemented his solo career by joining Alexis Korner's Blues Incorporated. The singer appeared on *Red Hot From Alex* (1964), *Sky High* (1966) and *Blues Incorporated* (1967), during which time group members Jack Bruce (bass), Danny Thompson (bass) and Terry Cox (drums) assisted on several informal sessions later compiled on Power's *Innovations* set. Guitarist John McLaughlin also contributed to the album, before joined the vocalist's next project, Duffy's Nucleus. Power

Duffy Power

resumed his solo career late in 1967 when this short-lived attraction disbanded, but an ensuing fitful recording schedule did little justice to this under-rated artist's potential.

Albums: *Innovations* aka *Mary Open The Door* (1970), *Duffy Power* (1973), *Powerhouse* (1976).

Price, Walter (Big Walter)

b. 2 August 1917, Gonzales, Texas, USA. Like many other aspects of society today, the blues has personalities famous for being famous. Big Walter Price is one. Raised from the age of three by his uncle, C.W. Hull, and aunt, he moved with them to San Antonio in 1928. Throughout his schooling, he also worked in cottonfields, sold newspapers, shined shoes and washed dishes. Taking an interest in music, he played with the Northern Wonders gospel group. From school, he worked on the railroad until, in 1955, he made three records for TNT Records, the first 'Calling Margie' achieving local success. Thereafter, he cut 'Shirley Jean', on which his reputation rests, and four other singles for Peacock in Houston, several of them with Little Richard's old band, The Upsetters, masquerading as The Thunderbirds. In the next 10 years, he recorded for Goldband, Myrl, Jet Stream and Teardrop, while other tracks recorded for Roy Ames and featuring Albert Collins on guitar were issued later on Flyright and P.Vine. In July 1971, also for Ames, he recorded an album eventually issued in England 17 years later. His ebullient personality tended to minimise the effect of his rather wayward timing; though written of as an exponent of classic Texas piano blues, the influence is more geographical than musical.

Album: *Boogies From Coast To Coast* (1988).

Primer, John

b. 3 March c.1946, Camden, Mississippi, USA. Primer recalls hearing the music of Muddy Waters as a youngster, and he played a one-string instrument before moving to Chicago in 1963 and acquiring a guitar. He initially played in Jimmy Reed's style. He began to take music more seriously around 1973 and played at the famed Chicago club Theresa's (1974-80), usually with Sammy Lawhorn, who gave Primer many tips on playing blues guitar. In the early 80s he was a member of the Muddy Waters band, and after Muddy's death he replaced 'Alabama' Junior Pettis as second guitarist in Magic Slim's band the Teardrops. Slim allows his accompanist some of the spotlight, and Primer has recorded for Austrian label Wolf; he is highly rated for his pure blues playing (particularly slide guitar) and singing. Primer is a worthy bearer of the old Chicago blues traditions.

Album: *Chicago Blues Session, Volume Six - Poor Man Blues* (1991).

Professor Longhair

b. Henry Roeland Byrd, 19 December 1918, Bogalusa, Louisiana, USA, d. 30 January 1980. Byrd grew up in New Orleans where he was part of a novelty dance team in the 30s. He also played piano, accompanying John Lee 'Sonny Boy' Williamson. After wartime service, Byrd gained a residency at the Caldonia club, whose owner christened him Professor Longhair. By now, he had developed a piano style that combined rumba and mambo element with more standard boogie-woogie and barrelhouse rhythms. Particularly through his most ardent disciple, Dr John Longhair's has become recognised as the most influential New Orleans R&B pianist since Jelly Roll Morton. In 1949 he made the first record of his most famous tune, 'Mardi Gras In New Orleans' for the Star Talent label, which credited the artist as Professor Longhair & his Shuffling Hungarians. He next recorded 'Baldhead' for Mercury as Roy Byrd and his Blues Jumpers and the song became a national R&B hit in 1950. Soon there were more singles on Atlantic (a new version of 'Mardi Gras' and the well-known 'Tipitina' in 1953) and Federal. A mild stroke interrupted his career in the mid-50s and for some years he performed infrequently apart from at Carnival season when a third version of his topical song, 'Go To The Mardi Gras' (1958) received extensive radio play. Despite recording Earl King's 'Big Chief' in 1964, Longhair was virtually inactive throughout the 60s. He

Professor Longhair

returned to the limelight at the first New Orleans Jazz & Heritage Festival in 1971 when, accompanied by Snooks Eaglin, he received standing ovations. (A recording of the concert was finally issued in 1987). This led to European tours in 1973 and 1975 and to recordings with Gatemouth Brown and for Harvest. Longhair's final album, for Alligator, was completed shortly before he died of a heart attack in January 1980. In 1991 he was posthumously inducted into the Rock 'n' Roll Hall Of Fame.

Selected albums: *New Orleans Piano* (reissue, 1972), *Rock 'N' Roll Gumbo* (1977), *Live On The Queen Mary* (1978), *Crawfish Fiesta* (1980), *The London Concert* (1981), *The Last Mardi Gras* (1982), *Houseparty New Orleans Style* (1987).

Pryor, 'Snooky'

b. James Edward Pryor, 15 September 1921, Lambert, Mississippi, USA. After settling in Chicago in 1945 after US Army service, Pryor joined the Maxwell Street group of blues singers which included Johnny Young, Floyd Jones and Moody Jones, with whom he recorded in 1948. Their records were harbingers of the amplified downhome sound of post-war Chicago blues, although at this time Pryor's singing and harmonica were heavily influenced by John Lee 'Sonny Boy' Williamson. Pryor made his first record, 'Telephone Blues' with guitarist Moody Jones in 1949. There were later singles for J.O.B. ('Boogy Fool' 1950), Parrot (1953), Blue Lake (1954) and VeeJay Records ('Someone To Love Me' 1956). During the 50s Pryor also frequently toured the South. After making the dance novelty 'Boogie Twist', Pryor left the music business in 1963 but returned in the early 70s, touring and recording in Europe in 1973. A 1974 album was made with a New Orleans rhythm section including guitarist Justin Adams. In recent years he has benefited from the revived interest in blues, recording his 1992 album for Texas label Antone's.

Albums: *Snooky Pryor* (1969), *Snooky Pryor And The Country Blues* (1973), *Do It If You Want To* (1973), *Homesick James And Snooky Pryor* (1974), *Shake Your Moneymaker* (1984), *Too Cool To Move* (1992), with Johnny Shines (1993).

Pugh, Joe Bennie (Forest City Joe)

b. 10 July 1926, Hughes, Arkansas, USA, d. 3 April 1960, Horseshoe Lake, Arkansas, USA. An admirer of John Lee (Sonny Boy) Williamson, Forest City Joe only recorded two sessions 11 years apart, but these were enough to create a significant reputation. He lived most of his life in Crittenden County, which encompasses the sites of his birth and death. Like many other harmonica players growing up in the 30s, his idolisation of Williamson led to an imitiation not only of his instrumental style but also of the speech impediment that affected his 'tongue-tied' vocals. In the late 40s he travelled north to Chicago several times, earning a reputation in the clubs that he played. On 2 December 1948, six months after Williamson had been murdered with an ice-pick, Joe recorded eight titles for Aristocrat with a guitarist tentatively identified as J. C. Cole. Only one single was issued at the time, combining 'Memory Of Sonny Boy' and 'A Woman On Every Street'. The complete session was released in the late 80s. Returning to Arkansas, nothing was heard of him until August 1959, when Alan Lomax recorded him for the 'Southern Folk Heritage' series, both solo and with a band including guitarist Sonny Boy Rogers, performing Williamson songs and 'Red Cross Store', a piano blues. Nine months later, he died when the lorry in which he was travelling home from a dance overturned, killing him instantly.

Album: *Memory Of Sonny Boy* (1988).

Q

Quattlebaum, Doug

b. 22 January 1927, Florence, South Carolina, USA. It was after moving to Philadelphia in the early 40s that Quattlebaum took up the guitar seriously, and toured with a number of gospel groups, claiming to have recorded with the Bells Of Joy in Texas. In 1952, he recorded solo as a blues singer for local label Gotham. By 1961, he was accompanying the Ward Singers but, when discovered by a researcher, was playing blues and popular tunes through the PA of his ice-cream van, hence the title of his album. *Softee Man Blues* showed him to be a forceful singer, influenced as a guitarist by Blind Boy Fuller, and with an eclectic repertoire largely derived from records. Quattlebaum made some appearances on the folk circuit, but soon returned to Philadelphia, where he recorded a single in the late 60s. He is thought to have entered the ministry soon afterwards.
Albums: *Softee Man Blues* (1962), *East Coast Blues* (1988).

Queen, Ida (Guillory)

b. Ida Lewis, 15 January 1930, Lake Charles, Louisiana, USA. Lewis grew up singing Louisiana French songs and began playing accordion shortly after the World War II. When the family moved to San Francisco and Ida married, she had little to do with music until 1976. Ida and her brother Al Rapone played at parties, and she was then invited to perform at a Mardi Gras celebration, which subsequently led to more bookings. She signed with GNP Records in 1976 and has made numerous albums since then, and has been a frequent visitor to Europe with her Bon Ton Zydeco Band. Ida's brand of zydeco is more accessible than that of many Louisiana artists, and she enjoys huge popularity among the non-Louisiana audience.
Albums: *Zydeco* (1976), *Cooking With Queen Ida* (1989).

Quillian, Rufus And Ben

Rufus (b. 2 February 1900, Gainesville, Georgia, USA, d. 31 January 1946; piano/vocals) and Ben (b. 23 June 1907, Gainesville, Georgia, USA; vocals). They worked in various combinations, but mostly in a group named the Blue Harmony Boys. This group, which also included other singers or musicians at various times, such as guitarist James McCrary, was very rare in that they sang blues and related material in sweet, close harmonies. Ben was not with them at their first recording session in 1929, but was present at sessions in the following two years. The brothers were well-known as performers around Atlanta at this time and they had a regular spot on a local radio station. Although their material on record was of a good-time nature, Rufus was also known for composing religious songs.
Album: *Complete Recordings In Chronological Order* (1985).

R

Rachell, James 'Yank'

b. 16 March 1910, Brownsville, Tennessee, USA. Yank Rachell learned mandolin from his uncle Daniel Taylor and later extended his talents to include guitar, harmonica and violin. He worked on the L&N railroad as a track hand in his early years, supplementing his income by playing local dances and parties in the company of local artists such as Hambone Willie Newbern. Rachell seems to have been doubling as a talent scout when he recorded with Sleepy John Estes in 1929. Later, he formed a partnership with Dan Smith and worked on record with John Lee Sonny Boy Williamson. Recordings under his own name appeared on labels such as Victor, Vocalion and Banner and between 1938 and 1941 he recorded 24 titles for the famous Bluebird label. Despite all this activity Yank was never able to survive as a full-time musician and often worked as a farmer. He returned to music, along with Estes and Hammie Nixon, with the revival of interest in

blues in the early 60s. During that period he appeared at festivals, clubs and concerts and made quite a name as a showman. He recorded again for Delmark in 1964.
Albums: *Complete Recordings In Chronological Order Volume 1 (1934-1938) Vol 2 (1938-1941)* (1986), *Yank Rachell* (1964).

Radcliff, Bobby
b. 1951, Bethesda, Maryland, USA. Radcliff started to play guitar at 12 years old. In the 60s and 70s he worked on the Washington DC blues scene, associating with veterans such as Thomas 'TNT' Tribble and Bobby Parker. By the end of the 60s he spent some time in Chicago, meeting and absorbing the music of bluesmen such as Magic Sam, Otis Rush, and Jimmy Dawkins. Radcliff moved to New York in 1977 and in the early 80s he recorded a little edition album for the A-OK label. Towards the end of the decade he was recommended to his present label, Black Top Records, by Ronnie Earl, and his first album for them was highly acclaimed. Radcliff is a strong singer and a powerful, rhythmic guitarist who utilizes elements of soul and funk in his playing.
Album: *Dresses Too Short* (1989).

Rainey, Gertrude 'Ma'
b. Gertrude M. Pridgett, 26 April 1886, Columbus, Georgia, USA, d. 22 December 1939. After working as a saloon and tent show singer around the turn of the century, Rainey began singing blues. She later claimed that this occurred as early as 1902 and however much reliance is placed upon this date she was certainly amongst the earliest singers to bring blues songs to a wider audience. By the time of her first recordings, 1923, she was one of the most famous blues singers in the deep south and was known as the 'Mother of the Blues'. Although many other singers recorded blues songs before her, she eschewed the refining process some of them had begun, preferring instead to retain the earthy directness with which she had made her name. Her recordings, sadly of generally inferior technical quality, show her to have been a singer of great power, while her delivery has a quality of brooding majesty few others ever matched. A hard-living, rumbustious woman, Rainey influenced just about every other singer of the blues, notably

Bessie Smith whom she encouraged during her formative years. Although Rainey continued working into the early 30s her career at this time, like that of her protege, Smith, was overshadowed by changes in public taste. She retired in 1935 and died in 1939. In the late 80s a musical show, *Ma Rainey's Black Bottom*, was a success on Broadway and in London.
Compilations: *Blues The World Forgot* (1923-24), *Complete Recordings Vol. 1* (1923-24), *Oh My Babe Blues* (1923-24), *Complete Recordings Vol. 2* (1924-25).

Raitt, Bonnie
b. 8 November 1949, Burbank, California, USA. Born into a musical family, her father, John Raitt, starred in Broadway productions of **Oklahoma!** and **Carousel**. Having learned guitar as a child, Bonnie became infatuated with traditional blues, although her talent for performing did not fully flourish until she attended college in Cambridge, Massachusetts. Raitt initially opened for John Hammond, before establishing her reputation with prolific live appearances throughout the east coast circuit on which she was accompanied by longtime bassist Dan 'Freebo' Friedberg. Bonnie then acquired the management services of Dick Waterman, who guided the career of many of the singer's mentors, including Son House, Mississippi Fred McDowell and Sippie Wallace. She often travelled and appeared with these performers and *Bonnie Raitt* contained material drawn from their considerable lexicon. Chicago bluesmen Junior Wells and A.C. Reed also appeared on the album, but its somewhat reverential approach was replaced by the contemporary perspective unveiled on *Give It Up*. This excellent set included versions of Jackson Browne's 'Under The Falling Sky' and Eric Kaz's 'Love Has No Pride' and established the artist as an inventive and sympathetic interpreter. *Taking My Time* features assistance from Lowell George and Bill Payne from Little Feat and included an even greater diversity, ranging from the pulsating 'You've Been In Love Too Long' to the traditional 'Kokomo Blues'. Subsequent releases followed a similar mixture, and although *Streetlights* was a minor disappointment, *Home Plate*, produced by veteran Paul A. Rothchild, reasserted her talent. Nonetheless Raitt refused to embrace a

Bonnie Raitt

conventional career, preferring to tour in more intimate surroundings. Thus the success engendered by *Sweet Forgiveness* came as a natural progression and reflected a genuine popularity. However its follow-up, *The Glow*, failed to capitalize on this newfound fortune and while offering a spirited reading of Mable John's 'Your Good Thing', much of the material was self-composed and lacked the breadth of style of its predecessors. Subsequent releases, *Green Light* and *Nine Lives* proved less satisfying and Raitt was then dropped by Warner Brothers, her outlet of 15 years.

Those sensing an artistic and personal decline were proved totally wrong in 1989 when *Nick Of Time* became one of the year's most acclaimed and best-selling releases. Raitt herself confessed slight amazement at winning a Grammy award. The album was highly accomplished and smoothed some of the rough bluesier edges for an AOR market. The emotional title track became a US hit single and this notable set was produced by Don Was of Was (Not Was), featured sterling material from John Hiatt and Bonnie Hayes. Raitt also garnered praise for her contributions to John Lee Hooker's superb 1990 release, *The Healer*, and that same year reached a wider audience with her appearance of the concert for Nelson Mandela at Wembley Stadium. She continued in the same vein with the excellent *Luck Of The Draw* featuring strong material from Paul Brady, Hiatt and Raitt herself. The album was another million-plus seller and demonstrated Raitt's new mastery in singing smooth emotional ballads; none better than the beautifully evocative 'I Can't Make You Love Me'. Her personal life became stable following her marriage in 1991, and after years of singing about broken hearts, faithless lovers and 'no good men' Raitt entered the 90s at the peak of her already lengthy and impressive career.

Albums: *Bonnie Raitt* (1971), *Give It Up* (1972), *Takin' My Time* (1973), *Streetlights* (1974), *Home Plate* (1975), *Sweet Forgiveness* (1977), *The Glow* (1979), *Green Light* (1982), *Nine Lives* (1986), *Nick Of Time* (1989), *Luck Of The Draw* (1991). Compilation: *The Bonnie Raitt Collection* (1990).

Rankin, R.S.

b. 22 February 1933, Royse City, Texas, USA. Rankin's uncle was 'T-Bone' Walker, who encouraged the youngster to play blues guitar and then took him on the road as a valet in the late 40s. He worked and recorded with Walker during the 50s, and was dubbed 'T-Bone' Walker Jnr. around 1955, and it was under this name that he recorded for the Midnite label in 1962. He has been less active on the music scene since the mid-60s but did surface to play at the T-Bone Walker Memorial Concert in Los Angeles, California in May 1975, when *Blues Unlimited* reported that 'he did a fantastic job on his uncle's classics'.
Compilation: (one 1962 recording only) *Texas Guitar - From Dallas To L.A.* (1972).

Ray, Harmon

b. 1914, Indianapolis, Indiana, USA. Ray grew up in St. Louis, where he took up blues singing in the 30s, adopting the vocal style of Peetie Wheatstraw, with whom he worked as a double act from 1935 until Wheatstraw's death in 1941. In 1942, Ray recorded as 'Peetie Wheatstraw's Buddy'. After military service he settled in Chicago, singing in clubs, and recording for J. Mayo Williams, who may have been the source of a Hy-Tone 78 release. Ray's last recordings were made in 1949, one song being in the manner of Charles Brown, and the other three in Wheatstraw's style; two of these were covers of Wheatstraw songs, but 'President's Blues' was an original tribute to Truman. Ray continued to work in Chicago clubs until the early 60s, when cancer forced him to retire.
Album: *Chicago Blues* (1985).

Red Nelson

b. Nelson Wilborn, 31 August 1907, Sumner, Mississippi, USA. Red Nelson was a Chicago based vocalist, and possibly a guitarist, but not a pianist, despite frequent reports to that effect. He was given interesting and varied accompanists during his recording career, which began in 1935, and was a fine singer with a telling falsetto, although he often held himself emotionally in check, possibly to accommodate the 30s fashion for the laconic. His 1935/6 Decca recordings with Cripple Clarence Lofton, though less considered, are outstanding, with 'Crying Mother Blues' an unquestionable masterpiece, while his 1947 titles for Aladdin, with James Clark on piano are almost as good. Last seen working with Muddy Waters in the

60s, Nelson was an amiable alcoholic with a penchant for *double entendres*, as might be inferred from the ebullient 'Dirty Mother Fuyer', which he recorded in 1947 under the pseudonym 'Dirty Red'.
Albums: *Blues Uptown* (1969), *The Piano Blues Vol. 9 Lofton/Noble* (1979), *Red Nelson* (1989).

Reed, A.C.

b. Aaron Corthen Reed, 9 May 1926, Wordell, Missouri, USA. Reed was attracted to the saxophone by hearing a Jay 'Hootie' McShann record. On moving to Chicago at the age of 15, he bought a saxophone and studied music, although he was tutored in the blues by J.T. Brown. He spent much of the 50s touring the southwestern states with blues musician Dennis Binder. The following decade he re-established himself in Chicago, recording in his own right for several small labels, even enjoying a minor hit with 'Talkin' 'Bout My Friends' on Nike Records in the mid-60s. He became an in-demand session musician for over three decades. He has had long spells in the bands of Buddy Guy and Albert Collins but now has a successful solo career. Reed's vocals, powerful saxophone playing and often witty songwriting have been recorded for the white collector market by Alligator and Wolf, and he also runs his own Ice Cube label.
Album: *Take These Blues And Shove 'Em* (1984).

Reed, Jimmy

b. Mathis James Reed, 6 September 1925, Leland, Mississippi, USA, d. 29 August 1976, Oakland, California, USA. Jimmy Reed was a true original, he sang in a lazy mush-mouthed ramble, played limited, if instantly recognizable harmonica, and even more minimal guitar. He produced a series of hits in the 50s that made him the most successful blues singer of the era. He was born into a large sharecropping family and spent his early years on Mr. Johnny Collier's plantation situated near Dunleith, Mississippi. Here, he formed a childhood friendship with Eddie Taylor which was to have a marked effect on his later career. Reed sang in church and learned rudimentary guitar along with Taylor, but while Eddie progressed Jimmy never became more than basically competent on the instrument. Jimmy left school in 1939 and found work farming around Duncan and Meltonia,

Mississippi. Around 1943-44 he left the south to find work in Chicago where opportunities abounded due to the war effort. He was drafted in 1944 and served out his time in the US Navy. Discharged in 1945 he returned briefly to Mississippi before gravitating north once more to the Chicago area. Working in the steel mills, Reed gigged around in his leisure time with a friend named Willie Joe Duncan, who played a one-string guitar, or Diddley-bow. He also re-established contact with Eddie Taylor who had also moved north to try his luck. This led to his becoming known on the local club scene and after appearances with John and Grace Brim Reed secured a recording contract with VeeJay Records in 1953. His initial sessions, though highly regarded by collectors, produced no hits and VeeJay were considering dropping him from their roster when in 1955 'You Don't Have To Go' took off. From then on, his success was phenomenal as a string of hits such as 'Ain't That Lovin' You Baby', 'You've Got Me Dizzy', 'Bright Lights Big City', 'I'm Gonna Get My Baby' and 'Honest I Do' carried him through to the close of the decade. Many of these timeless blues numbers were adopted by every white R&B beat group during the early 60s. Two of his songs are now standard and often used as rousing encores by name bands; 'Baby What You Do You Want Me To Do' closed the Byrds' live performances for many years and 'Big Boss Man' is arguably the most performed song of its kind. Much of the credit for this success must be attributed to his friend Eddie Taylor, who played on most of Reed's sessions, and his wife, Mama Reed, who wrote many of his songs and even sat behind him in the studio reciting the lyrics into his forgetful ear as he sang. On some recordings her participation is audible. Jimmy's songs had little to do with the traditional blues, but they were eminently danceable and despite employing the basic blues line-up of harmonica, guitars and drums were generally classed as R&B. His hits were 'crossovers' appealing to whites as well as blacks. Perhaps this contributed to his continuing success as the blues entered its post-rock 'n' roll hard times. In his later days at VeeJay, various gimmicks were tried such as dubbing an album's worth of 12-string guitar solos over his backing tracks, faking live performances and introducing a commentary between album cuts; none were

Jimmy Reed

too successful in reviving his flagging sales. To counter the positive elements in his life, Reed was continually undermined by his own unreliability, illness (he was an epileptic) and a fascination for the bottle. He visited Europe in the early 60s by which time it was obvious that not all was well with him. He was supremely unreliable and prone to appear on stage drunk. By the mid-60s his career was in the hands of the controversial Al Smith and his recordings were appearing on the Bluesway label. Inactive much of the time due to illness, Reed seemed on the road to recovery and further success, having controlled his drink problem. Ironically he died soon after of respiratory failure. He was buried in Chicago. Reed is an important figure who has influenced countless artists through his songs. Steve Miller recorded *Living In The 20th Century* with a segment of Reed songs and dedicated the album to him. The Rolling Stones, Pretty Things and the Grateful Dead also acknowledge a considerable debt to him.

Selected albums: *At Carnegie Hall* (1961), *Just Jimmy Reed* (1962), *The Boss Man Of The Blues* (1964), *Now Appearing* (1966), *T'ain't No Big Thing* (1968), *High And Lonesome* (1981), *Funky Funky Soul* (1981), *I'm The Man Down There* (1985), *Ride 'Em On Down* (1989), Compilations: *Cold Chills 1967-70* (1985), *Upside Your Head* (1985), *Big Boss Blues* (1986), *12 Greatest Hits* (1987), *Rockin' With Reed* (1987), *Got Me Dizzy* (1988), *Honest I Do* (1988).

René Brothers

Otis (b. 1898, New Orleans, Louisiana, USA, d. 1968) and Leon (b. 1902, Covington, Louisiana, USA, d. 1982). Formed their Exclusive Records in Los Angeles, California, in 1942. Otis generally worked outside the music business before the 30s, whereas Leon had studied music and piano at night school and formed his own orchestra, the Southern Syncopators, in the mid-20s. The brothers' greatest successes came in the 30s when, as songwriters, they composed ASCAP standards such as 'When It's Sleepy Time Down South' (1931) and 'When The Swallows Come Back To Capistrano' (1939), the royalties from which helped to fund their new venture in 1942. They continued to pen big sellers such as 'Gloria', 'Someone's Rocking My Dreamboat' and 'I Left My Sugar in Salt Lake City'. Exclusive had early successes with ex-Duke Ellington band balladeers Ivie Anderson and Herb Jeffries, but hit its stride in 1945 with the inauguration of the 200 R&B series, resulting in some of the earliest R&B hits by Joe Liggins ('the Honeydripper'), Ivory Joe Hunter ('Blues At Sunrise'), and Johnny Moore's Three Blazers ('Sunny Road', 'Merry Christmas Baby', 'Soothe Me'). Otis formed a companion label, Excelsior, in 1944 which issued records by Nat 'King' Cole, Johnny Otis, and Big Joe Turner, but by 1949 both Excelsior and Exclusive were in difficulties and the masters were sold to fund new projects - the short-lived Excellent and Selective labels. In 1953, Leon returned to incorporate his new label, Class, which had big hits in the rock 'n' roll era by Oscar McLollie, Richard Berry and Bobby Day - Leon penned the classic 'Rockin' Robin' - and lasted until 1962.

Reynolds, Blind Joe

b. 1900, Arkansas, USA, d. 10 March 1968, Monroe, Louisiana, USA. Reynolds also recorded as Blind Willie Reynolds. He was a wild and violent man with an extensive criminal record, who carried a gun even after he was blinded by a shotgun during an argument in the mid-20s. He played widely in Mississippi and Louisiana, and recorded in 1929 and 1930; the two 78s on which he recorded feature fierce singing and slide guitar, closely allied to the blues styles of Mississippi. His lyrics are caustic, misogynistic, bawdy and sometimes hastily self-censored. His signature tune, 'Outside Woman Blues' was recorded by Cream in the 60s, at which time Reynolds, was still performing in his original milieu, perhaps the last important blues singer of his generation to do so.

Album: *Son House And The Great Delta Blues Singers* (1990).

Rhodes, Eugene

Rhodes' blues singing and guitar were recorded in the Indiana State Penitentiary in the early 60s. As a youth, he had been a travelling one-man-band, and claimed to have met Blind Lemon Jefferson, Buddy Moss and Blind Boy Fuller, being particularly impressed and influenced by the latter pair. Rhodes' repertoire consisted largely of the commercially recorded blues of the late 20s and the 30s, with a few well-known

spirituals; his performance of them was marred by his erratic timing and uncertain pitch.
Album: *Talkin' About My Time* (1963).

Rhodes, Sonny

b. Clarence Edward Smith, 3 November 1940, Smithville, Texas, USA. Rhodes received his first electric guitar at the age of nine and began emulating 'T-Bone' Walker, Chuck Willis (Rhodes still wears a turban), Junior Parker and Bobby Bland. He first recorded in 1961 in Austin, then moved to California two years later and recorded for Galaxy in 1965. In the 70s and 80s he made several mediocre albums for European companies and some interesting singles for Blues Connoisseur, Cleve White's Cherrie label, and his own Rhodes-Way label. In 1991 Rhodes made the best album of his career for Ichiban, highlighting his vocals and songwriting skills in addition to his prowess on both regular and lap steel guitars.
Album: *Disciple Of The Blues* (1991).

Rhodes, Walter

Reportedly from Cleveland, Mississippi, USA, Rhodes was unusual, possibly unique, coming from that state, to be a blues singing accordionist. He had one record issued, cut in 1927, and it seems certain that Charley Patton knew either Rhodes personally or his record; for Patton's 'Banty Rooster Blues' is a cover of Rhodes' 'The Crowing Rooster'. Rhodes played in a band that included two guitars and a fiddle, though only a guitar duo backs him on record. He is said to have died in the 40s after being struck by lightning.
Album: *Memphis Blues* (1987).

Ridgley, Tommy

b. 30 October 1925, New Orleans. Originally a pianist, Ridgley played with a dixieland group and Earl Anderson's band in 1949 before his powerful R&B voice made him one of New Orleans most respected singers for nearly three decades. His first record was 'Shrewsbury Blues', named after a district of the city and produced by Dave Bartholomew for Imperial in 1949. He also recorded the humorous 'Looped' before Ahmet Ertegun's Atlantic label came to record in New Orleans in 1953. The label recorded Ridgley singing 'I'm Gonna Cross That River' and 'Ooh Lawdy My Baby', with Ray Charles on piano. Both were highly popular locally. 'Jam Up', an instrumental with Ridgley on piano, later appeared on anthology albums. In 1957, it was the turn of Al Silver of the New York-based Ember label to fish in the New Orleans talent pool. He recorded Ridgley in a more mellow blues ballad style on 'When I Meet My Girl' and 'I've Heard That Story Before'. At this point, Ridgley turned down a booking at New York's Apollo because 'the money they was offering didn't match up to the money down here'. By now, Ridgley and his band the Untouchables were resident at the New Orleans Auditorium, backing touring rock 'n' roll package shows when they reached Louisiana. Several young singers also started their careers with his group, notably Irma Thomas. In the early 60s, Ridgley recorded for the local Ric label, owned by Joe Ruffino. Among his singles were 'In The Same Old Way' and and Ivory Joe Hunter's 'I Love You Yes I Do'. Later tracks were produced by Wardell Quezergue while in 1973, Ridgley turned to production, having a local hit with 'Sittin' And Drinkin'' by Rose Davis. He remained a familiar figure on the New Orleans music scene throughout the 70s and 80s when Rounder recorded him.
Albums: *Through the Years* (reissue 1984), *New Orleans King Of The Stroll* (1988).

Robey, Don

b. 1 November 1903, Houston, Texas, USA, d. 16 June 1975, Houston, Texas, USA. Houston businessman and impresario Don Robey bought his nightclub, the Bronze Peacock, in 1945, and it soon became a centre for developing local talent as well as bringing in big names from across the country. Soon after, he opened a record shop, which was also to become the base of operations for his Peacock Records, one of the first labels ever in the US to have a black owner. Peacock developed as one of the most important R&B and gospel labels, featuring artists such as Gatemouth Brown, Johnny Ace and Big Mama Thornton, as well as the Dixie Hummingbirds and Five Blind Boys. Robey then bought the Duke label from Memphis, which became another major outlet, especially for Bobby Bland and Junior Parker. Another label, Songbird, also issued gospel records for many years.

Robinson, Banjo Ikey

b. 28 July 1904, Dublin, Virginia, USA. Despite a brief stint with Jelly Roll Morton, recording with Clarence Williams, and providing superb single-string guitar on the records of Georgia White, most of Robinson's work was on the borderline between jazz and popular music. He worked for Wilbur Sweatman and Noble Sissle in New York, and was a member of the Hokum Boys. In Chicago, he played with Carroll Dickerson and Erskine Tate before forming his own band in the 40s. He has continued to be active in music, though on a diminishing scale. Robinson's guitar and banjo work is fast, precise and elaborate, and his singing is likewise clearly enunciated. An all-round entertainer, Robinson, though black, is reminiscent of such black-influenced white musicians as Ukulele Ike (Cliff Edwards).
Album: *Banjo Ikey Robinson* (1986).

Robinson, Bobby

Robinson opened a record shop in Harlem, New York City, USA shortly after World War II, and became an authority on the music scene. His advice was sought by many independent labels. In November 1951 he formed his first record company, Robin Records - which swiftly became Red Robin Records when a southern independent of the same name threatened legal action. He began producing and releasing records by such artists as Morris Lane, Tiny Grimes and Red Prysock, but found greater success with the birth of the New York doo-wop groups, and such acts as the Mello Moods, Vocaleers and the Du Droppers. Red Robin was dissolved in 1956, but many more labels were to follow through to the 60s - Whirlin Disc, Fury, Fire, Fling, Enjoy, and Everlast - mainly issuing classic vocal group numbers by such as the Channels, Velvets, Scarlets, Teenchords, the Delfonics and Gladys Knight And the Pips. These labels occasionally achieved success with single R&B stars like Wilbert Harrison ('Kansas City'), Buster Brown ('Fannie Mae'), Bobby Marchan ('There Is Something On Your Mind'), Lee Dorsey ('Ya Ya'), Lightnin' Hopkins, Elmore James and King Curtis.
In the early 70s Bobby Robinson started a new label, Front Page Records and reactivated his Enjoy label.

Robinson, Fenton

b. 23 September 1935, Greenwood, Mississippi, USA. Although held in high regard by both his peers and audiences, Robinson's mellow voice and jazz-oriented guitar-playing remains a rare pleasure. Robinson took an interest in guitar on hearing T-Bone Walker's Black & White records in 1946 and was helped by local musician, Sammy Hampton. In 1951 he moved to Memphis and received tuition from Charles McGowan, guitarist in Billy 'Red' Love's band. In 1953 he moved to Little Rock, Arkansas to play with Love and Eddie Snow. He formed a band with Larry Davis, then a drummer but later a bass player and guitarist. Robinson made his recording debut in Memphis in 1955, 'Tennessee Woman', for Lester Bihari's Meteor. Two years later, he and Davis recorded for Duke Records in Houston, playing on each other's tracks. Robinson's four Duke records included a remake of 'Tennessee Woman', 'Mississippi Steamboat' and the first version of his most famous song, 'As The Years Go By'. In the 60s, he moved to Chicago and made singles for U.S.A., Palos (his other blues standard, 'Somebody Loan Me A Dime'), Giant and Sound Stage 7. During the 70s, he made two critically-acclaimed albums for Alligator, *Somebody Loan Me A Dime* and *I Hear Some Blues Downstairs*, before personal problems and disillusionment kept him out of music. One album, *Blues In Progress* was made in 1984 with guitarist/arranger Reggie Boyd. In 1989, he headlined the Burnley Blues Festival and recorded the *Special Road* in Holland. Not just a bluesman, Robinson seems too individual a musician to pander to blunatic audiences and his career suffers thereby.
Selected albums: *Somebody Loan Me A Dime* (1974), *I Hear The Blues Downstairs* (1977), *Special Road* (1989).

Robinson, Freddie

b. c.30s, Arkansas, USA. As 'Fred Robertson' he recorded with Little Walter (Jacobs) in the late 50s and by the early 60s he had become a noted guitarist in Chicago, where he recorded for the Queen, M-Pac/One-Der-Ful, and Chess labels. After moving to Los Angeles around 1968, he maintained his links with producer/musician Milton Bland (aka Monk Higgins) and recorded in a jazz context for World Pacific in 1969 and

Rockin' Sidney

as blues and soul guitarist for Enterprise (the Stax subsidiary label) a few years later. In 1977 he recorded for ICA, with which he also worked as a session guitarist, writer, and arranger, mostly in a soul vein. In the 80s he toured and record with Louis Myers.
Albums: *The Coming Atlantis* (1969), *At The Drive-In* reissued as *Black Fox* (1972), *Off The Cuff* (1973).

Robinson, L.C. 'Good Rockin''
b. Louis Charles Robinson, 15 May 1915, Brenham, Texas, USA, d. 26 September 1976. Robinson began playing guitar at nine-years-old, and was reputedly taught to play bottleneck style by Blind Willie Johnson. Western swing musician Leon McAuliffe introduced him to the steel guitar, and Robinson was also a blues fiddler of note and gave Sugarcane Harris some lessons on the instrument. L.C. moved to the San Francisco area around 1939, where he often played together with his brother A.C. Robinson. They recorded for the Black And White label in 1945 as the Robinson Brothers. L.C. recorded for Rhythm in the early 50s, for World Pacific in the 60s, and for Arhoolie and Bluesway in the 70s, and he accompanied Mercy Dee Walton and John Lee Hooker on records. He died of a heart attack in September 1976.
Albums: *Ups And Down* (1971), *House Cleanin' Blues* (1974).

Robinson, 'Lonesome' Jimmy Lee
b. 30 April 1931, Chicago, Illinois, USA. In the 40s, Robinson played blues guitar on Chicago's Maxwell Street, occasionally working with Eddie Taylor. In the 50s he worked in the clubs, associating with artists including Freddie King, Elmore James, and Magic Sam. He became an in-demand session player, both as a bassist and guitarist, and recorded under his own name for the Bandera label in the early 60s. He toured Europe with the *American Folk Blues Festival* in 1965 and again in 1975 with the *American Blues Legends*, recording on both occasions.
Albums: *Chicago Jump* (1979, Bandera recordings), two tracks, plus backing other artists *American Blues Legends '75* (19

Rockin' Sidney
b. Sidney Semien, 9 April 1938, Lebeau, Louisiana, USA. The full range of black South Louisiana music - blues, R&B, swamp pop and zydeco - can be found in the work of Rockin' Sidney, who was born and grew up in the French-speaking part of that state. Many of his records are characterized by a light approach, even his blues tracks frequently opt for melody rather than emotional expression. Nevertheless, he has recorded regularly for over 30 years, from early singles on the local Jin and Goldband labels to albums self-produced in his own studio. In the early 80s, he achieved a wider profile through the success of his song 'Toot Toot'. So far he has not managed to recapture its novelty appeal, despite evident hard work his recent recordings have featured Semien playing all of the instruments. His infectious and accessible songs have done much to widen the appeal of zydeco music in Europe.
Albums: *They Call Me Rockin'* (1975), *Boogie Blues 'N' Zydeco* (1984), *My Toot Toot* (1986), *Creola* (1987), *Crowned Prince Of Zydeco* (1987), *Give Me A Good Time Woman* (1987), *A Celebration Holiday* (1987), *Hotsteppin'* (1987), *My Zydeco Shoes* (1987), *Live With The Blues* (1988).

Rodgers, Sonny
b. Oliver Lee Rodgers, 4 December 1939, Hughes Arkansas, USA, d. 7 May 1990. He learned guitar from his father and was influenced by B.B. King, Robert Nighthawk, and Muddy Waters. After forming his first band at the age of 17, he recorded as accompanist to Forest City Joe Pugh in 1959. Two years later, Rodgers settled in Minneapolis, beginning a long association with Mojo Burford. He also recorded with Burford and Lazy Bill Lucas. In the early 70s Rodgers had a spell as guitarist in Muddy Waters' band, and after some years out of music, he formed his own band in the 80s, winning several music awards in Minnesota. His Blue Moon single 'Big Leg Woman/Cadillac Blues' was voted 'Blues Single Of 1990' in the international W.C. Handy awards. Rodgers only made one full album, which was highly-acclaimed on its release, which tragically coincided with his death on 7 May 1990, just prior to a tour of the UK.
Album: *They Call Me The Cat Daddy* (1990).

Rogers, Jimmy
b. James A. Lane, 3 June 1924, Ruleville, Mississippi, USA. Self-taught on both harmonica

and guitar, Rogers began working at local house parties in his early teens. He then followed an itinerant path, performing in Mississippi and St. Louis, before moving to Chicago in 1939. Rogers frequently took work outside of music, but having played for tips on the city's famed Maxwell Street, began appearing in several clubs and bars. Although he worked as a accompanist with pianist Sunnyland Slim, Rogers established his reputation with the Muddy Waters Band with whom he remained until 1960. The guitarist thus contributed to many of urban blues' finest performances, including 'Hoochie Coochie Man', 'I Got My Mojo Workin'' and the seminal *At Newport*. Rogers also enjoyed a moderately successful career in his own right. 'That's All Right' (1950), credited to Jimmy Rogers And His Trio, featured Waters, Little Walter (harmonica) and Big Crawford (bass) and its popularity around the Chicago area engendered a new group, Jimmy Rogers And His Rocking Four. Several more sessions ensued over the subsequent decade, but the guitarist only enjoyed one national R&B hit when 'Walkin' By Myself' reached number 14 in 1957.

By the 60s Rogers found himself eclipsed by a new generation of guitarists, including Buddy Guy and Magic Sam. Despite enjoying work supporting Sonny Boy Williamson and Howlin' Wolf, he spent much of the decade in seclusion and only re-emerged during the blues revival of the early 70s. He was signed to Leon Russell's Shelter label for whom he completed *Gold Tailed Bird*, a low-key but highly satisfying set. It inspired a period of frenetic live activity which saw Rogers tour Europe on two occasions, with the American Folk Blues Festival (1972) and the Chicago Blues Festival (1973). Appearances in the USA were also well-received, but the artist retired from music during the middle of the decade to work as the manager of an apartment building. However Rogers rejoined Muddy Waters on *I'm Ready* (1977), one of the excellent selections recorded under the aegis of Johnny Winter. These releases brought Waters new dignity towards the end of his career and invested Rogers with a newfound confidence. He continues to perform on the contemporary blues circuit and his 1990 release, *Ludella*, named after the artist's guitar, was produced by Kim Wilson from the Fabulous Thunderbirds.

Albums: *Gold Tailed Bird* (1971), *That's All Right* (1974), *Jimmy Rogers And Left Hand Frank* (1979), *Live: Jimmy Rogers* (1982), *Chicago Blues* (1982), *Feelin' Good* (1985), *Dirty Dozens* (1985), *Ludella* (1990). There have been several compilations and archive releases, including: *Chicago Bound, Golden Years* (1976), *Chess Masters* (1982), *Chicago Blues* (1982), *That's All Right* (1989 - different from above), *Jimmy Rogers Sings The Blues* (1990).

Roland, Walter

b. Birmingham, Alabama, USA, d. c.1970. Although a somewhat obscure character Walter Roland saw something like 40 recordings issued under his own name during the period 1933-35. He is also justly famous for the work he did accompanying Lucille Bogan (Bessie Jackson) and Sonny Scott around the same time. Roland was a skilled pianist, capable of providing sympathetic support to his own and other people's vocal performances as well as displaying a considerable ability in the 'barrel house' style. His own voice was expressive and his blues ran the whole gamut from the deeply introspective through to the cheerfully obscene. Although often only discussed in relationship to the outstanding Bogan, Roland stands on his own as a blues singer and pianist of the first rank whose work deserves to be much better known and appreciated. His 1933 recording 'Jook It, Jook It', a piano solo issued as by the Jolly Jivers, has appeared on many anthologies.

Albums: *The Piano Blues Volume 6: Walter Roland* (1978), *Walter Roland* (1988).

Roomful Of Blues

Formed as a seven-piece band in the Boston, Massachusetts, area in the late 70s. Roomful Of Blues quickly established first a national reputation in the USA with their very authentic-sounding, swing big band R&B, and then broke through on the international scene in the 80s. The group honed their first-hand knowledge of the music by playing with many of the originators, as well as having numerous recordings in their own right. The also recorded behind Big Joe Turner, Eddie 'Cleanhead' Vinson, and Earl King. The group's main successful alumni include guitarists Duke Robillard and Ronnie Earl, vocalist Curtis Salgado, pianist Al Copley, and saxophonist

Greg Piccolo. Despite personnel changes, the group continues to work, though their impact has lessened, due to the plethora of similar groups that have followed in their wake.
Albums: *Hot Little Mama* (1981), *Live At Lupo's Heartbreak Hotel* (1987).

Ross, Doctor

b. Charles Isiah Ross, 21 October 1925, Tunica, Mississippi, USA. Ross had American Indian ancestry. He learned harmonica at the age of nine and was performing with Willie Love and on radio stations in Arkansas and Mississippi in the late 30s. He served in the US Army from 1943-47. His paramedical training there earned Ross the soubriquet of Doctor when he returned to music, leading his Jump And Jive Band and appearing on radio in the *King Bicuit Time Show*. Ross also developed a one-man-band act, which he frequently performed in the 50s and 60s. His Memphis recordings for Sam Phillips in the early 50s included 'Country Clown' and 'The Boogie Disease'. In 1954, he moved to Flint, Michigan to work in an auto factory. Ross continued to perform and in 1958

set up his own DIR label. In the early 60s, Ross benefited from the growing white interest in blues, recording for Pete Welding's Testament label and touring Europe with the 1965 Folk Blues Festival. He returned there during the 70s, recording in London and performing at the Montreux Jazz Festival with Muddy Waters' band.
Albums: *The Flying Eagle* (1966), *Dr Ross, The Harmonica Boss* (1972), *Jivin' The Blues* (1974), *Live At Montreux* (1975), *First Recordings* (reissue 1981).

Rupe, Art

Originally from Pittsburgh and the son of Hungarian immigrants, Rupe had moved to Los Angeles as a teenager to attend University of California at Los Angeles. His first involvement in the record business was as a partner in the small Atlas Records, which was notable for being the first label to record Johnny Moore's Three Blazers and Frankie Laine. Despite this, Atlas failed in its first year, and with diminished savings Rupe founded Jukebox Records in 1944. The first release on Jukebox, 'Boogie #1'

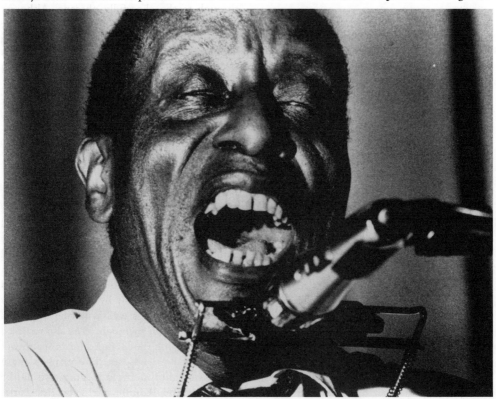

Doctor Ross

by the Sepia Tones, sold about 70,000 copies. While the following year the label added Roy Milton's Solid Senders to its roster and had immediate success with 'R.M. Blues' in 1946, at which point Jukebox became Specialty Records. Specialty went from strength to strength throughout the late 40s with records by Jimmy Liggins And His Drops Of Joy, Camille Howard and, at the turn of the decade, Joe Liggins and Percy Mayfield. The label also recorded some of the era's finest In early 1952 Rupe made his first trip to New Orleans to find a 'Fats Domino' for Specialty Records, and instead he came away with Lloyd Price and 'Lawdy, Miss Clawdy', which shot to number 1 on the R&B charts and became one of the first funky R&B records to be bought in large quantities by white Americans. Later in the 50s, this New Orleans connection led to artists such as of Larry Williams, Earl King, Art Neville, Guitar Slim and, of course, Little Richard. Owing mainly to the success of Little Richard and his many hit records, Specialty continued to flourish during the rock 'n' roll years with secular recordings by Sam Cooke among others, but after the

departure of Richard and Cooke in the late 50s, Rupe began to direct his business acumen towards movies and real estate. However, he and his family have maintained the Specialty label, whose treasured reissues continue to sell to R&B, rock 'n' roll and gospel fans, to this day.

Rush, Otis

b. 29 April 1934, Philadelphia, Mississippi, USA. A left-handed blues guitarist, Rush moved to Chicago where his impassioned singing and playing on 'I Can't Quit You Baby' brought a Top 10 R&B hit in 1956. This and other Cobra recordings ('Double Trouble', 'All Your Love') from the same era inspired British guitarists such as Peter Green and Mick Taylor who strived to re-create the starkly emotive quality of his solos. In the early 60s, Rush recorded for Chess and Duke where 'So Many Roads' and 'Homework' were his best-known songs. As blues declined in popularity with black audiences, he turned increasingly to college concerts and collaborations with white blues artists such as Mike Bloomfield, with whom he made an album for Cotillion in 1969. During the 70s,

Otis Rush

Rush toured Europe and Japan, recording in Sweden, France and Japan as well as making two albums for Chicago-based label Delmark. *Right Place Wrong Time* had been made in 1971 for Capitol with producer Nick Gravenites, but was only issued on the independent Bullfrog label five years later. He performed and toured less frequently in the 80s, although an album made at the 1985 San Francisco Blues Festival showed him to be on top form.

Albums: *Chicago - The Blues - Today !* (1964), *Mourning In The Morning* (1969), *Cold Place In Hell* (1975), *Right Place, Wrong Time* (1976), *So Many Roads* (1978), *Troubles, Troubles* (1978), *Screamin' And Cryin'* (1979), *Tops* (1985).

S

Sane, Dan

b. c.1895, Hernando, Mississippi, USA, d. c.1971, Osceola, Arkansas, USA. Sane, sometimes identified as Dan Sain and also as Dan Sing, was an unobtrusive, but important member of the Memphis blues community up to the 50s. He only ever sang on an unissued recording, and it was as a ragtime-influenced guitarist that he made his mark. He recorded as a member of the band led by Jack Kelly, accompanying the singing of violinist Will Batts, a fellow band member, and guitarist Frank Stokes. He recorded fairly extensively, with the latter producing percussive but effortlessly nimble flat-picked figures that meshed with Stokes' rhythm guitar to form one of the most impressive series of two-guitar arrangements in blues.

Albums: *The Beale Street Sheiks* (1990), *Frank Stokes* (1990), *Jack Kelly & His South Memphis Jug Band* (1990).

Savoy Brown

Formed in 1966 as the Savoy Brown Blues Band, this institution continues to be led by founding guitarist Kim Simmonds. The original line-up comprising Simmonds, Brice Portius (vocals), Ray Chappell (bass), John O'Leary (harmonica), Bob Hall (piano) and Leo Mannings (drums), were featured on early sessions for producer Mike Vernon's Purdah label, before a second guitarist, Martin Stone, joined in place of O'Leary. The re-shaped sextet then secured a recording deal with Decca. Their debut *Shake Down*, was a competent appraisal of blues favourites, featuring material by Freddie King, Albert King and Willie Dixon.

Unhappy with this reverential approach, Simmonds pulled the group apart, retaining Hall on an auxiliary basis and adding Chris Youlden (vocals), Dave Peverett (guitar/vocals), Rivers Jobe (bass) and Roger Earl (drums). The new line-up completed 'Getting To The Point' before Jobe was replaced by Tone Stevens. The restructured unit was an integral part of the British blues boom. In Youlden they possessed a striking frontman, resplendent in bowler hat and monocle, whose confident, mature delivery added panache to the group's repertoire. Their original songs matched those they chose to cover, while the Simmonds/Peverett interplay added fire to Savoy Brown's live performances. 'Train To Nowhere', from *Blue Matter*, has since become one of the genre's best-loved recordings. Youlden left the group following *Raw Sienna*, but the inner turbulence afflicting the group culminated at the end of 1970 when Peverett, Stevens and Earl walked out to form Foghat.

Simmonds meanwhile toured America with a restructured line-up - Dave Walker (vocals), Paul Raymond (keyboards), Andy Pyle (bass) and Dave Bidwell (drums) - setting a precedent for Savoy Brown's subsequent development. Having honed a simple, blues-boogie style, the guitarist now seemed content to repeat it and the group's ensuing releases are of decreasing interest. Simmonds later settled in America, undertaking gruelling tours with musicians who become available, his determination both undeterred and admirable.

Albums: *Shake Down* (1967), *Getting To The Point* (1968), *Blue Matter* (1969), *A Step Further* (1969), *Raw Sienna* (1970), *Looking In* (1970), *Street Corner Talking* (1971), *Hellbound Train* (1972), *Lion's Share* (1972), *Jack The Toad* (1973), *Boogie Brothers* (1974), *Wire Fire* (1975),

Skin 'N' Bone (1976), *Savage Return* (1978), *Rock 'N' Roll Warriors* (1981), *Just Live* (1981), *A Hard Way To Go* (1985), *Make Me Sweat* (1988). Compilations: *The Best Of Savoy Brown* (1977), *Blues Roots* (1978), *Highway Blues* (1985).

Sayles, Charlie

b. 4 January 1948, Woburn, Massachusetts, USA. Sayles only became acquainted with the blues when he heard a record by B.B. King during his US military service in Vietnam, and began to take a serious interest in playing harmonica in 1971. During the 70s he played frequently on the streets in cities across the country, and was put on the bill of several folk festivals. His original blues compositions, raw, amplified harmonica and direct singing were captured on vinyl in 1976, when he was playing in New York. Sayles began working with a small band around 1980, but he still remains largely an uncompromising street and solo performer. In 1990 he recorded for the JSP label, to coincide with a British tour.
Albums: *The Raw Harmonica Blues Of Charlie Sayles* (1976), *Night Ain't Right* (1990).

Scott, Isaac

b. 11 June 1945, Pine Bluff, Arkansas, USA. Scott's family moved to the west coast in the late 40s, settling in Portland, Oregon, and Isaac was exposed to both gospel music and blues as a youngster. Until the 70s he worked with gospel groups, but in 1974 he chose to concentrate on blues, while he was living in Seattle, Washington. His guitar playing reflects the influence of Albert Collins, and his singing and repertoire reveal strong elements of blues, soul, and gospel. Scott has had two albums released by Red Lightnin' and live material has been issued by Solid Smoke and Criminal.
Albums: *Isaac Scott Blues Band* (1978), *Big Time Blues Man* (1983).

Scott, Marylin

Other than her records, almost nothing is known about Marylin Scott. One of her record companies had an address for her in Norfolk, Virginia, USA, and her first recording session was held in Charlotte, North Carolina, so an origin in the South Eastern states of the USA seems probable. Between 1945-51 she recorded blues and R&B as Scott, and gospel as Mary

Deloach. There was also a further gospel record in the mid-60s. Some of her records feature acoustic instruments and a fairly traditional sound, while others are in a more contemporary vein, with a small band for the R&B numbers, and organ and backing vocals for the gospel. In whatever setting, she performed with skill and conviction, and seemed to have few problems reconciling the sacred and secular sides of her musical personality.
Albums: *The Uneasy Blues* (1988), *I Got What Daddy Like* (1988).

Seals, Son

b. Frank Seals Jnr., 13 August 1942, Osceola, Arkansas, USA. Son Seals was one of 13 children of Jim Seals, an entertainer and club owner in rural Arkansas. Son began his musical education on the drums and worked with many of the later famous musicians who travelled through the area. Having taught himself to play the guitar, he formed his own band to work around the city of Little Rock. He moved to Chicago in 1971, initially to work outside music, although he soon began to appear at local clubs. In 1973, he signed to the Alligator label and recorded his first album. Since then, he has become well-known on the blues scene both in the USA and in Europe. Edging towards the 'soul blues' category his career has gained strength, particularly with the release of the well-received album *Bad Axe*, although he has not yet fully-achieved the attention he deserves.
Albums: *Son Seals* (1973), *Midnight Son* (1975), *Chicago Fire* (1980), *Bad Axe* (1984), *Live 'N' Burnin'* (1988), *Living In The Danger Zones* (1991).

Sears, Zenas 'Daddy'

A respected white Atlanta, Georgia, jazz and pop disc jockey, Sears began programming jump blues and R&B records in January 1946. In 1948, he took a job at the state-owned radio station WGST, on the condition that he would be allowed a nightly blues show, *The Blues Caravan*. Due to his success with this format, he was able to expand the show to include talent shows which he broadcast live from Atlanta theatres such as Decatur Street's 81 Theatre. Here he discovered local singers such as Tommy Brown, Billy Wright, Chuck Willis (whom he managed in the early to mid-50s, and got him

Son Seals

his first recording contract with OKeh Records) and Little Richard. These artists were invariably backed by the Blues Caravan All Stars, a group of local musicians which included John Peek and Roy Mays. In 1954, Georgia's new governor banned Sears' programme from the WGST, and Sears formed WAOK (where he remains to this day). He continued with his policy to play the best of black music - in 1959 he recorded Ray Charles' set at the WAOK 5th Anniversary Party which Atlantic issued as the best-selling *Ray Charles In Person*. In the late 50s and 60s, Sears became involved with Dr Martin Luther King and the SCLC, and his position with the radio station allowed him to spread his views on integration and equal rights.

Sellers, Brother John

b. 27 May 1924, Clarksdale, Mississippi, USA. Raised by his godmother after his family broke up in the aftermath of a flood, Sellers moved to Chicago in the 30s, and began his professional career in gospel. He subsequently toured with Mahalia Jackson in the 40s. His religious convictions never excluded blues, and he recorded in both genres from 1945. He was quick to see the growing market among whites for black music, and was working festivals and white clubs by the early 50s. In 1957 he came to Europe with Big Bill Broonzy. After Broonzy's death his star began to wane as research uncovered more intuitive blues singers, whose approach was regarded as more 'authentic' than Sellers' stagey and rather inflexible singing. He has continued to make solo appearances, and has been with the Alvin Ailey Dance Company (as a musician) since the early 60s.
Albums: *Brother John Sellers Sings Blues And Folk Songs* (1954), *In London* (1957), *Big Boat Up The River* (1959), *Baptist Shouts And Gospel Songs* (1959).

Semien, 'Ivory' Lee

b. 13 September 1931, Washington, Louisiana, USA. Having played music from his early years, Ivory Lee settled in Houston in his teens and began to play in the blues clubs in that city, making his first records as a vocalist in the early 50s. He took up as drummer with the great slide guitarist Hop Wilson, and they made a number of records together, some with Wilson as leader, others - including his best known song 'Rockin'

In The Coconut Top' with Semien himself on vocals. In the early 60s, he started his own record label, Ivory Records, whose best known releases featured some magnificent blues by Wilson. He remained an active musician in Houston, at least on a semi-professional basis, although making little impact outside.
Albums: *Rockin' Blues Party* (1987), *Steel Guitar Flash* (1988).

Seward, Alec

b. 16 March 1902, Charles City, Virginia, USA, d. 11 May 1972, New York City, New York, USA. Raised in Newport News, Virginia, Seward was a semi-professional blues singer and guitarist from the age of 18. In 1923, he moved to New York, where he became an associate of Sonny Terry and Brownie McGhee. He recorded with Louis Hayes under a variety of colourful pseudonyms, including Guitar Slim & Jelly Belly, the Blues King and the Back Porch Boys, and with Terry and Woody Guthrie for the nascent folk audience. His music was typical of the southeast, being gentle, relaxed, and ragtime influenced. By 1960, when mental illness ended Hayes' musical career, Seward was also largely retired. He recorded again in the mid-60s, but was little heard of thereafter.
Albums: *Creepin' Blues* (1965), *Carolina Blues* (c.1972), *Late One Saturday Evening* (1975).

Shad, Bob

b. 12 February 1920, New York City, New York, USA, d. 13 March 1985, Los Angeles, California, USA. Shad entered record production in the 40s, producing jazz (including Charlie Parker) and blues and R&B (including Dusty Fletcher) for Savoy, National and other companies. In 1948 he founded Sittin' In With, initially recording jazz, but concluded that there was a bigger market for blues, which the majors were neglecting; he cut material by Lightnin' Hopkins, Sonny Terry and Brownie McGhee, and the last sides by Curley Weaver. On field trips to the South, Shad recorded Smokey Hogg and Peppermint Harris (including his hit 'Rainin' In My Heart') on portable equipment. In 1951, he joined Mercury as A&R director, producing Patti Page, Vic Damone and the Platters as well as blues sessions by Hopkins, Big Bill Broonzy and others, and launching the jazz marque Emarcy, for which he made important sessions with Sarah Vaughan, Maynard Ferguson, Dinah Washington (her first with strings) and many others. After leaving Mercury, Shad founded Mainstream, which issued, besides his Sittin' In With material, jazz by such as Shelly Manne and Dizzy Gillespie, and Sarah Vaughan's collaborations with Michel Legrand. Shad also produced rock artists, making the first recordings of Janis Joplin and Ted Nugent, and remained active with Mainstream through the 70s.

Shade, Will
b. 5 February 1898, Memphis, Tennessee, USA, d. 18 September 1966, Memphis, Tennessee, USA. Although named after his father, Will Shade was raised by his grandmother Annie Brimmer and was often known around Memphis as Son Brimmer. He took an early interest in music and played guitar and harmonica. He worked as a musician in and around Memphis, sometimes joining the medicine shows which visited the city. Sometime in the 20s he formed the Memphis Jug Band, a shifting conglomeration of local talent that included at different times Charlie Burse, Will 'Casey Bill' Weldon, Furry Lewis, Jab Jones, and Ben Ramey. The popularity of this group, whose work ranged from knock-about, good-time dance numbers to moving blues performances, was at its peak during the years 1927-34 after which they ceased to record but remained mainstays of the local scene. The group often supported singers such as Jenny Mae Clayton, Shade's wife, and Memphis Minnie, at one time married to Will Weldon. Shade enjoyed a brief second career when, in the company of Charlie Burse, he recorded for the Folkways and Rounder labels in the early 60s. He death was due to pneumonia.
Albums: *Memphis Jug Band 1927-1930 (3 volumes)*(1991), *Memphis Jug Band 1932-34* (1991).

Shakey Jake
b. James D. Harris, 12 April 1921, Earle, Arkansas, USA, d. 2 March 1990, Pine Bluff, Arkansas, USA. A professional gambler when not playing harmonica (his nickname was derived from the crapshooters' call 'Shake 'em, Jake'), Harris began playing in Chicago blues bands during the late 40s. He recorded a single

in 1958, on which his contribution was overshadowed by that of his nephew Magic Sam. During the 60s he recorded two albums that did not do him justice, as club recordings with Sam make evident. His encouragement of younger musicians brought about the recording debut of, among others, Luther Allison, with whom Jake recorded his best album after moving to Los Angeles. In later years, occasional recordings appeared, including some on his own label, and Harris ran a blues club for a while, but was dogged by poor health, and isolated by neighbourhood gang violence.
Albums: *Good Times* (1960), *Mouth Harp Blues* (1961), *Further On Up The Road* (1969), *The Devil's Harmonica* (1972), *Magic Rocker* (1980), *Magic Touch* (1983), *The Key Won't Fit* (c.1985).

Shaw, Allen
b. c.1890, Henning, Tennessee, USA, d. 1940, Tipton County, Tennessee, USA. A travelling man, remembered all through western Tennessee and in Memphis, Shaw played forceful steel guitar, and sang the blues in an exultant voice on his one issued record, cut in 1934 with Willie Borum on second guitar. On one title, Shaw played impeccably sensitive yet very powerful slide guitar. Shaw and Borum also backed Hattie Hart at this session. Shaw's son, Willie Tango, reckoned to be a better guitarist than his father, never recorded (though he was the subject of a song recorded by Memphis Minnie).
Compilation: *Memphis Blues* (1990).

Shaw, Eddie
b. 20 March 1937, Benoit, Mississippi, USA. Shaw grew up in neighbouring Greenville and learned to play clarinet and trombone before choosing the saxophone. He played with local jump-blues bands (including one led by Ike Turner) and sat in with Muddy Waters in 1957. Muddy hired him immediately and he moved to Chicago. Once there he associated with Howlin' Wolf and Magic Sam, and recorded with both. He also fronted his own band on vocals and saxophone. Eddie also ran the 1815 Club in Chicago, wrote and arranged songs for other artists, learned to play blues harmonica, and has recorded as bandleader for Mac Simmons' label, for Alligator's *Living Chicago Blues* project, and for Isabel and Rooster.

Albums: *Have Blues - Will Travel* (1979), *Movin' And Groovin' Man* (1982).

Shaw, Robert

b. 9 August 1908, Staffons, Texas, USA. One of the great Texas barrelhouse piano players, Shaw was raised on his father's cattle ranch. His mother played piano and guitar. From his mid-20s he started playing for local parties. Eventually he left home to work as an itinerant pianist in bordellos, juke-joints and barrelhouses throughout Texas and up as far as Kansas City, Missouri. In 1935 he settled in Austin, Texas working outside music running a food market, with occasional private party work, into the 70s. He played the Berlin Jazz Festival in 1974 and Montreux in 1975. Nat Hentoff referred to him as a 'gruff easeful blues singer telling stories that came out of his audience's lives.
Album: *Texas Barrelhouse Piano* (1980).

Shaw, Thomas

b. 4 March 1908, Brenham, Texas, USA, d. 24 February 1977, San Diego, California, USA. Shaw was taught harmonica and guitar by relatives while still quite young, developing his blues style through his collaborations with more famous artists of the day, Blind Lemon Jefferson and Ramblin' Thomas. Having spent much of his youth travelling throughout Texas, he settled in California in 1934. There he continued his musical activities, appearing on radio and setting up his own club, which ran for many years. In the 60s, he became a minister at a San Diego church, but he was also taken up by the blues revival, and made his first recordings, in which the Jefferson influence was especially notable. He appeared at folk festivals and toured in Europe in 1972.
Album: *Born In Texas* (1974).

Shines, John Ed 'Johnny'

b. 26 April 1915, Frayser, Tennessee, USA, d. 20 April 1992. Johnny Shines was taught to play the guitar by his mother and sometimes worked the streets of Memphis for tips with a group of other youths. In 1932 he set up as a sharecropper in Hughes, Arkansas, but still worked part time as a musician. During the 30s he hoboed around the work camp and juke joint circuit in the company of such men as Robert Johnson, with whom he appeared on a

radio show in 1937. His ramblings took him as far as Canada. In 1941 he took the trail north to Chicago where he sometimes performed in the famous Maxwell Street market before forming his own group to play the clubs; he sometimes doubled as house photographer. Despite being respected by his fellow musicians and occasionally recording under the name Shoe Shine Johnny, his career did not take off until the 60s when his slide guitar and strong, emotive vocals were seen as a direct link with Delta blues, then much in vogue. From then on Johnny Shines went from strength to strength, touring the USA, Europe and Japan, with great success often in the company of Robert Lockwood. Shines was an intelligent and articulate man who was fully aware of his position in the blues world and made the most of his late opportunities. Concerned about the quality of life offered to his children in the northern cities, he moved back to the south where he suffered a heart attack that affected his playing. His recovery was slow and although still played guitar he was unable to return to the dazzling proficiency of his earlier days.
Albums: *Masters Of The Modern Blues* (1966), *Last Night Dream* (1968), *With Big Walter Horton* (1970), *Standing At The Crossroads* (1970), *Sitting On Top Of The World* (1972), *Nobody's Fault But Mine* (1973), *Hey Ba Ba Re Bop* (1978), *Johnny Shines Live 1974* (1989), with Snooky Pryor *Back To The Country* (1993).

Short, J.D.

b. 26 December 1902, Port Gibson, Mississippi, USA, d. November 1962. Short grew up in various parts of Mississippi where he learned guitar from Willie Johnson and piano from Son Harris. In 1923, Short moved to St Louis where he was discovered by Jessie Stone. He recorded country blues for Paramount (1930) and Vocalion (1932), but spent most of the 30s playing clarinet in a St Louis jazz group. Short was crippled by a wartime injury but continued performing after 1945, often as a guitar/harmonica/bass drum one-man-band and sometimes with his cousin Big Joe Williams. The duo worked together on Short's final recording for Sonet, recreating on tracks like 'Starry Crown Blues', the music of their early years in the South. Short died a few months later, in November 1962.

Albums: *The Legacy Of The Blues Vol 8* (1962).

Shower, 'Little' Hudson
b. 6 September 1919, Anguilla, Mississippi, USA. Little Hudson (as he was known on records) had been playing guitar for some years when he moved to Chicago at the age of 20. There he began to play on the flourishing blues scene, and eventually started his own group, the Red Devils Trio. He made some records in 1953, for the JOB label with his band including pianist Lazy Bill Lucas, but otherwise remained obscure. A very short recording, originally made as a radio advertisement, has been unearthed and issued in more recent years.
Albums: *John Brim And Little Hudson* (1981), *Southside Screamers* (1984).

Siegal-Schwall Blues Band
Corky Siegel (vocals/harmonica) and Jim Schwall (guitar/vocals) began working as a duo in April 1965. As such they made several appearances in Chicago's south-side clubs, prior to securing a date at the prestigious *Pepper's*. Here they used a temporary rhythm section - Bob Anderson (bass) and Billy Davenport (drums) before replacing them with Jos Davidson and Russ Chadwick. Although an electric ensemble, the group's early albums were less intense than those of contemporaries, the Paul Butterfield Blues Band and Charlie Musselwhite's South Side Blues Band. Siegal-Schwall offered a lighter perspective, reliant on a collective effort rather than virtuoso soloing. Siegal was, nonetheless, an accomplished harmonica player and the group retained an in-concert popularity throughout the 60s. The two founder members remained at the helm through several line-up alterations, but the band split up in 1974 following the release of the highly unusual *Three Pieces For Blues Band And Orchestra* by William Russo. Siegal and Schwall were reunited 14 years later to celebrate the 15th anniversary of radio station WXRT-FM, on which the group had performed during its inauguration.
Albums: *The Siegal-Schwall Band* (1966), *Say Siegal-Schwall* (1967), *Shake!* (1968), *Siegal-Schwall 70* (1970), *Siegal-Schwall Band* (1971), *Sleepy Hollow* (1972), *953 West* (1973), *Three Pieces For Blues Band And Orchestra* (1973), *Live Last Summer* (1974), *RIP Siegal-Schwall* (1974), *Siegal-Schwall Reunion Concert* (1988). Compilation: *The Best Of The Siegal-Schwall Band* (1974).

Simmons, 'Little' Mac(k)
b. 25 January 1934, Twist, Arkansas, USA. Simmons is one of the stalwarts of the Chicago club scene; he taught himself harmonica as a youngster and in the early 50s sometimes worked with bluesman on the Saint Louis, Missouri, club circuit, before settling in Chicago in 1954. Since the late 60s he has recorded for many small local labels, and occasionally larger companies such as Checker. He has run his own label and club from time to time and has recorded blues, gospel (he was known for a time as 'Reverend Mac Simmons') and soul. His version of 'Rainy Night In Georgia', performed as a harmonica instrumental, was a local hit in the early 70s. He toured Europe in 1975.
Album: *Blue Lights* (1976).

Sims, Clarence 'Guitar'
b. New Orleans, Louisiana, USA. Sims was initially inspired to sing the blues on hearing Tommy McClennan's recording of 'Bottle Up And Go', and later vocal influences included Nappy Brown, Fats Domino, Louis Jordon and Lloyd Price. In 1955 Sims moved to Los Angeles, where he appeared on talent shows and in clubs. Two years later, he moved to San Francisco's Fillmore district and assumed the profession name 'Fillmore Slim' and recorded for the Dooto, Kent, and Dore labels. In the late 60s he also appeared on disc as 'Ron Silva'. However, Sims was incarcerated between 1980 and 1985; it was during this time that he began to play guitar seriously. Following his release, he recorded a promising album for Troyce Keys's label in February 1987 and continues to play around the west coast. His age at the time of recording was given as 53 years old.
Album: *Born To Sing The Blues* (1987).

Sims, Frankie Lee
b. 30 April 1917, New Orleans, Louisiana, USA, d. 10 May 1970. Despite his birthplace, Sims' music is very much in the blues vein of Texas, where he moved in childhood. On his earliest records, for the Blue Bonnet label, in 1947-48, he played a traditional fingerstyle guitar, but later developed an electric style of his

own, riffing behind the vocals, filling the breaks with exciting, often distorted flashes of lead. His best known song was 'Lucy Mae', which he recorded several times, most successfully with Specialty in 1953. Later recordings on Ace and Vin developed his rocking style still further with a small band, but they marked the end of his brief period of success. A New York session in 1960 remained unissued until well after his death.
Albums: *Lucy Mae Blues* (1970), *Walking With Frankie* (1985).

Singer, Harold 'Hal'
b. 8 October 1919, Tulsa, Oklahoma, USA. After beginning his musical tuition on the violin at the age of eight, Singer switched to clarinet and, finally, tenor saxophone which he played with various big bands in the 40s - notably Ernie Fields and Tommy Douglas (both 1941), Nat Towles (1942), Jay McShann (1942-43), Roy Eldridge (1944) and Lucky Millinder and Oran 'Hot Lips' Page (both 1947). After appearing on various jazz and R&B records in the late 40s - he played tenor on Wynonie Harris' 'Good Rocking Tonight' - he was recommended to Savoy Records by his close friend, Don Byas, and began a run of instrumental hits in 1948 with a tune that would furnish him with a life-long nickname - 'Cornbread'. He later went to Mercury (1950), Coral (1951-52), returning to Savoy in 1952 to play as both session musician and to usher in the new musical era with his own 'Rock & Roll' and 'Hot Rod'. In the late 50s he recorded R&B for Time, DeLuxe and King and blues and jazz for Prestige and in the 60s recorded a jazz album for Strand before moving to France where he maintained a steady, if unexciting, living recording for French Polydor, Black & Blue and Futura. In the 80s, Hal made a comeback with guest spots on records by Booker T. Laury, Jimmy Witherspoon, and Rocket 88, as well his own excellent *Swing On It*, on England's JSP Records.
Albums: with Charlie Shavers *Blue Stompin'* (1959), *Shades Of Blue* (1963), with Milt Buckner *Milt And Hal* (1966), *Paris Soul Food* (1969), *Blues And News* (1971), with Paul Williams, Big Jay McNeely, Sam 'The Man' Taylor and Lee Allen *Honkers & Screamers - Roots Of Rock 'N' Roll Vol. 6* (1979), *Swing On It*

(1981), *Rent Party* (1984).

Small, Drink
b. c.1934, Bishopville, South Carolina, USA. Small began playing guitar at the age of four and began his musical career while in high school, playing in secular groups and singing bass in a church choir. In the 50s he worked and recorded with the Spiritualaires of Columbia, South Columbia and *Metronome* magazine voted him Top Gospel Guitarist during his time with the group. In 1959 he returned to South Carolina and began working as a blues musician, recording the same year for the Sharp label. He has since recorded for his own Bishopville label, and for the Southland company, and he enjoyed a lot of attention following the release of a cassette album (from folk-blues to disco-blues), and followed it up with another well-received set a year later.
Albums: *The Blues Doctor* (1990), *Round Two* (1991).

Smith, Bessie
b. 15 April 1894, Chattanooga, Tennessee, USA, d. 26 September 1937. In her childhood, Smith sang on street corners before joining a touring black minstrel show as a dancer. Also in the show was Ma Rainey and before long the young newcomer was also singing the blues. The older woman encouraged Smith, despite the fact that even at this early stage in her career her powerful voice was clearly heralding a major talent who would one day surpass Rainey. By 1920 Smith was headlining a touring show and was well on the way to becoming the finest singer of the blues the USA would ever hear. Despite changing fashions in music in the northern cities of New York and Chicago, Smith was a success wherever she performed and earning her billing as the Empress of the Blues. For all her successes elsewhere, however, her real empire was in the South, where she played theatres on the Theatre Owners' Booking Association circuit, packing in the crowds for every show. Although she was not among the first blues singers to make records, when she did they sold in huge numbers, rescuing more than one recording company from the brink of bankruptcy. The records, on which her accompanists included Louis Armstrong and Joe Smith, consolidated her position as the leading

Bessie Smith

blues singer of her generation, but here too fashion dictated a shift in attitude. By 1928 her recording career was effectively over and personal problems, which stemmed from drink and poor judgement over her male companions, helped begin a drift from centre-stage. It was during this fallow period that she made her only film appearance, in *St Louis Blues* (1929), with James P. Johnson and members of the recently disbanded Fletcher Henderson Orchestra. She continued to perform, however, still attracting a faithful if diminished following. In 1933 John Hammond organized a record date, on which she was accompanied by, amongst others, Jack Teagarden and Coleman Hawkins, which proved to be her last. The following year she was in a highly successful touring show and in 1935 appeared at the Apollo Theatre in New York to great acclaim. In her private life she had a new companion, a showbiz-loving bootlegger named Richard Morgan, an uncle of Lionel Hampton, who brought her new stability. With the growing reawakening of interest in the earlier traditions of American music and another film planned, this should have been the moment for Smith's career to revive, but on 26 September 1937 she was fatally injured while being driven by Morgan to an engagement in Mississippi.

Smith's recordings range from uproarious vaudeville songs to slow blues; to the former she brought a reflection of her own frequently bawdy lifestyle, while the latter are invariably imbued with deeply felt emotions. All are delivered in a rich contralto matched by a majestic delivery. Every one of her recordings is worthy of attention, but especially important to an understanding of the blues and Smith's paramount position in its history are those made with Armstrong and Smith. Even in such stellar company, however, it is the singer who holds the attention. She was always in complete control, customarily refusing to work with a drummer and determinedly setting her own, usually slow, tempos. Indeed, on some recordings her entrance, after an opening chorus by her accompanists, noticeably slows the tempo. On her final record date she makes a gesture towards compromise by recording with musicians attuned to the imminent swing era, but she is still in charge. Her influence is impossible to measure, so many of her

contemporaries drew from her that almost all subsequent singers in the blues field and in some areas of jazz have stylistic links with the 'Empress of the Blues'. Many years after her death she was still the subject of plays and books, several of which perpetuated the myth that her death was a result of racial prejudice or used her to promulgate views not necessarily relevant to the singer's life. Fortunately, one of the books, Chris Albertson's *Bessie,* is an immaculately researched and well-written account of the life, times and music of one of the greatest figures in the history of American music.

Selected albums: *Any Woman's Blues (1923-30)* (1974), *Nobody's Blues But Mine (1925-27)* (1979), *St Louis Blues (1929)* (1981, film soundtrack), *The Bessie Smith Collection - 20 Golden Greats* (1985), *The Empresss (1924-28)* (1986), *Jazz Classics In Digital Stereo* (1986), *The World's Greatest Blues Singer* (1987), *The Bessie Smith Story (1924-33)* (1989).

Further reading: *Bessie,* Chris Albertson.

Smith, Byther

b. 17 April 1933, Monticello, Mississippi, USA. Smith began playing guitar in church, but after settling in Chicago in 1958 he started singing blues and was tutored on guitar by Herbert Sumlin and Freddie Robinson. He recorded for several local labels (including, reputedly, Cobra and VeeJay), and worked with numerous gospel and blues groups, occasionally sitting in with his cousin JB Lenoir.In the late 60s he left music, returning in the early 70s as house guitarist at the famed Theresa's Lounge in Chicago, and enjoying a minor hit for CJ Records with 'Give Me My White Robe'. In 1983, Smith recorded an acclaimed album for Grits, with the Follow-up two years later being reissued in 1991; Byther has also recorded for JSP. Smith is a modern, though traditionally-rooted Chicago bluesman with a very large repertoire.

Selected albums: *Tell Me How You Like It* (1985), *Addressing The Nation With The Blues* (1989), *Housefire* (1991, reissue).

Smith, Carrie

b. 25 August 1941, Fort Gaines, Georgia, USA. Smith appeared at the 1957 Newport Jazz Festival as a member of a New Jersey church choir, but her solo professional career did not take off until the early 70s. An appearance with

Dick Hyman and the New York Jazz Repertory Orchestra at Carnegie Hall in 1974 should have alerted audiences to her exceptional qualities, but for the rest of the decade she was much better received in Europe than in the USA. Her tours of festivals and concert halls were sometimes as a single, but also in company with NYJRO, Tyree Glenn, the World's Greatest Jazz Band and others. Smith's style is rooted in the blues and gospel but her repertoire is wide, encompassing many areas of 20th-century popular music. Her voice is deep and powerful and she is especially effective in live performances. Although her reputation has grown throughout the 80s, she still remains much less well known than her considerable talent warrants.

Albums: with Dick Hyman *Satchmo Remembered* (1974), *Do Your Duty* (1976), *When You're Down And Out* (1977), *Carrie Smith* (1978), with others *Highlights In Jazz Anniversary Concert* (1985).

Smith, Clara

b. c.1894, Spartanburg, South Carolina, USA, d. 2 February, 1935. Singing professionally from her mid-teens in theatres and tent shows throughout the Deep South, by 1923 Smith was a big name in New York. She sang in Harlem clubs, opening her own very popular and successful Clara Smith Theatrical Club. She was signed by Columbia to make records, on some of which she duetted with Bessie Smith (a partnership that ended when they came to blows). Her instrumental accompanists on record included Louis Armstrong, Lonnie Johnson and James P. Johnson. She worked constantly throughout the late 20s and into the early 30s, mostly in New York but with occasional short tours and residencies at clubs in other cities. She died suddenly from a heart attack on 2 February 1935. Smith sang the blues in a lowdown, dragging manner, creating dirge-like yet often deeply sensual interpretations.

Album: *Clara Smith, Vols. 1-7 (1923-32)* (1974).

Smith, Clarence 'Pine Top'

b. 11 January 1904, Troy, Alabama, USA, d. 15 March 1929, Chicago, Illinois, USA. Often considered to be the founder of the boogie woogie style of piano playing, Smith was actually a vaudeville performer. From his mid-teens, he toured tent shows and theatres as a

pianist and dancer. He gradually concentrated on piano and, encouraged by Charles 'Cow Cow' Davenport, made a handful of records. Smith's style was largely in the mould of humorous songs backed up by vigorous two-handed playing. His small list of recordings also included blues but his fame rests, more than anything, on his recording of 'Pine Top's Boogie Woogie' (1928). This song represents, possibly, the first documented use of the term. His work on the circuits took him all over the south with such artists as Butterbeans And Susie and Ma Rainey, but it was in Chicago that his promising career was cut short when he was accidentally shot by a man named David Bell during a skirmish in a dance hall. He was 25 and left a wife and two children. He has been recorded by many artists over the years, 'Pine Top's boogie woogie' remains as satisfying today as it was when it made its initial impact in 1928.

Album: *Pine Top Smith And Romeo Nelson* (1987).

Smith, George

b. 22 April 1924, Helena, Arkansas, USA, d. 2 October 1983, Los Angeles, USA. A master of amplified and chromatic blues harmonica, Smith made a stunning debut in 1954 with 'Telephone Blues'/'Blues In The Dark', but failed to capture the audience which elevated Little Walter to stardom. This may have been because his west coast record label tended to back him with saxophones rather than the guitar-based sound of Chicago. Smith had worked in Chicago and Kansas City, but resided in Los Angeles from 1955, where he worked as a name act and accompanied Big Mama Thornton for many years. He continued to make recordings of variable quality, and was briefly a member of the Muddy Waters band. He toured Europe, during the 70s and was a member with J.D. Nicholson of the mainly white blues band Bacon Fat.

Albums: *Blues With A Feeling* (1969), *Arkansas Trap* (1970), *No Time For Jive* (1970), *Blowin' The Blues* (c. 1979), *Boogiein' With George* (c. 1983), *Harmonica Ace* (1991).

Smith, J.B.

Johnnie B. Smith was recorded in the Texas State Penitentiary in the 60s while serving his fourth prison term, one of 45 years for murder. He was a powerful worksong leader, but his most important recordings were nine long unaccompanied solos, which he thought of as parts of a single song. Their 132 stanzas use essentially the same melody, at varying tempos, and with varying amounts of decoration. This melody, which appears to be unique to Smith, carries a four-line stanza, usually ABB'A' with B'A' a reversal of AB, leading to some striking poetic effects; indeed, Smith was a remarkable poet of the prison experience, using some traditional lines and verses, but working them into songs that are largely original compositions, thematically coherent, and full of poignant images of confinement, loneliness and the slow passage of time. Smith was paroled in 1967, and did some preaching in Amarillo, but returned to prison for a parole violation.

Albums: *Ever Since I Have Been A Man Full Grown* (c.1970), *I'm Troubled With A Diamond* (1990), *Old Rattler Can't Hold Me* (1990).

Smith, J.T. 'Funny Papa'

b. c.1890, Texas, USA. Very little is known about the life of this blues guitarist and singer, although he reportedly played in New York in 1917, and worked in Texas and Oklahoma in the 20s and 30s. In 1930, he recorded. One of his albums provided him with a nickname (or possibly reflected an existing one), 'The Howling Wolf', pre-dating the more famous blues artist of that name by about 20 years, on record. His steady, rhythmic picking and warm baritone helped sell sufficient albums for him to record again the following year, including another 'Howling Wolf' track, and a dozen more. Following this, he served a prison sentence for murder. In 1935, he recorded at four long sessions in Fort Worth, Texas, along with Black Boy Shine and Bernice Edwards, although almost nothing from these was released. Smith's date of death is unrecorded.

Selected album: *The Original Howling Wolf* (1971).

Smith, Joe

b. 28 June 1902, Ripley, Ohio, USA, d. 2 December 1937. With his father, six brothers and a cousin all playing trumpet, it is hardly surprising that Smith too played this instrument. By his late teens, Smith was playing in New York, where he became a big attraction as musical director and featured soloist with a Noble Sissle and Eubie Blake show. He also established a reputation as a sensitive accompanist to singers, playing and recording with Bessie Smith, Mamie Smith, Ma Rainey and Ethel Waters. He was hired by Fletcher Henderson in 1925, staying three years, later rejoining the band for occasional club and recording dates. (During this period his brother, Russell Smith, was Henderson's lead trumpeter). In the late 20s and early 30s, he was also frequently in and out of McKinney's Cotton Pickers. He was one of the first trumpeters to intelligently explore the possibilities of mutes other than to create barnyard effects. Despite a reputation for leading a wild lifestyle, Smith's playing was always tasteful and often deeply moving. Preferring to remain in the middle register, he rarely used the spectacular high notes with which his contemporaries pleased their audiences. In his introspective approach to his solos, and his habitually relaxed and unhurried accompaniments to singers, he prefigured the manner in which trumpet players of a later generation would conceive of the instrument. In 1930, while touring with the Cotton Pickers, he was driving a car which was involved in an accident. A passenger in the car, his only close friend, George 'Fathead' Thomas, was killed. Subsequently, Smith's mental state deteriorated and in 1933 he was confined to an institution, where he died in December 1937.

Selected albums: with Ethel Waters *Oh Daddy!* (1921-24), with Waters *Jazzin' Baby Blues* (1921-27), with Fletcher Henderson *A Study In Frustration* (1923-38), with Ma Rainey *Blame It On The Blues* (1920s), *The Bessie Smith Story* (1925-27).

Smith, Mabel 'Big Maybelle'

b. 1 May 1924, Jackson, Tennessee, USA, d. 23 January 1972. After singing in the choir of her home town church, Smith began working in Memphis with local bands. In the late 30s she joined a touring show headlined by the International Sweethearts Of Rhythm. She sang briefly with Tiny Bradshaw and then went solo. A powerful, gutsy performer with a dangerous edge to her singing style, Big Maybelle, as she was billed, startled many of her younger audiences, who were accustomed to rather pale imitations of the real thing. In 1956 she appeared at the Newport Jazz Festival, filmed as

Jazz On A Summer's Day (1958). In the 60s she appeared in a blues package show at New York's Carnegie Hall and also sang at Birdland. During this period, which should have been the most artistically successful of her life, she suffered persistent ill-health and died in January 1972.
Selected albums: *The OKeh Sessions* (1952-55), *The Last Of Big Maybelle* (c. 1960s).

Smith, Mamie

b. 26 May 1883, Cincinnati, Ohio, USA, d. 30 October 1940. Despite beginning her show business career as a dancer, before the outbreak of World War I Smith was established as a singer. Although she was, essentially, a vaudeville singer, in 1920 she recorded 'Crazy Blues', thus becoming the first black singer to record the blues as a soloist. The enormous success of this and her subsequent recordings established her reputation and thereafter she was always in great demand. Her accompanying musicians, on record and on tour, included Willie 'The Lion' Smith, Joe Smith, Johnny Dunn, Bubber Miley and Coleman Hawkins. She lived extravagantly, squandering the enormous amount of money she earned, and when she died on 30 October 1940 after a long illness, she was bankrupt.
Compilations: with others *Jazz Sounds Of The Twenties Vol. 4: The Blues Singers* (1923-31).

Smith, Moses 'Whispering'

b. 25 January 1932, Union Church, Mississippi, USA, d. 19 April 1984, Baton Rouge, Louisiana, USA. Smith is more associated with the blues of Louisiana, where he moved in his 20s, than that of his birth state. He learned harmonica in his teens and was playing regularly while still in Mississippi, but it was following his relocation in Baton Rouge, and taking up with Lightnin' Slim, that he made his first records. His harmonica work was uncomplicated but effective, and his voice had a distinctive, almost hoarse quality, with an extraordinary power that gave him his sardonic nickname. The handful of singles recorded in 1963 and 1964, earned him a reputation that he was able to capitalize on during the blues revival some years later. There were a few more recordings on albums in the 70s, and a single in the early 80s showed he was still a convincing blues performer.
Album: *Louisiana Blues* (1984).

Smith, Robert Curtis

b. c.1930, Mississippi, USA. This accomplished guitarist, was influenced by Big Bill Broonzy. A wistful but committed blues singer, Smith was encountered by chance in Wade Walton's barber shop. Smith worked as a farm labourer, and raised a large family in considerable poverty. He was recorded again in 1962, but failed to achieve success with the new white audience. In 1969 he was reported to have joined the church and abandoned the blues.
Albums: *The Blues Of Robert Curtis Smith* (1963), *I Have To Paint My Face* (1969).

Smith, Trixie

b. 1895, Atlanta, Georgia, USA, d. 21 September 1943. Unlike many of her contemporaries, Smith attended university before going on the road as a singer. She worked the vaudeville circuit, singing popular songs of the day interspersed with blues songs. By the early 20s she was making records and had embarked upon a parallel career as an actress. A highly polished performer, her records include several outstanding examples of the blues on which she is accompanied by artists such as James P. Johnson, Fletcher Henderson and Freddie Keppard.
Selected album: *Trixie Smith And Her Down Home Syncopators* (1925).

Smokey Babe

b. Robert Brown, 1927, Itta Bena, Mississippi, USA, d. 1975, Louisiana, USA. Smokey Babe led a hard life of farmwork and migrant labour before and after settling in Baton Rouge, Louisiana. Here he entertained, and jammed with, his neighbours and friends, and was recorded in the early 60s. He was one of the most talented acoustic blues guitarists located by folkloric research, singing and playing both swinging, energetic dance music and moving personal blues. However, he never achieved the acclamation and wider exposure his talent merited.
Selected Albums: *Country Negro Jam Session* (1960), *Hot Blues* (1961), *Hottest Brand Goin'* (1963).

Smothers, Otis (Smokey)

b. 21 March 1929, Lexington, Mississippi, USA. Raised in the Tchula area, Smothers learned

Mamie Smith

harmonica and guitar from an aunt before moving north to Chicago in 1946. His first stage appearance came five years later, with Johnny Williams and Johnny Young at the Square Deal Club. Other musicians with whom he played, on and off the street, included Big Boy Spires, Earl Hooker, Henry Strong and cousin, Lester Davenport. He also played with Bo Diddley, and claims to be on 'Bring It To Jerome'. In 1956 he joined Howlin' Wolf's band, playing second guitar on 'The Natchez Burning' and 'I Asked For Water'. Later, he was in a Muddy Waters' junior band, along with Freddie King, Mojo Elem and drummer T.J. McNulty. Having been refused by Chess, he recorded for Federal in August 1960. Encouraged by producer Sonny Thompson to emulate Jimmy Reed, he recorded 'Honey, I Ain't Teasin'' as part of a marathon 12-title session whose second half was immeasurably improved by the addition of Freddie King, the day before his own Federal debut. Another 1962 Federal session, with harmonica player Little Boyd, produced 'Twist With Me Annie', a bizarre updating of Hank Ballard's original. Sometime later, while a member of Muddy Waters' band, he recorded 'I Got My Eyes On You' for the obscure Gamma label. By the 70s, he had almost forsaken music, saying with more equanimity than some in his position, 'Everybody can't be president'.
Album: *The Complete Sessions* (1982).

Sons Of Blues (aka the S.O.B. Band)

This young, Chicago-based band originally comprised Lurrie Bell, Billy Branch, bassist Freddie Dixon (son of Willie Dixon), and drummer Jeff Ruffin. They garnered international acclaim for their recordings on Volume Three of the Alligator label's ground-breaking *Living Chicago Blues* series. Bell left in the early 80s and so Branch assumed leadership. The band's 1983 album for the Red Beans label included solid Chicago blues and some contemporary R&B. The line-up of Branch, guitarist Carlos Johnson, bassist J.W. Williams and drummer Moses Rutues was augmented by several guests, including Jimmy Walker. In recognition of William's own former band, the group is now known as The Sons Of Blues/Chi-Town Hustlers, under which name they recorded in 1987.
Album:*Where's My Money* (1983).

Spand, Charlie

Details on Spands early history and later life is scant. What is known is that he recorded in excess of 20 tracks for the Paramount label between 1929-31 and a further eight for OKeh Records in 1940. He was a friend and working partner of Blind Blake, with whom he recorded the classic 'Hastings Street' and appeared on the Paramount sampler disc 'Home Town Skiffle'. Spand's piano work was in the powerful Detroit style and his writing skills were considerable. His first recording 'Soon This Morning' became something of a staple for blues pianists. Working mainly in Chicago he was known to artists such as Little Brother Montgomery and Jimmy Yancey but after the war he disappeared. It is speculated, by Francis Wilford Smith, that Spand was born around the turn of the century in Ellijay, Georgia and retired to Los Angeles.
Compilations: *Piano Blues, Vol. 1* (1977), *Piano Blues, Vol. 5* (1978), *Piano Blues, Vol. 16* (1981).

Spann, Lucille

b. Mahalia Lucille Jenkins, 23 June 1938, Bolton, Mississippi, USA. Lucille sang gospel to start with, both in Mississippi and later in Chicago, where she moved in her early teens. In the 60s, she met the great blues pianist Otis Spann, and they began a musical partnership and later married. They recorded together, but tragically their collaboration came to an end with Otis's early death in 1970. Lucille continued to work in music and made a number of further recordings.
Album: *Cry Before I Go* (1974).

Spann, Otis

b. 21 March 1930, Jackson, Mississippi, USA, d. 24 April 1970, Chicago, Illinois, USA. One of the finest pianists of post-war blues, Spann learned the instrument as a child. He initially played in his step-father's church, but by the age of 14 was a member of a small, local combo. Having pursued careers in football and boxing, Otis moved to Chicago where he returned to music through work with several established attractions, including Memphis Slim and Roosevelt Sykes, before fronting the houseband at the city's Tick Tock club. In 1952 the pianist made his first recordings with Muddy Waters and the following year he became a permanent member of this seminal artist's group, where he

Otis Spann

remained for most of his professional life. Spann did complete a solo session in 1955 with the assistance of Willie Dixon and Robert 'Junior' Lockwood, but session appearances for Bo Diddley and Howlin' Wolf apart, is recalled for the subtle yet complimentary support he imparted on Waters' music. Otis supported the singer on his ground-breaking UK tour of 1958 and was an integral part of the group which appeared at the 1960 Newport Jazz Festival. He subsequently completed an album for the Candid label, before resuming his association with Waters with a series of successful tours. British concerts during 1963 and 1964 proved highly influential on the emergent R&B scene and on the second visit Spann recorded two tracks, 'Pretty Girls Everywhere' and 'Stirs Me Up', with Yardbirds' guitarist Eric Clapton. Otis began a thriving solo career on returning to the US, completing a series of albums for several different labels, including Prestige and Bluesway. These releases not only showcased his remarkable talent on piano, they also offered a skilled composer and vocalist and featured sterling support from such contemporaries as

Waters, James Cotton (harmonica) and S.P. Leary (drums). The latter also appeared on *The Biggest Thing Since Colossus*, Spann's collaboration with Fleetwood Mac stalwarts Peter Green, Danny Kirwan and John McVie. Barring contributions to a session by Junior Wells and the film *Blues Like Showers Of Rain*, this excellent set was the artist's last significant work. Increasingly debilitated by illness, Otis Spann entered Chicago's Cook County Hospital, where he died of cancer in 1970.

Albums: *Otis Spann Is The Blues* (1960), *Blues Is Where It's At* (1963), *Portrait In Blues* (1963), *Piano Blues* (1963), *The Blues Of Otis Spann* (1964), *Nobody Knows My Troubles* (1967), *Bottom Of The Blues* (1968), *Raw Blues* (1968), *Cracked Spanner Head* (1969), *Blues Never Die* (1969), *Cryin' Time* (1970), *The Everlasting Blues* (1970). Compilations: *Walking Blues* (1972), *Chicago Blues* (1964), *Candid Spann, Volume 1* (1983), *Candid Spann, Volume 2* (1983), *Nobody Knows Chicago Like I Do* (1983), *Rarest* (1984), *Take Me Back Home* (1984), *Walking The Blues* (1987).

Sparks Brothers

Twin brothers, Aaron 'Pinetop' Sparks and Marion (aka Milton) 'Lindberg' Sparks (b. 22 May 1910, Tupelo, Mississippi, USA) were constantly in trouble with the law for fighting, gambling and theft, although Milton gradually reformed after a jail sentence for manslaughter in 1937. Pinetop was an accomplished pianist, equally adept at slow numbers and mid-tempo boogies, in which his style recalls Big Maceo. Lindberg's singing was more nasal, but equally attractive. Maceo and Lindberg played the rowdy houseparties of St. Louis, and recorded, separately and together, from 1932-35, leaving an impressive body of work, including what appear to be the original versions of '61 Highway' and 'Every Day I Have The Blues'. Their lyrics make poetry from the realities of their lives: travel, lowlife, prison and sex. Aaron died in c.1938, while Milton passed away on 25 May 1963, St. Louis, Missouri, USA.
Album: *Sparks Brothers* (1989).

Spires, Arthur (Big Boy)

b. 1912, Yazoo City, Mississippi, USA. One of eight children in a family that, save for his uncle Robert, was unmusical, Spires remembers watching Henry Stuckey perform around his hometown. Teaching himself guitar in his late teens, he accompanied Lightnin' Hopkins when the latter made forays into Mississippi in the early 40s, playing in Yazoo City's Beer Garden. Spires moved to Chicago in 1943, studied guitar with Eddie El, and played in a group with El and fellow guitarist Earl Dranes. In 1952 the group submitted demos to Leonard Chess, who made one single (Checker 752) with Spires' vocals; 'Murmur Low' is a faithful reworking of Tommy Johnson's 1928 recording of 'Big Fat Mama', the vibrato in Spires' voice akin to that of Arthur 'Big Boy' Crudup, indicating the provenance of his nickname. The following year, he recorded 'About To Lose My Mind' (Chance 1137) which featured John Lee Henley on harmonica. A further session for United (referred to below) was split between Spires and Willie 'Long Time' Smith. Putting aside music at the end of the 50s, Spires didn't record again until 1965, taping a session for Pete Welding's Testament label with Johnny Young, which remains largely unissued.
Album: *Wrapped In My Baby* (1989).

Spivey, Addie 'Sweet Peas'

b. 22 August 1910, Houston, Texas, USA, d. 1943, Detroit, Michigan, USA. Like her sister Elton ('The Za Zu Girl'), Addie probably owed her recording career to the success of the third sister, Victoria Spivey. A less mannered singer than Victoria, Sweet Peas possessed a big, rich voice that was deployed to good effect, accompanied by a quartet led by Henry 'Red' Allen. Later recordings were less successful, and in the late 30s Addie Spivey retired from showbusiness.
Albums: Henry *'Red Allen Volume 2* (1975), *Blues Box 2* (1976), *Super Sisters* (1982).

Spivey, Victoria

b. 15 October 1906, Houston, Texas, USA, d. 3 October 1976, New York City, New York, USA. Spivey was recording at the age of 19, and had early hits 'Black Snake Blues' and 'T.B. Blues', sung in her unmistakable nasal, acidic tones. She recorded until 1937, appeared in the early black film musical *Hallelujah*, and worked in vaudeville until her retirement in the early 50s. In 1960, she made a comeback, still writing remarkable songs, which she usually accompanied on piano or - less happily - ukulele. She founded the Spivey label in 1962, issuing some valuable recordings, and the first featured Bob Dylan as an accompanist Others were by inferior artists and/or poorly recorded. She was invaluable in coaxing her contemporaries like Lucille Hegamin and Alberta Hunter back to recording. Self-styled 'The Queen', Spivey was the Madonna of the blues, hyper-energetic, propelled by total self-belief, always performing, and drawn to themes of drugs, violence and sexual deviance.
Albums: *Idle Hours* (1961), *Songs We Taught Your Mother* (1962), *Basket Of Blues* (1962), *Victoria And Her Blues* (1963) *The Queen And Her Knights* (1965), *The Victoria Spivey Recorded Legacy Of The Blues* (c.1970), *Victoria Spivey* (1990).

Stackhouse, Houston

b. 28 September 1910, Wesson, Mississippi, USA, d. 1981. Despite his colourful name and his reputation among his peers, Stackhouse only received interest and acclaim towards the end of his life, although he played a contributory role in the development of delta blues. He became an active musician in his teens, learning first

harmonica, violin, then mandolin and guitar. Moving to Crystal Springs, Mississippi, he came under the influence of Tommy Johnson and his brothers, Clarence and Mager. He in turn taught his first cousin, Robert Nighthawk, and on one occasion the pair worked with Jimmy Rodgers in Jackson, Mississippi. During the 30s, with Carey 'Ditty' Mason and Cootsie Thomas, he worked in a band modelled on the Mississippi Sheiks, with whom he occasionally played. In April 1946, Nighthawk summoned him to Helena, Arkansas, where he was advertising Mother's Best flour on station KFFA, with a band that included Pinetop Perkins and Kansas City Red. Stackhouse then became a member of the King Biscuit Boys, led by Peck Curtis when Sonny Boy Williamson (Rice Miller) was out of town. A day job with Chrysler and gigs with the Biscuit Boys continued through the 50s. He was not recorded until August 1967, in a session that also included Nighthawk and Curtis. A week later, he recorded with 'Ditty' Mason. Tracks from these sessions appeared on anthologies released by Testament, Arhoolie, Matchbox and Flyright. During the 70s, Stackhouse became a regular participant in blues festivals throughout the US. As befitted the station he'd taken for himself, his death in 1981 went unrecorded.
Album: *Mississippi Delta Blues Vol. 1* (1968).

Stidham, Arbee

b. 9 February 1917, Devalls Bluff, Arkansas, USA. Following a highly musical childhood, during which he learnt to play harmonica, clarinet and alto saxophone and formed his own band, Arbee Stidham moved to Chicago and met Lester Melrose who signed the young blues singer to RCA-Victor in 1947. His biggest hit, 'My Heart Belongs to You', was recorded at the first session in September of that year, and Stidham spent the rest of his career trying to emulate its success. After Victor (1947-50), he recorded for Sittin' In With (1951), Checker (1953), Abco (1956) and States (1957) as a vocalist, but took up the guitar in the 50s under the tutelage of Big Bill Broonzy. In 1960-61, Stidham recorded one album for Bluesville (which included a remake of his big hit) and two for Folkways, in which his singing was accompanied by his guitar. He also accompanied Memphis Slim on one of the pianist's Folkways sessions. In 1965 Stidham again recut 'My Heart

Belongs To You' for Sam Phillips. In the 70s he saw the release of a single on Blues City and a brace of albums on Mainstream and Folkways.
Selected albums: *There's Always Tomorrow* (70s), *My Heart Belongs To You* (1982).

Stokes, Frank

b. 1 January 1888, Whitehaven, Tennessee, USA, d. 12 September 1955, Memphis, Tennessee, USA. Stokes was raised in Mississippi, taking up the guitar early. He worked on medicine shows, and in the streets of Memphis in the bands of Will Batts and Jack Kelly. By 1927, when Stokes and his fellow guitarist Dan Sane made their first records as the Beale Street Sheiks, they were one of the tightest guitar duos in blues, much influenced by ragtime, and also performing medicine show and minstrel songs. Stokes was the vocalist, and played second guitar. They recorded together until 1929. However, Stokes also recorded solo, and with Will Batts on fiddle. Stokes' recorded personality is that of the promiscuous rounder, by turns macho and pleading for another chance. His singing is forthright, with impressive breath control. Stokes and Sane worked together until illness forced Stokes to retire from music in 1952.
Albums: *The Beale Street Sheiks* (1990), *Frank Stokes* (1990).

Stovall, Jewell (Babe)

b. 4 October 1907, Tylertown, Mississippi, USA, d. 21 September 1974, New Orleans, Louisiana, USA. More properly regarded as a songster in the tradition of Mance Lipscomb, Stovall emerged in the blues revival of the mid-60s. The last of 12 children in a sharecropping family, he taught himself to play the guitar, encouraged by his schoolteacher. He learned his first tune, later twice recorded as 'Maypole March', from oldest brother Myrt Holmes. During the 20s, Stovall became part of a group of musicians, congregated around an older man, Herb Quinn, that played for both black and white audiences. In the mid-30s, Tommy Johnson married a local girl, Rosa Youngblood, and stayed in the area for some years. Stovall, along with Arzo Youngblood, O.D. Jones and Roosevelt Holts, learned Johnson's 'Big Road Blues' and copied his style. Around this time, he married, and moved to Franklinton, Louisiana.

In 1957, he began to play on the streets of New Orleans' French Quarter. He was recorded, twice in 1958, and once with brother Tom on mandolin in 1961, by Larry Borenstein. The tapes remaining unissued until 1988. A full session, with accompaniment from banjo and string bass, was recorded in 1964, and issued but poorly distributed by Verve. Stovall joined the folk circuit thereafter, appearing at the first five New Orleans Jazz & Heritage Festivals from 1970 to 1974.

Album: *Babe Stovall 1958 - 1964* (1990).

Stovepipe No.1

b. Sam Jones. He was a Cincinnati-based black one-man band, playing guitar, rack harmonica, and the length of chimney that gave him his nickname, and produced booming, fruity bass lines. He recorded as early as 1924, with a repertoire of gospel, blues, ballads and white dance tunes. Jones was associated with the guitarist and harmonica player David Crockett, who accompanied Jones on recordings in 1927, and led King David's Jug Band; Jones was the band's lead singer on its 1930 recordings, and his stovepipe provided the 'jug' sound.

Album: *Stovepipe No. 1 & David Crockett* (1988).

Stuckey, Henry

b. 11 April 1897, Bentonia, Mississippi, USA, d. 9 March 1966, Jackson, Mississippi, USA. Stuckey is best known as the apparent originator of a local style of blues guitar playing and singing, mostly associated with Skip James, also from Bentonia. He had taught himself guitar in childhood, which may account partly for the rather odd uses of open tunings that James was to exploit so effectively on his records. The two men played together frequently in the 20s, but Stuckey did not make any records when James did in 1931. He claimed later to have recorded in 1935, but no trace of these has been found. He remained sporadically active in music, mainly on a local basis, although he also worked for a while in Omaha, Nebraska.

Sumlin, Hubert

b. 16 November 1931, Greenwood, Mississippi, USA. Renowned for his guitar work, particularly in support of his mentor Howlin' Wolf, Hubert Sumlin began his career in the Mississippi juke joints. He joined Jimmy Cotton

and met Wolf in Memphis where he worked with him briefly before following him to Chicago in 1954. His occasional stormy relationship with Wolf lasted until the latter's death although on Wolf's obsequies he is listed as a son. He was in Europe with Wolf on the AFBF of 1964 and later worked with other bluesmen including Eddie Taylor and Muddy Waters. Since Wolf's death Hubert has pursued his career under his own name, often working with alumni of Wolf's band. Never a strong singer, he has relied on his guitar playing prowess to see him through, but his work has been patchy and some feel that he has yet to regain his original stature.

Albums: *The Rocking Chair Album (Howlin Wolf)* (1962), *Blues Party* (1987), *Blues Guitar Boss* (1991).

Sunnyland Slim

b. Albert Luandrew, 5 September 1907, Vance, Mississippi, USA. A seminal figure in the development of the post-war Chicago blues, Sunnyland Slim taught himself piano and organ as a child in Mississippi and spent many years playing around the South, before settling in Chicago in 1942. There, he established his reputation with older musicians such as Lonnie Johnson, Tampa Red and Peter J. 'Doctor' Clayton (some of his earliest records were issued under the pseudonym Doctor Clayton's Buddy), but more importantly with the new breed of blues singers and musicians that included figures such as Muddy Waters and Little Walter. In the company of artists such as these, his powerful piano work was to set the standard for underpinning the hard, electric sound associated with Chicago blues in the 50s. He recorded extensively under his own name for many important labels of the period, like Chess, J.O.B., VeeJay and Cobra, as well as smaller labels, producing such classic Chicago blues sides as 'Johnson Machine Gun', 'Going Back To Memphis' and 'Highway 51'. He is also to be heard accompanying many other important artists of the time, including Robert Lockwood, Floyd Jones and J.B. Lenoir, as well as those already mentioned. He is often credited as having helped younger musicians to get their careers started. Throughout the 60s and 70s, he recorded prolifically and toured widely both in the US and overseas. In the 80s he produced

Roosevelt Sykes

albums on his own Airway label, and lent assistance to young players such as Eddie Lusk and Lurrie Bell.

Albums: *Devil Is A Busy Man* (1989), *Be Careful How You Vote* (1989), *House Rent Party* (1992).

Sykes, Roosevelt

b. 31 January 1906, Elmar, Arkansas, USA. Sykes learned piano at 12 and by the early 20s was playing in local barrelhouses. Sykes moved to St. Louis in 1928 and his first records for Ikeh and Victor were in 1929-31. During the 30s, Sykes recorded for Decca and acted as a talent scout for the label. Among his most popular compositions were 'Night Time Is The Right Time' and 'The Honeydripper', which was Sykes' nickname. He settled in Chicago in the early 40s, becoming the piano accompanist on numerous city blues records by artists such as St Louis Jimmy and Lonnie Johnson. In 1954, he moved to New Orleans continued to record prolifically for Decca, Prestige, Spivey, Folkways, Delmark and other labels. The Prestige album, *Honeydripper*, included King Curtis on saxophone. His versatility in different piano styles made Sykes well placed to take advantage of the increased European interest in blues and he made his first visit to the UK in 1961, performing with Chris Barber's jazz band. He returned in 1965 and 1966 with the Folk Blues Festival package and he played many US blues and jazz festivals in the 70s. As a result of his popularity with these new audiences, much of his pre-1945 work was reissued in the 70s and 80s.

Albums: *Big Man Of The Blues* (1959), *Return Of Roosevelt Sykes* (1960), *Honeydripper* (1961), *Blues* (1963), *Blues From Bar Rooms* (1967) *Feel Like Blowing My Horn* (1973), *Dirty Double Mother* (1973).

T

Taggart, Joel 'Blind Joe'

Blind Joe Taggart was second in popularity to only Blind Willie Johnson as a 'guitar evangelist'. Like Johnson he often employed a female voice on his sessions and although he did not have Johnson's vocal range or his guitar skills, he did produce many recordings that are as effective today as when they were recorded. These range from his earlier, often unaccompanied duets with his wife Emma (some made before Johnson got to record) to his later days when his own guitar work had much improved and he was often aided by a very young Josh White. He also used the voices of his son James and daughter Bertha and had his work issued under the pseudonyms Blind Jeremiah Taylor, Blind Tim Russell and Blind Joe Donnell. It is generally accepted that the singer who recorded 'C and O Blues' at one of his sessions in 1927 under the name of Blind Joe Amos was also Taggart disguising his involvement with the 'devil's music'.
Selected albums: *Blind Joe Taggart: A Guitar Evangelist* (1972), *Blind Joe Taggart 1926 - 1934* (1984)

Tampa Red

b. Hudson Woodbridge aka Whittaker, c.8 January 1904, Smithville, Georgia, USA; d. 19 March 1981, Chicago, Illinois, USA. Tampa Red was raised in Tampa, Florida by his grandmother Whittaker's family, hence his nickname. By the time of his 1928 recording debut for Vocalion, he had developed the clear, precise bottleneck blues guitar style that earned him his billing, 'The Guitar Wizard'. He teamed with Thomas A. Dorsey in Chicago in 1925, and they were soon popular, touring the black theatre circuit. 'It's Tight Like That', recorded in late 1928, was a huge hit, fuelling the hokum craze. They recorded extensively, often in *double entendre* vein, until 1932, when Dorsey finally moved over to gospel. Tampa also recorded with his Hokum Jug Band, featuring Frankie 'Half Pint' Jaxon, and alone, in which capacity he cut a number of exquisite guitar solos. By 1934, when Tampa signed with Victor, he had ceased live work outside Chicago. He was with Victor for nearly 20 years, recording a great many titles. During the 30s, many of them were pop songs with his Chicago Five, often featuring his kazoo. Usually a live solo act, he worked on record with various piano players. He was also an accomplished pianist, in a style anticipating that of Big Maceo, who became his regular recording partner in 1941. In the late 40s, Tampa was still keeping up with trends, leading a recording band whose rhythmic force foreshadows the post-war Chicago sound.

Tampa Red's wife Frances was his business manager, and ran their home as a lodging house and rehearsal centre for blues singers. Her death in the mid-50s had a devastating effect on Tampa, leading to excessive drinking and a mental collapse. In 1960, he recorded two under-produced solo albums for Bluesville, also making a few appearances. However, he had no real wish to make a comeback, and lived quietly with a woman friend, and from 1974 in a nursing home. In a career that ranged from accompanying Ma Rainey to being backed by Walter Horton, he was widely admired and imitated, most notably by Robert Nighthawk, and wrote many blues standards, including 'Sweet Black Angel', 'Love Her With A Feeling', 'Don't You Lie To Me' and 'It Hurts Me Too' (covered respectively by B.B. King, Freddy King, Fats Domino and Elmore James among others).
Albums: *Don't Tampa With The Blues* (1960), *Don't Jive Me* (1961), *Bottleneck Guitar* (1974), *Guitar Wizard* (1975), *The Guitar Wizard* (c.1976), *Crazy With The Blues* (1981), *Tampa Red i* (1982), *Tampa Red ii* (1983), *Midnight Blues* (1988), *Get It Cats'* (1989), *Volume 2* (1990).

Tarheel Slim

b. Alden Bunn, 24 September 1924, Bailey, North Carolina, USA, d. 21 August 1977. Tarheel Slim was a blues, gospel and doo-wop singer and guitarist who took his sobriquet from the popular nickname of North Carolina - Tarheel State. Bunn learned guitar at the age of 12 and sang in church by the age of 20. He began working with the Gospel Four following World War II and then joined the Selah Jubilee Singers, with whom he first recorded, in the late

40s. As the gospel group could not record secular music, they also worked under the names the Four Barons and the Larks, recording the R&B hits 'Eyesight To The Blind' and 'Little Side Car' for Apollo Records in 1951. Bunn recorded under his real name for Apollo and also with the group the Wheels in 1956 on Premium Records. That was followed by a partnership with his wife as the Lovers for Lamp Records in 1958. They then recorded for the Fire label as Tarheel Slim and Little Ann, a name they kept until 1962. After a spell outside the music business, Slim returned in 1970, when he recorded for Trix Records, an association which lasted until his death in August 1977.
Album: *Lock Me In Your Heart* (1989).

Taste

A popular blues-rock attraction, Taste was formed in Cork, Eire in 1966 when Eric Kittringham (bass) and Norman Damery (drums) joined Rory Gallagher (b. 2 March 1949, Ballyshannon, Co. Donegal, Eire), erstwhile guitarist with the Impact Showband. The new group became a leading attraction in Ireland and in Germany, but in 1968 Gallagher replaced the original rhythm section with Charlie McCracken (bass) and John Wilson (ex-Them) on drums. The new line-up then became a part of London's burgeoning blues and progressive circuit. Their debut, *Taste*, was one of the era's most popular releases, and featured several in-concert favourites, including 'Same Old Story' and 'Sugar Mama'. *On The Boards* was another commercial success, and the group seemed poised to inherit the power-trio mantle vacated by Cream. However, the unit broke up in October 1970 following a rancorous split between Gallagher and his colleagues. The guitarist then began a fruitful solo career.
Albums: *Taste* (1969), *On The Boards* (1970), *Live Taste* (1971), *Live At The Isle Of Wight* (1972). Compilation: *The Greatest Rock Sensation* (1978).

Tate, Baby

b. 28 January 1916, Elberton, Georgia, USA, d. 17 August 1972, Columbia, South Carolina, USA. Tate moved to Greenville, South Carolina at the age of 10, and there took up with Blind Boy Fuller. He learned guitar, and his music developed along similar lines to Fuller's, in the distinctively southeastern style. He continued to play, at least on a part-time basis, in the local area, broken only by military service in World War II. He partnered Pink Anderson for several years, and this connection led to his making an album in 1962, in which he demonstrated a wide traditional repertoire, although the Fuller sound also came across strongly. He recorded again 10 years later, with harmonica player Peg Leg Sam.
Album: *See What You Done* (1962).

Taylor, Eddie 'Playboy'

b. 29 January 1923, Benoit, Mississippi, USA. A self-taught musician, Taylor found early inspiration in the work of Charley Patton, Son House and Robert Johnson. His formative years were spent playing guitar at local social gatherings and clubs but in 1948 he travelled to Chicago to pursue a full-time career. Taylor's combo became a popular attraction and in 1953 he auditioned for the city's VeeJay label. Paradoxically, the company preferred the style of back-up guitarist Jimmy Reed and their roles were consequently reversed. Eddie appeared on the majority of masters Reed recorded between 1953-64, including 'You Don't Have To Go' (1955), 'Ain't That Lovin' You Baby' (1956) and 'Honest I Do' (1957), each of which reached the R&B Top 10. Taylor's sessions as a leader commenced in 1955 and he later achieved a local hit with 'Big Town Playboy'. Despite such success, further recordings were sporadic, and only six more titles were issued, the last of those in 1964. Taylor meanwhile sought employment as an accompanist with other VeeJay acts, including John Lee Hooker and Sunnyland Slim. In 1968 he joined Hooker and Reed on a successful European tour, but positive reviews did not engender a new recording deal. The guitarist continued sporadic studio work until 1972 when he completed *I Feel So Bad* for a west coast independent label. This in turn inspired a second transatlantic tour, during which Taylor recorded *Ready For Eddie* for the Birmingham-based Big Bear company. He then endured a further low-key period, but a collection of masters from the VeeJay era, released in 1981, rekindled interest in this accomplished, yet underrated, bluesman's career. Eddie Taylor was never a self-promoter and he has probably sold more records since his death

than while he was alive.
Albums: *I Feel So Bad* (1972), *Ready For Eddie* (1972), *My Heart Is Bleeding* (1988), *Still Not Ready For Eddie* (1988). Compilation: *Big Town Playboy* (1981).

Taylor, Eva

b. Irene Gibbons, 22 January 1895, St. Louis, Missouri, USA; d. 31 October 1977, Mineola, New York, USA. On stage from the age of three, Taylor had toured the Antipodes and Europe before her teens. In 1921 she settled in New York and married the bandleader, pianist and composer Clarence Williams. She pursued a prolific career in musical theatre, recording and especially radio until 1942, when she virtually retired, although she made a few European appearances in the late 60s and 70s. Taylor's singing lacked much jazz or blues feeling; it seems likely that her husband's position as 'race' records manager for OKeh Records accounts for the frequency with which Taylor recorded. Not surprisingly, it was often a Clarence Williams composition that was selected.
Compilations: *Sidney Bechet Memorial Album* (c.1960), *Jazz Sounds Of The Twenties, Volume 4* (c.1962), *Clarence Williams* (c.1962), *Eva Taylor & Clarence Williams* (c.1985), *1925-26* (1988).

Taylor, Koko

b. Cora Walton, 28 September 1935, Memphis, Tennessee, USA. Taylor is one of the few major figures whom post-war Chicago blues has produced. Her soulfully rasping voice has ensured her popularity in the Windy City, and latterly further afield, for 30 years, since she recorded her first single for the local USA label. Pacted by the leading black music independent label Chess, she scored their last blues hit in 1966 with the Willie Dixon song 'Wang Dang Doodle', whose cast of low-life characters suited her raucous delivery (guitar work supplied by Buddy Guy). In the 70s and 80s a series of well-produced and sometimes exciting albums with her band the Blues Machine, as well as such prestigious gigs as Carnegie Hall and the Montreux International Jazz Festival, have confirmed her position as the world's top-selling female blues artist. Though she admits that 'It's not easy to be a woman out there', she has succeeded on her own terms and without compromising the raunchy, bar-room quality of

her outstanding music.
Albums: *Koko Taylor* (1968), *Basic Soul* (c.1970), *Chicago Baby* (1974), *I Got What It Takes* (1975), *Earthshaker* (1978), *From The Heart Of A Woman* (1981), *Queen Of The Blues* (1985), *An Audience With The Queen - Live From Chicago* (1987), *Blues In Heaven* (1988), *Jump For Joy* (1990). Compilation: *Koko Taylor* (1990, rec. 1965-69)

Taylor, 'Little' Johnny

b. Johnny Young, 11 February 1943, Memphis, Tennessee, USA. After relocating to Los Angeles, this expressive singer joined a respected gospel group, the Mighty Clouds Of Joy, where he struck up friendships with Ted Taylor and Clay Hammond. The latter composed 'Part Time Love', an emotional blues-ballad, which gave Young, now called Little Johnny Taylor, a number 1 US R&B and national Top 20 single in 1963. The song has since become a soul standard. Despite further excellent releases, each of which were in a similar mould, it was not until 1971 that Johnny recaptured something of his erstwhile standing with 'Everybody Knows About My Good Thing'. Several later singles were minor hits, but Taylor did not find it easy to live up to that early success, although he nevertheless continued to perform and occasionally record.
Album: *Part Time Love* (1962), *Little Johnny Taylor* (1963), *Everybody Knows About My Good Thing* (1970), *Open House At My House* (1973), with Ted Taylor *The Super Taylors* (1974), *L.J.T.* (1974), *Stuck In The Mud* (1988), *Ugly Man* (1989). Compilations: *I Should'a Been A Preacher* (1981), *Part-Time Love* (1981), *The Galaxy Years* (1991).

Taylor, Melvin

b. 13 March 1959, Jackson, Mississippi, USA. At three years old Taylor moved with his family to Chicago, and began playing guitar around the age of six, inspired by an uncle who played blues. He was influenced by a variety of guitarists, including B.B. King, Albert King, Jimi Hendrix, and particularly Wes Mongomery. In the early 70s Taylor played on Maxwell Street, Chicago's open air street market, and in his mid-teens was with a group call the Transistors. He has also worked with Carey Bell, (and son Lurrie Bell), and was a member of Eddie Shaw's group (he also recorded with Shaw) and the

Koko Taylor

Legendary Blues Band. He made his debut recording for the French label in 1982, and a follow-up appeared in 1984. He also recorded on Alligator's 'New Bluebloods' anthology. Taylor is a fleet-fingered player who now plays with feel and technique.

Album: *Melvin Taylor Plays The Blues For You* (1984).

Taylor, Mick

b. Michael Taylor, 17 January 1948, Welwyn Garden City, Hertfordshire, England. A rock and blues guitarist, much influenced by B.B. King, Muddy Waters and jazz saxophone giant John Coltrane, Taylor taught himself to play after leaving school at 15. His first band, the Welwyn-based Gods, also featured Ken Hensley (later of Uriah Heep) and John Glascock (Jethro Tull). In August 1965, Taylor deputized for absentee Eric Clapton in John Mayall's Bluesbreakers, and joined the band on a permanent basis from June 1967. He was the longest-serving of Mayall's guitarists by the time he left to join the Rolling Stones in 1969, as a replacement for Brian Jones. Taylor had minimal involvement with their *Let It Bleed*, but his controlled and tasteful blues playing brought a rare lyricism to the band's early 70s' releases. He left the Stones in December 1975, working initially with Jack Bruce and Carla Bley, and appearing on two albums by jazz-rockers Gong. The well-received *Mick Taylor* put him back in

Mick Taylor

the limelight temporarily; he spent much of the early 80s as part of Bob Dylan's band, appearing on three albums and touring with him in 1984. *Stranger In This Town* met with little success, and Taylor subsequently joined informal band the Bluesmasters (with Junior Wells and Steve Jordan) on *Win Or Lose* (1991), the debut release by American Brian Kramer.

Albums: with John Mayall And The Bluesbreakers *Crusade* (1967), *Diary Of A Band Vol. 1* (1968), *Diary Of A Band Vol 2* (1968), *Bare Wires* (1968), *Blues From Laurel Canyon* (1969), *Back To The Roots* (1971); with the Rolling Stones *Let It Bleed* (1969), *Get Yer Ya-Ya's Out* (1970), *Sticky Fingers* (1971), *Exile On Main Street* (1972), *Goat's Head Soup* (1973), *It's Only Rock 'N' Roll* (1974); with Bob Dylan *Infidels* (1983), *Real Live* (1984); solo *Mick Taylor* (1979), *Stranger In This Town* (1990).

Taylor, Montana

b. Arthur Taylor, 1903, Butte, Montana, USA. Nicknamed after his birthplace, Taylor was raised in Indianapolis, where he learned piano in 1919. He played cafes and rent parties there and in Chicago, before recording two 78s for Vocalion in 1929. Although one record was partially spoiled by the vocal antics of the Jazoo Boys, Taylor's percussive, inventive piano playing was of the highest order. Shortly afterwards he stopped playing, discouraged by the absence of royalties. Located by jazz fans in 1946, Taylor made a series of recordings that not only showed he retained all his instrumental abilities, both solo and as accompanist to Bertha 'Chippie' Hill, but revealed him to be a moving singer as well, particularly on slow, introspective pieces like 'I Can't Sleep'. Discouraged anew, however, Taylor dropped out of sight again, and his subsequent whereabouts are unknown.

Album: *Montana's Blues* (1977).

Taylor, Theodore 'Hound Dog'

b. 12 April 1917, Natchez, Mississippi, USA, d. 17 December 1975, Chicago, Illinois, USA. Taylor had an early apprenticeship playing guitar around Mississippi with musicians such as Elmore James and John Lee 'Sonny Boy' Williamson. In 1942, he moved to Chicago, where he worked the clubs, as well as the market on Maxwell Street. Two singles from the early 60s underlined the raw vitality of his

music, especially the high-energy 'Five Take Five'. Later in that decade, he won a new following among young blues enthusiasts and toured in Europe as well as throughout North America. In 1971, he made his first album for Alligator Records and this and further recordings on that label established a reputation for intense bottleneck guitar blues and rocking R&B. Sadly, he did not live long enough to exploit his burgeoning reputation.

Album: *And His Houserockers* (1971), *Beware Of The Dog* (1975).

Temple, Johnny

b. 18 October 1906, Canton, Mississippi, USA, d. 22 November 1968, Jackson, Mississippi, USA. Johnny Temple learned guitar from his stepfather Slim Duckett, a well known performer from the Jackson area who later recorded for OKeh Records in 1930. Temple could also play the mandolin and often worked at house parties and juke joints. In 1932 he moved to Chicago where he worked as a general all-round-musician and recorded blues for both Decca and Vocalion. He worked with the famous McCoy brothers and recorded as part of the knockabout jazz group the Harlem Hamfats. He continued to work in Chicago until well into the post-war period, appearing with artists such as Billy Boy Arnold and Walter Horton, as well as forming his own group, the Rolling Four. In the mid-60s he returned to Jackson where, after a period of ill health, he died from cancer at the age of 62.

Compilations: *Chicago Blues* (1985), *Johnny Temple* (1986).

Terry, Sonny

b. Saunders Terrell, 24 October 1911, Greensboro, North Carolina, USA, d. 12 March 1986, New York City, New York, USA. By the age of 16, Sonny Terry was virtually blind following two accidents, which encouraged his concentration on music. After his father's death, Terry worked on medicine shows, and around 1937 teamed up with Blind Boy Fuller, moving to Durham, North Carolina, to play the streets with Fuller, Gary Davis and washboard player George Washington (Bull City Red). Terry made his recording debut in December 1937 as Fuller's harmonica player. His vocalized tones were interspersed with a distinctive falsetto

Sonny Terry

whoop, and he continued in this fashion until Fuller's death in 1941. By Terry's good luck, Fuller was in jail when John Hammond came to recruit him for the 1938 *Spirituals To Swing* concert, and Terry took his place. His inextricably interwoven harmonica playing and singing were a sensation, but had little immediate effect on his career, although OKeh Records did record him as a name artist. In 1942, Terry was to appear at a concert in Washington, DC, and J.B. Long, who managed them both, suggested that Brownie McGhee should lead Terry. This led to a booking in New York, where both men relocated, and to the formation of their long-term musical partnership. In New York Terry recorded, as leader and sideman, for many black-orientated labels; but his first New York sides were made for Moses Asch of Folkways with accompaniment by Woody Guthrie, and this was a pointer to the future. By the late 50s, Terry and McGhee had effectively ceased to perform for black audiences, and presented their music as 'folk-blues'. This was seen as a sell-out by those who demanded uncompromisingly 'black' music from blues singers. However an objective examination of their repertoire shows a large number of songs that had been recorded for black audiences in an R&B setting, while the children's songs and country dance music Terry recorded for Asch remain a valuable documentation. Even so Terry's singing voice, (now no longer falsetto), was rather coarse, and sometimes badly pitched. McGhee and Terry were not close friends, and in the latter days actively disliked one another even to the point of bickering on stage; nevertheless, their partnership brought the blues to a vast audience worldwide.

Albums: *Harmonica And Vocal Solos* (c.1958), *Sonny Terry's New Sound* (1958), *On The Road* (c.1959), *Washboard Band Country Dance Music* (1963), *Sonny's Story* (1960), *Hometown Blues* (1969), *Wizard Of The Harmonica* (1972), *Whoopin'* (c.1985), *Whoopin' The Blues* (1986), *Old Town Blues Vol. 1* (1986), *Sonny Terry* (1987), *Toughest Terry And Baddest Brown* (1987), *Sonny Terry* (1988), *Brownie McGhee & Sonny Terry Sing* (1990), *The Folkways Years* (1991).

Thomas, Chris (US)

b. 14 October 1962, Baton Rouge, Louisiana,

USA. The son of bluesman Tabby Thomas, Chris grew up with the music of his father and other local artists including Slim Harpo, Silas Hogan, and Henry Gray, Although he includes Prince, Jimi Hendrix, and Bob Marley among his major influences. He has toured and recorded with his father, and material under his own name has appeared on Bluebeat (his father's label), Arhoolie, and Wolf. He is now under contract to Hightone/Warner Brothers Records. *Living Blues* described Thomas as 'One of the most versatile young artists around, grounded in the blues...'.

Album: *The Beginning* (1986), with various artists *Louisiana Blues Live At Tabby's Blues Box* (1989, one track only).

Thomas, George

b. c.1885, Houston, Texas, USA, d. March 1930, Chicago, Illinois, USA (1936, Washington, DC, USA also cited). Thomas was the pianist head of an important Texas blues clan which included his daughter Hociel Thomas, his siblings Beuluh 'Sippie' Wallace and Hersal Thomas, plus Bernice Edwards, not a blood relative, but raised with the family. Thomas was an important composer (of 'New Orleans Hop Scop Blues' and 'Muscle Shoals Blues' among other tunes), and a publisher, for a time in partnership with Clarence Williams. On disc, he made 'The Rocks' in 1923 (as Clay Custer), a solo which contains the earliest recording of a walking bass, accompanied Sippie's friend Tiny Franklin, and made one record under his own name, and a few with his jazz group, the Muscle Shoals Devils.

Album: *The Thomas Family* (1977).

Thomas, Hersal

b. 1910, Houston, Texas, USA, d. 3 July 1926, Detroit, Michigan, USA. A child prodigy on piano, Thomas was tutored by his brother George, but soon exceeded him for invention. In mid-20s Chicago, his reputation, alike for technique and feeling, made other pianists wary of playing at parties where he was present. He cut 'Hersal Blues' and his celebrated 'Suitcase Blues', an enduring standard of blues piano, in 1925, and was accompanying his sister Beuluh 'Sippie' Wallace (with Joe 'King' Oliver and Louis Armstrong!) before he was 15. In 1925-6 he was heavily in demand for recording, backing

his niece Hociel Thomas among others. He was working at Penny's Pleasure Inn in Detroit, an engagement arranged by Sippie, when he died of food poisoning, aged only 16.
Album: *The Thomas Family* (1977).

Thomas, Hociel

b. 10 July 1904, Houston, Texas, USA, d. 22 August 1952, Oakland, California, USA. Sister of George Thomas, and niece of Beuluh 'Sippie' Wallace and Hersal Thomas, Hociel Thomas was a direct and effective blues singer, as she showed when she recorded during 1925-26; her records always featured Hersal on piano, and his sudden death in 1926 devastated Hociel, who abandoned her musical career. Discovered in California by jazz fans, she recorded some fine sides in 1946 with her own capable Texas piano, and Mutt Carey on trumpet, and appeared with Kid Ory in 1948, but soon retired again. In about 1950, she was acquitted of manslaughter after a fight with a sister, in which the sister died and Hociel was blinded.
Albums: *Hot Society LP 1001* (untitled) (c.1970), *Louis And The Blues Singers* (1972), *The Piano Blues, Vol. 4* (1977), *The Thomas Family* (1977).

Thomas, James 'Son'

b. 14 October 1926, Eden, Mississippi, USA. Until his discovery by a blues music researcher in 1967, Thomas had never travelled more than 100 miles from Leland, Mississippi. As such, he was a valuable source of lore on the creative processes of Delta blues, and made a number of satisfying recordings, accompanying his dark singing with the typically hypnotic guitar of the region. In subsequent years, he travelled more widely, including Europe, and recorded again. Greater exposure has revealed him to be a likeable performer, but one with few original themes, as is often typical of blues singers of his generation. Thomas is also a story teller and folk sculptor. In late 1991 he was dangerously ill.
Albums: *The Blues Are Alive And Well* (1970), *Down On The Delta* (1981), *Delta Blues Classics* (1981), *Highway 61 Blues* (1983), *Good Morning School Girl* (1986), *Bottomlands* (1990).

Thomas, Jesse 'Babyface'

b. 3 February 1911, Logansport, Louisiana, USA. Although he was the younger brother of blues guitarist Willard Ramblin' Thomas, Jesse

was not influenced by his style. On his 1929 debut records, he imitated Lonnie Johnson and Blind Blake but by the time of his next recordings in 1948, he had developed an individual electric guitar style of great fluency. This stemmed from formal training, an acquaintance with jazz, and his serious attempts to transfer his piano playing to the guitar. His singing and playing were still firmly within Texan blues traditions. Thomas recorded intermittently on the west coast until 1957, when he returned to Louisiana. while there, he occasionally released records on his self-operated Red River label, a successor to Club, which had briefly traded in the early 50s. A mid-60s soul recording was less successful than a blues single released on Red River in 1989. This showed that Thomas remained a capable and sophisticated musician.
Album: *Down Behind The Rise* (1979).

Thomas, Kid

b. Louis Thomas Watts, 20 June 1934, Sturgis, Mississippi, USA, d. 13 April 1970, Beverley Hills, California, USA. Watts was also known as Tommy Lewis/Louis. Chicago based from 1941, he played harmonica and sang blues from the end of the 40s, recording for Federal in 1955, and seeing occasional releases on small labels until the end of his life. This came shortly after his location by a music researcher in California, where Thomas had settled in 1960. He had killed a child in a road accident and was shot by the boy's father after manslaughter charges were dismissed. The strong feelings this aroused among blues enthusiasts should not be allowed to mask the fact that Thomas was a minor and derivative performer, albeit an impressively energetic one, especially when imitating Little Richard.
Albums: *Rockin' This Joint Tonite* (1979), *Here's My Story* (1991).

Thomas, Lafayette Jerl

b. 13 June 1928, Shreveport, Louisiana, USA, d. 20 May 1977, Brisbane, California, USA. One of the few postwar guitarists to develop a personal style from an early admiration of T-Bone Walker, Thomas was encouraged by uncle, Jesse 'Babyface' Thomas. The family moved to San Francisco soon after his birth and there he learned to play both piano and guitar.

His first gig in 1947 was with Al Simmons' Rhythm Rockers. In 1948 he replaced guitarist Robert Kelton in Jimmy McCracklin's band, with whom he remained intermittently for the rest of his career. He made his first record while on tour with McCracklin. 'Baby Take A Chance With Me', recorded in Memphis in 1951 for Sam Phillips, was issued on Chess as by 'L.J. Thomas & His Louisiana Playboys'. He also worked with Bob Geddins, playing on many Jimmy Wilson sessions leased to Aladdin, 7-11, Big Town and Irma. His own records were made for small labels such as Jumping, Hollywood (unissued) and Trilyte but more often he cut odd titles at McCracklin's 50s sessions for Modern, Peacock and Chess, to be discovered and issued on album three decades later. Moving briefly to New York in 1959, he made 'Lafayette's A-Comin'' for Savoy with pianist Sammy Price, before returning to the West Coast. He worked outside music for most of the 60s, sharing one album session with pianist Dave Alexander and L.C. 'Good Rocking' Robinson in September 1968. The comeback was brief and he spent his last years working as a hose assembler. His best work is to be found on the records of McCracklin and Wilson, providing the biting solos for which he'll be remembered.
Album: *Everybody Rock! The Best Of Jimmy McCracklin* (1989).

Thomas, Ramblin'

b. Willard Thomas, 1902, Logansport, Louisiana, USA, d. c.1945, Memphis, Tennessee, USA. According to his younger brother Jesse 'Babyface' Thomas, Willard Thomas was nicknamed by Paramount when he recorded in 1928. He was peripatetic and spent much of his time between Dallas (where he played with Blind Lemon Jefferson) and Shreveport, where he probably acquired the slide guitar technique heard on many of his records. Thomas also travelled east of Shreveport into Louisiana, where he associated with King Solomon Hill. Although echoes of Jefferson, Blind Blake and Lonnie Johnson are audible, both Thomas's sour-edged playing and his cynical, hard-bitten singing are instantly recognizable. Thomas was an inventive lyricist who drew on his life for his songs, singing of being locked up for 'vag', of 'Hard Dallas', and

of the alcoholism which may have hastened his death from tuberculosis.
Album: *Ramblin' Thomas* (1983).

Thomas, Tabby

b. 5 January 1929, Baton Rouge, Louisiana, USA. Thomas's first musical influences came from radio and records, and he started to play music himself while in the airforce. He sang with an R&B band during the early 50s and his first records were in that style, with strong touches of Roy Brown's sound. A release on the Feature label in 1954 marked the beginning of a long, if intermittent association with producer Jay Miller, during which they tried a wide range of styles, including blues and soul. Their most successful collaboration was 'Hoodoo Party', on Excello in 1962. In 1981, Thomas opened the Blues Box in Baton Rouge to present local artists; this has achieved an international reputation for regular appearances by Silas Hogan, Henry Gray and others, including Thomas's own son Chris.
Album: *25 Years With The Blues* (1979), *Hoodoo Party* (1990).

Thomas, Willie B.

b. 25 May 1912, Lobdell, Mississippi, USA. Thomas was permanently disabled by a back injury he received in his early teens during his family's migration to Louisiana. He partnered the fiddler James 'Butch' Cage on kazoo for 10 years before taking up the guitar, on which he recorded with Thomas after their discovery in 1959. Thomas was unusual in seeing no conflict between his secular music and his activities as a street preacher. His guitar playing, though limited, was an ideal complement to Cage's fiddle, and they formed an unmistakable, raucous vocal duo.
Albums: *Country Negro Jam Session* (1960), *I Have To Paint My Face* (1969), *Raise A Rukus Tonight* (1979).

Thompson, Joe And Odell

b. 9 December 1918 and 9 August 1911 respectively, Mebane, North Carolina, USA. Joe (fiddler) and Odell Thompson (banjoist) are first cousins whose fathers were musicians on the same instruments. Odell took up blues and the guitar in the 20s, but continued to play the older repertoire with his cousin in local stringbands until the 40s. As this style lost popularity, they retired until the early 70s, when a folklore researcher persuaded them to perform in public once more. Much of their repertoire was derived from their fathers, so that they preserved the music of the pre-World War I black string band; as possibly the last black fiddle-banjo duo performing, it was an unexpected bonus that they were still vigorous and skilful musicians.

Album: *Old Time Music From The North Carolina Piedmont* (1989).

Thornton, Willie Mae 'Big Mama'

b. 11 December 1926, Montgomery, Alabama, USA, d. 25 July 1984. Thornton was the daughter of a minister and learned drums and harmonica as a child. By the early 40s she was singing and dancing in Sammy Green's Hot Harlem Revue throughout the southern states. Basing herself in Texas, she made her first records as Big Mama Thornton for Peacock in 1951. Two years later she topped the R&B charts with the original version of 'Hound Dog', the Leiber and Stoller song which Elvis Presley would later make world famous. The backing was by Johnny Otis' band with Pete Lewis contributing a memorable guitar solo. Thornton toured with Otis and recorded less successfully for Peacock until 1957 when she moved to California. There she made records for Bay-Tone (1961) Sotoplay (1963) and Kent (1964). Her career took a new turn when she joined the 1965 Folk Blues Festival troupe and entranced audiences in Europe. The next year, Arhoolie recorded her in Chicago with Muddy Waters, James Cotton and Otis Spann. A 1968 live album for the same label included 'Ball And Chain' which inspired Janis Joplin's notable version of the song. She sang some pop standards on the 1969 Mercury album and in the 70s she recorded for Backbeat, Vanguard and Crazy Cajun. *On Jail*, recorded before prison audiences, she performed new versions of 'Hound Dog' and 'Ball And Chain'. Thornton died in Los Angeles in July 1984.

Albums: *In Europe* (1965), *Big Mama Thornton, Vol. 2* (1966), *With Chicago Blues* (1967), *She's Back* (1968), *Ball & Chain* (1968), *Stronger Than Dirt* (1969), *The Way It Is* (1970), *Maybe* (1970), *She's Back* (1970), *Saved* (1973), *Jail* (1975), *Sassy Mama* (1975), *Mama's Pride* (1978), *Live Together* (1979).

Thorogood, George

b. 31 December 1952, Wilmington, Delaware, USA. White blues guitarist George Thorogood first became interested in music, notably Chicago blues, when he saw John Paul Hammond performing in 1970. Three years later he formed the Destroyers in Delaware before moving them to Boston where they backed visiting blues stars. The Destroyers comprised Thorogood (guitar), Michael Lenn (bass), and Jeff Simon (drums). School friend Ron Smith played guitar on and off to make up the quartet. In 1974 they recorded some demos which were released later. They made their first album in 1975 after blues fanatic John Forward spotted them playing at Joe's Place in Cambridge, Massachusetts and put them in touch with the folk label Rounder. The album was not released immediately as Blough replaced Lenn and his bass parts had to be added. It was eventually released in 1978 (on Sonet in the UK) and the single 'Move It On Over' was Rounder's first release. Smith left in 1980 and was replaced by saxophonist Hank Carter. Thorogood, a former semi-professional baseball player, took time away from music that season to play ball but by 1981 was back in the fold as the band opened for the Rolling Stones at several of their American gigs. The venues were unfamiliar to Thorogood as normally he shunned large arenas for smaller clubs, even going to the extent of playing under false names to prevent the smaller venues being overcrowded. After three albums with Rounder they signed to Capitol and continued to record throughout the 80s. In 1985 they appeared at Live Aid playing with blues legend Albert Collins.

Albums: *George Thorogood And The Destroyers* (1978), *Move It On Over* (1978), *Better Than The Rest* (1979), *More George Thorogood And The Destroyers* (1980), *Bad To The Bone* (1982), *Maverick* (1985), *Live* (1986), *Born To Be Bad* (1988).

Tinsley, John

b. 10 February 1920, Chestnut Mountain, Virginia, USA. Tinsley learned guitar at the age of 11, and from 18 played for social events. He acquired much of his repertoire from, and was stylistically influenced by, the records of Blind Boy Fuller and Buddy Moss. He also composed

Willie Mae 'Big Mama' Thornton

George Thorogood

personal blues, including one arising from a 1949 incident when he shot and wounded his stepfather. In 1952 Tinsley recorded a 78 with Fred Holland for a local label, but its failure to sell induced him to stop playing blues by 1955. In 1977, he resumed playing with the encouragement of blues music researchers, made some likeable recordings and visited Europe a couple of times, despite a dispute with a Danish promoter on the first occasion.

Albums: *Country Blues Roots Revived* (1978), *Home Again Blues* (c.1980), *Sunrise Blues* (1982).

Toscano, Eli

Toscano ran three important record labels, issuing blues and R&B in Chicago in the 50s. The first was Abco, which ran for eight issues, most notably by Arbee Stidham and Louis Myers, then the most important, Cobra, which issued over 30 discs including classic sides by Otis Rush, Ike Turner, Harold Burrage and Magic Sam. Finally, there was Artistic, whose five issues included two by Buddy Guy and another by Turner.

Townsend, Henry

b. 27 October 1909, Shelby, Mississippi, USA.

Townsend was raised in Cairo, Illinois, then moved to St. Louis in the late 20s. He took up guitar at about the age of 15, and was a forceful and accomplished player by the time of his recording debut in 1929. He was closely associated with Walter Davis, touring with him and providing accompaniment on his recordings. In the early 30s, Townsend added piano to his skills. He worked and recorded with Robert Lee McCoy, John Lee 'Sonny Boy' Williamson and Big Joe Williams, as well as making further records under his own name. After World War II, he appeared on Davis's last sessions (playing imaginative electric guitar), and teamed with Roosevelt Sykes for a time. Following his retirement Townsend was discovered by a new, white audience and recorded intermittently. He continued to develop his music and compose new songs, concentrating now on piano, and sometimes duetting with his wife, Vernell.

Albums: *The Blues In St Louis* (1961), *Mule* (1980), *Hard Luck Stories* (1981), *Henry Townsend & Henry Spaulding* (1986).

Trenier Twins

b. 14 July 1919, Mobile, Alabama, USA. Claude

(d. 2 March 1983) and Cliff Trenier formed their first band, the Alabama State Collegians, in college during the 30s and took it on the road after graduating in 1941. Claude left in 1943 to replace Dan Grissom as ballad singer with Jimmie Lunceford's Orchestra, and Cliff joined him the following year. Claude also sang on sessions headed by Barney Bigard and Charles Mingus in 1946. After going solo in 1947 with their own small group including Don Hill on alto saxophone and Gene Gilbeaux on piano, they began recording for Mercury going on to record for Chord (1949), London (1950), OKeh/Epic (1951-55), RCA's Vik subsidiary (1956), Brunswick (1957) and Dot (1958). After becoming the visual act of the early rock 'n' roll era and inspiring clones like the Comets and the Bellboys, the Treniers appeared in several major rock 'n' roll movies (notably *Don't Knock The Rock* and *The Girl Can't Help It*) and visited Europe in 1958, where they were the support act on the ill-fated Jerry Lee Lewis tour. Increasingly becoming a supper-club act in the 60s, they made albums for Hermitage, TT and their own Mobile Records. Cliff died in 1983, but Claude is still active and continues to lead the Treniers with older brother Buddy, nephew Skip and Don Hill on alto saxophone.
Albums: *Go! Go! Go! The Treniers On TV* (1955), *The Treniers Souvenir Album* (1958), *After Hours With The Fabulous Treniers* (1962), *The Treniers By The Sea* (1962), *Popcorn Man* (60s), *Live And Wild At The Flamingo* (70s), *The Fabulous Treniers* (70s), *Those Crazy Treniers* (70s), *Rockin' Is Our Bizness* (1983), *You're Killin' Me* (1985), *Hey Sister Lucy* (1988), *Cool It Baby* (1988).

Tribble, Thomas E., 'TNT'

b. 5 August 1921, Ferrel, Pennsylvania, USA. Tribble took up the drums upon moving to Washington, DC in the late 30s and carried his musical studies through his army service until his demobilization in 1946, when he joined his brother Floyd's band, the Treble Clefs, and later formed his own group. In 1949, Tribble joined Frank Motley's Motley Crew who were signed to the local DC label as 'name' act and houseband. Their session tapes were then leased or sold to other record companies, and releases resulted on Gotham and other independent labels. Tribble had records on Gotham both in

his own right and as singer/drummer with the Motley Crew, as well as separate sessions recorded for RCA Victor in 1951. In 1952 he split from Motley and DC and became an exclusive Gotham artist until 1955 when he embarked upon a lengthy tour of the eastern seaboard and Cuba, recording for Miami's Chart label in 1957, Atlantic's East-West subsidiary in 1960, and the tiny Frandy label in 1961. He has managed to eke out a fairly satisfying living as a live act since the late 50s and continues to lead a rock 'n' roll and soul revival revue in Washington, DC.
Albums: *T.N.T. Tribble* (1987), *T.N.T. Tribble Vol. 2: Red Hot Boogie* (1988), with Frank Motley *The Best Of Washington, D.C. R 'N' B* (1991).

Trice, Richard

b. 16 November 1917, Hillsborough, North Carolina, USA. Born into a very musical family, Trice learned guitar early, and was partnering his brother Willie Trice, playing blues for dances by his early teens. In the 30s, he took up with Blind Boy Fuller, and his music developed very much in Fuller's mould. In the late 30s he made records; two sides solo and two supporting his brother, very much in the eastern states style of the time. In the 40s, he moved to Newark, New Jersey and not long afterwards made a solo record under the pseudonym Little Boy Fuller. In the 50s he moved back south, and his music moved in a religious direction, as he joined a gospel quartet. He was interviewed by researchers in the 70s, but refused to play blues guitar again.
Album: *Bull City Blues* (1972).

Trice, Willie

b. 10 February, 1910, Hillsborough, North Carolina, USA, d. 10 December, 1976, Durham, North Carolina, USA. Trice's parents played music and he learned guitar from an uncle, but one of his principal influences as a blues guitarist was Blind Gary Davis. In the 30s he formed a partnership with his younger brother, Richard Trice, playing the ragtime-influenced blues style prevalent in the Carolinas at that time. In 1937 he made a record, with Richard playing second guitar, but it can have had little success as he did not record again until the 70s. He lived his whole life in the same area, and continued to play music. In his retirement he made some new recordings, and saw an album released shortly before his death at the age of 66.

Albums: *Bull City Blues* (1972), *Blue And Rag'd* (1975).

Trout, Walter, Band

This highly talented and experienced blues guitarist finally formed and recorded with his own band in 1989. With the help of Jim Trapp (bass), Leroy Larson (drums) and Dan Abrams (keyboards) he debuted with *Life In The Jungle* in 1990. This showcased Trout's remarkable feel and dexterity and courted Jimi Hendrix, Robin Trower and Gary Moore comparisons. Klas Anderhill took over the drumstool on *Prisoner Of A Dream* and saw the band move in a more commercial direction. Much of the soulful passion had evaporated, leaving almost identikit Europe, Whitesnake and Bon Jovi style songs. These average songs were rescued by the occasional inspired guitar break.

Albums: *Life In The Jungle* (1990), *Prisoner Of A Dream* (1991), *Transition* (1992).

Tucker, Luther

b. 20 January 1936, Memphis, Tennessee, USA. Tucker moved to Chicago, Illinois, at the age of nine and is still probably best-known as one of Little Walter's backing guitarists both on stage and on record in the 50s. He also worked with other musicians such as Junior Wells, Muddy Waters and Sonny Boy 'Rice Miller' Williamson in the same decade. Tucker has remained an in-demand backing guitarist and has recorded with numerous blues artists, including James Cotton, Otis Rush and John Lee Hooker. He settled in California in 1969 and has occasionally led a group under his own name. He is known for the speed of his playing and has recorded in his own right for Messaround and Paris Albums. He lived in the Netherlands for some years but is now back in California.

Compilations: *Blue Bay* (1976, three tracks only), *San Francisco Blues Festival European Sessions* (1980, three tracks only).

Turner, 'Big' Joe

(aka: Big Vernon) b. Joseph Vernon Turner, 18 May 1911, Kansas City, Missouri, USA, d. 24 November 1985, Los Angeles, California, USA.

He began singing in the local KC clubs in his early teens upon the death of his father, and at the age of 15 teamed up with pianist Pete Johnson. Their professional relationship lasted on and off for over 40 years. During the late 20s and early 30s Turner toured with several of KC's best black bands, including those led by George E. Lee, Bennie Moten, Andy Kirk and Count Basie. However, it was not until 1936 that he left his home ground and journeyed to New York City. Making little impression on his debut in the Big Apple, Turner and Johnson returned in 1938 to appear in John Hammond's *From Spirituals To Swing* concerts and on Benny Goodman's *Camel Caravan* CBS radio show and this time they were well-received. They teamed up with Albert Ammons and Meade Lux Lewis as the Boogie Woogie Boys and sparked the boogie-woogie craze that subsequently swept the nation and the world with their Vocalion recording of the classic 'Roll 'Em Pete'. Boogie-woogie was only a small part of Turner's repertoire. His early recordings depicted him as both a fine jazz singer and, perhaps more importantly, a hugely influential blues-shouter. He appeared on top recording sessions by Benny Carter, Coleman Hawkins and Joe Sullivan as well as his own extensive recording for Vocalion (1938-40) and Decca (1940-44), which featured accompaniment by artists such as Willie 'The Lion' Smith, Art Tatum, Freddie Slack or Sammy Price, when Johnson, Ammons or Lewis were unavailable. After World War II, Turner continued to make excellent records in the jazz-blues/jump-blues styles for the burgeoning independent labels - National (1945-47), Aladdin (1947, which including a unique *Battle Of The Blues* session with Turner's chief rival, Wynonie 'Mr Blues' Harris), Stag and RPM (1947), Down Beat/Swing Time and Coast/DooTone (1948), Excelsior and Rouge (1949), Freedom (1949-50), and Imperial/Ba'you (1950), as well as a west coast stint in 1948-49 with new major MGM Records.

As the 40s wore on these recordings, often accompanied by the bands of Wild Bill Moore, Maxwell Davis, Joe Houston and Dave Bartholomew, took on more of an R&B style which began to appeal to a young white audience by the early 50s. In 1951 Big Joe started the first of 13 years with the fledgling

Walter Trout

Atlantic Records, where he became one of the very few jazz/blues singers of his generation who managed to regain healthy record sales in the teenage rock 'n' roll market during the mid-to-late 50s. His early Atlantic hits were largely blues ballads like 'Chains Of Love' and 'Sweet Sixteen', but 1954 witnessed the release of Turner's 'Shake Rattle And Roll' which, covered by artists such as Bill Haley and Elvis Presley, brought the 43-year-old blues shouter some belated teenage adoration. This was maintained with such irresistible (and influential) classics as 'Hide And Seek' (1954), 'Flip, Flop And Fly', 'The Chicken And The Hawk' (1955), 'Feelin' Happy' (1956) and 'Teenage Letter' (1957). At the height of the rock 'n' roll fever, Atlantic had the excellent taste to produce a retrospective album of Turner singing his old KC jazz and blues with a peerless band featuring his old partner Pete Johnson. The album, *The Boss Of The Blues*, has since achieved classic status.

In the late 50s, Atlantic's pioneering rock 'n' roll gave way to over-production, vocal choirs and symphonic string sections. In 1962 Turner left this fast-expanding independent company and underwent a decade of relative obscurity in the clubs of Los Angeles, broken by the occasional film appearance or sporadic single releases on Coral and Kent. The enterprising Bluesway label reintroduced Big Joe to the general public. In 1971 he was signed to Pablo Records, surrounded by old colleagues like Count Basie, Eddie Vinson, Pee Wee Crayton, Jay McShann, Lloyd Glenn and Jimmy Witherspoon. He emerged irregularly to produce fine one-off albums for Blues Spectrum and Muse, and stole the show in Bruce Ricker's essential jazz film *The Last Of The Blue Devils*. Turner's death in 1985 was as a result of 74 years of hard-living, hard-singing and hard-drinking, but he was admired and respected by the musical community and his funeral included musical tributes by Etta James and Barbara Morrison.

Albums: *The Boss Of The Blues* (1956, reissued 1976), *Big Joe Rides Again* (1959, reissued 1988), *Big Joe Singing The Blues* (1967), *Texas Style* (1971), *The Best Of Big Joe Turner, His Greatest Recordings, Early Big Joe* (70s), with Count Basie *The Bosses* (1975), *The Things That I Used To Do* (1975), with Pee Wee Crayton *Every Day I Have The Blues* (1976), *Midnight Special* (1976), with Basie and Eddie Vinson *Kansas City Shout* (1978), *Jumpin' The Blues* (1981), *Great R&B Oldies* (1981), with Jimmy Witherspoon *Nobody In Mind* (1982), *In The Evening* (1982), *Best Of Joe Turner* (1982), *The Trumpet Kings Meet Joe Turner* (1982), *Boogie Woogie Jubilee* (1982), *Big Joe Turner With Knocky Parker & His Houserockers* (80s), *Big Joe Turner & Roomful Of Blues* (1983), *Have No Fear, Joe Turner Is Here* (1982), *Life Ain't Easy* (1983), *Kansas City, Here I Come* (1984), *Have No Fear, Big Joe Is Here* (198), *Jumpin' With Joe* (1984), *Rock This Joint* (1984), *Jumpin' Tonight* (1985), *Blues Train* (1986), with Witherspoon *Patcha Patcha* (1986), *I Don't Dig It* (1986), *The Rhythm & Blues Years* (198), *Greatest Hits* (1987), *Big Joe Turner Memorial Album* (1987), *Boogie Woogie And More* (198), *Honey Hush* (1988), *Steppin' Out* (1988), *Big Joe Turner* (1989), with 'T-Bone' Walker *Bosses Of The Blues* (1989), *The Complete 1940-1944 Recordings* (1990), *I've Been To Kansas City* (1991).

Turner, Other

b. 2 June 1907, Jackson, Mississippi, USA. A sharecropper most of his life, from 1970 Turner managed to buy some land of his own. A player of the fife, and of the bass and snare drums that accompany the fife, Turner kept up the practice of singing while working in the fields, which dates from slavery, and was uncommon by the time he was recorded. His guitar-accompanied blues singing was derived from his field hollers, and was both overwhelmingly intense and remarkably uninfluenced by commercial recordings. Turner's daughter Bernice continued the tradition as a player of the drum.

Albums: *Traveling Through The Jungle* (1974), *Afro-American Music From Tate And Panola Counties, Mississippi* (1978).

Turner, Titus

A US, Georgia-born singer and songwriter, he made his first records for OKeh in 1951, but his first big success came in 1955 when Little Willie John had a Top 10 R&B hit with the Turner composition, 'All Around The World'. The song was revived as 'Grits Ain't Groceries' by Little Milton in 1969. Turner made other singles for Wing and Atlantic before in 1959 he had his first hits with a pair of 'answer' songs to current bestsellers by Lloyd Price, a singer with a similar style to Turner's. 'The Return Of Stag-O-Lee'

(King) was a follow-up to 'Staggerlee' while
Turner's 'We Told You Not To Marry'
(Glover), was a riposte to 'I'm Gonna Get
Married'. In 1961, Turner had a minor pop hit
with a revival of 'Sound Off', produced by Al
Gallico on Jamie, but this was overshadowed by
Ray Charles' success with 'Sticks And Stones',
the powerful gospel blues which is Turner's
best-known composition. During the 60s,
Turner discovered blues singer Tommy Tucker
and worked with producer Herb Abramson. He
continued to record a range of blues, soul,
novelty and disco material for such companies as
Josie, Atco, Philips and Mala.
Album: *Sound Off* (1961).

T.V. Slim

b. Oscar Wills, 10 February 1916, Houston,
Texas, USA. d. 21 October 1969, Kingman,
Arizona, USA. A musician from the late 30s,
Wills was resident and recording in Louisiana
during the 50s, playing guitar (and harmonica,
though not on record), and singing blues in a
voice that was rich and laidback on slow songs,
hoarse and exciting on uptempo ones. He
operated his own Speed label, but recorded the
humorous tale of 'Flat Foot Sam' ('always in a
jam') for Cliff; when Cliff went out of business,
Slim acquired the tape and leased it to Checker,
for whom it was a novelty hit. Wills moved to
California in 1959, and did some touring and
recording, but was chiefly occupied running the
television repair shop that gave him his
nickname. He died in a car crash while
returning from a gig in Chicago.
Albums: *Goin' To California* (1979), *Flat Foot
Sam* (c.1984).

V

Vanguard Records

Formed in 1950 in New York City, Vanguard Records became one of the most important US folk and blues labels of the 50s and 60s. Brothers Maynard and Seymour Solomon founded the company and signed primarily classical and international/ethnic artists until 1954, when they began signing jazz acts. Among the jazz artists who recorded for the label were Louis Armstrong, Larry Coryell, Count Basie, Stephane Grappelli, Ruby Braff, Buck Clayton, Sadao Watanabe and Stomu Yamash'ta. In 1957 they recruited the Weavers, the most important folk group of its era. In 1959 they signed folk singer Joan Baez, who became their biggest selling artist. During the early 60s Vanguard hit its peak with a roster that included blues performers Mississippi John Hurt, Buddy Guy, Big Mama Thornton, Junior Wells, James Cotton, Skip James, Jimmy Rushing, Otis Spann, Pee Wee Crayton, Otis Rush, John Hammond, Johnny Shines and J.B. Hutto. In addition to Baez, the company's folk artists included Ian & Sylvia, Buffy Sainte-Marie, Eric Andersen, Mimi and Richard Farina, Odetta, Doc and Merle Watson, Paul Robeson and Tom Paxton. Vanguard also released country and bluegrass records, including performers Jerry Jeff Walker, the Clancy Brothers, Kinky Friedman and the Country Gentlemen.

Their catalogue also featured instrumentalists whose meditative music prefigured new age, such as John Fahey, Sandy Bull and Oregon. In the mid-60s Vanguard signed political protest-rockers Country Joe And The Fish, who became one of the label's most popular acts. Their 60s roster also included the Siegel-Schwall Blues Band and the Jim Kweskin Jug Band. In the early 70s the label ceased signing new acts, and briefly shifted direction at the end of that decade. During the 80s dance artists such as Alisha, who had a strong regional disco hit in the New York clubs with her 'Baby Talk', joined the organization. In 1986, the Solomon brothers sold Vanguard to the Welk Group, a company run by the son of bandleader Lawrence Welk, who did not take an active part in the running of the company. Vanguard has since reissued most of its original album catalogue on compact disc and began signing new artists again in 1990.

Compilations: *The Best Of The Chicago Blues Volume One* (1988), *Greatest Folksingers Of The Sixties* (1988).

Van Walls, Harry

b. Harold Eugene Vann Walls, 24 August 1918, Millersboro, Kentucky, USA. Van Walls was raised in Charleston, West Virginia by his music teacher mother, and learnt to play piano at a very early age, accompanying the local church choir. His attention switched to blues and jazz in his teens with Jay McShann becoming a particularly potent influence. Soon he began playing dates locally, both with bands and as a solo piano/vocalist. In 1949 Van Walls and his band travelled to New York to back tenor saxophonist Frank 'Floorshow' Culley at his debut session for the fledgling Atlantic label, and there he remained to provide the distinctive piano part to the famed Atlantic R&B Sound on the records of Granville 'Stick' McGhee, Ruth Brown, Joseph 'Joe' Morris, the Drifters, the Clovers and Big Joe Turner. In 1954 Van Walls eased up on the session work to join a band, the Nite Riders, who had a solid career recording for Grand, Apollo (for whom they recorded the classic 'Women And Cadillacs'), Teen/Sound and a host of other licensees. In 1963 Van Walls left the group to settle in Canada, but was rediscovered by *Whiskey, Women And Song* magazine in 1987 and was persuaded to record again.

Album: *They Call Me Piano Man* (1989).

Vaughan, Jimmie

b. 20 March 1951, Dallas, Texas, USA. Vaughan began playing rock music as an adolescent and worked with several local bands, moving nearer to the blues with each one, finally establishing a formidable reputation as a guitar player. In 1968 he saw Muddy Waters, and from then on concentrated almost exclusively on blues. He moved to Austin, Texas in 1970 and formed the Fabulous Thunderbirds in 1975. The band were often cited as one of the prime movers in the blues revival in 80s America, with Vaughan's stylish, pared-down and economical guitar playing a major factor. He recorded on many sessions and left the Thunderbirds in 1990 to work with his brother Stevie Ray Vaughan, shortly before the latter's death.

Album: with Stevie Ray Vaughan as the Vaughan Brothers *Family Style* (1990).

Vaughan, Stevie Ray

b. 3 October 1954, Dallas, Texas, USA, d. 27 August 1990, East Troy, Wisconsin, USA. This blues guitarist was influenced by his older brother Jimmie Vaughan (of the Fabulous Thunderbirds), whose record collection included such key Vaughan motivators as Albert King, Otis Rush and Lonnie Mack. He honed his style on his brother's hand-me-down guitars in various high school bands, before moving to Austin in 1972. He joined the Nightcrawlers, then Paul Ray And The Cobras, with whom he recorded 'Texas Clover' in 1974. In 1977 he formed Triple Threat Revue with vocalist Lou Ann Barton. She later fronted Vaughan's most successful project, named Double Trouble after an Otis Rush standard, for a short period after its inception in 1979. The new band also featured drummer Chris Layton and ex-Johnny Winter bassist Tommy Shannon. Producer Jerry Wexler, an early fan, added them to the bill of the 1982 Montreux Jazz Festival, where Vaughan was spotted and hired by David Bowie for his forthcoming *Let's Dance* (1983). Vaughan turned down Bowie's subsequent world tour, however, to rejoin his own band and record *Texas Flood* with veteran producer John Hammond. *Couldn't Stand The Weather* showed the influence of Jimi Hendrix, and earned the band its first platinum disc; in February 1985, they picked up a Grammy for their contribution to the *Blues Explosion* anthology.

Soul To Soul saw the addition of keyboards player Reese Wynans; Vaughan, by this point a much sought-after guitarist, could also be heard on records by James Brown, Johnny Copeland, and his mentor, Lonnie Mack. The period of extensive substance abuse that produced the lacklustre *Live Alive* led to Vaughan's admittance to a Georgia detoxification centre. His recovery was apparent on *In Step*, which won a second Grammy. In 1990 the Vaughan brothers worked together with Bob Dylan, on their own *Family Style*, and as guests on Eric Clapton's American tour. Vaughan died in 1990, at East Troy, Wisconsin, USA when, anxious to return to Chicago after Clapton's Milwaukee show, he switched helicopter seats and boarded a vehicle which crashed, in dense fog, into a ski hill. Vaughan was a magnificent ambassador for the blues, whose posthumous reputation is likely to increase. Plans to erect an 9-foot bronze statue to the guitarist in his hometown of Austin are to go ahead for October 1992.

Albums: *Texas Flood* (1983), *Couldn't Stand The Weather* (1984), *Soul To Soul* (1985), *Live Alive* (1986), *In Step* (1989), as the Vaughan Brothers *Family Style* (1990), *The Sky Is Crying* (1991, previously unreleased recordings from 1984-89), with Double Trouble *In The Beginning* (1992, rec. 1980).

Vernon, Mike

b. 20 November 1944, Harrow, Middlesex, England. Vernon's early interest in blues, R&B and jazz inspired *R&B Monthly*, an influential publication he founded with fellow-enthusiast Neil Slaven in 1964. Having secured a position at Decca Records as a production assistant, Vernon worked with such disparate artists as Kenneth McKellar, Benny Hill and David Bowie, but he is renowned for his relationship with the company's blues acts. He oversaw sessions by John Mayall, Savoy Brown and the Artwoods and, in partnership with Slaven, established several independent labels including Purdah, Outasite and the original Blue Horizon. The last named was established as a fully-fledged concern in 1967 when Vernon secured a distribution deal with CBS Records on the strength of their early signing, Fleetwood Mac. This exceptional group was the producer's major attraction and he drew just commercial desserts when their 1968 single 'Albatross' sold in excess of one million copies. Further success with Chicken Shack and Duster Bennett accompanied a series of judicious reissues from B.B. King, Elmore James and Otis Rush which together consolidated Blue Horizon's role as a premier blues outlet. The loss of Fleetwood Mac in 1969 prompted Vernon's departure from Decca. Free to concentrate fully on his label, he began planning to expand its repertoire and having switched distribution to Polydor in 1971, enjoyed hits with Dutch progressive-rock band Focus. Vernon also nurtured British talent, including Mighty Baby and Jellybread, as well as

Stevie Ray Vaughan

recording in his own right, but latterly dissolved the company to pursue a career as an independent producer. 'Natural High' became a million-selling single for protégés Bloodstone; he later enjoyed fruitful partnerships with Freddy King and Jimmy Witherspoon. Vernon drew plaudits for work with Pete Wingfield and the Olympic Runners while his studio at Chipping Norton in rural Oxfordshire was another successful venture. A series of demos recorded there by Level 42 helped launch this highly popular group. Mike retained his affection for blues with recordings for Dana Gillespie, and he relaunched the Blue Horizon name during the late 80s with releases by Charlie Musselwhite and Blues And Trouble. This respected entrepreneur has since continued to forge his independent path by forming a new label, Indigo, among which the first releases include Jimmy Witherspoon's *The Blues, The Whole Blues And Nothin' But The Blues*.

Albums: *Bring It Back Home* (1971), *Moment Of Madness* (1973).

Vincent, Johnny

b. John Vincent Imbragulio, Laurel, Mississippi, USA. Johnny Vincent owned a successful record company operating in Jackson, Mississippi, from the 40s to the 60s. His first label was Champion, which issued an obscure disc by Arthur Crudup. Better known was the Ace label, responsible for a large number of excellent blues, R&B and rock 'n' roll by artists such as Frankie Lee Sims, Sammy Myers, Earl King and Huey 'Piano' Smith. Vincent resurrected the label in later years, but the revival was short-lived.

Vincent, Monroe

b. 9 January, Woodville, Mississippi, USA, d. April 1982, Oakland, California, USA. Also known throughout his career as Vince Monroe, Polka Dot Slim and Mr. Calhoun, Vincent was 40 years old and living in Baton Rouge, Louisiana before he made his first records, although he had been playing harmonica and singing blues since his young days in Mississippi. Having developed a style that mixed elements of Sonny Boy 'Rice Miller' Williamson and Louisiana R&B, he seems to have been something of an all purpose performer at J.D. 'Jay' Miller's Crowley studio in the late 50s, recording in slightly different styles, using two

different names, with the resulting records appearing on two different labels. He was resident in New Orleans for many years, playing in local bars and clubs, and making more records, under yet another pseudonym, in the early 60s. Later in his life, he moved to the west coast.

Album: *Gonna Head For Home* (1976).

Vinson, Eddie 'Cleanhead'

b. 18 December 1917, Houston, Texas, USA, d. 2 July 1988, Los Angeles, California, USA. Taking up the alto saxophone as a child, his proficiency at the instrument attracted local bandleaders even while young Vinson was still at school, and he began touring with Chester Boone's territory band during school holidays. Upon his graduation in 1935, Vinson joined the band full-time, remaining when the outfit was taken over by Milton Larkin the following year. During his five year tenure with the legendary Larkin band he met T-Bone Walker, Arnett Cobb, and Illinois Jacquet, who all played with Larkin in the late 30s. More importantly the band's touring schedule brought Vinson into contact with Big Bill Broonzy, who taught him how to shout the blues, and Jay 'Hootie' McShann's Orchestra whose innovative young alto player, Charlie Parker, was 'kidnapped' by Vinson for several days in 1941 in order to study his technique. After being discovered by Cootie Williams in late 1941, Vinson joined the Duke Ellington trumpeter's new orchestra in New York City and made his recording debut for the OKeh label in April 1942, singing a solid blues vocal on 'When My Baby Left Me'.

With Williams' Orchestra, Vinson also recorded for Hit Records (1944), Capitol Records (1945) and appeared in a short film, *Film Vodvil*, before leaving to form his own big band in late 1945 and recording for Mercury Records. At Mercury he recorded small group bop and blasting band instrumentals, but his main output was the fine body of suggestive jump-blues sung in his unique wheezy Texas style. Hits such as 'Juice Head Baby', 'Kidney Stew Blues' and 'Old Maid Boogie' were the exceptions, however, as most of Vinson's no-holds-barred songs, including 'Some Women Do', 'Oil Man Blues' and 'Ever-Ready Blues', were simply too raunchy for airplay. After the 1948 union ban, Vinson began recording for King Records in a largely unchanged style ('I'm Gonna Wind Your Clock', 'I'm Weak But Willing', 'Somebody Done Stole My Cherry Red'), often with all-star jazz units. However, his records were not promoted as well as King's biggest R&B stars, like Wynonie Harris and Roy Brown, and he left to return to Mercury in the early 50s, rejoining Cootie Williams' small band briefly in the mid-50s. In 1957 he toured with Count Basie's Orchestra and made some recordings with a small Basie unit for King's jazz subsidiary, Bethlehem Records, after which he retired to Houston. In 1961 he was rediscovered by fellow alto saxophonist, Cannonball Adderley, and a fine album resulted on Riverside Records with the Adderley brothers' small band. From then until his death in 1988, Vinson found full-time employment at worldwide jazz and blues festivals, a steady international touring schedule and dozens of credible albums on such jazz and blues labels as Black & Blue, Bluesway, Pablo, Muse and JSP.

Albums: *Cleanhead's Back In Town* (1957), *Back Door Blues* (1961), *Cherry Red* (1967), *Wee Baby Blues* (1969), *Kidney Stew* (1969), *Live!* (1969), *The Original Cleanhead* (1969), *You Can't Make Love Alone* (1971), *Jammin' The Blues* (1974), *Eddie 'Cleanhead' Vinson In Holland* (1976), *Cherry Red Blues* (1976), *Live In Blue Note, Göttingen* (1976), *Great Rhythm & Blues Volume 2* (1977), *The Clean Machine* (1978), *Hold It Right There!* (1978), *Live At Sandy's* (1978), *Fun In London* (1980), *I Want A Little Girl* (1981), with Count Basie and Big Joe Turner *Kansas City Shout* (1982), *Eddie 'Cleanhead' Vinson And A Roomful Of Blues* (1982), *Mr Cleanhead's Back In Town* (1982), *Kidney Stew* (1984), *Mr Cleanhead Steps Out* (1985), *Sings The Blues* (1987), with Etta James *Blues In The Night: The Early Show* (1988), *Cleanhead & Cannonball* (1988), *The Real 'Mr Cleanhead'* (1989), *Meat's Too High* (1989), *Midnight Creeper* (1989), with James *Blues In The Night: The Late Show* (1989).

Vinson, Walter

b. 2 February 1901, Bolton, Mississippi, USA, d. 22 April 1975, Chicago, Illinois, USA. An accomplished guitarist in his teens, Vinson became a close associate of the Chatman family, and especially of fiddler Lonnie Chatman. Vinson and Chatman issued most of their records issued under the name the Mississippi Sheiks. Vinson had a high regard for his partner's playing, but unfortunately his view that the guitar was merely a back-up instrument led him to over-simplify his playing (which at times could be remarkable). As well as recording with Lonnie, Vinson made records under his own name up to 1940. His career was interrupted from 1936-40 from the effects of a stroke. In the early 70s, he was briefly a member of a re-formed Mississippi Sheiks which included Sam Chatman.

Albums: *The New Mississippi Sheiks* (1972), *Rats Been On My Cheese* (c.1978).

Von Battle, Joe

Von Battle was a record store owner in the Detroit ghetto, recording local black talent in 1948 and issuing material spasmodically on a confusing variety of labels. Artists included himself (backed by two out-of-tune harmonicas, piano and bass), Iverson 'Louisiana Red' Minter, L.C. Green and One String Sam. However, Von Battle's most important recordings were early blues tracks by John Lee Hooker, gospel by Rev. C.L. Franklin and the first recordings of Franklin's 14-year-old daughter, Aretha Franklin. Like much other material, the Franklin recordings were leased to Chess to bring in some cash, for Von Battle operated on a shoestring, which meant poor distribution, and often poor sound quality for his own releases which, though sometimes superb, are usually very rare. Modern, King and Gotham also benefited from Von Battle material. By the 70s he had retired from recording, but was still operating a shop.

W

Walker, Charles

b. 26 July 1922, Macon, Georgia, USA, d. 24 June 1975, New York City, New York, USA. Walker's career as a blues singer and guitarist began in Newark, New Jersey in 1955, and he recorded for a number of small labels in the late 50s and early 60s. Changing audience tastes and marriage prompted him to retire from music in 1962, but after his wife's death in 1968 he began to perform and record again, and was beginning to be promoted to white audiences at the time of his death.
Albums: *Blues From The Apple* (1974), *New York Rhythm 'N' Blues* (1974), *Blow By Blow* (c.1980), *Wild Jimmy Spruill The Hard Grind Bluesman* (1984).

Walker, Eddie

b. 31 October 1948, England. This singer, guitarist and songwriter specialized in ragtime and country blues. His work encompasses the styles of artists such as Big Bill Broonzy, Mississippi John Hurt and Rev. Gary Davis. Between 1977-82 Walker released four albums, the second of which was a compilation of residency appearances at the Cutty Wren Folk Club in Redcar, Cleveland. This included Walker's song 'Candy'. Another Walker original, 'Stolen My Heart Away', was joint winner of the Tyne Tees television programme *Songwriter* in 1982. Eddie has now teamed up with the highly-respected guitarist John James in the duo Carolina Shout. James was earlier featured playing guitar on Walker's 1985 release *Picking My Way*. The album included a tribute to songwriter Steve Goodman. Walker has played the Hong Kong Folk Music Festival, in addition to regular dates in Europe, and continues to play the folk circuit, though more often these days as part of Carolina Shout.
Albums: *Everyday Man* (1977), *Folk At The Wren* (1978), *Castle Cafe* (1981), *Red Shoes On My Feet* (1983), *Picking My Way* (1985), as Carolina Shout *Carolina Shout* (1989).

Walker, Jimmy

b. 8 March 1905, Memphis, Tennessee, USA. Raised in Chicago, Walker learned piano in his teens, and later played for dances and house rent parties. He abandoned blues in the mid-30s, as he felt it to be incompatible with playing in church. However, resumed in the early 50s, working in the clubs as a name act, and as accompanist for Homesick James, Billy Boy Arnold, Elmore James and Little Walter. He has made occasional recordings from the 60s onwards, usually in duet with Erwin Helfer, his own 'rough and ready piano' being somewhat affected by age and his inherent limitations.
Albums: *Rough And Ready Piano* (1964), *Jimmy Walker & Erwin Helfer* (c.1974), *Original South Side Blues Piano* (1983).

Walker, Joe Louis

b. 26 December 1949, San Francisco, California, USA. Although born in the city and raised during the era of 'flower power' Joe Louis had a strong and realized sense of the blues tradition. He was also a musician of considerable accomplishment. His albums are superior examples of modern blues, generally being consisting of songs that are fluent and witty and sacrifice none of their 'bluesiness' in their awareness of contemporary trends. Formal musical training allows him to write and arrange his own material, including the horn charts. He usually produces lyrics alone or in various combinations made up from the impressive team of Amy and (Dennis) Walker and Henry Oden. On one of his finest songs, 'I'll Get To Heaven On My Own', he performs solo accompanying himself with some delta-styled slide guitar. Yet even this number, which has the pure feel and power of the early blues does not take refuge in re-cycling traditional verses. In an interview with M.K. Aldin he expressed his ideas on other people's material: 'I don't do cover songs (on recordings). I do some of them live. I have a real theory about 'em. I can't do 'em any better than they've been done but. . . I change them'. Another statement: 'And my style is not all playing 90 miles-an-hour,' indicates another reason why, in the heavily rock-influenced modern scene, Joe Louis Walker is a man to watch.
Albums: *Cold Is The Night* (1986), *The Gift* (1988), *Blue Soul* (1989), *Live At Slim's* (1991),

Live At Slims, Volume Two (1992).

Walker, Johnny 'Big Moose'

b. 27 June 1929, Greenville, Mississippi, USA. Walker learned to play several instruments in his teens but is known primarily as a pianist. He began touring with blues bands from 1947, playing piano and organ, and worked with many Mississippi artists in the 40s and early 50s, including Ike Turner, Sonny Boy 'Rice Miller' Williamson, Lowell Fulson and Choker Campbell. Walker's most enduring associations were with Elmore James and Earl Hooker, to whose recordings he made telling contributions on piano, although his organ work was less successful. He served in the US Army between 1952-55 and recorded in his own right for Ike Turner in 1955, though the results were not released until the late 60s. Tracks that Walker made the same year for the Ultra label were released under the name 'Moose John'. In the late 50s he settled in Chicago, and became an in-demand session players (most notably recording with Elmore James as 'Bushy Head'), and is widely regarded as one of the best blues pianists still active.

Selected albums: *To Know A Man* (1969), *Rambling Woman* (1970), *Some Old Folks Boogie* (1978), *Going Home Tomorrow* (1980). Compilation: *Swear To Tell The Truth* (1991).

Walker, Philip

b. 11 February, 1937, Welsh, Louisiana, USA. Originating from the Port Arthur area of Louisiana, Walker worked in many bands building a reputation as a performer of note. Moving to Los Angeles he recorded for the small Elko label before finally having an album made up from tracks recorded for producer Bruce Bromberg during 1969-72. These were released on Hugh Hefner's Playboy label. Later albums confirmed promise and Walker has become one of the most effective of the 'Modern' blues performers. His varied background renders him capable of playing in many styles, from the Texas blues of Lightnin' Hopkins through the Louisiana 'swamp' sound, up to the most sophisticated offering of writers like Dennis Walker. He is married to blues singer Ina Beatrice 'Be Bop' Walker.

Albums: *Blues* (1973), *Someday You'll Have These Blues* (1977), *Tough As I Want To Be* (1984), *The Bottom Of The Top* (1990), with Otis Grand *Big Blues From Texas* (1992). Compilations: *All Night Long They Play The Blues* (1979), *Mr. Fullbright's Blues, Volume 1* (1990).

Walker, 'T-Bone'

b. Aaron Thibeault Walker, 28 May 1910, Linden, Texas, USA, d. 16 March 1975, Los Angeles, California, USA. Walker was raised in Dallas where his parents operated an 'open house' to all the touring blues musicians. During his childhood, Walker was brought into contact with artists such as Blind Lemon Jefferson, and in fact he became Jefferson's 'eyes' around the streets of Dallas whenever the blind musician was in town. Inspired by the more sophisticated blues and singing style of pianist Leroy Carr, Walker took up the guitar, and began performing himself. During the mid-20s he toured Texas as a musician/comedian/dancer with Dr. Breeding's Big B Tonic Show, before joining a travelling revue led by singer Ida Cox. By 1929 he had made a solitary country blues record for Columbia Records as 'Oak Cliff T-Bone'. His recording career may very well have started and finished there, had he not travelled to Oklahoma City and met Chuck Richardson, the man who was teaching young Charlie Christian (a boyhood friend of Walker's) to play single string solos on the new electrified instrument - 'T-Bone' began his instruction alongside Christian that same day. Developing his act as a singer and dancer in the style of Cab Calloway (with whose band he toured for a week in 1930 as first prize in a talent contest), Walker was introduced to the slick world of jazz and big band swing. He moved to Los Angeles in 1934 and obtained a job with 'Big' Jim Wynn's band in Little Harlem. Walker's popularity steadily grew throughout the late 30s and in 1940 he took a job with Les Hite's Orchestra. His amplified guitar, still a novelty, brought a distinctive touch to the ensemble's overall sound while an undoubted showmanship increased the attention lavished upon the artist. Upon arriving in New York with Hite, Varsity Records recorded the orchestra and Walker's feature 'T-Bone Blues' became a great success - although Frank Pasley and not 'T-Bone' played the electric guitar accompaniment. Leaving Hite, upon his return to California, Walker co-led a band with Big Jim Wynn at the top Los

'T-Bone' Walker

Angeles nightspots, honing his provocative act which included playing the guitar behind his head whilst doing the splits - a sense of showmanship that would later influence Chuck Berry and Jimi Hendrix.

In 1942-44 Walker recorded for Capitol Records with Freddie Slack's band. Slack repaid the compliment by supporting the Walker on the first release under the guitarist's name. The two tracks, 'Mean Old World' and 'I Got A Break Baby' rapidly became standards for the next generation of electric blues guitarists. During 1945-46 Walker was in Chicago, starring at the Rhumboogie Club with Milt Larkin's or Marl Young's Orchestras (Young's band accompanied T-Bone on the recordings he made in Chicago for the club's own Rhumboogie label and for disc jockey Al Benson's Swingmaster Records). Upon his return to the west coast, Walker was in great demand, both in concert and with his new records released on the Black & White label and its jazz subsidiary Comet (1946-47 - later purchased and released by Capitol Records). These included classics such as 'I'm Gonna Find My Baby', 'T-Bone Shuffle' and 'Call It Stormy Monday'. The latter melancholic ballad, also known as 'Stormy Monday' and 'Stormy Monday Blues', has since been the subject of numerous interpretations by artists as disparate as Chris Farlowe, Bobby 'Blue' Bland and the Allman Brothers.

In the late 40s the second musician's union ban and a heavy touring schedule with his old partner Big Jim Wynn prevented T-Bone from recording, but in 1950 he secured a four-year contract with Imperial Records where he demonstrated a harder, funkier style of his blues with sessions utilizing T.J. Fowler's band in Detroit and Dave Bartholomew's band in New Orleans as well as his own working unit from Los Angeles. These experiments continued after moving to Atlantic Records between 1955-59 where he teamed-up with blues harmonica player Junior Wells in Chicago and modern jazz guitarist Barney Kessel in Los Angeles. Although nominally versed in blues, Walker often sought the accompaniment of jazz musicians who allowed free rein to the guitarist's fluid style. He continued to record prolifically throughout the early 50s, but gradually eased such strictures in favour of regular concert appearances. He visited Europe on several occasions and performed successfully at many large-scale jazz and blues festivals. Later albums, including *The Truth* and *Funky Town*, showcased a virtually undiminished talent, still capable of incisive playing. However, by the early 70s his powers were diminished through ill-health, and at personal appearances he often played piano instead of his guitar. In 1974 he suffered a severe stroke from which he never made a recovery. T-Bone Walker died of bronchial pneumonia on 16 March 1975, his reputation as a giant of blues music assured.

Selected albums: *Classics In Jazz* (1953), *T-Bone Walker* I (1956), *Sings The Blues* (1959), *T-Bone Blues* (1959), *Singing The Blues* (1960), *I Get So Weary* (1961), *The Great Blues, Vocals And Guitar* (1963), *T-Bone Walker* II (1964, UK release), *I Want A Little Girl* (1967), *The Truth* (1968), *Blue Rocks* (1968), *Funky Town* (1969), *Feeling The Blues* (1969), *Very Rare* (1974), *Stormy Monday Blues* (1978), *Dirty Mistreater* (1973), *T-Bone Jumps Again* (1981), *Good Feelin'* (1982), *Plain Ole Blues* (1982), *The Natural Blues* (1983), *Hot Leftovers* (1985), *Low Down Blues* (1986), with Big Joe Turner *Bosses Of The Blues* (1989). Compilations: *The Blues Of T-Bone Walker* (1965), *Stormy Monday Blues* (1968), *Classics Of Modern Blues* (1975), *T-Bone Walker Jumps Again* (1980), *Plain Ole Blues* (1982), *The Natural Blues* (1983), *Collection - T-Bone Walker* (1985), *The Inventor Of The Electric Guitar Blues* (1983), *I Don't Be Jivin'* (1987), *The Bluesway Sessions* (1988), *The Hustle Is On: Imperial Sessions, Volume 1* (1990), *The Complete 1940 - 1954 Recordings Of T-Bone Walker* (1990), *The Complete Imperial Recordings, 1950-54* (1991).

Walker, Willie

b. 1896, South Carolina, USA, d. 4 March 1933, Greenville, South Carolina, USA. Blind from birth, Walker worked only as a musician, and was playing guitar in a string band with Rev. Gary Davis by 1911. Josh White said that Blind Blake was fast but Walker was like Art Tatum.' This is no exaggeration, as Walker's issued 1930 recordings, especially the two takes of 'South Carolina Rag', ably confirm. He was a strong singer, but it is his guitar that immediately astonishes; lightning fast but impeccably clear (and admirably accompanied by Sam Brooks). At least some at least of Walker's playing appears to be a transfer to the guitar of mandolin

figurations. It has been speculated that on 'Dupree Blues' he flatpicks the bass strings and simultaneously fingerpicks the treble; certainly his abilities were held in awe by former associates even 40 years after his death from congenital syphilis.
Album: *Ragtime Blues Guitar* (1982).

Wallace, Beulah 'Sippie'
b. Beulah Thomas, 1 November 1898, Houston, Texas, USA, d. 1 November 1986, Detroit, Michigan, USA. Blues singer Sippie Wallace was a sister to Hersal and George Thomas (both piano players of some renown), and an aunt of George's blues singing daughter Hociel Thomas. Beulah left Houston to join George in Chicago in 1923 and recorded her first single, 'Up The Country Blues' in October of that year. It was a hit and led to an career that, intermittently, spanned four decades. Her initial period of success on record and in vaudeville came to a close when she moved to Detroit in 1929 to work in the church. Sippie did not work in music again until 1937 when she sang with Jimmy Noone's Orchestra. After the war, in 1946, she recorded again and later began working on the revived blues circuit playing colleges and clubs. In 1966 she toured Europe with the AFBF. In 1983 she saw her last album nominated for a Grammy award.
Selected albums: *Sippie Wallace* (1982), *Sings The Blues* (1988). Compilation: *The Piano Blues, Volume 4* (1977).

Wallace, Wesley
Wallace was a blues pianist who recorded a few accompaniments to St. Louis singers in 1929, and made one 78 rpm record under his own name, on which his fame rests. 'Fannie Lee' is an excellent instrumental, but 'No. 29' has a good enough claim to being one of the finest of all train/railroad tunes. Wallace plays an absolutely even, unaccented 6/4 bass, and describes, in speech and with a dazzling, onomatopoeic right hand.
Compilation: *The Piano Blues Vol. 1 Paramount* (1977).

Walton, Wade
b. 10 October 1923, Lombardy, Mississippi, USA. Walton is best known as a musical barber, entertaining visitors to his shop in Clarksdale,

Mississippi, but he started in music in his youth, and was touring with minstrel shows in his teens. He formed the Kings Of Rhythm with Clarksdale's most famous R&B artist, Ike Turner, but preferred to stay with his steady work when Turner moved on to a career as a professional musician. Paul Oliver recorded Walton in his shop in 1960, singing and playing or stropping his razor in rhythm, and he made an album two years later. Since then he has made a number of recordings, and appeared in short films, and often acts as unofficial host for blues fans visiting the town.
Album: *The Blues Of Wade Walton* (1962).

Warren, Robert Henry (Baby Boy)
b. 13 August 1919, Lake Providence, Louisiana, USA, d. 1 July 1977, Detroit, Michigan, USA. Baby Boy Warren made exactly 10 records, mostly for tiny storefront labels, but the quality of his lyrics and plaintive vocal sincerity made them all memorable. The youngest of eight children (hence the sobriquet), Robert was raised in Memphis by his mother, Beulah, after father, Lee, died in March 1920. Learning guitar from older brothers, Jack and Willie, Robert spent his weekends working the Arkansas joints with Howling Wolf and Sonny Boy Williamson (Rice Miller). Moving to Detroit in 1941, Warren made his first records with pianist Charley Mills for Staff; 'My Special Friend', 'Nervy Woman' and 'Don't Want No Skinny Woman' revealed affinities with John Lee (Sonny Boy) Williamson. 'Please Don't Think I'm Nosey' was later recorded by Eddie Kirkland. Rice Miller was a frequent visitor and recorded with Warren and Washboard Willie for Joe Von Battle; 'Hello Stranger', 'Sanafee' and the instrumental 'Chicken' are Warren's most famous tracks and hark back to the musicians' country origins. The first two tracks were also recorded for Blue Lake, with Calvin Frazier on second guitar. Warren retired through ill-health and disillusionment during the 60s. He was rediscovered in 1967, and spent the decade until his death appearing at blues festivals, and, with Boogie Woogie Red, toured Europe in 1972.
Album: *Baby Boy Warren* (1991).

Washboard Doc
b. Joseph Doctor, 8 September 1911,

Charleston, South Carolina, USA, d. 16 September 1988, New York City, New York, USA. A street musician from his arrival in New York in 1935, Washboard Doc was on the fringes of black musical life thereafter, claiming to have recorded alongside Ralph Willis and Sonny Terry. He certainly provided backing for Alec Seward, and played, with varying degrees of appropriateness, on many Victoria Spivey albums. Full albums by his trio led to a European visit in 1980.
Selected albums: *Washboard Doc And His Hep 3* (1978), *Early Morning Blues* (1979).

Washboard Slim
b. Robert Young, 5 June 1900, Marshall, Texas, USA, d. 2 June 1990, Philadelphia, Pennsylvania, USA. Young was a trumpeter, trombonist, guitarist, drummer, singer and comedian on travelling circuses and medicine shows, settling in North Carolina in the 30s. A stroke temporarily limited his musical scope, and he concentrated on the washboard, which he adorned with frying pans and cowbells. He played with Blind Boy Fuller, Buddy Moss, Sonny Terry and Brownie McGhee, recording behind the last three in 1941. He settled in Philadelphia in the 40s, playing in the streets and occasionally at coffee houses and festivals.
Selected album: *Brownie McGhee* (1988).

Washboard Willie
b. William Paden Hensley, 24 July 1909, Phoenix City, Alabama, USA. Raised in Georgia, where he began drumming at the age of six, Washboard Willie moved to Detroit in 1945, and soon became a fixture on the city's blues scene, playing the bars with his Super Suds Of Rhythm, and making occasional records for independent record producer Joe Von Battle. These are of limited interest because Von Battle could only fund limited accompaniment (guitar, piano and bass guitar), rather than the horn section which Willie's jump blues needed. His back-up work on 'Brother Will' Hairston's 'Alabama Bus', about the early 60s, civil rights Montgomery bus boycott, is a demonstration of what the washboard and its associated kitchen implements can achieve. In 1973 he appeared in Europe, confirming in person that he was a lively and extrovert entertainer.
Selected albums: *Detroit Blues - The Early 1950s*

(1966), *Whuppin' That Board* (1969), *American Blues Legends '73* (1973), *Motor Town Boogie* (1982).

Washington, George
b. 18 October 1907, Brunswick, Georgia, USA. Raised in Jacksonville, Florida. Washington began learning to play trombone at the age of 10, against his parents wishes. After playing professionally with the local band led by Calvin 'Eagle Eye' Shields, Washington went north to Philadelphia in 1925 to play with J.W. Pepper's band, and then went to New York City. There he studied trombone and arrangement at the New York Conservatory of Musical Art by day and played jazz by night with the bands of Luckey Roberts (1926), Charlie 'Fess' Johnson (various times between 1926 and 1929), Don Redman (1931), Benny Carter (1933), Mills Blue Rhythm Band (various times between 1932 and 1936), Fletcher Henderson (1937), and Louis Armstrong (1937-43). In the mid-40s, Washington moved to Los Angeles where he did several stints with Horace Henderson and Benny Carter before joining Johnny Otis's Orchestra in 1945, with whom he demonstrated his other talent; as a vocalist on jump tunes like 'Good Boogie Googie' (1946) and 'It Ain't The Beauty' (1951). Washington remained with Otis throughout the 50s and left to play with Joe Darensbourg's jazz band in 1960, thereafter working freelance in the music and movie industries.

Washington, Walter 'Wolfman'
b. Edward Washington, 20 December 1943, New Orleans, Louisiana USA. Wolfman began his musical career singing gospel music in church and was a self-taught guitarist. He has a very long association with singer Johnny Adams, who gave him music and singing advice. Washington's music tended towards the silky smooth, soulful side of the blues. In the 60s, he spent over two years touring with Lee Dorsey, and met up with B.B. King and Jimi Hendrix during this time; both of them were to influence him. After this he worked with Irma Thomas and several other bands before forming his own unit. He recorded a few singles and made his first album in 1981 and has had regular album releases since, signing with Rounder in 1985. In 1991, he recorded for the Pointblank label.

Albums: *Leader Of The Pack* (1981), *Wolfman* (1987), *Wolf Tracks* (1987), *Out Of The Dark* (1988), *Rainin' My Life* (1988), *Good And Juicy* (1989), *Sada* (1991).

Waterford, Charles 'Crown Prince'

b. 21 October 1919, Jonesboro, Arkansas, USA. Waterford's parents, who were both musicians, taught him to sing. His first professional jobs were with Andy Kirk's 12 Clouds Of Joy and Leslie Sheffield's Rhythmaires, Waterford became known as 'the Crown Prince Of The Blues' during his brief stay with Jay McShann's Orchestra, during which he recorded for Philo/Aladdin and Premier/Mercury. Usurped by Jimmy Witherspoon, Waterford went solo in 1946 to record in Chicago for Hy-Tone and the following year recorded his most celebrated tracks in Los Angeles for Capitol Records with Pete Johnson's band. These included the salacious 'Move Your Hand Baby'. Waterford rejoined McShann at a 1949 recording session for Jack Lauderdale and made four superb tracks for King with young Harold Land And His All-Stars, and another four with the Joe Thomas Orchestra. A mid-50s session for Excello resulted in two tracks of prime blues shouting, but later records for Orbit and Stampede tried to appeal to the twist craze and sank into obscurity. By contrast, Waterford's earlier sides show him to be an original blues singer, most of his songs were self-penned and featured highly original and evocative lyrics. It is reported that Waterford is still alive and his time is now devoted to the church.
Compilation: *Shoutin' The Blues* (1985).

Waters, Ethel

b. 31 October 1896, Chester, Pennsylvania, USA, d. 1 September 1977. One of the most influential of popular singers, Water's early career found her working in vaudeville. As a consequence, her repertoire was more widely based and popularly angled than those of many of her contemporaries. It is reputed that she was the first singer to perform W.C. Handy's 'St Louis Blues' in public, and she later popularized blues and jazz-influenced songs such as 'Stormy Weather' and 'Travellin' All Alone', also scoring a major success with 'Dinah'. She first recorded in 1921 and on her early dates she was accompanied by artists such as Fletcher Henderson, Coleman Hawkins, James P. Johnson and Duke Ellington. Significantly, for her acceptance in white circles, she also recorded with Jack Teagarden, Benny Goodman and Tommy Dorsey. In the 30s she was a star of the Cotton Club, which is where she regularly stopped the show with 'Stormy Weather'. During the same decade she was heard frequently on the radio and also appeared on television. In later life she became an actress, distinguishing herself on the Broadway stage, in films such as *Cabin In The Sky* (1943), *Pinky* (1949) and *The Member Of The Wedding* (1953), and starring on television in *Beulah* in 1950-51.

Throughout the 60s and on into the mid-70s she sang as a member of the organization which accompanied evangelist Billy Graham. Although less highly regarded in blues and jazz circles than either Bessie Smith or Louis Armstrong, in the 30s Waters transcended the boundaries of these musical forms to far greater effect than either of these artists and spread her influence throughout popular music. Countless young hopefuls emulated her sophisticated, lilting vocal style and her legacy lived on in the work of outstanding and, ironically, frequently better-known successors, such as Connee Boswell, Ruth Etting, Adelaide Hall, Mildred Bailey, Lee Wiley, Lena Horne and Ella Fitzgerald. Even Billie Holiday (with whom Waters was less than impressed, commenting, 'She sings as though her shoes are too tight'), acknowledged her influence. A buoyant, high-spirited singer with a light, engaging voice that frequently sounds 'whiter' than most of her contemporaries, Waters' career was an object lesson in determination and inner drive. Her appalling childhood problems and troubled early life, recounted in the first part of her autobiography, *His Eye Is On The Sparrow*, were overcome through grit and the application of her great talent. She died in 1977.
Selected albums: *His Eye Is On The Sparrow* (c.1963), *Ethel Waters Reminisces* (c.1963). Compilations: *Ethel Waters* (1979), *The Complete Bluebird Sessions (1938-39)* (1986), *On The Air (1941-51)* (1986), *Ethel Waters On Stage And Screen (1925-40)* (1989), *Who Said Blackbirds Are Blue?* (1989).
Further reading: *His Eye Is On The Sparrow*, Ethel Waters, London, 1951.

Ethel Waters

Waters, Muddy

b. McKinley Morganfield, 4 April 1915, Rolling
Fork, Mississippi, USA, d. 30 April 1983,
Chicago, Illinois, USA. One of the dominant
figures of post-war blues, Muddy Waters was
raised in the rural Mississippi town of Clarksdale,
in whose juke-joints he came into contact with
the legendary Son House. Having already
mastered the rudiments of the guitar, Waters
began performing and this early, country blues
period was later documented by Alan Lomax.
Touring the South making field recordings for
the Library Of Congress, this renowned archivist
taped Muddy on three occasions between 1941-
42. The following year Waters moved to
Chicago where he befriended Big Bill Broonzy

whose influence and help proved vital to the
younger performer. Muddy soon began using
amplified, electric instruments and by 1948 had
signed a recording deal with the newly-founded
Aristocrat label, the name of which was later
changed to Chess Records. Waters' second
release, 'I Feel Like Goin' Home'/'I Can't Be
Satisfied', was a minor R&B hit and its
understated accompaniment from bassist Big
Crawford set a pattern for several further singles,
including 'Rollin' And Tumblin'', 'Rollin'
Stone' and 'Walking Blues'.
By 1951 the guitarist was using a full backing
band and among the musicians who passed
through its ranks were Otis Spann (piano),
Jimmy Rogers (guitar), Little Walter, Walter

Muddy Waters

'Shakey' Horton and James Cotton (all harmonica). This pool of talent ensured that the Muddy Waters Band was Chicago's most influential unit and a score of seminal recordings, including 'Hoochie Coochie Man', 'I've Got My Mojo Working', 'Mannish Boy', 'You Need Love' and 'I'm Ready', established the leader's abrasive guitar style and impassioned singing. Waters' international stature was secured in 1958 when he toured Britain at the behest of jazz trombonist Chris Barber. Although criticized in some quarters for his use of amplification, Muddy's effect on a new generation of white enthusiasts was incalculable. Cyril Davies and Alexis Korner abandoned skiffle in his wake and their subsequent combo, Blues Incorporated, was the catalyst for the Rolling Stones, the Graham Bond Organisation, Long John Baldry and indeed British R&B itself. Paradoxically, while such groups enjoyed commercial success, Waters struggled against indifference. Deemed 'old-fashioned' in the wake of soul music, he was obliged to update his sound and repertoire, resulting in such misjudged releases as *Electric Mud*, which featured a reading of the Rolling Stones' 'Let's Spend The Night Together', the ultimate artistic *volte-face*. The artist did complete a more sympathetic project in *Fathers And Sons* on which he was joined by Paul Butterfield and Mike Bloomfield, but his work during the 60s was generally disappointing. *The London Sessions* kept Waters in the public eye, as did his appearance in the Band's *The Last Waltz*, but it was an inspired series of collaborations with guitarist Johnny Winter that signalled a dramatic rebirth. This pupil produced and arranged four excellent albums which recaptured the fire and purpose of Muddy's early releases and bestowed a sense of dignity to this musical giant's legacy. Waters died of heart failure in 1983, his stature as one of world's most influential musicians secured.

Selected albums: *Muddy Waters At Newport* (1960), *Muddy Waters, Folk singer* (1964), *Muddy Waters Sings Big Bill Broonzy* (1964), *Muddy Brass And The Blues* (1965), *Down On Stovall's Plantation* (1966), *Electric Mud* (1968), *After The Rain* (1969), *Fathers And Sons* (1969), *They Call Me Muddy Waters* (1970), *The London Sessions* (1971), *Live At Mister Kelly's* (1971), *Experiment In Blues* (1972), *Sail On* (1972), *Can't Get No*

Grinding (1973), *Mud In Your Ear* (1973), *London Revisited* (1974), *Woodstock Album* (1975), *Unk In Funk* (1977), *Hard Again* (1977), *Muddy Waters Live* (1977), *Live* (1977), *I'm Ready* (1978), *King Bee* (1981), *Muddy Waters In Concert 1958* (1982). Compilations: *The Best Of Muddy Waters* (1964), *Real Folk Blues* (1965), *More Real Folk Blues* (1967), *Vintage Mud* (1970), *McKinley Morganfield* aka *Muddy Waters* (1972), *Back In The Early Days* (1977), *Chess Masters* (1981), *Trouble No More* (1989).

Watkins, John 'Mad Dog'
b. 19 July 1953, Chicago, Illinois, USA. As a youngster, Watkins was exposed to his parents' blues record collection and later taught himself to play bass and drums. Around 1967-68 his mother finally bought him a guitar and by 1969 he was playing with Buddy Guy at Theresa's Lounge in Chicago. From there, he went on to play with Koko Taylor, Son Seals, Junior Wells and others. He toured with Willie Dixon for seven years and then joined James Cotton's band, recording with both artists. He made his own debut album in France in 1984 and also recorded one track for Alligator's *New Bluebloods* anthology in 1987. He spent two years working with his uncle, blues guitarist Jimmy Johnson, but formed his own band in 1987 to showcase his crisp guitar-playing and soulful blues singing. Album: *Here I Am* (1984).

Watson, Johnny 'Guitar'
b. 3 February 1935, Houston, Texas, USA. Before Watson made a name for himself in the 70s playing funk R&B, he had a long career going back to the early 50s. Watson's father played piano, which also became Watson's first instrument. On seeing Clarence 'Gatemouth' Brown perform, he convinced himself that he had to play guitar. He inherited a guitar from his grandfather, a sanctified preacher, on one condition that he did not play the blues on it - 'that was the first thing I played', Watson later said. In the early 50s his family moved to Los Angeles, which is where he started playing piano in the Chuck Higgins band and was billed as 'Young John Watson'. Switching to guitar, he was signed to Federal and recorded 'Space Guitar', an instrumental way ahead of its time in the use of reverberation and feedback. He also played 'Motorhead Baby' with an enthusiasm

that was to become his trademark. He recorded the same track for Federal with the Amos Milburn band in tow. Watson became in-demand as a guitarist and in the late 50s toured and recorded with the Olympics, Don And Dewey and Little Richard. Johnny 'Guitar' Watson was from the same mould of flamboyance that motivated another of Little Richard's guitarists: Jimi Hendrix. Watson later stated: 'I used to play the guitar standing on my hands, I had a 150 foot cord and I could get on top of the auditorium - those things Jimi Hendrix was doing, I *started* that shit!'.

Moving to the Modern label in 1955, he immediately hit with a bluesy ballad, 'Those Lonely, Lonely Nights', (US R&B Top 10), but failed to follow-up on the label. In 1957 the novelty tune 'Gangster Of Love' (later adopted by Steve Miller) gave him a minor hit on the west coast. A partnership with Larry Williams was particularly successful and in 1965 they toured England and recorded an album for Decca. Watson did not return to the charts until 1962, when on the King label he hit with 'Cuttin' In' (US R&B number 6), which was recorded with strings accompaniment. The following year he recorded *I Cried For You*, a 'cocktail-lounge' album with hip renditions of 'Polkadots And Moonbeams' and 'Witchcraft'. The Beatles invasion signified hard times for the inventors of rock 'n roll. Watson cut two soulful funk albums for the Fantasy label (*Listen* and *I Don't Want To Be Alone, Stranger*) with keyboardist Andre Lewis (later to tour with Frank Zappa). As if to repay his enthusiasm for Watson's guitar playing, of which Zappa had often said was amongst his favourite, Watson was recruited for Zappa's *One Size Fits All* in 1975. In 1976 Watson released *Ain't That A Bitch* on DJM Records, a brilliant marriage of 50s rockin' R&B, Hollywood schmaltz and futuristic funk. Watson produced, played bass, keyboards and drums. It went gold, and a further six albums appeared on DJM to the same formula. In 1981 he quit the label for A&M Records, but the production diluted Watson's unique sound and the record was a failure. One positive side-effect was a characteristic solo on Herb Alpert's *Beyond*. Watson retired to lick his wounds, emerging with the hilarious *Strike On Computers* at the end of the 80s and an appearance at London's Town & Country Club in 1987. Apart from cameo appearances on Frank Zappa albums, Watson seems to have retired: this is a shame because dance music can always use his innovative production and uniquely humorous approach.

Albums: *Gangster Of Love* (1958), *Johnny Guitar Watson* (1963), *I Cried For You* (1963), *The Larry Williams Show* (1965), *The Blues Soul of Johnny Guitar Watson* (1965), *Bad* (1966), with Larry Williams *Two For The Price Of One* (1967), *In The Fats Bag* (1967), *Listen* (1973), *I Don't Want To Be Alone, Stranger* (1975), *Captured Live* (1976), *Ain't That A Bitch* (1976), *A Real Mother For Ya* (1977), *Funk Beyond The Call Of Duty* (1977), *Gangster Of Love* (1977), with the Watsonian Institute *Master Funk* (1978), *Giant* (1978), with Papa John Creach *Inphasion* (1978), with the Watsonian Institute *Extra Disco Perception* (1979), *What The Hell Is This?* (1979), *Love Jones* (1980), *Johnny 'Guitar' Watson And The Family Clone* (1981), *That's What Time It Is* (1981), *Strike On Computers* (1984). Compilations: *Gettin' Down With Johnny 'Guitar' Watson* (c.80s), *I Heard That!* (1985), *Hit The Highway* (1985), *Three Hours Past Midnight* (1991), *Listen/I Don't Want To Be Alone, Stranger* (1992).

Wayne, Wee Willie

b. New Orleans, Wayne was a blues singer and drummer who was discovered by Stan Lewis. As James Waynes, he recorded for Bob Shad's Sittin In With label in Houston in 1950. Among the titles released by Shad were 'Junco Partner' and 'Tend To Your Business', a big R&B hit in 1951. Wayne next joined Imperial, recording with Lee Allen's studio band in New Orleans from 1951-52. These tracks, including 'When Night Falls' and 'Two Faced Woman' were issued under the name Wee Willie Wayne. After a 1954 session in Los Angeles for Aladdin where he sang 'Crying In Vain', Wayne recorded 'Travelin' Mood' (Imperial 1955) which became popular in the New Orleans area. He continued to perform locally and in 1961 made a new version of 'Tend To Your Business' for Imperial which issued an album of his work the following year. Wayne subsequently left the music business and in the late 60s was reported to be hospitalised, suffering from a mental illness.

Albums: *Travelin' Mood* (1962), *Travelin' From New Orleans* (reissue 1988).

Weaver, Curley James

b. 25 March 1906, Covington, Georgia, USA, d. 20 September 1960, Almon, Georgia, USA. Weaver's mother taught him his first lessons on guitar, and he moved to Atlanta in the 20s, where he played with musicians such as Charlie and Robert Hicks (aka Charley Lincoln and Barbecue Bob). He made his first records in 1928, and recorded frequently up to 1935 as a solo artist, and also as an accompanist to other artists including Eugene 'Buddy' Moss and 'Blind' Willie McTell. He also appeared in the groups the Georgia Cotton Pickers and the Georgia Browns. These show him as a versatile and skilled musician, whose work encompassed a range of styles from ragtime-flavoured numbers to tough bottleneck blues. In the 40s and early 50s, Weaver continued to be musically active and made a few more records, which rank among the best country blues recordings of the period.

Albums: *Georgia Guitar Wizard* (1988), *1933-1950* (1990).

Webb, 'Boogie' Bill

b. 1926, Jackson, Mississippi, USA, d. 23 August 1990, New Orleans, Louisiana, USA. Among Webb's first guitar teachers was Roosevelt Holts, and he later played with Tommy Johnson and Ishmon Bracey. He retained the ability to play in the South Mississippi blues style throughout his life, but in the 40s he extended his musical points of reference when he teamed up with a young Chuck Berry, and later in New Orleans, when he played with Fats Domino's band. In 1952, he recorded four tracks, of which only two were issued, and he did not record again until the 60s. In the meantime, he lived for a period in Chicago, where he played with some of the big names of the time, including Muddy Waters. In 1966, he made the first of a number of recordings aimed at the blues revival, although he was not to make an album until 1989.

Album: *Drinkin' And Stinkin'* (1989).

Webster, Katie

b. Kathryn Thorne, 1 September 1939, Houston, Texas, USA. Webster learned to play the piano as a child, playing hymn tunes when her mother was within earshot and Fats Domino and Chuck Berry tunes when she was not. She developed, in her words, 'A funky left hand and a rollin' right', which talent led to her becoming house pianist at Jay Miller's studio in Crowley, Louisiana from 1959-66. During that period, she

Katie Webster

backed swamp blues artists such as Lazy Lester, Lonesome Sundown and Lightnin' Slim. She also recorded under her own name, or with billing shared with Ashton Conroy (Ashton Savoy). These showed her to be a versatile performer, covering tough downhome blues, rocking R&B, soul and pop ballads and revealed a sweet, but sassy voice. She played with Otis Redding's touring band from 1966 until Redding's death the following year, after which her career took a downturn and she played only local gigs during the 70s. In 1982 she toured Europe, the first of many such tours. Currently her career is on the upturn as she continues to tour with her band, Silent Partners, and lay down her two-fisted playing and no-nonsense singing on a succession of fine albums.

Albums: *Katie Webster Has The Blues* (1979), *You Can Dig It* (early 80s), *Live And Well* (early 80s), *200% Joy* (mid-80s), *You Know That's Right* (1985), *Swamp Boogie Queen* (1988), *Two Fisted Mama* (1990), *No Foolin'* (1991). Compilations: *Whooee Sweet Daddy* (1977), *Katie Webster* (1991), *The Many Faces Of Katie Webster* (1988).

Weldon, Casey Bill

b. 10 July 1909, Pine Bluff, Arkansas, USA. Weldon was briefly married to Memphis Minnie in the 20s, and made his recording debut with the Memphis Jug Band in 1927, also recording under the name of Will Weldon. He sang in a high, straining voice, and played chugging guitar which, in duet with Vol Stevens, emulated the playing of Charley Jordan. Weldon reappeared in Chicago in 1935, having allegedly made his way there via Kansas City (hence his nickname, a version of 'K.C.'). His singing became deeper and warmer, embellished with falsetto, while his guitar had changed even more radically. Sometimes billed as 'the Hawaiian Guitar Wizard', he now played steel guitar with a slide. He was evidently influenced by Hawaiian players like Sol Hoopii (and possibly by western swing guitarists like Leon McAuliffe), but he remained firmly rooted in blues. Extensively recorded, Weldon composed the standards 'Gonna Move To The Outskirts Of Town' and 'Somebody Changed The Lock On My Door'. His songs often featured a trademark melody, but when he broke away from this he played highly inventive, swinging guitar. He disappeared from the music scene after 1938,

reportedly moving to California, and later to Detroit.

Albums: *Bottleneck Guitar Trendsetters Of The 1930s* (1975), *Casey Bill Weldon (1935-37)* (1988).

Wellington, Valerie

b. 14 November 1959, Chicago, Illinois, USA. Wellington trained as an opera singer at Chicago's American Conservatory of Music for three years. She learned piano as a youngster and played with local bluesman Lee 'Shot' Williams at the age of 15. In 1982 she came to the notice of the blues audience as a singer by portraying Ma Rainey in a local musical stage play and, two years later, she recorded her debut album for the Rooster label, which received 'rave' reviews from the critics, all of who commented on the power of Wellington's voice. In 1987 she contributed one track to Alligator Records' *The New Bluebloods*, an anthology of younger blues artists as well as providing music to several television commercials.

Album: *Million Dollar Secret* (1984).

Wells, Junior

b. Amos Blackmore, 9 December 1934, Memphis, Tennessee, USA. Having eschewed parental pressure to pursue a career in gospel music, Wells began playing harmonica in the streets of West Memphis, inspired by local heroes Howlin' Wolf and Junior Parker. Having followed his mother to Chicago in 1946, the young musician won the respect of senior figures of the blues fraternity, including Tampa Red, Big Maceo and Sunnyland Slim. Wells formed a trio, initially known as the Little Chicago Devils, then the Three Deuces, with Louis Myers (guitar) and David Myers (bass). Later known as the Three Aces, the group became a popular attraction, especially with the addition of drummer Fred Below. Their reputation reached Little Walter, harmonica player with Muddy Waters, who was about to embark on a solo career. Walter appropriated the Aces as his backing group, while Junior joined Muddy on tour. The exchange was not irrevocable as the Aces accompanied Wells on his first solo sessions, credited to Junior Wells And His Eagle Rockers, which included the original version of 'Hoodoo Man', a song the artist would return to over the years. A spell in

Junior Wells

the US Army then interrupted his progress, but Wells resumed recording in 1957 with the first of several releases undertaken for local entrepreneur Mel London. These included 'Little By Little' (1960) and the excellent 'Messin' With The Kid' (1960) the latter which featured guitarist Earl Hooker, but Wells's most fruitful partnership was forged in 1965 when he began a long association with Buddy Guy. *Hoodoo Man Blues* consummated their relationship and this superb set, one of the finest Chicago blues albums, featured Wells's sterling harmonica work and Guy's exemplary, supportive guitar playing. Subsequent releases, including *On Tap*, *Southside Blues Jam* and *It's My Life Baby*, although less fiery, were nonetheless impressive, and the group became popular with both black and white audiences, the latter through appearances on the rock circuit. In the *Billboard* R&B chart he scored well with 'Up In Heah' (1966) and 'You're Tuff Enough' (1968). By the end of the 60s Wells and Guy were sharing top billing, while a release as Buddy And The Juniors denoted their association with pianist Junior Mance. However, Guy's growing reputation resulted in a diminution of this democratic approach and the harmonica player's role was increasingly viewed as supportive. By the early 90s, the partnership was dissolved. Wells is still an impressive stylist and he remains, with Little Walter and Sonny Boy 'Rice Miller' Williamson a leading practitioner of post-war blues harmonica.

Albums: *Hoodoo Man Blues* (1965), *On Tap* (1966), *It's My Life Baby* (1966), *Southside Blues Jam* (1967), *Comin' At You* (1968), *You're Tuff Enough* (1968), *Junior Wells Sings At The Golden Bear* (1968), *Buddy And The Juniors* (1970), *Buddy Guy And Junior Wells Play The Blues* (1972), with Buddy Guy *Alone And Acoustic* (1981, reissued in 1991 with extra tracks), with Guy *Drinkin' TNT 'N' Smokin' Dynamite* (1982), with James Cotton, Carey Bell and Billy Branch *Harp Attack* (1991). Compilations: *Blues Hit Big Town* (1969), *In My Younger Days* (1971), *Chiefly Wells* (1986), *Universal Rock* (1986), *Messing With The Kid* (1986).

Wells, Viola 'Miss Rhapsody'

b. 14 December 1902, Newark, New Jersey, USA, d. 22 December 1984, New York City, USA. Touring the TOBA circuit as a classic blues singer in the 30s Wells met and married guitarist Harold Underhill. She was a much-admired jazz and blues singer in her day, winning substantial respect, and envy, from her fellow singers and musicians. In the early-to-mid-40s, billed as 'The Ebony Stick Of Dynamite', she became a huge success at Harlem's Apollo Theatre, on 125th Street and had her own radio shows as both performer and disc jockey. Despite such exposure she recorded only three times in her heyday (for Savoy Records in 1944-45) and retired from music in 1946 as a result of diabetes. In the mid-60s she was rediscovered by blues historian Sheldon Harris, who persuaded her to test for Columbia Records and reunited her with Victoria Spivey, who recorded a handful of sides by 'Miss Rhapsody'. She remained in obscurity until April 1972 when she was again brought out of retirement to record a jazz-blues album for the Saydisc-Matchbox label in New York City. Her last years were, happily, employed touring as singer with Clyde Bernhardt's Harlem Blues & Jazz Band.

Selected albums: *Miss Rhapsody* (1972), with Little Esther Phillips, Albinia Jones and Linda Hopkins *Ladies Sing The Blues* (1977).

Wheatstraw, Peetie

b. William Bunch, 21 December 1902, Ripley, Tennessee, USA. d. 21 December 1941, East St. Louis, Illinois, USA. Wheatstraw, also known as the Devil's Son-In-Law was an influential and popular blues artist of the 20s and 30s. He opened a club with Big Joe Williams in 1929. An accomplished guitarist, pianist and singer he was tragically killed in a car accident at a comparatively young age. Throughout his recordings, usually with Vocalion or Decca, he was accompanied by musicians such as Kokomo Arnold, Lonnie Johnson and Lil Armstrong. Although he recorded many tracks, little of his work has been available for some time, giving fuel to the argument that his importance and influence is on the wane.

Compilation: *Peetie Wheatstraw And Kokomo Arnold* (1975).

Further reading: *The Devil's Son-In -Law*, Paul Garon.

Wheeler, Golden

b. 16 December 1929, Baconton, Georgia,

Peetie Wheatstraw

USA. Wheeler became interested in the blues during the 30s and learned to play harmonica from Buster Brown in the early 50s Wheeler moved to Chicago in 1954 and began to play seriously the following year, inspired by Junior Wells and Little Walter. He formed his first band but after a few years of low pay and problems with other musicians, he performed less and less, and did not resume an active musical career again until 1987. Wheeler is a solid Chicago blues singer and player, and has recorded for the Mr. Blues label in 1976 (issued by Rooster in 1988) and for Wolf Records under his own name and as accompanist to Eddie King and Artie 'Blues Boy' White. Compilations: *Low Blows: An Anthology Of Chicago Harmonica Blues* (1988, two tracks by Wheeler), *Chicago Blues Session, Volume 14* (1989, contains four tracks by Wheeler).

White, Artie 'Blues Boy'

b. 1937, Vicksburg, Mississippi, USA. White began singing gospel at the age of 11 and, after moving to Chicago in 1956, he sang with the Full Gospel Wonders. He began singing blues in the early 60s and later recorded singles for small labels such as Gamma, World-Wide, PM and Sky Hero (both owned by 'Little' Mac

Simmons), and Altee ('Leanin' Tree' was a local hit for the latter company). For some time he ran a Chicago club called Bootsy's Lounge and in 1985 he made his debut album for the Ronn label. In 1987 he signed with Ichiban and has had a regular album and single releases since then, all of a consistently high standard, spotlighting White's soul-drenched blues singing, which, transferred to the stage, reveals White as a dynamic performer. Albums: *Nothing Takes The Place Of You* (1987), *Where It's At* (1989), *Thangs Got To Change* (1989). Compilation: *Tired Of Sneaking Around* (1990).

White, Bukka

b. Booker T. Washington White, 12 November 1906, Houston, Mississippi, USA, d. 26 February 1977, Memphis, Tennessee, USA. White learned guitar and piano in his teens, and hoboed from 1921, playing blues with artists such as George 'Bullet' Williams. In the mid-30s White was a boxer and baseball pitcher. White recorded for Victor in 1930, a largely unissued session including spirituals and the first of his breakneck train imitations. Returning to Vocalion in 1937, he recorded his composition 'Shake 'Em On Down' and was given the

Bukka White

misspelt billing which he always disliked. By the time 'Shake 'Em On Down' was a hit, White had been imprisoned in Parchman Farm for assault. There, he recorded two songs for the Library of Congress, and claimed to have had an easy time as a prison musician. However, when he recorded commercially again in 1940, he was clear that he had been traumatized by his experience. The result was a remarkable series of recordings, obsessed with prison, trains, drink, and death. The songs were poetic, complete and coherent, often with deep insights into their topics, their heavy vocal delivery perfectly complemented by fierce, percussive slide guitar. After his US Navy service during World War II, White settled in Memphis from 1944 onwards. In 1946, his second cousin B.B. King lived with him, learning perhaps less about music than about the blues singer's life. As white interest in blues increased, 'Fixin' To Die Blues' and 'Parchman Farm Blues' became cult songs. Rediscovered in 1963, White had retained most of his abilities, and was extensively recorded (including, for the first time, on piano). At his best, he could still produce stunningly inventive lyrics. White joined the folk club and festival circuit, performing across the USA, Canada, Mexico and Europe until the mid-70s, when illness enforced his retirement.

Album: *Big Daddy* (1974). Compilations: *The Complete Sessions 1930-1940* (1990), *Sky Songs* (1990), *The Legacy Of The Blues Vol. 1* (1991), *Aberdeen Mississippi Blues (1937-40)* (90s).

White, Georgia

b. 9 March 1903, Sandersville, Georgia, USA. The birth date was supplied by Big Bill Broonzy and it is not known if Georgia White is still alive at the time of writing. Her first record was recorded for Vocalion in 1930 in the company of Jimmie Noone, but she enjoyed considerably greater success during the late 30s when she recorded almost 100 tracks for the Decca label. A excellent blues singer with an easy style, she was also a competent pianist and may, indeed, have worked for Decca as a house musician at one time. She worked, but did not record with, Bumble Bee Slim and during the late 40s formed an all-girl band. Around 1950 she was working as pianist in Big Bill's Laughing Trio and her last recorded appearance was at a Chicago club in 1959. Her blues were often

humorous and she could play first-rate boogie-woogie but she also had a more sober side and blues pundits do not seem to have afforded her the attention that her talent deserves.

Album: *Georgia White Sings And Plays The Blues* (1982).

White, Josh

b. Joshua White, 11 February 1915, Greenville, South Carolina, USA, d. 5 September 1969, Manhasset, New York, USA. A grounding in church music stood Josh White in good stead, as it was something to which he returned at various points in a long career as blues singer and, later, folk entertainer. He learned guitar acting as a guide for blind street singers, and began his recording career at a young age. Between 1932-36, he recorded prolifically. The results often demonstrated a notable versatility, covering blues in local or more nationally popular idioms (sometimes under the pseudonym Pinewood Tom) or sacred material as the Singing Christian. In the mid-30s he moved to New York, where he found a new audience interested in radical politics and folk music. In retrospect, it seems as if he was diluting as well as tailoring his music for the consumption of white listeners who were at this time unused to hearing authentic black music. As the years went on, he learned a lot of new material, and turned his repertoire into an odd mixture, encompassing everything from traditional ballads like 'Lord Randall' to popular songs like 'Scarlet Ribbons', as well as protest songs and blues. He toured overseas in the post-war years and recorded extensively.

Selected albums: *The World Of Josh White* (1969), *Josh White With Molly Malone* (1974), with the Ronnie Sisters *Blues And Spirituals* (early 80s), *Joshua White 1936-41* (1989), *Joshua White (Pinewood Tom) Vol. 2* (1989).

White, 'Schoolboy' Cleve

b. 10 June 1928, Baton Rouge, Louisiana, USA. White taught himself to play harmonica as a youngster and received his stage name because of his youthful appearances. In the mid-50s he recorded with Lightnin' Slim and in his own right for J.D. 'Jay' Miller's Feature label, and in 1957 for Ace Records. In 1960 he moved to Los Angeles, California and retired from music, although in 1970 he relocated to San Francisco

Josh White

'Big' Joe Williams

and began to perform again. He has since recorded for Blues Connoisseur and his own Cherrie label, whose roster also includes J.J. Malone.
Album: *Lightnin' Slim Volume Three: The Feature Sides 1954* (1981, although credited to Lightnin' Slim, the title includes compositions and backings by White).

Whiting, James 'Sugar Blue'
b. James Whiting, 1949, New York City, New York, USA. Whiting's initial inspiration for both vocals and harmonica was Stevie Wonder, but he was attracted to blues through seeing shows by such acts as B.B. King and Albert King at the Apollo Theatre. He began playing seriously at the age of 17 and later worked with local bluesmen Charles Walker and Washboard Doc. Whiting was based in Paris, France for a time but finally settled in Chicago in the 80s. He recorded in his own right for various compilations and had two full albums released in France, and has recorded with many artists, including the Rolling Stones, Willie Dixon, Syl Johnson, Booker T Laury and Johnny Shines. His fluid, jazz-influenced playing has been heard on film soundtracks and 'Sugar Blue' is now rated one of the world's best blues harmonica players.
Selected albums: *Cross Roads* (1979), *From Chicago To Paris* (1982).

Wilkins, Joe Willie
b. 7 January 1923, Davenport, Mississippi, USA, d. 28 March 1979, Memphis, Tennessee, USA. His reputation as a guitarist, higher among his fellow musicians that it is with even those possessed examples of his work, Wilkins has apologists who maintain that his influence reached further and deeper than is currently recognised. His father, Frank, bought him a guitar when he was 12 and already proficient on the harmonica. He learned more from Bob Williams, Pat Rhodes and Sam Harris, members of a string band that included his father. Soon he took to the road, working in cottonfields and playing on street corners, earning the name 'Joe Willie The Walking Seeburg'. He encountered Sonny Boy Williamson (Rice Miller) and Robert Lockwood during his travels, trading ideas with the latter. He linked up with them in 1942 in Helena, Arkansas, broadcasting on

station KFFA. He was one of the King Biscuit Boys with Sonny Boy, and promoted Mother's Best Flour alongside Lockwood. He also met and worked with Robert Nighthawk and B.B. King in West Memphis. In Jackson, Mississippi in 1951, he played on sessions for Sonny Boy and Willie Love, and in Memphis in 1953 was on Albert Williams' session for Sun. He continued to work with Sonny Boy until the latter's death in 1965. During the 70s, despite being hampered by illness, he worked the Memphis area with his own King Biscuit Boys and recorded a single and album, though neither are currently available.
Album: *Goin' In Your Direction* (1991).

Wilkins, Robert, Rev.
b. 16 January 1896, Hernando, Mississippi, USA, d. 30 May 1987, Memphis, Tennessee, USA. Wilkins moved to Memphis during World War I, and by the 20s was playing his guitar and singing in the blues joints of Beale Street. Between 1928-34, he made a series of excellent recordings, which showed a carefully crafted approach, tailoring his fingerpicked accompaniments to suit the lyrics as well as the tunes. Some of his records were issued under his middle name, Tim. There was a 30-year gap before he recorded again, following rediscovery in the days of the folk/blues boom. By this time he had renounced blues and played only religious music, having been ordained a minister in 1950. His overall style was much the same, and 'Prodigal Son', was later covered by the Rolling Stones.
Albums: *Memphis Gospel Singer* (1964), *Before The Reverence* (1973), *The Original Rolling Stone* (1980).

Williams, 'Big' Joe
b. Joe Lee Williams, 16 October 1903, Crawford, Mississippi, USA, d. 17 December 1982, Macon, Mississippi, USA. Big Joe Williams was one of the most important blues singers to have recorded and also one whose life conforms almost exactly to the stereotyped pattern of how a 'country' blues singer should live. He was of partial Red Indian stock, his father being 'Red Bone' Williams a part Cherokee. 'Big Joe' took his musical influences from his mother's family, the Logans. He made the obligatory 'cigar box' instruments when a

child and took to the road when his step-father threw him out around 1918. He later immortalized this antagonist in a song that he was still performing at the end of his long career. Joe's life was one of constant movement as he worked his way around the lumber camps, turpentine farms and juke joints of the south. Around 1930 he married and settled, in St. Louis, Missouri, but still took long sweeps through the country as the rambling habit never left him. This rural audience supported him through the worst of the depression when he appeared under the name 'Poor Joe'. His known recordings began in 1935 when he recorded six tracks for Bluebird in Chicago. From then on he recorded at every opportunity. He stayed with Bluebird until 1945 before moving to Columbia. He formed a loose partnership on many sessions with John Lee 'Sonny Boy' Williamson which have been likened to that of Muddy Waters and Little Walter. In 1952, he worked for Trumpet in Jackson, Mississippi, then went back to Chicago for a session with Vee Jay. Other recordings made for smaller companies are still being discovered. During 1951-52, he also made recordings of other singers at his St. Louis base. Williams found a wider audience when blues came into vogue with young whites in the 60s. He continued to record, and tour, adding Europe and Japan to his itinerary. He still used cheap, expendable guitars fixed up by himself with an electrical pick-up and usually festooned with extra machine heads to accommodate nine strings. With his gruff, shouting voice and ringing guitar - not to mention his sometimes uncertain temper - he became a great favourite on the club and concert circuit. He had come full circle and was living in a caravan in Crawford, Mississippi, when he died. The sheer volume of easily accessible albums recorded during his last years tended to obscure just how big a blues talent Joe's really was.

Selected albums: *Piney Woods Blues* (1958), *Tough Times* (1960), *Nine String Guitar Blues* (1961), *Blues On Highway 49* (1961), *Mississippi's Big Joe Williams* (1962), *Blues On Highway 49* (1962), *Blues For Nine Strings* (1963), *Big Joe Williams At Folk City* (1963), *Studio Blues* (1964), *Starvin' Chain Blues* (1966), *Classic Delta Blues* (1966), *Hellbound And Heaven Sent* (1967), *Big Joe Williams* (1969), *Legacy Of The Blues,*

Volume 6 (1974), *Tough Times* (1981), *Thinking Of What They Did* (1981), *Big Joe Williams 1974* (1982). Compilations: *Field Recordings 1973-80* (1988), *Malving My Sweet Woman* (1988), *Complete Recorded Works In Chronological Order Volumes 1 & 2* (1991), with Luther Huff and Willie Love *Delta Blues - 1951* (1991).

Williams, Bill

b. 28 February 1897, Richmond, Virginia, USA, d. 6 October 1973, Greenup, Kentucky, USA. Williams claimed to have played 'Yankee Doodle Dandy' within 15 minutes of picking up a guitar in 1908, and his awesome abilities when aged over 70 with an arthritic wrist lend his claim credibility. By 1922, he had settled in Greenup to work as a trackliner after a period of wandering, and played thereafter for the local white audience. His repertoire included the 'blues, rags and ballads' of his posthumous album, songster material like 'Chicken' and 'Railroad Bill', and white fiddle pieces transposed to guitar, pop songs like 'Darktown Strutters' Ball' and 'Up A Lazy River'. There was even a ragtime version of 'The Star-Spangled Banner'. Discovered in 1970, he had a brief, and professedly reluctant, career playing concerts and television shows.

Albums: *Low And Lonesome* (1971), *Blues, Rags And Ballads* (1974).

Williams, Blind Connie

b. c.1915, Florida, USA. Williams was recorded in 1961 in Philadelphia, having been found by a folklorist singing spirituals to his accordion accompaniment. He proved also to have a repertoire of the better known blues, and to be an accomplished guitarist. As a result of studying at the St. Petersburg School for the Blind, he had a sophisticated grasp of harmony, and used many passing notes and altered chords. Williams' technique was also influenced by an association with Rev. Gary Davis in New York (though his dating of it to the late 30s is confusing, since Davis did not move to New York until 1944). Williams was also a quartet singer, though not recorded as such. He was still known to be alive in 1974, though frail and seldom performing in the streets.

Compilation: *Philadelphia Street Singer* (1974).

Williams, J. Mayo

b. 1894, Monmouth, Illinois, USA, d. 2 January 1980, Chicago, Illinois, USA. A college graduate, Williams was nicknamed 'Ink' by musicians; he was the first, and in his time the most successful, black executive in the US record industry. In 1924, he joined Paramount, which he made perhaps the most successful of all 'race' labels in terms of both quality and quantity of output, recording Blind Lemon Jefferson, Papa Charlie Jackson and Ma Rainey among others. Williams was careful to find out what black purchasers wanted; when replies to market research indicated overwhelming demand for blues, he abandoned his own preference for the likes of Paul Robeson. In 1927, Williams resigned to found the short-lived Black Patti label, moving on immediately to Vocalion, to whom he brought Georgia Tom, Tampa Red and Jim Jackson. In 1934, he became responsible for black A&R at Decca, recording Mahalia Jackson's debut sides. After World War II, Williams operated a series of small labels, all of which suffered from undercapitalization and a loss of touch by Williams (as may be heard on Muddy Waters' first commercial recording). As an executive, his income came from a share of publishing royalties and from padding his expense accounts; but said that 'I was better than 50% honest, and in this business that's pretty good'.

Williams, Johnny

b. 15 May 1906, Alexandria, Louisiana, USA. Williams learned guitar in 1918, and divided his time between Mississippi and Chicago until 1938. He moved north permanently, and became a professional musician in 1943. He worked with many Chicago blues singers, most closely with Theodore 'Hound Dog' Taylor, Big Boy Spires and his cousin Johnny Young. In the late 40s, Williams played guitar behind Young on an Ora-Nelle 78, singing on one side. He and Young also recorded for Al Benson's Planet/Old Swingmaster labels, and Williams shared a 1953 session with Spires for the Chance label, on which his serious, committed delivery is perhaps indicative of the Baptist minister he became in 1959.

Albums: *Chicago Boogie* (1974), *Going Back Home* (1984).

Williams, Joseph (Jo Jo)

b. 1920, Coahoma, Mississippi, USA. One of a legion of musicians whose name and record follow one another with Pavlovian accuracy, Williams played in bands whose members sometimes worked with better-known artists. Raised in northwest Mississippi and on the outskirts of Memphis, his first steps in music were with baling wire strung on the wall. During the 30s he witnessed Son House and Willie Brown playing for country suppers. He developed his guitar playing in Memphis in the early 40s before moving on to Chicago. In 1953 he played his first professional gig, with pianist Lazy Bill Lucas. Two years later, Williams formed his own group with Lucas, drummer Johnny Swanns and Lucas' niece, 'Miss Hi Fi', singing. He then teamed up with harmonica player Mojo Buford in a band with Dave Members and Cadillac Sam Burton. With Buford, he became a member of Muddy Waters' Junior Band, playing Smitty's Corner when Muddy was out of town. In 1959, he made two records, the first un-numbered, for the Atomic-H label. 'All Pretty Wimmens' epitomises raucous, impromptu blues at its best, all the better for being obscure, as was the follow-up, 'Afro Shake Dance'. In 1962, he moved, with Lucas and Buford, to Minneapolis, playing bass in a group that recorded as Mojo & The Chi Fours, the material released on Folk Art and Vernon. Two years later, the band had two singles released on Adell. Williams recorded with Lazy Bill for Lucas' own label in 1970, and retired from music sometime in the 70s.

Album: *Lazy Bill And His Friends* (1970).

Williams, Joseph Leon (Jody)

b. 3 February 1935, Mobile, Alabama, USA. More people are familiar with Jody Williams' guitar work than they are with his name. Anyone with Bo Diddley's 'Who Do You Love' or Billy Boy Arnold's 'I Wish You Would' (Jody wrote 'I Was Fooled', the B side of the original Vee Jay single) or Billy Stewart's 'Billy's Blues' (the trial run for 'Love Is Strange'), has a sample of his ringing, nervy guitarwork. Though making only a handful of singles, few of them under his own name, he was an extremely busy session and house musician throughout the 50s. He arrived in Chicago in 1941, first taking up the harmonica before learning guitar with Ellas

Robert Pete Williams

McDaniel (Bo Diddley) but to greater effect than the future star. By 1951, they and tub bass player Roosevelt Jackson, had formed a band. Williams quickly became a proficient and in-demand musician, touring the US in Charles Brown's band before he was 20. That year (1955), he played on Bo's 'Diddy Wah Diddy', Arnold's 'I Wish You Would' and soloed alongside B.B. King on Otis Spann's 'Five Spot'. Inevitably, his own career was incidental to his other work. Singles appeared on Blue Lake, Argo and Herald as Little Papa Joe or Little Joe Lee or Sugar Boy Williams, since Joe Williams already sang with Count Basie's band. In the mid-60s, he quit music to study electronics, and later, computer maintenance. He has made sporadic appearances since then but cannot be tempted back.

Williams, L.C.

b. 12 March 1930, Crockett, Texas, USA, d. 18 October 1960, Houston, Texas, USA. Another artist whose given names are initials, Williams grew up in Mullican, Texas, before moving to Houston about 1945. There he worked in dance halls and bars as both singer and dancer. He also learned to play drums. Having made the acquaintance of Lightnin' Hopkins, he recorded for Bill Quinn's Gold Star label, nicknamed 'Lightnin' Jr.', with Hopkins backing him on guitar and piano on three singles, and pianists Leroy Carter and Elmore Nixon on one side each of a fourth, all subsequently reissued. He also recorded for Freedom, another Houston label owned by Solomon Kahal, making six records, one combining 'My Darkest Hour' and 'I Want My Baby Back' reissued on Imperial, mostly with Conrad Johnson's Conney's Combo. In 1951 he recorded at least four titles, including 'Baby Child' and 'Fannie Mae', for Sittin In With, owned by New Yorker Bob Shad. Shad probably produced Williams' final commercial session, made the same year for Mercury with backing by saxman Henry Hayes And His Rhythm Kings. Williams, addicted to cheap wine, also suffered from tuberculosis. Just prior to his death, he recorded one title with Hopkins and harmonica player Luke 'Long Gone' Miles. When asked the significance of his initials, Williams' reply was 'love crazy'. Ironic then that his death was from lung collapse.
Albums: *Texas Blues - The Gold Star Sessions*

(1992), *The Big Three* (1992).

Williams, Lester

b. 24 June 1920, Groveton, Texas, USA, d. 13 November 1990, Houston, Texas, USA. Raised in Houston on the records of Blind Lemon Jefferson and Lonnie Johnson, Williams was inspired to take up the electric guitar after hearing fellow Texan 'T-Bone' Walker. His debut recording on the small, local Macy's Records - 'Wintertime Blues' - was to be his biggest hit. His last records were made for Imperial Records in 1956, although he continued to perform locally, and was rediscovered in 1986 for a tour of Europe.
Albums: *Dowling Street Hop* (1982), *Texas Troubador* (1987).

Williams, Robert Pete

b. 14 March 1914, Zachary, Louisiana, USA, d. 31 December 1980, Rosedale, Louisiana, USA. Although he had been playing and singing blues since he was a young man, Williams first came to wider notice when he was recorded in 1958 by folklorist Harry Oster. At the time, Williams was serving a sentence for murder at the Penitentiary at Angola. His sombre vocals and gentle, understated guitar accompaniments were impressive in themselves, but more significant was his unique ability to sing long, partially extemporized songs, sometimes based around a traditional formula, sometimes remarkably original and intensely personal. This exposure led to his being taken up by a younger audience and on his release from prison he made many appearances at concerts and festivals in the USA and overseas. He also made many more records, most of which testify to his great creative imagination and artistry.
Albums: *Angola Prisoners Blues* (1958), *Blues From Bottoms* (1973), *Those Prison Blues* (1981), *Live* (1988), *With Big Joe Williams* (1988), *Roberts Pete Williams And Roosevelt Sykes* (1988). Compilation: *Legacy Of The Blues* (1973).

Williamson, John Lee 'Sonny Boy'

b. 30 March 1914, Jackson, Tennessee, USA, d. 1 June 1948, Chicago, Illinois, USA. Williamson learned harmonica as a child, and as a teenager in Tennessee was associated with the group of musicians around Sleepy John Estes. 'Sonny Boy' had been in Chicago for three years

Sonny Boy (Rice Miller) Williamson

when he came to record in 1937, but his early records retained the plaintive sound, and often the songs, of Estes' circle. From the first, however, Williamson was an unmistakable musician, partly through his 'Tongue-tied' singing style (probably a controlled version of his stammer), but chiefly for his harmonica playing. He worked almost invariably in 'cross-note' tuning, in which the key of the harmonica is a fourth above that of the music. This technique encourages drawn rather than blown notes, thus facilitating the vocalization, slurring and bent notes that are basic, in conjunction with intermittent hand muting, and various tonguing and breath control effects, to most blues harmonica playing.

In his time, Williamson was the greatest master of these techniques, and of blending voice and harmonica into a continuous melodic line; he reached a peak of technical and emotional perfection that sets the standard and defines the aesthetic for blues harmonica players to this day. Williamson recorded prolifically, as both leader and accompanist. His music developed continuously, and by the end of his life featured a powerful ensemble sound with amplified guitar. Williamson was equally adept at the expression of emotional intensity and the provision of rocking, exuberant dance music; in the musically rather bland years of the 40s, he preserved these qualities in the blues of Chicago, as if to prophesy the changes that were taking place by the time of his death. Universally liked, despite his enthusiasm for fighting when drunk, Williamson was greatly respected by his fellow musicians; he was enormously influential on more than one generation of harmonica players, from his contemporaries like Walter Horton and Drifting Slim to youngsters like Junior Wells and Billy Boy Arnold, and a remarkable proportion of his songs became blues standards. In Forrest City Joe, he acquired a devoted imitator, but perhaps the best indication of John Lee Williamson's importance, notwithstanding the monetary considerations that were doubtless his initial motivation, was the stubborn insistence of Sonny Boy 'Rice Miller' Williamson, a harmonica genius in his own right, that he was 'the original Sonny Boy Williamson'. On 1 June 1948, Williamson's life came to a tragic end following a serious assault. Selected albums: *Big Bill & Sonny Boy* (1964), *Volume 1* (c. 1965), *Volume 2* (c. 1968), *Volume 3* (c. 1972), *Bluebird, Number. 1* (c. 1982), *Bluebird, Number. 15* (c. 1985), *Sonny Boy Williamson* (c. 1986), *Rare Sonny Boy* (1988): *Volume 1* (1991).

Williamson, Sonny Boy 'Rice Miller'

b. Aleck/Alex Ford, 5 December 1899, Glendora, Mississippi, USA. d. 25 May 1965, Helena, Arkansas, USA. Being a man never to compromise a good story by affording undue attention to veracity, and mischievous to boot, Sonny Boy's own various accounts of his life were never to be trusted and led to much confusion. Often referred to as 'Sonny Boy Williamson II' he was, in fact, older than John Lee 'Sonny Boy' Williamson whose name, and associated glory, he appropriated sometime in the late 30s or early 40s. Why he felt the need to do so is odd in light of the fact that he owed John Lee Williamson nothing in style or ability, and along with that worthy and Little Walter Jacobs was one of the most innovatory and influential exponents of the blues harmonica. He was the illegitimate child of Millie Ford, but he took to using his stepfather's name and by common association became 'Rice Miller'. He mastered his chosen instrument (he could also play guitar and drums) early in his life and seems to have taken to the road as soon as he was able, relying on his skill for a livelihood. His wanderings throughout the south brought him into contact with many blues artists.

The list includes Robert Johnson, Robert 'Junior' Lockwood, Elmore James and Howlin' Wolf, whose half sister, Mary, he married sometime in the 30s. During this period Sonny Boy used many names, working as 'Little Boy Blue', Willie Williamson, Willie Williams and Willie Miller (after his brother) and known to his friends as 'Foots' because of his habit of razoring his shoes, no matter how new they might be, to make them comfortable. He was cashing in on the popularity of John Lee Williamson (safely out of the way in Chicago) when he got a job broadcasting over KFFA radio out of Helena on the *King Biscuit Show* in 1941. The show was heard all over the south and made Sonny Boy famous. He continued to travel but now sought radio stations to advertise his activities. In the early 50s he recorded for Lillian McMurray's Trumpet label in Jackson,

Mississippi along with friends Willie Love and Elmore James. His work on this label includes many outstanding performances with 'Mighty Long Time' being perhaps the greatest of all. On the strength of his increased popularity he extended his area of work and began to appear in the bars of Detroit, where he worked with Baby Boy Warren, and in Chicago (John Lee Williamson was dead by this time).

He began his career with Chess Records of Chicago in 1955 with his hit 'Don't Start Me Talkin'' and became a mainstay of the label almost until his death. In 1963, he took Europe by storm as a result of his appearances with the AFBF. His impressive appearance; tall and stooped in his famous grey/blue suit (quartered like a jester's doublet) and sporting a bowler hat and umbrella, along with his hooded eyes and goatee beard, hypnotized audiences as he weaved back and forth snapping his fingers and clicking his tongue in a display of perfect rhythmic control. His skill on the harmonica was augmented by many tricks of showmanship such as playing two instruments at once (one with his large and plastic nose) or holding the harp end on in his mouth and manoeuvring it with his tongue. If Europe took to him, Sonny Boy seems to have enjoyed Europe. He stayed over when the tour ended and played his way around the burgeoning blues clubs, travelling as far as Poland!.

He recorded for the Storyville label in Denmark and with Chris Barber in Britain. He returned to Europe, often stating his intention to to take up permanent residence. He never lived to see the days when Chess tried to convert their roster of blues singers into pop stars, by uniting them with the most unlikely material and musical support, but in earlier days he had been quite happy to follow a similar route, by recording with such groups as the Yardbirds and the Animals; and a jazz combo led by Brian Auger. Some of these efforts stand up better than others but Sonny Boy did not care - as long as he got paid. Despite all this moving around he still maintained a home in the USA, with his second wife Mattie Lee Gordon. He was back in Helena, appearing on the *King Biscuit Show* when he died in his sleep in 1965. Apart from his skill as a harmonica player and singer Sonny Boy was also a 'character' and anecdotes about him are legion, both among the blues fraternity

and his fans in Europe. If he was difficult, contentious, and unreliable he was also a charming man who played upon his reputation as an evil, dangerous, hard-living blues troubadour. His music reveals that he was also capable of being both sensitive and humorous. He will always remain something of a conundrum but as an artist his stature is recognised and his fame deserved.

Selected albums: *Down And Out Blues* (1959), *Portrait In Blues* (1964), *The Real Folk Blues* aka *In Memorium* (1965), *Don't Send Me No Flowers* (1966), *More Real Folk Blues* (1967), *Sonny Boy Williamson And The Yardbirds* (1966), *One Way Out* (1968), *Bummer Road* (1969), *King Biscuit Time* (1989), *The Animals With Sonny Boy Williamson* (1989, rec. 1963). Compilations: with Willie Love *Clowning With The World* (1989), *The Chess Years* (1991), *Boppin' With Sonny* (1992).

Willis, Aaron (Little Sonny)

b. 6 October 1932, Greensboro, Alabama, USA. Despite the claims of his first album, its evidence shows that Little Sonny Willis is an adequate harmonica player and reluctant singer whose music career has been at best intermittent. With little experience in music apart from singing in church choirs, Willis moved to Detroit in 1954. Working as a photographer in the bars of the Hastings Street area, he also picked up the rudiments of the harmonica. His first gig was in the Good Time Bar with Washboard Willie's band. Willis gained some harmonica tuition from Sonny Boy Williamson (Rice Miller), from whom he adopted his nickname. In March 1956, he formed his own band with pianist Chuck Smith, guitarist Louis (Big Bo) Collins and drummer Jim Due Crawford. Two years later Smith, Crawford and Eddie Burns backed Willis on his debut record, 'I Gotta Find My Baby', for Duke Records. Another record, 'Love Shock', recorded by Joe Von Battle, was leased to Excello. An unissued 1961 session for Chess resaged a five-year record silence, followed by singles for Speedway, Revilot (including the instrumental 'The Creeper') and Wheel City at the end of the decade. In 1969 he recorded his first album for the Stax subsidiary, Enterprise. *New King Of The Blues Harmonica*, an album of mostly uninventive instrumentals, evoked the Hans Christian Andersen fairy tale.

A second album released in 1973, *Hard Goin' Up*, was a more honest, balanced exercise. Albert King recorded Willis' 'Love Shock' and 'Love Mechanic' for Tomato in 1978. The album, *King Albert*, was recorded in Detroit and used Willis' songs, Aaron Jnr., Anthony and Eddie in the backup band. Perhaps their father had read *King Lear*.
Selected album: *New King Of The Blues Harmonica/Hard Goin' Up* (1991).

Willis, Chick

b. Robert L. Willis, 24 September 1934, Atlanta, Georgia, USA. Willis primary influence was Eddie 'Guitar Slim' Jones, who he saw numerous times in Atlanta. As a guitarist he toured with many R&B acts in the 50s, including Nappy Brown, Ray Charles, and Big Joe Turner, and for several years he was on tour with his cousin Chuck Willis. In the 60s he began fronting his own band. He had made his recording debut around 1956, but for many years he was confined to working for small singles' companies. In 1972, he had a huge hit with the *risqué* 'Stoop Down Baby' achieved without any airplay, and he is still often billed as 'the Stoop Down Man'. He can still produce pure 50s style blues and R&B from time to time.
Albums: *Stoop Down Baby, Let Your Daddy See* (1972), *Back To The Blues* (1991).

Willis, Ralph

b. 1910, Alabama, USA, d 1957, New York City, New York, USA. Ralph Willis moved to North Carolina in the 30s, and met Blind Boy Fuller, Eugene 'Buddy' Moss and Brownie McGhee; he was closely associated with McGhee in New York after relocated there in 1944, and his recordings often have McGhee on second guitar. They range from delicate guitar duets to driving dance music, with a nice line in bawdy humour, although he could also be lazily wistful, as on his solo cover of Luke Jordan's 'Church Bells'. Despite his connection with McGhee and Sonny Terry, Willis did not make contact with the burgeoning folk revival. He was known as 'Bama' for his rural ways, he perhaps lacked the drive or the self-confidence to achieve mainstream success.
Albums: *Faded Picture Blues* (1970), *Carolina Blues* (1974), *East Coast Blues* (1988).

Wilson, Edith Goodall

b. 6 September 1896, Louisville, Kentucky, USA, d. March 1981. Edith Wilson was a blues singing stage star whose career credits include a long list of revues beginning with *Put And Take* in 1921. In the same year she made her first records in the company of Johnny Dunn And His Original Jazz Hounds. Never just a blues singer, she continued to work after the initial interest in the so-called classic blues had declined appearing on stage and films, both as a singer and as an actress. She later appeared advertising cookies in the assumed role of 'Aunt Jemima'. She never really retired and took advantage of the increased interest in blues during the 60s to float a second career that saw her recording an album for the Delmark label in 1970 and performing at the Newport Jazz Festival in 1980. As a blues singer, what she lacked of the rawness and power associated with performers such as Bessie Smith and Ma Rainey she made up for in urbanity and wit.
Compilation: *Edith Wilson With Johnny Dunn's Jazz Hounds (1921-22)* (1979).

Wilson, Harding 'Hop'

b. 27 April 1921, Grapeland, Texas, USA, d. 27 August 1975, Houston, Texas, USA. Although his nickname is a corruption of 'Harp', reflecting early prowess on the harmonica, it is as a slide guitarist that Wilson will be remembered. As well as playing conventional guitar, he played steel guitar placed horizontally on a stand, a manner usually associated with C&W musicians. He played and sang with great skill and expression, encompassing a range of rhythms and moods from rocking R&B to tormented slow blues. Working in East Texas and Louisiana, he made singles for the Goldband company in 1958, and the small label Ivory (owned by drummer 'Ivory' Lee Semien) in 1960 and 1961. These, plus a handful of tracks unissued at the time, but released on an album after his death, account for his entire recorded legacy, but they are sufficient to establish Wilson as one of the most original blues artists of his time.
Album: *Steel Guitar Flash* (1988).

Wilson, Jimmy

b. 1921, Louisiana, USA, d. 1965, Dallas, Texas, USA. Wilson was singing in California with a

gospel quartet when his distinctive, bluesy lead was noticed by impresario, Bob Geddins, who recorded Wilson as the blues singer with his band, Bob Geddins' Cavaliers, and in his own right, for his Cava Tone label, often in the company of legendary Bay Area guitarist, Lafayette Thomas. Some of these tracks created just enough of a stir for Aladdin Records to take an interest and purchase some of Wilson's masters from Geddins, and later during 1952 Wilson began recording for Aladdin and its small subsidiary 7-11. In 1953 Jimmy Wilson again signed with Geddins to record for his new Big Town label, and the first release, 'Tin Pan Alley', although not a Wilson original, was a tremendous success and has since become synonymous with his name. Most of Wilson's mid-50s output was issued on Big Town, although odd releases appeared on Irma and Elko (the latter under guitarist Jimmy Nolan's name), and four tracks were issued on the Chart label. Later recordings did not match up to the doomy Bay Area sound of his Geddins' tracks, despite a couple of attempts at the 'Tin Pan Alley' sound and a good local seller 'Please Accept My Love' on Goldband which was covered successfully by B.B. King. Wilson died in 1965 of drink-related problems virtually forgotten by the record-buying public.
Albums: *Trouble In My House* (1984), *Jimmy Wilson - San Francisco 1952-53* (1985).

Wilson, 'Kid' Wesley

b. 1 October 1893, Jacksonville, Florida, USA, d. 10 October 1958, Cape May Court House, New Jersey, USA. With his wife, Leola B. 'Coot' Grant, Wilson formed a long-established and very popular black vaudeville team, who were on stage from 1912 to the mid-30s. They recorded extensively, using a number of pseudonyms, and featuring comic dialogues of marital strife in the manner of Butterbeans And Susie. Both also recorded solo, and Wilson duetted with Harry McDaniels (as Pigmeat Pete & Catjuice Charlie). Their songwriting was also important, and they produced over 400 numbers, including 'Gimme A Pigfoot', and the other three songs recorded at Bessie Smith's last session. They reappeared briefly in the late 40s, recording and writing for Mezz Mezzrow's King Jazz label, and playing a few concerts, but had retired by the end of the decade.

Selected albums: *Great Blues Singers Vol. 1* (1970), *Leola B. Wilson & 'Kid' Wesley Wilson* (1989).

Wilson, Up

b. Huary Wilson, 4 September 1935, Shreveport, Louisiana, USA. Wilson learned to play on his grandmother's guitar and after moving to Dallas, Texas in the early 50s he became acquainted with local bluesmen Mercy Baby, Zuzu Bollin, and Frankie Lee Sims. Around 1954 he recorded behind Bollin, though the tracks remain unissued. In the late 50s Wilson played on a regular basis with Robert Ealey. During the 70s and early 80s he only occasionally played professionally, due to family commitments. In 1988 he recorded a session for Pee Wee Records, who released one single; 'Red Lightnin''. They later released a full album. *Blues And Rhythm* magazine called Wilson's music 'superb Texas blues from one of the discoveries of the 80s'.
Albums: *On My Way* (1988), *Wild Texas Guitar* (1989, CD only).

Wingfield, Pete

b. 7 May 1948, Kiphook, Hampshire, England. Wingfield was a pianist who previously led Pete's Disciples and played sessions with Top Topham, Graham Bond, and Memphis Slim. He was also an acknowledged soul music expert who started the *Soul Beat* fanzine in the late 60s, and in the 70s would write for *Let It Rock* magazine. While at Sussex University he met fellow students Paul Butler (guitar), John Best (bass), and local teacher Chris Waters (drums) and formed the band Jellybread. With Wingfield doing most of the singing they made an album for their own Liphook label which they used as a demo and got themselves a deal with Blue Horizon Records. Although they gained some plaudits from the media they were generally unsuccessful and Wingfield left in the summer of 1971. He next played in Keef Hartley's band but that liaison ended when Hartley was invited to drum for John Mayall. Wingfield did further sessions for Freddie King, then joined Colin Blunstone's band, and also backed Van Morrison for a spell. With Joe Jammer, he became the core of the session band the Olympic Runners, who were the brainchild of Blue Horizon boss Mike Vernon. The Runners also included

DeLisle Harper (bass) and Glen LeFleur (drums) who acted as the rhythm section on Wingfield's own 1975 album *Breakfast Special* which included the hit single '18 With A Bullet'. The Olympic Runners had some success in their own right late in the 70s. Wingfield still does sessions and various studio projects, putting out the occasional single. However, he is now better known for his production credits (like Dexys Midnight Runners' *Searching For The Young Soul Rebels*, plus Blue Rondo A La Turk and the Kane Gang).
Album: *Breakfast Special* (1975).

Winter, Edgar

b. 28 December 1946, Beaumont, Texas, USA. Although at times overshadowed by his brother, Johnny Winter, Edgar has enjoyed an intermittently successful career. The siblings began performing together as teenagers, and were members of several itinerant groups performing in southern-state clubs and bars. Edgar later forsook music for college, before accepting an offer to play saxophone in a local jazz band. He rejoined his brother in 1969, but the following year Edgar released *Entrance*. He then formed an R&B revue, Edgar Winter's White Trash, whose live set *Roadwork*, was an exciting testament to this talented ensemble. Winter then fronted a slimmer group - Dan Hartman (vocals), Ronnie Montrose (guitar) and Chuck Ruff (drums) - which appeared on the artist's only million-selling album, *They Only Come Out At Night*. This highly successful selection included the rousing instrumental, 'Frankenstein', which became a hit single in its own right. Guitarist Rick Derringer, who had produced Winter's previous two albums, replaced Montrose for *Shock Treatment*, but this and subsequent releases failed to maintain the singer's commercial ascendancy. He rejoined his brother in 1976 for the *Together* album, since which Edgar Winter's professional profile has been considerably lean.
Albums: *Entrance* (1970), *Edgar Winter's White Trash* (1971), *Roadwork* (1972), *They Only Come Out At Night* (1972), *Shock Treatment* (1974), *Jasmine Nightdreams* (1975), *Edgar Winter Group With Rick Derringer* (1975), with Johnny Winter *Together* (1976), *Recycled* (1977), *The Edgar Winter Album* (1979), *Standing On The Rock* (1981). Compilation: *Rock Giants* (1982).

Winter, Johnny

b. 23 February 1944, Leland, Mississippi, USA. Raised in Beaumont, Texas with younger brother, Edgar Winter, Johnny was a child prodigy prior to forging a career as a blues guitarist. He made his recording debut in 1960, fronting Johnny and the Jammers, and over the next eight years completed scores of masters, many of which remained unreleased until his success prompted their rediscovery. By 1968 the guitarist was leading Tommy Shannon (bass) and John Turner (drums) in a trio entitled Winter. The group recorded a single for the Austin-based Sonobeat label, consigning extra tracks from the same session to a demonstration disc. This was subsequently issued by United Artists as *The Progressive Blues Experiment*. An article in **Rolling Stone** magazine heaped effusive praise on the guitarist's talent and led to lucrative recording and management deals. *Johnny Winter* ably demonstrated his exceptional dexterity while *Second Winter*, which included rousing versions of 'Johnny B. Goode' and 'Highway 61 Revisited', suggested a newfound emphasis on rock. This direction was confirmed in 1970 when Winter was joined by the McCoys, a group struggling to shed a teeny-bop image. Billed as Johnny Winter And - with guitarist Rick Derringer acting as a foil - the new line-up proclaimed itself with a self-titled studio collection and a fiery live set. These excellent releases brought Winter a much-deserved commercial success. Chronic heroin addiction forced him into partial retirement and it was two years before he re-emerged with *Still Alive And Well*. Subsequent work was bedevilled by indecision until the artist returned to his roots with *Nothing But The Blues* and *White Hot And Blue*. At the same time Winter assisted Muddy Waters by producing and arranging a series of acclaimed albums which recaptured the spirit of the veteran blues artist's classic recordings. Winter's recent work has proved equally vibrant and three releases for Alligator, a Chicago-based independent label, included the rousing *Guitar Slinger*, which displayed all the passion apparent on those early, seminal recordings. His career may have failed to match initial, extravagant expectations, but his contribution to the blues should not be underestimated; he remains an exceptional talent.
Albums: *Johnny Winter* (1969), *The Progressive*

Johnny Winter

Blues Experiment (1969), *Second Winter* (1969), *Johnny Winter And* (1970), *Johnny Winter And Live* (1971), *Still Alive And Well* (1973), *Saints And Sinners* (1974), *John Dawson Winter III* (1974), *Captured Live!* (1976), with Edgar Winter *Together* (1976), *Nothin' But The Blues* (1977), *White Hot And Blue* (1978), *Raisin' Cain* (1980), *Raised On Rock* (1981), *Guitar Slinger* (1984), *Serious Business* (1985), *Third Degree* (1986), *Winter Of '88* (1988), *Let Me In* (1991), *Hey, Where's Your Brother?* (1992). Compilations: *The Johnny Winter Story* (1969), *First Winter* (1970), *Early Times* (1971), *About Blues* (1972), *Before The Storm* (1972), *Austin Texas* (1972), *The Johnny Winter Story* (1980), *The Johnny Winter Collection* (1986), *Birds Can't Row Boats* (1988).

Witherspoon, Jimmy

b. 8 August 1923, Gurdon, Arkansas, USA. Witherspoon has crossed over into rock, jazz and R&B territory, but his deep and mellow voice places him ultimately as one of the finest ever blues singers. He sang in his local Baptist church from the age of seven. From 1941-43 he was in the Merchant Marines and, during stopovers in Calcutta, he found himself singing the blues with a band led by Teddy Weatherford. In 1944, he replaced Walter Brown in the Jay McShann band at Vallejo, California, and toured with him for the next four years. In 1949 he had his first hit, 'Tain't Nobody's Business If I Do', which stayed on the *Billboard* chart for 34 weeks. Other recordings at the time with bands led by Jimmy 'Maxwell Street' Davis are fine examples of rollicking west coast R&B (collected as *Who's Been Jivin' You*). Witherspoon's popularity as an R&B singer faded during the course of the 50s, but he made a great impression on jazz listeners at the Monterey Jazz Festival in October 1959, performing with a group that included Ben Webster. Other collaborations with jazz artists included *Some Of My Best Friends Are The Blues*, with horns and strings arranged and conducted by Benny Golson, and a guest performance on Jon Hendricks's *Evolution Of The Blues Song*. He won the *Downbeat* critics' poll as a 'new star' in 1961. Frequent tours of Europe followed, beginning in 1961 with a Buck Clayton group and later with Coleman Hawkins, Roy Eldridge, Earl Hines and Woody Herman. He also did community work, including singing in prisons. In the early 70s he gave up touring for a sedentary job as a blues disc jockey on the radio station KMET in Los Angeles, but resumed active music thanks to the encouragement of Eric Burdon, During his touring with Burdon he introduced a young Robben Ford as his guitarist and toured Japan and the Far East. In 1974 his 'Love Is A Five Letter Word' was a hit, though some fans regretted his neglect of the blues. A record with the Savoy Sultans in 1980 was a spirited attempt to recall a bygone era. 1992's *The Blues, The Whole Blues And Nothin' But The Blues* was the first album release for Mike Vernon's new label, Indigo. Witherspoon has been revered by generations during different eras, his name was often cited as a major influence during the 60s beat boom; his work is destined to endure.

Albums: *New Orleans Blues* (1956), *Goin' To Kansas City Blues* (1958), with Eddie Vinson *Battle Of The Blues, Volume 3* (1959), *At The Monterey Jazz Festival* (1959), with Gerry Mulligan *Mulligan With Witherspoon* (1959), *Feelin' The Spirit* (1959), *Jimmy Witherspoon At The Renaissance* (1959), *Singin' The Blues* (1959), *There's Good Rockin' Tonight* (1961), *Spoon* (1961), *Hey, Mrs. Jones* (1962), *Roots* (1962), *Baby, Baby, Baby* (1963, reissued as *Mean Old Frisco*), *Evenin' Blues* (1964), *Goin' To Chicago Blues* (1964), *Blue Spoon* (1964), *Some Of My Best Friends Are The Blues* (1964), *Take This Hammer* (1964), *Blues For Spoon And Groove* (1965), *Spoon In London* (1965), *Blues Point Of View* (1966), *Blues For Easy Livers* (1967), *Ain't Nobodys Business* (1967), *A Spoonful Of Soul* (1968), *The Blues Singer* (1969), *Love Is A Five Letter Word* (1975), *Hunh!* (1970), *Handbags & Gladrags* (1970), *Blues Singer* (1970), with Eric Burdon *Guilty* (1971), *Jimmy Witherspoon And Ben Webster (That's Jazz)* (1977), with Buck Clayton *Live In Paris, Big Blues* (1981), with New Savoy Sultans *Sings The Blues* (1980), *Call My Baby* (1991), *The Blues, The Whole Blues And Nothin' But The Blues* (1992). Compilations: *The Best Of Jimmy Witherspoon* (1969), *Never Knew This Kind Of Hurt Before: The Bluesway Sessions* (1988, recorded 1969-71), *Meets The Jazz Giants* (1989, recorded 1959).

Woodfork, 'Poor' Bob

b. 13 March 1925, Lake Village, Arkansas, USA,

d. June 1988, Chicago, Illinois, USA. Woodfork learned guitar as a youngster, but his musical career began in the US Army during World War II, when the USO spotted him in Swansea, Wales. Back in Chicago, he worked as a sideman for Otis Rush, and later for Jimmy Rogers, Howlin' Wolf, George Smith and Little Walter. Some mid-60s recordings under his own name were released on albums for the new European blues audience, but did not advance his career. Woodfork continued to work as a sideman, and occasional leader, in the Chicago clubs.

Selected albums: *Blues Southside Chicago* (1966), *Have A Good Time* (1971).

Woods, Oscar 'Buddy'

b. 1900, Shreveport, Louisiana, USA, d. c.1956, Shreveport, Louisiana, USA. Little is known about Oscar Woods who was one of the most impressive of the pre-war slide guitar blues stylists. He was closely associated with Ed Schaffer with whom he recorded as the Shreveport Home Wreckers in Memphis in 1930. In 1932, he and Schaffer took part in what was probably one of the first integrated sessions when they lent their vocal and instrumental talents to support *risqué* country singer Jimmie Davis, later Governor of Louisiana and famous for 'You Are My Sunshine'. Woods recorded some master sole tracks in 1936, in New Orleans, under the pseudonym of the Lone Wolf and later featured with Kitty Gray and others as the Wampus Cats. Finally, in 1940, he recorded five tracks for Alan Lomax of the Library Of Congress. He also worked with B.K. Turner, 'The Black Ace', and was last heard of working in Shreveport area around the late 40s/early 50s.

Album: *Complete Recordings: Oscar 'Buddy' Woods 1930-1938* (1987).

Wrencher, Big John

b. 12 February 1924, near Sunflower, Mississippi, USA, d. 15 July 1977, Clarksdale, Mississippi, USA. A self-taught harmonica player and singer, Wrencher recalled seeing many leading bluesman during his teens. He left Mississippi in 1947, though he returned frequently and on one trip was involved in a car crash which resulted in the loss of his left arm. He lived in Detroit, Michigan and St. Louis,

Missouri before settling in Chicago during 1962, where he often worked for gratuities on Maxwell Street. He recorded for the Testament, Ja-Wes and Barrelhouse labels in the 60s and toured Europe in the early 70s, establishing a loyal following for his excellent harmonica playing and mellow vocals; he also recorded for Big Bear Records.

Albums: *Big John's Boogie* (1974), *Maxwell St. Alley Blues* (1978).

Wright, Billy

b. 21 May 1932, Atlanta, Georgia, USA, d. 28 October 1991, Atlanta, Georgia, USA. A promising gospel singer as a child, he would often sneak into Atlanta's famous 81 Theater to watch the secular shows and eventually turned to performing the blues. His soulful voice came to the attention of Savoy Records, who secured a US R&B Top 5 hit with his debut record 'Blues For My Baby' in 1949. Other less successful releases followed, but Wright's strength was in his live performances, earning him the nickname - Prince Of The Blues. After his Savoy tenure, Wright recorded for Peacock in 1955 and then passed on the baton to his devoted admirers Little Richard, James Brown and Otis Redding. In the late 50s he made his final recordings for Bobby Robinson's Fire Records and tiny local labels, Carrollton and Chris, before settling down in Atlanta, where he continued to perform and introduces acts as a compere until his death in 1991.

Albums: *Stacked Deck* (1980), *Goin' Down Slow* (1984), with Little Richard *Hey Baby, Don't You Want A Man Like Me?* (1986).

Wynn, 'Big' Jim

b. 1912, El Paso, Texas, USA, d. 1976, Los Angeles, California, USA. After moving to Los Angeles as a child, Wynn began his musical tuition on clarinet before switching to tenor sax and playing professionally with the band of Charlie Echols. In 1936, Wynn had his own unit and began to link up with the young 'T-Bone' Walker this association would last until the end of the famous blues musician's life, with the Wynn band regularly touring and recording with him. The Wynn band's own recording career lasted through R&B's golden years, when records were released on 4 Star/Gilt Edge (1945 - including his biggest hit 'Ee-Bobaliba', which was lucratively covered in various disguises by the likes of Helen Humes and Lionel Hampton), Modern (1946), Specialty and Supreme (1948), Mercury and Recorded In Hollywood (1951) and Million (1954). By the late 40s, Wynn had increasingly eschewed his tenor in place of a beefy baritone saxophone, and its deep honking coupled with his own histrionic stage act was the role model for the next generation of west coast R&B saxophonists. A respected session musician from the late 50s into the 70s, Wynn often played with the bands of his good friends 'T-Bone' Walker and Johnny Otis.

Album: *Blow Wynn Blow* (1985).

Yancey, Jimmy

b. c.1894, Chicago, Illinois, USA, d. 17 September 1951. While still a small child Yancey appeared in vaudeville as a tap dancer and singer. After touring the USA and Europe he abandoned this career and, just turned 20, settled in Chicago where he taught himself to play piano. He began to appear at rent parties and informal club sessions, gradually building a reputation. Nevertheless, in 1925, he decided that music was an uncertain way to earn a living and took a job as groundsman with the city's White Sox baseball team. He continued to play piano and was one of the prime movers in establishing the brief popularity of boogie-woogie. He made many records and played clubs and concerts, often accompanying his wife, singer Estella 'Mama' Yancey, but retained his job as groundsman until shortly before his death in 1951. Although Yancey's playing style was elementary, he played with verve and dash, and if he fell behind such contemporaries as Albert Ammons and Pete Johnson in technique, he made up most of the deficiencies through sheer enthusiasm.

Compilations: *Piano Solos* (1939), *The Immortal*

Jimmy Yancey (1940-43).

Young, Ernie

Based in Nashville, USA, Young was a jukebox operator, record retailer and disc jockey. A move into production was therefore logical, given his access to retail outlets. Nashboro was founded in 1951 to record gospel, and Excello in 1952. Using the band led by Skippy Brooks for backing, Excello recorded many local blues artists, while Nashboro acquired a distinguished roster, including Edna Gallmon Cooke, Morgan Babb, the Consolers and the Swanee Quintet. Although there was occasional national chart success, Excello's predominant market was in the south. In 1955, Young finalized a deal with Jay Miller, whereby Miller recorded blues in his Crowley studio for Excello. A steady stream of classics was released, Excello's greatest chart success was Slim Harpo. In 1966, Young sold the label and retired, as by now he was elderly and unwell.

Young, Johnny (Man Young)

b. 1 January 1918, Vicksburg, Mississippi, USA, d. 18 April 1974, Chicago, Illinois, USA. Although he was a more than competent guitarist, Young regarded mandolin as his main instrument. He learned both, as well as harmonica, from uncle Anthony Williams, while living with him in Rolling Fork, birthplace of Muddy Waters. When he returned to Vicksburg, he played house parties with cousin Henry Williams, influenced by the records of Charlie McCoy and the Mississippi Sheiks. He also claimed to have worked with Robert Nighthawk and Sleepy John Estes before moving to Chicago in 1940. He joined the musicians who frequented the Maxwell Street market area, with Floyd Jones, Snooky Pryor and another cousin, Johnny Williams. In 1947 he made his first record, 'Money Takin' Woman', with Williams, for Ora Nelle, run by Maxwell Radio Shop owner, Bernard Abrams. A year later, with Williams and Pryor, he recorded 'My Baby Walked Out' and 'Let Me Ride Your Mule' for Planet, as Man Young. Apart from two unissued songs for JOB, Young did not record again until the 60s, when he taped a number of sessions for Testament, Arhoolie, Vanguard, Milestone, Blues On Blues, Bluesway and Blue Horizon, in the company of men like Otis Spann, Walter Horton, Little Walter and James Cotton. From 1969 until his death, he was a member of the Bob Riedy Chicago Blues Band. In 1972 he toured Europe as a part of the American Folk Blues Festival.

Selected albums: *Johnny Young & His Chicago Blues Band* (1965), *Fat Mandolin* (1969), *Chicago Boogie!* (1974).

Young, 'Mighty' Joe

b. 23 September 1927, Shreveport, Louisiana, USA. Blues guitarist 'Mighty' Joe Young grew up in the northern state of Wisconsin but later relocated to Louisiana before settling in Chicago in the 50s. There he briefly joined a group called Joe Little And His Heart Breakers before joining ex-Muddy Waters harmonica player Billy Boy Arnold in his band. He next went to guitarist Jimmy Rogers' blues band in 1959, meanwhile recording several unsuccessful singles on his own. Young played with guitarist Otis Rush from 1960-63, still recording solo with no luck. He built a reputation as a session guitarist in the 60s, recording with artists such as Magic Sam, Willie Dixon and Tyrone Davis. Young recorded several albums in the early 70s and became a popular blues nightclub act in Chicago. Since 1976 he has been absent from the recording scene.

Albums: *Blues With A Touch Of Soul* (1970), *Legacy Of The Blues Volume Four* (1972), *Chicken Heads* (1974), *Mighty Joe Young* (1976), *Live At The Wise Fools Pub* (1990).

The Guinness Encyclopedia of Popular Music

Compiled and Edited by Colin Larkin

' A landmark work. As much as the history of popular music deserves. ★★★★★' *Q Magazine*

'This is an absolutely invaluable addition to any musicologist's shelf.' *Vox*

The most comprehensive and authoritative guide to popular music that has ever been published, *The Guinness Encyclopedia of Popular Music* covers every important artist, band, genre, group, event, instrument, publisher, promoter, record company and musical style from the world of popular music in four 832-page volumes in a slipcase. Price £225.00

The product of over four years of intensive labour by an international group of more than 100 skilled writers, musicologists and advisors, its scope is truly global. Compiled in an A-Z format, it covers all forms of popular music from 1900 to 1992 and contains almost 10,000 entries varying in length from 100 to 5,000 words.

A bibliography of over 4,000 entries is included along with a full index of artists' names.

For further details of this essential reference work, please write to:
Section D,
The Marketing Department,
Guinness Publishing,
33 London Road,
Enfield,
Middlesex EN2 6DJ,
England.

Proposed Titles for Inclusion in the

'Guinness Who's Who of Popular Music Series'

Compiled and Edited by Colin Larkin

The Guinness Who's Who of 50s Music
The Guinness Who's Who of 60s Music★
The Guinness Who's Who of 70s Music★
The Guinness Who's Who of 80s Music
The Guinness Who's Who of Indie and New Wave Music★
The Guinness Who's Who of Blues Music★
The Guinness Who's Who of Folk Music
The Guinness Who's Who of Reggae
The Guinness Who's Who of Soul Music
The Guinness Who's Who of Country Music★
The Guinness Who's Who of Jazz★
The Guinness Who's Who of Heavy Metal Music★
The Guinness Who's Who of Gospel Music
The Guinness Who's Who of UK Rock and Pop
The Guinness Who's Who of USA Rock and Pop
The Guinness Who's Who of Danceband Pop
The Guinness Who's Who of World Music
The Guinness Who's Who of Stage Musicals

★ Already published

For further information on any of these titles please write to:
Section D,
The Marketing Department,
Guinness Publishing,
33 London Road,
Enfield,
Middlesex EN2 6DJ,
England